# Switching *to the* Mac *Leopard Edition*

## THE MISSING MANUAL

*The book that
should have been
in the box*®

# Switching *to the* Mac *Leopard Edition*

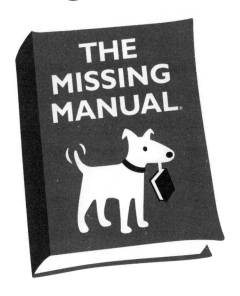

David Pogue

POGUE PRESS™
O'REILLY®

*Beijing • Cambridge • Farnham • Köln • Paris • Sebastopol • Taipei • Tokyo*

## Switching to the Mac: The Missing Manual, Leopard Edition

by David Pogue

Copyright © 2008 David Pogue. All rights reserved.
Printed in the United States of America.

Published by O'Reilly Media, Inc., 1005 Gravenstein Highway North,
Sebastopol, CA 95472.

O'Reilly Media books may be purchased for educational, business, or sales
promotional use. Online editions are also available for most titles: *safari.oreilly.*
*com.* For more information, contract our corporate/institutional sales department:
800-998-9938 or *corporate@oreilly.com.*

February 2008:     First Edition.

RepKover™ This book uses RepKover™, a durable and flexible lay-flat binding.

ISBN-13:  978-0-596-51412-9

# Table of Contents

**Introduction** ...................................................................................... **1**

What Mac OS X Gives You.............................................................. 3

What Mac OS X Takes Away ......................................................... 5

About This Book ........................................................................... 6

The Very Basics............................................................................ 8

## *Part One: Welcome to Macintosh*

**Chapter 1: How the Mac Is Different**.................................... **11**

Power On, Dude............................................................................ 11

That One-Button Mouse............................................................... 12

On, Off, and Sleep........................................................................ 13

The Menu Bar ............................................................................... 15

Finder = Windows Explorer .......................................................... 15

Dock = Taskbar ............................................................................ 16

Menulets = Tray............................................................................ 16

Keyboard Differences ................................................................... 19

Disk Differences............................................................................ 24

Where Your Stuff Is ...................................................................... 25

Window Controls........................................................................... 28

Terminology Differences ............................................................... 36

**Chapter 2: Folders, Dock, & Windows**................................ **37**

Getting into Mac OS X.................................................................. 37

The Four Window Views ............................................................... 39

Icon View...................................................................................... 41

List View....................................................................................... 47

Column View................................................................................. 52

Cover Flow View........................................................................... 55

Quick Look ................................................................................... 57

The Dock....................................................................................... 60

The Finder Toolbar ....................................................................... 69

Getting Help in Mac OS X............................................................. 70

## Chapter 3: Files, Icons, & Spotlight ......................................... 75

Renaming Icons .................................................................. 75
Selecting Icons .................................................................. 77
Moving and Copying Icons ................................................. 79
Aliases: Icons in Two Places at Once ................................... 84
Color Labels ..................................................................... 85
The Trash ......................................................................... 88
Get Info ........................................................................... 91
The Spotlight Menu ........................................................... 94
The Spotlight Window ........................................................ 100
Customizing Spotlight ........................................................ 107
Smart Folders ................................................................... 109

## Chapter 4: Documents, Programs, & Spaces ......................... 111

Opening Mac OS X Programs ............................................... 112
The New, Improved "Alt-Tab" ............................................. 115
Exposé: Death to Window Clutter ........................................ 116
Spaces: Your Free Quad-Display Mac .................................... 122
Hiding Programs the Old-Fashioned Way ............................... 127
How Documents Know Their Parents .................................... 129
Keyboard Control .............................................................. 134
The Save and Open Dialog Boxes ......................................... 136
Two Kinds of Programs: Cocoa and Carbon ........................... 141
The Cocoa Difference ......................................................... 142
Universal Apps (Intel Macs) ................................................ 145
Installing Mac OS X Programs ............................................. 146
Dashboard ....................................................................... 150
Web Clips: Make Your Own Widgets ..................................... 154

# Part Two: Moving In

## Chapter 5: Eight Ways to Transfer Your Files ..................... 159

Transfer by Apple Genius .................................................... 160
Transfers by iTornado ........................................................ 161
Transfers by Disk .............................................................. 162
Transfers by Network ......................................................... 163
Transfers by File-Sending Web Site ...................................... 163
Transfers by Email ............................................................ 164
Transfers by iDisk ............................................................. 164
Transfers by Bluetooth ....................................................... 164
Where to Put Your Copied Files ........................................... 165
Document-Conversion Issues ............................................... 167

## Chapter 6: Transferring Email and Contacts ..................................... 171

A Reminder That Could Save You Hours ............................................................. 172
Transferring Your Outlook Mail ......................................................................... 172
Transferring Your Outlook Address Book ........................................................... 180
Transferring from Outlook Express .................................................................... 184
Transferring Your Eudora Mail ........................................................................... 184
Transferring Your Eudora Address Book ............................................................. 187
Email Settings ................................................................................................... 188

## Chapter 7: Special Software, Special Problems ................................. 191

ACDSee ............................................................................................................. 191
Acrobat Reader ................................................................................................. 192
ACT ................................................................................................................... 192
Ad Subtract (Pop-up Stopper) ........................................................................... 193
Adobe [your favorite program here] ................................................................... 194
America Online .................................................................................................. 194
AIM (AOL Instant Messenger) ............................................................................ 195
Children's Software ........................................................................................... 195
Earthlink Total Access ....................................................................................... 196
Easy CD Creator ................................................................................................ 196
Encarta ............................................................................................................. 196
Eudora .............................................................................................................. 197
Excel ................................................................................................................. 197
Firefox .............................................................................................................. 197
Games .............................................................................................................. 197
Google Desktop Search ..................................................................................... 197
ICQ ................................................................................................................... 198
Internet Explorer ............................................................................................... 198
iTunes ............................................................................................................... 198
Kazaa ................................................................................................................ 198
Limewire ........................................................................................................... 198
MacAfee VirusScan ............................................................................................ 198
Microsoft Access ............................................................................................... 199
Microsoft Money ............................................................................................... 200
Microsoft Office ................................................................................................ 201
Microsoft Publisher ........................................................................................... 203
Microsoft Visio .................................................................................................. 203
Minesweeper ..................................................................................................... 203
MSN Messenger ................................................................................................ 203
NaturallySpeaking ............................................................................................. 203
Netscape ........................................................................................................... 204
Newsgroup Readers .......................................................................................... 204
Norton AntiVirus ............................................................................................... 204
Norton Utilities ................................................................................................. 204
Notepad ............................................................................................................ 204
Outlook/Outlook Express ................................................................................... 204

Paint Shop Pro ............................................................................................... 205
Palm Desktop .............................................................................................. 205
Picasa ........................................................................................................ 205
Pocket PC ................................................................................................... 205
PowerPoint ................................................................................................. 206
QuickBooks ................................................................................................. 206
Quicken ...................................................................................................... 206
RealPlayer ................................................................................................... 207
RssReader ................................................................................................... 207
Skype ......................................................................................................... 207
SnagIt ........................................................................................................ 207
Solitaire ..................................................................................................... 208
Street Atlas USA .......................................................................................... 209
TaxCut, TurboTax ......................................................................................... 209
WinAmp, MusicMatch ................................................................................... 209
Windows Media Player .................................................................................. 209
WinZip ....................................................................................................... 210
Word .......................................................................................................... 210
WordPerfect ................................................................................................ 210
Yahoo Messenger ......................................................................................... 210

**Chapter 8: Windows on Macintosh** .......................................................... **211**
Boot Camp ................................................................................................. 212
Windows in a Window ................................................................................... 220

**Chapter 9: Hardware on the Mac** .............................................................. **223**
Printers and Printing .................................................................................... 223
Managing Printouts ..................................................................................... 229
Faxing ........................................................................................................ 232
PDF Files .................................................................................................... 236
Fonts—and Font Book ................................................................................... 237
Digital Cameras ........................................................................................... 242
Disks .......................................................................................................... 243
Burning CDs and DVDs .................................................................................. 245
iTunes: The Digital Jukebox ........................................................................... 250
DVD Movies ................................................................................................. 258
Keyboard .................................................................................................... 261
Mouse ........................................................................................................ 262
Monitors ..................................................................................................... 263
Time Machine .............................................................................................. 263
.Mac Sync ................................................................................................... 275

# Part Three: The Mac Online

## Chapter 10: Internet Setup ................................................................. 279
Network Central—and Multihoming ........................................... 279
Broadband Connections............................................................. 281
Dial-up Modem Connections...................................................... 287
Switching Locations .................................................................. 291
Internet Sharing........................................................................ 292
.Mac Services ........................................................................... 295
Internet Location Files .............................................................. 300

## Chapter 11: Mail & Address Book ......................................................... 301
Checking Your Mail .................................................................. 301
Writing Messages ..................................................................... 304
Stationery ................................................................................ 308
Reading Email .......................................................................... 310
The Anti-Spam Toolkit............................................................... 324
RSS Feeds ................................................................................ 325
Notes ...................................................................................... 327
To Dos ..................................................................................... 328
Address Book ........................................................................... 331

## Chapter 12: Safari & iChat ................................................................. 339
Safari ...................................................................................... 340
Tips for Better Surfing............................................................... 346
Tabbed Browsing...................................................................... 350
iChat ....................................................................................... 356
Text Chats ............................................................................... 363
Audio Chats............................................................................. 365
Video Chats ............................................................................. 366
Sharing Your Screen.................................................................. 370
iChat Theater............................................................................ 372

# Part Four: Putting Down Roots

## Chapter 13: Accounts, Parental Controls, & Security ......................... 377
Introducing Accounts................................................................ 377
Creating an Account ................................................................. 379
Parental Controls...................................................................... 387
Editing Accounts ...................................................................... 395
Setting Up the Login Process ..................................................... 396
Signing In, Logging Out............................................................ 398
Sharing Across Accounts ........................................................... 399
Fast User Switching................................................................... 400
Four Mac OS X Security Shields ................................................. 401

## Chapter 14: Networking, File Sharing, & Screen Sharing ............... 413
Wiring the Network........................................................................... 413
File Sharing ...................................................................................... 416
Accessing Shared Files..................................................................... 422
Networking with Windows............................................................... 426
Screen Sharing.................................................................................. 431

## Chapter 15: System Preferences............................................. 437
The System Preferences Window...................................................... 437
.Mac.................................................................................................. 439
Accounts ........................................................................................... 440
Appearance....................................................................................... 440
Bluetooth .......................................................................................... 442
CDs & DVDs...................................................................................... 444
Date & Time...................................................................................... 445
Desktop & Screen Saver ................................................................... 447
Displays............................................................................................. 454
Dock .................................................................................................. 456
Energy Saver ..................................................................................... 456
Exposé & Spaces............................................................................... 460
International........................................................................................ 460
Keyboard & Mouse ........................................................................... 464
Network ............................................................................................ 469
Parental Controls............................................................................... 469
Print & Fax ........................................................................................ 469
QuickTime ......................................................................................... 469
Security ............................................................................................. 469
Sharing............................................................................................... 469
Software Update................................................................................ 471
Sound................................................................................................. 471
Speech .............................................................................................. 473
Spotlight............................................................................................. 475
Startup Disk....................................................................................... 475
Time Machine.................................................................................... 475
Universal Access............................................................................... 475

## Chapter 16: The Free Programs............................................... 479
Address Book..................................................................................... 480
AppleScript........................................................................................ 480
Automator ......................................................................................... 481
Calculator .......................................................................................... 482
Chess................................................................................................. 484
Dashboard.......................................................................................... 485
Dictionary .......................................................................................... 485
DVD Player ........................................................................................ 487
Exposé............................................................................................... 487

Font Book ............................................................................................ 487

Front Row ........................................................................................... 487

GarageBand ........................................................................................ 489

iCal ...................................................................................................... 489

iChat ................................................................................................... 498

iDVD ................................................................................................... 498

iMovie, iPhoto .................................................................................... 498

iTunes ................................................................................................. 498

Mail ..................................................................................................... 498

Photo Booth ....................................................................................... 498

Preview ............................................................................................... 502

QuickTime Player ............................................................................... 507

Safari ................................................................................................... 509

Stickies ............................................................................................... 509

System Preferences ............................................................................ 511

TextEdit .............................................................................................. 511

Time Machine .................................................................................... 517

Utilities: Your Mac OS X Toolbox ..................................................... 517

## *Part Five: Appendixes*

### Appendix A: Installation & Troubleshooting ........................................ 537

Getting Ready to Install ..................................................................... 537

Four Kinds of Installation ................................................................... 538

The Basic Installation ......................................................................... 538

The Upgrade Installation .................................................................... 540

The Clean Install ("Archive and Install") ........................................... 540

Erase & Install .................................................................................... 541

The Setup Assistant ............................................................................ 541

Troubleshooting .................................................................................. 544

### Appendix B: The "Where'd It Go?" Dictionary .................................... 555

### Appendix C: The Master Mac OS X Secret Keystroke List ................ 569

THE MISSING CREDITS

# The Missing Credits

## About the Author

 **David Pogue** is the weekly tech columnist for the *New York Times*, an Emmy-winning correspondent for *CBS News Sunday Morning*, weekly CNBC contributor, and the creator of the Missing Manual series. He's the author or co-author of 45 books, including 20 in this series and six in the "For Dummies" line (including *Macs, Magic, Opera,* and *Classical Music*). In his other life, David is a former Broadway show conductor, a magician, and a pianist. News, photos, links to his columns, blog, and weekly videos await at *www.davidpogue.com*.

He welcomes feedback about his books by email at *david@pogueman.com*.

## About the Creative Team

**Sarah Friedlander** (production miracle worker) is a graduate of Rochester Institute of Technology and lives in Campbell, California. She works in high-tech marketing in Silicon Valley and keeps her hands on creative projects as often as she can. When not working, she enjoys interior decorating, sushi, traveling and spending time with her fiancé, Ryan. Her online musings can be found at *www.sarahfriedlander.com*.

**Adam Goldstein** (coauthor, previous edition) is the author of *AppleScript: The Missing Manual*, and has contributed to a number of other titles, including *Mac OS X: The Missing Manual, Mac OS X Power Hound*, and *Google: The Missing Manual*. In his ample free time, Adam attends M.I.T. Web: *www.goldfishsoft.com*

**Phil Simpson** (design and layout) works out of his office in Southbury, Connecticut, where he has had his graphic design business since 1982. He is experienced in many facets of graphic design, including corporate identity, publication design, and corporate and medical communications. Email: *pmsimpson@earthlink.net*.

## Acknowledgments

The Missing Manual series is a joint venture between the dream team introduced on these pages and O'Reilly Media. I'm grateful to all of them, and also to a few people who did massive favors for this book. The prose of Joseph Schorr and Adam Goldstein, contributors to earlier editions, lives on in this one; John Rizzo and Winn Schwartau served as technical editors for previous editions. Teresa Noelle Roberts did some last-minute copyediting of new material; and Lesa Snider King put in a gruelling yet somehow satisfying day helping me create the index. Thanks to David Rogelberg for believing in the idea, and above all, to Jennifer, Kelly, Tia, and Jeffrey, who make these books—and everything else—possible.

—*David Pogue*

## The Missing Manual Series

Missing Manuals are witty, superbly written guides to computer products that don't come with printed manuals (which is just about all of them). Each book features a handcrafted index; cross-references to specific page numbers (not just "see Chapter 14"); and RepKover, a binding that lies flat without the assistance of cinder blocks.

Here's a sampling of current titles.

- *Mac OS X Leopard: The Missing Manual* by David Pogue
- *iMovie '08 & iDVD: The Missing Manual* by David Pogue
- *iPhoto '08: The Missing Manual* by David Pogue and Derrick Story
- *iPhone: The Missing Manual* by David Pogue
- *AppleScript: The Missing Manual* by Adam Goldstein
- *iPod: The Missing Manual,* 6th Edition by J.D. Biersdorfer
- *Office 2008 for Macintosh: The Missing Manual* by Jim Elferdink et al.
- *FileMaker Pro 9: The Missing Manual* by Geoff Coffey and Susan Prosser
- *CSS: The Missing Manual* by David Sawyer McFarland
- *Creating Web Sites: The Missing Manual* by Matthew MacDonald
- *Dreamweaver CS3: The Missing Manual* by David Sawyer McFarland
- *Flash CS3: The Missing Manual* by E. A. Vander Veer and Chris Grover
- *eBay: The Missing Manual* by Nancy Conner
- *Wikipedia: The Missing Manual* by John Broughton
- *Google: The Missing Manual,* 2nd Edition by Sarah Milstein and Rael Dornfest
- *Home Networking: The Missing Manual* by Scott Lowe
- *Windows Vista: The Missing Manual,* by David Pogue
- *FrontPage 2003: The Missing Manual* by Jessica Mantaro
- *Office 2007: The Missing Manual* by Chris Grover, M. MacDonald, et al.
- *Word 2007: The Missing Manual* by Chris Grover
- *Excel 2007: The Missing Manual* by Matthew MacDonald
- *PowerPoint 2007: The Missing Manual* by Emily A. Vander Veer
- *Access 2007: The Missing Manual* by Matthew MacDonald
- *Microsoft Project 2007: The Missing Manual* by Bonnie Biafore
- *PCs: The Missing Manual* by Andy Rathbone
- *Photoshop Elements 6: The Missing Manual* by Barbara Brundage
- *QuickBooks 2008: The Missing Manual* by Bonnie Biafore

# Introduction

What's going on with the Mac these days?

Its market share has tripled since 2005. At the 2008 Macworld Expo, there were 475 booths and 50,000 attendees—both up 25 percent over the previous year. And Mac book sales are up about 35 percent over a year ago (woo-hoo!).

And then there's you, possibly the most significant statistic of all, sitting there reading this book—because, obviously, you intend to switch to (or add on) a Mac.

What's going on?

Maybe the coolness of all those iPods and iPhones is rubbing off onto the rest of Apple's product line. Maybe people have grown weary of boring beige and black boxes. Maybe it was the "I'm a Mac/ I'm a PC" ads on TV, or the convenience of the Apple stores. Maybe potential switchers feel more confident to take the plunge now that Macs (because they contain Intel chips) can run Windows programs.

Or maybe people have just spent one Saturday too many dealing with viruses, worms, spyware, crapware, excessive startup processes, questionable firewalls, inefficient permissions, and all the other land mines strewn across the Windows world.

In any case, there's never been a better time to make the switch. Mac OS X version 10.5 (Leopard) is gorgeous, easy to understand, and virus-free. Apple's computers are in top form, too, complete with features like built-in video cameras, built-in Ethernet, DVD burners, and two different kinds of wireless connections. If you're talking laptops, the story is even better: Apple's laptops generally cost less than similarly outfitted Windows laptops, yet weigh less. Plus, they look a lot cooler.

And then there's that Intel processor that sizzles away inside today's Macs. Yes, it lets you *run Windows*—and Windows programs—at blazing speed, right there on your Macintosh. (Hell really has frozen over.) Chapter 8 has the details.

That's not to say, however, that switching to the Mac is all sunshine and bunnies. The Macintosh is a different machine, running a different operating system, and built by a company with a different philosophy—a fanatical perfectionist/artistic zeal. When it comes to their missions and ideals, Apple and Microsoft have about as much in common as a melon and a shoehorn.

In any case, you have three challenges before you. First, you'll probably want to copy your Windows stuff over to the new Mac. Some of that is easy to transfer (photos, music, Microsoft Office documents), and some is trickier to extract (email messages, address books, buddy lists).

Second, you have to assemble a suite of Macintosh programs that do what you're used to doing in Windows. Most programs from Microsoft, Adobe, and other major players are available in nearly identical Mac and Windows formats. But occasionally, it's more difficult: Many second-tier programs are available only for Windows, and it takes some research (or Chapter 7 of this book) to help you find Macintosh replacements.

Finally, you have to learn Mac OS X itself. In some respects, it resembles the latest versions of Windows: There's a taskbar-like thing, a Control Panel–like thing, and, of course, a Trash can. At the same time, hundreds of features you thought you knew have been removed, replaced, or relocated. (If you ever find yourself groping for an old favorite feature, see Appendix B, the "Where'd It Go?" Dictionary.)

---

**Note:** In Mac OS X, the X is meant to be a Roman numeral, pronounced "ten." Unfortunately, many people see "Mac OS X" and say "Mac Oh Ess Sex." That's a sure way to get funny looks in public.

---

**FREQUENTLY ASKED QUESTION**

## All About "Leopard"

*What's this business about Leopard?*

Like Microsoft, Apple develops its wares in secret, giving new products code names to throw outsiders off the scent. Apple's code names for Mac OS X and its descendants all refer to big cats: Mac OS X was Cheetah, 10.1 was Puma, 10.2 was Jaguar, 10.3 was Panther, 10.4 was Tiger, and 10.5 is Leopard.

Usually, software code names are dropped when the products are complete, at which time the marketing department

provides the real names. In Mac OS X's case, though, Apple thinks that its cat names are cool enough to retain for the finished product.

It makes you wonder what Apple plans to call future versions. Since Apple only increases the decimal point with each major upgrade, it's got four big cats to go before it hits Mac OS XI.

Let's see: Bobcat, Lion, Cougar…um…Ocelot?

# What Mac OS X Gives You

These days, a key attraction of the Mac—at least as far as switchers are concerned—is its security features. There isn't yet a single widespread Mac OS X virus. (Even Microsoft Word macro viruses don't run in Mac OS X.) For many people, that's a good enough reason to move to Mac OS X right there.

Along the same lines, there have been no reported sightings of *adware* (software that displays annoying ads when you use your Web browser) or *spyware* (malicious software that tracks your computer use and reports it back to a shady company) for Mac OS X. Mail, Mac OS X's built-in email program, deals surprisingly well with *spam*—the unsolicited junk email that's become the scourge of the Internet.

If you ask average people why the Mac isn't overrun by viruses and spyware, as Windows is, they'll probably tell you, "Because the Mac's market share is too small for the bad guys to write for."

That may be true (although 45 million machines isn't too shabby, as targets go). But there's another reason, too: Mac OS X is a very young operating system. It was created only a few years ago, and with security in mind. (Contrast with Windows, whose original versions were written before the Internet even existed.) Mac OS X is simply designed better. Its built-in firewall makes it virtually impossible for hackers to break into your Mac, and the system insists on getting your permission before *anything* gets installed on your Mac. Nothing can get installed behind your back, as it can in Windows.

But freedom from gunkware and viruses is only one big-ticket item. Here are a few other joys of becoming a Mac fan:

- **Stability.** Underneath the shimmering, translucent desktop of Mac OS X is Unix, the industrial strength, rock-solid OS that drives many a Web site and university. It's not new by any means; in fact, it's decades old, and has been polished by generations of programmers. That's precisely why Apple CEO Steve Jobs and his team chose it as the basis for the NeXT operating system, which Jobs worked on during his 12 years away from Apple and which Apple bought in 1997 to turn into Mac OS X.

- **No nagging.** Unlike Windows, Mac OS X isn't copy-protected. You can install the same copy on your desktop and laptop Macs, if you have a permissive conscience. When you buy a new Mac, you're never, ever asked to type in a code off a sticker. Nor must you "register," "activate," sign up for ".NET Passport," or endure any other friendly suggestions unrelated to your work. And you won't find any cheesy software demos from other companies clogging up your desktop when you buy a new Mac, either. In short, Mac OS X leaves you alone.

- **Sensational software.** Mac OS X comes with several dozen useful programs, from Mail (for email) to a 3-D, voice-activated Chess program. The most famous programs, though, are the famous Apple "iApps": iTunes for working with audio files, iMovie for editing video, iPhoto for managing your digital photos, GarageBand for creating and editing digital music, and so on. You also get iChat (an AOL-, Jabber-, and Google Talk-compatible instant messaging program that also offers videoconferencing) and iCal, a calendar program.

- **Simpler everything.** Most applications in Mac OS X show up as a single icon. All of the support files are hidden away inside, where you don't have to look at them. There's no Add/Remove Programs program on the Macintosh; in general, you can remove a program from your Mac simply by dragging that one application icon to the Trash, without having to worry that you're leaving scraps behind.

- **Desktop features.** Microsoft is a neat freak. Windows XP, for example, is so opposed to your using the desktop as a parking lot for icons, it actually interrupts you every 60 days to sweep all your infrequently used icons into an "Unused" folder.

The Mac approach is different. Mac people often leave their desktops absolutely littered with icons. As a result, Mac OS X offers a long list of useful desktop features that will be new to you, the Windows refugee.

For example, *spring-loaded* folders let you drag an icon into a folder within a folder within a folder with a single drag, without leaving a wake of open windows. An optional second line under an icon's name tells you how many items are in a folder, what the dimensions of a graphic are, and so on. And there's a useful column view, which lets you view the contents of many nested folders at a glance. (You can think of it as a horizontal version of Windows Explorer.)

When your screen gets cluttered with windows, you can temporarily hide all of them with a single keystroke. If you want to see *all* the windows on your screen without any of them overlapping, Mac OS X's Exposé feature is your best friend (page 116).

A speedy, system-wide Find command called Spotlight is accessible from any program. It searches not only the names of your files and folders, but also the words *inside* your documents, and can even search your email, calendar, address book, Web bookmarks, and about 100 other kinds of data, all at once.

Finally, Mac OS X offers the Dashboard (which inspired the Sidebar in Windows Vista). It lets you summon dozens of miniprograms—a calculator, weather forecaster, dictionary, and so on—with a single keystroke, and dismiss them just as easily. You can download thousands more of these so-called widgets from the Internet, making it even easier to find TV listings, Google search results, local movie showtimes, and more, no matter what program you're using at the moment.

- **Advanced graphics.** Mac programmers get excited about the set of advanced graphics technologies called *Quartz* (for two-dimensional graphics) and *OpenGL* (for three-dimensional graphics). For the rest of us, these technologies translate into a beautiful, translucent look for the desktop, smooth-looking (*antialiased*) onscreen lettering, and the ability to turn any document on the screen into an Adobe Acrobat (PDF) file. And then there are the slick animations that permeate every aspect of Mac OS X: the rotating-cube effect when you switch from one logged-in person to another, the "genie" effect when you minimize a window to the Dock, and so on.

- **Advanced networking.** When it comes to hooking up your computer to others, including those on the Internet, few operating systems can touch Mac OS X. It offers advanced features like *multihoming*, which lets your laptop switch automatically from its cable modem settings to its wireless or dial-up modem settings when you take it on the road.

    If you're not so much a switcher as an *adder* (you're getting a Mac but keeping the PC around), you'll be happy to hear that Macs and Windows PCs can "see" each other on a network automatically, too. As a result, you can open, copy, and work on files on both types of machines as though the religious war between Macs and PCs had never even existed.

- **Voice control, keyboard control.** You can operate almost every aspect of every program entirely from the keyboard—or even by voice. These are terrific timesavers for efficiency freaks. In fact, the Mac can also read aloud *any text in any program*, including Web pages, email, your novel, you name it.

- **Full buzzword compliance.** You can't read an article about Mac OS X without hearing certain technical buzzwords that were once exclusively the domain of computer engineers: *preemptive multitasking, multithreading, symmetrical multiprocessing, dynamic memory allocation,* and *memory protection,* for example.

    What it all adds up to is that Mac OS X is very stable; that a crashing program can't crash the whole machine; that the Macintosh can exploit multiple processors; and that the Mac can easily do more than one thing at once—downloading files, playing music, and opening a program, for example—all simultaneously.

- **A command-line interface.** In general, Apple has completely hidden from you every trace of the Unix operating system that lurks beneath Mac OS X's beautiful skin. For the benefit of programmers and other technically oriented fans, however, Apple left uncovered a tiny passageway into that far more complex realm: Terminal, a program in your Applications→Utilities folder.

    This isn't a Unix book, so you'll find only the basics of using Terminal here. Still, if the idea of an all-text operating system gets you going, you can capitalize on the *command-line interface* of Mac OS X by typing out commands in the Terminal window, which the Mac executes instantly and efficiently. Think DOS prompt, just faster and more useful.

## What Mac OS X Takes Away

Besides quirks like viruses, spyware, and the Start menu, there are some substantial things on a PC that you lose when you switch to the Mac:

- **Programs.** As mentioned above, there are certain programs that are stubbornly Windows-only. You can always search for replacements—using Chapter 7 of this book as a guide, for example—but you may end up having to pay for them. And, of course, there are *certain* programs—like some proprietary accounting and laboratory software, and lots of games—where the Windows versions are simply irreplaceable. For those, you have to keep a PC around or run Windows on your Mac (Chapter 8).

• **Peripherals.** Most add-on devices nowadays work equally well on both Windows PCs and Macs. That includes printers, scanners, digital cameras (still- and video-varieties), and "multifunction" devices that incorporate several of those attributes into one machine.

Unfortunately, not every company is that enlightened. If you have a device made by an obscure manufacturer—especially if the device is more than a few years old—it may not work with your Mac at all.

Still, all hope is not lost. Chapter 9 can get you out of any hardware ruts you may find yourself in while making the Big Switch.

## About This Book

*Switching to the Mac: The Missing Manual* is divided into five parts, each containing several chapters:

• Part 1, **Welcome to Macintosh,** covers the essentials of the Macintosh. It's a crash course in everything you see onscreen when you turn on the machine: the Dock, Sidebar, icons, windows, menus, scroll bars, Trash, aliases,  menu, and so on.

• Part 2, **Moving In,** is dedicated to the actual process of hauling your software, settings, and even peripherals (like printers and monitors) across the chasm from the PC to the Mac. It covers both the easy parts (copying over your documents, pictures, and music files) and the harder ones (transferring your email, address books, buddy lists, and so on). It also covers the steps for running Windows on your Mac, which is an extremely attractive option.

• Part 3, **The Mac Online,** walks you through the process of setting up an Internet connection on your Mac. It also covers Apple's Internet software suite: Mail, Address Book, Safari, and iChat.

• Part 4, **Putting Down Roots,** deals with more advanced topics—and aims to turn you into a Macintosh power user. It teaches you how to set up private accounts for people who share a Mac, create a network for file sharing and screen sharing, navigate the System Preferences program (the Mac equivalent of the Windows Control Panel), and operate the 50 freebie bonus programs that come with Mac OS X.

---

**Note:** Some of the material in this book is adapted from the bestselling *Mac OS X: The Missing Manual,* Leopard Edition. That book is a much fatter, more in-depth guide to Mac OS X (and a worthy investment if you grow into a true Macoholic).

---

- Part 5. At the end of the book, you'll find three appendixes. The first covers installation and troubleshooting. The second is the "Where'd It Go?" Dictionary—an essential reference for anyone who occasionally (or frequently) flounders to find some familiar control in the new, alien Macintosh environment. The last is a master keyboard-shortcut list for the entire Mac OS X universe.

## About→These→Arrows

Throughout this book—and throughout the Missing Manual series—you'll find sentences like this one: "Open the System→Libraries→Fonts folder." That's shorthand for a much longer instruction that directs you to open three nested folders in sequence, like this: "On your hard drive, you'll find a folder called System. Open that. Inside the System folder window is a folder called Libraries; double-click it to open it. Inside *that* folder is yet another one called Fonts. Double-click to open it, too."

Similarly, this kind of arrow shorthand helps to simplify the business of choosing commands in menus, as shown in Figure I-1.

**Figure I-1:**
*In this book, arrow notations help to simplify folder and menu instructions. For example, "Choose ⌘→Dock →Position on Left" is a more compact way of saying, "From the ⌘ menu, choose Dock; from the submenu that then appears, choose Position on Left," as shown here.*

## About MissingManuals.com

If you visit *www.missingmanuals.com*, click the "Missing CD-ROM" link, and then click the title of this book, you'll find a neat, organized, chapter-by-chapter list of the shareware and freeware mentioned in this book. (As noted on the inside back cover, having the software online instead of on a CD-ROM saved you $5 on the cost of the book.)

The Web site also offers corrections and updates to the book (to see them, click the book's title, and then click Errata). In fact, you're encouraged to submit such corrections and updates yourself. In an effort to keep the book as up-to-date and accurate as possible, each time we print more copies of this book, we'll make any confirmed corrections you've suggested. We'll also note such changes on the Web site, so that you can mark important corrections into your own copy of the book, if you like.

## The Very Basics

To use this book, and indeed to use a Macintosh, you need to know a few basics. This book assumes that you're familiar with a few terms and concepts:

- **Clicking.** This book gives you three kinds of instructions that require you to use the Mac's mouse. To *click* means to point the arrow cursor at something on the screen and then—without moving the cursor—press and release the clicker button on the mouse (or your laptop trackpad). To *double-click,* of course, means to click twice in rapid succession, again without moving the cursor at all. And to *drag* means to move the cursor while holding down the button.

  When you're told to ⌘-*click* something, you click while pressing the ⌘ key (which is next to the Space bar). *Shift-clicking, Option-clicking,* and *Control-clicking* work the same way—just click while pressing the corresponding key.

- **Menus.** The *menus* are the words at the top of your screen: , File, Edit, and so on. Click one to make a list of commands appear.

  Some people click and release to open a menu and then, after reading the choices, click again on the one they want. Other people like to press the mouse button continuously after the initial click on the menu title, drag down the list to the desired command, and only then release the mouse button. Either method works fine.

- **Keyboard shortcuts.** If you're typing along in a burst of creative energy, it's disruptive to have to grab the mouse to use a menu. That's why many Mac fans prefer to trigger menu commands by pressing certain combinations on the keyboard. For example, in word processors, you can press ⌘-B to produce a **boldface** word. When you read an instruction like "press ⌘-B," start by pressing the ⌘ key, then, while it's down, type the letter B, and finally release both keys.

---

***Tip:*** You know what's really nice? The keystroke to open the Preferences dialog box in every Apple program—Mail, Safari, iMovie, iPhoto, TextEdit, Preview, and on and on—is always the same: ⌘-comma. Better yet, that standard is catching on with other software companies, too; Word, Excel, Entourage, and PowerPoint use the same keystroke, for example.

---

- **Icons.** The colorful inch-tall pictures that appear in your various desktop folders are the graphic symbols that represent each program, disk, and document on your computer. If you click an icon one time, it darkens, indicating that you've just *highlighted* or *selected* it. Now you're ready to manipulate it by using, for example, a menu command.

# Part One:
# Welcome to Macintosh

**Chapter 1: How the Mac Is Different**

**Chapter 2: Folders, Windows, & Dock**

**Chapter 3: Files, Icons, & Spotlight**

**Chapter 4: Programs & Documents**

1

# How the Mac Is Different

When you get right down to it, the job description of every operating system is pretty much the same. Whether it's Mac OS X, Windows Vista, or Billy Bob's System-Software Special, any OS must serve as the ambassador between the computer and you, its human operator. It must somehow represent your files and programs on the screen so that you can open them; offer some method of organizing your files; present onscreen controls that affect your speaker volume, mouse speed, and so on; and communicate with your external gadgets, like disks, printers, and digital cameras.

In other words, Mac OS X offers roughly the same features as recent versions of Windows. That's the good news.

The bad news is that these features are called different things and parked in different spots. As you could have predicted, this rearrangement of features can mean a good deal of confusion for you, the Macintosh foreigner. For the first few days or weeks, you may instinctively reach for certain familiar features that simply aren't where you expect to find them, the way your tongue keeps sticking itself into the socket of the newly extracted tooth.

To minimize the frustration, therefore, read this chapter first. It makes plain the most important and dramatic differences between the Windows method and the Macintosh way.

## Power On, Dude

As a critic might say, Apple is always consistent with its placement of the power button: It's different on every model.

---

On iMacs and Mac Minis, the power button is on the back panel. On tower Macs (Mac Pro, Power Mac), it's on the front panel. And on laptop Macs, the button is near the upper-right corner of the keyboard. (Then again, if you have a laptop, you should get into the habit of just closing the lid when you're done working, and opening it to resume; the power button rarely plays a role in your life.)

In every case, though, the power button looks the same (Figure 1-1): it bears the ⏻ logo.

**Figure 1-1:**
*Every Mac's power button looks like this, although it might be hard to find. The good news: Once you find it, it'll pretty much stay in the same place.*

## That One-Button Mouse

You can get terrific mileage out of *shortcut menus* on the Mac, just as in Windows (Figure 1-2).

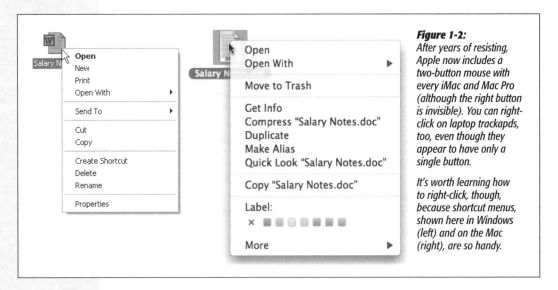

**Figure 1-2:**
*After years of resisting, Apple now includes a two-button mouse with every iMac and Mac Pro (although the right button is invisible). You can right-click on laptop trackapds, too, even though they appear to have only a single button.*

*It's worth learning how to right-click, though, because shortcut menus, shown here in Windows (left) and on the Mac (right), are so handy.*

But for years, it took two hands to open a Mac shortcut menu. You did it by *Control-clicking* something on the screen—and you can still do that. But Windows veterans have always preferred the one-handed method: right-clicking. That is, clicking something by pressing the *right* mouse button on a two-button mouse.

"Ah, but that's what's always driven me nuts about Apple," goes the common refrain. "Their refusal to get rid of their stupid one-button mouse!"

Well, not so fast.

First of all, you can attach any old $6 USB two-button mouse to the Mac, and it'll work flawlessly.

Furthermore, if you bought a desktop Mac since late 2005, you probably already *have* a two-button mouse—but you might not realize it. Take a look: Is it a white shiny plastic capsule with tiny, gray, scrolling track-pea on the far end? Then you have a Mighty Mouse, and it has a *secret* right mouse button. It doesn't work until you ask for it.

To do that, choose  →System Preferences. Click Keyboard & Mouse. Click the Mouse tab. There, in all its splendor, is a diagram of the Mighty Mouse. (There's a picture on page 465.)

Your job is to choose *Secondary Button* from the pop-up menu that identifies the right side of the mouse. (The reason it's not called "right button" is because left-handers might prefer to reverse the right and left functions.)

From now on, even though there aren't two visible mouse buttons, your Mighty Mouse does, in fact, register a left-click or a right-click depending on which *side* of the mouse you push down. It works a lot more easily than it sounds like it would.

The old Control-clicking technique still works. But in this book, you'll be instructed to "right-click" things, since that's probably what you're used to.

---

*Tip:* You can right-click using a Mac laptop's trackpad, too. See page 467.

---

# On, Off, and Sleep

If you're the only person who uses your Mac, finishing up a work session is simple. You can either turn off the machine or simply let it go to sleep, in any of several ways.

## Sleep Mode

It's clear that Apple expects its customers *not* to shut down their machines between sessions, because the company has gone to great lengths to make doing so inconvenient. (For example, you have to save your work in all open programs before you can shut down.)

That's OK. *Sleep mode* (called Standby on the PC) consumes very little power, keeps everything you were doing open and in memory, and wakes the Mac up almost immediately when you press a key or click the mouse. To make your machine sleep, use any of these techniques:

- Choose  →Sleep. (The  menu, available no matter what program you're using, is at the upper-left corner of your screen.)

- Press the Power button on your machine—or, if you don't have one easily accessible, press Control-⏏ key. On some models, doing so makes the Mac sleep immediately; on others, you have to click Sleep in the dialog box that appears (Figure 1-3).

- Just walk away, confident that the Energy Saver control panel described on page 456 will send the machine off to dreamland automatically at the specified time.

**Figure 1-3:**
*Once the Shut Down dialog box appears, you can press the S key instead of clicking Sleep, R for Restart, Esc for Cancel, or Enter for Shut Down.*

## Restart

You shouldn't have to restart the Mac very often. But on those rare occasions, including severe troubleshooting mystification, here are a few ways to do it:

- Choose  →Restart. Click Restart (or press Enter) in the confirmation dialog box.

- Press the Power button or Control-⏏ to summon the dialog box shown in Figure 1-3, if your Mac doesn't automatically go to sleep. Click Restart (or type R).

- If all else fails, press Control-⌘-Power key. (On newer keyboards that lack a power key, use Control-⌘-⏏ instead.) That restarts the Mac instantly, but you lose any chance to save changes in your open documents.

## Shut Down

To shut down your machine completely (when you don't plan to use it for more than a couple of days or when you plan to transport it, for example), do one of the following:

- Choose  →Shut Down. A simple confirmation dialog box appears; click Shut Down (or press Enter).

- Press Control-Option-⌘-⏏. (It's not as complex as it looks—the first three keys are all in a tidy row to the left of the Space bar.)

- Press the Power key or Control-⏏ to summon the dialog box shown in Figure 1-3; click Shut Down (or press Enter).

- As a last resort, hold down the Power key for about five seconds. The Mac will shut down in a snap, but you'll lose any unsaved work.

**Note:** The Macintosh a Hibernate mode, just like the modern Windows PC, but you can't trigger it on command. It kicks in only when you change a laptop's battery.

## Log Out

If you share your Mac with other people, you should *log out* when you're done. Doing so ensures that your stuff is safe from the evil and the clueless when you're out of the room. To do it, choose  →Log Out (or press Shift-⌘-Q). When the confirmation dialog box appears, click Log Out (or press Enter), or just wait for two minutes. The Mac hides your world from view and displays the login dialog box, ready for the next victim.

Another option is to use *fast user switching*—a feature that lets you switch from one user to another without actually logging out, just as in Windows XP or Vista. With fast user switching turned on, your Mac can have several people logged in at once, although only one person at a time actually sees his own desktop.

In either case, this whole accounts system is described in much more detail in Chapter 13.

**Tip:** If you press the Option key as you release the mouse when choosing the Restart, Shut Down, or Log Out commands, you eliminate the "Are you sure?" confirmation dialog box. The mouse clicks you save each time can really add up.

## The Menu Bar

It won't take you long to discover that on the Macintosh, there's only one menu bar. It's always at the top of the screen. The names of these menus, and the commands inside them, change to suit the window you're currently using. That's different from Windows, where a separate menu bar appears at the top of *every* window.

**Note:** Out of the box, Leopard's menu bar is slightly transparent. If that drives you crazy, see page 447.

Mac and Windows devotees can argue the relative merits of these two approaches until they're blue in the face. All that matters, though, is that you know where to look when you want to reach for a menu command. On the Mac, you always look upward.

## Finder = Windows Explorer

In Mac OS X, the "home base" program—the one that appears when you first turn on the machine and shows you the icons of all your folders and files—is called the Finder. This is where you manage your folders and files, throw things away, manipulate disks, and so on. (You may also hear it called the *desktop,* since the items you find there mirror the files and folders you might find on a real-life desktop.)

Getting used to the term Finder is worthwhile right up front, because it comes up so often. For example, the first icon on your Dock is labeled Finder, and clicking it always takes you back to your desktop.

## Dock = Taskbar

At the bottom of almost every Mac OS X screen sits a tiny row of photorealistic icons. This is the Dock, a close parallel to the Windows taskbar. (As in Windows, it may be hidden or placed on the left or right edge of the screen instead—but those are options primarily preferred by power users and eccentrics.)

The Dock displays the icons of all your open windows and programs, which are denoted by small glowing dots beneath their icons. Clicking these icons opens the corresponding files, folders, disks, documents, and programs. If you click and hold (or right-click) an open program's icon, you'll see a pop-up list of the open windows in that program, along with Quit and a few other commands.

When you close a program, its icon disappears from the Dock (unless you've secured it there for easy access, as described on page 66).

---

*Tip:* You can cycle through the various open programs on your Mac by holding down the ⌘ key and pressing Tab repeatedly. (Sound familiar? It's just like Alt-Tabbing in Windows.) And if you just *tap* ⌘-Tab, you bounce back and forth between the two programs you've used most recently.

---

What you may find confusing at first, though, is that the Dock also performs one function of the Windows Start menu: It provides a "short list" of programs and files that you use often, for easy access. To add a new icon to the Dock, just drag it there (put programs to the left of the divider line; everything else goes on the right). To remove an icon from the Dock, just drag the icon away from the Dock. As long as that item isn't actually open at the moment, it disappears from the Dock with a little animated puff of smoke when you release the mouse button.

The bottom line: On the Mac, a single interface element—the Dock—exhibits characteristics of *both* the Start menu (it lists frequently used programs) and the taskbar (it lists currently open programs and files).

If you're still confused, Chapter 2 should help clear things up.

## Menulets = Tray

Most Windows fans refer to the row of tiny status icons at the lower-right corner of the screen as the *tray,* even though Microsoft's official term is the *notification area.* (Why use one syllable when eight will do?)

Macintosh fans wage a similar battle of terminology when it comes to the little menubar icons shown in Figure 1-4. Apple calls them Menu Extras, but Mac fans prefer to call them *menulets.*

In any case, these menu-bar icons are cousins of the Windows tray—that is, each is both an indicator and a menu that provides direct access to certain settings in System Preferences. One menulet lets you adjust your Mac's speaker volume, another lets you change the screen resolution, another shows you the remaining power in your laptop battery, and so on.

**Figure 1-4:**
*These little guys are the direct descendants of the controls once found on the Mac OS 9 Control Strip or the Windows system tray.*

Making a menulet appear usually involves turning on a certain checkbox. These checkboxes lurk on the various panes of *System Preferences* (Chapter 15), which is the Mac equivalent of the Control Panel. (To open System Preferences, choose its name from the  menu, or click the gears icon on the Dock.)

Here's a rundown of the most useful Apple menulets, complete with instructions on where to find this magic on/off checkbox for each.

*Tip:* The following descriptions indicate the official, authorized steps for installing a menulet. There is, however, a folder on your hard drive that contains *25 of them* in a single window, so that you can install one with a quick double-click. To find them, open your hard drive→System→Library→CoreServices→Menu Extras folder.

- **AirPort** lets you turn your AirPort card on or off, join existing AirPort wireless networks, and create your own private ones. *To find the "Show" checkbox:* Open System Preferences→Network. From the "Show" pop-up menu, choose AirPort.

- **Battery** shows how much power remains in your laptop's battery. *To find the "Show" checkbox:* Open System Preferences→Energy Saver→Options tab.

- **Bluetooth** connects to Bluetooth devices, "pairs" your Mac with a cellphone, and so on. *To find the "Show" checkbox:* Open System Preferences→Bluetooth. The "Show Bluetooth status in the menu bar" checkbox appears at the bottom of the Settings tab.

- **Clock** is the standard menu-bar clock that's been sitting at the upper-right corner of your screen from Day 1. Click it to open a menu where you can check today's date, convert the menu-bar display to a tiny analog clock, and so on. *To find the*

*"Show" checkbox:* Open System Preferences→Date & Time. On the Clock tab, turn on "Show the date and time."

- **Displays** adjusts screen resolution. On Macs with a projector or second monitor attached, it lets you turn screen mirroring on or off—a tremendous convenience to anyone who gives PowerPoint or Keynote presentations. *To find the "Show" checkbox:* Open System Preferences→Displays→Display tab.

- ⏏ is the oddball: There's no checkbox in System Preferences to make this menulet appear. The fact that it even exists is something of a secret.

  To make it appear, open your System→Library→CoreServices→Menu Extras folder as described above, and double-click the Eject.menu icon. That's it! The ⏏ menulet appears.

  You'll discover that its wording changes: "Open Combo Drive," "Close DVD-ROM Drive," "Eject [Name of Disc]," or whatever, to reflect your particular drive type and what's in it at the moment.

- **Fax** reveals the current status of a fax you're sending or receiving, so you're not kept in suspense. *To find the "Show" checkbox:* Open System Preferences→Print & Fax, and then click Faxing.

- **iChat** is a quick way to let the world know, via iChat and the Internet (Chapter 12), that you're away from your keyboard, or available and ready to chat. Via the Buddy List command, it's also a quick way to open iChat itself. *To find the "Show" checkbox:* Open iChat; it's in your Applications folder. Choose iChat→Preferences, click the General button, and turn on "Show status in menu bar."

- **PPP** lets you connect or disconnect from the Internet. *To find the "Show" checkbox:* Open System Preferences→Network. From the "Show" pop-up menu, choose Internal Modem. Click the Modem tab button.

- **Script menu** lists a variety of useful, ready-to-run AppleScript programs (see page 480). *To find the "Show" checkbox:* Open your Applications folder, and then open the program called AppleScript Utility.

- **Sync** is useful only if you have a .Mac account (page 295)—but in that case, it's *very* handy. It lets you start and stop the synchronization of your Mac's Web bookmarks, calendar, address book, Keychains, and email with another Mac across the Internet, and it always lets you know the date of your last sync. (Syncing is described in more detail in Chapter 9.) *To find the "Show" checkbox:* Open System Preferences→.Mac, and then click Sync.

- **TextInput** (officially named the Input Menu) makes it easy for you to switch among different *text input modes.* You're probably most familiar with the normal keyboard. But what if your language uses a different alphabet, like Russian, or thousands of characters, like Chinese? This menulet summons and dismisses the alternative keyboards and input methods needed for these other systems. Details on page 460. *To find the "Show" checkbox:* Open System Preferences→International. Click the Input Menu tab.

***Note:*** You also use this menulet when you're trying to figure out how to type a certain symbol like ¥ or §
or ♥. You use the menulet to open the Character Palette and Keyboard Viewer—two great character-finding
tools that are described in Chapter 9.

- **User** identifies the account holder (Chapter 13) who's logged in at the moment.
  To make this menulet appear (in bold, at the far right end of the menu bar), turn
  on *fast user switching,* which is described on page 400.

- **Volume,** of course, adjusts your Mac's speaker or headphone volume. *To find the
  "Show" checkbox:* Open System Preferences→Sound.

To remove a menulet, ⌘-drag it off of your menu bar, or turn off the corresponding
checkbox in System Preferences. You can also rearrange them by ⌘-dragging them
horizontally.

These little guys are useful, good-looking, and respectful of your screen space. The
world could use more inventions like menulets.

# Keyboard Differences

Mac and PC keyboards are subtly different, too. Making the switch involves two big
adjustments: Figuring out where the special Windows keys went (like Alt and Ctrl)—
and figuring out what to do with the special Macintosh keys (like ⌘ and Option).

## Where the Windows Keys Went

Here's how to find the Macintosh equivalents of familiar PC keyboard keys:

- **Ctrl key.** The Macintosh offers a key labeled Control (or, on laptops, "ctrl"), but
  it isn't the equivalent of the PC's Ctrl key. The Mac's Control key is primarily for
  helping you "right-click" things, as described earlier.

  Instead, the Macintosh equivalent of the *Windows* Ctrl key is the ⌘ key. It's right
  next to the Space bar, bearing the cloverleaf symbol and, on older Macs, the 
  logo. It's pronounced "command," although novices can often be heard calling it
  the "pretzel key," "Apple key," or "clover key."

  Most Windows Ctrl-key combos correspond perfectly to ⌘ key sequences on the
  Mac. The Save command is now ⌘-S instead of Ctrl-S, Open is ⌘-O instead of
  Ctrl-O, and so on.

***Note:*** Mac keyboard shortcuts are listed at the right side of each open menu, just as in Windows. Unfortunately, they're represented in the menu with goofy symbols instead of their true key names. Here's your
cheat sheet to the menu keyboard symbols: ⇧ represents the Shift key, ⌥ means the Option key, and ^
refers to the Control key.

• **Alt key.** On most Mac keyboards, a key on the bottom row of the Macintosh keyboard is labeled both Alt and Option (at least on Macs sold in the U.S.). This is the closest thing the Mac offers to the old Alt key.

In many situations, keyboard shortcuts that involve the Alt key in Windows use the Option key on the Mac. For example, in Microsoft Word, the keyboard shortcut for the Split Document Window command is *Alt*-Ctrl-S in Windows, but *Option*-⌘-T on the Macintosh.

Still, these two keys aren't exactly the same. Whereas the Alt key's most popular function is to control the menus in Windows programs, the Option key on the Mac is a "miscellaneous" key that triggers secret functions and secret characters.

For example, when you hold down the Option key as you click the Close or Minimize button on a Macintosh window, you close or minimize *all* open desktop windows. And if you press the Option key while you type R, G, or 2, you get the ®, ©, and ™ symbols in your document, respectively. (See page 463 to find out how you can see which letters turn into which symbols when you press Option.)

• **⊞ key.** As you probably could have guessed, there is no Windows-logo key on the Macintosh. Then again, there's no Start menu to open by pressing it, either.

---

*Tip:* Just about any USB keyboard works on the Mac, even if the keyboard was originally designed to work with a PC. Depending on the manufacturer of the keyboard, the Windows-logo key may work just like the Mac's ⌘ key.

---

• **Backspace and Delete.** On the Mac, the backspace key is labeled Delete, although it's in exactly the same place as the Windows Backspace key.

The Delete key in Windows (technically, the *forward delete* key, because it deletes the character to the right of the insertion point) is a different story. On a desktop Macintosh, it's labeled with the word *Del* and the ⌦ symbol.

On small Mac keyboards (like laptop keyboars), this key is missing. You can still perform a forward delete, however, by pressing the regular Delete key while pressing the Fn key in the corner of the keyboard.

• **Enter.** Most full-size Windows keyboards have *two* Enter keys: one at the right side of the alphabet keyboard, and one at the lower-right corner of the number pad. They're identical in function; pressing either one serves to "click" the OK button in a dialog box, for example.

On the Mac, the big key on the number pad still says Enter, but the key on the alphabet keyboard is labeled Return. Most of the time, their function is identical—once again, either can "click" the OK button of a dialog box. Every now and then, though, you'll run across a Mac program where Return and Enter do different things. In Microsoft Word for Mac OS X, for example, Shift-*Return* inserts a line break, but Shift-*Enter* creates a page break.

---

*Note:* See page 261 for a summary of the Mac's text-navigation keystrokes.

---

## What the Special Mac Keys Do

So much for finding Windows keys you're used to. There's another category of keys worth discussing, however: keys on the modern Macintosh keyboard that you've never seen before.

To make any attempt at an explanation even more complicated, Apple's keyboards keep changing. The one you're using right now is probably one of four models:

- The standard white desktop keyboard, made of plastic.

- The new, superthin aluminum keyboard that comes with the iMac (Figure 1-5).

- The new, superthin aluminum *wireless* Bluetooth keyboard that you can buy as an option. It has no separate block of number keys, so it's almost exactly like the Apple laptop keyboard. In the following discussion, in fact, any references to the Mac laptop keyboards also include this Bluetooth wireless one.

- The Apple laptop keyboard, which has no numeric keypad, either.

**Figure 1-5:**
*The aluminum Mac keyboards turn the F-keys on the top row into completely different buttons—according to a scheme that's different from most Mac laptops.*

*Here, you can see that tapping the F1 through F4 keys correspond to Screen Dimmer, Screen Brighter, Exposé, and Dashboard.*

*(The Exposé key works three different ways, depending on what modifier key you're pressing. See page 116.)*

Here, then, is a guided tour of the non-typewriter keys on modern Mac keyboard.

- **Fn.** How are you supposed to pronounce Fn? Not "function," certainly; after all, the F-keys on the top row are already known as function keys. And not "fun"; goodness knows, the Fn key isn't particularly hilarious to press.

  What it does, though, is quite clear: It changes the purpose of certain keys. That's a big deal on laptops, which don't have nearly as many keys as desktop keyboards. So for some of the less commonly used functions, you're supposed to press Fn and a regular key. (For example, Fn turns the ↑ key into a Home key, which scrolls to the top of a window or a list.)

  You'll find many more Fn examples in the following paragraphs.

• **Numeric keypad.** The number-pad keys do exactly the same thing as the numbers at the top of the keyboard. But with practice, typing things like phone numbers and prices is much faster with the number pad, since you don't have to look down at what you're doing.

Now, at first glance, only desktop keyboards appear to have these blocks of number keys. But if you look at some Mac laptops closely, you may see that the numbers 0 through 9 have actually been painted onto a block of *letter* keys near the right side. (1, 2, and 3 are J, K, and L, for example.)

You can turn those letter keys into their numeric alter egos in either of two ways. First, you can press the NumLock key at the top of the keyboard, which turns on the numbers and keeps them on until you press NumLock again. Or, for just a couple of quick numbers, you can hold down the Fn key with your left hand.

---

*Note:* Apple is phasing out this "embedded keypad" effect, mainly because there are more people who hit that NumLock key accidentally (thus turning off all their alphabet keys) than there are people who actually type numbers with that embedded number pad.

---

• ◀, ◀», and ◀»)). These three buttons control your speaker volume. The ◀ key represents the Mute button; tap it once to cut off the sound completely, and again to bring it back to its previous level. Tap the ◀» repeatedly to make the sound level lower, the ◀»)) key to make it louder.

With each tap, you see a big white version of each key's symbol on your screen, your Mac's little nod to let you know that it understands your efforts.

• ⏏. This is the Eject key. When there's a CD or DVD in your Mac, tap this key to make the computer spit it out. If your Mac has a sliding CD/DVD tray (rather than just a slot), hold down this button for about a second to make the tray slide open.

• **Home, End.** "Home" and "End" mean "jump to the top or bottom of the window." If you're looking at a list of files, the Home and End keys jump to the top or bottom of the list. In iPhoto, they jump to the first or last photo in your collection. In iMovie, the Home key rewinds your movie to the very beginning. In Safari, it's the top or bottom of the Web page.

(In Word, they jump to the beginning or end of the line. But then again, Microsoft has always had its own ways of doing things.)

On laptops, you get these functions by holding down Fn as you tap the ← and → keys.

• **Pg Up, Pg Down.** These keys scroll up or down by one screenful. The idea is to let you scroll through word processing documents, Web pages, and lists without having to use the mouse.

On laptops, you get these functions by holding down Fn as you tap the ↑ and ↓ keys.

- **Clear.** Clear gets rid of the you've highlighted, but without putting a copy on the invisible Clipboard, as the Cut command would do.

- **Esc.** Esc stands for Escape, and just as in Windows, it means "Cancel." It's fantastically useful. It closes dialog boxes, closes menus, and exits special modes like Quick Look, Front Row, slideshows, screen savers, and so on. Get to know it.

- **Delete.** The backspace key.

- ⌦. If you're used to Windows keyboards, you already know about this delightful little key: the Forward Delete key.

  Whereas Delete backspaces over whatever letter is just *before* the insertion point, this one (labeled Del on some keyboards) deletes whatever is just to the *right* of the insertion point. It really comes in handy when, for example, you've clicked into some text to make an edit—but wound up planting your cursor in just the wrong place.

  On laptops, you get this function by holding down Fn as you tap the regular Delete key.

- ⌘. This key triggers keyboard shortcuts for menu items, as described above.

- **Control.** The Control key triggers shortcut menus, as described above.

- **Option.** The Option key (labeled Alt on keyboards in some countries) is sort of a "miscellaneous" key. It's the equivalent of the Alt key in Windows.

  It lets you access secret features—you'll find them described all through this book—and type special symbols. For example, you press Option-4 to get the ¢ symbol, and Option-y to get the ¥ yen symbol.

- **Help.** In the Finder, Microsoft programs, and a few other places, this key opens up the electronic help screens. But you guessed that.

- **F1, F2, F3...** OK, here's where things start to get really complicated.

  In the beginning, the F1, F2, F3, and F4 keys corresponded to the Undo, Cut, Copy, and Paste menu commands. And on Apple's traditional plastic keyboards, they still do. But Apple discovered that not many people were using them for anything. So today, modern Mac keyboards come with those keys reassigned to other functions.

  On laptops, F1 through F4 govern screen brightness (☼ and ☀) and speaker volume (◀, ◀), and ◀))).

  On the aluminum desktop-Mac keyboards, F1 and F2 govern screen brightness, F3 triggers Exposé (page 116), and F4 opens Dashboard (page 150), as shown in Figure 1-5. The ◀, ◀), and ◀)) volume keys have been moved to F10 through F12.

  So the question is: What if you don't *want* to trigger the hardware features of these keys? What if you want pressing F1 to mean "F1" (which opens the Help window in most programs)?

For that purpose, you're supposed to press the Fn key. The Fn key (lower-right on laptops and Bluetooth keyboards, center block of keys on the big aluminum one) switches the function of the function keys.

*Tip:* You can reverse the logic, too, so that pressing the F-keys usually triggers software functions, and governs brightness and audio only when you're pressing Fn. See page 464.

The aluminum keyboards also have playback controls (◄◄, ►/II, and ►►) painted on the F7 through F9 keys. They work in QuickTime Player, DVD Player, iTunes, and other programs where it's handy to have Rewind, Play/Pause, and Fast Forward buttons.

## Disk Differences

Working with disks is very different on the Mac. Whereas Windows is designed to show the names (letters) and icons for your disk *drives,* the Mac shows you the names and icons of your *disks.* You'll never, ever see an icon for an empty drive, as you do on Windows.

As soon as you insert, say, a CD, you see its name and icon appear on the screen. In fact, *every* disk inside, or attached to, a Macintosh is represented on the desktop by an icon (see Figure 1-6). That's why the icon for your primary hard drive has been sitting in the upper-right corner of your screen since the first time you turned on the Mac. (It's usually named Macintosh HD.)

If you prefer the Windows look, in which no disk icons appear on the desktop, it's easy enough to re-create it on the Mac; choose Finder→ Preferences and turn off the four checkboxes you see there ("Hard disks," "External disks," "CDs, DVDs, and iPods," and "Connected servers."

**Figure 1-6:**
*You may see all kinds of disks on the Mac OS X desktop (shown here: hard drive, CD, iPod, iDisk)—or none at all, if you've chosen to hide them using the Finder→Preferences command. But chances are pretty good you won't be seeing many floppy disk icons.*

*If you do decide to hide your disk icons, you can always get to them as you do in Windows: by opening the Computer window (Go→Computer).*

Ejecting a disc from the Mac is a little bit different, too, whether it's a CD, DVD, USB flash drive, shared network disk, iDisk, iPod, or external hard drive. You can go about it in any of these ways:

- Hold down the ⏏ key on your keyboard (CDs and DVDs only).

- Right-click the disk's desktop icon. From the shortcut menu that appears, choose "Eject [whatever the disk's name is]."

- Click the disk's icon and then choose File→"Eject [disk's name]" (or press ⌘-E).

- Drag the icon of the disk onto the Trash icon at the end of the Dock. (You'll see its icon turn into a giant ⏏ symbol, the Mac's little acknowledgment that it knows what you're trying to do.)

For you, the Windows veteran, the main thing to remember here is that you *never eject a Macintosh disk by pushing the Eject button* on the disk drive itself (if there even is one). Doing so usually has no effect, but on the rare occasion that it does, you could end up seriously confusing Mac OS X.

# Where Your Stuff Is

The icon for your hard drive (usually called Macintosh HD) generally appears in the upper-right corner of your screen. If you double-click it, all you'll find in the Macintosh HD window is a set of folders called Applications, Library, and Users.

Most of these folders aren't very useful to you, the Mac's human companion. They're there for Mac OS X's own use (which is why the Finder→Preferences dialog box offers a checkbox that hides their icons entirely). Think of your main hard drive window as storage for the operating system itself, which you'll access only for occasional administrative purposes.

In fact, the folders you really do care about boil down to these:

## Applications Folder

*Applications* is Apple's word for *programs*.

When it comes to managing your programs, the Applications folder (which you can open by choosing Go→Applications) is something like the Program Files folder in Windows—but without the worry. You should feel free to open this folder and double-click things. In fact, that's exactly what you're supposed to do. This is your complete list of programs. (What's on your Dock is more like a Greatest Hits subset.)

Better yet, on the Mac, programs bear their real, plain-English names, like *Microsoft Word,* rather than eight-letter abbreviations, like *WINWORD.EXE.* Most are self-contained in a single icon, too (rather than being composed of hundreds of little support files), which makes copying or deleting them extremely easy.

# Home Folder

Your documents, files, and preferences, meanwhile, sit in an important folder called your *Home folder*. Inside (Figure 1-7) are folders that closely resemble the My Documents, My Pictures, and My Music folders on Windows—except that on the Mac, they don't say "My."

What's in the hard drive window     A Home folder for each account holder     What's in your Home folder

**Figure 1-7:**
*This is it: the folder structure of Mac OS X. It's not so bad, really. For the most part, what you care about are the Applications folder in the main hard drive window and your own Home folder. You're welcome to save your documents and park your icons almost anywhere on your Mac (except inside the System folder or other people's Home folders). But keeping your work in your Home folder makes backing up and file sharing easier.*

Mac OS X is rife with shortcuts for opening this all-important folder.

- Choose Go→Home.

- Press Shift-⌘-H.

- Click the Home icon in the Sidebar (page 32).

- Click the Home icon on the Dock. (If you don't see one, consult page 60 for instructions on how to put one there.)

Within your Home folder, you'll find another set of standard Mac folders. (You can tell that the Mac considers them holy because they have special logos on their folder icons.) Except as noted, you're free to rename or delete them; Mac OS X creates the following folders solely as a convenience:

- **Desktop.** When you drag an icon out of a folder or disk window and onto your Mac OS X desktop, it may appear to show up on the desktop. But that's just an optical illusion, a visual convenience. In truth, nothing in Mac OS X is really on the desktop. It's actually in this Desktop folder, and mirrored on the desktop area.

  You can entertain yourself for hours by proving this point to yourself. If you drag something out of your Desktop folder, it also disappears from the actual desktop. And vice versa. (You're not allowed to delete or rename this folder.)

- **Documents.** Apple suggests that you keep your actual work files in this folder. Sure enough, whenever you save a new document (when you're working in Keynote or Word, for example), the Save As box proposes storing the new file in this folder, as described in Chapter 4.

  Your programs may also create folders of their own here. For example, you may find a Microsoft User Data folder for your Entourage email, a Windows folder for use with Parallels or VMWare Fusion (Chapter 8), and so on.

- **Library.** The main Library folder (the one in your main hard drive window) contains folders for your Mac's system-wide fonts, preferences, help files, and so on.

  You have your *own* Library folder, too, right there in your Home folder. It stores the same kinds of things—but they're *your* fonts, your preferences, and so on.

- **Movies, Music, Pictures.** These folders, of course, are designed to store multimedia files. The various Mac OS X programs that deal with movies, music, and pictures will propose these specialized folders as storage locations. For example, when you plug a digital camera into a Mac, the iPhoto program automatically begins to download the photos on it—and stores them in the Pictures folder. Similarly, iMovie is programmed to look for the Movies folder when saving its files, and iTunes stores its MP3 files in the Music folder.

- **Public.** If you're on a network, or if others use the same Mac when you're not around, this folder can be handy: It's the "Any of you guys can look at these files" folder. Other people on your network, as well as other people who sit down at this machine, are allowed to see whatever you've put in here, even if they don't have your password. (If your Mac isn't on an office network and isn't shared, you can throw away this folder.) Details on sharing the Mac are in Chapter 13, and those on networking are in Chapter14.

- **Sites.** Mac OS X has a built-in Web server: software that turns your Mac into a Web site that people on your network—or, via the Internet, all over the world—can connect to. This Mac OS X feature relies on a program called the Apache Web server, which is so highly regarded in the Unix community that programmers lower their voices when they mention it. This is the folder where you will put the actual Web pages you want to make available to the Internet at large.

The rationale for forcing you to keep all of your stuff in a single folder is described in Chapter 13. (Windows 2000, XP, and Vista work very similarly.) For now, it's enough to note that the approach has some major advantages. Most notably, by keeping such tight control over which files go where, Mac OS X keeps itself pure—and very, very stable.

## System Folder

This folder is the same idea as the Windows or WINNT folder on a PC, in that it contains hundreds of files that are critical to the functioning of the operating system. These files are so important that moving or renaming them could render the computer useless, as it would in Windows. And although there are thousands of files within, many are hidden for your protection.

For maximum safety and stability, you should ignore Mac OS X's System folder just as thoroughly as you ignored the old Windows folder.

## Window Controls

As in Windows, a window on the Mac is framed by an assortment of doodads and gizmos (Figure 1-8). You'll need these to move a window, close it, resize it, scroll it, and so on. But once you get to know the ones on a Macintosh, you're likely to be pleased by the amount of thought those fussy perfectionists at Apple have put into their design.

Close button
Minimize button
Zoom button    Toolbar    Folder proxy icon    Search box    "Old Finder mode" button

Sidebar    Status bar    Scroll bar    Resizing handle

*Figure 1-8:*
*When Steve Jobs unveiled Mac OS X at a Macworld Expo in 1999, he said that his goal was to oversee the creation of an interface so attractive, "you just want to lick it." Desktop windows, with their juicy, fruit-flavored controls, are a good starting point.*

Here's an overview of the various Mac OS X window-edge gizmos and what they do.

### Title Bar

When several windows are open, the darkened window name and colorful upper-left controls tell you which window is *active* (in front). Windows in the background have gray, dimmed lettering and gray upper-left control buttons. As in Windows, the title bar also acts as a *handle* that lets you move the entire window around on the screen.

**Tip:** Here's a nifty keyboard shortcut with no Windows equivalent: You can cycle through the different open windows in one program without using the mouse. Just press ⌘-` (that's the tilde key, to the left of the number 1 key). With each press, you bring a different window forward within the current program. It works both in the Finder and in your programs.

Perhaps more usefully, you can use Control-F4 to cycle through the open windows in *all* programs.

After you've opened one folder inside another, the title bar's secret *folder hierarchy menu* is an efficient way to backtrack—to return to the enclosing window. Figure 1-9 reveals everything about the process after this key move: pressing the ⌘ key as you click the name of the window. (You can release the ⌘ key immediately after clicking.)

**Tip:** Instead of using this title bar menu, you can also jump to the enclosing window by pressing ⌘-up arrow. Pressing ⌘-down arrow takes you back into the folder you started in. (This makes more sense when you try it than when you read it.)

**Figure 1-9:**
*Right-click (or ⌘-click) a Finder window's title bar to summon the hidden folder hierarchy menu.*

*This trick also works in most other Mac OS X programs. For example, you can ⌘-click a document window's title to find out where the document is actually saved on your hard drive.*

One more title bar trick: By double-clicking the title bar, you *minimize* the window (see the page 31).

**Tip:** The Option key means "apply this action to all windows." For example, Option-double-clicking any title bar minimizes *all* desktop windows, sending them flying to the Dock. Option-clicking the Close button closes all open desktop windows, and so on. (The Option-key trick doesn't close all windows in every program, however—only those in the current program. Option-closing a Safari window closes *Safari* windows, but your desktop windows remain open. Moreover, Option-closing doesn't work at all in Microsoft Office programs.)

## The Folder Proxy Icon

Virtually every Macintosh title bar features a small icon next to the window's name (Figure 1-10), representing the open window's actual folder or disk icon. In the Finder, dragging this tiny icon (technically called the *folder proxy icon*) lets you move or copy the folder to a different folder or disk, to the Trash, or into the Dock, without having to close the window first. (When clicking this proxy icon, hold down the mouse button for a half second, or until the icon darkens. Only then are you allowed to drag it.) It's a handy little function with no Windows equivalent.

---

**Tip:** In some programs, including Microsoft Word, dragging this proxy icon lets you move the *actual file* to a different disk or folder—without even leaving the program. It's a great way to make a backup of the document that you're working on without interrupting your work.

---

**Figure 1-10:**
When you find yourself confronting a Finder window that contains useful stuff, consider dragging its proxy icon to the Dock. You wind up installing its folder or disk icon there for future use. That's not the same as minimizing the window, which puts the window icon into the Dock, and only temporarily at that. (Note: Most Mac OS X document windows also offer a proxy-icon feature, but produce only an alias when you drag the proxy to a different folder or disk.)

## Close Button

As the tip of your cursor crosses the three buttons at the upper-left corner of a window, tiny symbols appear inside them: x, –, and +. The most important window gadget is the Close button, the red, droplet-like button in the upper-left corner (see Figure 1-10). It closes the window, exactly like the X button at the upper-*right* corner in Windows. Learning to reach for the upper-left corner instead of the upper-right will probably confound your muscle memory for the first week of using the Macintosh.

If you can't break the old habit, you can avoid the frustration entirely by learning the keyboard shortcut: ⌘-W (for *window*)—an easier keystroke to type than the

Windows version (Alt+F4), which for most people is a two-handed operation. If you get into the habit of dismissing windows with that deft flex of your left hand, you'll find it far easier to close several windows in a row, because you don't have to aim for successive close buttons.

*Tip:* If, while working on a document, you see a tiny dot in the center of the Close button, Mac OS X is trying to tell you that you haven't yet saved your work. The dot goes away when you save the document.

## Minimize Button

Click this yellow drop of gel to minimize any Mac window, sending it shrinking, with a genie-like animated effect, into the right end of the Dock, where it now appears as an icon. It's exactly like minimizing a window in Windows, except that the window is now represented by a Dock icon rather than a taskbar button (Figure 1-11). To bring the window back to full size, click the newly created Dock icon. See Chapter 2 for more on the Dock.

*Tip:* If you enjoy the ability to roll up your windows in this way, remember that you actually have a bigger target than the tiny minimize button. The entire striped title bar becomes a giant minimize button when you double-click anywhere on it.

Better yet, you can minimize a window from the keyboard (in most programs) by pressing ⌘-M. That's a keystroke worth memorizing on Day One.

*Figure 1-11:*
*Clicking the Minimize button sends a window scurrying down to the Dock, collapsing in on itself as though being forced through a tiny, invisible funnel. A tiny icon appears on the lower-right corner of its minimized image to identify the program it's running in.*

## Zoom Button

A click on this green geltab (see Figure 1-8) makes a desktop window just large enough to show you all of the icons inside it. If your monitor isn't big enough to show all the icons in a window, the zoom box resizes the window to show as many as possible. In either case, a second click on the zoom button restores the window to its original size. (The Window→Zoom Window command does the same thing.)

This should sound familiar: It's a lot like the Maximize button at the top right of a Windows window. On the Macintosh, however, the window rarely springs so big that it fills the *entire* screen, leaving a lot of empty space around the window contents; it only grows enough to show you as much of the contents as possible.

## The Finder Sidebar

The Sidebar is the pane at the left side of every Finder window (and, by the way, also at the left side of every Open dialog box and full-sized Save dialog box). It's a list (identified in Figure 1-8) with as many as four different sections, each preceded by a collapsible heading:

- **Devices.** This section lists every storage device connected to, or installed inside, your Mac: hard drives, CDs, DVDs, iPods, memory cards, USB flash drives, and so on. The removable ones (CDs, DVDs, iPods, and so on) bear a little gray ⏏ logo, which you can click to eject that disk.

- **Shared.** It took 20 years for an operating system to list all the other computers on the home or small-office network, right there in every window, without any digging, connecting, button-clicking, or window-opening. But here it is: a complete list of the other computers on your network whose owners have turned on File Sharing, ready for access. See Chapter 14 for complete details.

- **Places.** This primary section of the sidebar lists *places* (in this case, folders) where you might look for files and folders. Into this list, you can stick the icons of anything at all—files, programs, folders, disks, or whatever—for easy access.

  Each icon is a shortcut. For example, click the Applications icon to view the contents of your Applications folder in the main part of the window. And if you click the icon of a file or program here, it opens.

- **Searches.** The "folders" in this Sidebar section are actually canned searches that execute instantly when you click one. If you click Today, for example, the main window fills with all files and folders on your computer that you've changed today. Yesterday and Past Week work the same way.

  The All Images, All Movies, and All Documents searches round up everything in those file-type categories, no matter what folders they're actually sitting in.

  These insta-searches are very useful all by themselves, but what's even better is how easy it is to make your *own* search folders to put here. Page 109 has the details.

### Fine-tuning the Sidebar

The beauty of this parking lot for containers is that it's so easy to set up with *your* favorite places. For example:

- **Remove** an icon by dragging it out of the Sidebar entirely. It vanishes with a puff of smoke (and even a little *whoof* sound effect). You haven't actually removed anything from your *Mac;* you've just unhitched its alias from the Sidebar.

---

***Tip:*** You can't drag Shared items out of the list. Also, if you drag a Devices item out of the list, you'll have to choose Finder→Preferences to put it back in.

---

- **Rearrange** the icons by dragging them up or down in the list. (You're not allowed to rearrange the computers listed in the Shared section, though.)

- **Install a new icon** by dragging it off your desktop (or out of a window) into any spot in the Places list of the Sidebar.

---

***Tip:*** You can also highlight an icon wherever it happens to be and then choose File→Add to Sidebar, or just press ⌘-T.

---

- **Adjust the width** of the Sidebar by dragging its *right edge*—either the skinny divider line or the extreme right edge of the vertical scroll bar, if there is one. You "feel" a snap at the point when the line covers up about half of each icon's name. Any covered-up names sprout ellipses (…) to let you know (as in "Secret Salaries Spreadsh…").

- **Hide the Sidebar** by clicking the Old Finder Mode button, a white, capsule-like button in the upper-right corner of the window, or using its menu equivalent (View→Hide Toolbar).

## Window Management

Mac OS X prefers to keep only one Finder window open at a time. That is, if a window called United States is filled with folders for the individual states, double-clicking the New York folder doesn't open a second window. Instead, the New York window replaces the United States window. Modern versions of Windows work exactly the same way.

So what if you've now opened inner folder B, and you want to backtrack to outer folder A? In that case, just click the tiny ◀ (Back) button or use one of these alternatives:

- Choose Go→Back.

- Press ⌘-[ (left bracket).

- Press ⌘-up arrow.

None of that helps you, however, if you want to copy a file from one folder into another, or compare the contents of two windows. In such cases, you'll probably want to see both windows open at the same time.

You can open a second window using any of these techniques:

- Choose File→New Finder Window (⌘-N).

---

**Tip:** The window that appears when you do this is your Home folder by default, but you can change that setting in Finder→Preferences→General.

---

- ⌘-double-click a disk or folder icon.

- Choose File→Preferences, and turn on "Always open folders in a new window." Now when you double-click a folder, it always opens into a new window.

Another alternative is to switch to "Old Finder mode" (not the official Apple terminology). The upper-right corner of every Finder window contains a little button

**Figure 1-12:**
*To help you avoid window clutter, Apple has designed Mac OS X windows so that double-clicking a folder in a window (top) doesn't actually open another window (bottom). Every time you double-click a folder in an open window (except in column view), its contents replace whatever was previously in the window. If you double-click three folders in succession, you still wind up with just one open window.*

that looks like a half-inch squirt of Crest toothpaste. When you click it, you enter a hidden-toolbar, hidden-Sidebar mode. (You can also enter this mode by pressing Option-⌘-T, the equivalent for the View→Hide Toolbar command.)

In this mode, two things happen. First, the Finder window toolbar slides out of sight, along with the Sidebar on the left. Second, double-clicking a folder now opens a new corresponding window.

You can return to regular Mac OS X mode by clicking the toolbar button again, by pressing Option-⌘-T again, or by choosing View→Show Toolbar.

*Note:* You'll find this little white toolbar-control nubbin in a number of toolbar-endowed programs, including Mail, Preview, and others. Clicking it always makes the toolbar go away.

## Scroll Bars

In general, scroll bars work on the Mac just as they do in Windows.

*Tip:* One key difference: Out of the box, the Mac's scroll-up arrow and scroll-down arrow are nestled together, at the same end of the scroll bar. To "fix" them so that they sit at opposite ends as in Windows, choose ⌘→System Preferences. Click Appearance. Where it says "Place scroll arrows," click "At top and bottom."

Mac OS X, however, offers an option called "Scroll to here." Ordinarily, when you click into the scroll-bar track above or below the gelatinous handle, the window scrolls by one screenful. But your other option is to turn on "Scroll to here" mode in the Appearance panel of your System Preferences (see page 440). Now when you click in the scroll-bar track, the Mac considers the entire scroll bar a proportional map of the document and scrolls directly to the spot you clicked. That is, if you click at the very bottom of the scroll-bar track, you see the very last page.

It's worth noting, however, that the true speed expert eschews scroll bars altogether. The Mac has the usual complement of navigation keys: Page Up, Page Down, Home, and End. And if your mouse has a scroll wheel on the top, you can use it to scroll windows, too, without pressing any keys at all.

## Resize Box

The lower-right corner of every standard Mac OS X window is ribbed, a design that's meant to imply that you can grip it by dragging. Doing so lets you resize and reshape the window, just as on the PC. Unfortunately, you can't also change the shape of a Macintosh window by dragging its *edges,* as you can in Windows.

## Path Bar

This little item appears when you choose View→Show Path Bar. It's a tiny map at the bottom of the window that shows where you are in the folder hierarchy. If it says Casey▸Pictures▸Picnic, well, then, by golly, you're looking at the contents of the Picnic folder, which is inside Pictures, inside your Home folder.

*Tip:* Each tiny folder icon in this display is fully operational. You can double-click it to open it, right-click it to open a shortcut menu, or even drag things into it.

## Status Bar

The information strip at the bottom of a window tells you how many icons are in it ("14 items," for example) and the amount of free space remaining on the disk.

# Terminology Differences

There are enough other differences between Mac and Windows to fill 15 pages. Indeed, that's what you'll find the end of this book: an alphabetical listing of every familiar Windows feature and where to find its equivalent on the Mac.

As you read both that section of the book and the chapters that precede it, however, you'll discover that some functions are almost identical in Mac OS X and Windows, but have different names. Here's a quick-reference summary:

| **Windows term** | **Macintosh term** |
|---|---|
| Control Panel | System Preferences |
| Gadget | Widget |
| Drop-down menu | Pop-up menu |
| Program | Application |
| Properties | Get Info |
| Recycle Bin | Trash |
| Search command | Spotlight |
| Shortcuts | Aliases |
| Sidebar | Dashboard |
| Taskbar | Dock |
| Tray (notification area) | Menulets |
| Windows Explorer | Finder |
| Windows folder | System folder |

With that much under your belt, you're well on your way to learning the ways of Mac OS X.

# Folders, Dock, & Windows

## Getting into Mac OS X

When you first turn on a Mac that's running Mac OS X 10.5, an Apple logo greets you, soon followed by an animated, rotating "Please wait" gear cursor—and then you're in. No progress bar, no red tape.

**Figure 2-1:**
*Left: On Macs configured to accom-modate different people at different times, this is one of the first things you see upon turning on the computer. Click your name. (If the list is long, you may have to scroll to find your name—or just type the first few letters of it.)*

*Right: At this point, you're asked to type in your password. Type it, and then click Log In (or press Return or Enter; pressing these keys usually "clicks" any blue, pulsing button in a dialog box). If you've typed the wrong password, the entire dialog box vibrates, in effect shaking its little dialog-box head, suggesting that you guess again. (See Chapter 13.)*

## Logging In

What happens next depends on whether you're the Mac's sole proprietor or have to share it with other people in an office, school, or household.

- **If it's your own Mac,** and you've already been through the Mac OS X setup process described in Appendix A, no big deal. You arrive at the Mac OS X desktop.

- **If it's a shared Mac,** you may encounter the Login dialog box, shown in Figure 2-1. Click your name in the list (or type it, if there's no list).

If the Mac asks for your password, type it and then click Log In (or press Return). You arrive at the desktop. Chapter 13 offers much more on this business of user accounts and logging in.

## The Elements of the Mac OS X Desktop

The *desktop* is the shimmering, three-dimensional Mac OS X landscape shown in Figure 2-2. On a new Mac, it's covered by a starry galaxy photo that belongs to Leopard's overall outer-space graphic theme.

If you've ever used a computer before, most of the objects on your screen are nothing more than updated versions of familiar elements. Here's a quick tour.

Apple menu   Menu bar   Desktop   Menulets

Dock   Divider   Trash

**Figure 2-2:**
*The Mac OS X landscape looks like a more futuristic version of the operating systems you know and love. This is just a starting point, however. You can dress it up with a different background picture, adjust your windows in a million ways, and, of course, fill the Dock with only the programs, disks, folders, and files you need.*

### Disk icons

In the Mac world, the icons of your hard drive and any other disks attached to your Mac generally appear on your desktop for quick access.

---

**Note:** If you prefer the setup in Windows, where disks remain safely caged in the My Computer window— Leopard can accommodate you. Choose Finder→Preferences, click General, and turn off the checkboxes of the disks whose icons you don't want on the desktop: Hard disks, External disks, and so on.

From now on, you'll have to look in the Sidebar (page 32) or the Computer window (Go→Computer) to find those disk icons.

---

### The Dock

This row of translucent, almost photographic icons is a launcher for the programs, files, folders, and disks you use often—and an indicator to let you know which programs are already open. In Leopard, they now rest on what appears to be a polished, highly reflective shelf.

Because the Dock is such a critical component of Mac OS X, Apple has decked it out with enough customization controls to keep you busy experimenting for months. You can change its size, move it to the sides of your screen, hide it entirely, and so on. Page 60 begins a complete discussion of using and understanding the Dock.

### The  menu

The  menu at the top left of the screen houses important Mac-wide commands like Sleep, Restart, and Shut Down. In a sense, it's like the Start menu on a diet: It lists recent programs, system-wide functions, and includes a quick way to jump to System Preferences.

### The menu bar

The first menu in every program, in boldface, tells you at a glance what program you're in. The commands in this Application menu include About (which tells you what version of the program you're using), Preferences, Quit, and others like Hide Others and Show All (which help you control window clutter, as described on page 127).

The File and Edit menus come next, exactly as in Windows. The last menu is almost always Help. It opens a miniature Web browser that lets you search the online Mac Help files for explanatory text.

## The Four Window Views

You can view the files and folders in a desktop window in any of four ways: as icons; as a single, tidy list; in a series of neat columns; or as giant document icons that you flip through like they're CDs in a record-store bin (called Cover Flow view). Figure 2-3 shows the four different views.

Every window remembers its view settings independently. You might prefer to look over your Applications folder in list view (because it's crammed with files and folders), but you may prefer to view the Pictures folder in icon or Cover Flow view, where the larger icons serve as previews of the photos.

To switch a window from one view to another, just click one of the four corresponding icons in the window's toolbar, as shown in Figure 2-3.

**Figure 2-3:**
*From the top: The same window in icon view, list view, column, and Cover Flow views. Very full folders are best navigated in list or column views, but you may prefer to view emptier folders in icon or Cover Flow views, because larger icons are easier to preview and click.*

*Remember that in any view (icon, list, column, or Cover Flow), you can highlight an icon by typing the first few letters of its name. In icon, list, or Cover Flow view, you can also press Tab to highlight the next icon (in alphabetical order), or Shift-Tab to highlight the previous one.*

You can also switch views by choosing View→as Icons (or View→as Columns, or View→as List, or View→as Cover Flow), which can be handy if you've hidden the toolbar. Or, for less mousing and more hardbodied efficiency, press ⌘-1, ⌘-2, ⌘-3, or ⌘-4 for icon, list, column, or Cover Flow view, respectively.

The following pages cover each of these views in greater detail.

**Note:** One common thread in the following discussions is the availability of the View Options palette, which lets you set up the sorting, text size, icon size, and other features of each view, either one window at a time or for *all* windows.

Apple gives you a million different ways to open View Options. You can choose View→Show View Options, or press ⌘-J, or choose Show View Options from the ✿ menu at the top of every window.

# Icon View

In an icon view, every file, folder, and disk is represented by a small picture—an *icon*. This humble image, a visual representation of electronic bits and bytes, is the cornerstone of the entire Macintosh religion. (Maybe that's why it's called an icon.)

## Icon View Options

Mac OS X offers a number of useful icon-view options, all of which are worth exploring. Start by opening any icon view window, and then choose View→Show View Options (⌘-J).

### Always open in icon view

In Mac OS X Leopard, it's easy to set up your preferred look for *all folder windows* on your entire system. With one click on the "Use as Defaults" button (described below), you can change the window view of 20,000 folders at once—to icon view, list view, or whatever you like.

The "Always open in icon view" option lets you *override* that master setting, just for *this* window.

For example, you might generally prefer a neat list view with large text. But for your Pictures folder, it probably makes more sense to set up icon view, so you can see a thumbnail of each photo without having to open it.

That's the idea here. Open Pictures, change it to icon view, and then turn on "Always open in icon view." Now every folder on your Mac is in list view *except* Pictures.

**Note:** The wording of this item in the View Options dialog box changes according to the view you're in at the moment. In a list-view window, for example, it says "Always open in list view." In a Cover Flow–view window, it says "Always open in Cover Flow." And so on. But the function is the same: to override the *default* (master) setting.

### Icon size

Mac OS X draws the little pictures that represent your icons using sophisticated graphics software. As a result, you (or the Mac) can scale them to almost any size without losing any quality or clarity.

In the View Options window (Figure 2-4), drag the Icon Size slider back and forth until you find a size you like. (For added fun, make little cartoon sounds with your mouth.)

### Grid spacing

You can control how closely spaced icons are in a window. If you want see a lot of them without making the window bigger, you can pack 'em in like sardines. Figure 2-4 shows all.

**Figure 2-4:**
*Drag the "Grid spacing" slider to specify how tightly packed you want your icons to be. At the minimum setting (top), they're so crammed that it's almost ridiculous; you can't even see their names. But sometimes, you don't really need to. At more spacious settings (bottom), you get a lot more "white space."*

### Text size

Using this slider, you can adjust the type *size* for your icons And for people with especially big or especially small screens—or people with aging retinas—this feature is handy indeed.

### Label position

Click either Bottom or Right to indicate where you want an icon's *name* to appear, relative to its *icon.* As shown in Figure 2-5, it lets you create, in effect, a multiple-column list view in a single window.

### Show item info

While you've got the View Options palette open, try turning on "Show item info." Suddenly you get a new line of information (in tiny blue type) for certain icons, saving you the effort of opening up the folder or file to find out what's in it. For example:

- **Folders.** The info line lets you know how many icons are inside each without having to open it up. Now you can spot empties at a glance.

- **Graphics files.** Certain other kinds of files may show a helpful info line, too. For example, graphics files display their dimensions in pixels.

- **Sounds and QuickTime movies.** The light-blue bonus line tells you how long the sound or movie takes to play. For example, an MP3 file might say "03' 08," which means three minutes, eight seconds.

- **.zip files.** On compressed archives like .zip files, you get to see the archive's total size on disk (like "48.9 MB").

You can see some of these effects illustrated in Figure 2-5.

**Figure 2-5:**
*The View Options dialog box for an icon view window offers the chance to create colored backgrounds for certain windows or even to use photos as window wallpaper (bottom). Using a photo may have a soothing, annoying, or comic effect—like making the icon names completely unreadable. (Note, by the way, how the icon's names have been set to appear beside the icons, rather than underneath. You now have all the handy, freely draggable convenience of an icon view, along with the more compact spacing of a list view.)*

### Show icon preview

This option pertains primarily to graphics, which Mac OS X often displays only with a generic icon (stamped with the file type, like JPEG, TIFF, or PDF). But if you turn on "Show icon preview," Mac OS X turns each icon into a miniature display of the image itself, as shown in Figures 2-5. It's ideal for working with folders full of digital photos.

---

*Tip:* A small but delicious point: You can tell just by looking at a PDF file's icon whether it's longer than one page. The icon for a one-page PDF has a curled upper-right corner. But on a multi-page PDF, only the first page's corner curls down. And in the gap it reveals, you can see a tiny bit of the *actual* page 2 showing!

---

### Arrange by

For a discussion of this pop-up menu, see the next section.

### Background

Here's another Mac OS X luxury that other operating systems can only dream about: You can fill the background of any icon view window on your Mac with a certain color—or even a photo.

Color-coordinating or "wallpapering" certain windows is more than just a gimmick. In fact, it can serve as a timesaving psychological cue. Once you've gotten used to the fact that your main Documents folder has a sky-blue background, you can pick it out like a sharpshooter from a screen filled with open windows. Color-coded Finder windows are also especially easy to distinguish at a glance when you've minimized them to the Dock.

---

**Note:** Background colors and pictures disappear in list, column, and Cover Flow views.

---

Once a window is open, choose View→View Options (⌘-J). The bottom of the resulting dialog box offers three choices, whose results are shown in Figure 2-5.

- **White.** This is the standard option (not shown).

- **Color.** When you click this button, you see a small rectangular button beside the word Color. Click it to open the Color Picker (page 148), which you can use to choose a new background color for the window. (Unless it's April Fool's Day, pick a light color. If you choose a dark one—like black—you won't be able to make out the lettering of the icons' names.)

- **Picture.** If you choose this option, a Select button appears. Click it to open the Select a Picture dialog box, already open to your Library→Desktop Pictures folder. Now choose a graphics file—one of Apple's in the Desktop Pictures folder, or one of your own. When you click Select, you see that Mac OS X has superimposed the window's icons on the photo. As you can see in Figure 2-5, low-contrast or light-background photos work best for legibility.

Incidentally, Mac OS X makes no attempt to scale down a selected photo to fit neatly into the window. If you have a high-res digital camera, therefore, you see only the upper-left corner of a photo in the window. Use a graphics program to scale the picture down to something smaller than your screen resolution for better results.

### Use as Defaults

This harmless-looking button can actually wreak havoc—or restore order to your kingdom—with a single click. It applies the changes you've just made in the View Options dialog box to *all* windows on your Mac (instead of only the *frontmost* window).

If you set up the frontmost window with a colored background, big icons, small text, and a tight grid, and then you click Use as Defaults, you'll see that look in *every* disk or folder window you open.

You've been warned.

Fortunately, there are two auxiliary controls that can give you a break from all the sameness.

First, you can set up individual windows to be weirdo exceptions to the rule; see "Always open in icon view," above.

Second, you can *remove* any departures from the default window view—after a round of disappointing experimentation on a particular window, for example—using a secret button. To do so, choose View→Show View Options to open the View Options dialog box. Now hold down the Option key. The Use as Defaults button magically changes to say "Restore to Defaults," which means "Abandon all the changes I've foolishly made to the look of this window."

## Keeping Icons Neat and Sorted

In general, you can drag icons anywhere within a window. For example, some people like to keep current project icons at the top of the window and move older stuff to the bottom.

If you'd like Mac OS X to impose a little discipline on you, however, it's easy enough to request a visit from an electronic housekeeper who tidies up your icons by aligning them neatly to an invisible grid. In Leopard, you can even specify how tight or loose that grid is.

### Grid alignment

Mac OS X offers an enormous number of variations on the "snap icons to the underlying rows-and-columns grid" theme:

- **Aligning individual icons to the grid.** Press the ⌘ key while dragging an icon or several highlighted icons. (Don't press the key until after you begin to drag.) When you release the mouse, the icons you've moved all jump into neatly aligned positions.

- **Aligning all icons to the grid.** Choose View→Clean Up (if nothing is selected) or View→Clean Up Selection (if some icons are highlighted). Now all icons in the window, or those you've selected, jump to the closest positions on the invisible underlying grid.

  These same commands appear in the shortcut menu when you right-click anywhere inside an icon-view window, which is handier if you have a huge monitor.

---

***Tip:*** If you press Option, you swap the wording of the command. Clean Up changes to read Clean Up Selection, and vice versa.

---

Note, by the way, that the grid alignment is only temporary. As soon as you drag icons around, or add more icons to the window, the newly moved icons wind up just as sloppily positioned as before you tidied up.

---

If you want the Mac to lock *all* icons to the closest spot on the grid *whenever* you move them, choose View→Show View Options (⌘-J); from the "Arrange by" pop-up menu, choose Snap to Grid.

## The Go to Folder Command

Sometimes a Unix tentacle pokes through the user-friendly Mac OS X interface. Every now and then, you find a place where you can use Unix shortcuts instead of the mouse.

One classic example is the Go→Go to Folder command (Shift-⌘-G). It brings up a box like the one shown here.

The purpose of this box is to let you jump directly to a certain folder on your Mac by typing its Unix *folder path.* Depending on your point of view, this special box is either a shortcut or a detour.

For example you want to see what's in the Documents folder of your Home folder, you could choose Go→Go to Folder and type this:

*/Users/chris/Documents*

Then click Go or press Return. (In this example, of course, *chris* is your short account name.)

In other words, you're telling the Mac to open the Users folder in your main hard drive window, then your Home folder inside that, and then the Documents folder inside that. Each slash means "and then open." (You can leave off the name of your hard drive if your path begins with a slash.) When you press Enter, the folder you specified pops open immediately.

Of course, if you really wanted to jump to your Documents folder, you'd be wasting your time by typing all that. Unix (and therefore Mac OS X) offers a handy shortcut that means "home folder." It's the tilde character (~) at the upper-left corner of your keyboard.

To see what's in your Home folder, then, you could type just that ~ symbol into the Go To Folder box and then press

Return. Or you could add some slashes to it to specify a folder inside your Home folder, like this:

*~/Documents*

You can even jump to someone *else's* Home folder by typing a name after the symbol, like this:

*~chris*

If you get into this sort of thing, here's another shortcut worth noting: If you type nothing but a slash (/), and then press Return, you jump immediately to the Computer window, which provides an overview of all your disks.

Note, too, that you don't have to type out the full path—only the part that drills down from the *window you're in*. If your Home folder window is already open, for example, you can open the Pictures folder just by typing *Pictures.*

But the Go to Folder trick really turns into a high-octane timesaver if you use *auto completion*. Here's how it works: After each slash, you can type only enough letters of a folder's name to give Mac OS X the idea—*de* instead of *desktop,* for example—and then wait a fraction of a second (or, if you're late for a plane, press the Tab key). Mac OS X instantly and automatically fills in the rest of the folder's name. It even auto-capitalizes the folder names for you. (In Unix, capitalization matters.)

For example, instead of typing */Applications/Microsoft Office/ clipart/standard,* you could type nothing more than */ap/mi/ cl/st,* remembering to press Tab after each pair of letters. Now *that's* a way to feel like a Unix programmer.

Even then, though, you'll soon discover that none of these grid-snapping techniques move icons into the most compact possible arrangement. If one or two icons have wandered off from the herd to a far corner of the window, they're merely nudged to the grid points closest to their current locations. They aren't moved all the way back to the group of icons elsewhere in the window.

To solve that problem, use one of the sorting options described next.

---

*Tip:* You can always override the grid setting by pressing the ⌘ key when you drag. In other words, when grid-snapping is turned *off*, ⌘ makes your icons snap into position; when grid-snapping is turned *on*, ⌘ lets you drag an icon freely.

---

### Sorted alignment

If you'd rather have icons sorted and bunched together on the underlying grid—no strays allowed—make a selection from the View menu:

- **Sorting all icons for the moment.** If you choose View→Arrange By→Name, all icons in the window snap to the invisible grid *and* sort themselves alphabetically. Use this method to place the icons as close as possible to each other within the window, rounding up any strays.

  The other subcommands in the View→Arrange By menu work similarly (Size, Date Modified, Label, and so on), but sort the icons according to different criteria.

  As with the Clean Up command, View→Arrange By serves only to reorganize the icons in the window at this moment. If you move or add icons to the window, they won't be sorted properly. If you'd rather have all icons remain sorted *and* clustered, try this:

- **Sorting all icons permanently.** You can also tell your Mac to maintain the sorting and alignment of all icons in the window, present *and* future. Now if you add more icons to the window, they jump into correct alphabetical position; if you remove icons, the remaining ones slide over to fill in the resulting gap. This setup is perfect for neat freaks.

  To make it happen, open the View menu, hold down the Option key, and choose from the "Keep Arranged By" submenu (choose Name, Date Modified, or whatever sorting criterion you like). Your icons are now locked into sorted position, as compactly as the grid permits.

## List View

In windows that contain a lot of icons, the list view is a powerful weapon in the battle against chaos. It shows you a tidy table of your files' names, dates, sizes, and so on. In Leopard, alternating blue and white background stripes help you read across the columns in a list-view window.

You have a great deal of control over your columns, in that you get to decide how wide they should be, which of them should appear, and in what order (except that Name is always the first column). Here's how to master these columns:

## Sorting the List

Most of the world's list-view fans like their files listed alphabetically. It's occasionally useful, however, to view the newest files first, largest first, or whatever.

When a desktop window displays its icons in a list view, a convenient new strip of column headings appears (Figure 2-6). These column headings aren't just signposts; they're buttons, too. Click Name for alphabetical order, Date Modified to view newest first, Size to view largest files at the top, and so on.

**Figure 2-6:**
*You control the sorting order of a list view by clicking the column headings (top). Click a second time to reverse the sorting order (bottom).*

*You'll find the identical ▲ or ▼ triangle—indicating the identical information—in email programs, in iTunes, and anywhere else where reversing the sorting order of the list can be useful.*

It's especially important to note the tiny, dark gray triangle that appears in the column you've most recently clicked. It shows you *which way* the list is being sorted.

When the triangle points upward, the oldest files, smallest files, or files beginning with numbers (or the letter A) appear at the top of the list, depending on which sorting criterion you have selected.

*Tip:* It may help you to remember that when the *smallest* portion of the triangle is at the top (▲), the *smallest* files are listed first when viewed in size order.

To reverse the sorting order, click the column heading a second time. Now the newest files, largest files, or files beginning with the letter Z appear at the top of the list. The tiny triangle turns upside-down.

## Flippy Triangles

One of the Mac's most attractive features is the tiny triangle that appears to the left of a folder's name in a list view. In its official documents, Apple calls these buttons *disclosure triangles;* internally, the programmers call them *flippy triangles.*

Either way, these triangles are very useful: When you click one, the list view turns into an outline, which displays the contents of the folder in an indented list, as shown in Figure 2-7. Click the triangle again to collapse the folder listing. You're saved the trouble and clutter of opening a new window just to view the folder's contents.

By selectively clicking flippy triangles, you can, in effect, peer inside two or more folders simultaneously, all within a single list view window. You can move files around by dragging them onto the tiny folder icons.

*Figure 2-7:*
*Click a "flippy triangle" (left) to see the list of the folders and files inside that folder (right). Or press the equivalent keystrokes: ⌘-> (to open) and ⌘-< (to close).*

## Your Choice of Columns

Choose View→Show View Options. In the dialog box that appears, you're offered on/off checkboxes for the different columns of information Mac OS X can show you: Date Modified, Size, Kind, and so on.

## Other View Options

The View Options for a list view include several other useful settings; choose View→ Show View Options, or press ⌘-J.

- **Always open in list view.** Turn on this option to override your system-wide preference setting for all windows. See "Always open in icon view" on page 41 for details.

- **Icon size.** These two buttons offer you a choice of icon size for the current window: either standard or tiny. Unlike icon view, list view doesn't give you a size slider.

  Fortunately, even the tiny icons aren't so small that they show up blank. You still get a general idea of what they're supposed to look like.

- **Text size.** As described on page 42, you can change the type size for your icon labels, either globally or one window at a time.

- **Show columns.** Turn on the columns you'd like to appear in the current window's list view, as described in the previous section.

---

**FREQUENTLY ASKED QUESTION**

### Calculate All Sizes

*When I sort my list view by size, I see only dashes for folder sizes. What am I doing wrong?*

Nothing at all; that's normal. When viewing a Finder window, you see a Size statistic for each file. For folders and disks, however, you're shown only an uninformative dash.

Most Mac fans study this anomaly only momentarily, scratch their chins, and then get back to their work. Former Windows users don't even scratch their chins; Windows PCs *never* show folder-size or disk-size information in list views.

Here's what's going on: It can take a computer a long time to add up the sizes of all files inside a folder. Your System→ Library folder alone, for example, contains over 1,500 files. Instead of making you wait while the Mac does all of this addition, Mac OS X simply shows you a dash in the Size column for a folder.

On occasion, however, you really do want to see how big your folders are. In such cases, choose View→Show View Options and turn on "Calculate all sizes." You see the folder sizes slowly begin to pop onto the screen, from the top of

the window down, as the Mac crunches the numbers of the files within.

In fact, you can even turn on the "Calculate all sizes" option *globally*—that is, for all windows. In the Mac operating systems of days gone by, this act would have caused a massive slowdown of the entire computer. But remember that Mac OS X is multithreaded—that is, it has the opposite of a one-track mind. It's perfectly capable of devoting all of its attention to calculating your folder sizes and all of its attention to whatever work you're doing in the foreground.

Now consider this anomaly: Suppose you've opted to sort a particular window by folder size—in other words, you've clicked the word Size at the top of the column. Turning on "Calculate all sizes" bewilders the unprepared, as folders arbitrarily begin leaping out of order, forcing the list to rearrange itself a couple of times per second.

What's happening, of course, is that all folders begin at the bottom of the list, showing only dashes in the Size column. Then, as the Mac computes the size of your folders' contents, they jump into their correct sorted order at what may seem to be random intervals.

---

- **Use relative dates.** In a list view, the Date Modified and Date Created columns generally display information in a format like this: "Sunday, March 9, 2008." (As noted below, the Mac uses shorter date formats as the column gets narrower.) But when the "Use relative dates" option is turned on, the Mac substitutes the word "Yesterday" or "Today" where appropriate, making recent files easier to spot.

- **Calculate all sizes.** See the box on the facing page.

- **Show icon preview.** Exactly as in icon view, this option turns the icons of graphics files into miniatures of the photos or images within.

- **Use as Defaults.** Click to make your changes in the View Options box apply to *all* windows on your Mac. (Option-click this button to restore a wayward window *back* to your defaults.)

## Rearranging Columns

You're stuck with the Name column at the far left of a window. However, you can rearrange the other columns just by dragging their gray column headers horizontally. If the Mac thinks you intend to drop a column to, say, the left of the column it overlaps, you'll actually see an animated movement—indicating a column reshuffling—even before you release the mouse button.

## Adjusting Column Widths

If you place your cursor carefully on the dividing line between two column headings, you'll find that you can drag the divider line horizontally. Doing so makes the column to the *left* of your cursor wider or narrower.

What's delightful about this activity is watching Mac OS X scramble to rewrite its information to fit the space you give it. For example, as you make the Date Modified (or Created) column narrower, "Sunday, March 9, 2008, 2:22 PM" shrinks first to "Sun, Mar 9, 2008, 2:22 PM," then to "3/9/08, 2:22 PM," and finally to a terse "3/9/08."

If you make a column too narrow, Mac OS X shortens the file names, dates, or whatever by removing text from the *middle*. An ellipsis (…) appears to show you where the missing text would have appeared. (Apple reasoned that truncating the *ends* of file names, as in some other operating systems, would hide useful information like the number at the end of "Letter to Marge 1," "Letter to Marge 2," and so on. It would also hide the three-letter *extensions*, such as Thesis.*doc,* that may appear on file names in Mac OS X.)

For example, suppose you've named a Word document "Ben Affleck—A Major Force for Humanization and Cure for Depression, Acne, and Migraine Headache." (Yes, file names can really be that long.) If the Name column is too narrow, you might see only "Ben Affleck—A Major…Migraine Headache."

*Tip:* You don't have to make the column mega-wide just to read the full text of a file whose name has been shortened. Just point to the icon's name without clicking. After a moment, a yellow, floating balloon appears—something like a tooltip in Windows—to identify the full name.

And if you don't feel like waiting, hold down the Option key. As you whip your mouse over truncated file names, their tooltip balloons appear instantaneously. (Both of these tricks work in list, column, or Cover Flow views—and in Save and Open dialog boxes, for that matter.)

## Column View

The goal of column view is simple: to let you burrow down through nested folders without leaving a trail of messy, overlapping windows in your wake.

The solution is shown in Figure 2-8. It's a list view that's divided into several vertical panes. The first pane (not counting the Sidebar) shows whatever disk or folder you first opened.

*Figure 2-8:*
*If the rightmost folder contains pictures, sounds, Office documents, or movies, you can look at them or play them, right there in the Finder. You can drag this jumbo preview icon anywhere—into another folder or the Trash, for example.*

When you click a disk or folder in this list (once), the second pane shows a list of everything in it. Each time you click a folder in one pane, the pane to its right shows what's inside. The other panes slide to the left, sometimes out of view. (Use the horizontal scroll bar to bring them back.) You can keep clicking until you're actually looking at the file icons inside the most deeply nested folder.

If you discover that your hunt for a particular file has taken you down a blind alley, it's not a big deal to backtrack, since the trail of folders you've followed to get here is still sitting before you on the screen. As soon as you click a different folder in one of the earlier panes, the panes to its right suddenly change, so that you can burrow down a different rabbit hole.

Furthermore, the Sidebar is always at the ready to help you jump to a new track; just click any disk or folder icon there to select a new first-column listing for column view.

The beauty of column view is, first of all, that it keeps your screen tidy. It effectively shows you several simultaneous folder levels, but contains them within a single window. With a quick ⌘-W, you can close the entire window, panes and all. Second, column view provides an excellent sense of where you are. Because your trail is visible at all times, it's much harder to get lost—wondering what folder you're in and how you got there—than in any other window view.

**Note:** In Leopard, for the first time, you can change how Column view is sorted; it doesn't have to be alphabetical. Press ⌘-J to open the View Options dialog box, and then choose the sorting criterion you want from the "Arrange by" pop-up menu (like Size, Date Created, or Label).

## Manipulating the Columns

The number of columns you can see without scrolling depends on the width of the window. In no other view are the zoom and resize controls as important as they are here.

That's not to say, however, that you're limited to four columns (or whatever fits on your monitor). You can make the columns wider or narrower—either individually or all at once—to suit the situation, according to this scheme:

To make a single column wider or narrower, drag its right-side handle (circled in Figure 2-9).

**Figure 2-9:**
*What you want to do most of the time is adjust one column. Adding the Option key as you drag the handle lets you adjust all columns at once.*

To make *all* the columns wider or narrower simultaneously, hold down the Option key as you drag that right-side handle.

And here's the tip of the week: *Double-click* one of the right-side handles to make the column *precisely* as wide as necessary to reveal all the names of its contents.

Best of all, you can *Option*-double-click any column's right-side handle to make *all* columns just as wide as necessary.

## View Options

Just as in icon and list view, you can choose View→Show View Options to open a dialog box—a Spartan one, in this case—offering additional control over your column views.

- **Always open in column view.** Once again, this option lets you override your system-wide preference setting for all windows. See "Always open in icon view" on page 41 for details.

- **Text size.** Whatever point size you choose here affects the type used for icons in *all* column views.

- **Show icons.** For maximum speed, turn off this option. Now you see only file names—not the tiny icons next to them—in all column views.

- **Show icon preview.** In Leopard, you can request that the tiny icons in column view display their actual contents—photos show their images, Word and PDF documents show the first page, and so on. Of course, this feature isn't always terrifically useful, since the icons are the size of a hydrogen atom; but now and then, you can get the general gist of what's in a file just by its overall shape and color.

- **Show preview column.** The far-right Preview column can be handy when you're browsing graphics, sounds, or movie files. Feel free to enlarge this final column when you want a better view of the picture or movie; you can make it *really* big. Almost Quick Look big.

  The rest of the time, though, the Preview column can get in the way, slightly slowing down the works and pushing other, more useful columns off to the left side of the window. If you turn off this checkbox, the Preview column doesn't appear.

---

**GEM IN THE ROUGH**

### Multiple Views, Same Folder

If you've read this section carefully, you may have discovered a peculiar quirk of the Mac OS X Finder: By choosing File→New Finder Window (or ⌘-double-clicking a disk or folder icon), you open a second, completely independent Finder window. If you stop to think about it, therefore, there's nothing to stop you from opening a third, fourth, or fifth copy of *the same folder window.* Once they're open, you can even switch them into different views.

Try this, for example: Choose Go→Applications. Choose File→New Finder Window (⌘-N), and then choose Go→Applications *again.* Using the View menu or the con-

trols in the toolbar, put one of these windows into list view, and the other into icon view.

This phenomenon has its advantages. For example, you might decide to open the same window twice while doing some hard drive housekeeping. By keeping a list view open, you can check the Size column as you move your files into different folders (so you can make sure the folders fit onto a blank CD, for example). By keeping a *column* view open, on the other hand, you gain quicker navigational access to the stuff on your drive.

---

*Tip:* No matter what view you're in, remember this if you ever start dragging an icon and then change your mind: Press the Esc key or ⌘-period, even while the mouse button is still down. The icon flies back to its precise starting place. (Too bad real life doesn't have a similar feature.)

# Cover Flow View

As you can sort of see from Figure 2-10, Cover Flow is a visual display that Apple stole from its own iTunes software, where Cover Flow simulates the flipping "pages" of a jukebox, or the CDs in a record-store bin. There, you can flip through your music collection, marveling as the CD covers flip over in 3-D space while you browse.

The idea is the same in Mac OS X, except that now it's not CD covers you're flipping; it's gigantic file and folder icons.

To fire up Cover Flow, open a window. Then click the Cover Flow button identified in Figure 2-10, or choose View→as Cover Flow, or press ⌘-4.

**Figure 2-10:**
*The bottom half of a Cover Flow window is identical to list view. The top half, however, is an interactive, scrolling "CD bin" full of your own stuff. It's especially useful for photos, PDF files, Office documents, and text documents. And when a movie comes up in this virtual data jukebox, you can point to the little ▶ button and click it to play the video, right in place.*

Now the window splits. On the bottom: a traditional list view, complete with sortable columns, exactly as described above.

On the top: the gleaming, reflective, black Cover Flow display. Your primary interest here is the scroll bar. As you drag it left or right, you see your own files and folders float by and flip in 3-D space. Fun for the whole family!

The effect is spectacular, sure. It's probably not something you'd want to set up for every folder, though, because browsing is a pretty inefficient way to find something. But in folders containing photos or movies (that aren't filled with hundreds of files), Cover Flow can be a handy and satisfying way to browse.

And now, notes on Cover Flow:

- **You can adjust the size of Cover Flow display** (relative to the list-view half) by dragging up or down on the grip strip area just beneath the Cover Flow scroll bar.

- **Multipage PDF documents are special.** When you point to one, circled arrow buttons appear on the jumbo icon. You can click them to page through the document—without even opening it for real (Figure 2-11).

**Figure 2-11:**
*When you point to a PDF file without clicking, you get special arrow buttons that let you turn pages.*

- **QuickTime movies are special, too.** When you point to its jumbo display, a ▶ button appears. Click it to play the movie, right there in the Cover Flow window (Figure 2-10).

- **You can navigate with the keyboard, too.** Any icon that's highlighted in the list view (bottom half of the window) is also front and center in the Cover Flow view. Therefore, you can use all the usual list-view shortcuts to navigate both at once. Use the up or down arrow keys, type the first few letters of an icon's name, press Tab or Shift-Tab to highlight the next or previous icon alphabetically, and so on.

- **Cover Flow shows whatever the list view shows.** If you expand a flippy triangle to reveal an indented list of what's in a folder, the contents of that folder now become part of the cover flow.

- **The previews are actual icons.** When you're looking at a Cover Flow minidocument, you can drag it with your mouse—you've got the world's biggest target—anywhere you'd like to drag it: another folder, the Trash, whatever.

## Quick Look

As the preceding several thousand pages make clear, there are lots of ways to view and manage the seething mass of files and folders on a typical hard drive. Some of them actually let you see what's in a document without having to open it—the Preview column in column view, the giant icons in Cover Flow, and so on.

Quick Look, a star feature of Leopard, takes this idea to another level. It lets you open and browse a document nearly at full size—without switching window views or opening any new programs. You highlight an icon (or several), and then press the Space bar (or click the eyeball icon at the top of the window).

*Figure 2-12:*
*Once the Quick Look window is open, you can play the file (movies and sounds), study it in more detail (most kinds of graphics files), or even read it (PDF, Word, and Excel documents).*

*You can also click another icon, and another, and another, without ever closing the preview; the contents of the window simply change to reflect whatever you've just clicked.*

*Supertip: Quick Look even works on icons in the Trash, too, so you can figure out what something is before you nuke it forever.*

Quick Look

Full Screen   Add to iPhoto

The Quick Look window now opens, showing a nearly full-size preview of the document (Figure 2-12). Rather nice, eh?

The idea here is that you can check out a document without having to wait for it to open in the traditional way. For example, you can find out what's in a Word, Excel, or PowerPoint document without actually having to *open* Word, Excel, or PowerPoint, which saves you about 45 minutes.

## What Quick Look Knows

You might wonder: How, exactly, is Quick Look able to display the contents of a document without opening it? Wouldn't it have to somehow understand the internal file format of that document type?

Exactly. And that's why Quick Look doesn't recognize *all* documents. If you try to preview, for example, a Final Cut Pro video project, a sheet-music file, a .zip archive, or a database file, all you'll see is a six-inch-tall version of its generic icon. You won't see what's inside.

Over time, people will write plug-ins for those nonrecognized programs. Already, plug-ins that let you see what's inside folders and .zip files await at *www.qlplugins.com*. In the meantime, here's what Quick Look recognizes right out of the box:

- **Graphics files and photos.** This is where Quick Look can really shine, because it's often useful to get a quick look at a photo without having to haul iPhoto or Photoshop out of bed. Quick Look recognizes all common graphics formats, including TIFF, JPEG, GIF, PNG, RAW, and Photoshop documents.

- **PDF and text files.** Using the scroll bar, you can page through multipage documents, right there in the Quick Look window.

- **Audio and movie files.** They begin to play instantly when you open them into the Quick Look window. Most popular formats are recognized (MP3, AIFF, AAC, MPEG4, H.264, and so on). A scroll bar appears so that you can jump around in the movie or song.

- **Microsoft Word, Excel, and PowerPoint documents.** Because these formats are so common, Mac OS X comes with a Quick Look plug-in to recognize them. Move through the pages using the vertical scroll bar; switch to a different Excel spreadsheet page using the Sheet tabs at the bottom.

- **Fonts.** Totally cool. When you open a font file in Quick Look, you get a crystal-clear, huge sampler that shows every letter of the alphabet in that typeface.

- **vCards.** A *vCard* is an address-book entry that people can send by email to each other to save time in updating their Rolodexes. When you drag a name out of Apple's or Microsoft's address books and onto the desktop, for example, it turns into a vCard document. In Quick Look, the vCard opens up as a handsomely formatted index card that displays all of the person's contact information.

- **Pages, Numbers, Keynote, and TextEdit documents.** Naturally, since these are Apple programs, Quick Look understands the document formats.

- **HTML (Web pages).** If you've saved some Web pages to your hard drive, here's a great way to inspect them without firing up your Web browser.

To exit the Quick Look display, press the Space bar again.

## Fun with Quick Look

Here are some stunts that make Quick Look even more interesting.

- **Zoom in or out.** Option-click the preview to magnify it; drag inside the zoomed-in image to scroll; Shift-Option-click to zoom back out. Or press Option as you turn your mouse's scroll wheel. (PDF documents have their own zoom in/zoom out keystrokes: ⌘-plus and ⌘-minus.)

- **Full screen.** When you click the Full Screen arrows (identified in Figure 2-12), your screen goes black, and the Quick Look window expands to fill it. Keep this trick in mind when you're trying to read Word, Excel, or PDF documents, since the text is usually too small to read otherwise. (When you're finished with the closeup, click the Full Screen button again to restore the original Quick Look window, or the ⊗ button to exit Quick Look altogether.)

---

***Tip:*** How's *this* for an undocumented shortcut?

If you *Option-click* the eyeball icon in any Finder window, you go straight into Full Screen mode without having to open the smaller Quick Look window first. Kewl.

---

**Figure 2-13:**
*Once the slideshow is underway, you can use this control bar. It lets you pause the slideshow, move forward or backward manually, enlarge the current "slide" to fill the screen, or end the show.*

*The Index view is especially handy. (You can press ⌘-Return to "click" the Index View button.) It displays an array of labeled miniatures, all at once—a sort of Exposé for Quick Look. Click a thumbnail to jump directly to the Quick Look document you want to inspect.*

Previous  Pause  Next  Index View  Add to iPhoto  Exit Full Screen  Exit Quick Look

- **Add to iPhoto.** This icon appears in the Quick Look windows of graphics files that you're examining. Click it to add the picture you're studying to your iPhoto photo collection.

- **Keep it going.** Once you've opened Quick Look for *one* icon, you don't have to close it before inspecting *another* icon. Just keep clicking different icons; the Quick Look window changes instantly with each click to reflect the new document.

### The Quick Look Slideshow

Highlight a *bunch* of icons, and then open Quick Look. The screen goes black, and the documents begin their slideshow. Each image appears on the screen for about three seconds before the next one appears. (Press the Esc key or ⌘-period to end the show.)

It's a useful enough feature when you've just downloaded or imported a bunch of photos or Office documents and want a quick look through them. Use the control bar shown in Figure 2-13 to manage the playback.

*Note:* This same slideshow mechanism is available for graphics in Preview and Mail.

# The Dock

For years, most operating systems maintained two different lists of programs. One listed *unopened* programs until you needed them, like the Start menu in Windows. The other kept track of which programs were *open* at the moment for easy switching, like the Windows taskbar.

In Mac OS X, Apple combined both functions into a single strip of icons called the *Dock*.

### Setting Up the Dock

Apple starts the Dock off with a few icons it thinks you'll enjoy: Dashboard, QuickTime Player, iTunes, iChat, Mail, the Safari Web browser, and so on. But using your Mac without putting your own favorite icons in the Dock is like buying an expensive suit and turning down the free alteration service. At the first opportunity, you should make the Dock your own.

The concept of the Dock is simple: Any icon you drag onto it (Figure 2-14) is installed there as a button.)

A single click, not a double-click, opens the corresponding icon. In other words, the Dock is an ideal parking lot for the icons of disks, folders, documents, programs, and Internet bookmarks that you access frequently.

Here are a few aspects of the Dock that may throw you at first:

- **It has two sides.** See the whitish dotted line running down the Dock? That's the divider (Figure 2-14). Everything on the left side is an application—a program.

Everything else goes on the right side: files, documents, folders, disks, and minimized windows.

It's important to understand this division. If you try to drag an application to the right of the line, for example, Mac OS X teasingly refuses to accept it. (Even aliases observe that distinction. Aliases of applications can go only on the left side, and vice versa.)

**Figure 2-14:**
*To add an icon to the Dock, simply drag it there. You haven't moved the original file; when you release the mouse, it remains where it was. You've just installed a pointer—like a Macintosh alias or Windows shortcut.*

Divider

←—— Programs side | Everything else ——→

Open programs      Minimized document windows

• **Its icon names are hidden.** To see the name of a Dock icon, point to it without clicking. You'll see the name appear above the icon.

When you're trying to find a certain icon in the Dock, run your cursor slowly across the icons without clicking; the icon labels appear as you go. You can often identify a document just by looking at its icon.

• **Folders and disks sprout** *stacks.* If you click a folder or disk icon in the right side of the Dock, a list of its contents sprouts from the icon. It's like X-ray vision without the awkward moral consequences. Turn the page for details on stacks.

• **Programs appear there unsolicited.** Nobody but you (and Apple) can put icons on the right side of the Dock. But program icons appear on the left side of the Dock automatically whenever you open a program, even one that's not listed in the Dock. Its icon remains there for as long as it's running.

## Organizing and Removing Dock Icons

You can move the tiles of the Dock around by dragging them horizontally. As you drag, the other icons scoot aside to make room. When you're satisfied with its new position, drop the icon you've just dragged.

To remove a Dock icon, just drag it away. (You can't remove the icons of the Finder, the Trash, the Dock icon of an open program, or any minimized document window.) Once your cursor has cleared the Dock, release the mouse button. The icon disappears, its passing marked by a charming little puff of animated cartoon smoke. The other Dock icons slide together to close the gap.

## Stacks

A *stack* is what you get when you click a disk or folder icon on the Dock—and it's one of Leopard's marquee new features. The effect is shown in Figure 2-15.

---

**Tip:** If you press Shift as you click, the stack opens in slow motion. Amaze your friends.

---

In essence, Mac OS X is fanning out the folder's contents so you can see all of them. If it could talk, it would be saying, "Pick a card, any card."

### Fan vs. grid vs. list

Sometimes there are too many icons in a folder to fit in a fan. In that case, the stack becomes a grid instead (Figure 2-15, bottom). The grid, of course, holds many more icons than the fan, although it's not as pretty.

But you can force a certain Dock folder to sprout a fan or a grid *all the time,* rather than letting Mac OS X decide. From the Dock folder's shortcut menu (page 66), choose "View content as"→Fan or "View content as"→Grid (instead of the factory setting, "View content as"→Automatic).

From now on, you'll always get the fan, or always get the grid.

---

**Note:** When your Dock is positioned on a side of the screen instead of the bottom, you *always* get the grid, never the fan. The View As command doesn't even appear in the shortcut menu.

---

Truth is, though, that both the grid and the fan have limited storage space for icons; the exact number depends on your monitor size. In any case, if there are too many icons to display at once, the last icon says, "24 more in Finder" (or whatever the number is). Click that icon to open the folder's regular window, where all the contents are available.

Of course, then you've defeated the fan's step-saving purpose.

Maybe that's why many Mac fans choose View Content As→List from each Dock folder's shortcut menu (an option in version 10.5.2 and later). Now, when you click a folder in the Dock, you get a simple pop-up list of *everything* in that folder.

### Ready-made stacks

When you first install Mac OS X 10.5, you get a couple of starter stacks just to get you psyched. One is called Downloads; the other is Documents. (Both of these folders are physically inside your Home folder. But you may well do most of your interacting with them on the Dock.)

The Downloads folder, new in Leopard, collects three kinds of Internet arrivals:

• Files you download from the Web using Safari

• Files you receive in an iChat file-transfer session

• File attachments you get via email using Mail.

Unless you intervene, they're sorted by the date you downloaded them.

It's handy to know where to find your downloads, and nice not to have them all cluttering your desktop.

**Figure 2-15:**
Top: When you click the icon of a folder or disk on the Dock (just one single click), you get this effect: a rainbow that shows what's inside. Click an icon to open it, just as though you'd double-clicked it in a window. You can even Option-click one icon after another, opening them all while the stack remains arrayed before you.

Or grab an icon and drag it right out of the stack—into another window, say.

Bottom: If there are too many icons to fit in the arc (as determined by your monitor size), you get this grid instead. Alas, here, too, space is limited. If there are more than fits on the grid, click the "35 more in Finder" icon at the lower right. You go to the folder's standard Finder window, where you can see the complete list of icons.

### Creating and removing stacks

Creating a new stack is easy. Just drag *any* folder or disk icon onto the right end of the Dock. That's right: *All* folders and disks become stacks when clicked on the Dock.

Therefore, to get a stack off the Dock, drag its folder icon away from the Dock and let go. You're not deleting the actual folder—just its Dock shortcut.

---

*Tip:* When you first add a folder icon to the Dock, its shortcut menu (page 66) starts out saying "Display as" →Stack. In this condition, folder icons on the Dock start out *change* to reflect their contents. The Downloads folder, for example, takes on the icon of whatever was most recently added to it. That can be a little disorienting, since you can't get to know a folder by its icon—it keeps changing!

The solution is simple: From the "Display as" section of the Dock folder's pop-up menu, choose Folder.

---

## Three Ways to Get the Dock Out of Your Hair

The bottom of the screen isn't necessarily the ideal location for the Dock. All Mac screens are wider than they are tall, so the Dock eats into your limited vertical screen space. You have three ways out: Hide the Dock, shrink it, or rotate it 90 degrees.

### Auto-hiding the Dock

To turn on the Dock's auto-hiding feature, choose  →Dock→Turn Hiding On (or press Option-⌘-D).

When the Dock is hidden, it doesn't slide into view until you move the cursor to the Dock's edge of the screen. When you move the cursor back to the middle of the screen, the Dock slithers out of view once again. (Individual Dock icons may occasionally shoot upward into Desktop territory when a program needs your attention—cute, very cute—but otherwise, the Dock lies low until you call for it.)

On paper, an auto-hiding Dock is ideal; it's there only when you summon it. In practice, however, you may find that the extra half-second the Dock takes to appear and disappear makes this feature slightly less appealing.

Many Mac fans prefer to hide and show the Dock at will by pressing the hide/show keystroke, Option-⌘-D. This method makes the Dock pop on and off the screen without requiring you to move the cursor.

### Shrinking and enlarging the Dock

Depending on your screen's size, you may prefer smaller or larger Dock buttons. The official way to resize them goes like this: Choose  →Dock→Dock Preferences. In the resulting dialog box, drag the Dock Size slider, as shown in Figure 2-16.

There's a much faster way to resize the Dock, however: Just position your cursor carefully in the Dock's divider line, so that it turns into a double-headed arrow. Now drag up or down to shrink or enlarge the Dock.

You may not be able to *enlarge* the Dock, especially if it contains a lot of icons. But you can make it almost infinitely *smaller*. This may make you wonder: How can you distinguish between icons if they're the size of molecules?

The answer lies in the ⌘→Dock→Turn Magnification On command. What you've just done is trigger the swelling effect shown in Figure 2-16. Now your Dock icons balloon to a much larger size as your cursor passes over them. It's a weird, magnetic, rippling, animated effect that takes some getting used to. But it's another spectacular demonstration of the graphics technology in Mac OS X, and it can actually come in handy when you find your icons shrinking away to nothing.

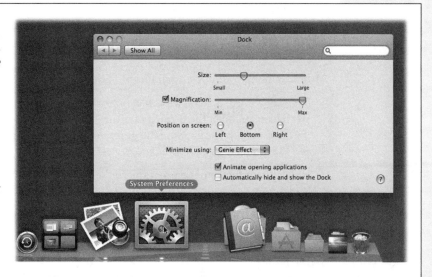

**Figure 2-16:**
*To find a comfortable setting for the Magnification slider, choose ⌘→Dock→Dock Preferences. Leave the Dock Preferences window open on the screen, as shown here. After each adjustment of the Dock Size slider, try out the Dock (which still works when the Dock Preferences window is open) to test your new settings.*

### Moving the Dock to the sides of the screen

Yet another approach to getting the Dock out of your way is to rotate it, so that it sits vertically against a side of your screen. You can rotate it in either of two ways:

- **The menu way.** From the ⌘→Dock submenu, choose "Position on Left," "Position on Right," or "Position on Bottom," as you see fit.

- **The mouse way.** While pressing Shift, drag the Dock's divider line, like a handle, to the side of the screen you want.

You'll probably find that the right side of your screen works better than the left. Most Mac OS X programs put their document windows against the left edge of the screen, where the Dock and its labels might get in the way.

---

**Note:** When you position your Dock vertically, the "right" side of the Dock becomes the bottom of the vertical Dock. In other words, the Trash now appears at the bottom of the vertical Dock. So as you read references to the Dock in this book, mentally substitute the phrase "bottom part of the Dock" when you read references to the "right side of the Dock."

---

# Using the Dock

Most of the time, you'll use the Dock as either a launcher (you click an icon once to open the corresponding program, file, folder, or disk) or as a status indicator (the tiny, shiny reflective spot, identified in Figure 2-14, indicate which programs are running).

But the Dock has more tricks than that up its sleeve. You can use it, for example, to pull off any of the following stunts.

### Switch applications

The Dock isn't just a launcher; it's also a switcher. For example, it lets you:

- Jump among your open programs by clicking their icons.

- Drag a document (such as a text file) onto a Dock application (such as the Microsoft Word icon) to open the former with the latter. (If the program balks at opening the document, yet you're sure the program *should* be able to open the document, add the ⌘ and Option keys as you drag.)

- Hide all windows of the program you're in by Option-clicking another Dock icon.

- Hide all *other* programs' windows by Option-⌘-clicking the Dock icon of the program you *do* want (even if it's already in front).

### Secret menus

Each Dock icon has its own very useful shortcut menu (Figure 2-17). For example:

- [**Window names.**] The secret Dock menu of a *running program* usually lists at least one tiny, neatly labeled window icon, like those shown in Figure 2-17. This useful feature means that you can jump directly not only to a certain program, but to a certain *open window* in that program—just as though you were using the Windows taskbar.

- **Keep In Dock/Remove From Dock.** Whenever you open a program, Mac OS X puts its icon in the Dock—marked with a shiny, white reflective spot—even if you don't normally keep its icon there. As soon as you quit the program, its icon disappears again from the Dock.

  If you understand that much, then the Keep In Dock command makes a lot of sense. It means, "Hello, I'm this program's icon. I know you don't normally keep me in your Dock, but I *could* stay here even after you quit my program. Just say the word." If you find that you've been using, for example, Terminal a lot more often than you thought you would, this command may be the ticket.

  On the other hand, what if a program's icon is always in the Dock (even when it's not running) and you *don't* want it there? In that case, this command says Remove From Dock instead. It gets the program's icon off the Dock, thereby returning the space it was using to other icons. (You can achieve the same result by dragging the icon away from the Dock, but evidently too many Mac fans weren't aware of this trick.)

Use this command on programs you rarely use. When you *do* want to run those programs, you can always use Spotlight to fire them up.

**Figure 2-17:**
*Left: Right-click a Dock icon, or click and hold on it, to open the secret*

*Right: Right-click the divider bar to open a different hidden menu. This one lists a bunch of useful Dock commands, including the ones listed in the  ≤→Dock submenu.*

- **Open at Login.** This command lets you specify that you want this icon to open itself automatically each time you log into your account. It's a great way to make sure that your email Inbox, your calendar, or the Microsoft Word thesis you've been working on is fired up and waiting on the screen when you sit down to work.

  To make this item *stop* auto-opening, choose this command from its Dock icon again, so that the check mark no longer appears.

- **Show In Finder.** This command highlights the actual icon (in whatever folder window it happens to sit) of the application, alias, folder, or document you've clicked. You might want to do this when, for example, you're using a program that you can't quite figure out, and you want to jump to its desktop folder in hopes of finding a Read Me file there.

---

***Tip:*** Once again, there's a much faster way to reveal a Dock icon in its enclosing window: ⌘-click its Dock icon.

---

- **Hide/Show.** This operating system is crawling with ways to hide or reveal a selected batch of windows. Here's a case in point: You can hide all traces of the program you're using by choosing Hide from its Dock icon. (You could accomplish the same thing in many other ways, of course; see page 127.)

  What's cool here is that (a) you can even hide the Finder and all *its* windows, and (b) if you press Option, the command changes to say Hide Others. This, in its way, is a much more powerful command. It tells all the programs you're *not* using—the ones in the background—to get out of your face. They hide themselves instantly.

- **Quit.** You can quit any program directly from its Dock shortcut menu. (Finder and Dashboard are exceptions.) You don't have to switch into a program in order to access its Quit command.

  You might be thankful for this quick-quitting feature when your boss is coming down the hallway and the Dilbert Web site is on your screen where a spreadsheet is supposed to be.

---

**Tip:** If you hold down the Option key—even after you've opened the pop-up menu—the Quit command changes to say Force Quit. That's your emergency hatch for jettisoning a locked-up program.

---

- **Sort by, Display as, View content as.** If you right-click a folder on the Dock, you get a shortcut menu containing these three sections. They govern how the folder's contents are listed in the pop-out display, as described on page 64 (grid, fan, or list, for example), and how they're sorted.

## Drag and Drop

Dock icons are spring-loaded. That is, if you drag any icon onto a Dock icon and pause—or, if you're in a hurry, tap the Space bar—the Dock icon *opens* to receive the dragged file.

---

**Note:** It opens, that is, *if* the spring-loaded folder feature is turned on in Finder→Preferences.

---

This technique is most useful in these situations:

- **Drag a document icon onto a Dock folder icon.** The folder's Finder window pops open, so that you can continue the drag into a subfolder.

- **You drag a document into an application.** The classic example is dragging a photo onto the iPhoto icon. When you tap the Space bar, iPhoto opens automatically. Since your mouse button is still down, and you're technically still in mid-drag, you can now drop the photo directly into the appropriate iPhoto album or Event. You can drag an MP3 file into iTunes or an attachment into Mail or Entourage the same way.

## Do Your Filing

Once you've tried stashing a few important folders on the right side of your Dock, there's no going back. The folders you care about are always there, ready for opening with a single click.

Better yet, they're easily accessible for *putting away* files; you can drag files directly into the Dock's folder icons as though they were regular folders.

In fact, you can even drag a file into a *subfolder* in a Dock folder. That's because in Leopard, the Dock's folders are spring-loaded. When you drag an icon onto a Dock folder and pause, the folder's window appears around your cursor, so you can continue the drag into an inner folder (and even an *inner* inner folder, and so on). Page 81 has the details on spring-loaded folders.

Page 81 has the details on spring-loaded folders.

**Tip:** When you try to drag something into a Dock folder icon, the Dock icons scoot out of the way; the Dock assumes that you're trying to put that something *onto* the Dock. But if you press the ⌘ key as you drag an icon to the Dock, the existing Dock icons freeze in place. Without the ⌘ key, you wind up playing a frustrating game of chase-the-folder.

## The Finder Toolbar

At the top of every Finder window is a small set of function icons, all in a gradient-gray row (Figure 2-18). The first time you run Mac OS X 10.5, you'll find only these icons on the toolbar:

- **Back, Forward.** The Finder works something like a Web browser. Only a single window remains open as you navigate the various folders on your hard drive.

  The Back button (◀) returns you to whichever folder you were just looking at. (Instead of clicking ◀, you can also press ⌘-[, or choose Go→Back—particularly handy if the toolbar is *hidden*, as described below.)

  The Forward button (▶) springs to life only after you've used the Back button. Clicking it (or pressing ⌘-]) returns you to the window you just backed out of.

**Figure 2-18:**
If you ⌘-click the upper-right toolbar button repeatedly, you cycle through six combinations of large and small icons and text labels. (Three examples are shown here.) Tip: This same ⌘-clicking business cycles through the same toolbar variations in Mail, Preview, and other programs that have toolbars.

- **View controls.** The four tiny buttons next to the ▶ button switch the current window into icon, list, column, or Cover Flow view, respectively. And remember, if the toolbar is hidden, you can get by with the equivalent commands in the View menu at the top of the screen—or by pressing ⌘-1, ⌘-2, ⌘-3, or ⌘-4 (for icon, list, column, and Cover Flow view, respectively).

- **Quick Look.** The eyeball icon opens the Quick Look preview for a highlighted icon (or group of them).

- **Action (✿).** This little pop-up menu contains the same commands you'd see if you right-clicked something.

- **Search bar.** This little round-ended text box is yet another entry point for the Spotlight feature described in Chapter 3.

## Removing or Shrinking the Toolbar

Between the toolbar, the Dock, the Sidebar, and the large icons of Mac OS X, it almost seems like there's an Apple conspiracy to sell big screens.

Fortunately, the toolbar doesn't have to contribute to that impression. You can hide it by choosing View→Hide Toolbar or pressing Option-⌘-T. (The same keystroke, or choosing View→Show Toolbar, brings it back.)

But you don't have to do without the toolbar altogether. If its consumption of screen space is your main concern, you may prefer to collapse it—to delete the pictures but preserve the text buttons; see Figure 2-18.

## Rearranging or Removing Toolbar Icons

You can drag toolbar icons around, rearranging them horizontally, by pressing ⌘ as you drag. Taking an icon off the toolbar is equally easy. While pressing the ⌘ key, just drag the icon clear away from the toolbar. It vanishes in a puff of cartoon smoke. (If the Customize Toolbar sheet is open, you can perform either step *without* the ⌘ key.)

You can also get rid of a toolbar icon by right-clicking it and choosing Remove Item from the shortcut menu.

# Getting Help in Mac OS X

It's a good thing you've got a book about Mac OS X in your hands, because the only user manual you get with Mac OS X is the Help menu. You get a Web browser–like program that reads a set of help files that reside in your System→Library folder.

---

*Tip:* In fact, you may not even be *that* lucky. In Leopard, the general-information Help page about each topic is on your Mac, but thousands of more nichey or more technical pages actually reside online, and require an Internet connection to read.

---

You're expected to find the topic you want in one of these three ways:

- **Use the new Search box.** When you click the Help menu , a tiny search box appears just beneath your cursor (Figure 2-19). You can type a few words here to specify what you want help on: "setting up printer," "disk space," whatever.

*Tip:* You can also hit ⌘-Shift-/ (that is, ⌘-?) to open the Help search box.

**Figure 2-19:**
*In Leopard, you don't have to open the Help program to begin a search. No matter what program you're in, typing a search phrase into the box shown here produces an instantaneous list of help topics, ready to read.*

---

**GEM IN THE ROUGH**

## Menu Help in the Help Menu

Mac OS X Leopard contains a weird, wonderful little enhancement to its online help system. It helps you find menu commands you can't find.

You're floundering in some program. You're *sure* there's a Page Numbering command in those menus somewhere. But there are 11 menus and 143 submenus hiding in those menus, and you haven't got time for the pain.

That's when you should think of using the Help menu. When you type *page number* (or whatever) into its Search box, the results menu lists, at the top, the names of any menu commands in that program that contain the words you typed. Better still, it actually *opens that menu* for you, and displays a big, blue, animated, floating arrow pointing to the command you wanted. You'd have to have your eyes closed to miss it.

Slide your cursor over, click the menu command, and get

on with your life.

Supertip: This feature is especially helpful in Web browsers like Safari and Firefox, because it even finds entries in your Bookmarks and History menus!

In Safari, for example, you can pluck a recently visited site out of the hundreds in the daily History submenus, like the "Wednesday, January 9" submenu. You've just saved yourself a *lot* of poking around menus, trying to find the name of a site you know you've seen recently.)

Ultratip: If you think about it, this feature also means that you have complete keyboard power over every menu in every program in the world. Hit ⌘-Shift-? to open the Help search box, type a bit of the command's name, and then use the arrow keys to walk down the results. Hit Enter to trigger the command you want

---

The menu now becomes a list of Apple help topics pertaining to your search. Click one to open the Help browser described next; you've just saved some time and a couple of steps.

---

***Tip:*** The results menu does not, however, show *all* of Help's results—only the ones Apple thinks are most relevant. If you choose Show All Results at the bottom of the menu, the Help browser opens (described below). It shows a more complete list of Help-search results.

---

- **Drill down.** Alternatively, you can begin your quest for assistance the old-fashioned way: by opening the Help browser first. To do that, choose Help→Mac Help. (This works only in the Finder, and only when nothing is typed in the Search box. To empty the Search box, click the ⊗ button at the right end.)

After a moment, you arrive at the Help browser program shown in Figure 2-20. The starting screen offers several "quick click" topics that may interest you. If so, keep clicking text headings until you find a topic that you want to read.

You can backtrack by clicking the ◄ button at the top of the window. And you can always return to the starting screen by clicking the little Home icon at the top.

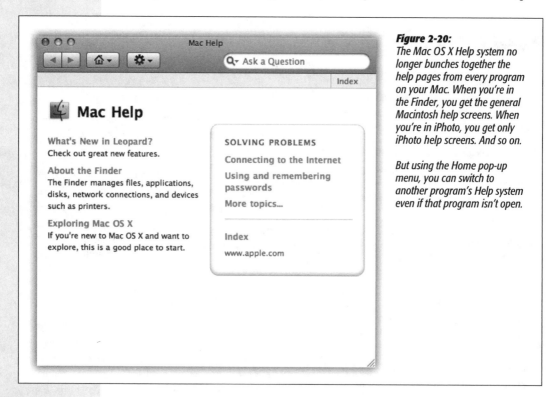

**Figure 2-20:**
*The Mac OS X Help system no longer bunches together the help pages from every program on your Mac. When you're in the Finder, you get the general Macintosh help screens. When you're in iPhoto, you get only iPhoto help screens. And so on.*

*But using the Home pop-up menu, you can switch to another program's Help system even if that program isn't open.*

**Tip:** Annoyingly, the Leopard Help window insists on floating in front of all other windows; you can't send it to the back like any normal program. Therefore, consider making the window tall and skinny, so you can put it *beside* the program you're working in. Drag the ribbed lower-right corner to change the window's shape.

- **Use the "Ask a Question" blank.** Type the phrase you want, such as *printing* or *switching applications*, into the Search box at the top of the window, and then press Return. The Mac responds by showing you a list of help-screen topics that may pertain to what you need (Figure 2-21).

  This Search box usually gives you a more complete list of results than you'd have gotten by using the Search box in the Help *menu*, as described above.

**Note:** Actually, there's one more place where Help has cropped up in Leopard: in System Preferences dialog boxes. Click the blue, circled question-mark button in the lower-right corner of each System Preferences panel to open a Help page that identifies each control.

***Figure 2-21:***
*The bars indicate the Mac's "relevance" rating—how well it thinks each help page matches your search. Double-click a topic's name to open the help page. If it isn't as helpful as you hoped, click the ◄ button at the top of the window to return to the list of relevant topics. Click the little Home button to return to the Help Center's welcome screen.*

# Files, Icons, & Spotlight

E very document, program, folder, and disk on your Mac is represented by an *icon:* a colorful little picture that you can move, copy, or double-click to open. In Mac OS X, icons look more like photos than cartoons, and you can scale them to practically any size.

This chapter is all about manipulating those icons—that is, your files, folders, and disks. It's all about naming them, copying them, deleting them, labeling them—and then, maybe most important of all, finding them, using the Mac's famous Spotlight instant-search feature.

## Renaming Icons

A Mac OS X icon's name can have up to 255 letters and spaces. If you're accustomed to the 31-character or even 8-character limits of older computers, that's quite a luxurious ceiling.

As a Windows veteran, futhermore, you may be delighted to discover that in Mac OS X, you can name your files using letters, numbers, punctuation—in fact, any symbol except for the colon (:), which the Mac uses behind the scenes for its own folder-hierarchy designation purposes. And you can't use a period to *begin* a file's name.

To rename a file, click its name or icon (to highlight it) and then press Return or Enter. (Or, if you have time to kill, click once on the name, wait a moment, and then click a second time.)

In any case, a rectangle now appears around the name (Figure 3-1). At this point, the existing name is highlighted; just begin typing to replace it. If you type a very long name, the rectangle grows vertically to accommodate new lines of text.

*Tip:* If you simply want to add letters to the beginning or end of the file's existing name, press the left or right arrow key immediately after pressing Return or Enter. The insertion point jumps to the corresponding end of the file name.

When you're finished typing, press Return, Enter, or Tab—or just click somewhere else—to make the renaming rectangle disappear.

As you edit a file's name, remember that you can use the Cut, Copy, and Paste commands in the Edit menu to move selected bits of text around, just as though you're word processing. The Paste command can be useful when, for instance, you're renaming many icons in sequence (*Quarterly Estimate 1, Quarterly Estimate 2,* and so on).

**Figure 3-1:**
*Click an icon's name (top left) to produce the renaming rectangle (top right), in which you can edit the file's name. Leopard is kind enough to highlight only the existing name, and not the suffix (like .jpg or .doc).*

*Now just begin typing to replace the existing name (bottom left). When you're finished typing, press Return, Enter, or Tab to seal the deal, or just click somewhere else.*

And now, a few tips about renaming icons:

- When the Finder sorts files, a space is considered alphabetically *before* the letter A. To force a particular folder to appear at the top of a list view window, insert a space before its name.

- Older operating systems sort files so that 10 and 100 come before 2, the numbers 30 and 300 come before 4, and so on. You wind up with alphabetically sorted files like this: "1. Big Day," "10. Long Song," "2. Floppy Hat," "20. Dog Bone," "3. Weird Sort," and so on. Generations of computer users have learned to put zeros in front of their single-digit numbers just to make the sorting look right.

    In Mac OS X, though, you get exactly the numerical list you'd hope for: "1. Big Day," "2. Floppy Hat," "3. Weird Sort," "10. Long Song," and "20. Dog Bone." At long last, you can get out of the habit of putting zeros in front of file names to make them sort properly.

# Selecting Icons

To highlight a single icon in preparation for printing, opening, duplicating, or deleting, click the icon once. Both the icon and the name darken in a uniquely Leopardish way.

---

***Tip:*** You can change the color of the oval highlighting that appears around the name of a selected icon. Choose  →System Preferences, click Appearance, and use the Highlight Color pop-up menu.)

---

That much may seem obvious. But lots of people have no idea how to manipulate *more* than one icon at a time—an essential survival skill. These techniques are essentially the same as in Windows, except that the keys you hold down are different.

## Selecting by Clicking

To highlight multiple files in preparation for moving or copying, use one of these techniques:

- **To highlight all the icons.** To select all the icons in a window, press ⌘-A (the equivalent of the Edit→Select All command).

- **To highlight several icons by dragging.** You can drag diagonally to highlight a group of nearby icons, as shown in Figure 3-2. In a list view, in fact, you don't even have to drag over the icons themselves—your cursor can touch any part of any file's row, like its modification date or file size.

---

***Tip:*** If you include a particular icon in your diagonally dragged group by mistake, ⌘-click it to remove it from the selected cluster.

---

**Figure 3-2:**
*You can highlight several icons simultaneously by dragging a box around them. To do so, drag from outside of the target icons diagonally across them (right), creating a translucent gray rectangle as you go. Any icons or icon names touched by this rectangle are selected when you release the mouse. If you press the Shift or ⌘ key as you do this, any previously highlighted icons remain selected.*

Start dragging here

- **To highlight consecutive icons in a list.** If you're looking at the contents of a window in list view or column view, you can drag vertically over the file and folder names to highlight a group of consecutive icons, as described above. (Begin the drag in a blank spot.)

There's a faster way to do the same thing: Click the first icon you want to highlight, and then Shift-click the last file, just as in Windows. All the files in between are automatically selected, along with the two icons you clicked.

- **To highlight random icons.** If you want to highlight only the first, third, and seventh icons in a window, for example, start by clicking icon No. 1. Then ⌘-click each of the others (or ⌘-drag new rectangles around them). Each icon darkens to show that you've selected it.

If you're highlighting a long string of icons and click one by mistake, you don't have to start over. Instead, just ⌘-click it again, so that the dark highlighting disappears. (If you do want to start over, you can deselect all selected icons by clicking any empty part of the window—or by pressing the Esc key.)

The ⌘ key trick is especially handy if you want to select *almost* all the icons in a window. Press ⌘-A to select everything in the folder, then ⌘-click any unwanted icons to deselect them.

Once you've highlighted multiple icons, you can manipulate them all at once. For example, you can drag them en masse to another folder or disk by dragging any *one* of the highlighted icons. All other highlighted icons go along for the ride. This technique is especially useful when you want to back up a bunch of files by dragging them onto a different disk, delete them all by dragging them to the Trash, and so on.

When multiple icons are selected, the commands in the File and Edit menus—such as Duplicate, Open, and Make Alias—apply to all of them simultaneously.

## Selecting Icons from the Keyboard

For the speed fanatic, using the mouse to click an icon is a hopeless waste of time. Fortunately, you can also select an icon by typing the first couple letters of its name.

When looking at your Home window, for example, you can type *M* to highlight the Movies folder. And if you actually intended to highlight the Music folder instead, press the Tab key to highlight the next icon in the window alphabetically. Shift-Tab highlights the previous icon alphabetically. Or use the arrow keys to highlight a neighboring icon.

(The Tab-key trick works only in icon, list, and Cover Flow views—not column view, alas. You can always use the ← and → keys to highlight adjacent columns, however.)

After highlighting an icon this way, you can manipulate it using the commands in the File menu or their keyboard equivalents: open (⌘-O), put it into the Trash (⌘-Delete), Get Info (⌘-I), duplicate (⌘-D), or make an alias, as described later in this chapter (⌘-L). By turning on the special disability features described on page 304, you can even *move* the highlighted icon using only the keyboard.

# Moving and Copying Icons

In Mac OS X, there are two ways to move or copy icons from one place to another: by dragging them, or by using the Copy and Paste commands.

## Copying by Dragging

You can drag icons from one folder to another, from one drive to another, from a drive to a folder on another drive, and so on. (When you've selected several icons, drag any *one* of them; the others tag along.) While the Mac is copying, you can tell that the process is still under way even if the progress bar is hidden behind a window, because the icon of the copied material shows up *dimmed* in its new home, darkening only when the copying process is over. (You can also tell because Leopard's progress box is a lot clearer and prettier than it used to be.) You can cancel the process by pressing either ⌘-period or the Esc key.

---

***Tip:*** If you're copying files into a disk or folder that already contains items with the same names, Mac OS X asks you individually about each one. ("An older item named 'Fiddlesticks' with extension '.doc' already exists in this location.") Note that, thank heaven, Mac OS X tells you whether the version you're replacing is *older* or *newer* than the one you're moving.

Turn on "Apply to all" if all of the incoming icons should (or should not) replace the old ones of the same names. Then click Replace or Don't Replace, as you see fit, or Stop to halt the whole copying business.

---

Understanding when the Mac *copies* a dragged icon and when it *moves* it bewilders many a beginner. However, the scheme is fairly simple when you consider the following:

- Dragging from one folder to another on the same disk *moves* the icon.

---

**UP TO SPEED**

## The Wacky Keystrokes of Leopard

Mac OS X offers a glorious assortment of predefined keystrokes for jumping to the most important locations on your Mac: your Home folder, the Applications folder, the Utilities folder, the Computer window, your iDisk, the Network window, and so on.

Better yet, the keystrokes are incredibly simple to memorize: Just press Shift-⌘ and the first letter of the location you want. Shift-⌘-H opens your Home folder, Shift-⌘-A opens the Applications folder, and so on. You learn one, you've learned 'em all.

The point here is that Shift-⌘, in Leopard, means *places*.

The other system-wide key combo, Option-⌘, means *functions*. For example, Option-⌘-D hides or shows the Dock, Option-⌘-H is the Hide Others command, Option-⌘-+ magnifies the screen (if you've turned on this feature), Option-⌘-Esc brings up the Force Quit dialog box, and so on. Consistency is always nice.

---

- Dragging from one disk (or disk partition) to another *copies* the folder or file. (You can drag icons either into an open window or directly onto a disk or folder *icon*.)

- If you press the Option key as you release an icon you've dragged, you *copy* the icon instead of moving it. Doing so within a single folder produces a duplicate of the file called "[Whatever its name was] copy."

- If you press the ⌘ key as you release an icon you've dragged from one disk to another, you *move* the file or folder, in the process deleting it from the original disk.

---

***Tip:*** This business of pressing Option or ⌘ *after* you begin dragging is a tad awkward, but it has its charms. For example, it means that you can change your mind about the purpose of your drag in mid-movement, without having to drag back and start over.

---

And if it turns out you just dragged something into the wrong window or folder, a quick ⌘-Z (the shortcut for Edit→Undo) puts it right back where it came from.

## Copying by Using Copy and Paste

Dragging icons to copy or move them probably feels good because it's so direct: You actually see your arrow cursor pushing the icons into the new location.

But you pay a price for this satisfying illusion. You may have to spend a moment or two fiddling with your windows to create a clear "line of drag" between the icon to be moved and the destination folder. (A background window will courteously pop to the foreground to accept your drag. But if it wasn't even open to begin with, you're out of luck.)

There's a better way. Use the Copy and Paste commands to move icons from one window into another (just as you can in Windows—except you can only copy, not cut, Mac icons). The routine goes like this:

---

**NOSTALGIA CORNER**

### Printing a Window—or a List of Files

*Hey, in Mac OS 9, I could print a Finder window. I'd get a neat list of the files, which I could use as a label for a CD I was going to burn, or whatever. How do I print a Finder window in Mac OS X? (The File→Print command prints a selected document, not the list of files in a window.)*

It's easy enough to make a list of files for printing. Once the window is open on your screen, choose Edit→Select All. Choose Edit→Copy. Now switch to a word processor and paste. (If you're using TextEdit, use Edit→Paste and Match Style instead.) You get a tidy list of all the files in that window, ready to format and print.

This simple file name list still isn't the same as printing a window, that's true; you don't get the status bar showing how many items are on the disk and how full the disk is. For that purpose, you can always make a screenshot of the window (page 570), and print that. Of course, that technique's no good if the list of files is taller than the window itself.

Really, what you want is Print Window, a handy shareware program dedicated to printing out your Finder windows, without any of these workarounds or limitations. You can download it from the "Missing CD" page at *www.missingmanuals.com*.

---

1. **Highlight the icon or icons you want to move.**

   Use any of the techniques described on page 63.

2. **Choose Edit→Copy.**

   Or press the keyboard shortcut: ⌘-C.

---

**Tip:** You can combine steps 1 and 2 by right-clicking an icon and choosing the Copy command from the shortcut menu that appears—or by using the ✿ menu. If you've selected several icons, say five, the command will say "Copy 5 items."

---

3. **Open the window where you want to put the icons. Choose Edit→Paste.**

   Once again, you may prefer to use the keyboard equivalent: ⌘-V. And once again, you can also right-click inside the window and then choose Paste from the shortcut menu that appears, or you can use the ✿ menu.

A progress bar may appear as Mac OS X copies the files or folders; press Esc or ⌘-period to interrupt the process. When the progress bar goes away, it means you've successfully transferred the icons, which now appear in the new window.

## Spring-Loaded Folders: Dragging Icons into Closed Folders

Here's a common dilemma: You want to drag an icon not just into a folder, but into a folder nested *inside* that folder. This awkward challenge would ordinarily require you to open the folder, open the inner folder, drag the icon in, and then close both of the windows you opened. As you can imagine, the process is even messier if you want to drag an icon into a sub-subfolder or even a *sub*-sub-subfolder.

Fortunately, there's a better waky: *spring-loaded folders* feature (Figure 3-3).

With a single drag, drag the icon onto the first folder—but keep your mouse button pressed. After a second, the window opens automatically, centered on your cursor.

Still keeping the button down, drag onto the inner folder; its window opens, too. Now drag onto the *inner* inner folder—and so on. (If the inner folder you intend to open isn't visible in the window, you can scroll by dragging your cursor close to any edge of the window.)

---

**Tip:** You can even drag icons onto disks or folders whose icons appear in the Sidebar (Chapter 1). When you do so, the main part of the window flashes to reveal the contents of the disk or folder you've dragged onto. When you let go of the mouse, the main window changes back to reveal the contents of the disk or folder where you *started* dragging.

In short, Sidebar combined with spring-loaded folders make a terrific drag-and-drop way to file a desktop icon from anywhere to anywhere—without having to open or close any windows at all.

---

When you finally release the mouse, you're left facing the final window. All the previous windows closed on the way. You've neatly placed the icon into the core of the nested folders.

## Making Spring-Loaded Folders Work

That spring-loaded folder technique sounds good in theory, but can be disconcerting in practice. For most people, the long wait before the first folder opens is almost enough wasted time to negate the value of the feature altogether. Furthermore, when the first window finally does open, you're often caught by surprise. Suddenly your cursor—mouse button still down—is inside a window, sometimes directly on top of another folder you never intended to open. But before you can react, its window, too, has opened, and you find yourself out of control.

**Figure 3-3:**
*Top: To make spring-loaded folders work, start by dragging an icon onto a folder or disk icon. Don't release the mouse button. Wait for the window to open automatically around your cursor.*

*Bottom: Now you can either let go of the mouse button to release the file in its new window or drag it onto yet another, inner folder. It, too, will open. As long as you don't release the mouse button, you can continue until you've reached your folder-within-a-folder destination.*

Fortunately, you can regain control of spring-loaded folders using these tricks:

• Choose Finder→Preferences. On the General pane, adjust the "Spring-loaded folders and windows" Delay slider to a setting that drives you less crazy. For example, if you find yourself waiting too long before the first folder opens, drag the slider toward the Short setting.

- You can turn off this feature entirely by choosing Finder→Preferences and turning off the "Spring-loaded folders and windows" checkbox.

- Tap the Space bar to make the folder spring open at your command. That is, even with the Finder→Preferences slider set to the Long delay setting, you can force each folder to spring open when *you* are ready by tapping the Space bar as you hold down the mouse button. True, you need two hands to master this one, but the control you regain is immeasurable.

---

*Tip:* The Space bar trick works even when "Spring-loaded folders and windows" checkbox (in Finder→Preferences) is turned off. That's a handy arrangement, because it means that folder windows never pop open accidentally.

---

- Whenever a folder springs open into a window, twitch your mouse up to the newly opened window's title bar or down to its information strip. Doing so ensures that your cursor won't wind up hovering on, and accidentally opening up, an inner folder. With the cursor parked on the gradient gray, you can take your time to survey the newly opened window's contents, and plunge into an inner folder only after gaining your bearings.

---

*Tip:* Email programs like Entourage and Mail have spring-loaded folders, too. You can drag a message out of the list and into one of your filing folders, wait for the folder to spring open and reveal its subfolders, and then drag it directly into one of them.

---

**POWER USERS' CLINIC**

## Designing Your Own Icons

You don't have to be content with the icons provided by Microsoft, Apple, or whoever else wrote your software. You can paste new icons onto your file, disk, and folder icons to help you pick them out at a glance.

The easiest way to replace an icon is to copy it from another icon. To do so, highlight the icon, hold down the Option key and choose File→Show Inspector (see page 93). In the resulting window, click the existing icon, and then choose Edit→Copy.

Next, click the icon to which you want to transfer the copied picture. Its icon now appears in the Info dialog box that's still open on the screen. Click the icon in the dialog box, and this time choose Edit→Paste.

If you'd rather introduce all-new icons, you're welcome to steal some of the beautifully designed ones waiting at *www.iconfactory.com* and the icon sites linked to it.

Once you've downloaded these special icon files, you can copy their images from the Get Info window as you would any icon.

To design a Mac OS X icon from scratch, use a graphics program like Photoshop or the shareware favorite Graphic-Converter.

Once you've saved your icon file, select it, and then copy and paste its icon using the Show Inspector method described above.

Note that you can't change certain folder icons that Mac OS X considers important, such as Applications or System.

You can, however, change the special Mac OS X folder icons in your Home folder—Pictures, Documents, and so on, and your hard drive icon. You're also not allowed to change icons that belong to other people who share your Mac and sign in under a different name (Chapter 13).

# Aliases: Icons in Two Places at Once

Highlighting an icon and then choosing File→Make Alias (or pressing ⌘-L), generates an *alias,* a specially branded duplicate of the original icon (Figure 3-4). It's not a duplicate of the *file*—just of the *icon;* therefore it requires negligible storage space. When you double-click the alias, the original file opens. A Macintosh alias, in other words, is essentially the same as a Windows *shortcut.*

Because you can create as many aliases as you want of a single file, aliases let you, in effect, stash that file in many different folder locations simultaneously. Double-click any one of them, and you open the original icon, wherever it may be on your system.

---

***Tip:*** You can also create an alias of an icon by Option-⌘-dragging it out of its window. (Aliases you create this way lack the word *alias* on the file name—a distinct delight to those who find the suffix redundant and annoying.) You can also create an alias by right-clicking a normal icon and choosing Make Alias from the shortcut menu that appears, or by highlighting an icon and then choosing Make Alias from the ✿ menu.

---

Elbow Grease

Elbow Grease alias

The alias "Elbow Grease alias" could not be opened, because the original item cannot be found.

[ Delete Alias ]   [ Fix Alias... ]   [ OK ]

**Figure 3-4:**
*Top: You can identify an alias by the tiny arrow badge on the lower-left corner. (Longtime Mac fans should note that the name no longer appears in italics.)*

*Bottom: If the alias can't find the original file, you're offered the chance to hook it up to a different file.*

## What's Good about Aliases

An alias takes up almost no disk space, even if the original file is enormous. Aliases are smart, too: even if you rename the alias, rename the original file, move the alias, and move the original around on the disk, double-clicking the alias still opens the original icon.

Here are a few ways you can put aliases to work:

- You may want to file a document you're working on in several different folders, or place a particular folder in several different locations.

- You can use the alias feature to save you some of the steps required to access another hard drive on the network. (Details on this trick in Chapter 13.)

---

**Tip:** Mac OS X makes it easy to find the file to which an alias "points" without actually having to open it. Just highlight the alias and then choose File→Show Original (⌘-R), or choose Show Original from the ✿ menu. Mac OS X immediately displays the actual, original file, sitting patiently in its folder, wherever that may be.

---

## Broken Aliases

An alias doesn't contain any of the information you've typed or composed in the original. Don't email an alias to the Tokyo office and then depart for the airport, hoping to give the presentation upon your arrival in Japan. When you double-click the alias, now separated from its original, you'll be shown the dialog box at bottom in Figure 3-4.

If you're on a plane 3,000 miles away from the hard drive on which the original file resides, click Delete Alias (to delete the orphan alias you just double-clicked) or OK (to do nothing, leaving the orphaned alias where it is).

In certain circumstances, however, the third button—Fix Alias—is the most useful. Click it to summon the Fix Alias dialog box, which you can use to navigate your entire Mac. When you click a new icon and then click Choose, you associate the orphaned alias with a different original icon.

Such techniques become handy when, for example, you click your book manuscript's alias on the desktop, forgetting that you recently saved it under a new name and deleted the older draft. Instead of simply showing you an error message that says "'Enron Corporate Ethics Handbook' can't be found," the Mac displays the box that contains the Fix Alias button. By clicking it, thus reassociating it with the new document, you can save yourself the trouble of creating a new alias. From now on, double-clicking your manuscript's alias on the desktop opens the new draft.

---

**Tip:** You don't have to wait until the original file no longer exists before choosing a new original for an alias. You can perform alias reassignment surgery any time you like. Just highlight the alias icon and then choose File→Get Info. In the Get Info dialog box, click Select New Original. In the resulting window, find and double-click the file you'd now like to open whenever you double-click the alias.

---

## Color Labels

This feature lets you tag selected icons with one of seven different labels, each of which has both a text label and a color associated with it.

To do so, highlight the icons. Open the File menu (or the ✿ menu, or the shortcut menu that appears when you right-click the icons). There, under the heading Color Label, you'll see seven colored dots, which represent the seven different labels you can use. Figure 3-5 shows the routine.

---

## What Labels Are Good For

After you've applied labels to icons, you can perform some unique file-management tasks—in some cases, on all of them simultaneously, even if they're scattered across multiple hard drives. For example:

**Figure 3-5:**
Use the File menu, ✿ menu, or shortcut menu to apply label tags to highlighted icons.

Instantly, the icon's name takes on the selected shade. In a list or column view, the entire row takes on that shade, as shown in Figure 3-6. (If you choose the little X, you're removing any labels that you may have applied.)

## Compressing, Zipping, and Archiving

Mac OS X comes with a built-in command that compresses a file or folder down to a single, smaller icon—an archive—suitable for storing or emailing.

It's just like using StuffIt in previous Mac OS versions, except for two big changes. First, Mac OS X creates .zip files, the same compression format used in Windows. That means that you can now send .zip files back and forth to PC owners without worrying that they won't be able to open them. In Leopard, these files open even more reliably in Windows. (Pre-Panther/Tiger/Leopard Mac owners can open .zip files, too. They just use the free StuffIt Expander as usual.)

Second, the software that does the compressing is built right in. Right-click a file or folder, and choose "Compress [the icon's name]" from the shortcut menu. (Of course, you can use the File menu or ✿ menu instead.)

Mac OS X thoughtfully creates a .zip archive, but leaves the original behind so you can continue working with it.

Opening a .zip file somebody sends you is equally easy: Just double-click it. Zip!—it opens.

On the other hand, Leopard does not come with StuffIt Expander, the free unstuffing program that recognizes .zip files, .sit files, and just about any other form of compressed files.

If you don't already have a copy of Expander from a previous Mac OS version, you can download and install it yourself, which is worth doing. You can get it from, for example, this book's "Missing CD" page at *www.missingmanuals.com.*

- **Round up files with Find.** Using the Find command described in Chapter 3, you can round up all icons with a particular label. Thereafter, moving these icons at once is a piece of cake—choose Edit→Select All, and then drag any one of the highlighted icons out of the results window and into the target folder or disk.

  Using labels in conjunction with Find this way is one of the most useful and inexpensive backup schemes ever devised—whenever you finish working on a document that you'd like to back up, right-click it and apply a label called, for example, Backup. At the end of each day, use the Find command to round up all files with the Backup label—and then drag them as a group onto your backup disk.

- **Sort a list view by label.** No other Mac sorting method lets you create an arbitrary order for the icons in a window. When you sort by label, the Mac creates alphabetical clusters *within* each label grouping, as shown in Figure 3-6.

**Figure 3-6:**
*Sorting by label lets you create several different alphabetical groups within a single window. In Leopard, in fact, you can sort by labels in any view (icon, column, whatever), using the View→Show View Options palette.*

*In a list view, the quickest way to sort by label is to first make the label column visible. Do so by choosing View→Show View Options and turning on the Label checkbox.*

This technique might be useful when, for example, your job is to process several different folders of documents; for each folder, you're supposed to convert graphics files, throw out old files, or whatever. As soon as you finish working your way through one folder, flag it with a label called Done. The folder jumps to the top (or bottom) of the window, safely marked for your reference pleasure, leaving the next unprocessed folder at your fingertips, ready to go.

- **Track progress.** Use different color labels to track the status of files in a certain project. The first drafts have no labels at all. Once they've been edited and approved, make them blue. Once they've been sent to the home office, they turn purple. (Heck, you could have all kinds of fun with this: Money-losing projects get red tints; profitable ones get green; things that make you sad are blue. Or maybe not.)

## Changing Labels

When you first install Mac OS X, the seven labels in the File menu are named for the colors they show: Red, Orange, Yellow, and so on. Clearly, the label feature would be much more useful if you could rewrite these labels, tailoring them to your purposes.

Doing so is easy. Choose Finder→Preferences. Click the Labels button. Now you see the dialog box shown in Figure 3-7, where you can edit the text of each label.

**Figure 3-7:**
*Top left: In the Labels tab of the Preferences dialog box, you can change the predefined label text. Each label can be up to 31 letters and spaces long.*

*Bottom right: Now your list and column views reveal meaningful text tags instead of color names.*

## The Trash

No single element of the Macintosh interface is as recognizable or famous as the Trash can, which now appears at the end of the Dock. It is, of course, the inspiration for Windows's own Recycle Bin.

You can discard almost any icon by dragging it onto the Trash icon (actually a wastebasket, not a trash can, but let's not quibble). When the tip of your arrow cursor touches the Trash icon, the little wastebasket turns black. When you release the mouse, you're well on your way to discarding whatever it was you dragged. As a convenience, Mac OS X even replaces the empty-wastebasket icon with a wastebasket-filled-with-crumpled-up-papers icon, to let you know there's something in there.

---

*Tip:* Learn the keyboard alternative to dragging something to the Trash: Highlight the icon, and then press ⌘-Delete. This technique is not only far faster than dragging, but requires far less precision, especially if you have a large screen. Mac OS X does all the Trash-targeting for you.

---

## Rescuing Files and Folders from the Trash

File and folder icons sit in the Trash forever—or until you choose Finder→Empty Trash, whichever comes first.

If you haven't yet emptied the Trash, you can open its window by clicking the wastebasket icon once. Now you can review its contents: icons that you've placed on the waiting list for extinction. If you change your mind, you can rescue any of these items by dragging them out of the Trash window.

## Emptying the Trash I: Quick and Easy

If you're confident that the items in the Trash window are worth deleting, use any of these three options:

- Choose Finder→Empty Trash.

- Press Shift-⌘-Delete. Or, if you'd just as soon not bother with the "Are you sure?" message, throw the Option key in there, too.

- Right-click the wastebasket icon; choose Empty Trash from the shortcut menu.

---

*Tip:* This last method has two advantages. First, the Mac doesn't bother asking "Are you sure?" (If you're clicking right on the Trash and choosing Empty Trash from the pop-up menu, it's pretty darned obvious you *are* sure.) Second, this method nukes any locked files without making you unlock them first.

---

If you use either of the first two methods, the Macintosh asks you to confirm your decision. Click OK. (Figure 3-8 shows both this message and the secret for turning it off forever.)

Either way, Mac OS X now deletes those files from your hard drive.

## Emptying the Trash II: Secure and Forever

When you empty the Trash as described above, each Trashed icon sure looks like it disappears. The truth is, though, that the data *in* each file is still on the hard drive.

---

**GEM IN THE ROUGH**

### Opening Things in the Trash

Now and then, it's very useful to see what some document in the Trash *is* before committing it to oblivion—and the only way to do that is to open it.

Trouble is, you can't open it by double-clicking; you'll get nothing but an error message.

Or at least that's what Apple *wants* you to think.

There is, of course, a workaround or two. First of all, you can use Quick Look (page 58) to inspect something in the Trash.

Or, if Quick Look can't open the file—or if you want to *edit* it instead of just reading it—drag the document onto the icon of a program that can open it. That is, if a file called Don't Read Me.txt is in the Trash, you can drag it onto, say, the Word or TextEdit icon in your Dock.

The document dutifully pops open on the screen. Inspect, close, and *then* empty the Trash (or rescue the document).

---

Yes, the space occupied by the dearly departed is now marked with an internal "This space available" message, and in time, new files that you save may overwrite that spot. But in the meantime, some future eBay buyer of your Mac—or, more imminently, a savvy family member or office mate—could use a program like Norton Utilities to resurrect those deleted files. (In more dire cases, companies like DriveSavers.com can use sophisticated clean-room techniques to recover crucial information—for several hundred dollars, of course.)

That notion doesn't sit well with certain groups, like government agencies, international spies, and the paranoid. As far as they're concerned, deleting a file should *really, really* delete it, irrevocably, irretrievably, and forever.

Mac OS X has a command, therefore, called *Secure* Empty Trash. When you choose this command from the Finder menu, the Mac doesn't just obliterate the parking spaces around the dead file. It actually records *new* information over the old—random 0's and 1's. Pure static gibberish.

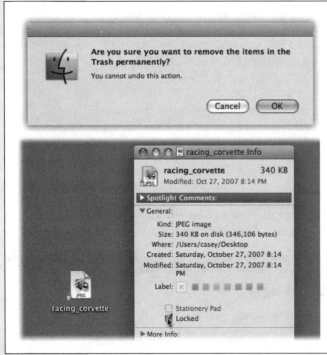

**Figure 3-8:**
*Top: Your last warning. Mac OS X doesn't tell you how many items are in the Trash or how much disk space they take up.*

*If you'd rather not be interrupted for confirmation every time you empty the Trash, you can suppress this message permanently.*

*To do that, choose File→Preferences, click Advanced, and turn off "Show warning before emptying the Trash."*

*Bottom: The Get Info window for a locked file. Locking a file in this way isn't military-level security by any stretch–any passing evildoer can unlock the file in the same way. But it does trigger an "operation cannot be completed" warning when you try to put it into the Trash–or indeed when you try to drag it into any other folder–providing at least one layer of protection against mistakes.*

The process takes longer than the normal Empty Trash command, of course. But when it absolutely, positively has to be gone from this earth for good (and you're absolutely, positively sure you'll never need that file again), Secure Empty Trash is secure indeed.

## Locked Files: The Next Generation

By highlighting a file or folder, choosing File→Get Info, and turning on the Locked checkbox, you protect that file or folder from accidental deletion (see Figure 3-8 at bottom). A little padlock icon appears on the corner of the full-size icon, also shown in Figure 3-8.

Mac OS X doesn't even let you put a locked icon *into* the Trash—or *any* other folder. You can't put the icon of an open program into the Trash, either.

If something that's already *in* the Trash turns out to be locked, click and hold on the Trash itself. Now, when you choose Empty Trash from its shortcut menu, Mac OS X empties the Trash without warnings, locked files and all.

Of course, the other alternative is to unlock what's in the Trash. Fortunately, there's a quick way to do so. Click the Trash icon to open its window, then highlight the icons you want to unlock (or choose Edit→Select All).

Now press Option-⌘-I (or press Option as you choose File→Show Inspector). Turn off the Locked checkbox in the resulting Info window. (Yes, you can lock or unlock a mass of files at once.) Now you can send the newly unprotected files to data heaven without any fancy tricks.

# Get Info

By clicking an icon and then choosing File→Get Info, you open an important window like the one shown in Figure 3-9. It's a collapsible, multipanel screen that provides a wealth of information about a highlighted icon. In essence, this is the Properties window for the icon. For example:

- For a document icon, you see when it was created and modified, and what programs it "belongs" to.

- For an alias, you learn the location of the actual icon it refers to.

- For a program, you see whether or not it's been updated to run on Intel-based Macs. If so, the Get Info window says *Kind: Universal.* If not, it says *Kind: PowerPC,* and will probably run slower than you'd like because it must be translated by Rosetta (page 145).

- For a disk icon, you get statistics about its capacity and how much of it is full.

- If you open the Get Info window when *nothing* is selected, you get information about the desktop itself (or the open window), including the amount of disk space consumed by everything sitting on or in it.

- If you highlight 11 icons or more simultaneously, the Get Info window shows you how many you highlighted, breaks it down by type ("23 documents, 3 folders," for example), and adds up the total of their file sizes. That's a great opportunity to change certain file characteristics on numerous files simultaneously, such as locking or unlocking them, hiding or showing their filename extensions (page 131), changing their ownership or permissions (page 418), and so on.

If you highlight fewer than 11 icons, Mac OS X opens up individual Get Info windows for each one.

## The Get Info Panels

Apple built the Get Info window out of a series of collapsed "flippy triangles," as shown in Figure 3-9. Click a triangle to expand a corresponding information panel.

Depending on whether you clicked a document, program, disk, alias, or whatever, the various panels may include the following:

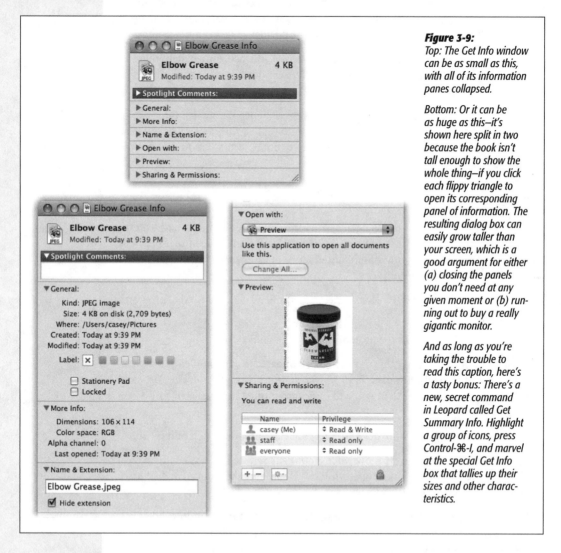

**Figure 3-9:**
*Top: The Get Info window can be as small as this, with all of its information panes collapsed.*

*Bottom: Or it can be as huge as this—it's shown here split in two because the book isn't tall enough to show the whole thing—if you click each flippy triangle to open its corresponding panel of information. The resulting dialog box can easily grow taller than your screen, which is a good argument for either (a) closing the panels you don't need at any given moment or (b) running out to buy a really gigantic monitor.*

*And as long as you're taking the trouble to read this caption, here's a tasty bonus: There's a new, secret command in Leopard called Get Summary Info. Highlight a group of icons, press Control-⌘-I, and marvel at the special Get Info box that tallies up their sizes and other characteristics.*

- **Spotlight Comments.** Here, you can type in random comments for your own reference. Later, you can view these remarks in any list view, if you display the

Comments column (see page 49)—and find them when you conduct Spotlight searches.

- **General.** Here's where you can view (and edit) the name of the icon, and also see its size, creation date, most recent change date, locked status, and so on.

  If you click a disk, this info window shows you its capacity and how full it is. If you click the Trash, you see how much stuff is in it. If you click an alias, this panel shows you a Select New Original button and reveals where the original file is. The General panel always opens the first time you summon the Get Info window.

- **More Info.** Just as the name implies, here you'll find more info, most often the dimensions and color format (graphics only) and when the icon was last opened. These morsels are also easily Spotlight-searchable.

- **Name & Extension.** On this panel, you can read and edit the name of the icon in question. The "Hide extension" checkbox refers to the suffix on Mac OS X file names (the last three letters of *Letter to Congress.doc,* for example).

  Many Mac OS X documents, behind the scenes, have filename extensions of this kind—but Mac OS X comes factory-set to hide them. By turning off this checkbox, you can make the suffix reappear for an individual file. (Conversely, if you've elected to have Mac OS X *show* all file name suffixes, this checkbox lets you hide filename extensions on individual icons.)

- **Open with.** This section is available for documents only. Use the controls on this screen to specify which program will open when you double-click this document, or all documents of its type. (Details on page 132.)

- **Preview.** When you're examining pictures, text files, PDF files, Microsoft Office files, sounds, clippings, and movies, you see a magnified thumbnail version of what's actually *in* that document. This Preview is like a tiny version of Quick Look (page 57). A controller lets you play sounds and movies, where appropriate.

- **Languages.** The menus and dialog boxes of well-written Mac OS X programs (iMovie and iPhoto, for example) appear by magic in whatever language you choose. The trouble is, your hard drive carries a lot of baggage as a result; it must store the wording for every menu and dialog box in every language.

  If you're pretty sure you do most of your computing in just one language, expand the Languages tab, select all of the languages you *don't* speak, and click Remove. You can reclaim a *lot* of hard-drive space this way.

- **Sharing & Permissions.** This is available for all kinds of icons. If other people have access to your Mac (either from across the network or when logging in, in person), this panel lets you specify who is allowed to open or change this particular icon. See Chapter 14 for a discussion of this hairy topic.

Here and there, you may even see other panels in the Get Info window, especially when you get info on application icons. For example, iPhoto and iDVD each offer a Plugins panel that lets you manage add-on software modules.

## The Spotlight Menu

Every computer offers a way to find files. And every system offers several different ways to open them. But Spotlight, a star feature of Mac OS X, combines these two functions in a way that's so fast, so efficient, so spectacular, it reduces much of what you've read in the previous chapters to irrelevance.

That may sound like breathless hype, but wait till you try it. You'll see.

See the little magnifying-glass icon in your menu bar? That's the mouse-driven way to open the Spotlight search box.

The other way is to press ⌘-Space bar. If you can memorize only one keystroke on your Mac, that's the one to learn. It works both at the desktop and in other programs.

In any case, the Spotlight text box appears just below your menu bar (Figure 3-10).

Begin typing to identify what you want to find and open. For example, if you're trying to find a file called *Pokémon Fantasy League.doc,* typing just *pok* or *leag* would probably suffice. (Spotlight doesn't find text in the *middles* of words, though; it searches from the beginnings of words.)

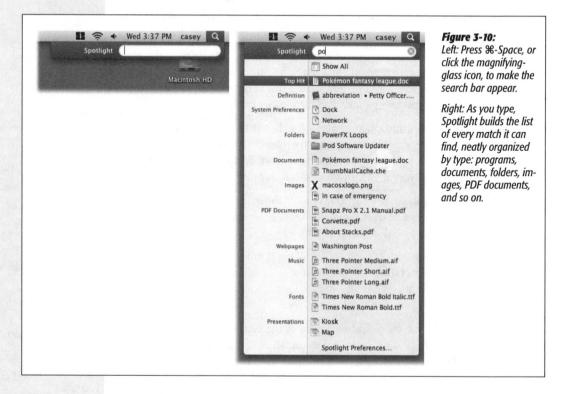

*Figure 3-10:*
*Left: Press ⌘-Space, or click the magnifying-glass icon, to make the search bar appear.*

*Right: As you type, Spotlight builds the list of every match it can find, neatly organized by type: programs, documents, folders, images, PDF documents, and so on.*

A menu immediately appears below the search box, listing everything Spotlight can find containing what you've typed so far. (This is a live, interactive search; that is, Spotlight modifies the menu of search results *as you type.*) The menu lists every file, folder, program, email message, address book entry, calendar appointment, picture, movie, PDF document, music file, Web bookmark, Microsoft Office (Word, PowerPoint, Excel, Entourage) document, System Preferences panel, To Do item, chat transcript, Web site in your History list, and even font that contains what you typed, regardless of its name or folder location.

If you see the icon you were hoping to dig up, just click it to open it. Or use the arrow keys to "walk down" the menu, and then press Return or Enter to open it.

If you click an application, it pops onto the screen. If you select a System Preferences panel, System Preferences opens and presents that panel. If you choose an appointment, the iCal program opens, already set to the appropriate day and time. Selecting an email message opens that message in Mail or Entourage. And so on.

Spotlight is so fast, it eliminates a lot of the folders-in-folders business that's a side effect of modern computing. Why burrow around in folders when you can open any file or program with a couple of keystrokes?

## Spotlight-Menu Tips

It should be no surprise that a feature as important as Spotlight comes loaded with options, tips, and tricks. Here it is—the official, unexpurgated Spotlight Tip-O-Rama:

- If the very first item—labeled Top Hit—is the icon you were looking for, just press Return or Enter to open it. This is a huge deal, because it means that in most cases, you can perform the entire operation without ever taking your hands off the keyboard.

  To open Safari in a hurry, for example, press ⌘-Space bar (to open the Spotlight bar), type *safa,* and hit Enter, all in rapid-fire sequence, without even looking. Presto: Safari is before you.

  And what, exactly, is the Top Hit? Mac OS X chooses it based on its *relevance* (the importance of your search term inside that item) and timeliness (when you last opened it).

---

***Tip:*** Spotlight makes a spectacular application launcher. That's because Job #1 for Spotlight is to display the names of matching *programs* in the results menu. Their names appear in the list nearly instantly—long before Spotlight has built the rest of the menu of search results.

If some program on your hard drive doesn't have a Dock icon, for example—or even if it does—there's no faster way to open it than to use Spotlight.

---

- To jump to a search result's Finder icon instead of opening it, ⌘-click its name.
- Spotlight's menu shows you only 20 of the most likely suspects, evenly divided among the categories (Documents, Applications, and so on). The downside: To see the complete list, you have to open the Spotlight *window* (page 100).

The upside: It's fairly easy to open something in this menu from the keyboard. Just press ⌘-down arrow (or ⌘-up arrow) to jump from category to category. Once you've highlighted the first result in a category, you can walk through the remaining four by pressing the arrow key by itself. Then, once you've highlighted what you want, press Return or Enter to open it.

In other words, you can get to anything in the Spotlight menu with only a few keystrokes.

• The Esc key (top-left corner of your keyboard) offers a two-stage "back out of this" method. Tap it once to close the Spotlight menu and erase what you've typed, so that you're all ready to type in something different. Tap Esc a *second* time to close the Spotlight text box entirely, having given up on the whole idea of searching.

(If you just want to cancel the whole thing in *one* step, press ⌘-Space bar again, or ⌘-period, or ⌘-Esc.)

• Think of Spotlight as your little black book. When you need to look up a number in Address Book, don't bother opening Address Book; it's faster to use Spotlight. You can type somebody's name or even part of someone's phone number.

• Spotlight is also a quick way to adjust one of your Mac's preference settings. Instead of opening up the System Preferences program, type the first few letters of, say, *volume* or *network* or *clock* into Spotlight. The Spotlight menu lists the appropriate System Preferences panel, so you can jump directly to it.

• If you point to an item in the Spotlight menu without clicking, a tooltip balloon appears. It tells you the item's actual name—which is useful if Spotlight listed something because of text that appears *inside* the file, not its name—and its folder path (that is, where it is on your hard drive).

• The Spotlight menu lists 20 found items. In the following pages, you'll learn about how to see the rest of the stuff. But for now, note that you can eliminate some of the categories that show up here (like PDF Documents or Bookmarks), and even rearrange them, to permit more of the *other* kinds of things to enjoy those 20 seats of honor. Details on page 107.

• Spotlight shows you only the matches from *your account* and the public areas of the Mac (like the System, Application, and Developer folders)—but not what's in anyone else's Home folder. If you were hoping to search your spouse's email for phrases like "meet you at midnight," forget it.

• If Spotlight finds a different version of something on each of two hard drives, it lets you know by displaying a faint gray hard drive name after each such item in the menu.

• Spotlight works by storing an *index,* a private, multimegabyte Dewey Decimal system, on each hard drive, disk partition, or USB flash (memory) drive. If you have some oddball type of disk, like a hard drive that's been formatted for Windows, Spotlight doesn't ordinarily index it—but you can turn on indexing by using the File→Get Info command on that drive's icon.

- If you point to something in the results list without clicking, you can press ⌘-I to open the Get Info window for that item.

## Advanced Menu Searches

Most people just type the words they're looking for into the Spotlight box. But if that's all you type, you're missing a lot of the fun.

### Use quotes

If you type more than one word, Spotlight works just the way Google does. That is, it finds things that contain both words *somewhere* inside.

But if you're searching for a phrase where the words really belong together, put quotes around them. You'll save yourself from having to wade through hundreds of results where the words appear *separately*.

For example, searching for *military intelligence* rounds up documents that contain those two words, but not necessarily side-by-side. Searching for *"military intelligence"* finds documents that contain that exact phrase. (Insert your own political joke here.)

### Limit by kind

You can confine your search to certain categories using a simple code. For example, to find all photos, type *kind:image*. If you're looking for a presentation document, but you're not sure whether you used Keynote, iWork, or PowerPoint to create it, type *kind:presentation* into the box. And so on.

Here's the complete list of kinds. Remember to precede each keyword type with *kind* and a colon.

| To find this: | Use one of these keywords: |
| --- | --- |
| A program | app, application, applications |
| Someone in your address book | contact, contacts |
| A folder | folder, folders |
| A message in Mail | email, emails, mail message, mail messages |
| An iCal appointment | event, events |
| An iCal task | to do, to dos, todo, todos |
| A graphic | image, images |
| A movie | movie, movies |
| A music file | music |
| An audio file | audio |
| A PDF file | pdf, pdfs |
| A System Preferences control | preferences, system preferences |
| A Safari bookmark | bookmark, bookmarks |
| A font | font, fonts |
| A presentation (PowerPoint, etc.) | presentation, presentations |

You can combine these codes with the text you're seeking, too. For example, if you're pretty sure you had a photo called "Naked Mole-Rat," you could cut directly to it by typing *mole kind:images* or *kind:images mole*. (The order doesn't matter.)

### Limit by recent date

You can use a similar code to restrict the search by chronology. If you type *date: yesterday*, Spotlight limits its hunt to items that you last opened yesterday.

Here's the complete list of date keywords you can use: *this week, this month, this year; today, yesterday, tomorrow; next week, next month, next year*. (The last four items are useful only for finding upcoming iCal appointments. Even Spotlight can't show you files you haven't created yet.)

### Limit by metadata

If your brain is already on the verge of exploding, now might be a good time to take a break.

In Leopard, you can limit Spotlight searches by *any* of the 125 different info-morsels that may be stored as part of the files on your Mac: Author, Audio bit rate, City, Composer, Camera model, Pixel width, and so on. Here are a few examples:

---

**GEM IN THE ROUGH**

## Sweet Spotlight Serendipity: Equations and Definitions

In Mac OS X 10.5, Spotlight has been given two quiet enhancements that turn it into a different beast altogether.

First, it's a tiny pocket calculator, always at the ready. Click in the Search box, type or paste *38*48.2-7+55*, and marvel at the first result in the Spotlight menu: *1879.6*. There's your answer—and you didn't even have to fire up the Calculator.

(For shorter equations—only a few characters long—the first result in the Spotlight menu shows the *entire* equation, like *.15*234=35.1*.)

And it's not just a four-function calculator, either. It works with square roots: Type *sqrt(25)*, and you'll get the answer 5. It also works with powers: Type

*pow(6,6)*—that is, 6 to the power of 6—and you'll get 46656. You can even type *pi* to represent—you know, pi.

Second, the Spotlight menu is now a full-blown English dictionary. Or, more specifically, it's wired directly into Mac OS X's *own* dictionary, which sits in your Applications folder.

So if you type, for example, *schadenfreude* into the Spotlight box, you'll see, to your amazement, the beginning of the actual definition right there in the menu. Click it to open Dictionary and read the full-blown entry. (In this example, that would be: "noun: pleasure derived by someone from another person's misfortune.")

---

- *author:casey.* Finds all documents with "casey" in the Author field. (This presumes that you've actually *entered* the name Casey into the document's Author box. Microsoft Word, for example, has a place to store this information.)

- *width:800.* Finds all graphics that are 800 pixels wide.

- *flash:1.* Finds all photos that were taken with the camera's flash on. (To find photos with the flash *off,* you'd type *flash:0.* A number of the yes/no criteria work this way: Use 1 for yes, 0 for no.)

- *modified:3/7/08-3/10/08.* Finds all documents modified between March 7 and March 10.

  You can also type *created:=6/1/08* to find all the files you created on June 1, 2008. Type *modified:<=3/9/08* to find all documents you edited *on or before* March 9, 2008.

  As you can see, three range-finding symbols are available for your queries: <, >, and -. The < means "before" or "less than," the > means "after" or "greater than," and the hyphen indicates a range (of dates, size, or whatever you're looking for).

---

**Tip:** Here again, you can string words together. To find all PDFs you opened today, use *date:today kind:PDF.* And if you're looking for a PDF document that you created on July 4, 2008 containing the word *wombat*, you can type *created:=7/4/08 kind:pdf wombat,* although at this point, you're not saving all that much time.

---

Now, those examples are just a few representative searches out of the dozens that Leopard makes available.

It turns out that the search criteria codes that you can type into the Spotlight box (*author:casey, width:800,* and so on) correspond to the master list that appears when you choose Other in the Spotlight *window,* as described on page 100. In other words, there are *125 different* search criteria.

### Boolean searches

Mac OS X 10.5 adds another layer of sophistication to Spotlight searches by permitting what Comp Sci professors call *Boolean* searches. These are search terms that round up results containing *either* of two search terms, or *both* search terms, or one term but *not* another.

To go Boolean, you're supposed to incorporate terms like AND, OR, or NOT into your search queries.

For example, you can round up a list of files that match *two* terms by typing, say, *vacation AND kids.* (That's also how you'd find documents coauthored by two specific people—you and a pal, for example. You'd search for *author:Casey AND author:Chris.* Yes, you have to type Boolean terms in all capitals.)

---

**Tip:** You can use parentheses instead of AND, if you like. That is, typing *(vacation kids)* finds documents that contain both words, not necessarily together.

---

If you use OR, you can find icons that match *either* of two search criteria. Typing *kind:jpeg OR kind:pdf* turns up photos and PDF files in a single list.

The minus sign (hyphen) works, too. If you did a search for *dolphins,* hoping to turn up sea-mammal documents, but instead find your results contaminated by football-team listings, by all means repeat the search with *dolphins -miami.* Mac OS X eliminates all documents containing "Miami."

---

*Tip:* The word NOT works the same way. You could type *dolphins NOT miami* to achieve the same effect. But the hyphen is faster to type.

---

# The Spotlight Window

As you may have noticed, the Spotlight menu doesn't list *every* match on your hard drive. Unless you own one of those extremely rare 60-inch Apple Skyscraper Displays, there just isn't room.

Instead, Spotlight uses some fancy behind-the-scenes analysis to calculate and display the *20 most likely* matches for what you typed. But at the top of the menu, you usually see that there are many other possible matches; it says something like "Show All," meaning that there are other candidates. (Mac OS X no longer tells you how *many* other results there are.)

There is, however, a second, more powerful way into the Spotlight labyrinth. And that's to use the Spotlight *window,* shown in Figure 3-11.

### Spotlight Window from Spotlight Menu

If the Spotlight menu—its Most Likely to Succeed list—doesn't include what you're looking for, click Show All. You've just opened the Spotlight window.

Now you have access to the *complete* list of matches, neatly listed in what appears to be a standard Finder window.

### Opening the Spotlight Window Directly

When you're in the Finder, you can also open the Spotlight window *directly*, without using the Spotlight menu as a trigger.

Actually, there are three ways to get to the Spotlight window (Figure 3-11):

- ⌘-F (for *Find*, get it?). When you choose File→Find (or press ⌘-F), you get an *empty* Spotlight window, ready to fill in for your search.

- **Option-⌘-Space bar**. This keystroke opens the same window. But instead of starting empty and filling up, this window starts with a list of *every single thing* on your Mac and winnows down as you type a search query.

- **Open any desktop window, and type something into the Search box at upper-right.** Presto—the mild-mannered folder window turns into the Spotlight window, complete with search results.

Once you type something to search for, the results are identical.

## The Basic Search

When the Spotlight window opens, you can start typing whatever you're looking for into the Search box at the upper right.

As you type—or, more realistically, a second or two after you type each letter—the window changes to reveal a list of the files and folders whose names contain what you typed. It's just like the Spotlight menu, but in a window with no 20-item results limit (Figure 3-11, bottom).

While the searching is going on, a sprocket icon whirls away in the lower-right corner. To cancel the search in progress, click the ⊗ button next to the phrase you typed. That button also clears the box so you can type a different word or phrase.

**Figure 3-11:**
The Spotlight window either lists nothing *(top)*—or everything *on your hard drive (bottom)*, depending on how you open it. Either way, it's ready to search your entire hard drive (except other people's Home folders). But Spotlight has many tricks up its software sleeve.

## Power Searches

The real beauty of the Spotlight window, though, is that it can hunt down icons using extremely specific criteria; it's much more powerful (and complex) than the Spotlight menu. If you spent enough time setting up the search, you could use this feature to find a document whose name begins with the letters *Cro,* is over one megabyte in size, was created after 10/1/07 but before the end of the year, was changed within the last week, has the file name suffix *.doc,* and contains the phrase "attitude adjustment." (Of course, if you knew *that* much about a file, you'd probably know where it is without having to use the Search window. But you get the picture.)

To use the Search window, you need to feed it two pieces of information: *where* you want it to search, and *what* to look for. You can make both of these criteria as simple or complex as you like.

## Where to Look

The three phrases at the top of the window—This Mac, "Folder Name," and Shared—are buttons. Click one of these to tell Spotlight where to search:

- **This Mac** means your *entire* computer, including secondary disks attached to it (or installed inside).

- **"Letters to Congress"** (or whatever the current window is) limits the search to whatever window was open when you called up the Spotlight window. So, for example, if you want to search your Pictures folder, open it first and *then* hit ⌘-F. You'll see the "Pictures" button at the top of the window, and you can click it to restrict the search to that folder.

*Note:* If no folder window is open when you press ⌘-F, this button says "Casey" (or whatever); it identifies your Home folder. That is, Spotlight is prepared to search *all* your stuff on this Mac.

- **Shared.** Click this button to expand the search to your *entire network* and all the computers on it. (This assumes, of course, that you've brought their icons to your screen as described in Chapter 14. If there aren't any shared folders or disks, this button doesn't appear at all.)

If the other computers are Macs running Leopard, Spotlight can even search their files just the way it does on your own Mac—finding words inside the files, for example. If they're any other kind of computer, Spotlight can only search for files by name.

*Tip:* If the object of your quest doesn't show up, you can adjust the scope of the search with one quick click on another button at the top of the window, like This Mac or Shared. Spotlight updates the results list.

## Search by Name/Search by Contents

The two other buttons at the top of the Spotlight window are also very powerful:

- **Contents.** This button, the factory setting, works just the way Spotlight usually does. It's prepared to search for the words *inside* your files, along with all the metadata attached to them.

- **File Name.** All of this searching-inside-files business is well and good. But there's no denying that sometimes, you already know a file's *name*—you just don't know where it is. In this case, it's far faster to search by name, just as people did before Spotlight came along. The list of results will be far shorter, and you'll spot what you want much faster. That's why this button is so welcome.

***Tip:*** If you press Shift as you open the File menu (or as you press ⌘-F), the Find command changes to Find by Name. It opens the Find window, preset to search for icons by name. What a shortcut!

## Complex Searches

If all you want to do is search your entire computer for files containing certain text, you may as well use the Spotlight *menu* described at the beginning of this chapter.

The power of the Spotlight *window,* though, is that it lets you design much more specific searches, using over 125 different search criteria: date modified, file size, the "last opened" date, color label, copyright holder's name, shutter speed (of a digital photo), tempo (of a music file), and so on. Figure 3-12 illustrates how detailed this kind of search can be.

To set up a complex search like this, you'll use the second row of controls at the top of the window.

And third, and fourth, and fifth. Each time you click one of the + buttons at the right end of the window, a new criterion row appears, whose pop-up menus you can use to specify *what* date, *what* file size, and so on. Figure 3-12 shows how you might build, for example, a search for all photo files that you've opened within the last week that contain a Photoshop layer named *Freckle Removal.*

***Figure 3-12:***
*By repeatedly clicking the + button, you can turn on as many criteria as you'd like; each additional row further narrows the search.*

To delete a row, click the – button at its right end.

Here's a rundown of the ways you can restrict your search, according to the options you find in the first pop-up menu of a row. Note that after you choose from that first pop-up menu (Last Opened, for example), you're supposed to use the additional pop-up menus to narrow the choice ("within last," "2," and "weeks," for example).

### Kind

When the first pop-up menu says Kind, you can use the second pop-up menu to indicate what kind of file you're looking for: Applications, Documents, Folders, Images, Movies, Music, PDF files, Presentations, Text files, or Other.

For example, when you're trying to free up some space on your drive, you could round up all your movie files, which tend to be huge. Choosing one of these file types makes the window begin to fill with matches automatically and instantly.

### Last opened date/Last modified date/Created date

When you choose one of these options from the first pop-up menu, the second pop-up menu lets you isolate files, programs, and folders according to the last time you opened them, the last time you changed them, or when they were created.

---

**Tip:** You're allowed to add *two* Date rows—a great trick that lets you round up files that you created or edited between two dates. Set up the first Date row to say "is after," and the second one to say "is before."

In fact, if it doesn't hurt your brain to think about it, how about this? You can even have *more* than two Date rows. Use one pair to specify a range of dates for the file's creation date, for example, and two *other* rows to limit when it was modified.

Science!

---

### Name

The beauty of Spotlight is that it finds text *anywhere* in your files, no matter what their *names* are. That's why Apple demoted this option—the icon's name—to such a low position in the pop-up menu.

Anyway, when you want to search for an icon by the text that's only in its *name*, this is your ticket. Capitalization doesn't matter.

Of course, if all you want to do is find files whose names include *Sales*, you may as well save yourself all of this reading and use the Spotlight menu (or click the File Name button at the top of the window). But using the Search window offers you far more control, thanks to the second pop-up menu that offers you options like Contains, Starts with, Ends with, and so on.

### Contents

You can think of this option as the opposite of Name. It finds *only* the text that's inside your files, and *completely* ignores their icon names.

That's a handy function when, for example, a document's name doesn't match its contents. Maybe a marauding toddler pressed the keys while playing KidPix, inadvertently renaming your doctoral thesis "xggrjpO#$5%////." Or maybe you just can't remember what you called something.

**Other**

If this were a math equation, it might look like this: *options x options=overwhelming.*

Choosing Other from the first pop-up menu opens a special dialog box containing at least 125 *other* criteria. Not just the big kahunas like Name, Size, and Kind, but far more targeted (and obscure) criteria like "Bits per sample" (so you can round up MP3 music files of a certain quality), "Device make" (so you can round up all digital photos taken with, say, a Canon camera), "Key signature" (so you can find all the GarageBand songs you wrote in the key of F sharp), "Pages" (so you can find all Word documents that are really long), and so on. As you can see in Figure 3-13, each one comes with a short description.

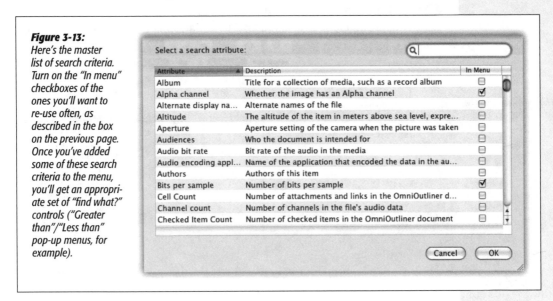

**Figure 3-13:**
*Here's the master list of search criteria. Turn on the "In menu" checkboxes of the ones you'll want to re-use often, as described in the box on the previous page. Once you've added some of these search criteria to the menu, you'll get an appropriate set of "find what?" controls ("Greater than"/"Less than" pop-up menus, for example).*

You may think that Spotlight is offering you a staggering array of file-type criteria. In fact, though, big bunches of information categories (technically called *metadata)* are all hooks for a relatively small number of document types. For example:

- **Digital photos and other graphics files** account for the metadata types *alpha channel, aperture, color space, device make, device model, EXIF version, exposure mode, exposure program, exposure time, flash, FNumber, focal length, ISO speed, max aperture, metering mode, orientation, pixel height, pixel width, red eye, resolution height, resolution width,* and *white balance.*

- **Digital music files** have searchable metadata categories like *album, audio bit rate, bits per sample, channel count, composer, duration, General MIDI sequence, key signature, lyricist, musical genre, recording date, sample rate, tempo, time signature, track number,* and *year recorded.* There's even a special set of parameters for GarageBand and Soundtrack documents, including *instrument category, instrument name, loop descriptors, loop file type, loop original key,* and *loop scale type.*

---

- **Microsoft Office documents** can contain info bits like *authors, contributors, fonts, languages, pages, publishers,* and contact information (*name, phone number,* and so on).

This massive list also harbors a few criteria you may use more often, like Size, Label, and Visibility (which lets you see all the invisible files on your hard drive).

Now, you could argue that in the time it takes you to set up a search for such a specific kind of data, you could have just rooted through your files and found what you wanted manually. But hey—you never know. Someday, you may remember *nothing* about a photo you're looking for except that you used the flash and an F-stop of 1.8.

## What to Do with Search Results

The Spotlight window is a regular old Finder window, with all the familiar views and controls (Figure 3-14).

**Figure 3-14:**
Click a result once to see where it sits on your hard drive (very bottom). If the window is too narrow to reveal the full folder path, run your cursor over them without clicking. As your mouse moves from one folder to another, Leopard briefly reveals its name, compressing other folders as necessary to make room. (Sub-tip: You can drag icons into these folders, too.)

You can work with anything in the results window exactly as though it's a regular Finder window: Drag something to the Trash, rename something, drag something to the desktop to move it there, drag something onto a Dock icon to open it with a certain program, Option-⌘-drag it to the desktop to create an alias, and so on.

You can move up or down the list by pressing the arrow keys, scroll a "page" at a time with the Page Up and Page Down keys, and so on. You can also highlight multiple icons simultaneously, the same way you would in a Finder list view: Highlight all of them by choosing Edit→Select All; highlight individual items by ⌘-clicking them; drag diagonally to enclose a cluster of found items; and so on.

Or you can proceed in any of these ways:

- **Change the view** by clicking one of the View icons or choosing from the View menu. You can switch between icon, list, or Cover Flow views (see Chapter 2). Actually, Cover Flow is a *great* view for search results; since this list is culled from folders all over the computer, you otherwise have very little sense of context as you examine the file names.

- **Sort the results** by clicking the column headings (not available in icon view). It can be especially useful to sort by Kind, so that similar file types are clustered together (Documents, Images, Messages, and so on).

- **Get a Quick Look at one result** by clicking it and then hitting the Space bar. If it's a document type that Mac OS X understands, you get the big, bold Quick Look preview window.

- **Find out where it is.** It's nice to see all the search results in one list, but you're not actually seeing them in their native habitats: in the Finder folder windows where they physically reside.

  If you click once on an icon in the results, the bottom edge of the window becomes a folder map that shows you where that item is.

- **Open the file (or open one of the folders it's in).** If one of the found files is the one you were looking for, double-click it to open it (or highlight it and press either ⌘-O or ⌘-down arrow). In many cases, you'll never even know or care where the file was—you just want to get into it.

- **Move or delete the file.** You can drag an item directly out of the found-files list and into a different folder, window, or disk—or straight to the Dock or the Trash.

- **Give up.** If none of these avenues suits your fancy, you can close the window as you would any other (⌘-W).

## Customizing Spotlight

You've just read about how Spotlight works fresh out of the box. But you can tailor its behavior, both for security reasons and to fit it to the kinds of work you do.

Here are three ways to open the Spotlight preferences center:

- **Choose Spotlight Preferences** at the bottom of the Spotlight menu just after you've performed a search.

- **Use Spotlight itself.** Hit ⌘-Space bar, type *spotl,* and press Enter.

- **Choose** 🍎→**System Preferences.** Click Spotlight.

In any case, you wind up face-to-face with the dialog box shown in Figure 3-15. You can tweak Spotlight in three ways here, all very useful:

- **Turn off categories.** The list of checkboxes identifies all the kinds of things that Spotlight tracks. If you find that Spotlight uses up valuable menu space listing, say, Web bookmarks or fonts—stuff you don't need to find very often—turn off their checkboxes. Now the Spotlight menu's precious 20 slots are allotted to icon types you care more about.

- **Prioritize the categories.** This dialog box also lets you change the *order* of the category results; just drag an individual list item up or down to change where it appears in the Spotlight menu.

- **Change the keystroke.** Ordinarily, pressing ⌘-Space bar highlights the Spotlight search box in your menu bar, and Option-⌘-Space bar opens the Spotlight window described above. If these keystrokes clash with some other key assignment in your software, though, you can reassign them to almost any other keystroke you like.

Click inside the white box that lists the keystroke and then press *any* key combination—Control-S, for example—to choose something different. Whatever keystroke you choose *must* include at least one of the modifier keys (Option, Control, or ⌘) or one of the F-keys (such as F4).

**Figure 3-15:**
*Here's where you can specify what categories of icons you want Spotlight to search, which order you want them listed in the Spotlight menu, and what keystroke you want to use for highlighting the Spotlight bar.*

---

***Note:*** Apple assumes no responsibility for your choosing a keystroke that messes up some other function on your Mac. ⌘-S, for example, would not be a good choice.

---

## Privacy Settings

Ordinarily, Spotlight doesn't consider any corner of your hard drive off-limits. It looks for matches wherever it can except in other people's Home folders. (That is, you can't search through other people's stuff).

But even within your own Mac world, you can hide certain folders from Spotlight searches. Maybe you have privacy concerns—for example, you don't want your spouse Spotlighting your stuff while you're away from your desk. Maybe you just want to create more focused Spotlight searches, removing a lot of old, extraneous junk from its database.

Either way, the steps are simple. Open the Spotlight panel of System Preferences, as described above. Click the Privacy tab. Figure 3-16 explains the remaining steps.

Once you've built up the list of private disks and folders, close System Preferences. Spotlight now pretends the private items don't even exist.

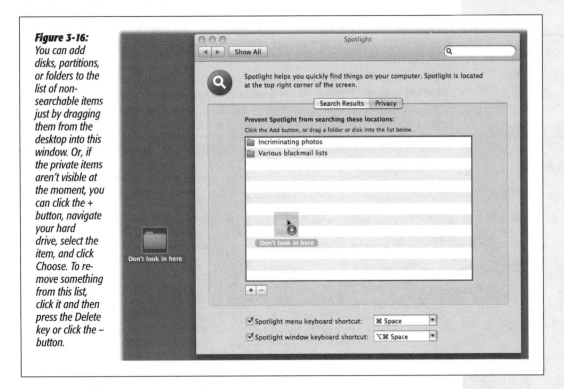

**Figure 3-16:**
*You can add disks, partitions, or folders to the list of non-searchable items just by dragging them from the desktop into this window. Or, if the private items aren't visible at the moment, you can click the + button, navigate your hard drive, select the item, and click Choose. To re-move something from this list, click it and then press the Delete key or click the – button.*

## Smart Folders

You may remember from Chapter 1 (or from staring at your own computer) that the Sidebar at the left side of every Leopard desktop window contains a set of little folders under the Searches heading. Each is actually a *smart folder*—a self-updating folder that, in essence, performs a continual, 24/7 search for the criteria you specify.

(Smart folders are a lot like smart albums in iPhoto and iTunes, smart mailboxes in Mail, and so on.)

*Note:* In truth, the smart folder performs a search for the specified criteria *at the moment you open it.* But because it's so fast, and because it's always up to date, it feels as though it's been quietly searching all along.

As it turns out, the ones installed there by Apple are meant to serve as inspiration for you to create your *own* smart folders. The key, as it turns out, is the little Save button in the upper-right corner of the Spotlight window.

Here's a common example of how you might use it. You choose File→Find. You set up the pop-up menus to say "last opened date" and "this week." You click Save. You name the smart folder something like Current Crises, and you turn on "Add to Sidebar" (Figure 3-17).

From now on, whenever you click that smart folder, it reveals all of the files you've worked on in the last week or so. The great part is that these items' *real* locations may be all over the map, scattered in folders all over your Mac and your network. But through the magic of the smart folder, they appear as though they're all in one neat folder.

*Tip:* If you decide your original search criteria need a little fine-tuning, click the smart folder. From the Action menu, choose Show Search Criteria. You're back on the original setting-up-the-search window. Use the pop-up menus and other controls to tweak your search setup, and then click the Save button once again.

To *delete* a smart folder, just drag its icon out of the Sidebar. (Or if it's anywhere else, like on your desktop, drag it to the Trash like any other folder.)

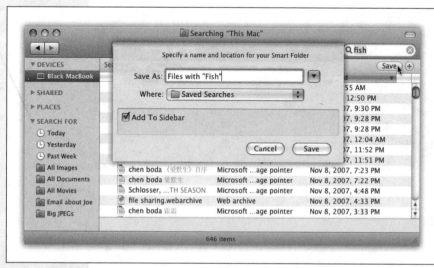

**Figure 3-17:**
*Mac OS X can preserve your search as a smart folder listed in the Sidebar (lower left)—at least, it does as long as "Add To Sidebar" is turned on. You can stash a smart folder in your Dock, too, although it doesn't display a stack of its contents, as normal folders do.*

# Documents, Programs, & Spaces

T he beauty of life in the Era of Switchers is that most of the big-boy programs are available in nearly identical versions for both the Mac and Windows. Word, Excel, and PowerPoint; Photoshop, Illustrator, and InDesign; FileMaker Pro; Dreamweaver; and many other programs are available for both Mac and Windows. Sometimes you have to buy the Mac version separately; sometimes it's on the same CD.

The best part: The documents you create with the Mac versions are generally *identical in format* to the ones created in Windows. A Microsoft Word document, for example, requires no conversion when transferred from a Mac to a PC or vice-versa. It is what it is—a .doc or .docx file.

---

**UP TO SPEED**

### Carbon, Cocoa, and Classic (R.I.P.)

There are two chief kinds of Mac OS X–compatible programs, known by the geeks as *Carbon* and *Cocoa* programs. These terms refer to the programming tools that were used to create them, which also have a small effect on how well they run in Mac OS X. Page 141 covers them in more detail, but the point is that this chapter describes how Carbon and Cocoa programs work—these are true Mac OS X programs.

Now, until Leopard came along, there was a third software category. Older Macs (pre-Intel Macs) could also run the very old, pre-2001 operating system known as Mac OS 9, and all of its programs. Mac OS X came with a built-in Mac OS 9 *simulator* called Classic.

Now, a handful of G4 Leopard-capable Mac models can still *restart* into Mac OS 9, which is better than nothing.

But Classic is gone. Leopard is all Mac OS X, all the time, making life simpler for Apple—and more complicated for anyone who used to rely on some of those older programs.

---

Same thing with Excel spreadsheets (.xls), PowerPoint slideshows (.ppt), Photoshop documents (.psd), and on and on. You may occasionally encounter a tiny formatting difference—a line thickness change, a movie file that requires a plug-in—but most documents open flawlessly when moved between Macs and PCs. (Chapter 7 offers more detail on finding Mac versions of your favorite PC programs.)

But even if switching to the Mac OS X versions of your programs is relatively easy, learning how Mac OS X programs *in general* operate may require some study. As this chapter makes clear, the relationship between programs and their documents differs in several substantial ways from the way things work in Windows.

## Opening Mac OS X Programs

Many of the techniques for launching (opening) a program work just as they do in Windows. For example:

- Click a program's icon on the Dock, the Sidebar, or the Finder toolbar.

- Use Spotlight. Hit ⌘-Space bar, type the first letters of the program's name, and then press Return or Enter.

- Double-click an application's icon in the Finder.

- Highlight an application icon and then press ⌘-O (short for File→Open) or ⌘-down arrow.

- Use the submenus of the  menu's Recent Items→Applications command.

- Open a *document* icon in any of these ways, or drag a document onto the icon of a program that can open it (whether in the Dock, the Finder toolbar, the Sidebar, or in a folder window).

---

**FREQUENTLY ASKED QUESTION**

### What's with the Big "Duh"?

*So, I've just installed Leopard, I'm all excited, and I double-click an Excel document. And now the Mac asks me: "You are opening Microsoft Excel for the first time. Do you want to continue?" Well, HELLO! I double-clicked the icon, didn't I? Does Apple think I'm some kind of idiot?*

It's not you Apple's worried about. It's the silent parade of evil hackers, lurking out there in Internet Land, waiting for the right moment to bring down the Mac.

See, in the Windows world, spyware authors have to be sneaky about how they install their stuff on your PC. You wouldn't be so stupid as to double-click an application called Spyware Installer™, of course. So the spyware tricks you into

running its installer. It commandeers a certain document type (like MP3 or JPEG), reassigning it to its installer. You innocently double-click some document, but an unanticipated program opens—and you've just opened Pandora's box.

In Mac OS X, that can't happen. When double-clicking some document opens a program for the first time, this dialog box appears, just to let you know what's about to happen. If the program that's about to open isn't the one you were expecting, well, you've got a chance to back out of it.

And if it *is* the program you were expecting, click Continue. You won't be asked again about this version of this particular program.

---

*Tip:* If you press Option as you open an application (or anything else) in the Finder, you automatically close the window that contains its icon. Later, when you return to the Finder, you'll find a neat, clean desktop—no loitering windows.

When you launch a program, the Mac reads its computer code, which lies on your hard drive's surface, and feeds it quickly into RAM (memory). During this brief interval, the icon of the opening program jumps up and down eagerly in your Dock.

*Tip:* Want to see *multithreading* in action? Launch a program that takes a long time to open—that is, whose icon in the Dock does a lot of bouncing.

You don't have to wait for the application to finish bouncing—you're wasting perfectly good computing time. Just switch to another program and get to work; the newly opened program keeps right on launching in the background. Multithreading means that Mac OS X can crunch more than one process at a time.

What happens next depends on the program you're using. Most present you with a new, blank, untitled document. Some, like iDVD, automatically open the last file you worked on. Some, like FileMaker and PowerPoint, ask if you want to open an existing document or create a new one.

And a few oddball programs don't open any window at all when first launched.

## The Application Menu

In each case, however, the very first menu after the  appears with bold lettering and identifies the program you're using. It might say iTunes, or Microsoft Word, or Stickies.

This Application menu (Figure 4-1) offers a number of commands pertaining to the entire program and its windows, including About, Quit, and Hide.

**Figure 4-1:**
*The first menu in every program lets you know, at a glance, which program you're actually in. It also offers overall program commands like Quit and Hide.*

## Quitting Programs

In Macintosh lingo, you don't "exit" a program when you're finished with it, you "quit" it. And the command to do so isn't in the File menu—it's at the bottom of the Application menu.

But Mac OS X offers two much more fun ways to quit a program:

- Right-click a program's Dock icon and then choose Quit from the pop-up menu.

- When you've pressed ⌘-Tab to summon Leopard's "heads-up display" of open programs (page 115), type the letter Q without releasing the ⌘ key. The highlighted program quits without further ado.

## Force Quitting Programs

Mac OS X is a rock-solid operating system, but that doesn't mean that *programs* never screw up. Individual programs are as likely as ever to freeze—or, rather, to *hang* (to

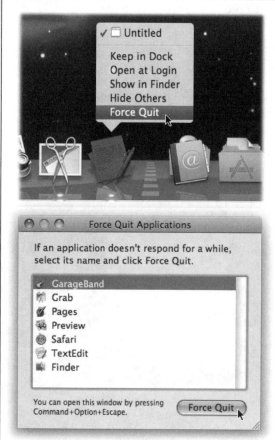

**Figure 4-2:**
*Top: You can force quit a program from the Dock, thanks to the Option key.*

*Bottom: When you press Option-⌘-Esc or choose Force Quit from the ⌘ menu, a tidy box listing all open programs appears. Just click the one you want to abort, click Force Quit, and click Force Quit again in the confirmation box. Often, you may have to force quit a program twice to make it really go away. (Using more technical tools like the Unix kill command, there are other ways to jettison programs. But this is often the most convenient.)*

lock up and display the "spinning beach ball of death" cursor). In such cases, you have no choice but to *force quit* the program—or, in Windows lingo, to terminate it or "end its task."

Doing so doesn't destabilize your Mac; you don't have to restart it. In fact, you can usually reopen the very same program and get on with your life.

You can force quit a stuck program in any of several ways:

- Right-click its Dock icon, or just hold your mouse down on it. Once the shortcut menu appears, press Option so that the Quit command now says Force Quit (see Figure 4-2). Bingo—that program is outta here.

- Press Option-⌘-Esc, the traditional Mac force quit keystroke.

- Choose  →Force Quit.

Either way, proceed as shown in Figure 4-2.

Again, force quitting is not bad for your Mac. The only downside to force quitting a program is that you lose any unsaved changes to your open documents, along with any preference settings you may have changed while the program was open.

## The New, Improved "Alt-Tab"

Only one program can be in front, or active, at a time. Just as in Windows, there's a handy keystroke for switching from one to another; it's the ⌘-Tab keystroke (see Figure 4-3).

**Figure 4-3:**
*Apple calls this row of open program icons a "heads-up display," named after the projected data screens on a Navy jet windshield that lets pilots avoid having to look down at their instruments.*

You can use this feature in three different ways, which are well worth learning:

- If you keep the ⌘ key pressed, each press of the Tab key highlights the Dock icon of another program, in left-to-right Dock order. Release both keys when you reach the one you want. Mac OS X brings the corresponding program to the front. (To move backward through the open programs, press Shift-⌘-Tab.)

- If you leave the ⌘ key pressed, you can choose a program by clicking its icon with your mouse.

- A single press of ⌘-Tab takes you to the program you used most recently, and another, separate ⌘-Tab bounces back to the program you started in.

Imagine that, for example, you're doing a lot of switching between two programs— your Web browser and your email program, for example. If you have five other programs open, you don't waste your time ⌘-Tabbing your way through all open programs just to "get back" to your Web browser.

---

*Tip:* Here's a related keystroke, equally awesome. If you press ⌘-tilde (the ~ key next to the 1 key), you switch to the next *window* in the *same* program.

---

## Exposé: Death to Window Clutter

In its day, the concept of overlapping windows on the screen was brilliant, innovative, and extremely effective. (Apple borrowed this idea from a research lab called Xerox PARC.) In that era before digital cameras, MP3 files, and the Web, managing your windows was easy this way; after all, you had only about three of them.

These days, however, managing all the open windows in all the open programs can be like herding cats. Off you go, burrowing through the microscopic pop-up menus of your taskbar buttons (Windows) or the Dock (Mac OS X 10.5), trying to find the window you want. And heaven help you if you need to duck back to the desktop—to find a newly downloaded file, for example, or eject a disk. You'll have to fight your way through 50,000 other windows on your way to the bottom of the "deck."

---

**TROUBLESHOOTING MOMENT**

### A Tedious Sidebar about the Aluminum Apple Keyboards

Do you have the superthin aluminum Apple keyboard (the wireless one, or the aluminum iMac one)? If so, the keystrokes described in this chapter don't not work.

On that keyboard, the F9, F10, and F11 keys—the keys you need for Exposé—are mapped to the Mac's speaker volume!

Fortunately, the most often used Exposé function, the one that exposes all open windows at once, has its *own* special key on this keyboard: the F3 key.

So you're covered there: press F3 instead of F9. But what about the other two Exposé functions, normally triggered by F10 and F11?

**Method 1:** Add the Control key (to Exposé one application's windows only) or the ⌘ key (to see the desktop).

That is, instead of F11 to expose the desktop, you should press ⌘-F3.

**Method 2:** Hold down the Fn key. If you do that, then you can use the F9, F10, and F11 keys like everybody else. (Lots of Fn details are on page 9.)

Kind of a drag, right?

**Method 3:** Actually, there's a final twist to all this. In System Preferences → Keyboard & Mouse, you'll find a checkbox that reverses this logic. It's called "Use all F1, F2, etc. keys as standard function keys."

If that checkbox is *on,* then you can use F9, F10, and F11 to trigger Exposé exactly as described in this chapter. Now you need the Fn key only when you want those keys to adjust the *volume.*

---

Exposé represents the first fresh look at this problem in decades. The concept is delicious: With the press of the F9 key, Mac OS X shrinks all windows in all programs to a size that fits on the screen (Figure 4-4), like index cards on a bulletin board. You click the one you want, and you're there. It's fast, efficient, animated, and a lot of fun.

**Figure 4-4:**
Top: Quick! Where's the Apple Web page in all this mess?

Bottom: With a tap of the F9 key, you can spot that window, shrunken but not overlapped. As your cursor passes over each thumbnail, the window darkens and identifies itself, courtesy of the floating label in its center. What's especially cool is that these aren't static snapshots of the windows at the moment you Exposé'd them. They're live, still-updating windows, as you'll discover if one of them contains a QuickTime movie during playback or a Web page that's still loading. If you're not pointing to a window, tapping F9 again turns off Exposé without changing anything; if you're pointing to a window, tapping F9 again brings it forward.

*Note:* On the superthin aluminum Apple keyboards, use the F3 key instead of F9. The painful details are in the box below.

## More Ways to Exposé

That business about finding a buried window on your screen is probably the way you'll use Exposé most often. But it's actually only one of three Exposé functions. The other options:

### Find one window in the current program

A second Exposé keystroke is designed to help you find a certain window only in the *program you're using*—great when you're Web browsing or word processing. When you tap F10 (the factory setting), all of the windows in the frontmost program spread out and shrink, if necessary, so you can see all of them simultaneously, in full—and so you can click the one you want (see Figure 4-5, top).

*Note:* As noted in the box on page 116, you may have to add the Fn key (that is, press Fn+F9) if you have Apple's superthin, iMac-style keyboard.

And now, tips:

- While your application windows are arrayed before you, tap the Tab key to switch to the *next* running program. All of *its* windows spring to the fore, and all of the *other* programs' windows grow dim. (Shift-Tab, as usual, cycles through the programs in the opposite direction.)

- Suppose you pressed F9 to shrink *all* programs' windows, but you decide that what you really meant to do was press F10 to see only *one* program's windows. The solution is to press the Tab key, which switches you *into* F10 mode, dimming (and restoring to full size) all programs' windows but one. At this point, you can press Tab or Shift-Tab to cycle through the open programs as described in the preceding paragraph.

Here's another way to change programs once you've "F10'ed" your windows: Press ⌘-Tab to bring up the "heads-up display" application switcher (yes, even while your windows are shrunken). Tab your way through the program icons (Figure 4-5) until the one you want is selected, and then release the keys. That program's windows spring to the front, still miniaturized and arrayed for your selection pleasure.

### Return to the desktop

The third keystroke (F11 is the factory setting) is surprisingly handy. It sends *all* windows in *all* programs cowering to the edges of your screen, revealing the desktop beneath in all its uncluttered splendor (Figure 4-5, bottom). There they remain—forever, or until you tap F11 again, click a visible window edge, double-click an icon, or take some other window-selection step.

**Note:** Once again: On Apple's superthin, iMac-style keyboard, press Fn+F11 instead. See the box on page 116.

*Figure 4-5:*
*Top: When you press the F10 key, you get a clear shot at any window in the current program (Safari, in this example). In the meantime, the rest of your screen attractively dims, as though someone has just shined a floodlight onto the windows of the program in question. It's a stunning effect.*

*Bottom: Tap the F11 key when you need to duck back to the desktop for a quick administrative chore. Here's your chance to find a file, throw something away, eject a disk, or whatever, without having to disturb your application windows.*

*In either case, tap the same function key again to turn off Exposé. Or click one of the window edges, which you can see peeking out from all four edges of the screen.*

This is a spectacular opportunity to save headache and hassle in situations like these:

- You're writing an email message, and you want to attach a file. Tap F11, root around in the Finder until you locate the file you want. Begin to drag it, and then tap F11 again to bring back your email window. Move your cursor, with the file in mid-drag, directly over the outgoing message window; release the cursor to create the attachment.

---

**Tip:** You can apply the same life-changing shortcut to dragging a graphic into some page-layout program, a folder of photos into iPhoto, a sound or graphic into iMovie, and so on.

---

- You want to open a different document. For many people, having access to the entire Finder beats the pants off having to use the Open dialog box. Double-clicking the icon you want automatically opens it and turns off Exposé.

- You're on the Web, and you want to see if some file has finished downloading. Tap F11 to survey the situation on your desktop.

In essence, Apple has finally realized that the desktop really *isn't* "just another program." If the layer of open programs is the atmosphere, the Finder is the earth below—and the ability to teleport you back and forth is a huge time saver.

---

**Tip:** You can switch among the three Exposé modes (F9, F10, or F11), even after you've triggered one. For example, if you press F10 to shrink only *one* program's windows, you can then press F11 to see the desktop, and then press F9 to shrink *all* programs' windows.

---

### Another way to Exposé

Most of the time, you'll probably use Exposé in two steps. You'll tap the function key once to get the windows out of the way, and tap it again to bring them back (if, indeed, you haven't *clicked* a window to bring them back).

In some cases, though, you may find it easier to *hold down* the relevant key. For example, hold down F11 to see if a file is finished copying to the desktop, then release the key to bring back all of the windows. For quick window-clearing situations, that method saves you the step of having to press the key a second time to turn off Exposé.

## Three Triggers for Exposé

Exposé is wonderful and all, but the standard keys for triggering its three functions—F9 to expose all windows, F10 for current-application windows, F11 for show-me-the-desktop—may leave something to be desired. For one thing, they may already be "taken" by other functions in your programs (like Microsoft Word) or even by your computer (like certain PowerBook G4 models, whose F9 and F10 keys adjust the keyboard illumination). For another thing, those keys are at the top of the keyboard where your typing fingers aren't used to going, and you may have to hunt to make sure you're pressing the right one.

Fortunately, you can reassign the Exposé functions to a huge range of other keys, with or without modifiers like Shift, Control, and Option. To view your options, choose  →System Preferences and then click the Exposé & Spaces icon (Figure 4-6).

Here, you'll discover that you can trigger Exposé's functions in any of three ways:

### Screen corners

The four pop-up menus (Figure 4-6) represent the four corners of your screen. Using these menus, you can assign an Exposé trigger to each corner; for example, if you choose Desktop from the first pop-up menu, when your pointer hits the upper-left corner of the screen, you'll hide all windows and expose the desktop. (To make the windows come back, click any visible edge of a window, or twitch the cursor back into the same corner.)

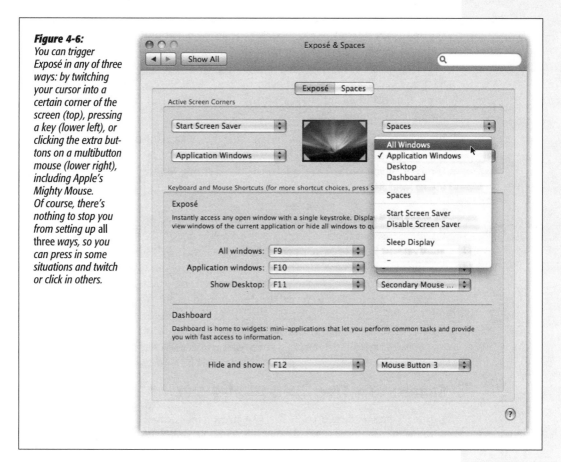

**Figure 4-6:**
*You can trigger Exposé in any of three ways: by twitching your cursor into a certain corner of the screen (top), pressing a key (lower left), or clicking the extra buttons on a multibutton mouse (lower right), including Apple's Mighty Mouse. Of course, there's nothing to stop you from setting up all three ways, so you can press in some situations and twitch or click in others.*

Depending on the size of your screen, this option can feel awkward at first. But if you've run out of keystrokes that aren't assigned to other functions, be glad that Apple offers you this alternative.

### Keystrokes

Also in the Dashboard & Exposé preferences, you'll find three pop-up menus—"All windows," "Application windows," and "Show Desktop"—that correspond to the three functions of Exposé as described above. (The fourth pop-up menu, Dashboard, is described at the end of this chapter.) You can't assign *any* old keystroke to Exposé, but you have far more options than the puny F9, F10, and F11 keys.

Within each pop-up menu, for example, you'll discover that all of your F-keys are available as triggers: F1, F2, F3, and so on. If, while the pop-up menu is open, you press one or more of your modifier keys (Shift, Option, Control, or ⌘), all of these F-key choices *change* to reflect the key you're pressing; now the pop-up menu says Shift-F1, Shift-F2, Shift-F3, and so on. That's how you can make *Shift*-F1 trigger the hide-all-windows function, for example.

These pop-up menus also contain choices like Left Shift, which refers to the Shift key on the left side of your keyboard. That is, instead of pressing F9 to make all your windows shrink, you could simply tap the Shift key. (This is only an example. Repeat: This is only an example. *Actually* using the Shift key to shrink all your windows is a terrible, terrible idea, as you'll quickly discover the next time you try to type a capital letter. This feature is intended exclusively for hunt-and-peck typists who never use the Shift key on one side.)

If you have a laptop, you'll also find out that the Fn key is also available for Exposé—and this time, it's a *great* choice, because Fn otherwise has very little direction in life. (Fn is the neglected key in the lower-left corner of a Mac laptop keyboard, or in the top middle cluster of Apple's aluminum keyboard.)

### Multiple-button mouse clicks

If your mouse has more than one button, you see a second column of pop-up menus in System Preferences. Each pop-up menu offers choices like Right Mouse Button, Middle Mouse Button, and so on. Use these pop-up menus to assign the three Exposé modes (or Dashboard) to the various clickers on your mouse: right-click to hide *all* windows, left-side click to reveal the desktop, and so on.

---

*Tip:* No matter how you trigger Exposé, try holding down the Shift key as you do it. You'll enjoy watching all your windows shift around with Mac OS X's patented slow-motion animation, which can be quite a sight.

---

## Spaces: Your Free Quad-Display Mac

Exposé is pretty darned cool. But Leopard offers another radical step forward in window management that you may even come to prefer. It's called Spaces.

This feature gives you two, four, six, eight, or even sixteen *full-size monitors*. Ordinarily, of course, attaching so many screens to a single computer would be a massively expensive proposition, not to mention the number it would do on your living space and personal relationships.

But the bonus monitors that Spaces gives you are *virtual*. They exist only in the Mac's little head. You can look at only one at a time; you switch using a keystroke, a menu, or the mouse. Instead of shuffling through your windows using Exposé, you can now leave them all spread out over a much larger virtual desktop.

Just because the Spaces screens are simulated doesn't mean they're not useful, though. You can dedicate each one to a different program or *kind* of program. Screen 1 might contain your email and chat windows, arranged just the way you like them. Screen 2 can hold Photoshop, with an open document and the palettes carefully arrayed. On Screen 3: your Web browser in full-screen mode.

You can also have the *same* program running on multiple screens—but different documents or projects open on each one.

Now, virtual screens aren't a new idea—this sort of software has been available for the Mac and Windows for years. But it's never before been a standard feature of an operating system, and rarely executed with such finesse.

## Turning on Spaces

To "install" your new monitors, start by choosing  →System Preferences. Click the Exposé & Spaces icon, then click the Spaces tab. You see something like Figure 4-7.

The setup ritual goes like this:

- **Turn Spaces on.** The "Enable Spaces" checkbox is the master on/off switch.

- **Add the menulet.** Turn on "Show Spaces in menu bar" to make a menu of your virtual screens appear in the menu bar. It not only lets you switch screens, but the numeral on it also reminds you which screen you're *on*.

---

***Tip:*** Consider turning on this option, if only at first, as a safety net. Otherwise, if you don't remember the keystroke for switching screens, you might lose one of your programs on another screen and not be able to find it!

---

- **Add rows or columns.** Click the + and – buttons to add rows or columns of virtual monitors. There's a difference between rows and columns, by the way. Not only will you eventually learn to sense where your various window setups live, but you can also move from one screen to another by bumping the mouse against the corresponding edge of your *current* screen—and you'll need to know which edge.

- **Set up program auto-screen assignments.** Spaces starts to become truly useful only when you make it part of your routine. You'll eventually memorize where everything is: Web stuff, top left. Email, top right. Photoshop, lower left. Finder with Applications folder open, lower right.

  For that reason, you can use the controls in the center of the System Preferences pane to specify onto which screen certain programs *automatically* go when they open. Click the + button to view your Applications folder. Double-click a program's icon to make it appear in the list. Now use the pop-up menu in the Space column to indicate which space you want this program to live on, as shown in Figure 4-7.

*Tip:* You can also choose All Spaces, meaning that this program's windows are available on *every* virtual screen. That's handy if it's something you use constantly, like a stock ticker or your phone-book program.

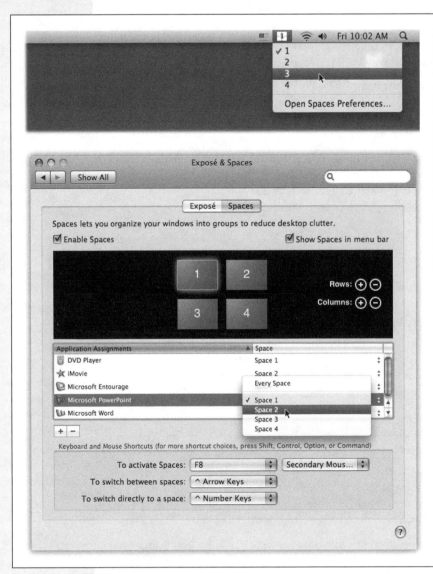

**Figure 4-7:**
*Use the controls at the top to specify how many virtual screens you want– how many rows, how many columns, up to 16 in all. Use the middle section to specify where you want particular programs to appear (that is, on which screen) when they open. Use the bottom controls to set up how you want to move from one screen to another.*

To make a program stop opening into a certain screen, click its name, and then click the – button.

- **Set up keyboard or mouse triggers.** Once you've got your majestic array of Cineplex Displays assembled, you need a way to move among them.

Spaces comes set up with the Control key as the "I'm switching screens" key. For example, press Control-↑ to move up one screen, Control-→ to move one screen to the right, and so on. Or, if you have tons of screens, you can jump to one by number (as indicated in the map shown in Figure 4-7): Control-1, Control-4, Control-9, or whatever.

You're welcome to change these keyboard assignments, however, especially if you're already using the Control key for other functions. Use the two bottom pop-up menus.

For example, suppose you want to switch screens by pressing the Option key rather than Control. In that case, you'd open the "To switch between Spaces" pop-up menu, press Option, and choose "⌥ Arrow Keys." (In these pop-up menus, ⌥ means the Option key, ⇧ is the Shift key, and ^ means Control.)

---

**Tip:** The pop-up menu at the bottom of the window, "To activate Spaces," lets you choose a keystroke that opens up the master map of all your screens. (See Figure 4-9.) For tips on choosing a trigger, see page 121.

---

## Using Spaces

Once you've got Spaces set up and turned on, the fun begins. Start by moving to the virtual screen you want. Here are some ways to do that:

- Choose a virtual screen's number from the Spaces menulet, shown in Figure 4-7.

- Press Control-arrow key, or whatever keystroke you set up as described above. Or hold down Control and keep tapping the arrow key to scroll through all your screens.

- Press Control-number key to jump to a screen without having to scroll.

- Use the heads-up switcher (page 115), or the Dock, to select a program; Spaces switches to the proper screen automatically.

When you make a switch, you see a flash of animation as one screen flies away and another appears. You also see the display shown in Figure 4-8 to help you orient yourself among your magnificent array of virtual monitors.

---

**Figure 4-8:**
*This display appears momentarily when you switch screens. The arrow shows you the screens you're moving to and from.*

*You can even move diagonally. While pressing Control, press two arrow keys on your keyboard at once (like ↓ and →).*

---

Now that you're "on" the screen you want, open programs and arrange windows onto it as usual.

### The big picture

The F8 key opens up a gigantic miniature (if there is such a thing) of your entire Spaces universe (Figure 4-9).

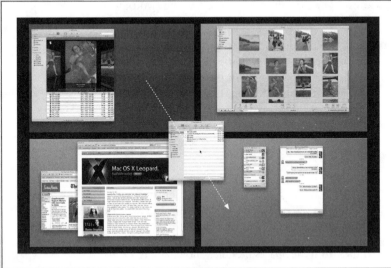

*Figure 4-9:*
*Press F8, or click Spaces in your Dock, to open this live master view of all the windows on all the screens. (The windows update in real time—if you're in a chat or playing a movie, for example.) You can actually drag individual windows from one of these "window panes" (actually virtual screens) to another. In fact, you can even use the Exposé keystrokes to make all the windows on all the screens visible at once, for ease in moving them around the screens.*

Clicking the Spaces icon in the Dock brings up the same display.

**Note:** As usual, you may run into trouble with this key if you're using Apple's aluminum, superflat keyboard. See the box on page 116.

So what can you do here?

- **Get oriented.** You could have sworn you opened your favorite Web site—where the heck is it? Pressing F8 gives you an instant readout of where all your windows are sitting at the moment.

- **Switch screens.** Click any "pane" of the big-picture view to jump to the screen. Or just press its number on your keyboard (4 to open the fourth screen, for example).

- **Reorder the screens.** Using any blank background spot as a handle, you can drag the actual panes of the big-picture view around to rearrange them. If you decide that your email screen should really be at top left, drag it there.

- **Move windows around.** Here's the real power of the big-picture view. As shown in Figure 4-9, you can actually drag windows from one screen to another. You can use any part of the window as a handle, not just the title bar.

***Tip:*** If you press Shift as you drag, you move *all* windows that belong to the same program simultaneously.

- **Hit an Exposé keystroke.** You can actually use the F9 and F10 Exposé keystrokes *while* you're in the F8 big-picture view.

  Yes, this gets kind of meta, but it's useful when you're trying to arrange your windows and programs among your screens. Once you're in the F8 big-picture view, for example, you can hit F9 to see *all* windows on *all* screens scurry apart, so that nothing is covered up. Then start dragging windows onto different screens as necessary.

***Tip:*** Once the big-picture view is open, pressing the letter C key rounds up all of your open windows, from all virtual screens, into the first space—a handy way to consolidate your world in times of disorientation. Press C again to send them back where they started.

### Moving windows among screens

One way to move a particular window to a different screen is to drag it in big-picture view, as shown in Figure 4-9.

But there are two other ways that don't require entering the F8 big-picture view:

- Drag a window (using its title bar as a handle) all the way to the edge of the screen. Stay there with the mouse button still down. After about a second, you'll see the adjacent screen slide into view; you've just moved the window.

- Click anywhere inside a window, and keep the mouse button down. Now press your screen-switching keystroke (Control-←, for example, or Control-3). You've just moved the window to the designated screen.

To be sure, these are power-user techniques that may not come naturally. But the F8 big-picture view is always waiting should you become befuddled.

***Tip:*** What if you want to drag something from one screen (like a photo in iPhoto) into a window that's on a different screen (like an outgoing email message)?

Two ways; take your pick. First, you can start dragging whatever it is—and then, in mid-drag, press F8 to open the big-picture view, and complete the drag directly onto the other Space (and even into the relevant window *in* that Space).

Another approach: Start dragging. With the mouse still down, press ⌘-Tab to open the application switcher. Continue the drag onto the *icon* of the receiving program, and still keep the mouse button down. Mac OS X switches to the appropriate virtual screen automatically.

# Hiding Programs the Old-Fashioned Way

When it comes to getting windows out of your way, nothing can touch Exposé and Spaces for speed and entertainment value. Once you've mastered those features, the traditional rituals of hiding windows will seem charmingly quaint. "When I was your age," you'll tell your grandchildren, "we used to have to *hold down the Option key* to hide windows!"

But you know the drill at software companies: They addeth, but they never taketh away. All of the old techniques are still around.

## Hiding the Program You're Using

For the purposes of this discussion, when a program is *hidden,* all of its windows, tool palettes, and button bars disappear. You can bring them back only by bringing the program to the front again (by clicking its Dock icon again, for example).

If your aim is to hide only the program you're currently using, Mac OS X offers a whole raft of approaches to the same problem. Many of them involve the Option key, as listed here:

- **Option-click any visible portion of the desktop.** The program you were in vanishes, along with all of its windows.

- **Option-click any other program's icon on the Dock.** You open that program (or bring all of its windows to the front) *and* hide all the windows of the one you were using.

- **Option-click any visible portion of another program's windows.** Once again, you switch programs, hiding the one you were using at the time.

- **From the Application menu, choose Hide iPhoto (or whatever the program is).** The Application menu is the boldfaced menu that bears the program's name.

- **When you've highlighted a Dock icon by pressing ⌘-Tab to rotate through the running programs, press the letter H key.** The program hides itself instantly. Leave the ⌘ key down the whole time, and after pressing the H, press Tab again to move on to the next program. If you release the keys while "stopped" on the program instead, you'll bring it forward rather than hiding it.

- **Press ⌘-H.** This may be the easiest and most useful trick of all (although it doesn't work in every program). Doing so hides the program you're in; you then "fall down" into the next running program.

To un-hide a program and its windows, click its Dock icon again, choose the Show All command in the Application menu, or press ⌘-Tab to summon the heads-up application display.

## Hiding (Minimizing) Individual Windows

In Mac OS X, there's more to managing your window clutter than simply hiding entire programs. You can also hide or show *individual windows* of a single program. In fact, Apple must believe that hiding a window will become one of your favorite activities, because it offers at least four ways to do so:

- Choose Window→Minimize Window, if your program offers such a command, or press ⌘-M.

- Click the Minimize button on the window's title bar, as shown in Figure 4-10.

- Double-click the window's title bar.

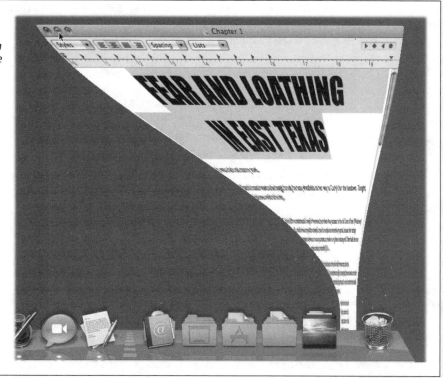

**Figure 4-10:**
*When you click the center button on a window title bar, double-click the title bar, or press ⌘-M, you minimize that window, getting it out of your way and off your screen. Minimizing on the Mac is a lot like minimizing in Windows; the minimized window is now represented by an icon on your Dock, which you can click to reopen the window.*

In any case, the affected window shrinks down until it becomes a new icon in the right side of the Dock. Click that icon to bring the window back.

## How Documents Know Their Parents

Every operating system needs a mechanism to associate documents with the applications that created them. When you double-click a Microsoft Word document icon, for example, it's clear that you want Microsoft Word to launch and open the document.

So how does Mac OS X know how to find a document's mommy?

It actually has four different mechanisms.

- **Your preferences.** If you've used the "Always Open with" command to *specify* a program (page 132), that's the one that opens.

- **Type/Creator codes.** First, it checks to see if the document has an invisible, four-letter *Type code* and *Creator code*. It does that because that's how Mac OS 9 used to recognize documents, and Mac OS X wants to ensure compatibility. (Apple used to monitor and track these four-letter codes, in conjunction with the various Mac software companies, so that no two creator codes were alike.)

The Creator code is the same for a program and the *documents* it creates—MSWD for Microsoft Word, FMP7 for FileMaker Pro, and so on. That's the entire point: The creator code tells the Mac which program to open when you double-click a particular document.

The Type code, meanwhile, specifies the document's file format: GIF, JPEG, TIFF, and so on.

When you double-click a document, Mac OS X checks to see if it has a creator code. If so, it then consults an invisible database of icons and codes, the master index that lists the correspondence between creator codes and the applications that generate them.

If the desktop file discovers a match, then the corresponding program opens the document, which now appears on your screen.

- **Unix database.** If the document doesn't have Type or Creator codes (and documents created by Cocoa programs—see page 141—generally don't), Mac OS X consults a second internal Mac OS X database, one that's inherited from Unix systems. The only real interaction you have with it is when you change a document's parent to

---

## Using the Dock or Sidebar for Drag-and-Drop

The Mac is smart about the relationship between documents and applications. If you double-click a TextEdit document icon, for example, TextEdit opens automatically and shows you the document.

But it's occasionally useful to open a document using a program *other* than the one that created it. Perhaps, as is often the case with downloaded Internet graphics, you don't *have* the program that created it, or you don't know which one was used. This technique is also useful when opening a Read Me file into your word processor, such as Word, instead of the usual TextEdit program.

In such cases, the Dock is handy: Just drag the mystery document onto one of the Dock's tiles, as shown here. Doing so forces the program to

open the document—if it can. (Dragging onto a program's icon in the Sidebar or even the Finder toolbar works just as well.)

Incidentally, in general, only the Dock icons of programs that can, in fact, open the file you're dragging become highlighted. The others just shrug indifferently or even scoot aside, thinking you're trying to drag the file *into* the dock.

Pressing Option-⌘ as you drag forces Dock icons to be more tolerant. Now *all* of them "light up" as your document touches them, indicating that they'll *try* to open your file. Even so, a "could not be opened" error message may result. As they say in Cupertino, sometimes what a can really needs is a can opener.

---

a different program, as described on the following pages. (Actually, you can open and examine the database—if you're a programmer/geek.)

- **Filename extensions.** A *filename extension* is a suffix following a period in the file's name, as in *Letter to Mom.doc.* (It's usually three letters long, but doesn't have to be.) These, too, play a role in determining which documents open into which programs—as the operating system's last resort.

That's how Windows identifies its documents. If you double-click something called *memo.doc,* it opens in Microsoft Word. If you double-click *memo.wri,* it opens in Microsoft Write, and so on.

---

**Note:** Mac OS X comes set to hide most filename extensions, on the premise that they make the operating system look more technical and threatening. If you'd like to see them, however, choose Finder→Preferences, click the Advanced button, and then turn on "Show all file extensions." Now examine a few of your documents; you'll see that their names now display the previously hidden suffixes.

You can hide or show these suffixes on an icon-at-a-time basis, too (or a clump-at-a-time basis). Just highlight the icon or icons you want to affect, and then choose File→Get Info. In the resulting Info window, proceed as shown in Figure 4-11.

---

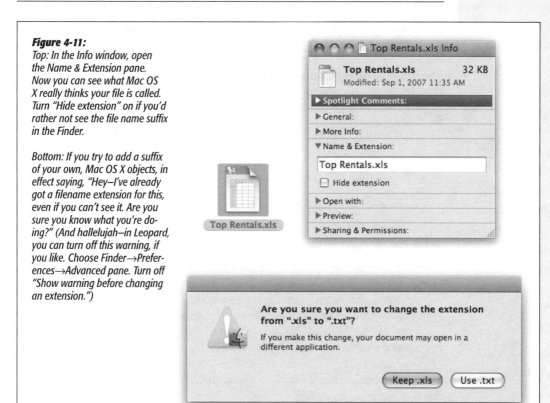

*Figure 4-11:*
*Top: In the Info window, open the Name & Extension pane. Now you can see what Mac OS X really thinks your file is called. Turn "Hide extension" on if you'd rather not see the file name suffix in the Finder.*

*Bottom: If you try to add a suffix of your own, Mac OS X objects, in effect saying, "Hey—I've already got a filename extension for this, even if you can't see it. Are you sure you know what you're doing?" (And hallelujah—in Leopard, you can turn off this warning, if you like. Choose Finder→Preferences→Advanced pane. Turn off "Show warning before changing an extension.")*

It's possible to live a long and happy life without knowing anything about these codes and suffixes. Indeed, the vast majority of Mac fans may never even encounter them. But if you're prepared for a little bit of technical bushwhacking, you may discover that understanding creator/type codes and file name suffixes can be useful in troubleshooting, keeping your files private, and appreciating how Mac OS X works.

## Reassigning Documents to Programs

Unfortunately, Type and Creator codes aren't of much use when you encounter a document created by a program that you don't have. If someone emails you a MIDI file (a file-exchange format for music) that she exported from the Finale sheet-music program, you won't be able to open it by double-clicking, unless you, too, have Finale installed. Even if you have a different sheet-music program on your hard drive, just double-clicking the MIDI file won't, by itself, open it.

Filename extensions, meanwhile, have problems of their own. Filename extensions are even less likely to pinpoint which parent program should open a particular document. Suppose you've downloaded a graphic called Sunset.jpg. Well, almost any program these days can open a JPEG graphic—Photoshop, Word, Preview, Safari, and so on. How does Mac OS X know which of these programs to open when you double-click the file?

Fortunately, *you* can decide. You can *reassign* a document (or all documents of its kind) to a specific program. Here's the rundown.

### Reassigning a certain document—just once

Double-clicking a graphics file generally opens it in Preview, the graphics viewer included with Mac OS X. Most of the time, that's a perfectly good arrangement. But Preview has only limited editing powers. What if you decide to edit a graphics file more substantially? You'd want it to open, just this once, into a different program—Photoshop Elements, for example.

To do so, you must access the Open With command. You can find it in two places:

- Highlight the icon, and then choose File→Open With.

- Right-click the file's icon. Or, in a Finder window, highlight the icon and then open the Action menu. In the shortcut menu, choose Open With.

Study the submenu for a moment (Figure 4-12, top). The program whose name says "(default)" indicates which program *usually* opens this kind of document. From this pop-up menu, choose the name of the program you'd *rather* open this particular file, right now, just this once.

### Reassigning a certain document—permanently

After opening a TIFF file in, say, Photoshop Elements for editing, you haven't really made any changes in the fabric of your Mac universe. The next time you double-click that file, it opens once again in Preview.

If you wish this particular file would *always* open in Photoshop Elements, the steps are slightly different. In fact, there are three different ways:

- In the Choose an Application dialog box, turn on "Always Open With" (shown at bottom in Figure 4-12).

*Figure 4-12:*
*Top: The shortcut menu offers a list of programs capable of opening an icon. If you were to press the Option key right now, the words Open With would suddenly change to say Always Open With.*

*Bottom: If you choose Other, you're prompted to choose a different program. Turn on Always Open With if you'll always want this document to open in the new parent program. Otherwise, this is a one-time reassignment.*

- Start out with one of the previously described techniques (File→Open With, or right-click the file's icon and choose Open With)—but after you see the menu, press the Option key, too. Before your very eyes, the Open With command changes to say *Always* Open With.

- Highlight the icon, and then choose File→Get Info. Open the "Open with" panel. Choose a new "parent" program's name from the pop-up menu. You'll see that the word "(default)" changes position, now tacking itself onto the name of the new program you've chosen.

### Reassigning all documents of one type

So much for reassigning one document (or group of documents) at a time. What if you're writing, say, a book about Mac OS X, and you've been taking a lot of screenshots? Mac OS X saves each captured screen illustration as a graphics file in something called PNG format. That's all fine, except that every time you double-click one of these, it opens into Preview, where you can't paint out unwanted details.

You could reassign all of these files, one at a time, to a different program, but your grandchildren would have grandchildren by the time you finish. In this case, you want to tell Mac OS X, "For heaven's sake, make *all* PNG files open in Photoshop from now on!"

To make it happen, start by highlighting *any* PNG file. Choose File→Get Info. (The shortcut menus won't help you in this case.) Open the "Open with" panel.

From its pop-up menu, choose the program you want to open this kind of document from now on. (If the one you prefer isn't listed, use the Other option, which opens the Choose an Application dialog box so that you can navigate to the one you want. Find and double-click the program.)

This time, follow up by clicking Change All beneath the pop-up menu. (This button is dimmed until you've actually selected a different program from the pop-up menu.) Mac OS X asks you to confirm by clicking Continue or pressing Enter.

From now on, double-clicking any similar kind of document opens it in the newly selected program.

# Keyboard Control

In Windows, of course, you can operate every menu in every program from the keyboard—and every control in every dialog box—thanks to the power of the Alt key.

Mac OS X offers full keyboard control, too. You can operate every control in every dialog box from the keyboard, including pop-up menus and checkboxes. And you can even *redefine* many of the keyboard shortcuts in Mac OS X and even your programs. In short, if you were a keyboard power-user in Windows, you'll feel right at home in Mac OS X.

Here are some of the ways you can control your Mac mouselessly. In the following descriptions, you'll encounter the factory settings for the keystrokes that do the magic—but as you'll note in a moment, you can change these key combos to anything you like. (That's fortunate, since many of them, out of the box, conflict with canned brightness and volume keystrokes for laptops.)

## Control the Menus

When you press Control-F2, the  menu is highlighted. At this point, you can "walk" to another menu by pressing the ← or → keys (or Tab and Shift-Tab). When you reach the menu you want, open it by pressing ↓, Space, Return, or Enter.

Walk down the commands in the menu by pressing ↑ or ↓, or jump directly to a command in the menu by typing the first couple letters of its name. Finally, "click" a menu command by pressing Enter, Return, or the Space bar.

You can also close the menu without making a selection by pressing Esc or ⌘-period.

## Control the Dock

Once you've pressed Control-F3, you can highlight *any* icon on the Dock by pressing the appropriate arrow keys (or, once again, Tab and Shift-Tab).

Then, once you've highlighted a Dock icon, you "click it" by pressing Enter or the Space bar. Again, if you change your mind, press Esc or ⌘-period.

---

**Tip:** Once you've highlighted a disk or folder icon, you can press the ↑ or ↓ keys to make its shortcut menu appear. (If you've positioned the Dock vertically, use the left or right arrow instead!)

---

## Cycle Through Your Windows

Every time you press Control-F4, you bring the next window forward, eventually cycling through *every window in every open program.* Add the Shift key to cycle through them in the opposite order.

You may remember that Mac OS X offers a different keystroke for cycling through the different windows in your *current* program (it's ⌘-~, the tilde symbol at the upper-left of your keyboard). Control-F4, on the other hand, tours all windows in *all* programs. Both keystrokes are useful in different situations.

## Control the Toolbar

This one is on the unpredictable side, but it more-or-less works in most programs that display a Mac OS X–style toolbar: the Finder, System Preferences, and so on.

When you press Control-F5, you highlight the first button on that toolbar. Move the "focus" by pressing the arrow keys or Tab and Shift-Tab. Then tap Enter or the Space bar to "click" the highlighted button.

## Control Tool Palettes

In a few programs that feature floating tool palettes, you can highlight the frontmost palette by pressing Control-F6. At this point, use the arrow keys to highlight the various buttons on the palette. You can see the effect when, for example, you're editing text in TextEdit and you've also opened the Font palette. Pressing Control-F6 highlights the Font palette, taking the "focus" off your document.

## Control Dialog Boxes

You can also navigate and manipulate any *dialog box* from the keyboard.

See the dialog box shown in Figure 4-13? If you turn on "All controls" at the bottom, then pressing the Tab key highlights the next control of any type, whatever it may be—radio button, pop-up menu, and so on. Press the Space bar to "click" a button or open a pop-up menu. Once a menu is open, use the arrow keys (or type letter keys) to highlight commands on it, and the Space bar to "click" your choice.

---

***Tip:*** Press Control-arrow keys to "click" the different tabs of a dialog box.

---

**Figure 4-13:**
*Turn off any checkboxes for keystrokes that you never use—especially if they seem to conflict with identical keyboard shortcuts in your programs. In fact, there's even a keystroke that turns off all of the "full keyboard access" keystrokes (the ones that let you control menus, Dock, toolbars, palettes, and so on) all at once: Control-F1. (Don't mean to hurt your brain, but you can actually turn off even that keystroke.)*

# The Save and Open Dialog Boxes

When you choose File→Save, you're asked where you want the new document stored on your hard drive. The resulting dialog box is crystal-clear—more than ever, it's a miniature Finder. All of the skills you've picked up working at the desktop come into play here.

To give it a try, launch any Mac OS X program that has a Save or Export command—TextEdit, for example. Type a couple of words, and then choose File→Save. The Save sheet appears (Figure 4-14).

*Tip:* In Mac OS X, a quick glance at the Close button in the upper-left corner of a document window tells you whether it's been saved. When a small dot appears in the red button, it means you've made changes to the document that you haven't saved yet. (Time to press ⌘-S!). The dot disappears as soon as you save your work.

**Figure 4-14:**
*Top: The Save dialog box, or sheet, often appears in its compact form.*

*Right (inset): If you open the Where pop-up menu, you'll find that Mac OS X lists all the places it thinks you might want to save your new document: on the hard drive or iDisk, in a folder that you've put into your Sidebar (page 21), or into a folder you've recently opened.*

*Bottom: If you want to choose a different folder or create a new folder, click the ▼ button shown above to expand the dialog box. Here, you see the equivalent of the Finder—with a choice of icon, list, or column view. Even the Sidebar is here, complete with access to other disks on the network.*

*Supertip: Even in the Save or Open dialog box, you can highlight an icon (or several) and then press ⌘-I. You switch back to the Finder, where the Get Info box is waiting with the date, size, and other details about the selected icons.*

Compact Save sheet

Computer places
Sidebar places
Recent places

Expanded Save sheet

The big triangle button

## Sheets

In the days of operating systems gone by, the Save dialog box appeared dead center on the screen, where it commandeered your entire operation. Moreover, because it seemed stuck to your *screen* rather than to a particular *document*, you couldn't actually tell which document you were saving—a real problem when you quit out of a program that had three unsaved documents open.

In most Mac OS X programs, there's no mystery regarding which document you're saving, because a little Save dialog box called a *sheet* slides directly out of the document's title bar. Now there's no mistaking which document you're saving.

Better still, this little Save box is a sticky note attached to the document. It stays there, neatly attached and waiting, even if you switch to another program, another document, the desktop, or wherever. When you finally return to the document, the Save sheet is still there, waiting for you to type a file name and save the document.

## The Mini Finder

Of course, *you,* O savvy reader, have probably never saved a document into some deeply nested folder by accident, never to see it again. But millions of novices (and even a few experts) have fallen into this trap.

When the Save sheet appears, however, a pop-up menu shows you precisely where Mac OS X proposes putting your newly created document: usually in the Documents folder of your own Home folder. For many people, this is an excellent suggestion. If you keep everything in your Documents folder, it will be extremely easy to find, and you'll be able to back up your work just by dragging that single folder to a backup disk.

As shown at top in Figure 4-14, the Where pop-up menu gives you direct access to some other places you might want to save a newly created file. (The keystrokes for the most important folders work here, too—Shift-⌘-H for your Home folder, for example.)

In any case, when you save a file, the options in the Where pop-up menu have you covered 90 percent of the time. Most people work with a limited set of folders for active documents.

But when you want to save a new document into a new folder, or when you want to navigate to a folder that isn't listed in the Where pop-up menu, all is not lost. Click the ▾ button identified in Figure 4-14. The Save sheet expands miraculously into a very familiar sight: a miniature version of the Finder.

There's your Sidebar, complete with access to the other computers on your network. There's the Back button. There's your toggle switch between views; in Leopard, you can even switch to *icon* view here, in addition to the traditional list and column views.

---

*Tip:* In column view, your first instinct should be to widen this window, making more columns available. Do so by carefully dragging the lower-right corner of the dialog box. Mac OS X remembers the size you like for this Save sheet independently in each program.

---

Most of the familiar Finder-navigation shortcuts work here, too. For example, press the right and left arrow keys to navigate the columns, or the up and down arrow keys to highlight the disk and folder names *within* a column. Once you've highlighted a column, you can also type to select the first letters of disk or folder names.

Highlight the name of the folder in which you want to save your newly created document. Alternatively, you can click the New Folder button to create a new folder *inside* whatever folder is highlighted in the column view. (The usual New Folder keystroke works here, too: Shift-⌘-N.) You'll be asked to type the new name for the folder. After you've done so, click Create (or press Enter). The new folder appears in the rightmost pane of the column view. You can now proceed with saving your new document into it, if you like.

The next time you save a new document, the Save sheet reappears in whatever condition you left it. That is, if you used column view the last time, it's still in column view. At any time, you can collapse it into simplified view, shown at top in Figure 4-14, by clicking the ▲ button to the right of the Where pop-up menu.

---

*Tip:* The Save box always displays whatever places you've put in your Sidebar. (In compact view, the Where pop-up menu lists them; in expanded view, you see the Sidebar itself.)

The bottom line: If, on some project, you find yourself wanting to save new documents into the same deeply buried folder all the time, press F11 to duck back to the Finder, and add it to your Sidebar. From now on, you'll have quick access to it from the Save dialog box.

---

## Spotlight

The Search bar at the top of the Open and Save dialog box is a clone of the Finder's Search bar (Chapter 3). Press ⌘-F to make your insertion point jump there. Type a few letters of the name of the file or folder you're looking for, and up it pops, regardless of its actual hard-disk location.

Your savings: five minutes of burrowing through folders to find it, and several pages of reading about how to navigate the Save and Open boxes.

## The File Format Pop-up Menu

The Save dialog box in many programs offers a pop-up menu of file formats below the Save As box. Use this menu when preparing a document for use by somebody else—somebody whose computer doesn't have the same software. For example, if you've used a graphics program to prepare a photograph for use on the Web, this menu is where you specify JPEG format (the standard Web format for photos).

## The Open File Dialog Box

The dialog box that appears when you choose File→Open is almost identical to the expanded Save File sheet. Because you encounter it only when you're opening an existing file, this dialog box lacks the Save button, file name field, and so on.

---

*Note:* Furthermore, the Open dialog box shows you only icons for disks, folders, and documents that you can actually open at this moment. For example, when you're using GarageBand, picture files show up dimmed.

---

But it does have a new Sidebar category called Media (see Figure 4-15), which gives you direct access to all your photos, music, and movies. The premise is that Apple figures you might want to import these items *into* a document you're working on.

**Figure 4-15:**
*The new Media Browser is built right into the Open dialog box. That is, you get miniature listings of your iTunes, iPhoto, and movie files right in the Sidebar, for convenience in importing them into (for example) Keynote, PowerPoint, or a Web design program.*

Most of the other Save File dialog box controls, however, are equally useful here. That handy Spotlight search bar is still there, only a ⌘-F away. Once again, you can begin your navigation by seeing what's on the desktop (press ⌘-D) or in your Home folder (press Shift-⌘-H). Once again, you can find a folder or disk by beginning your quest with the Sidebar, and then navigate using either list or column view. And once again, you can drag a folder, disk, or file icon off your desktop directly into the dialog box to specify where you want to look. (If you drag a *file* icon, you're shown the folder that contains it.)

When you've finally located the file you want to open, do so by double-clicking it or highlighting it (which you can do from the keyboard), and then pressing Return, Enter, or ⌘-O.

In general, most people don't encounter the Open File dialog box nearly as often as the Save File dialog box. That's because the Mac offers many more convenient ways to *open* a file—double-clicking its icon in the Finder, choosing its name from the ⌘→Recent Items command, and so on—but only a single way to *save* a new file.

# Two Kinds of Programs: Cocoa and Carbon

Mac OS X was supposed to make life simpler. It was supposed to eliminate the confusion and complexity that the old Mac OS had accumulated over the years—and replace it with a smooth, simple, solid system.

Someday, that's exactly what Mac OS X will be. For the moment, however, you're stuck with running two different kinds of programs, each with different characteristics: *Cocoa and Carbon.*

The explanation involves a little bit of history and a little bit of logic. To take full advantage of Mac OS X's considerable technical benefits, software companies must write new programs for it from scratch. So what should Apple do—send out an email to the authors of the 18,000 existing Mac programs, suggesting that they throw out their programs and rewrite them from the bottom up?

At big companies like Microsoft and Adobe, such a suggestion would wind up on the Joke of the Week bulletin board.

Instead, Apple gave software companies a break. It wrote Mac OS X to let programmers and software companies choose precisely how much work they wanted to put into compatibility with the new system. The various levels include:

- **Update the existing programs (Carbon).** If software companies and programmers are willing to put *some* effort into getting with the Mac OS X program, they can simply adapt, or update, their existing software so that it works with Mac OS X.

  The resulting software looks and feels almost like a true Mac OS X program—you get the crash protection, the good looks, the cool-looking graphics, the Save sheets, and so on—but behind the scenes, the bulk of the computer programming is the same as it was in Mac OS 9. These are what Apple calls *Carbonized* programs, named for the technology (Carbon) that permits them to run on Mac OS X. (Examples of Carbonized programs include AppleWorks, Photoshop versions before CS3, FileMaker, Microsoft Office 2004, and, believe it or not, the Finder itself.)

  Most Carbonized programs don't offer all of the features available to Mac OS X, however. In the following pages, you'll discover which Mac OS X goodies you sacrifice when using programs adapted this way.

  On the other hand, such software offers a feature that software companies like *a lot:* A Carbon program is a lot easier to write concurrently with a Windows version of the same software. A Cocoa program, by contrast, is almost certainly locked into Macintosh-only Land.

- **Write new programs from scratch (Cocoa).** As Mac OS X becomes more popular, more software companies create new programs exclusively for it. The geeks call such programs *Cocoa* applications. Although they look exactly like Carbonized programs, they feel a little bit more smooth and solid. And they offer a number of special features that Carbonized programs don't offer.

Most of the programs that come on every Mac are true Cocoa applications, including iDVD, Safari, iChat, iPhoto, TextEdit, Stickies, Mail, Address Book, and so on.

## The Cocoa Difference

Here are some of the advantages Cocoa programs offer. It's worth reading—not to make you drool about a future when all Mac programs will fall into this category, but to help clear up any confusion you may have about why certain features seem to be present only occasionally.

---

**Note:** The following features appear in almost all Cocoa programs. That's not to say that you'll *never* see these features in Carbonized programs; the occasional Carbon program may offer one of these features or another. That's because programmers have to do quite a bit of work to bring them into Carbon applications—and almost none to include them in Cocoa ones.

---

### The Font Panel

The Mac has always been the designer's preferred computer, and Mac OS X only strengthens its position. For one thing, Mac OS X comes with over 200 absolutely beautiful fonts that Apple licensed from commercial type companies.

When you use a Carbon program, you usually access these fonts the same way as always: using a Font menu. But when you use a Cocoa program, you get the Font panel, which makes it far easier to organize, search, and use your font collection. Chapter 9 describes fonts, and the Font panel, in more detail.

### Services

Nestled in the Application menu of every Mac OS X program is a command called Services. These commands are dimmed when you use most *Carbonized* programs; they become available only when you use *Cocoa* programs.

Here's a sampling of the most useful commands in the Services menu.

---

**Note:** Not all of these Services work in all programs—even Cocoa programs. Implementing them is left to programmers' discretion.

---

#### Grab

Grab is a screen-capture program in your Applications→Utilities folder. You use it to turn what you see onscreen into graphics files. It's especially handy when writing computer books or training manuals.

The Grab service, in theory, lets you take your software snapshot from within any Cocoa application, without having to go find and launch Grab separately; unfortunately, it's available *only* in programs that can accept pasted graphics. You'll find details on Grab's submenu commands (Screen, Selection, Timed Screen) on page 526.

---

### Mail

This handy command springs to life only after you've highlighted some text in a Cocoa program—or a file in the Finder.

- **Send Selection.** In one step, the Mail Text command launches the Mail program and pastes the highlighted text into the body of a new, outgoing email message. You're saved the trouble of copying, launching Mail, creating a new message, and pasting. You might use this feature when, for example, you find something interesting on a Web page, and you'd like to email it to someone.

- **Send To.** This command is useful only if you've highlighted an email *address* in a text document. This command, too, switches to Mail and creates a new, outgoing message—but this time, Mac OS X pastes the text you've highlighted into the "To:" field.

### Make New Sticky Note

This command copies whatever text you've got highlighted, switches to your Stickies program (page 509), creates a new sticky note, and pastes your selected material in it. If you're the kind of person who keeps your life—lists, passwords, favorite URLs, to-do list, notes, and so on—in Stickies, this one can save you considerable hassle. No wonder Apple endowed it with its own keyboard shortcut: Shift-⌘-Y.

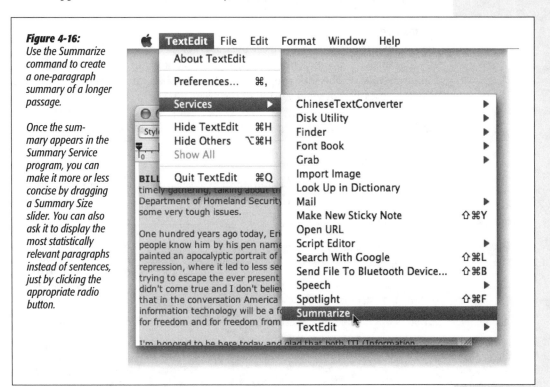

**Figure 4-16:**
Use the Summarize command to create a one-paragraph summary of a longer passage.

Once the summary appears in the Summary Service program, you can make it more or less concise by dragging a Summary Size slider. You can also ask it to display the most statistically relevant paragraphs instead of sentences, just by clicking the appropriate radio button.

### Open URL

When you highlight a Web address in any program, choosing this command fires up your Web browser and takes you to the indicated page.

### Search with Google

Never let it be said that inspiration is dead in the post-tech-bubble era. This unassuming command adds a powerful research assistant to every program where you can type. Highlight a phrase—*Picasso, electric curtains, Yankees game*—and hit this command. In seconds, you're online, in your Web browser, facing a list of Web pages from a Google search for that topic. It's a dictionary, thesaurus, news service, and stock ticker all in one.

The gang at Apple loves this one, too. They blessed it with its own keyboard shortcut: Shift-⌘-L (for *look up*).

### Spotlight

As you know from Chapter 3, Spotlight is always at your command, ready to find files, folders, or programs at the touch of a key. But the ⌘-Space bar trick requires you to type in a search phrase. This Service command (and its keystroke, Shift-⌘-F), on the other hand, triggers a Spotlight search for a word or phrase that's *already* typed—one that you've highlighted in whatever document is before you.

### Summarize

Talk about intriguing: When you choose this command after highlighting some text, the Mac analyzes the sentences you've highlighted and, after a moment, launches Summary Service. This little program, which you probably never even knew you had, displays a greatly shortened version of the original text.

---

*Tip:* To save the summarized document as a TextEdit document, choose File→Save As.

---

## Toolbar Tricks

The toolbar is an increasingly common sight at the top of modern application windows. In any thoughtfully written program, the Customize Toolbar command lets

**Figure 4-17:**
*By ⌘-clicking this button repeatedly, you can cycle among toolbar styles. In Mail, for example, you can cycle between six different toolbar styles: with icons and labels (large and small); with icons only (large and small); and with text labels only (large and small).*

you determine how you want this toolbar to show up—with icons, as icons with text labels beneath them, with text labels alone to save window space, and so on.

But in many Cocoa programs—including the Finder, OmniWeb, Mail, Address Book, and Xcode—there's a much faster way to switch among these toolbar styles: Just ⌘-click the white button shown in 5-19.

## Universal Apps (Intel Macs)

By the end of 2006, Apple had switched its entire Macintosh product line over to Intel's Core Duo processors (the successor to the Pentium).

Yes, *that* Intel. The company that Mac partisans had derided for years as part of the Dark Side. The company that Steve Jobs routinely belittled in his demonstrations of PowerPC chips (which IBM and Motorola supplied to Apple for more than a decade). The company whose marketing mascot Apple lit on fire in a 1996 attack ad on TV.

Why the change? Apple's computers can only be as fast as the chips inside them, and the chips that IBM had in the works just weren't keeping up with the industry. As one editorial put it, "Apple's doing a U-turn out of a dead-end road."

And sure enough, Intel-based Macs start up and run much faster than the old Macs, thanks to the endless march of speed improvements in the chip-making world. And thanks to that Intel chip, today's Macs can even run Microsoft Windows and all of the thousands of Windows programs. (Chapter 8 has details.)

At the time, though, there was a small glitch: *Existing Mac software didn't run on Intel chips.*

Apple would have to ask the world's software companies to rewrite their programs *yet again,* after already having dragged them through the Mac OS 9-to-Mac OS X transition only a few years earlier.

Fortunately, the transition wasn't as gruesome as you might expect. First, Apple had already secretly recompiled (reworked) Mac OS X itself to run on Intel chips.

Furthermore, Apple wrote an invisible translation program, code-named Rosetta, which permits the existing library of Mac OS X programs—Photoshop, Word, and so on—to run, unmodified, on Intel Macs.

They do not, however, run especially fast on Intel Macs. In fact, many of them run *slower* than they did on pre-Intel Macs.

To make their programs perform at *full speed* on Intel-based Macs, programmers have to update their wares. All the big software companies promised to make their programs into *universal binaries*—programs that run equally well on PowerPC- *and* Intel-based Macs with a double-click on the very same Finder icon.

It took two years for all the big-name programs to fall in line, but they finally did. Photoshop CS3, Microsoft Office 2008, Final Cut Pro, QuarkXPress, FileMaker, Firefox…one by one, the world's most popular Mac programs were reworked into Universal versions. (There's even a list of them—over 7,000 so far—at *http://guide. apple.com/universal.*)

You have only two indications that you're using a program originally designed for PowerPC-based Macs: first, you'll see a notation in the program's Get Info window (see Figure 4-18). Second, you'll probably discover that the program isn't as fast as it used to be.

If all this talk about architectures and chips makes your brain hurt, you can at least take comfort in one fact: No matter which kind of Mac you've got Leopard installed on, every feature, tip, and trick you've learned from this book will work exactly the same.

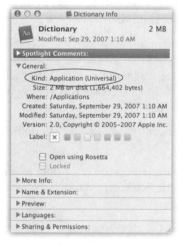

*Figure 4-18:*
*Here's a quick way to tell if a program is an old one that will run slowly on an Intel Mac (instead of a Universal one that won't require the Rosetta software translation). Highlight its icon and choose File→Get Info. Near the top, you'll see either "Application: PowerPC" (meaning "old and slow") or "Application: Universal" (meaning "runs fast on both Intel and PowerPC machines").*

# Installing Mac OS X Programs

In general, new programs arrive on your Mac via one of two avenues: on a CD or DVD, or via an Internet download. The CD method is slightly simpler; see "Performing the Installation" later in this section.

For help installing downloaded programs, on the other hand, read on.

## .sit, .zip, .tar, .gz, and .dmg

Programs you download from the Internet generally arrive in a specially encoded, compressed form. (And unless you've changed the settings, they arrive in the Downloads folder stack on your Dock.)

The downloaded file's name usually has one of these filename extensions:

- **.sit** indicates a *StuffIt* file, the standard Macintosh file-compression format of years gone by.

- **.zip** is the standard Windows compression file format. And because Leopard has a built-in Compress command right in the File menu (and *doesn't* come with StuffIt Expander), .zip is the *new* standard Macintosh compression format. It certainly makes life easier for people who have to exchange files with the Windows crowd.

- **.tar** is short for *tape archive,* an ancient Unix utility that combines (but doesn't compress) several files into a single icon, for simplicity in sending.

- **.gz** is short for *gzip,* a standard Unix compression format.

- **.tar.gz** or **.tgz** represents one *compressed* archive containing *several* files.

- **.dmg** is a disk image, described below.

*Figure 4-19:*
*Downloading a new program from the Internet may strew your desktop or Downloads folder with icons. A: These are the original downloaded files. Delete them after they're decompressed. B: The compressed file turns into this .dmg file. Double-click it to "mount" the disk image (if it didn't appear automatically). C: And now, the disk image itself. Double-click it to open the software installer window. "Eject" it after the installation is complete. D: Here's the actual software installer window. Drag the software's icon to your Applications folder, or double-click the installer, if you see one here. After the installation is complete, you can delete all of this stuff (except maybe the .dmg file, if you think you might want to install the software again later).*

Fortunately, if you use Safari (Chapter 12) as your Web browser, you don't have to worry about all this, because it automatically unzips and unstuffs them.

If you use some other browser, *StuffIt Expander* can turn all of them back into usable form when you download a file. (StuffIt Expander doesn't come with Mac OS X, but

---

## The Color Picker

Here and there—in System Preferences, iMovie, TextEdit, Microsoft Office, and many other programs—Mac OS X offers you the opportunity to choose a *color* for some element: for your desktop background, a window, and so on.

The dialog box that appears offers a miniature color lab that lets you dial in any color in the Mac's rainbow. Several color labs, actually, arrayed across the top, each designed to make color-choosing easier in certain circumstances:

**Color Wheel.** Drag the scroll bar vertically to adjust the brightness, and then drag your cursor around the ball to pick the shade.

**Color Sliders.** From the pop-up menu, choose the color-mixing method you prefer. *CMYK* stands for cyan, magenta, yellow, and black. People in the printing industry will feel immediately at home, because these four colors are the component inks for color printing. (These people may also be able to explain why *K* stands for *black*.)

*RGB* is how a TV or computer monitor thinks of colors: as proportions of red, green, and blue light. *Gray Scale* means shades of gray, like a black-and-white TV. And *HSB* stands for Hue, Saturation, and Brightness—a favorite color-specifying scheme in scientific circles.

In each case, just drag the sliders to mix up the color you want, or type in the percentages of each component.

**Color Palettes.** This option presents canned sets of color swatches. They're primarily for programmers who want

quick access to the standard colors in Mac OS X. The Web Safe Colors list is useful for Web designers, too; they can tell whether a color will display properly on other computers.

**Image Palettes.** Here's the visible rainbow arrayed yet another way: in cloudy, color-arranged streaks. (Cool tip: If you drag a graphics file directly into the dialog box, it appears in the spectrum's place. That's a handy trick if you're trying to identify the color of a certain spot of an image, for example. And don't miss the pop-up button at the bottom of the dialog box, which offers a few other stunts.)

**Crayons.** Now *this* is a good user interface. You can click each crayon to see its color name: Mocha, Fern, Cayenne, and so on. (Some interior decorator in Cupertino had a field day naming these crayons.)

In any of these color pickers, you can also "sample" a color that's outside the dialog box—a color you found on a Web page, for example. Just click the magnifying-glass icon and then move your cursor around the screen. You'll see the sliders and numbers change inside the dialog box automatically when you click.

Finally, note that you can store frequently used (or frequently admired) colors in the tiny palette squares at the bottom. To do that, drag the big rectangular color swatch (next to the magnifying glass) directly down into one of the little squares, where it will stay fresh for weeks.

If you don't have space for all the colors you want at the bottom of the window, you can drag the small circular dot down to make room for more.

---

you can download it for free from, for example, this book's "Missing CD" page at *www.missingmanuals.com.*)

## Disk Images (.dmg files)

Once you've unzipped a downloaded program, it often takes the form of a disk image file, whose name ends with the letters *.dmg* (second from top in Figure 4-19). Some files arrive as disk images straight from the Web, too, without having been compressed first.

Disk images are extremely common in Mac OS X. All you have to do is double-click the .dmg icon. After a moment, it magically turns into a disk icon on your desktop, which you can work with just as though it's a real disk (third from top in Figure 4-19). For example:

- Double-click it to open it. The software you downloaded is inside.

- Remove it from your desktop by dragging it to the Trash (whose icon turns into a big silver Eject key as you drag), highlighting it and pressing ⌘-E (the shortcut for File→Eject), clicking its ⏏ button in the Sidebar, or right-clicking it, and then choosing Eject from the shortcut menu. (You've still got the original .dmg file you downloaded, so you're not really saying goodbye to the disk image forever.)

## Cleaning Up after Decompression

When you've finished unzipping or unstuffing a downloaded file, you may have several icons on your desktop or in the Downloads folder. Some are useful; some you're free to trash:

- **The original compressed file.** It's safe to throw away the .sit, .tar, .gz, or .tgz file you originally downloaded (after it's decompressed, of course).

- **The .dmg file.** Once you've turned it into an actual disk-drive icon, installed the software from it, and "ejected" the disk-drive icon, you can delete the .dmg file. Keep it only if you think you might need to reinstall the software someday.

---

***Note:*** If you try to trash the .dmg file *before* removing the disk-drive icon from the screen, you'll get a "file in use" error message when you try to empty the Trash.

---

- **The disk image itself.** This final icon, the one that contains the actual software or its installer (third from top in Figure 4-19), doesn't exist as a file on your hard drive. It's a phantom drive, held in memory, that will go away by itself when you log out. So after installing its software, feel free to drag it to the Trash (or highlight it and press ⌘-E to "eject" it).

## Performing the Installation

Working with .tar, .gz, and .dmg files are all skills unique to downloading Mac OS X programs from the Internet. Installing software from a CD or DVD is much more straightforward.

In either case, once you've got a disk icon on your desktop (either a pseudo-disk from a disk image or a CD or DVD you've inserted), you're ready to install the software. You can install many Mac OS X programs just by dragging their icons or folders to your hard drive (usually the Applications folder). Others offer a traditional installer program that requires you to double-click, read and accept a license agreement, and so on.

In both cases, *where* you decide to install the new program is suddenly a big issue. You have the following two alternatives:

- **In the Applications folder.** Most programs, of course, sit in your Applications folder. Most of the time, this is where you'll want to install new programs. Putting them in the Applications folder makes them available to anyone who uses the Mac.

---

***Note:*** You can't put anything in your Applications folder unless you have an Administrator account, as described on page 379.

---

- **In your Home folder.** Suppose you share your Mac with other people, as described in Chapter 13. If that's your situation, you may occasionally want to install a program privately, reserving it for your own use only. In that case, just install or drag it into your Home folder, or a folder inside it. When other people log onto the machine, they won't even know that you've installed that new program, since it doesn't show up in the Applications folder.

If you don't have an Administrator account, in fact, this is your only option for installing new programs.

## Uninstalling Software

In Mac OS X, there's generally no Uninstall program, and no Add/Remove Programs window. To uninstall a program, you just drag it (or its folder) from the Applications folder (or wherever it is) to the Trash.

Some programs also leave harmless scraps of themselves behind; to check for them, look for preference files or folders bearing the dearly departed program's name in your Library folders (especially in Application Support) and your Home→Library→Preferences folder.

## Dashboard

The essence of using most operating systems is running *programs*, which often produce *documents*.

In Mac OS X, however, there's a third category: a set of weird, hybrid entities that Apple calls *widgets*. They appear, all at once, floating in front of your other windows, when your press the F12 key. Welcome to the Dashboard (Figure 4-20).

**Note:** On the thin aluminum Apple keyboard, the Dashboard has a different keystroke: F4. In fact, you can see a tiny Dashboard logo painted right on the key.

Either way, you can change this keyboard assignment, as described below. Also, on laptops where F12 is the Eject key, you have to hold down the Fn key (lower-left corner).

**Figure 4-20:**
*When you summon the Dashboard, you get a fleet of floating miniprograms that convey or convert all kinds of useful information. They appear and disappear all at once, on a tinted translucent sheet that floats in front of all your other windows. You get rid of Dashboard either by pressing the same key again (F12 or whatever) or by clicking anywhere on the screen except on a widget.*

What are these weird, hybrid entities, anyway? They're not really programs, because they don't create documents or have Dock icons (although Dashboard itself has a Dock icon). They're certainly not documents, because you can't name or save them. What they most resemble, actually, is little Web pages. They're meant to display information, much of it from the Internet, and they're written using Web programming languages like HTML and JavaScript. (Come to think of it, they're a lot like *gadgets* in Windows Vista.)

Mac OS X's starter widgets include a calculator, local movie showtimes database, current weather reporter, stock ticker, clock, White Pages and Yellow Pages phone books, and so on. (You may have to wait a few seconds for them to "warm up," go online, and display any meaningful information.) The real beauty of the Dashboard, though, is that you can take your pick of several thousand additional, free widgets that bring you games, shopping, information, TV and movie schedules, sports, searching tools, and much more. (You'll find them at *www.apple.com/downloads/dashboard*.)

Mastering the basics of Dashboard won't take you long at all:

- **To move a widget,** drag it around the screen. (Click anywhere but on a button, menu, or text box.)

- **To close a widget,** press the Option key as you move the mouse across the widget's face. You'll see the circled X button appear at the widget's top-left corner; click it.

---

***Tip:*** If the Widget Bar is open (as described below), every widget displays its X close button. You don't need the Option key.

---

- **To open a closed widget,** click the circled + button at the bottom of the screen. Now the entire screen image slides upward by about an inch to make room for the Widget Bar: a "perforated metal" tray containing the full array of widgets, even the ones that aren't currently on the screen (Figure 4-21). Open one by clicking its icon.

***Figure 4-21:***
*You'll probably have to scroll the Widget Bar to see all the widgets, by clicking the arrows at either end. When you're finished opening new widgets, close the Widget Bar by clicking its circled X button at the left side of your screen.*

A new widget appears by splashing down into the center of your screen, sending realistic pond ripples across the liquidy glass of your screen. These widgets really know how to make an appearance, don't they?

- **To hide one of Apple's widgets,** or delete one that you've installed yourself, use the Widget widget described in Figure 4-22.

- **To rearrange your widgets as they appear in the Widget Bar,** open your hard drive→Library→Widgets folder. Here you'll find the icons for the standard Apple

Dashboard widgets. To rearrange them, you have to rename them; they appear on the Widget Bar in alphabetical order. (You can also remove a widget for good by deleting it from this folder, if you must.)

---

***Tip:*** The Dashboard icon also appears in your Dock, just in case you forget the F12 keystroke. On the other hand, if you prefer the keystroke, you can remove the icon from your Dock to make room for more important stuff. Right-click the icon and, from the shortcut menu, choose Remove from Dock.

---

**Figure 4-22:**
*The Widget widget (whose icon appears at lower left in Figure 4-21) opens up this list of widgets. Turn off a check mark to hide a widget, or click – to completely uninstall any widget you installed yourself. The ones whose boxes aren't checked are the ones that no longer appear on the Widgets bar.*

## Dashboard Tips

Like most Leopard features, Dashboard is crawling with cool tips and tricks. Here are a few of the biggies:

- If you just *click* an icon on the Widget Bar, the widget appears right in the middle of your screen. But if you *drag* the widget's icon off the bar, you can deposit it anywhere you like on the screen.

- There's a great keystroke that opens and closes the Widget Bar: ⌘-equal sign (=). (This keystroke may be different on non-U.S. keyboard layouts.)

- To refresh a certain widget—for example, to update its information from the Internet—click it and press ⌘-R. The widget instantly *twist-scrambles* itself into a sort of ice-cream swirl (you've got to see it to believe it) and then untwists to reveal the new data.

- You can open more than one copy of the same widget. Just click its icon more than once in the Widget Bar. You wind up with multiple copies of it on your screen: three World Clocks, two Stock Trackers, or whatever. That's a useful trick when, for example, you want to track the time or weather in more than one city, or when you maintain two different stock portfolios.

- If you keep the Shift key pressed when you summon Dashboard, the widgets fly onto the screen in gorgeous, translucent, 3-D *slow motion.* Aren't you glad you're alive to see the day?

### Dashboard Preferences

To change the Dashboard keystroke to something other than F12, choose  →System Preferences, and then click Exposé & Spaces. In Leopard, they're combined in a single System Preferences pane because at their core, they serve similar functions: helping you herd your windows.

Here, you'll discover that you can choose almost any other keyboard combination to summon and dismiss the Dashboard, or even choose a screen corner that, when your mouse lands there, acts as the Dashboard trigger.

## Web Clips: Make Your Own Widgets

You don't have to be satisfied with Apple's 20 widgets *or* the several thousand that other people have written. Leopard introduces *Web clips,* a new way to make a Dashboard widget of your own—in about three clicks.

Web clips exploit an inescapable characteristic of widgets: An awful lot of them exist to deliver real-time information from the Web. That's the point of the Ski Report widget, Weather, Stocks, Flight Tracker, ESPN, and so on.

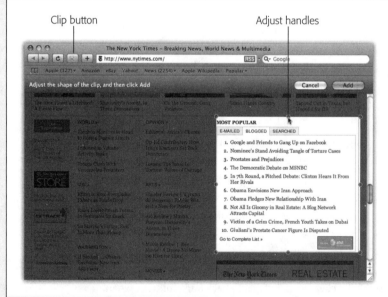

Clip button    Adjust handles

***Figure 4-23:***
*Drag the little round handles to make the white box just big enough to surround the part of the page you want to enshrine. Or drag inside the box to move the whole thing.*

But what if your interest isn't skiing, stocks, or sports? What if it's the *New York Times* front page? Or the bestselling children's books on Amazon? Or the most-viewed video on YouTube? Or some cool Flash game that you wish you could summon with the touch of a key?

That's the beauty of Web clips, a joint venture of Dashboard and the Safari Web browser. They let you turn *any section of any Web page* into a Dashboard widget that updates itself every time you open Dashboard. It's like having a real-time keyhole peek at all your favorite Web sites at once.

## Creating a Web Clip Widget

Here's how you go about creating a do-it-yourself widget:

**Figure 4-24:**
*Top: Click a frame style to give your widget better-looking edges. If the widget plays sound, it keeps playing sound when you close the Dashboard unless you turn on "Play audio in Dashboard only."*

*Bottom: Click Edit to return to the front of the widget, where you can adjust its position on the underlying Web page.*

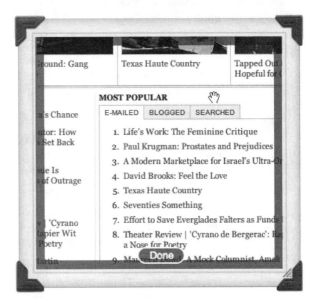

1. **Open Safari.**

   Safari is the Mac's Web browser. It's in your Applications folder.

2. **Navigate to the Web page that contains the information you want to snip. Click the Web clips button identified in Figure 4-23.**

   The screen goes dark, with only a small window of white. As you move your cursor around the page, the small white rectangle conveniently snaps to fit the various rectangular sections of the page.

   As shown in Figure 4-23, your job is to make a frame around the part of the page that usually shows the information you want. If the Web site ever redesigns its pages, it'll wreck your widget—but what the heck. It takes only five seconds to make it again.

3. **Adjust the corner or side handles to enclose the piece of page you want. When you're finished, click Add, or press Return or Enter.**

   Now Dashboard opens automatically. But wait—what's this? There's a new widget here that wasn't here before. At first, you might not even notice, because it's precisely centered *over* the piece of Web page that you enclosed. But if you drag it to one side, you'll see that it's a standalone, full-blown, real-time widget.

At this point, you can dress up your widget, adding a little polish to this raw clipping you've ripped out of a Web page. Click the ❶ button that appears when you move your mouse to the lower-right corner. The widget flips around to reveal the controls shown in Figure 4-24.

Here, you can click one of the frame styles to give your widget a better-looking border.

If you click Edit, the widget flips around to face you again, and here's where it gets weird: You can reposition your widget's contents as though they're a window on the Web page that's visible behind it. Drag the widget contents in any direction within the frame, or resize the frame using the lower-right resize handle. Click Done.

You can make as many Web-clip widgets as you want.

But here's a big screaming caution: If you close one of these homemade widgets, it's gone forever (or at least until you re-create it). They're never represented as icons on the Widget bar, as ordinariy widgets are.

Ah, well—easy come, easy go, right?

---

*Note:* If you're of the programmer persuasion–if you're handy in Javascript and HTML, for example–it's much easier to write custom widgets than ever before. (Not just Web-clip widgets; *real* widgets.)

That's because Leopard comes with Dashcode, an easy-to-use widget-assembly environment. You'll find the installer for it on your Leopard installation DVD (in the Optional Installs→XCode Tools folder), and you'll find tutorials and examples by typing *dashcode tutorial* into Google.

---

# Part Two: Moving In

**Chapter 5: Eight Ways to Transfer Your Files**

**Chapter 6: Transferring Email & Contacts**

**Chapter 7: Special Software, Special Problems**

**Chapter 8: Windows on the Mac**

**Chapter 9: Hardware on the Mac**

2

# Eight Ways to Transfer Your Files

A huge percentage of "switchers" do not, in fact, *switch*. Often, they just *add*. They may get a Macintosh (and get *into* the Macintosh), but they keep the old Windows PC around, at least for a while. If you're in that category, get psyched. It turns out that communicating with a Windows PC is one of the Mac's most polished talents.

That's especially good news in the early days of your Mac experience. You probably have a good deal of stuff on the Windows machine that you'd like to bring over to the Mac. Somewhere along the line, somebody probably told you how easy this is to do. In fact, the Mac's reputation for simplicity may even have played a part in your decision to switch.

In any case, this chapter describes the process of building a bridge from the PC to the Mac, so that you can bring all your files and settings into their new home. It also tells you where to *put* all of them. (The next chapter is dedicated to the slightly hairier process of getting your email and addresses copied over.)

As it turns out, files can take one of several roads from your old PC to your new Mac. For example, you can transfer them on a disk (such as a CD or iPod), by a network, or as an attachment to an email message.

---

*Tip:* The first part of this chapter covers the mechanical aspects of moving files and folders from your Windows PC to the Mac. On page 165, you'll find a more pointed discussion of where to put each kind of data (mail, photos, music, and so on) once it's on theMac.

---

# Transfer by Apple Genius

By far the easiest way to transfer all the stuff from your PC to your new Mac is to let Apple do it for you. Yes, that's right: those busy Geniuses who work at the 200 Apple stores around the world are prepared to bring your music, pictures, documents, address book, email, bookmarks, and other stuff to its new home on your Mac.

And believe it or not, you may be able to get this service for free.

It's important to understand, though, that there are two levels of this service:

• **Standard.** This lower-tier service requires some planning. You'll be instructed to put everything that you want rescued into a folder on your Windows desktop called Transfer. Put your Pictures, Music, and Documents folders in there, at the very least.

If you're smart, you'll also export your address book, email, calendar, and bookmarks from the various Windows programs they're in now, as described in this chapter and the next. Put those exported files into the Transfer folder, too.

The Apple store will copy that single Transfer folder to the desktop of your new Mac. That's it. They won't put those files in the right places for you (photos into iPhoto, music into iTunes, etc.); that's left for you to do.

In other words, the Standard service is a great value if you're tech-savvy enough to import and export data into the proper programs. (Although actually, this book describes those steps pretty well.)

The best part: if you bring in your old PC at the time you buy a new Mac, this service is *free.*

---

**Tip:** You don't necessarily have to bring in your PC the day you buy the Mac. If you bring a new Mac to the shop reasonably soon after buying it, even if you bought it online, the Geniuses are generally still willing to do the deed for you.

---

• **Complete.** Now we're talking. With the Complete service, you just hand over your PC, and the Apple dudes do everything. They take your entire Windows world and transfer everything into the appropriate programs on the Mac.

For example, all your Windows pictures (even if they're in Picasa or special photo-editing programs from HP or Kodak) get brought over to the Mac and imported into iPhoto. All your music is imported into iTunes on the Mac. Your documents and movies get copied to the Documents and Movies folders on the Mac. Your Web bookmarks from Internet Explorer or Firefox get transferred to Safari on the Mac. Even your email, address book, and calendar get transferred from Outlook or Outlook Express on the PC and brought into Mail and iCal on the Mac.

When they say complete, they mean complete.

*Tip:* Behind the scenes, the Apple geniuses use exactly the same techniques and tools described in this chapter, including the O2M shareware for transferring mail, calendar, and address book out of Outlook.

This service costs $50. However, it's free if you sign up for one of Apple's training services, like One to One (which gives you weekly private lessons—on any Mac topic—for $100 a year).

The rest of this chapter covers do-it-yourself ways to transfer your stuff. But man, there's nothing like having a professional do it for you.

## Transfers by iTornado

The iTornado is a special USB "smart cable" designed expressly for transferring stuff from a Windows PC to a Mac. You connect the USB cable to each machine, and that's it: you see a table-of-contents screen for each machine (Figure 5-1). You copy files back and forth simply by dragging their icons in either direction.

Using this technique, you can move your PC photos directly into theMac's Pictures folder, your iTunes library into the iTunes folder on the Mac, and so on.

It's fast and, goodness knows, simpler than any other do-it-yourself method. It does, however, cost money—the list price, at this writing, is $80. Fortunately, the special code at the back of this book lops 20 percent off the price (and throws in free shipping).

*Figure 5-1:*
*The iTornado is a retractable USB cable that doesn't require you to install any software. As soon as you connect it, you see the contents of both machines in folder-tree formation. You can drag and drop files from one computer to the other, with no fuss, accounts, or setup—only a knowledge of where you're supposed to put everything. (It works Mac-to-Mac and PC-to-PC, too.)*

# Transfers by Disk

Another way to transfer Windows files to the Mac is to put them onto a disk that you then pop into the Mac. (Although Windows can't read all Mac disks without special software, the Mac can read Windows disks.)

This disk can take any of these forms:

- **An external hard drive or iPod.** If you have an external hard drive (USB or IEEE 1394, what Apple calls *FireWire*), you're in great shape. While it's connected to the PC, drag files and folders onto it. Then unhook the drive from the PC, attach it to the Mac, and marvel as its icon pops up on your desktop, its contents ready for dragging to your Mac's built-in hard drive. (Most iPods work great for this process, too; they can operate as external hard drives—even the iPod Nano.)

- **A USB flash drive.** These small keychainy sticks are cheap and capacious, and they work beautifully on both Macs and PCs. Like a mini-external hard drive, a flash drive plugs directly into your USB port, at which point it shows up on your desktop just like a normal disk. You copy files to it from your PC, plug it into your Mac, and copy the files off, just like you would for any other disk. And, like an external hard drive, you're left with a backup copy of the data on the drive itself.

- **A CD or DVD.** If your Windows PC has a CD or DVD burner, here's another convenient method. Burn a disc in Windows, eject it, and then pop it into the Mac

**Figure 5-2:**
*Burned CDs generally show up with equal aplomb on both Mac and Windows, regardless of which machine you used to burn it. Here's a CD burned on a Windows XP machine (bottom), and what it looks like on the Mac (top)—same stuff, just a different look and different sorting order. Either way, you can drag files to and from it, rename files, delete files, and so on.*

(see Figure 5-2). As a bonus, you wind up with a backup of your data on the disc itself.

---

**Note:** If you're given a choice of file format when you burn the disc in Windows, choose ISO9660. That's the standard format that the Macintosh can read.

---

• **Move the hard drive itself.** This is a grisly, technical maneuver best undertaken by serious wireheads—but it can work. You can install your PC's hard drive directly into a Power Mac or Mac Pro, as long as it was prepared using the older FAT or FAT32 formatting scheme. (The Mac can handle FAT hard drives just fine, but chokes with NTFS hard drives.)

When you insert a Windows-formatted disk, whatever the type, its icon appears at the upper-right corner of your desktop, where Mac disks like to hang out. (If it doesn't appear, you or someone you love has probably fiddled with the "Show these items on the Desktop" settings in the Finder→Preferences→General tab.)

## Transfers by Network

Here's one of the best features of Mac OS X: It can "see" shared disks and folders on Windows PCs that are on the same network. Seated at the Mac, you can open or copy files from a PC. In fact, you can go in the other direction, too: Your old PC can see shared folders on your Mac.

This isn't a networking book, but Chapter 14 offers a crash course. When it's all over, you'll be seated at the Mac, looking at the contents of your Windows PC in a separate window. At that point, you can drag whatever files and folders you want directly to the proper places on the Mac.

## Transfers by File-Sending Web Site

There's a new breed of file-shuttling Web site prowling the Net—and a new option for transferring large amounts of data between machines.

They're free Web sites, like *yousendit.com* and *sendthisfile.com,* that are specifically designed for sending huge files from one computer to another, without worrying about email file attachments or size limits.

On the Windows PC, zip up your files into a great big .zip file. Upload it to one of these free sites, and provide your Mac's email address.

On the Mac, click the link that arrives by email—and presto, that huge zip file gets downloaded onto your Mac. It's free, there's no file-size limit, and you can download the big file(s) within three days of sending them. The only price you pay is a little bit of waiting while the stuff gets uploaded and then downloaded.

*Tip:* If you have your own Web site—a *.com* of your own, for example, or a free site through a university—you can also use *that* Web space as a transfer tool. Follow the uploading instructions that you were given when you signed up for the space. (Hint: It usually involves a so-called *FTP* program.) Then, once all your files are on the site, download them onto your Mac.

## Transfers by Email

Although sending files as email attachments might seem to be a logical plan, it's very slow. Furthermore, remember that most email providers limit your attachment size to 5 or 10 megabytes. Trying to send more than that at once will clog your system. If you've got a lot of stuff to bring over from your PC, use one of the disk- or network-based transfer systems described earlier in this chapter.

But for smaller transfer jobs or individual files, sending files as plain old email attachments works just fine.

If you have trouble, or if you can't open the attachments at the other end, consider the following potential snags.

## Transfers by iDisk

If your Windows PC isn't in the same building as the Mac, connecting the two using an Ethernet or a wireless network may not be a practical proposition. But even if you can't connect them into *a* network, you can still connect them via *the* network: the Internet.

It turns out that, for $100 per year, Apple will be happy to admit you to a club it calls *.Mac* ("dot-mac"). It offers a number of handy Internet features that tie in nicely to Mac OS X, as described on page 295.

For many people, the crown jewel of the .Mac services is the iDisk, which appears on your desktop as though it's a multi-gigabyte hard drive. Anything you drag into the folders inside this "drive" gets copied to Apple's secure servers on the Internet. (If that's not enough space for you, Apple will rent you a larger allotment in exchange for more money.)

Because you can use the iDisk as a go-between between Mac and Windows, anywhere in the world, it makes a handy universal transfer disk. Page 296 has details for pulling the iDisk onto the Mac's screen or the PC's screen.

## Transfers by Bluetooth

Bluetooth isn't really designed to be a networking technology; it's designed to eliminate cables between various gadgets. But if your Mac and a PC each have Bluetooth adapters, you can share files between them as though there's no language barrier at all. (Bluetooth is built into all Macs, and is available as a USB or internal card for Windows machines.)

Mac OS X comes with a nondenominational file-exchange program called Bluetooth File Exchange; not all Windows Bluetooth adapters come with such a program. But if yours does (3Com's adapters do, for example), you should be able to shoot files between the machines with the greatest of ease, if not the greatest of speed.

## Where to Put Your Copied Files

Just getting your PC files onto the Mac is only half the battle. Now you have to figure out where they *go* on the Mac.

The short answer: in your Home folder. (Choose Go→Home, or click the Home icon in your Sidebar.)

Some of the more specific "where to put it" answers are pretty obvious:

- **My Documents.** Put the files and folders from the PC's My Documents folder into your Home→Documents folder. Here's where you should keep all your Microsoft Office files, PDF files, and other day-to-day masterpieces, for example.

- **My Music.** In recent versions of Windows, a My Music folder is designed to hold all of your MP3 files, AIFF files, WAV files, and other music. As you could probably guess, you should copy these files into your Mac's Home→Music folder.

  After that, you can import the music directly into iTunes. If you used iTunes on your old PC, for example, just open iTunes on your Mac and choose iTunes→Preferences→Advanced. Then click Change, and navigate to the place where you moved your old iTunes library.

  If you used some *other* music program on your PC (like Windows Media Player or MusicMatch), things are a little different. On your Mac, choose iTunes→Import, and navigate to the folder that contains all your music. (In either case, click Choose in the resulting dialog box.)

- **My Pictures.** The latest Windows versions also offer a My Pictures folder, which is where your digital camera photos probably wound up. Mac OS X has a similar folder: the Home→Pictures folder.

  Here again, after copying your photos and other graphics faves over to the Mac, you're only halfway home. If you fire up iPhoto (in your Applications folder), choose File→Import, and choose the Pictures folder, you'll *then* be able to find, organize, and present your photos in spectacular ways.

- **My Videos.** The My Videos folder of Windows XP contains the video clips you've downloaded from your camcorder (presumably so that you can edit them with, for example, Microsoft's Movie Maker software). Once you've moved them to your Home→Movies folder, though, you're in for a real treat: You can now edit your footage (if it's *digital* footage) with iMovie, which, to put it kindly, runs rings around Movie Maker.

Other elements of your Windows world, though, are trickier to bring over. For example:

## Desktop Pictures (Wallpaper)

You can say whatever you like about Microsoft's sense of design (and devoted Macintosh fans have plenty to say on this topic). But especially in recent versions of Windows, the desktop pictures, better known in the Windows world as wallpaper, are pretty cool. Fortunately, you're welcome to bring them over to your Mac and use them on your own desktop.

To find the graphics files that make up the wallpaper choices in Windows XP, Windows Me, or Windows Vista, for example, proceed like this:

1. **Open My Computer, double-click your hard drive's icon, and open the WINDOWS or WINNT folder.**

   If you see a huge "These files are hidden" message at this point, or if the window appears empty, click "Show the contents of this folder" or "View the entire contents of this folder" at the left side of the window.

2. **In the Windows or WINNT window, open the Web folder.**

   You're looking for a folder inside it called Wallpaper.

3. **Open the Wallpaper folder.**

   It's filled with .bmp or .jpg files ready for you to rescue and use on the Mac. See page 447 for instructions on choosing wallpaper for your Mac.

---

**Note:** In Windows 95 or 98, the wallpaper files are in your Program Files→Plus!→Themes folder instead.

---

## Sound Effects

The Mac doesn't let you associate your own sound effects to individual system events, as Windows does (Low Battery Alarm, Maximize, Minimize, and so on). It lets you choose *one* sound effect for all of its attention-getting purposes, using the Sound pane of System Preferences (page 471).

Still, there's nothing to stop you from harvesting all of the fun little sounds from your Windows machine for use as the Mac's error beep.

To find them on the PC, repeat step 1 of the preceding instructions. But in the WINDOWS or WINNT folder, open the Media folder to find the .wav files (standard Windows sound files).

Once you've copied them to your Mac, you can double-click one to listen to it. (It opens up in something called QuickTime Player, which is the rough equivalent of Windows Media Player. Press the Space bar to listen to the sound.)

To use these sounds as error beeps, you'll have to convert them from the PC's .WAV format into the Mac's preferred .aiff format. You'll find step-by-step instructions in the free downloadable Appendix for this chapter, "Converting WAV Sounds to Mac Error Beeps.pdf."

You can find it on this book's "Missing CD" page at *www.missinmganuals.com*.

## Bookmarks (Favorites)

Moving your Favorites, or browser bookmarks, to a Mac is pretty easy. The hardest part is exporting them as a file, and that depends on which Web browser you've been using on the PC.

- **Internet Explorer.** Fire up Internet Explorer; choose File→Import and Export. (In the newer Internet Explorer 7, click the double-star icon in the upper-left corner of the window. From the pop-up menu, choose Import and Export.)

  When the Import/Export Wizard appears, click Next; on the second screen, click Export Favorites, and then click Next again.

  On the third screen, leave the Favorites folder selected, and click Next. Finally, click Browse to choose a location for saving the exported bookmarks file. For now, save it to your desktop.

  Click Next, Finish, and then OK.

- **Firefox.** In Firefox, choose Bookmarks→Manage Bookmarks. In the Bookmarks Manager window, choose File→Export. Save the Bookmarks file to your desktop.

Now you've got an exported Bookmarks file on your desktop. Transfer it to your Mac using any of the techniques described earlier in this chapter (network, email, whatever).

Now open the Mac's Web browser, Safari (it's in your Applications folder). Choose File→Import Bookmarks. Navigate to, and double-click, the exported Favorites file to pull in the bookmarks.

---

***Tip:*** Firefox is available for the Mac, too (*www.getfirefox.com*). If your bookmarks are already in Safari, you can import them by choosing File→Import. If not, you can import them from your exported Windows bookmarks file by choosing Bookmarks→Manage Bookmarks; then, in the Bookmarks Manager window, choose File→Import. Find and select the exported bookmarks file.

---

## Everything Else

See Chapter 6 for details on copying your email, address book, and Outlook calendar information to the Mac.

# Document-Conversion Issues

Most big-name programs are sold in both Mac and Windows flavors, and the documents they create are freely interchangeable.

Files in program-agnostic, standard exchange formats don't need conversion either. These formats include JPEG (the photo format used on Web pages), GIF (the cartoon/logo format used on Web pages), PNG (a newer image format used on Web pages),

HTML (raw Web-page documents), Rich Text Format (a word-processor exchange format that maintains bold, italic, and other formatting), plain text (no formatting at all), QIF (Quicken Interchange Format), MIDI files (for music), and so on.

Part of this blessing stems from the fact that both Windows and Mac OS X use file name extensions to identify documents. ("Letter to the Editor.doc", for example, is a Microsoft Word document on *either* operating system.) Common suffixes include:

| Kind of document | Suffix | Example |
| --- | --- | --- |
| Microsoft Word | .doc | Letter to Mom.doc |
| text | .txt | Database Export.txt |
| Rich Text Format | .rtf | Senior Thesis.rtf |
| Excel | .xls | Profit Projection.xls |
| PowerPoint | .ppt | Slide Show.ppt |
| FileMaker Pro | .fp5, fp6, fp7 … | Recipe file.fp7 |
| JPEG photo | .jpg | Baby Portrait.jpg |
| GIF graphic | .gif | Logo.gif |
| PNG graphic | .png | Dried fish.png |
| Web page | .htm | Index.htm |

**Note:** The latest versions of Microsoft Office for Mac and Windows offer an alternative, more compact file format ending with the letter x. For example, Word files are .docx, Excel files are .xlsx, and so on.

The beauty of Mac OS X is that most Mac programs add these file name suffixes automatically and invisibly—and recognize such suffixes from Windows with equal ease. You and your Windows comrades can freely exchange documents without ever worrying about this former snag in the Macintosh/Windows relationship.

You may, however, encounter snags in the form of documents made by Windows programs that don't exist on the Mac, such as Microsoft Access. Chapter 7 tackles these special cases one by one.

## FireWire Disk Mode (Target Disk Mode)

*FireWire Disk Mode* is by far the fastest method yet for transferring a lot of data—even faster than copying files over a network—but it works only between two Macs, which is why it occupies this lonely spot at the end of this chapter. FireWire Disk Mode is extremely useful in any of these situations:

- **You're traveling with a laptop.** You want to copy your life onto it from your main Mac, including your entire 2 GB email folder and project files, before taking it on a trip, and then unload it when you return.

**Note:** The MacBook Air doesn't have a FireWire jack, so it can't do this trick.

- **You have a new Mac.** You want to copy everything off the old one, without having to wait all night.

- **One Mac won't start up.** You want to repair it, using another Mac as a "front end."

In the following steps, suppose your main Mac is an iMac, and you want to use a MacBook Pro laptop as an external hard drive for it.

1. **Using a FireWire cable, connect the FireWire jacks of both computers.**

   For this trick, you need a *6-pin* FireWire cable—*not* the one that connects a camcorder to a Mac. The one you need has the same, large connector on both ends.

---

**Note:** If both Macs have Apple's new FireWire 800 jacks, use a 9-pin FireWire cable instead for much greater speed. If only one Mac has a FireWire 800 jack, use that computer's traditional FireWire 400 connector instead. Otherwise, you need either a special FireWire 800–to–FireWire 400 cable, or the 400-to-800 adapter that came with your Mac.

---

**UP TO SPEED**

# Moving Data Within the Mac

Most of this chapter concerns the act of moving files between *machines.* Once you've settled in on the Mac, though, you'll frequently want to move data between *documents.*

Fortunately, the Cut, Copy, and Paste commands work almost exactly as they do in Windows. You still can't paste a Web page into your image editor, and you can't paste MIDI music information into your word processor. But you *can* put graphics into your word processor, paste movies into your database, insert text into Photoshop Elements, and combine a surprising variety of seemingly dissimilar kinds of data. All you have to do is get used to the Macintosh keyboard shortcuts, which use the ⌘ key instead of the Ctrl key: ⌘-X for Cut, ⌘-C for Copy, and ⌘-V for paste.

You can also drag highlighted text or graphics to another place in the document, into a different window, or into a dif-

ferent application, as shown here—a satisfyingly direct feature that works in even more Macintosh programs than Windows programs. Just note that in some Mac OS X programs (*Cocoa* programs; see page 141), you must press the mouse button for half a second before beginning to drag.

You can also drag text, graphics, sounds, and even movie clips out of your document windows and directly onto the *desktop*. Once there, your dragged material generally becomes an icon called a *clipping file*. (In Windows, it's called a Scrap file.)

Later, when you drag a clipping from your desktop *back* into an application window, the material in that clipping reappears. Drag-and-drop, in other words, lets you treat your desktop itself as a giant, computer-wide pasteboard—an area where you can temporarily stash pieces of text or graphics as you work.

---

2. On the laptop, choose ➤→System Preferences. Click Startup Disk. Click Target Disk Mode. In the confirmation box, click Restart.

The MacBook Pro turns off, then on again. A giant, yellow, Y-shaped FireWire icon bounces around the laptop screen.

Now take a look at the iMac's screen: Sure enough, there's the MacBook Pro's hard drive icon on the desktop. You're ready to copy files onto or off of it, at extremely high speeds, and go on with your life.

3. When you're finished working with the laptop, eject it from the iMac's screen as you would any disk. Then turn off the laptop by pressing the power button.

The next time you turn on the MacBook Pro, it will start up from its own copy of Mac OS X, even if the FireWire cable is still attached. (You can disconnect the cable whenever.)

# Transferring Email and Contacts

I f you use your PC for email—hey, it could happen—there's good news: Switching to a Mac doesn't mean you have to lose your stash of messages, reconfigure your email accounts from scratch, or manually retype everything in your address book. This chapter covers the secrets of moving your entire email life over to the Mac— messages, addresses, settings, everything—with as little hassle as possible.

As you read this chapter, it's important to keep straight the two leading Windows email programs, which many people don't realize are actually two entirely different beasts:

- **Microsoft Outlook.** This program is part of Microsoft Office for Windows. It's a sprawling, network-based email, contact, and calendar program that's ubiquitous in corporate offices and many schools. You, or somebody who employs you, paid good money for this software.

- **Outlook Express.** This Windows program is a free, scaled-down version of Outlook. It comes with Microsoft Windows, and is therefore sitting on practically every PC sold. It doesn't have a calendar, a To Do list, or other bells and whistles of Outlook—but it's free.

---

***Note:*** *In Windows Vista, Microsoft renamed this program, calling it Windows Mail. Most people moving to the Mac these days are doing so to* avoid *having to do the whole Vista thing, so in this chapter, let's just use the old name: Outlook Express.*

---

Unfortunately, each Windows email program requires a different method of exporting its email and addresses. Each Macintosh email program requires a different piece of go-between Windows software to ease the transition, too.

---

There are so many permutations of the "to/from" issue, in fact, that you'd practically need a table or two to keep them straight. They might look something like this:

## Ways to Move Your Email

|  | **From Outlook** | **From Outlook Express** | **From Eudora** |
|---|---|---|---|
| **To Apple Mail** | O2M or Thunderbird | Thunderbird | Thunderbird |
| **To Entourage** | O2M or Thunderbird | Thunderbird | Thunderbird |
| **To Eudora for Mac** | O2M or Eudora for Windows | Thunderbird or Eudora for Windows | Copy files |

## Ways to Move Your Address Book

|  | **From Outlook** | **From Outlook Express** | **From Eudora** |
|---|---|---|---|
| **To Mac OS X Address Book** | O2M or Thunderbird | Thunderbird | Thunderbird |
| **To Entourage** | O2M or CSV Method | CSV Method | CSV Method |
| **To Eudora for Mac** | O2M or Eudora for Windows | Eudora for Windows | Copy files |

It's a complex matrix. But if you know what program you've been using on the PC, and which one you want to use on the Mac, you'll find the steps you need later in this chapter.

# A Reminder That Could Save You Hours

Remember: For $50, one of the Geniuses at an Apple store will transfer all your mail, settings, and address-book entries from your old PC into Mac OS X Mail for you. Truth is, the Geniuses use exactly the same methods described in this chapter—but the beauty of this concept is that *they* do the work, not you.

# Transferring Your Outlook Mail

If Microsoft Outlook has been your Windows address book/email program, you're in luck: You have two options for importing your stuff.

Both of these methods bring over your entire backlog of existing email—the contents of your Inbox, Sent items, archived mail and, perhaps, even deleted items that are still in your email program's Trash.

### O2M Method (Quick, Simple, $10)

If you value your time, buy O2M (short for Outlook2Mac)—a $10 utility that stream-lines the process of bringing Outlook data to your Mac. (You can download it right now from *www.littlemachines.com*.)

*Tip:* This, in fact, is the tool that the Geniuses use at the Apple Store when someone pays them to transfer their stuff from a PC to a new Mac.

With O2M, you're spared the lengthy, sometimes tricky steps required by the free conversion methods described in the following pages. The program takes a wizard-like approach to transferring your Outlook data, gently stepping you through the whole process, as shown in Figure 6-1. It saves all the exported data into one folder (called My_Outlook_Files), making it simple to grab the files you need and move them to your Mac.

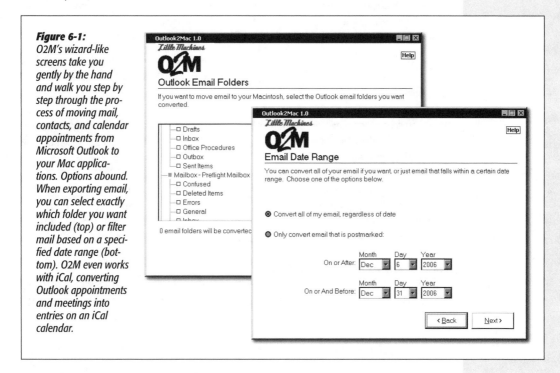

**Figure 6-1:**
*O2M's wizard-like screens take you gently by the hand and walk you step by step through the process of moving mail, contacts, and calendar appointments from Microsoft Outlook to your Mac applications. Options abound. When exporting email, you can select exactly which folder you want included (top) or filter mail based on a specified date range (bottom). O2M even works with iCal, converting Outlook appointments and meetings into entries on an iCal calendar.*

O2M also provides far more options than you get using other methods. For example, it lets you choose messages from only a specific date range—the last year's worth of email, for example, but nothing older. It lets you choose whether or not you want to include attachments with the transferred messages. It can even filter out certain attachments based on type.

O2M's other selling point is that it can handle more than just your email messages. It can also convert calendar entries and your address book, which can be imported directly into iCal, Entourage, or the Mac's Address Book.

As a final perk, the program moves email to and from just about any programs: *from* Outlook 97, 98, 2000, 2002, 2003, or 2007 *to* Apple Mail, Entourage, MailSmith, PowerMail, or iCal.

# Thunderbird Method (Time-Consuming, Free)

If you're on a *very* tight budget, too tight for a $10 piece of shareware, you can also transfer your email to the Mac for free. The trick is to import it first into—get this—Thunderbird for Windows.

Thunderbird is to email what Firefox is to Web browsers: a free, open-source, high-quality alternative to the Microsoft behemoths. It was put together by Mozilla.org and a team of volunteer programmers all over the world.

Thunderbird effortlessly imports email and address books from Outlook, Outlook Express, or Eudora. It even preserves any hierarchical folders you may have set up to sort and organize your messages. In other words, your email arrives on your Mac just as well organized as it was when it left your Windows machine.

Download your free copy of Thunderbird from *www.getthunderbird.com.* It works with Windows 98 or later. (If your machine has Windows 95, opt for the O2M method described earlier.)

---

**Note:** You don't need Thunderbird on the *Mac* for this process. Furthermore, when installing Thunderbird on Windows, you don't have to opt for any of the Custom install options–the default installation will give you everything you need.

---

When you've got Thunderbird installed on the PC, you're ready to follow the three big steps: First, you import your email into Thunderbird. Next, you copy the Thunderbird email to your Mac. You import the mail into Apple's Mail program—and then, optionally, Microsoft Entourage. Take a deep breath, and read on.

## Phase 1: Import to Thunderbird

Your first job is to bring your existing Outlook mail into Thunderbird. (This method also works for transferring Outlook Express or Eudora mail.) Here's how you do it:

1. **Open Thunderbird.**

   Actually, the very first time you open Thunderbird, it offers to do the importing described here. To avoid having to follow two slightly divergent s executivesof steps, though, decline that invitation. Go ahead into the program and then proceed as written here.

2. **Choose Tools→Import.**

   A dialog box opens, allowing you to select the type of information you want to import.

3. **Choose Mail. Click Next.**

   Don't worry about the Address Books or Settings options at this point. You can move those items over separately.

4. **Select the program from which you want to import messages.**

Thunderbird can handle email from Outlook, Outlook Express, Eudora, and easier versions of Netscape Communicator. Pick the appropriate program from among the ones listed.

5. **Click Next to start the import process—and be patient.**

Thunderbird now starts doing its thing, obediently sucking every last email message into its own email folder. If you've got a hefty stash of email—thousands of messages organized in lots of nested folders—this will take a while. It may even look as if Thunderbird has stalled, but it hasn't. Wait patiently as the progress bar creeps forward.

When the process is finally over, Thunderbird displays a dialog box listing all the different mailboxes, folders, and subfolders that it has successfully ingested, as shown in Figure 6-2. Click Finish to wrap things up.

**Figure 6-2:**
*This is Thunderbird's way of telling you that everything went OK when it imported all your mailboxes and messages. Review this list before forging ahead with your Mac migration to make sure Thunderbird grabbed all the mail you want brought over to your Mac.*

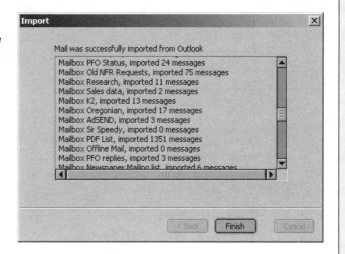

Now you see your imported mailboxes listed in the pane on the left (you might have to expand the Local Folders flippy triangle first). Clicking a mailbox icon displays the corresponding messages in the main window.

### Phase 2: Copy to the Mac

Your next task is to transfer Thunderbird's copy of your mail to your Mac.

1. **Open your Application Data folder.**

The steps depend on your version of Windows. For example:

*Windows 98 or 98SE:* Open the My Computer→your hard drive icon→Win98 →Application Data folder.

*Windows Me:* Open the My Computer→your hard drive icon→WINDOWS→ Application Data folder.

*Windows 2000:* Open the My Computer→your hard drive icon→Documents and Settings→*your name*→Application Data folder, where *your name* is your Windows user account name (the name you use to log into Windows at startup).

*Windows XP:* Microsoft's assumption is that you, the lowly, technically ignorant PC user, have no businesses mucking around in the important operating-system folders— so Windows hides them from you. To expose the hidden files, follow the steps shown in Figure 6-3.

**Figure 6-3:**
*You must uncloak the hidden folders lurking in Windows in order to copy your email files. Here's the trick: In any open folder window, choose Tools→Folder Options. Switch to the View tab, as shown here. In the Advanced settings, turn on "Show hidden files and folders," and then click OK. Now you can see all the previously hidden folders—including the Thunderbird ones.*

Once that's done, open the My Computer→your hard drive icon→Documents and Settings→*your name*→Application Data, where *your name* is your Windows user account name.

2. **Once you've opened the Application Data folder, open your Thunderbird→Profiles folder. Finally, open the folder that corresponds with the profile name you chose when you started running Thunderbird. (If you didn't set up a profile, it's just called something like "mx11bvdg. default".)**

Inside that folder, you'll find a folder called Mail. That's the one you want.

3. **Copy the Mail folder to your Mac.**

   Once again, Chapter 6 describes various ways to go about it.

Once the mail files are on your Mac, you're ready to bring them into the program of your choice. Exactly how you do this depends on the email program you're using; read on.

### Phase 3: Import into Mail

Mail, the email program that comes free with Mac OS X, does an elegant job of importing the files generated by Thunderbird. (If you plan to use Microsoft Entourage, you have to start with this step, too; that is, you must first bring the mail into Mail.)

Here are the steps for feeding the mail from your PC to the Mail program:

1. **Open Mail.**

   It's in the Applications folder, and its icon is probably on the Dock.

2. **In Mail, choose File→Import Mailboxes.**

   The Import Mailboxes dialog box appears.

3. **Click the Thunderbird/Mozilla radio button.**

   You can also import mail from a variety of *Mac* email programs, including Entourage, Outlook Express, and Eudora.

4. **Click the Continue button.**

   You're presented with a standard Open dialog box.

5. **Locate and select the Mail folder you brought over from your PC. Click the Choose button.**

   Mail displays a list of all the Thunderbird mailboxes it finds, as shown in Figure 6-4.

6. **Turn on the checkboxes of the email folders you want to bring into Mail.**

   All the checkboxes start out turned on, meaning that Mail will grab everything you brought over from Thunderbird (including RSS feeds and even what was in the Trash). But if you decide at this point that you don't want to include, say, the messages that were in the Trash folder, you can filter them out by turning off the appropriate checkboxes.

---

**Tip:** You can use the up and down arrow keys to navigate through a long list of mailboxes and folders in the Import Mailboxes window.

---

7. **Click Continue to start importing.**

   The import process now begins. Mail shows you the subject line of each message it brings in.

When the process is complete, your imported mailboxes appear in the Mailboxes column on the left side of the window, in a folder called Import. (See Chapter 11 for more on Mail.) By dragging messages, you can refile them into other mailbox folders, if you like.

### Phase 4: Import into Entourage (optional)

If you have Microsoft Office for Macintosh, you may prefer its more powerful Entourage email program. No problem: You can bring the Thunderbird files that you brought over from your PC—and then imported into Mail—into Microsoft Entourage.

**Figure 6-4:**
*When importing mail messages from Thunderbird, Mail first shows you all the mailboxes it found, ready for import. Turn off the checkboxes next to any folders that you don't want included during the import process.*

## From the Outlook Archives

*I've got about five years' worth of old Outlook email archived on my hard drive. Is there any way to get the contents of these archives into my Mac's email program?*

Absolutely.

When you're in Outlook (on your Windows PC), choose File→Open→Personal Folders File to open any of the Outlook-generated archive files that you want to bring over to your Mac. (Outlook archives have *.pst* file name extensions.) Once you open an archive file, a "mailbox"

icon called Archive Folders appears in Outlook's Folder List, allowing you to access any of the individual messages within the archive.

Simply import your Outlook mail into Thunderbird, as explained earlier in this chapter, *after* opening the archive files. Their contents will be included when you bring the mail into Thunderbird and when you later transfer your mail folders to your Mac.

1. **In Entourage, choose File→Import.**

   The Begin Import dialog box appears.

2. **Click the right arrow. Choose "Import information from a program."**

   Since your messages are already stored in Mail—with all the folders and subfolders intact—you can have Entourage go from there. Click the right arrow.

3. **Click the right arrow. Choose "Apple Mail."**

   Make sure Messages and Accounts are turned on. (The other two checkboxes are only useful if you've started customizing Mail as described in Chapter 11.) Click the right arrow again.

4. **Wait until the import is finished, and then click OK.**

   If everything went according to plan, your messages now show up in the main pane of Entourage's window.

## Alternative Method (Free, to Eudora Only)

O2M—the delightful $10 utility described earlier in this chapter—doesn't talk to Eudora for Mac.

Here's the convoluted workaround: Start by importing your Outlook (or Outlook Express) email and addresses into Eudora for *Windows*. (To import from Outlook Express, choose File→Import; to import from Outlook, choose File→Import and then click Advanced.) Use the most recent Eudora version, if possible.

Now that your mail and contacts are in Eudora for Windows, see page 184 for instructions on getting it all into Eudora for Mac OS X.

## Outlook and Exchange

If you run Microsoft Outlook on your office PC, you may be able to transfer the contents of your entire mailbox to your Mac *without* going through any of the import-export pyrotechnics described in this chapter.

On most office networks, Outlook accesses mail through a *Microsoft Exchange Server*—a central computer that stores all the email moving through the network. When you use Outlook in conjunction with Exchange, your mail, appointments, and contacts actually reside on the Exchange server itself—not on your PC's hard drive.

The same thing's possible in Entourage. To set up your Mac so that it checks your Exchange email, proceed like this:

1. **Open Entourage and choose Tools→Accounts.**

   This is the setup window for all your email accounts.

2. **Click the arrow next to New and choose Mail from the pop-up menu.**

   That's how you tell Entourage, "I want to input the settings for an email account."

3. **Turn on the "My account is on an Exchange server" checkbox.**

   If you had wanted to set up any other kind of email account—like one given by your Internet Service Provider—you'd leave the checkbox off.

4. **Call your network administrator over and ask her to give you information for all the required fields.**

   When you're done inputting everything and Entourage is satisfied, you should see a list of all your network-based email—the same messages you saw in Outlook.

---

**Tip:** If Entourage isn't your thing, you can tap into your network's Exchange Server with Mac OS X's built-in Mail program. In Mail, just choose File→Add Account, pick Exchange for the Account Type, and proceed with step 4 above.

Now you can download the contents of your Outlook folders directly to your Mac without having to manually copy them from machine to machine. You won't be able to see the Exchange Server's calendar or address book this way, but at least you'll get the messages.

---

# Transferring Your Outlook Address Book

The contents of your Contacts list may represent years of typing and compiling. The last thing you want to do is leave that valuable info behind or—heaven forbid—manually retype each entry as you set up your Mac email program.

Here are the steps for bringing all those names, phone numbers, email addresses, notes, and other details from Outlook into your favorite Mac contact manager.

## O2M Method (Easy, $10)

If you took the advice on page 172 and bought the O2M program, you're already done; this ingenious utility brings over both your email *and* your Outlook addresses to your choice of Mac programs.

## Thunderbird Method (Time-Consuming, Free)

Once again, Thunderbird for Windows comes to the rescue. Its address book module can extract contact info directly from the most popular PC email programs—not just Outlook, but also Outlook Express and Eudora. Better yet, it converts that data into a format that Apple's Address Book understands perfectly.

---

**Note:** These steps guide your little-black-book data into Mac OS X's built-in Address Book program. If your aim is to transfer it into Entourage on the Mac instead, see page 182.

---

When you've got Thunderbird installed, you're ready to transfer your contacts, like this:

1. **Import your Outlook contacts into Thunderbird.**

Follow the "Phase 1" steps described on page 174—but in Step 3, choose Address Books. Along the way, you'll be asked to choose the name of the email program whose addresses you want to snag (Figure 6-5). You can choose Outlook, Outlook Express, Eudora, or Communicator (an earlier version of the Thunderbird software).

With your contacts safely stored in Thunderbird, you're halfway home. Next, you need to get these contacts out of Thunderbird and onto your Mac. To do this, you must save them into an *LDIF* file. LDIF stands for Lightweight Directory Interchange Format—a text format mostly used by network administrators to synchronize directory information across large networks. It's also a format that Apple's Address Book recognizes.

**Figure 6-5:**
*Thunderbird, the Swiss Army software, is happy to open the address book of almost any email program, or even a text file containing addresses (such as tab- or comma-delimited text).*

2. **Click Address Book on the Thunderbird toolbar to view your imported contacts. Choose Tools→Export.**

   The Export dialog box appears.

3. **From the "Save as type" drop-down menu, choose LDIF. Type a name for the file, select a destination, and click Save.**

   Thunderbird writes all your contact data into a single self-contained file with an *.ldif* extension added to the end of its name.

4. **Copy the LDIF file to your Mac.**

   You can use any of the techniques described in Chapter 5.

5. **On the Mac, open Address Book (it's in the Applications folder, and its icon is probably on the Dock). Choose File→Import→LDIF.**

   The Open dialog box appears.

6. Locate and open the .ldif file you brought over from Windows.

Moments later, all the contacts you brought over from your Windows machine are converted into Address Book entries (see Figure 6-6).

**Figure 6-6:**
*Apple's Address Book program can slurp up your Windows contacts in one gulp by importing an LDIF file, which you can easily generate using Thunderbird on Windows.*

## CSV Method (Free, to Entourage Only)

If your email program of choice on the Mac is Microsoft Entourage, and you can't find the $10 you need to buy O2M (page 172), the Thunderbird method described above isn't enough. Entourage *can't* import LDIF files.

The best way to transfer contacts into Entourage, then, is to import them in *CSV* format. CSV is short for Comma-Separated Values, and it's a format that many contact programs can import and export these days. (In fact, *Address Book* can attempt to import CSV files, but it's picky to a fault about formatting—which is why the Thunderbird method described above is a lot more reliable if you use Address Book.)

Here's the procedure:

1. **On your PC, export your contacts in CSV format.**

   If you use Outlook Express, for example, choose File→Export Address Book and then select "Text File (Comma Separated Values)." Save the file. (Same goes if you use Outlook.)

   If you use Eudora on Windows, you're in for a bit more fun. Since Eudora can't directly export CSV files, you have to move your contacts into Thunderbird *first*, as described above. When you get to step 3 above, however, choose "Comma Separated" for the type of file you'd like to export, rather than LDIF. You now have a CSV file on your PC with your contacts inside, so read on.

2. **Move the CSV file to your Mac.**

   The file should end in .csv if you did everything right.

3. **Open Entourage and choose File→Import. Click "Import information from a text file."**

   Click the right arrow.

4. **Make sure "Import contacts from a tab- or comma-delimited text file" is selected.**

Again, click the right arrow.

5. **Select the CSV file you copied to your Mac in step 2.**

Press Return to dismiss the dialog box.

6. **"Map" any information that's confusing Entourage (Figure 6-7).**

Even though Entourage and Outlook are both made by Microsoft, there's still room for Entourage to get confused by your contacts—and mapping is how you fix it.

For instance, if you exported your contacts from Outlook Express, one field on the right might be called "E-mail Address" which confuses Entourage because it's not called "Email Address 1." To eliminate the confusion, drag the gray handle from the E-mail Address line on the right so it's next to the Email Address 1 line on the left. You've just told Entourage, in essence, "'E-mail' and 'Email' are the same thing, so let me get on with my life."

**Figure 6-7:**
*Drag the fields on the right to the matching fields on the left. Funny how Microsoft's quirks transcend operating systems.*

7. **Click Import.**

Dismiss the dialog box that appears by clicking Don't Save.

8. **Click Finish.**

Your contacts are now ready and waiting in Entourage.

## Eudora Method (Free)

If your aim is to get your contacts into Eudora for Macintosh, see "Alternative Method (Free, to Eudora Only)" on page 179. The instructions transfer your address book exactly the same way they transfer your messages.

# Transferring from Outlook Express

If you've been using Outlook Express (Microsoft's free email program) on the Windows PC, you'll have very little trouble moving into any of the Mac's email programs.

## Moving Your Address Book

You can use free Windows software as a go-between—but which Mac address book you've adopted will determine which program to use.

- To import your Outlook Express addresses into Apple's *Address Book,* follow the instructions in "Thunderbird Method (Time-Consuming, Free)" on page 174.

- To import them into *Microsoft Entourage* instead, see "CSV Method (Free, to Entourage Only)" on page 182.

## Moving Your Mail

Outlook Express is also a pleasant partner when it comes to moving the messages themselves over to the Mac. Here again, you use Thunderbird as a sort of translator. Follow the steps listed under "Thunderbird Method (Time-Consuming, Free)," beginning on page 174.

## To Eudora for Mac

Getting your mail and addresses from Outlook Express (Windows) into Eudora (Macintosh) involves moving it first into Eudora for Windows, and then into Eudora for Macintosh. See "Alternative Method (Free, to Eudora Only)" on page 179 for instructions; they cover moving both your messages and addresses out of Outlook Express.

# Transferring Your Eudora Mail

Eudora, an email program written at the University of Illinois in the eighties, used to be wildly popular because it was free and full-featured. Today, this venerable email client, now sold by Qualcomm, is available for both Windows and Mac OS X.

## Moving Email into Entourage or Mac OS X Mail

If you'd like your mail to wind up in a Mac email program like Entourage or Mail, it's good old Thunderbird to the rescue. Follow the steps in "Thunderbird Method (Time-Consuming, Free)," beginning on page 174.

## Moving Email to Eudora for the Mac

If you use Eudora on Windows and want to move your existing messages into the Mac version of Eudora, you can copy them straight over to your Mac. All you need to know is where to find the necessary files and how to set them up on your Mac.

Here's the most direct path for converting your Eudora mailboxes from Windows to Mac:

1. **Find the Eudora .MBX files on your PC.**

   The folder names depend on your version of Windows, but here's the gist:

   *Windows 98 or 98SE:* Open the My Computer→your hard drive icon→Win98 →Application Data→Qualcomm→Eudora folder.

   *Windows Me:* Open the My Computer→your hard drive icon→WINDOWS→ Application Data→Qualcomm→Eudora folder.

   *Windows 2000, Windows XP:* Turn on the hidden files, as shown in Figure 6-3. Then open the My Computer→your hard drive icon→Documents and Settings→*your name*→Application Data→Qualcomm→Eudora.

   *All versions:* In the Eudora folder, you'll find several mailbox files that—depending on your version of Eudora—may end with the filename extension .mbx: In, Out, and Trash, as shown in Figure 6-8. These are the files you want, whether they end in .mbx or not.

**Figure 6-8:**
*Drill down into the your PC's Applications Data folder to find the Eudora folder, where your Eudora mailbox files live. The Trash file contains messages you've already thrown into Eudora's trash can. There's no need to copy that file over to your Mac unless you want to preserve those trashed messages.*

**Note:** Can't find an Application Data folder inside your user folder? That's because Application Data is a hidden folder and you have the "Do not show hidden files and folders" option turned on in Windows. See the instructions for copying Thunderbird files on page 176 to learn how to change this setting.

1. **Copy the files to your Mac.**

   Don't worry about all the other stuff in the Eudora folder. The mailbox files contain all your messages, so they're the only ones you need to convert.

2. **Fix the carriage returns in the .mbx files.**

   Here's where things get a little bit ugly. While these mailbox files are really just text files containing your email messages, Windows handles *line breaks*—the invisible "this is the end of a line!" symbol—differently than the Mac. In order for the Mac version of Eudora to read the files correctly, you have to convert the *hard returns* in the text files into *line breaks*. You can accomplish this by doing a simple find-and-replace in a program like Microsoft Word, as shown in Figure 6-9.

**Tip:** If you don't have Microsoft Word, you can also run the mailbox files through a shareware conversion program like BBEdit, which is available on this book's "Missing CD" page at *www.missingmanuals.com*, among other places.

**Figure 6-9:**
*Here's how you'd use Word to convert Eudora mailbox (.mbx) files from Windows to Mac format. Open a mailbox file and choose Edit→Replace. Search for all paragraph marks and replace them all with manual line breaks—or, to be precise, search for ^p and replace with ^l. (You can also choose these symbols by name from the Special menu, as shown here.) Click Replace All to run the conversion, which may take some time; then save the modified text file.*

3. **Remove the .mbx extension from the file names.**

On the Mac side, Eudora expects the file to be called In, not In.mbx. Remove the extension, if it exists, from each of the mailbox files you've brought over.

4. **Drop the converted mailbox files into Eudora's Mail Folder folder on your Mac.**

   Starting from your Home folder, go to Documents→Eudora Folder→Mail Folder, and replace the existing mailbox files with the ones you copied and converted from your PC.

---

**Note:** If you don't see a folder called "Mail Folder" inside the Eudora folder, it's probably because you're looking in the Eudora application folder (in the *Applications* folder) instead of the Eudora folder inside your *Documents* folder.

---

5. **Launch Eudora and read your mail.**

   When you launch Eudora, your converted mail should now be accessible. Unfortunately, the status of each message (read, unread, forwarded, and so on) is not preserved, nor are any labels you may have applied to organize the messages within Eudora. Oh well.

# Transferring Your Eudora Address Book

Once again, the steps here depend on which program you'll be using as your Mac address book.

## Moving Contacts into Address Book

Fortunately, this one's easy. The Swiss Army Converter known as Thunderbird can convert your Eudora address book into a Mac-compatible format; see "Thunderbird Method (Time-Consuming, Free)" on page 174.

## Moving Contacts into Entourage

As noted earlier in this chapter, Thunderbird isn't enough if the landing site for your contacts is Microsoft Entourage. In that case, you should use the CSV format as a go-between. See "CSV Method (Free, Entourage Only)" on page 182.

## Moving Contacts into Eudora on the Mac

The easiest way to transfer your old Eudora contacts to the Mac is to *first* get your contacts into Mac OS X's Address Book program, as described above. Then, once that transfer is complete, open Eudora on your Mac and choose Eudora→ Preferences→Address Book. Turn on "Show OS X AddressBook."

Now all the contacts from your PC are in both Address Book *and* Eudora, which is extra convenient if you ever decide to switch from Eudora to Mail.

# Email Settings

Chapter 10 guides you through the painless process of plugging your Internet settings—whether by dial-up connection, cable modem, DSL, or network connection—from the PC to your Mac.

But even after you've done that, you can't start sending and receiving email on your Mac until you've transferred some vital email account *settings* from your PC.

Fortunately, there's only a handful of settings you need to grab—and hunting these down and moving them to your Mac is pretty quick work. Here's all the information you need to gather in order to get yourself set up:

- **Account name (or user name).** This is the name you use when you log into your email account, such as *Joe63* or *kjackson*.

- **Password.** This is the password that you have to enter along with your account name to get into your email account. Passwords can't be copied and pasted or directly exported, so you'll need to remember this password and type it in when configuring your Mac email software.

- **Account type.** There are two main kinds of email server protocols—*POP* (which stands for post-office protocol—by far most common) and IMAP (Internet Message Access Protocol). You'll need to know which type you've been using on your PC, so that you can set up accounts on your Mac the same way.

**Note:** *Exchange* servers are another choice popular in big organizations. If your email is stored on an Exchange server, see page 179.

- **Incoming and outgoing mail servers** are the names of the computers that route email to and from you, such as *mail.earthlink.net* or *mailserve.photorabbit.com*. (The incoming and outgoing servers sometimes have the same address, but they *can* be two different servers with different names.)

## Finding the Settings on Windows

Each of the popular Windows email programs stores these nuggets of email account info differently. Here's how to find the items you need:

### Outlook

If you're connected to a Microsoft Exchange Server computer—and you probably are if you're running Outlook in a corporate workplace—your user name and password are exactly the same as the ones you use to log into the network when you start up your computer. You'll have to check with your network administrator to get the name of the mail servers being used on the network.

If you're running Outlook in any other situation—at home, for example—choose Tools→E-mail Accounts. Click "View or change existing e-mail accounts," click Next, click your account's name on the E-mail Accounts page, and then click Change. You'll find your name, email address, incoming and outgoing servers, and other key settings staring you in the face. (Click Cancel after you've finished copying it down.)

### Outlook Express

Choose Tools→Accounts→Mail to open the dialog box containing the list of your current email accounts. Select the name of the account you want, then click the Properties button. In the Properties dialog box, click the Servers tab to reveal the Server Information pane, where you'll find all the info you need, as shown in Figure 6-10.

**Figure 6-10:**
Here's where Outlook Express for Windows keeps all the settings you need to harvest in order to configure your Mac email. Note that you can't copy the contents of the password field—that's prohibited for security reasons. You'll have to type your password in again when moving to your new machines.

### Eudora

Choose Tools→Options. Click the Getting Started icon, if it's not already selected, to find your incoming and outgoing mail server names. Then click the Incoming Mail icon to display the Server configuration setting—either POP or IMAP—at the top of the window.

### Thunderbird

Choose Tools→Account Settings. Each email account you use is listed in the field on the left side of the window. Click one to display its information on the right.

## Configuring the Settings on Your Mac

Once you've found and copied the email settings on your PC, you can plug them into the appropriate places in your Mac email programs:

### Apple Mail

Once you've opened Mail (in the Applications folder), choose File→Add Account. Proceed through the various screens, inputting the information from your old PC.

### Microsoft Entourage

Choose Tools→Accounts. Click the New button in the Accounts window to start the Account Setup Assistant. Follow the screen-by-screen directions to fill in the user name, password, and server information, as shown in Figure 6-11.

**Figure 6-11:**
*Once you've stepped through the five screens of the Entourage Account Setup Wizard, you end up here, with your account settings all in place and ready to connect up.*

### Eudora for Macintosh

Choose Eudora→Preferences and click the Checking Mail icon. Fill in the necessary details here, and then click Sending Mail to fill in the rest.

**Note:** The methods described in this chapter are the least technical ways to get mail, contacts, and settings from the various Windows email apps onto the Mac. But a quick Google search will reveal more technical ones that you may prefer. For example, if you can convert your email accout t an IMAP account, no biggie: your Mac email program reflects your email stash automatically.

# Special Software, Special Problems

Be glad you waited so long to get a Mac. By now, all the big-name programs look and work almost exactly the same on the Mac as they do on the PC. Once you've mastered the basic differences between the Mac and Windows (keyboard shortcuts, the menu bar, and so on), you'll find that programs from Microsoft, Adobe, and other major software companies feel distinctly familiar in their Mac incarnations. In fact, the documents that they create are in the same format and generally need no conversion.

But one fact is unassailable: There are more software programs available for Windows than for the Mac. Sooner or later, you'll probably run into a familiar Windows program for which there's no equivalent on the Mac.

One solution is simply to run those Windows programs *on* the Mac, as described in Chapter 8. For thousands of people, that's the screamingly obvious, and extremely convenient, approach. Each time you read, "There's no Mac equivalent of this program" in this chapter, add, in your head, "but you can always run the Windows version."

Still, in other cases, you may not want to fool around with Windows anymore. You may prefer to identify Mac replacements for your favorite Windows programs. That's the purpose of this chapter: to guide you in finding Mac equivalents for the most popular Windows programs (listed here alphabetically), and to guide you in bringing over your data and settings from Windows to the Mac whenever possible.

## ACDSee

As digital photography becomes more popular, so do programs like ACDSee, a popular Windows program that serves as a digital shoebox and basic retouching program for digital photos. Your Mac, of course, stands ready to run a far more elegant equivalent: iPhoto. It's one of the world's most pleasant photo-organizing programs—and it's free.

In its most recent incarnation, iPhoto has a pretty complete set of image-retouching features. Still, if you need more editing power, consider Photoshop Elements, a program that's available for both Mac and Windows and has won rave reviews on both platforms.

In any case, ACDSee doesn't have any documents of its own—it does all its work on your existing digital photos, wherever you keep them on your hard drive. All you have to do, then, is move the photos themselves to the Mac, using any of the techniques described in Chapter 5. From there, drag them into the iPhoto window to import them.

## Acrobat Reader

Acrobat Reader, which lets you read Acrobat (PDF) files, works precisely the same on the Mac as it does in Windows (except that it looks a little nicer on the Mac). If you like, you can download Acrobat Reader from *www.adobe.com.*

There are fewer and fewer reasons to use Acrobat Reader, though; you have a much nicer PDF-reading program right there in your Applications folder, called Preview.

Preview can read PDFs like the best of them—but it's also got Acrobat Reader covered on several other counts. Preview can annotate PDFs with virtual yellow sticky-notes— a great tool for marking up book layouts before they go to press, for example. Also, Preview's search feature is so fast and convenient, it blows Acrobat Reader out of the water. And finally, Preview opens in a matter of seconds, while Acrobat Reader can take a minute or so to launch. (For more on Preview, see page 502.)

## ACT

No Mac version of this address book/calendar program is available, but don't let that stop you. Export and Import commands are the bread and butter of address and calendar programs. Your ACT life can find a happy home in any of several Mac address books:

- Mac OS X's free, built-in Address Book.

- Palm Desktop for Mac OS X (a free address book/calendar/to-do program from *www.palm.com,* which works with—but doesn't require—an actual Palm organizer).

- Microsoft Entourage (part of Microsoft Office for Mac).

- Now Contact *(www.nowsoftware.com),* which is networkable. That is, if you have more than one computer in the house, you can check your Rolodex from any machine on the network (Mac or Windows).

In any case, here are the instructions for transferring your addresses from ACT (version 5 or later) to the Mac:

1. **In ACT for Windows, start by choosing File→Data Exchange→Export.**

   The Export Wizard dialog box appears.

2. **From the "File type" drop-down list, choose Text-Delimited. Specify a folder location and name for your exported file (call it Exported Contacts, for example). Click Next, and click Next on the next screen, too.**

   Now you're asked "Which contact or group records do you want to export?"

3. **Click "All records," and then click Next.**

   Now you see a list of the *fields* (information tidbits like City, State, and Zip) that ACT is prepared to export. You can save yourself time later if you take a moment now to remove the ones you don't need (click its name and then click Remove Field).

4. **Click Finish.**

   If you plan to import your addresses into a commercial program like Now Contact, transfer the Exported Contacts file to the Mac (see Chapter 5), and then import them into Now Contact. The tricky part is making sure that the order of the fields appears in the order Now Contact expects, which may entail some trial, error, and returning to the ACT Export Wizard screen described in step 3 (where you can rearrange the field order).

   If your aim is to import the addresses into Microsoft Entourage on the Mac, or Mac OS X's own Address Book program, though, read on.

5. **Open Outlook Express.**

   Yes, Outlook Express for Windows, the free program that comes on every PC. (The Windows Vista version is called Windows Mail.) You'll use it as a glorified converter program.

6. **Follow the instructions on page 184 for exporting the contacts into a format suitable for your Mac.**

   That page outlines two ways (one free, one fast) to get your contacts from Outlook Express into Mac OS X's Address Book—your ACT info's final resting place.

## Ad Subtract (Pop-up Stopper)

Nothing quite spoils the fun of the Web like pop-ups—those annoying miniature advertising windows that sprout in front of the Web page you're trying to read.

Safari, Mac OS X's Web browser, has a simple menu command for blocking pop-ups: Safari→Block Pop-Up Windows. Nowadays, so does just about every other Web browser made for the Mac—Firefox, Netscape, Camino, and so on. In other words, you don't even *need* Ad Subtract.

If you're interested in some of Ad Subtract's other features, like blocking animated ads or zapping all ads on Web pages, consider Pith Helmet (for Safari) or Adblock (for Firefox). Both are available for download from this book's "Missing CD" at *www. missingmanuals.com.*

## Adobe [your favorite program here]

Most of Adobe's bestsellers are available in Mac OS X versions, including Photoshop, Photoshop Elements, After Effects, Illustrator, InDesign, GoLive, Acrobat, Acrobat Reader, and so on. Even the Mac version of Premiere, the video-editing program, is back (after being abandoned by Adobe from 2003 to 2007).

You almost never have to do any document conversion. A Windows Photoshop document is exactly the same thing as a Macintosh Photoshop document, for example.

## America Online

America Online is available for both Windows and Mac OS X. In fact, the Mac OS X version may have come preinstalled on your Mac (look in the Applications folder). If not, you can download it from *http://downloads.channel.aol.com/macproducts.*

*Tip:* You don't actually need the AOL program on your Mac. You can access all of your AOL mail, as well as all of AOL's features, on the Web at *www.aol.com.*

When you use the Macintosh version of the software for the first time, just plug in your existing screen name and password.

The beauty of AOL is that it stores your mail, address book, buddy list, and favorites *online.* You can check your email one day at the office on a PC and the following night at home on the Mac, and you'll always see the same messages there. It makes no difference if you connect to the service using a Windows PC, a Macintosh, or a kerosene-powered abacus.

*Tip:* Your Favorites (bookmarks) are stored online only if you use AOL for Windows version 8 and later. If you've been using an earlier version on your PC, your Favorites won't be waiting for you when you switch the Mac.

If your PC meets the system requirements, you'd be wise to upgrade its copy of America Online to version 8 or later before switching to the Macintosh. (This is a free upgrade; you can download the software at *www. aol.com/downloads.*) If you do so, you'll find the Favorites waiting for you in AOL for Mac OS X.

This is all really good news, of course, but you may have one headache in performing the switch: your Personal Filing Cabinet. If you've been saving email messages into this virtual filing drawer, the news isn't quite as good: these messages are saved on the PC, not online. So when you switch to the Macintosh, your Personal Filing Cabinet will be empty.

Here are your options at this point:

- Be content with only the last 30 days' worth of old mail, and the last week's worth of new mail. This is what lives on the America Online computers, no matter what computer you use to access it. When you move to the Mac, that much email will immediately appear the first time you use AOL.

- Fire up your old PC and open each message in your Personal Filing Cabinet. Click the Forward button, and type in your own AOL address. You're basically emailing each message to yourself.

  Once the messages have arrived on the Mac, you can save them into *its* Personal Filing Cabinet. Of course, you were the sender, so you can no longer click Reply to send a response to whoever originally wrote you. (If that's ever necessary, you can always copy and paste the sender's address into your reply.)

Once all your information is in AOL for Mac OS X, you can, if you want, move the information into Apple's *own* Internet programs: iChat, Address Book, Mail, and Safari. Just download AOL Service Assistant from *http://downloads.channel.aol.com/ macproducts*, and click through the various steps.

By the final screen, all your bookmarks, contacts, screen names, and email settings will be waiting for you in Apple's programs, which are a lot more powerful (not to mention attractive) than the AOL software itself.

## AIM (AOL Instant Messenger)

If you're an online chat junkie, switching to the Mac involves very little disruption to your routine. AIM is available for the Mac, too, and it awaits your download at *www.aim.com.* Better yet, the minute you fire it up, you'll discover that your entire Windows-version buddy list is intact and ready to use. (That's because it actually lives on the America Online network, not on your Windows PC.)

---

*Tip:* Actually, you might have a lot more fun—and save a lot of effort—by just using iChat. It's a free Mac OS X chat program that's compatible with the whole AIM network, as described on page 356.

---

## Children's Software

Thanks to the vast number of Macs in schools, a huge percentage of educational software programs are available in both Mac and Windows versions—often on the same CD. That includes most programs from The Learning Company (including the Arthur, Carmen Sandiego, Little Bear, and Reader Rabbit series), Broderbund (Kid Pix, Mavis Beacon, Print Shop, and so on), Humongous Entertainment (series like Blue's Clues, Dora the Explorer, Putt-Putt, Backyard Sports), and other major educational publishers.

# Earthlink Total Access

If Earthlink is your Internet service provider, and you're a fan of its Total Access software (which provides access to email, blocks pop-up ads, lets you switch to other family members' accounts, and so on), you're in luck. Hie thee to *www.earthlink. net/home/software/mac* to download the Macintosh version, which includes a spam blocker, pop-up blocker, Address Book syncing with Earthlink's Web-based mail, and so on. (And then see Chapter 10 for details on transferring your Windows account settings to the Mac.)

# Easy CD Creator

You don't need any add-on software at all to burn CDs in Mac OS X. You can just drag files and folders onto the icon of a blank CD, as described on page 248.

If you want fancier features—recording less common disc formats, for example—what you need is Toast for the Macintosh. It comes from the same company that makes Easy CD Creator.

Its main rival is DiScribe *(www.charismac.com)*. Both programs can create audio CDs, video CDs, data DVDs, and so on. Both come with a program that helps you turn old vinyl records and tapes into digital CDs, too.

The only disappointment: Neither program can treat a CD as a glorified floppy disk, as Easy CD Creator for Windows can, so that you can add and delete files freely (rather than burning the CD all at once).

There's a workaround, though: Copy the contents of a rewriteable CD (a CD-RW disc) to a folder on your desktop; make whatever changes you like to the contents of this folder; and then burn the CD-RW again. (Use the Disk Utility program in your Applications→Utilities folder to erase the disc first.)

---

*Tip:* Ordinarily, the CD-burning feature of Mac OS X burns the entire CD each time, even if you've only filled a small portion of it. But if you download the handy $17 shareware program called CD Session Burner, you can perform additional "mini-burns" of new data to the CD until all the space is used up. Each such *session* shows up on your desktop with its own icon, as though it's a separate disc. You can download this program from *www.sentman.com/burner/*.

---

# Encarta

Microsoft's best-selling encyclopedia program isn't available for the Macintosh. The World Book Encyclopedia is, however. (Details at *www2.worldbook.com*.)

Of course, you can also use the Web-based versions of either encyclopedia (or Wiki-pedia, of course).

# Eudora

You want Eudora? You got Eudora! It's available on the Mac, as it is in Windows. Download it from *www.eudora.com*. Chapter 6 even tells you how to move your mail and address book over to the Mac version.

# Excel

See "Microsoft Office" in this chapter.

# Firefox

On Windows, Firefox is a faster, more secure, better-featured Web-browsing alternative to Internet Explorer. If you'd like, you can download the identical Mac version from *www.getfirefox.com,* and then follow the instructions on page 167 for transferring your bookmarks.

Alternatively, you can switch to Mac OS X's built-in, super-fast Safari browser, which offers a more Mac-like browsing experience. Chapter12 houses the coverage of the Safari adventure.

# Games

Nobody switches to the Mac to play games; of the top 250 computer games for Windows, only about 150 are available for the Macintosh.

Still, that number includes the majority of the big-name titles and series, including *Guitar Hero, Madden NFL, Tiger Woods PGA,* the various Sims games, *Civilization, Quake, Harry Potter, Spider-Man, Tomb Raider, WarCraft, Jedi Knight, Soldier of Fortune, Max Payne, Links Championship Edition, Age of Empires, Medal of Honor, Return to Castle Wolfenstein,* and hordes of others.

And once you do get these programs going on the Mac, you're likely to be impressed. Recent Macs generally come equipped with pleasantly high-horsepower graphics cards—the kind that serious computer games crave.

If you're a game nut, you can stay in touch with what's new and upcoming by reading the articles (and watching the game "trailers") at *www.apple.com/games,* not to mention *www.insidemacgames.com, macgamer.com,* and *macgamefiles.com.*

# Google Desktop Search

Mac OS X's Spotlight feature does everything that Google Desktop does—searching inside files, finding favorite Web sites, and so on. Spotlight just does it better.

# ICQ

If you're a fan of this Internet-wide chat program, look no further than ICQ for Mac or one of its many shareware rivals. To grab them, visit *www.versiontracker.com* and perform a search, on the Mac OS X tab, for *ICQ*.

## Internet Explorer

Internet Explorer is available for the Mac, but it's ancient, abandoned, and not worth it. Safari (Apple's built-in Web browser) blocks pop-up windows, loads pages more quickly, and doubles as an RSS reader for news sites. Coverage starts on page 339.

If some Web site (like a banking site) refuses to work with Safari, download Firefox for the Mac instead (*www.getfirefox.com*); it works with almost everything.

## iTunes

If you grew used to iTunes on Windows, you'll be glad to know that the Mac version is already sitting in your Applications folder. It works identically to the PC version.

Just move your iTunes Library folder from the Music folder of your old PC into the Music folder on your Mac. That's all there is to it!

## Kazaa

Kazaa, of course, is the "new Napster." People use it to swap music and video files online, hard drive to hard drive—illegally, in many cases. You know who you are.

If you visit *www.kazaa.com,* you won't find a Macintosh version of the Kazaa program that you need to do file swapping. There are such programs, however, including miMac, Poisoned, and others; you can find them at *www.versiontracker.com.* Or try Limewire, described next.

## Limewire

Limewire is the same idea as Kazaa (see above), but it runs on something called the Gnutella network—and there's a nice Mac version of the downloading program. You can get it at *www.limewire.com.*

## MacAfee VirusScan

The Mac version is called MacAfee Virex—but don't buy it. You don't even need a virus program for Mac OS X. (If you run Windows on your Mac, as described in the next chapter, then install your copy of VirusScan onto that side of the computer, by all means.)

# Microsoft Access

Microsoft has never been much interested in creating a Macintosh equivalent of its flagship database program (which comes with the higher-priced versions of Microsoft Office for Windows). FileMaker, a much easier-to-use database program, towers over the Macintosh database market like the Jolly Green Giant (and has a decent following on the Windows side, too). Resistance, Microsoft apparently assumes, is futile.

---

**Tip:** FileMaker's little brother, Bento (for the Mac), is even easier to use still.

---

It's easy enough to get your data out of Microsoft Access; just choose File→Export. In the resulting dialog box, you can choose from a number of common export formats that can serve as intermediaries between the Windows and Mac worlds (see Figure 7-1).

**Figure 7-1:**
*When you export your data from Access, you can choose from any of several formats. The idea is that you'll transfer the resulting exported file onto your Mac, and then import it into a proper database program there.*

Among them is Microsoft Excel—that is, you can turn your database into a spreadsheet. The beauty here is that FileMaker on the Macintosh can turn Excel documents into FileMaker databases without even batting an eye. You just drag the exported Excel document onto the FileMaker icon, and FileMaker does the rest.

Unfortunately, there's more to an Access database than just its data. Your database may well have fancy forms (layouts), complete with letterhead and other graphic elements, not to mention relational links between database files. In these situations, the situation isn't quite so hopeful—there's no way to export layouts and relational links to the Macintosh.

In this situation, your best bet might be to run Microsoft Access itself on the Macintosh, as described in Chapter 8.

---

# Microsoft Money

Microsoft doesn't make Money for the Macintosh (although it certainly makes money *from* the Macintosh). If you're looking for a home-finances program for Mac OS X, though, look no further than Quicken *(www.intuit.com)*.

You can even export your Money data into Quicken, although not every scrap of information comes through alive. You'll lose your Money abbreviations, comments, and Lifetime Planner information. Fortunately, the important stuff—your accounts and the transactions in them, including categories, classes, and stocks that you've set up—come through in one piece.

Unfortunately, you have to export one account at a time. Furthermore, you'll be creating something called a QIF (Quicken Interchange Format) file as an intermediary between Windows and the Mac—and this file format can't handle category names longer than 15 characters. Before you begin, then, you might want to take a moment either to shorten them or to make a note of which ones might get truncated in the transfer.

Ready? Fire up Money on your Windows PC and then proceed like this:

1. **Choose File→Export.**

   The Export dialog box appears. It wants to know if you are exporting your information to another version of Money ("Loose QIF") or to some other, rival financial program that shall, as far as Microsoft is concerned, remain nameless.

2. **In the resulting dialog box (Figure 7-2), choose Strict QIF, and then click OK.**

---

**UP TO SPEED**

## Viruses in Mac OS X (Not!)

One of the greatest perks of moving to Macintosh is that viruses are practically nonexistent. At this writing, in fact, not a *single virus* for Mac OS X has been reported in the wild.

The one kind of virus that manages to sneak into Mac OS X are Microsoft Word macro viruses that hide in ordinary Word files sent to you by your Windows friends.

Fortunately, on the Mac version of Word, most of these don't run at all. Second, whenever you try to open a document that contains macros that you didn't create yourself, you see the message shown here. All you have to do is click Disable Macros. The file opens normally, 100 percent virus free.

If you have Apple's .Mac service (described on page 295), you have free access to McAfee's antivirus software—just in case. Otherwise, it usually doesn't make financial sense to buy an antivirus program at all.

---

In the resulting dialog box, you're supposed to name and save the exported file. Make sure you give each account a descriptive name (like Citibank Savings).

3. **Specify a name and folder on your PC for the exported file, and then click OK.**

Repeat these three steps for each of your Money accounts.

**Figure 7-2:**
*Use the Strict QIF option. It lops off category names longer than 15 characters.*

4. **Transfer the exported files to the Mac.**

You can do it via network, burned CD, or any of the other techniques described in Chapter 5. Then move to the Macintosh, open Quicken 2003 or later, and create a new file (see the Quicken instructions). Then, once you've got an empty "check register" before you, continue like this:

5. **Choose File→Import QIF. In the "Select a QIF file" dialog box, navigate to, and open, the first exported account file.**

If all goes well, you should see a progress bar appear and then disappear. When the dust settles, you'll see your Money transactions safely ensconced in Quicken. (If you see a message that some transactions couldn't be completed, don't worry; it's usually just telling you that some of your category names were longer than 15 characters. and have been marked with asterisks to make them easier for you to find and correct.)

If you have more than one account, choose File→New Account to set it up, and then repeat step 5 to bring in your other Money accounts.

## Microsoft Office

Microsoft Office is available for the Mac in what some critics have declared to be a more attractive, less frustrating version than the Windows incarnation. At this writing, the current version is called Office 2008 for Macintosh.

As noted elsewhere in this book, the beauty of Microsoft Word, Excel, and Power-Point documents is that their format is the same on Mac and Windows. You can freely exchange files without having to go through any kind of conversion. (The big exception, as noted earlier, is Access; Microsoft doesn't make a database program for the Mac.)

In heavily formatted documents, you may occasionally see some strange differences: Windows documents containing many numbered paragraphs sometimes become confused on the Mac, for example. And if the Mac and the originating PC don't have the fonts installed, you'll see different fonts, too. Otherwise, documents look identical despite having been shuttled through the ether to a different kind of computer.

**Tip:** With Office 2007 for Windows, Microsoft introduced a set of new file formats (.docx for Word, .pptx for PowerPoint, and so on) that's more compact than the previous set (.doc, .ppt, and so on). When you save a document, you can choose which format you want to use: the old one, which 400 million other people can open on their Macs and PCs, or the new one, which nobody but recent upgraders can open.

Exactly the same conundrum presents itself on the Mac. Office 2008 can open and create those same new-fangled files, but the previous versions (like Office 2004 for the Mac) can open only the older formats.

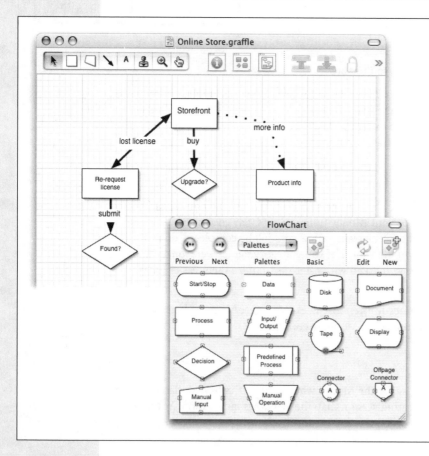

**Figure 7-3:**
OmniGraffle comes preinstalled in the Applications folders of many new Mac models, or you can download the latest version from www.omnigroup.com.

# Microsoft Publisher

Microsoft Publisher is a comprehensive page-layout program, complete with canned designs, clip art, and so on.

There's no Mac version of it, but you can perform most of the same tasks using Pages. (Pages is part of Apple's $80 iWork software suite; you can download a 30-day trial from *www.apple.com/iwork.*) Like Publisher, Pages offers dozens of attractive, ready-to-use page-design templates that you can adapt as you see fit.

There are also plenty of standalone page-design programs—this is the Mac, after all—including professional powerhouses like Adobe InDesign and QuarkXPress.

# Microsoft Visio

If flowcharts, org charts, network diagrams, family trees, project processes, office layouts and similar diagrams are part of your own personal workflow, you're in luck—at least some luck. Microsoft Visio isn't available in a Macintosh version, but you'll probably find that OmniGraffle for Mac OS X is a satisfactory, even delightful, replacement (see Figure 7-3). The Pro version even lets you import and export Visio documents.

# Minesweeper

Time wasters, rejoice! There are a number of free Minesweeper programs for Mac OS X, including CocoaMines and Aqua Mines. You can download them from a site like *www.versiontracker.com* (search for *minesweeper*).

# MSN Messenger

Online chat-aholics have nothing to worry about on the Mac. MSN Messenger, the instant-messaging program, is alive and well in a Mac OS X version that you can download from *www.microsoft.com/mac.* Like AOL Instant Messenger described earlier in this chapter, you don't even have to worry about your carefully assembled buddy list. From the instant you start up MSN Messenger for Mac OS X, you'll see your Buddy list in place (because the list is actually stored on the Internet, not on your computer).

# NaturallySpeaking

Speech-recognition programs have traditionally been far more advanced on Windows than on the Macintosh. Windows programs like Dragon NaturallySpeaking transcribe your dictated text with almost Star Trek–like accuracy, and even let you make corrections and manipulate the computer itself using all voice commands.

Fortunately, that same Dragon technology finally made it onto the Mac in early 2008 with the release of MacSpeech Dictate. It uses precisely the same "recognition engine" as Dragon Naturally Speaking (*www.macspeech.com*). If you just can't use the keyboard, or don't want to, you'll be amazed at its speed and accuracy.

## Netscape

Netscape comes in a Mac OS X version—free, of course, from *http://browser.netscape.com*. (Mozilla, which is like a Netscape cousin without all the AOL promotional material, is also available for the Mac, too, from *www.mozilla.org*. So is the Firefox Web browser, described earlier in this chapter.)

## Newsgroup Readers

If you're a fan of the online bulletin boards known as *newsgroups,* you've come to the right place. The Mac is crawling with newsgroup-reading programs. Microsoft Entourage, for instance, has one built in. In the shareware world (try searching *www.versiontracker.com),* you can take your pick of MT-NewsWatcher X, NewsHunter, and Halime, to name a few.

## Norton AntiVirus

You can buy Norton Antivirus for the Macintosh, no problem (*www.symantec.com*). The question is, why? See the box on page 200.

## Norton Utilities

This program, too, is available in a Mac OS X version. It does the same kinds of things it does in Windows: defragments your hard drive, helps recover files in case of disaster, and repairs disk problems.

In times of trouble, though, you may prefer Disk Warrior, a similar (and, many experts feel, superior) program that you can buy from *www.alsoft.com*.

## Notepad

If you're an aficionado of this beloved note-taking tool in the standard Windows Start menu, you're in luck. Mac OS X's Stickies program is even more powerful, because it offers formatting and even graphics. Or, for more of a word-processor effect, check out TextEdit.

## Outlook/Outlook Express

Mac OS X's built-in Mail program is similar to Outlook Express for Windows (or Windows Mail in Vista), just more powerful and a lot better-looking. Chapter 6 describes the process of switching, and Chapter 11 covers the rest of the Mail experience.

If you want all the features from *Outlook,* though, you'd probably be better off using Microsoft Entourage, which is available as part of Microsoft Office for Mac.

# Paint Shop Pro

If your goal is to retouch and edit digital photos, the closest you can come to Paint Shop on the Mac is probably Photoshop Elements, a sensational Mac OS X program (about $100) that belongs on the hard drive of any serious digital camera owner. (Any digital camera owner who doesn't also own the full-blown Photoshop program, that is.)

If your goal is to organize and *use* your photos, rather than paint on them, remember that the newest version of iPhoto is either already on your hard drive or available as part of Apple's iLife suite ($80).

Finally, if opening and converting graphics to other formats is your main concern, try Preview (page 502), whose exporting feature is surprisingly powerful. You may also want to investigate the beloved shareware program GraphicConverter (find and download it at *www.versiontracker.com*), which may be the last graphics editing/converting program you'll ever need.

# Palm Desktop

The CD that came with your Palm organizer included both Mac and Windows versions of this calendar/address book/to-do list/notepad program. Put another way, if you have a Palm, you probably already have Palm Desktop for Mac OS X.

# Picasa

Picasa, one of several Windows photo-organizers, isn't available for the Mac (at this writing, anyway; a Mac version is rumored to be in the works for late 2008). But don't worry. On Mac OS X, you can edit, organize, and order prints of your images with iPhoto.

# Pocket PC

The world of palmtop computers falls into two broad camps: Palm compatibles (from Palm, Sony, Kyocera, and others) and Pocket PC (from Dell, HP, ViewSonic, and others). Pocket PC machines are loaded with useful features. Unfortunately, they also run a tiny (but still confusing) version of Windows—and they can't exchange information with a Macintosh.

Or at least they can't right out of the box. Once you've added the program called PocketMac *(www.pocketmac.net)*, though, you can synchronize your Pocket PC with the appointments, calendar, and to do list from any of the popular Mac OS X programs that handle this kind of information: Microsoft Entourage, Address Book, and iCal. You can even load up the pocket PC with files from Word and Excel for viewing and editing on the road, and MP3 files for music listening in transit. (Depending on the features you want, you'll pay anywhere from $15 to $42.)

# PowerPoint

PowerPoint is available on the Mac; see "Microsoft Office" in this chapter. Remember, too, that Apple's own Keynote presentation program (available as part of iWork for $80) is the same idea as PowerPoint, but with much more spectacular graphic effects.

# QuickBooks

If you've been happily using QuickBooks for Windows to manage your small business—to prepare estimates and invoices, track bills, maintain lists of inventory and customers, and so on—there's good news and bad news. The good news is that QuickBooks is available on the Mac, and the steps for transferring your company files aren't difficult.

The bad news is that the transfer isn't perfect. Along the way, you might lose your memorized transactions, custom report designs, and reconciliations. Note, too, that you may not be able to send an older Windows file (like QuickBooks 2007) to an older version on the Mac (like QuickBooks 2006).

It's not especially hard; heck, there's a File→Utilities→Copy Company File for Quick-Books Mac command right in QuickBooks for Windows. You can find the rest of the step-by-step instructions in two places:

- Open the electronic Help for QuickBooks for Mac, and search for this topic: "Converting a QuickBooks file from Windows to Mac."

  - Follow the do-it-yourself procedure described on Intuit's Support Web page (here'sa short link to it: *http://tinyurl.com/2u8kmp/*).

# Quicken

If you've been keeping track of your personal finances in Quicken on your PC, you'll feel right at home when you move to the Mac. Quicken 2003 and later versions are available for Mac OS X.

In general, switching over is quick and painless. You can import into the Mac version of Quicken all of the actual transaction information, including accounts, the categories and classes you've used to group them, and stock holdings. Certain kinds of Windows Quicken information—like schedule transactions, QuickFill transactions, online account information, stock histories, and loan information—don't make it, however.

For the official manual on transferring your Quicken data from Windows to the Mac, download this chapter's free PDF Appendix from this book's "Missing CD" at *www.missingmanuals.com*.

If the technology gods are smiling, the Mac version of Quicken should take only a moment to import all of your Windows data, which now appears neatly in your Register windows, ready to use. Make sure the final balances match the final balances in Quicken for Windows. (If they don't, scan your Mac registers for duplicate or missing transactions.)

## RealPlayer

Want to listen to Internet music and watch Internet video in Real format, just as you did on your PC? No sweat. Visit *www.real.com* and download RealPlayer for Mac OS X, either in the free basic edition or the fancy paid version.

If you just want to listen to music on your *hard drive*, though, you'd be better off using iTunes (page 250).

## RssReader

RSS is a technology for reading quick Web site summaries, and it's taking the Net by storm. RSS returns the Internet to real utility, free from pop-up ads and the other annoyances of Web life.

To take advantage of RSS, however, you need a program to *subscribe* to Web sites that support RSS—and then to display the resulting summaries. On Windows, you might use a program like RssReader, or a Web site like *www.pluck.com.*

On Mac OS X, however, Apple's way ahead of you. Both Safari (Chapter 12), and Mail (Chapter 11) provide fantastic built-in RSS readers; both can subscribe to RSS sites with ease.

## Skype

For making Internet-based phone calls, it's hard to beat Skype. If you call from one computer to another, you pay absolutely nothing—no matter how far away your recipient is.

Luckily, you can download a Mac version from *www.skype.com.* From there, you can audio-chat with all your Mac- and PC-using Skype buddies until you lose your voice.

---

*Tip:* iChat, Apple's own instant-messaging program, also offers free audio chats. If you and your buddy both have Web cams or videocameras, in fact, you can make free, Internet *video* calls. See Chapter 12 for the details.

---

## SnagIt

If you prepare instructions for using any kind of computer or software—computer books, magazine articles, or how-to materials of any kind—you may already be familiar with this amazing screen-capture program. It captures any window, menu, or area of the Windows screen and saves it as a graphics file that you can print or pop into a layout program.

In Mac OS X, this feature is built right in. Here's how to capture:

- **The whole screen.** Press Shift-⌘-3 to create a picture file on your desktop, in PNG format, that depicts the entire screen image. A satisfying camera-shutter sound tells you that you were successful.

  The file is called *Picture 1*. Each time you press Shift-⌘-3, you get another file, called Picture 2, Picture 3, and so on. You can open these files in Preview, Photoshop, or another graphics program, in readiness for editing or printing.

- **One section of the screen.** You can capture only a rectangular *region* of the screen by pressing Shift-⌘-4. When you drag and release the mouse, you hear the camera-click sound, and the Picture file appears on your desktop as usual.

- **One menu, window, icon (with its name), or dialog box.** Once you've got your menu or window open onscreen, or the icon visible (even if it's on the Dock), press Shift-⌘-4. But instead of dragging diagonally, press the Space bar.

  Now your cursor turns into a tiny camera. Move it so that the misty highlighting fills the window or menu you want to capture—and then click. The resulting Picture file snips the window or menu neatly from its background. (Press the Space bar a second time to exit "snip one screen element" mode and return to "drag across an area" mode.)

---

***Tip:*** If you hold down the Control key as you click or drag (using any of the techniques described above), you copy the screenshot to your *clipboard,* ready for pasting, rather than saving it as a new graphics file on your desktop.

---

Mac OS X also offers another way to create screenshots: a program called Grab, which offers a timer option that lets you set up the screen before it takes the shot. It's in your Applications→Utilities folder.

But if you're really serious about capturing screenshots, you should opt instead for Snapz Pro X (*www.ambrosiasw.com*), which can capture virtually anything on the screen—even movies of onscreen procedures, along with your narration—and save it your choice of format.

## Solitaire

Ah yes, Solitaire: possibly the most overused Windows software in the world.

The Mac doesn't come with a preinstalled copy of Solitaire, but the Web is crawling with free and shareware solitaire games for the Mac. Luckily, there's a quick way to unearth the most popular 20 or so. On the Web, visit *www.versiontracker.com* (one of most popular sources for freeware and shareware Mac programs). Click the Mac OS X tab if it's not already selected, and then, in the Search box, type *solitaire.*

When you click Go or press Enter, you'll see a substantial list of solitaire games, ready to download: FreeCell, MacSolitaire, Klondike, and so on.

# Street Atlas USA

This popular mapping and routing software is also available for the Macintosh, although its features aren't quite as complete as they are in the Windows version.

And if it's Europe you want, it's Route 66 you need (*http://rs108.66.com/route66.*)

---

*Tip:* If you're looking for driving directions and maps, don't forget about Google Maps (*http://maps.google.com*). It's fast, it's convenient, it works the same on both Mac and Windows, and it's free.

Also, don't forget about the Yellow Pages feature of the Dashboard (page 150). It's ready to print directions and draw maps.

---

# TaxCut, TurboTax

TaxCut isn't available for the Mac; TurboTax is. You can even buy state versions of TurboTax for the states that require income tax returns. You can buy them wherever fine Mac programs are sold: *www.macmall.com, www.macwarehouse.com, www.macconnection.com,* and so on.

# WinAmp, MusicMatch

When it comes to playing MP3 files, creating MP3 files, burning music CDs, and otherwise organizing your music library, you'd be hard-pressed to beat iTunes, the free Mac OS X program that's already on your Mac (and a free download from *www.apple.com/itunes*).

# Windows Media Player

The Macintosh equivalent for Windows Media Player is, of course, QuickTime Player. It handily plays and shows almost any kind of movie, picture, or sound (although you'll want to use iTunes for most music playback).

There are a few entertainment sources that come in the Windows Media format, however, notably Windows Media Video (.wmv) movies that play on Web sites. By itself, QuickTime Player can't play them.

Microsoft actually went to the trouble of creating a Macintosh version of Windows Media Player (never mind the irony of its name). You can download it from *www.microsoft.com/mac,* but it's officially been abandoned.

The more modern, equally free solution is to download and install Flip4Mac. It's technically a plug-in for QuickTime Player, but you don't need to know that. All you need to know is that once you've installed it, you can suddenly play all those Web videos that you couldn't play before. You can download it from this book's "Missing CD" at *www.missingmanuals.com.*

# WinZip

In Mac OS X, you create a .zip file by right-clicking any Finder icon and choosing "Compress [the icon's name]" from the shortcut menu. You decompress a .zip file by simply double-clicking its icon in the Finder.

Sometimes, however, you'll encounter compressed files on the Mac that end in *.sit*. You decompress such files with StuffIt Expander, a free download from *www.stuffit.com*.

# Word

See "Microsoft Office" in this chapter.

# WordPerfect

Unfortunately, WordPerfect lost the battle with Microsoft Word on the Mac side pretty much the same way it did on the Windows side. If you're a die-hard WordPerfect fan, your best bet might be to invest in Microsoft Word and capitalize on its keystroke-customizing features to turn it into a living simulation of WordPerfect.

Or, if you'd rather not spend a significant portion of your life's savings on a word processor, use the free Word-importing and -exporting features of TextEdit (page 513).

# Yahoo Messenger

The equivalent chat program on the Mac is, of course, Yahoo Messenger for Mac OS X. It's a free download from *http://messenger.yahoo.com*.

# Windows on Macintosh

T he very moment Apple announced in 2006 that all new Mac models would come with Intel chips inside, the geeks and the bloggers started going nuts. "Let's see," they thought. "Macs and PCs now use exactly the same memory, hard drives, monitors, mice, keyboards, networking protocols, *and processors*. By our calculations, the Mac should be able to run Windows!"

Now, some in the Cult of Macintosh were revolted by the very idea. Who on earth, they asked, wants to pollute the magnificence of the Mac with a headache like Windows?

Lots of people, as it turns out. Millions of switchers have been tempted by the Mac's sleek looks, yet worried about leaving Windows behind entirely. Then there are the people who love Apple's iLife programs, but have jobs that rely on Microsoft Access, Outlook, or some other piece of Windows corporateware. Even true-blue Mac fans occasionally look longingly at some of the Windows-only games, Web sites, palmtop sync software, or movie download services they thought they'd never be able to use.

Today, there are two ways to run Windows on a Mac with an Intel chip:

- **Restart it in Boot Camp.** Boot Camp lets you *restart* your Mac into Windows. At that point, it's a full-blown Windows PC, with no trace of the Mac on the screen. It runs at 100 percent of the speed of a real PC, because it *is* one. Compatibility with Windows software is excellent. The only drag is that you have to restart the Mac *again* to return to the familiar world of Mac OS X and all your Mac programs and files.

- **Run Windows in a window.** For $80 or so, you can buy a program like Parallels or VMWare Fusion, which lets you run Windows *in a window.*

You're still running Mac OS X, and all your Mac files and programs are still available. But you've got a parallel universe—Microsoft Windows—running in a window simultaneously.

Compared with Boot Camp, this *virtualization software* offers only 90 percent of the speed and 90 percent of the software compatibility. But for thousands of people, the convenience of eliminating all those restarts—and gaining the freedom to copy and paste documents between Mac OS X and Windows programs—makes the Windows-in-a-window solution nearly irresistible.

---

**Tip:** There's nothing wrong with using *both* on the same Mac, by the way. In fact, the Parallels/VMWare-type programs can use the *same copy of Windows* as Boot Camp, so you save disk space and don't have to manage two different Windows worlds.

---

Both techniques require you to provide your own copy of Windows. And both are described on the following pages.

---

**Note:** Remember, running Windows smoothly and fast requires a Mac with an Intel chip inside. To find out if yours does, choose  →About This Mac. In the resulting dialog box, you'll see, next to the label Processor, either "Intel" something or "PowerPC."

If your Mac has a PowerPC chip, skip this chapter. There *are* programs that let you run Windows, but excruciatingly slowly. Frankly, it's not worth the effort.

---

# Boot Camp

To set up Boot Camp, you need the proper ingredients:

- **An Intel-based Mac.** All Mac models introduced in 2006 and later have Intel chips inside.

- **A copy of Windows XP or Windows Vista.** Windows XP needs Service Pack 2. If you have an earlier copy, you're not *totally* out of luck, but you'll need a hacky approach, which you can read about online. Let Google be your friend.

For Windows Vista, you need the Home Basic, Home Premium, Business, or Ultimate Edition. In both cases, an Upgrade disc won't work; you need a full-installation copy. Also, Boot Camp requires the normal 32-bit editions of Windows. The fancy 64-bit versions won't work.

- **At least 10 gigs of free hard drive space.**

Then you're ready to proceed.

## Installing Boot Camp

Open your Applications→Utilities folder. Inside, open the program called Boot Camp Assistant.

### Phase 1: Partition your drive

On the Introduction screen, you can print the instruction booklet, if you like (although the following pages contain the essential info). There's a lot of good, conservative legalese in that booklet: the importance of backing up your whole Mac before you begin, for example.

When you click Continue, you get the dialog box shown in Figure 8-1—the most interesting part of the whole process.

**Figure 8-1:**
How much hard drive space do you want to dedicate to your "PC"? It's not an idle question; whatever you give Windows is no longer available for your Mac. Drag the vertical handle between the Mac and Windows sides of this diagram.

You're being asked to *partition*—subdivide—your hard drive (which can't be partitioned already), setting aside a certain amount of space that will hold your copy of Windows and all the PC software you decide to install. This partitioning process doesn't involve erasing your whole hard drive; all your stuff is perfectly safe.

The dialog box offers handy buttons like Divide Equally and Use 32 Gigs, but it also lets you drag a space-divider handle, as shown in Figure 8-1, to divide up your drive space between the Mac and Windows sides.

Here's where things get tricky, though. If you choose an amount less than 32 gigabytes for the Windows partition, the Windows XP installer lets you choose between two Windows drive formats:

- **FAT32.** This unappetizingly named scheme is older and, if you ask power users and network nerds, more limited. For example, it's only available on disks smaller than 32 gigabytes.

  But the advantage of using FAT32 is that, when it's all over, you'll be able to drag files back and forth from the Windows side to the Mac side. (This works only when you're in Mac OS X; when you're in Windows, you can't see the Mac side of the hard drive without a commercial program like MacDrive [*www.macdrive.com*].)

- **NTFS.** If you choose a partition size *greater* than 32 GB, you *must* use the NT File System. It's a more modern, flexible formatting scheme—it offers goodies like file-by-file access permissions, built-in file compression and encryption, journaling (a safety feature), and so on.

  But on a Boot Camp Mac, NTFS is a drag. It means that when you're running from the Mac side, you can see what's on the Windows partition, but can't add, remove, or change any files.

*Note:* All this applies only to Windows XP. Windows Vista *always* uses NTFS. You don't have a choice.

Most people choose to dedicate a swath of the main internal hard drive to the Windows partition. But if you have a second internal hard drive, you can also choose one of these options:

- **Create a Second Partition.** The Boot Camp Assistant carves out a Windows partition from *that* drive.

- **Erase Disk and Create a Single Partition for Windows.** Just what it says.

## The Virus Question

*Doesn't running Windows on my Mac mean that I'll be susceptible to viruses and spyware, just like the rest of the Windows world?*

As a matter of fact, yes.

If you install Windows on your Mac, you should also install Windows antivirus and antispyware software to protect that half of the computer. The world is crawling with commercial programs that do the job; ironically, one of the easiest and least expensive is Microsoft's OneCare Live ($50 a year for up to three computers). There are also lots of free programs, like Microsoft Defender for spyware, and either AVG Antivirus (*www.free.grisoft.com*) or Avast Antivirus (*www.avast.com*) for viruses.

The good news is even if your Windows installation gets infected, the Mac side of your computer is unaffected. Just as Mac OS X can't run Windows-only software like, say, Microsoft Access, so it can't run Windows virus software.

Some people, therefore, run Windows naked—*without* virus protection (especially when using Windows-in-a-window programs like Parallels and VMWare Fusion). If a virus does strike, no big deal; they drag the infected copy of Windows to the Trash and just install a fresh one!

## Phase 2: Install Windows

On the Start Windows Installation screen, you're supposed to—hey!—start the Windows installation. Grab your Windows XP or Vista disc and slip it into the Mac. Its installer goes to work immediately.

Following the "I agree to whatever Microsoft's lawyers say" screen, Microsoft's installer asks partition you want to put Windows on. It's *really* important to pick the right one. Play your cards wrong, and you could erase your whole *Mac* partition. So:

- **Windows XP.** Choose the partition (by pressing the up or down arrow keys) called "C: Partition3 <BOOTCAMP>."

- **Windows Vista.** Choose the one called "Disk 0 Partition 3 BOOTCAMP."

When you press Enter, you now encounter another frightening-looking screen (Figure 8-2). Here, Windows invites you to format the new partition.

- **Windows XP.** If your Windows partition is less than 32 gigs, you get to choose between FAT32 or NTFS—a decision that, presumably, you've already made, having read the previous pages. Proceed as shown in Figure 8-2.

- **Windows Vista.** Click "Drive options (advanced)," click Format, click OK, and finally click Next. Your Windows partition is now formatted for NTFS, like it or not.

*Figure 8-2:*
*Use the arrow keys to highlight either "Format the partition using the NTFS file system (Quick)" or "Format the partition using the FAT file system (Quick)." Then press Enter. On the following screen, type F to confirm the formatting, then Enter to confirm the whole thing.*

```
Windows XP Professional Setup

   Setup will install Windows XP on partition

   C:  Partition1 <BOOTCAMP> [FAT32]        32326 MB ( 32307 MB free)

   on 99999 MB Disk 0 at Id 0 on bus 0 on atapi [MBR].

   Use the UP and DOWN ARROW keys to select the file system
   you want, and then press ENTER. If you want to select a
   different partition for Windows XP, press ESC.

   Format the partition using the NTFS file system (Quick)
   Format the partition using the FAT file system (Quick)
   Format the partition using the NTFS file system
   Format the partition using the FAT file system
   Convert the partition to NTFS
   Leave the current file system intact (no changes)

   ENTER=Continue   ESC=Cancel
```

## Phase 3: Install the drivers

Now a crazy, disorienting sight presents itself: Your Mac, running Windows. There's no trace of the familiar desktop, Dock, or  menu; it's Windows now, baby.

Walk through the Windows setup screens, creating an account, setting the time, and so on.

At this point, the Mac is actually a true Windows PC. You can install and run all your old Windows programs, utilities, and even games; you'll discover that they run *really* fast and well.

But as you probably know, every hardware feature of a Windows requires a *driver*—a piece of software that tells the machine how to communicate with its own monitor, networking card, speakers, and so on. And it probably goes without saying that Windows doesn't come with any drivers for *Apple's* hardware components.

That's why, at this point, you're supposed to insert your Leopard installation DVD; it contains all of the drivers for the Mac's graphics card, Ethernet and AirPort networking, audio input and output, AirPort wireless antenna, iSight camera, brightness and volume keys, Eject key, and Bluetooth transmitter. When this is all over, your white Apple remote control will even work to operate iTunes for Windows.

(It also installs a new Control Panel icon and system-tray pop-up menu, as described later in this chapter.)

---

**Note:** Unbeknownst to you, this DVD is actually a dual-mode disc. When you insert it into a Mac running Mac OS X, it appears as the Leopard installer you know and love. But when you slip it into a PC, its secret Windows partition appears–and automatically opens the Mac driver installer!

---

When you insert the Leopard disc, the driver installer opens and begins work automatically. Click past the Welcome and License Agreement screens, and then click Install. You'll see a lot of dialog boxes come and go; just leave it alone (and don't click Cancel).

A few words of advice:

- If you see, "The software you are installing has not passed Windows Logo testing," click Continue Anyway. (As if Apple's going to pay Microsoft to have its software certified for quality!)

- If the installation seems to stall, Windows may be waiting for you to click OK or Next in a window that's hidden behind other windows. Inspect the taskbar and look behind open windows.

---

**WORKAROUND WORKSHOP**

### How to Right-Click in Boot Camp

Page 12 offers the full details on right-clicking when your Mac is being a Mac. But how are you supposed to right-click when your Mac is running Windows?

You can use any USB two-button mouse, including the Apple Mighty Mouse (page 13) that comes with every desktop Mac since 2006.

If you're stuck with a one-button mouse or trackpad, you can highlight whatever you want to right-click and then press Shift-F10.

Or use the Apple Mouse Utility program for Windows. (You can download it from this book's "Missing CD" page at *www.missingmanuals.com.*) It lets you Control-click to simulate a right-click while you're running Windows.

---

- Windows XP concludes by presenting the Found New Hardware Wizard. Go ahead and agree to update your drivers.

When it's all over, a dialog box asks you to restart the computer; click Restart. When the machine comes to, it's a much more functional Windows Mac. (And it has an online Boot Camp Help window waiting for you on the screen.)

## Forth and Back, Windows/Mac

From now on, your main interaction with Boot Camp will be telling it what kind of computer you want your Mac to be today: a Windows machine or a Mac.

Presumably, though, you'll prefer one operating system *most* of the time. Figure 8-3 (top and middle) shows how you specify your favorite.

---

***Tip:*** If you're running Windows and you just want to get back to Mac OS X right now, you don't have to bother with all the steps shown in Figure 8-3. Instead, click the Boot Camp system-tray icon and, from the shortcut menu, choose Restart in Mac OS X.

---

From now on, each time you turn on the Mac, it starts up in the operating system you've selected.

If you ever need to switch—when you need Windows just for one quick job, for example—press Option key as the Mac is starting up. You'll see something like the icons shown in Figure 8-3 (bottom).

---

***Tip:*** To upgrade to Windows Vista: Restart your Mac using Windows. Insert your Vista installation or upgrade disc.

Follow the instructions that came with Vista.

---

## Keyboard Translation Guide

A Mac keyboard and a Windows keyboard aren't the same. Each has keys that would strike the other as extremely goofy. So if you're trying to trigger a familiar Windows keystroke, you might find this substitution guide handy:

| Windows Keystroke | Apple keyboard |
|---|---|
| Control-Alt-Delete | Control-Option-Delete |
| Alt | Option |
| Backspace | Delete |
| Delete (forward delete) | ⌦ (on laptops, Fn-Delete) |
| Enter | Return or Enter |
| Num lock | Clear (laptops: Fn-F6) |
| Print Screen | F14 (laptops: Fn-F11) |
| Print active window | Option-F14 (laptops: Option-Fn-F11) |
| Alt key | Option key |
| ⊞ key | ⌘ |

Similarly, the Alt key is the Windows equivalent of the Option key.

*Tip:* You know that awesome two-finger scrolling trick on Mac laptops (page 166)? Guess what? It works when you're running Windows, too.

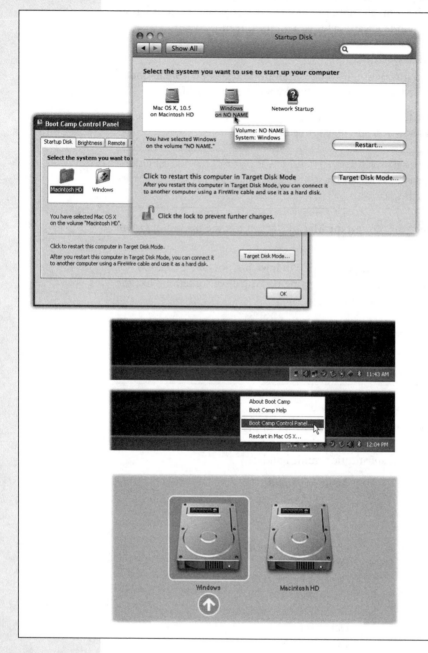

**Figure 8-3:**
*Top: To choose your preferred operating system—the one that starts up automatically unless you intervene—choose* ⌘→*System Preferences. Click Startup Disk, and then click the icon for either Mac OS X or Windows. Next, either click Restart (if you want to switch right now) or close the panel.*

*The identical controls are available when you're running Windows, thanks to the new Boot Camp Control Panel.*

*Middle: To open the Boot Camp control panel, choose its name from its new icon in the Windows system tray.*

*Bottom:This display, known as the Startup Manager, appears when you press Option during startup. It displays all the disk icons, or disk partitions, that contain bootable operating systems. Just click the name of the partition you want, and then click the Continue arrow.*

# Boot Camp Tip-O-Rama

And now, the finer points of Boot Camp...

- When you're running Mac OS X, you can get to the documents you created while you were running Windows, which is a huge convenience. Just double-click the Windows disk icon (called NO NAME or Untitled), and then navigate to the Documents and Settings→[your account name]→My Documents (or Desktop).

  If you formatted your Windows XP partition using the FAT format as described earlier, you can copy files to *or* from this partition, and even open them up for editing on the Mac side. If you used NTFS, though, you can only copy them *to* the Mac side, or open them without the ability to edit them.

---

***Tip:*** Actually, there's no reason your Windows "drive" has to be called NO NAME or Untitled. You can rename it as you would any other icon, either in Windows or in Mac OS X. (That's if you used the FAT format. If you used NTFS, you can't change the name in Mac OS X.)

---

- On the other hand, while you're running Windows, you generally can't access your *Mac* files; Windows doesn't even see the Mac hard drive.

  One way to around this is to buy a $50 program called MacDrive (*www.mediafour. com*).

---

**UP TO SPEED**

## Removing Windows

Maybe you're a switcher who held onto Windows because you were worried that you'd need it. Maybe you're finished with the project, the job, or the phase of life that required you to use Windows on your Mac. But one way or another, there may come a time when you want to get rid of your Windows installation and reclaim all the hard drive space it was using.

Fortunately, the process doesn't touch anything that's already on the Mac side. You don't have to erase your entire hard drive or anything—Leopard simply erases what's on the Windows partition of your hard drive, and then adds that disk space back to your main, *Mac* partition.

To do this, start by making sure you've rescued anything worth saving from the Windows side of your computer—it's about to be erased.

Start up in Mac OS X, quit all open programs, and make sure nobody's logged in but you. Now open up the Boot Camp

Assistant program in your Applications→Utilities folder.

On the welcome screen, click "Restore the startup disk to a single volume," and then click Continue. That's all there is to it.

Special notes for special setups: If you installed Windows on a separate hard drive, rather than a partition of your *main* hard drive, don't bother with all this. Just erase the Windows hard drive using Disk Utility, as described in Chapter 16, and format it as a Mac drive.

On the other hand, if your Mac has more than one internal hard drive, and you created a Windows partition on one of them (rather than taking it over completely), open Boot Camp Assistant as described above. This time, though, click "Create or remove a Windows partition," click Continue, click the Windows disk, and then click "Restore to a single Mac OS partition."

Another solution: use a disk that both Mac OS X and Windows "see," and keep your shared files on *that*. A flash drive works beautifully for this. So does your iDisk (page 295) or a shared drive on the network.

## Windows in a Window

The problem with Boot Camp is that every time you switch to or from Windows, you have to close down everything you were working on and restart the computer. You lose two or three minutes each way. And you can't copy and paste between Mac and Windows programs.

There is another way: an $80 utility called Parallels Workstation for Mac OS X (*www. parallels.com*), and its $80 rival, VMWare Fusion (*www.vmware.com*). These programs let you run Windows and Mac OS X *simultaneously;* Windows hangs out in a window of its own, while the Mac is running Mac OS X (Figure 8-4). You're getting about 90 percent of Boot Camp's Windows speed—not fast enough for 3-D games, but plenty fast for just about everything else.

**Figure 8-4:**
*The strangest sight you ever did see: Mac OS X and Windows XP. On the same screen. At the same time. Courtesy of VMWare Fusion. Parallels is very similar.*

Once again, you have to supply your own copy of Windows for the installation process. This time, though, it doesn't have to be Windows XP or Vista. It can be any version of Windows, all the way back to Windows 3.1—or even Linux, FreeBSD, Solaris, OS/2, or MS-DOS.

Virtualization software on an Intel Mac is a beautiful thing. You can be working on a design in iWork, duck into a Microsoft Access database (Windows only), look up an address, copy it, and paste it back into the Mac program.

And what if you can't decide whether to use Boot Camp (fast and feature-complete, but requires restarting) or Parallels/Fusion (fast and no restarting, but no 3-D games)? No problem—install both. They coexist beautifully on a single Mac, and can even use the same copy of Windows.

Together, they turn the Intel-based Macintosh into the Uni-Computer: the single machine that can run nearly 100 percent of the world's software catalog.

## Virtualization Tip-O-Rama

Mastering Parallels or Fusion means mastering Windows, of course, but it also means mastering these tips:

- You don't *have* to run Windows in a window. With one keystroke, you can make your Windows simulator cover the entire screen. You're still actually running two operating systems at once, but the whole Mac world is hidden for the moment so you can exploit your full screen. Just choose View→Full Screen.

---

***Tip:*** Or use the keystroke Alt-Enter (Parallels) or Ctrl-⌘-Return (Fusion) to enter and exit Full Screen mode.

---

- Conversely, both Parallels and Fusion offer something called *Coherence* or *Unity* mode, in which there's no trace of the Windows desktop. Instead, each Windows program floats in its own disembodied window, just like a Mac program; the Mac OS X desktop lies reassuringly in the background.

---

***Tip:*** In Fusion's Unity mode, you can access your Computer, Documents, Network, Control Panel, Search, and Run commands right from Fusion's Dock icon or launch palette, so you won't even care that there's no Start menu.

---

  In Parallels, press Alt+Ctrl+Shft to enter or exit Coherence mode. In Fusion, hit Ctrl-⌘-U for Unity mode.

---

***Tip:*** In Fusion, in Unity view, you can use the usual Mac keystrokes for Cut, Copy, and Paste within Windows applications (⌘-C, ⌘-X, ⌘-V). In Parallels, on the other hand, you can remap *all* Windows Control-key shortcuts to the ⌘ key in Preferences.

---

- To send the "three-fingered salute" when things have locked up in Windows (usually Ctrl+Alt+Delete), press Control-Option-⌦ (Fusion) or Ctrl+Fn+Alt+Delete (Parallels). Or use the Send Ctrl-Alt-Delete command in the menus.
- You can drag files back and forth between the Mac and Windows universes. Just drag icons into, or out of, the Windows window.

- If you have a one-button mouse, you can "right-click" in Parallels by Control-Shift-clicking. In Fusion, Control-click instead. On Mac laptops, you can right-click by putting two fingers on the trackpad as you click (page 467).

- When you quit the virtualization program, you're not really "shutting down" the PC; you're just *suspending* it, or putting it to sleep. When you double-click the Parallels/VMWare icon again, everything in your Windows world is exactly as you left it.

- Your entire Windows universe of files, folders, and programs is represented by a single file on your hard drive. In Parallels, it's in your Home→Library→Parallels folder. In Fusion, it's in your Home→Documents→Virtual Machines folder.

  That's super convenient, because it means that you can back up your entire Windows "computer" by dragging a single icon to another drive. And if your Windows world ever gets a virus or spyware infestation, you can drag the entire thing to the Trash—and restore the entire thing from that clean backup.

---

**POWER USERS' CLINIC**

## Beyond the Big Names

Parallels and VMWare Fusion are bloodthirsty rivals. New versions tumble out with alarming frequency, each designed to one-up its rival.

Both also let you specify which program—Mac *or* Windows—opens when you double-click documents of specific types (like JPEG or .DOC). That's yet another way Windows becomes a full player on the Mac team.

Still, these aren't the only options. A program called Virtual-Box (*www.virtualbox.org*) is not as polished or full-featured as its big-name rivals, but it's not as expensive, either; in fact, it's free. That's because it's open-source software, meaning that programmers around the world volunteer to collaborate on it.

Finally, several efforts are afoot to create software that lets you run Windows software *without Windows*. The most promising one is a $60 program called CrossOver (*www. codeweavers.com*).

Sure enough, CrossOver-compatible Windows programs open up and run in Mac OS X just as though they're real Mac programs—without your having to own, install, or fire up a copy of Windows itself.

Unfortunately, the list of compatible programs is tiny; fewer than 20 Windows programs work flawlessly in CrossOver. The list of programs that *mostly* work is longer, though, so check the list on CrossOver's Web site to see if what you need is CrossOver-friendly.

---

# Hardware on the Mac

M ost of the discussion in this book so far has covered *software*—not only the
Mac OS X operating system that may be new to you, but also the programs
and documents you'll be using on it. But there's more to life with a computer
than software. This chapter covers the finer points of using Macintosh-compatible
printers, cameras, disks, monitors, and keyboards—plus a guide to Time Machine,
Leopard's automatic backup feature.

## Printers and Printing

Printing has always been one of the Mac's strong suits—and you're about to find
out why.

### Setting Up a Printer

One beauty of Mac OS X is that setting up a printer for the first time is incredibly
easy. The first time you want to print something, follow this guide:

1. **Connect the printer to the Mac, and then turn the printer on.**

   Inkjet printers usually connect to your USB jack. Laser printers generally hook up
   to your Ethernet connector.

2. **Open the document you want to print. Choose File→Print. In the Print dialog
   box, choose your printer's name from the Printer pop-up menu (or one of its
   submenus, if any).**

   Cool! Wasn't that easy? Very nice how the Mac autodiscovers, autoconfigures,
   and autolists almost any USB, FireWire, Bluetooth, or Bonjour (Rendezvous)
   printer.

Have a nice afternoon. The End.

Oh—unless your printer *isn't* listed in the Printer pop-up menu. In that case, read on.

3. **From the Printer pop-up menu, choose Add Printer (Figure 9-1, top).**

A special setup window opens (Figure 9-1, bottom), which is even better at autodetecting printers available to your Mac. If you see the printer's name now, in the Printer Browser window, click it, and then click Add (Figure 9-1, bottom). You've just designated that printer as the *default* printer, the one that you'll print on most of the time.

*Figure 9-1:*
*Top: To introduce your Mac to a new printer, try to print something—and then choose Add Printer from this pop-up menu.*

*Bottom: Your Mac should automatically "see" any printers that are hooked up and turned on. Click the one you want, and then click Add.*

You're all set. Have a good time.

Unless, of course, your printer *still* isn't showing up. Proceed to step 4.

4. **Click the icon for the *kind* of printer you have: Windows, Bluetooth, AppleTalk, IP (that is, an Internet printer), or whatever.**

   Choose **AppleTalk** if you're connected to a laser printer via an Ethernet network cable or AirPort wireless network. Choose **Windows** if there's a Windows-only printer out there on your office network. And so on.

   After a moment, the names of any printers that are turned on and connected appear in the printer list. For most people, that means only one printer—but one's enough.

5. **Click the name of the printer you want to use.**

   As an optional step, you can open the Print Using pop-up menu at the bottom of the dialog box. Choose "Select a driver to use," and then, in the list that appears, choose your particular printer's model name, if you can find it. That's how your Mac knows what printing features to offer you when the time comes: double-sided, legal size, second paper tray, and so on.

6. **Click Add.**

   After a moment, you return to the main Printer Browser window (Figure 9-1, top), where your printer now appears. You're ready to print.

## The Printer List

If you're lucky enough to own several printers, repeat the steps above for each one. Eventually, you'll have introduced the Mac to all the printers available to it, so all their names show up in the printer list.

To see the printer list so far, open System Preferences→Print & Fax. You can have all kinds of fun here:

- **Choose a default printer.** As indicated by the Default Printer pop-up menu, Leopard intends, conveniently enough, to use whichever printer you used for the last printout for the next one. Most people, after all, don't switch printers much.

  Still, you can choose one particular printer from this pop-up menu to set it as the default printer—the one that the Mac uses unless you intervene by choosing from the Printer pop-up menu in the Print dialog box (Figure 9-1).

- **Recover a gig of drive space.** You know how Mac OS X comes with the necessary software for hundreds upon hundreds of printers? Unless you're in Oprah's tax bracket, you probably don't own that many printers—but their drivers are taking up nearly a gigabyte of hard drive space!

  To clean out the ones you don't need, open your hard drive→Library→Printers folder. Throw away the folders for printer companies that *didn't* make your printer. (Administrator account required.)

## Making the Printout

The experience of printing depends on the printer you're using—laser printer, inkjet, or whatever. In every case, however, all the printing options hide behind two commands: File→Page Setup, which you need to adjust only occasionally, and File→Print, which you generally use every time you print. You'll find these two commands in almost every Macintosh program.

### Page Setup

The Page Setup dialog box lets you specify some key characteristics about the document you're going to print: orientation, paper dimensions, and so on; see Figure 9-2.

The options here vary by program and printer. The Page Setup options for an Epson inkjet, for example, differ dramatically from those for a laser printer. Only your printer's user manual can tell you exactly what these choices do.

**Figure 9-2:**
*Here in Page Setup are the controls you need to print a document rotated sideways on the page, so it prints "the long way." The Scale control, which lets you reduce or enlarge your document, can be handy if the program you're using doesn't offer such a control. And the Paper Size pop-up menu, of course, specifies the size of the paper you're printing on—US Letter, US Legal, envelopes, or one of the standard European or Japanese paper sizes (A4 and B5).*

### The Print Command

Although you can grow to a ripe old age without ever seeing the Page Setup dialog box, you can't miss the Print dialog box. It appears, like it or not, whenever you choose File→Print in one of your programs.

Once again, the options you encounter depend on the printer you're using. They also depend on whether or not you *expand* the dialog box by clicking the ▼ button; doing so reveals a *lot* of useful options, including a handy preview; see Figure 9-3.

**Note:** The exact layout of this expanded Print dialog box differs by program.

If you expand the box, here's what you may find:

- **Printer.** If you have more than one printer connected to your Mac, you can indicate which you want to use for a particular printout by choosing its name from this pop-up menu.

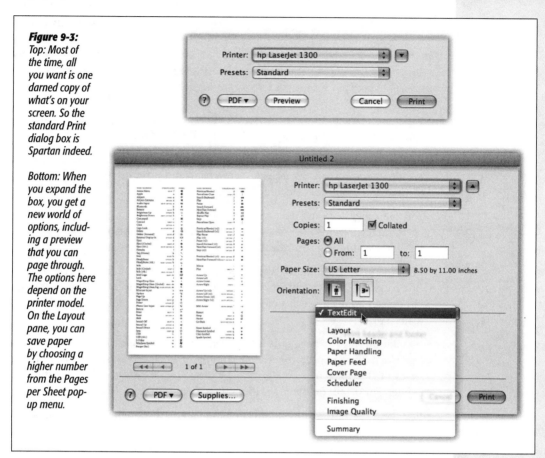

**Figure 9-3:**
*Top: Most of the time, all you want is one darned copy of what's on your screen. So the standard Print dialog box is Spartan indeed.*

*Bottom: When you expand the box, you get a new world of options, including a preview that you can page through. The options here depend on the printer model. On the Layout pane, you can save paper by choosing a higher number from the Pages per Sheet pop-up menu.*

- **Presets.** Here's a way to preserve your favorite print settings: Once you've proceeded through this dialog box, specifying the number of copies, which printer trays you want the paper taken from, and so on, you can choose Save As from the pop-up menu, and then assign your settings set a name (like "Borderless, 2 copies"). Thereafter, you'll be able to recreate that elaborate suite of settings simply by choosing its name from this pop-up menu.

- **Copies.** Type the number of copies you want printed. The Collated checkbox controls the printing order for the various pages. For example, if you print two copies of a three-page document, the Mac generally prints the pages in this order: 1, 2, 3, 1, 2, 3. If you turn off Collated, on the other hand, it prints in this order: 1, 1, 2, 2, 3, 3.

• **Pages.** You don't have to print an entire document—you can print, say, only pages 2 through 15.

---

***Tip:*** You don't have to type numbers into both the From and To boxes. If you leave the first box blank, the Mac assumes that you mean "from page 1." If you leave the second box blank, the Mac understands you mean "to the end." To print only the first three pages, in other words, leave the first box blank, and type 3 into the second box. (These page numbers refer to the physical pages you're printing, not to any fancy numbering you've set up in your word processor. As far as the Print dialog box is concerned, the first printed page is page 1, even if you've told your word processor to label it page 455.)

---

• **Paper Size, Orientation.** These options also appear in the Page Setup box, but it's convenient to have them duplicated right in the Print dialog box.

• **PDF.** A *PDF* file, of course, is an Adobe Acrobat document—a file that any Mac, Windows, Linux, or Unix user can view, read, and print using either Preview or the free Acrobat Reader (included with every PC).

You can easily save any document as a PDF file instead of printing it—a truly beautiful feature that saves paper, ink, and time. The document remains on your hard drive, and the text inside is even searchable using Spotlight.

But that's just the beginning. Apple has added a long list of additional PDF options (like password-protected PDFs, emailed ones, and so on). It faced a design quandary: How could it offer a new list of PDF-related options without junking up the Print dialog box?

Its solution was a strange little item called a pop-up *button,* shown in Figure 9-3, top. Use it like a pop-up menu. The command you'll use most often is probably Save as PDF, which turns the printout into a PDF file instead of sending it to the printer. For details on the other PDF-related options here, see page 237.

• **Preview.** This button, present only in the collapsed version of the Print dialog box (Figure 9-3, top), provides a print-preview function to almost every Mac OS X program on earth, which, in the course of your life, could save huge swaths of the Brazilian rain forest and a swimming pool's worth of ink in wasted printouts.

Technically, the Preview button sends your printout to Preview. Preview lets you zoom in or zoom out, rotate, or otherwise process your preview. When you're satisfied with how it looks, you can print it (File→Print), cancel it (File→Close), or turn it into a PDF file (File→Save as PDF).

• **Supplies.** This feature will strike you either as blissfully convenient or disgustingly mercenary: a button that takes you directly to a Web page where you can buy new cartridges for your specific printer model.

If you examine the unnamed pop-up menu just below the Presets pop-up menu, you find dozens of additional options. They depend on your printer model and the program you're using at the moment, but here are some typical choices:

- **Layout.** As described in Figure 9-3, you can save paper and ink or toner cartridges by printing several miniature "pages" on a single sheet of paper.

- **Paper Handling.** You can opt to print out your pages in reverse order so that they stack correctly, or you can print just odd or even pages so that you can run them through again for double-sided printing.

- **Cover Page.** Yes, that throwaway info page has made its way from the fax world into the hard-copy world.

- **Scheduler.** This option lets you specify *when* you want your document to print. If you're a freelancer, sitting at home with an inkjet on your desk, you might not immediately grasp why anyone wouldn't want the printouts *right now.* But try printing a 400-page catalog in a big office where other people on the network might conceivably resent you for tying up the laser printer all afternoon, and you'll get the idea.

- **ColorSync.** Most color printers offer this panel, where you can adjust the color settings—to add a little more red, perhaps. This is also where you indicate whose *color-matching system* you want to use: Apple's ColorSync, your printer manufacturer's, or none at all.

Then, below the light gray line in this pop-up menu, you'll find a few options that are unique to the chosen printer or program. Some HP printers, for example, offer Cover Page, Finishing, and other choices. Other likely guest commands:

- **Quality & Media** (inkjet printers only). Here's where you specify the print quality you want, the kind of paper you're printing on, and so on. (The name of this panel varies by manufacturer.)

- **[Program Name].** Whichever program you're using—Mail, Word, AppleWorks, or anything else—may offer its own special printing options on this screen.

## Printing

When all of your settings look good, click Print (or press Enter) to send your printout to the printer.

# Managing Printouts

After you've used the Print command, you can either sit there until the paper emerges from the printer, or you can *manage* the printouts-in-waiting. That option is attractive primarily to people who do a lot of printing, have connections to a lot of printers, or share printers with many other people.

Start by opening the printer's window. If you're already in the process of printing, just click the printer's Dock icon. If not, open  →System Preferences→Print & Fax, click the printer's name, and then click Open Print Queue.

At this point, you see something like Figure 9-4: The printouts that will soon be sliding out of your printer appear in a tidy list.

Here are some of the ways in which you can control these waiting printouts, which Apple collectively calls the *print queue:*

- **Delete them.** By clicking an icon, or ⌘-clicking several, and then clicking the Delete toolbar button, you remove items from the list of waiting printouts. Now they don't print.

- **Pause them.** By highlighting a printout and then clicking the Hold button, you pause that printout. It doesn't print out until you highlight it again and then click the Resume button. (Other documents continue to print.) This pausing business could be useful when, for example, you need time to check or refill the printer, or when you're just about to print your resignation as your boss drops by to offer you a promotion.

- **Halt them all.** You can stop all printouts from a printer by clicking Pause Printer. (They resume when you click the button again, which now says Resume Printer.)

*Tip:* As you now know, the icon for a printer's queue window appears automatically in the Dock when you print. Unfortunately, it *stays* in the Dock for the rest of the day; it doesn't disappear when the printing is complete.

If you wish it would, right-click) the printer's Dock icon; from the shortcut menu, choose Auto Quit.t

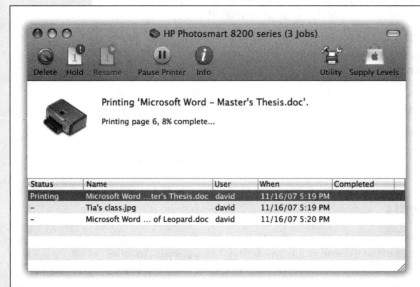

**Figure 9-4:**
*Waiting printouts appear in this window. You can sort the list by clicking the column headings (Name or Status), make the columns wider or narrower by dragging the column-heading dividers horizontally, or reverse the sorting order by clicking the column name a second time. The Supply Level button opens a graph that shows how much ink each cartridge has remaining (certain printer models only).*

## Printer Sharing

*Printer sharing* is for people (or offices) with more than one Mac, connected to a network, who'd rather not buy a separate printer for each machine. Instead, you connect the printer to one Mac, flip a couple of software switches, and then boom: The other

Macs on the network can send their printouts to the printer without actually being attached to it—even wirelessly attached, if they're on an AirPort network.

**Note:** Of course, this feature is most useful when you're sharing printers that can hook up to only one Mac at a time, like USB inkjet photo printers. Office laser printers are often designed to be networked from Day One.

Setting up printer sharing is easy; see Figure 9-5, top. Then, to make a printout from across the network, see the instructions in Figure 9-5, bottom.

**Figure 9-5:**
Top: On the Mac with the printer, open the Sharing panel of System Preferences. Turn on Printer Sharing. Turn on the checkbox for the printer(s) you want to share.

Bottom: To use a shared printer elsewhere on the network, open the document you want to print, and then choose File→Print. In the Print dialog box, choose Add Printer. The shared printer is clearly identified; click it and click Add, just as you'd add any printer (Figure 9-1). From now on, it shows up in the Printer pop-up menu just like any other printer.

If you're still using your Windows PC, you can install Bonjour for Windows (a free download from this book's "Missing CD" page at *www.missingmanuals.com*); then that machine can print to your Mac's shared printer, too.

*Tip:* Of course, your Mac (the one attached to the printer) must be turned on in order for the other computers to print. In part, that's because the documents-in-waiting from other people pile up on *your* hard drive.

## Faxing

Using the Mac as a fax machine is a terrific idea, for a lot of reasons. It saves money on paper and fax cartridges, and spares you the expense of buying a physical fax machine. Faxing from the Mac also eliminates the silly and wasteful ritual of printing something out just so you can feed it into a fax machine. And because your fax originates directly from the heart of Mac OS X instead of being scanned by a crummy 200-dpi fax-machine scanner, it blesses your recipient with a great-looking document.

Here's the basic idea: When faxes come in, you can read them on the screen, opt to have them printed automatically, or even have them emailed to you so that you can get them wherever you are in the world. (Try *that* with a regular fax machine.) And sending a fax is even easier on a Mac than on a regular fax machine: You just use the File→Print command, exactly like you're making a printout of the onscreen document.

*Figure 9-6:*
When you click the + button, this handy list of fax modems pops up. Chances are, you have only one—and it's either an old Apple Internal or a USB External model that you bought from Apple. Click its name, and then click Add.

# Setting Up Faxing

Open System Preferences. Click Print & Fax. Click the + button, and proceed as shown in Figure 9-6.

---

***Note:*** Unfortunately, Apple no longer builds fax modems into new Macs—not even laptops. You can buy an external dangly Apple USB Fax/Modem for $50, however. As soon as it's plugged into a USB port, its name appears in the Printers list.

---

If you intend to *send* faxes from the Mac, type in your return fax number in the Fax Number box.

---

***Tip:*** If you're smart, you'll also turn on "Show fax status in menu bar." It installs a fax menulet that lets you monitor and control your fax sending and receiving.

---

If you intend to *receive* faxes, click Receive Options, and turn on "Receive faxes on this computer." Then specify how soon the fax machine should pick up the call (after how many rings—you don't want it answering calls before *you* have a chance).

Finally, you can say how you want to handle incoming faxes, as described in Figure 9-7.

***Figure 9-7:***
*When your Mac answers the fax line, it can do three things with the incoming fax. Option 1: Save it as a PDF file that you open with Preview. (The Mac proposes saving these files into the Users→ Shared→Shared Faxes folder, but you can set up a more convenient folder.) Option 2: Print it out automatically, just like a real fax machine. Option 3: Email it to you, so you can get your faxes even when you're not home (and so you can forward the fax easily).*

## Sending a Fax

When you're ready to send a fax, type up the document you want to send. Choose File→Print. In the Print dialog box (Figure 9-3), open the PDF pop-up button and choose Fax PDF.

The dialog box shown in Figure 9-8 appears. Here are the boxes you can fill in:

- **To.** If you like, you can simply type the fax number into the To box, exactly the way it should be dialed: *1-212-553-2999,* for example. You can send a single fax to more than one number by separating each with a comma and a space.

   If you fax the same people often, though, you're better off adding their names and fax numbers to the Address Book (Chapter 11). That way, you can click the little silhouette button to the right of the To box and choose the recipient.

---

***Note:*** At this writing, the Address Book feature doesn't work when you're sending from Microsoft Word or Excel. You have to type in the fax number by hand.

---

***Figure 9-8:***
*When you send a fax, you get a modified Print dialog box. Here is where you specify a cover page (and what you want on it).*

*You can type a fax number into the To box, or you can click the silhouette head button to open a miniature version of Address Book. It lets you choose someone's name by double-clicking. All phone numbers appear here, so look for those identified as fax numbers. (Chances are that these listings don't include the 1- long-distance prefix, which is why Apple gave you a separate Dialing Prefix box.) If you've built groups in your address book, you can send to everyone in a group at once.*

- **Settings.** Most of the time, fiddling with the printing pop-up menu isn't relevant to sending a fax. But the standard printing controls are here for your convenience. You can use the Scheduler pane to specify a time for your outgoing fax, the Layout pane to print more than one "page" per sheet, and so on.

- **Use Cover Page, Subject, Message.** If you turn on this checkbox, you're allowed to type a little message into the Subject and Message boxes.

  Beware! Don't press the Return key to add a blank line to your message. Mac OS X thinks you intend to "click" the Fax button—and off it goes!

---

*Tip:* Choosing Save as PDF from the little PDF pop-up button, at this moment, is your only chance to keep a copy of the fax you're sending.

---

### Sending

When everything looks good, hit the Fax button. Although it may look like nothing is happening, check your Dock, where the icon for your fax/modem has appeared. If you click it, you'll see a clone of the dialog box shown in Figure 9-4, indicating the progress of your fax. Here you can pause the faxing, delete it, or hold it, exactly as you would a printout. (Your Fax menulet, if you've installed it, also keeps you apprised of the fax's progress.)

Otherwise, you don't get much feedback on the faxing process. Once the connection sounds are complete, you don't hear anything, see anything, or receive any notice that the fax was successful.

(If your fax was *not* successfully sent for some reason, the modem's window automatically reschedules the fax to go out in five minutes.)

### Checking the log, checking the queue

To see the log of all sent and received faxes, choose  →System Preferences→Print & Fax. Double-click your fax/modem's name; its fax-management window appears, but that's not what you're interested in. Instead, choose Jobs→Show Completed Jobs. You get a status window that looks a lot like the one for a printer.

## Receiving a Fax

A Mac that's been set up to answer calls does a very good impersonation of a fax machine. You don't even have to be logged in to get faxes, although the Mac does have to be turned on. In System Preferences→Energy Saver→Options, turn on "Wake when modem detects a ring" to prevent your Mac from being asleep at the big moment.

When a fax call comes in, the Mac answers it after the number of rings you've specified. Then it treats the incoming fax image in the way you've specified in System Preferences: by sending it to your email program, printing it automatically, or just saving it as a PDF file in a folder that you've specified.

# PDF Files

As a PC veteran, you've probably run into PDF (portable document format) files already. Many a software manual, Read Me file, and downloadable "white paper" comes in this format. In Windows, you needed the free program called Acrobat Reader to open or print these files, and some not-free-at-all software program to *create* them.

PDF files, however, are one of Mac OS X's common forms of currency. In fact, you can turn *any document* (in any program with a Print command) into a PDF file.

What's the big deal about PDF in Mac OS X? Consider these advantages:

- **Other people see your layout.** When you distribute PDF files to other people, they see precisely the same fonts, colors, page design, and other elements that you put in your original document. And here's the kicker: They get to see all of this even if they don't *have* the fonts or the software you used to create the document. (Contrast with the alternative. Say you're sending somebody a Microsoft Word document. If your correspondent doesn't have precisely the same fonts you have, then he'll see a screwy layout. And if he doesn't have Word or a program that can open Word files, he'll see nothing at all.)

- **It's universal.** PDF files are very common in the Macintosh, Windows, Unix/Linux, and even Palm and PocketPC organizer worlds. When you create a PDF file, you can distribute it (by email, for example) without worrying about what kinds of computers your correspondents are using.

- **It has very high resolution.** PDF files print at the maximum quality of any printer. A PDF file prints great both on cheapo inkjets and on high-quality image-setting gear at professional print shops. (Right now you're looking at a PDF file that was printed at a publishing plant.)

- **You can search it.** Although you may be tempted to think of a PDF file as something like a captured graphic of the original document, it has several key differences. Behind the scenes, its text is still text; Spotlight can find a PDF in a haystack in a matter of seconds. That's an especially handy feature when you work with electronic software manuals in PDF format.

## Opening PDF Files

There's nothing to opening up a PDF file: Just double-click it. Preview takes over from there, and opens the PDF file on your screen.

## Creating PDF Files

Opening, schmopening—what's really exciting in Mac OS X is the ability to create your *own* PDF files. The easiest way is to click the PDF pop-up button in the standard Print dialog box (visible in Figure 9-3). When you click it, you're offered a world of interesting PDF-creation possibilities, the most useful of which are these:

- **Save as PDF.** Mac OS X saves your printout-to-be to the disk as a PDF document instead of printing it.

- **Fax PDF** *faxes* a document instead of printing it, as described on the preceding pages.

- **Mail PDF** generates a PDF, and then attaches it to an outgoing message in Mail. Great for exchanging layout-intensive documents with collaborators who don't have the same fonts, layout software, or taste as you.

- **Save PDF to iPhoto** creates a PDF version of the document and then exports it to iPhoto. That's not such a bad idea; iPhoto is great at managing and finding any kind of graphics documents, including PDFs.

- **Save PDF to Web Receipts Folder** is one of the simplest and sweetest features in all of Mac OS X.

  You use it when you've just ordered something on a Web site, and the "Print This Receipt" screen is staring you in the face. Don't waste paper and ink (and, later, time trying to find it!). Instead, use this command. You get a perfectly usable PDF version, stored in your Home→Documents→Web Receipts folder, where you can use Spotlight to find it later, when you need to consult or print it because your gray-market goods never arrived.

- **Edit Menu** lets you prune this very list to remove the options you never use.

# Fonts—and Font Book

Mac OS X delivers type that is *all smooth, all the time.* Fonts in Mac OS X's formats—called TrueType, PostScript Type 1, and OpenType—always look smooth onscreen and in printouts, no matter what the point size.

Mac OS X also comes with a program that's *just* for installing, removing, inspecting, and organizing fonts. It's called Font Book (Figure 9-9), it's in your Applications folder, and it's been much improved in Leopard.

## Where Fonts Live

Brace yourself. In Mac OS X, there are *three* Fonts folders. The fonts you actually see listed in the Fonts menus and Font panels of your programs are combinations of these Fonts folders' contents.

They include:

- **Your private fonts (your Home folder→Library→Fonts).** This Fonts folder sits right inside your own Home folder. You're free to add your own custom fonts to this folder. Go wild—it's your font collection and yours alone. Nobody else who uses the Mac can use these fonts; they'll never even know that you have them.

- **Main font collection (Library→Fonts).** Any fonts in this folder are available to everyone to use in every program. (As with most features that affect everybody who shares your Macintosh, however, only people with Administrator accounts can change the contents of this folder.)

- **Essential system fonts** (System→Library→Fonts). This folder contains the 35 fonts that the Mac itself needs: the typefaces you see in your menus, dialog boxes, icons, and so on. You can open this folder to *see* these font suitcases, but you can't do anything with them, such as opening, moving, or adding to them. Remember that, for stability reasons, the System folder is sealed under glass forever.

With the exception of the essential system fonts, you'll find an icon representing each of these locations in your Font Book program, described next.

**Note:** And just to make life even more exciting, Adobe's and Microsoft' s software installers may donate even *more* fonts to your cause, in yet *another* folder: your Home→Application Support folder.

**Figure 9-9:**
*Each account holder can have a separate set of fonts; your set is represented by the User icon. You can drag fonts and font families between the various Fonts folders represented here— from your User account folder to the Computer icon, for example, making it available to all account holders.*

## Font Book: Installing and Managing Fonts

One of the biggest perks of Mac OS X is its preinstalled collection of over 50 great-looking fonts—"over $1,000 worth," according to Apple, which licensed many of them from type companies. In short, fewer Mac users than ever will wind up buying and installing new fonts.

But when you do buy or download new fonts, you're in luck. There's no limit to the number of fonts you can install.

### Looking over your fonts

Right off the bat, Font Book is great for one enjoyable pursuit: looking at samples of each typeface. Click Computer, for example, click the first font name, and then press the down arrow key. As you walk down the list, the rightmost panel shows you a sample of each font (Figure 9-9).

You can also click any font family's flippy triangle (or highlight its name and then press the right arrow) to see the font *variations* it includes: Italic, Bold, and so on.

---

***Tip:*** *When you first open Font Book, the actual text of the typeface preview (in the right panel) is pretty generic. Don't miss the Preview menu, though. It lets you substitute a full display of every character (choose Repertoire)—or, if you choose Custom, it lets you type your* own *text.*

---

### Printing a reference sheet

You can print a handy, whole-font sampler of any font. Click its name and then choose File→Print. In the Print dialog box, click the ▼ button to expand the dialog box, if necessary.

As shown in Figure 9-10, you can use the Report Type pop-up menu to choose from three reference-sheet styles: Catalog, Repertoire, or Waterfall. Choose each to view a preview of the report. When everything looks good, click Print.

### Eliminating duplicates

Since your Mac accesses up to three folders containing fonts, you might wonder what happens in the case of *conflicts.* For example, suppose you have two slightly different fonts, both called Optima, which came from different type companies, and are housed

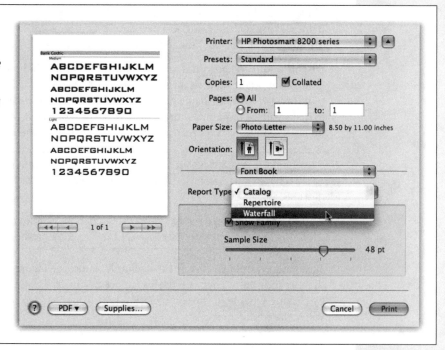

***Figure 9-10:***
*From the Report Type pop-up menu, choose the style you want. The preview screen shows you each one before you commit it to paper. Type-size controls always appear in the lower right.*

in different Fonts folders on your system. Which font do you actually get when you use it in your documents?

The scheme is actually fairly simple: Mac OS X proceeds down the list of Fonts folders in the order shown on page 237, beginning with your own home Fonts folder. It only acknowledges the existence of the *first* duplicated font it finds.

If you'd rather have more control, open Font Book. A bullet (•) next to a font's name is Font Book's charming way of trying to tell you that you've got copies of the same font in more than one of your Fonts folders. You might have one version of Comic Sans in your own Home→Library→Fonts folder, for example, and another in your Mac's main Fonts folder.

Click the one that you want to keep, and then choose Edit→Resolve Duplicates. Font Book turns off all *other* copies, and the bullet disappears.

### Adding, removing, and hiding fonts

Here's what you can do with Font Book:

- **Install a font.** When you double-click a font file's icon in the Finder, Font Book opens and presents the typeface for your inspection pleasure. If you like it, click Install Font. You've just installed it into *your account's* Fonts folder, so that it appears in the Font menus of all your programs. (If you'd rather install it so that it appears in *all* account holders' Fonts menus, see Figure 9-9.)

- **Remove a font.** Removing a font from your machine is easy: Highlight it in the Font Book list, and then press the Delete key. (You're asked to confirm the decision.) Before taking such a drastic and permanent step, however, keep in mind that you can simply *disable* (hide) the font instead. Read on.

- **Disable a font.** When you disable a font, you're simply hiding it from your programs. You might want to turn off a font so that you can use a different version of it (bearing the same name but from a different type company, for example), or to make your Font menus shorter, or to make programs like Microsoft Word start up faster. You can always turn a disabled font back on if you ever need it again.

---

*Tip:* How's this for a sweet feature? Mac OS X can activate fonts *automatically* as you need them. When you open a document that relies on a font it doesn't have, Leopard activates that font and keeps it available until that particular program quits.

Actually, it does better than that. If it doesn't see that font installed, it actually *searches your hard drive* on a quest to find the font—and then it asks you if you want it installed, so the document will look right.

---

To disable a font, just click it (or its family name; see Figure 9-9) and then click the checkbox button beneath the list (or press Shift-⌘-D). Confirm your decision by clicking Disable in the confirmation box. (Turn on "Do not ask me again," if you're the confident sort.)

The font's name now appears gray, and the word Off appears next to it, making it absolutely clear what you've just done. (To turn the font on again, highlight its name, and then click the now-empty checkbox button, or press Shift-⌘-D again.)

---

**Note:** When you install, remove, disable, or enable a font using Font Book, you see the changes in the Font menus and panels of your *Cocoa* programs immediately. You won't see the changes in older Carbon programs, however, until you quit and reopen them.

---

### Font libraries

A font library is a set of fonts *outside* Font Book that you can install or uninstall on the fly. They don't have to be in any of your Fonts folders; Font Book can install them from wherever they happen to be sitting on your hard drive (or even on the network). Font Book never copies or moves these font files as you install or remove them from libraries; it simply adds them to your Font menus by referencing them right where they sit.

---

**Tip:** That can be a handy arrangement if you periodically work on different projects for different clients. Why burden your day-to-day Font menu with the 37 fonts used by *Beekeeper Quarterly* magazine, when you need to work with those fonts only four times a year?

---

Once you've added some fonts to a library, you can even set up collections *within* that library.

To create a library, choose File→New Library; the library appears in the Collection list at the left side of Font Book. Now you can drag fonts into it right from the Finder, or set up collections inside it by highlighting the library's icon and choosing File→New Collection.

## The Fonts Panel

As noted in Chapter 4, some existing Mac programs have simply been touched up—Carbonized, in the lingo—to be Mac OS X–compatible. Choosing fonts in these programs works exactly as it always has on the Mac: You choose a typeface name from the Font menu or a formatting palette.

In many standard programs, though—like TextEdit, iMovie, Pages, Keynote, Numbers, iPhoto, and Mail—you get a standard Mac OS X feature called the Fonts panel. If you're seated in front of your Mac OS X machine now, fire up TextEdit or Pages and follow along.

### Choosing fonts from the Fonts panel

Suppose you've just highlighted a headline in TextEdit, and now you want to choose an appropriate typeface for it.

In TextEdit, you open the Fonts panel (Figure 9-11) by choosing Format→Font→Show Fonts (⌘-T). If you've ever used Font Book, this display should look familiar. The first column lists your Collections, as described above. The second column, Family, shows the names of the actual fonts in your system. The third, Typeface, shows the

---

various style variations—Bold, Italic, Condensed, and so on—available in that type family. (Oblique and Italic are roughly the same thing; Bold, Black, and Ultra are varying degrees of boldface.)

The last column lists a sampling of point sizes. You can use the size slider, choose from the point-size pop-up menu, or type any number into the box at the top of the Size list.

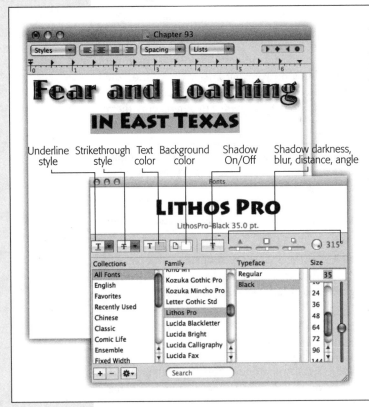

**Figure 9-11:**
*The Fonts panel, generally available only in Cocoa programs, offers elaborate controls over text color, shadow, and underline styles. It also contains some of the genetic material of old-style programs like Suitcase and Font Juggler.*

*See the handy font sample shown here above the font lists? To get it, choose Show Preview from the ✿ pop-up menu. Or use the mousy way: Place your cursor just below the title bar (where it says Fonts) and drag downward.*

# Digital Cameras

Just like Windows XP and Vista, Mac OS X is extremely camera-friendly. The simple act of connecting a digital camera to its USB cable stirs Mac OS X into action—namely, it opens iPhoto, Apple's digital-photo shoebox program.

If it's a digital *video* camera you plugged in, Mac OS X opens iMovie instead. (Both of these programs are described in this book's free 85-page iLife Appendix, which you can download from this book's "Missing CD" at *www.missingmanuals.com.*)

# Disks

Floppy drives disappeared from Macs beginning in 1997—and these days, they're absent from most Windows PCs, too.

In the meantime, there are all kinds of other disks you can connect to a Mac these days: CDs and DVDs, hard drives, iPods, USB flash drives, and so on.

When you insert a disk, its icon shows up in three places (unless you've changed your Finder preferences): on the right side of the screen, in the Computer window, and in the Sidebar (page 32). To see what's on a disk you've inserted, double-click its icon.

---

**Note:** You can make the Mac work like Windows, if you choose. For example, to open a single window containing icons of all currently inserted disks, choose Go→Computer (which produces the rough equivalent of the My Computer window).

To complete the illusion that you're running Windows, you can even tell Mac OS X not to put disk icons on the desktop at all. Just choose Finder→Preferences, click General, and turn off the four top checkboxes—"Hard disks," "External disks," "CDs, DVDs, and iPods," and "Connected servers." They'll no longer appear on the desktop—only in your Computer window. (You can stop them from appearing in the Sidebar, too, by clicking the Sidebar button in the Finder preferences and turning off the same checkboxes.)

---

To remove a disk from your Mac, use one of these methods:

---

**FREQUENTLY ASKED QUESTION**

## The Eject Button That Doesn't

*When I push the ⏏ key on my keyboard (or the Eject button on my CD-ROM drawer), how come the CD doesn't come out?*

There might be three things going on. First of all, some file on the disc might be open—that is, in use by one of your programs. You're not allowed to eject the disc until that file is closed.

Second, to prevent accidental pushings, the Eject key on the modern Mac keyboard is designed to work only when you hold it down steadily for a second or two. Just tapping it doesn't work.

Third, remember that once you've inserted a disk, the Mac won't let go unless you eject it in one of the official ways.

On Mac models with a CD tray (drawer), pushing the button on the CD-ROM door opens the drawer only when it's empty. If there's a disc in it, you can push that button till doomsday, but the Mac will simply ignore you.

That behavior especially confuses people who are used to working with Windows. (On a Windows PC, pushing the CD button does indeed eject the disc.) But on the Mac, pushing the CD-door button ejects an inserted disc only when the disc wasn't seated properly, or the Mac couldn't read the disc for some other reason, and the disc's icon never appeared onscreen.

The Eject key on the modern Mac keyboard, however, isn't so fussy. It pops out whatever CD or DVD is in the drive.

Oh—and if a CD or DVD won't come out at all (and its icon doesn't show up on the desktop), restart the Mac. Keep the mouse button pressed as the Mac restarts to make the disc pop out.

And if even that technique doesn't work, look for a tiny pinhole in or around the slot. Inserting a straightened paper clip, slowly and firmly, will also make the disc pop out.

---

- **Hold down the Eject key on your keyboard.** Mac keyboards, both on laptops and desktops, have a special Eject key (⏏), usually in the upper-right corner. Hold it down for a moment to make a CD or DVD pop out.

- **Drag its icon onto the Trash icon.** For years, this technique has confused and frightened first-time Mac users. Their typical reaction: Doesn't the Trash mean "delete"? Yes, but only when you drag *file or folder* icons there—not *disk* icons. Dragging a disk icon into the Trash (at the end of the Dock) makes the Mac spit the disk out. (If you've dragged a *disk image* icon or the icon of a networked disk, this maneuver *unmounts* them—that is, gets them off your screen.)

  The instant you begin dragging a disk icon, the Trash icon on the Dock changes form, as though to reassure the novice that dragging a disk icon there will only eject the disk. As you drag, the wastebasket icon morphs into a giant-sized ⏏ logo.

- **Highlight the disk icon, and then choose File→Eject (or press ⌘-E).** The disk pops out.

- **Right-click the disk icon.** Choose Eject from the shortcut menu.

- **Use the Sidebar.** Click the ⏏ button next to a disk's name in the Sidebar.

---

*Tip:* Any of these techniques also work to get network disks and disk images off your screen.

---

## Startup Disks

When you turn the Mac on, it hunts for a *startup disk*—that is, a disk containing a System folder. If you've ever seen the dispiriting blinking folder icon on a Mac's screen, you know what happens when the Mac *can't* find a startup disk. It blinks like that forever, or until you find and insert a disk with a viable System folder on it.

### Creating a startup disk

By installing the Mac OS onto a disk—be it a hard drive or a DVD—you can create a startup disk. Not all disks are capable of starting up the Mac, but any Leopard Mac can start up from an external FireWire hard drive.

### Selecting a startup disk

It's perfectly possible to have more than one startup disk simultaneously attached to your Mac. That's the deal, for example, whenever you've inserted the Mac OS X DVD into your Mac: Both your main hard drive and the DVD contain a System folder, and each is a startup disk. Some veteran Mac fans deliberately create other startup disks—using iPods, for example—so that they can easily start the Mac up from a backup disk, or from a different version of the OS. And if you've set up a Boot Camp partition (Chapter 8), of course, you essentially have a Mac startup disk and a Windows startup disk.

Only one System folder can be operational at a time. So how does the Mac know which to use as its startup disk? You make your selection in the Startup Disk pane of System Preferences (Figure 9-12).

*Tip:* If you're in a hurry to start the machine up from a different disk, just click the disk icon and then click Restart in the System Preferences window. You don't have to close the System Preferences window first.

**Figure 9-12:**
*In the Startup Disk pane of System Preferences, the currently selected disk—the one that will be "in force" the next time the machine starts up—is always highlighted. You also see the System folder's version, the name of the drive it's on, and its actual name.*

## Erasing a Disk

When you want to erase a disk (such as a DVD-RW disc), the only tool Apple gives you is Disk Utility, which sits in your Applications→Utilities folder.

Once you've opened Disk Utility, click the name of the disk (in the left-side list), click the Erase tab, and then click the Erase button.

## Burning CDs and DVDs

Who misses the floppy drive anymore? A blank DVD holds about 3,250 times as many files!

You can buy blank CDs incredibly cheaply in bulk—$20 for 100 discs, for example—via the Web. Blank DVDs are only slightly more expensive—about $30 for 100.

Burning a CD or DVD is great for backing stuff up, transferring stuff to another computer (like a Windows PC), mailing to somebody, or offloading (archiving) older files to free up hard drive space.

You can burn a disc in either of two ways: with the blank disc inserted or without.

# Burn Folders: Without the Disc

The *burn folder* is a special folder that you fill up by dragging file and folder icons to it. Then, when you're ready to burn, you just insert the blank disc and go.

The burn-folder concept has a lot going for it:

- **No wasted hard drive space.** The Mac just sets aside *aliases* of the files and folders you want to burn. Aliases take up negligible hard drive space. When you finally burn the disc, the designated material is copied directly onto the CD or DVD.

- **Easy reuse.** You can keep a burn folder on your desktop, prestocked with the folders you like to back up. Each time you burn a disc, you get the latest version of those folders' contents, and you're saved the effort of having to gather them each time.

**Figure 9-13:**
*Top: A burn folder looks like any ordinary folder—except that it has that radioactive logo on it. You can drag files and folders right into its window; Mac OS X displays only aliases for now, but when you burn the disc, the actual files and folders will be there.*

*If you open the burn folder, you find an unusual strip across the top. Its most important feature is the Burn button at the right.*

*Bottom: Ready to proceed, Captain.*

- **Prepare ahead of time.** You can get a CD or DVD ready to burn without having a blank disc on hand.

Here's how you use burn folders:

1. **Create a burn folder.**

To make a burn folder appear on your desktop, choose File→New Burn Folder. To create one in any other window, right-click a blank spot inside that window and, from the shortcut menu, choose New Burn Folder.

Either way, a new folder appears, bearing the universal Mac radioactive "burn" symbol (Figure 9-13).

**2. Rename it.**

Its name is highlighted, so you can just start typing to rename it. Press Enter when you're finished.

**3. Load up the folder by dragging files and folders onto it.**

If you double-click the burn folder to open its window (Figure 9-13), you'll notice that you're not actually copying huge files. You're simply making a list of aliases.

---

**Tip:** To check how many megabytes' worth of stuff you've added so far—so you don't overflow your CD or DVD—click the Burn button in the upper-right corner of the burn folder's window. The resulting message, shown at bottom in Figure 9-13, tells you the current total. (Hit the Enter key, or click Cancel, to close the dialog box.)

---

**4. Decorate the window, if you like.**

You can choose list view or icon view; you can drag the icons into an arrangement that you like; you can change the background color of the window; and so on. One nice feature of the Mac is that the look of a window is preserved when you burn it to CD.

**5. Click the Burn button in the upper-right corner of the window, or choose File→ Burn Disc.**

The message shown at bottom in Figure 9-13 appears.

**6. Insert a blank disc.**

If you have a slot-loading Mac, slip the disc into the slot. If your Mac has a sliding CD/DVD tray instead, open it first by pressing the button on the tray, or pressing your ⏏ key for about one second.

---

**Tip:** Once you've inserted a CD or DVD into your tray, you can close it either by pushing gently on the tray or by pressing the ⏏ key again.

---

One last confirmation box appears, where you can name the disc and choose a burning speed for it.

**7. Click Burn (or press Enter).**

The Mac's laser proceeds to record the CD or DVD, which can take some time. Feel free to switch into another program and continue using your Mac. When it's all over, you have a freshly minted CD or DVD, whose files and folders you can open on any Mac or Windows PC.

## Burn Folders: With a Blank Disc On Hand

If you have a blank disc ready to go, burn folders are even simpler to use. In fact, you may not even be aware that you're using them. The whole operation requires fewer steps.

Start by inserting a blank disc. After a moment, the Mac displays a dialog box asking, in effect, what you want to do with this blank disc (unless you've fiddled with your preference settings). See Figure 9-14 for instructions.

If you choose Open Finder, you'll see the disc's icon appear on the desktop after a

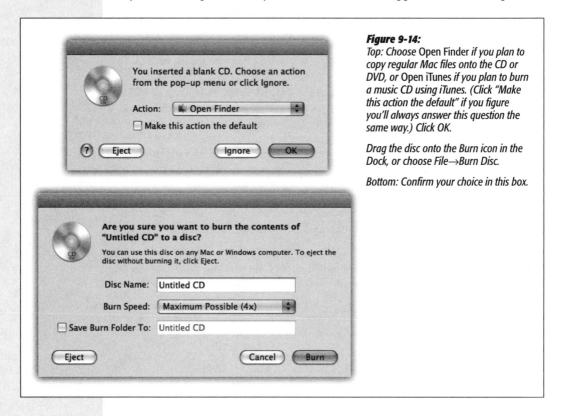

***Figure 9-14:***
*Top: Choose* Open Finder *if you plan to copy regular Mac files onto the CD or DVD, or* Open iTunes *if you plan to burn a music CD using iTunes. (Click "Make this action the default" if you figure you'll always answer this question the same way.) Click OK.*

*Drag the disc onto the Burn icon in the Dock, or choose File→Burn Disc.*

*Bottom: Confirm your choice in this box.*

moment; its icon also appears in the Sidebar, complete with a round Burn symbol that looks like a radioactivity logo.

At this point, you can begin dragging files and folders onto the disc's icon, or (if you double-click the icon) into its window. You can add, remove, reorganize, and rename the files on it just as you would in any standard Finder window. All you're really doing is dragging aliases around; the real files are left untouched on your hard drive. You can also rename the CD or DVD itself just as you would a file or folder.

*Tip:* The status bar at the bottom of the window gives you a running tally of the disk space you've filled up so far. (It may say, for example, "223.2 MB of 702.8 used on disc.") At last, you have an effortless way to exploit the blank disc's capacity with precision.

When the disk contains the files and folders you want to immortalize, do one of these things:

- Choose File→Burn Disc.

- Click the Burn button next to the disc's name in the Sidebar.

- Drag the disc's icon toward the Trash icon in the Dock. As soon as you begin to drag, the Trash icon turns into that yellow fallout-shelter logo. Drop the disc's icon onto it.

The dialog box shown at bottom left in Figure 9-14 now appears. Click Burn. When the recording process is over, you'll have yourself a DVD or CD that works in any other Mac or PC.

Here are a few final notes on burning CDs and DVDs at the desktop:

- Not sure what kinds of disks your Mac can burn? Open System Profiler (in your Applications→Utilities folder). Expand the Hardware triangle, and click the Disc Burning category. There it is, plain as day: a list of the formats your machine can read and write (that is, burn). For example, you might see: "CD-Write: -R, -RW. DVD-Write: -R, -RW, +R, +RW."

- If you do a lot of disc burning, a full-fledged CD-burning program like Toast Titanium (*www.roxio.com*) adds myriad additional formatting options that let you make startup CDs, video CDs, and so on.

- When you insert a CD-*RW* or DVD-*RW* disc that you've previously recorded, the box shown at top in Figure 9-14 doesn't appear. Instead, the disc's icon simply appears on the desktop as though it's an ordinary CD. Before you can copy new files onto it, you must erase it using Disk Utility as described in the previous section.

---

**FREQUENTLY ASKED QUESTION**

### Auto-Playing Music CDs

*How do I make my Mac play music CDs automatically when they're inserted?*

First, make sure iTunes is slated to open automatically when you insert a music CD. You do that on the CDs & DVDs panel of System Preferences (use the "When you insert a music CD" pop-up menu).

Then all you have to do is make sure iTunes knows to begin playing automatically once it launches. Choose iTunes→Preferences, click the General icon, and from the On CD Insert pop-up menu, choose Begin Playing. Click OK.

From now on, whenever you insert a music CD, iTunes will launch automatically and begin playing.

---

• The discs that your Mac burns work equally well on Macs and Windows (or Linux) PCs. If you plan to insert a CD or DVD into a PC, however, remember that Windows doesn't permit certain symbols in a Windows file name (\ / : * ? " < > |). You'll run into trouble if any of your file names contain these symbols. In fact, you won't be able to open any folders on your disc that contain illegally named files.

# iTunes: The Digital Jukebox

As a Windows veteran, you may already be familiar with iTunes. This program, which sits in your Applications folder, is the ultimate software jukebox (Figure 9-15). It can play music CDs, tune in to Internet radio stations, load up your iPod music player or iPhone, and play back digital sound files (including the Internet's favorite format, MP3 files) and other popular audio formats. It can also turn selected tracks from your music CDs *into* MP3 files, so that you can store favorite songs on your hard drive to play back anytime—without having to dig up the original CDs. iTunes also lets you record your own custom audio CDs that contain only the good songs. Finally, of course, iTunes is the shop window for the online iTunes Store ($1 a song).

iTunes can also burn *MP3 CDs:* music CDs that fit much more than the usual 74 or 80 minutes of music onto a disc (because they store songs in MP3 format instead of AIFF).

The first time you run iTunes, you're asked (a) whether you want iTunes to be the program your Mac uses for playing music files from the Internet, (b) whether you want it to ask your permission every time it connects to the Internet, and (c) whether you want the program to scan your Home folder for all music files already on it. (You can decline to have your hard drive scanned at this time. Later, you can always drag it, or any other folder, directly into the iTunes window for automatic scanning.)

---

*Tip:* The following pages present a mini-manual on iTunes. For the full scoop, plus coverage of the iPod and the iTunes Store, consult *iPod: The Missing Manual.*

---

## MP3 Files and Company

The iTunes screen itself is set up to be a list—a database—of every song you've got in formats like MP3, AIFF, WAV, AAC, and Apple Lossless. iTunes automatically finds, recognizes, and lists all such files in your Home folder→Music→iTunes→iTunes Music folder.

---

*Tip:* You can instruct iTunes to display the contents of other folders, too, by choosing File→Add to Library. It promptly copies any sound files from the folder you "show" it into your Home folder→Music→iTunes→ iTunes folder.

---

## Audio CDs

If you're not into collecting MP3 files, you can also populate the main list here simply by inserting a music CD. The songs on it immediately show up in the list.

---

At first, they may appear with the exciting names "Track 01," "Track 02," and so on. But after a moment, iTunes connects to the Internet and compares your CD with the listings at *www.gracenote.com*, a global database of music CDs and their contents. If it finds a match among the thousands of CDs there, it copies the album and song names into iTunes, where they reappear every time you use this particular CD.

*Tip:* If you connect an iTunes-compatible portable MP3 player to your Mac (the iPod isn't the only one), its name, too, shows up in the left-side Source list. You can add songs to your player (by dragging them onto its icon), rename or reorder them, and so on.

**Figure 9-15:**
*When the Library icon is selected in the Source list, you can click the Browse button (upper-right) to produce a handy, supplementary view of your music database, organized like a Finder column view. It lets you drill down from a performer's name (left column) to an album by that artist (right column) to the individual songs on that album (bottom half, beneath the browser panes).*

## The iPod and iPhone

Unless you're just off the shuttle from Alpha Centauri, you probably already know that the iPod is Apple's tiny, elegant music player. It, and its cellular pal the iPhone, are designed to integrate seamlessly with iTunes.

All you have to do is connect the iPod or iPhone to the Mac via its USB cable. You'll see the gadget's icon show up in the iTunes Source list. Click its icon to view its contents—and click the tabs (Music, TV Shows, Podcasts, and so on) to specify what Mac material you'd like copied over to it.

## The iTunes Store

The iTunes Store is incredibly easy to figure out. Right from within iTunes, you can search or browse for over 8 million pop songs, classical pieces, and even comedy excerpts—and then buy them for $1 apiece. Then there are the TV shows (episodes for $2 a piece, with no ads, from 500 series), movies (2,500), free podcasts (95,000), audiobooks (40,000), music videos (200,000), iPod games, and more. Sure, you may go broke, but at least you'll be entertained.

Besides, there are no monthly fees, and your downloads don't go *poof!* into the ether if you decide to cancel your subscription, as they do with some rival services.

Start by clicking the Store icon in the iTunes Source list. You go online and land on the home page, which looks and works like a Web page. Use the Search Store box (top right corner) to find the songs or performers you're interested in. Double-click a song or video to hear or view a 30-second excerpt. (For audio books, you get a 90-second excerpt.)

### Buying music

If you decide to buy a song, you need an Apple Account. Click the Account: Sign In button on the right side of the iTunes window to get started. (If you've ever bought or registered an Apple product on the company's Web site, signed up for AppleCare, ordered an iPhoto book, or have a .Mac membership, you probably have an Apple Account already. All you have to do is remember your name—usually your email address—and password.)

---

**GEM IN THE ROUGH**

## Playing Across the Network

If you've taken the trouble to set up a home network, you can share songs and playlists with up to five networked computers. You could, for example, tap into your old Windows jazz collection without getting up from your desk, or someone using it can sample the zydeco and tejano tunes from your Mac. The music you decide to share is streamed over the network to the other computer.

You can't share music across the Internet; only within your own home or office network. Technically speaking, the computers must be on the same subnet. (Open the Network panel of System Preferences to check your subnet number.)

To make your music available to others, choose iTunes→Preferences, click the Sharing icon, and turn on "Share my library on the local network." They'll find your iTunes collection listed in the Source pane, ready to play.

Unfortunately, you can't listen to a song from the iTunes Store across the network until you enter the Apple account name and user password that was used to purchase the song. Your Mac now takes one of the five spots on the song's authorized list. If you don't type in the owner's name and password for purchased songs, iTunes just skips those tracks.

---

When you click the Buy button next to a song's name, iTunes downloads it into your Home→Music→iTunes Music folder. It also shows up in the Purchased Music "playlist" in the Source list for convenient access.

### Restrictions

Most songs from the iTunes Store are copy-protected—gently. For example:

- **Maximum of five computers.** Apple lets you play your Store–bought songs on up to five computers at once. However, to prevent you from becoming a rampant music pirate, you must prove your honesty by *authorizing* these five machines.

  You authorized your first machine when you signed up for an Apple Account for the iTunes store. To authorize a song to play on another computer, copy it over from the first machine. Then, in iTunes, select the song and click the ▶ button. Type your Apple Account user name and password in the box that appears. This second computer is now authorized to play that song—and any other songs you bought using the same Apple Account.

---

***Tip:*** Thinking of putting that older computer up for sale? Before you wipe the drive clean and send it on its way, be sure to deauthorize it (choose Advanced→Deauthorize Computer), so that you're not wasting one of your five "authorized computer" slots. Erasing a hard drive, by itself, does not deauthorize a computer.

---

- **Maximum of 10 CDs per playlist.** You can also burn purchased tracks to blank CDs, so you can listen to them in the car or the big stereo rack in the living room. Here's another tiny form of copy protection: If you've added store-bought songs to a given playlist, you can't burn more than ten CD copies of it in a row without making at least one change to that list. Changing the song order slightly will do.

Music publisher EMI now offers its songs without any copy protection (at $1.30 instead of $1.00); Apple hopes to score similar deals with other record companies. Well, we can dream, can't we?

## Playing Music

To turn your Mac into a music player, click iTunes' Play button (▶) or press the Space bar. The Mac immediately begins to play the songs whose names have checkmarks in the main list (Figure 9-15), or the CD that's currently in your Mac.

---

***Tip:*** The central display at the top of the window shows not only the name of the song and album, but also where you are in the song, as represented by the diamond in the horizontal strip. Drag this diamond, or click elsewhere in the strip, to jump around in the song.

To view the current music's sound levels, click the tiny triangle at the left side of this display to see a pulsing VU meter, indicating the various frequencies.

---

## Playing with Playback

As music plays, you can control and manipulate the music and the visuals of your Mac in all kinds of interesting ways. Some people don't move from their Macs for months at a time.

### Turning on visuals

*Visuals* are onscreen light shows that pulse, beat, and dance in sync to the music. The effect is hypnotic and wild. (For real party fun, invite some people who grew up in the Sixties to your house to watch.)

To summon this psychedelic display, choose View→Turn On Visuals, or just press ⌘-T. The show begins immediately—although it's much more fun if you choose View→Full Screen (⌘-F) so the show takes over your whole monitor. True, you won't get a lot of work done, but when it comes to stress relief, visuals are a lot cheaper than a hot tub.

### Keyboard control

You can control iTunes' music playback using its menus, of course, but the keyboard can be far more efficient. Here are a few of the control keystrokes worth noting:

| Function | Keystroke |
|---|---|
| Play, Pause | Space bar |
| Next song/previous song | right arrow, left arrow |
| Next source/previous source | down arrow, up arrow |
| Louder | ⌘-up arrow |
| Quieter | ⌘-down arrow |
| Mute | Option-⌘-M |
| Fast-forward, rewind | Option-⌘-right arrow, -left arrow |
| Eject | ⌘-E |
| Turn Visuals on | ⌘-T |
| Turn Visuals off | ⌘-T or mouse click |
| Full-screen visuals | ⌘-F |
| Exit full-screen visuals | ⌘-T, ⌘-F, Esc, or mouse click |

*Tip:* You can also control CD playback from the Dock. right-click the iTunes icon (or click and hold on it) to produce a pop-up menu offering playback commands like Pause, Next Song, and Previous Song, along with a display that identifies the song currently being played.

### Playing with the graphic equalizer

If you choose Window→Equalizer, you get a handsome control console that lets you adjust the strength of each musical frequency independently.

### Preventing ear-blast syndrome

Here's a clever touch: In the iTunes→Preferences dialog box, if you click the Playback icon, you see a checkbox called Sound Check. Its function is to keep the playback volume of all songs within the same basic level, so that you don't have to adjust the volume to compensate for different recorded levels. (This setting, too, gets transferred to your iPod or iPhone.)

Come to think of it, you could wile away quite a few happy afternoons just poking through the Preferences dialog box. It grows richer with every successive version of iTunes.

## Copying (Ripping) CD Songs to Your Hard Drive

iTunes lets you convert your favorite songs from audio CDs into files on your hard drive. Once they've been transferred to your Mac, you can play them whenever you like, without needing the original CD.

To *rip* a CD (as aficionados would say) to your hard drive, make sure that only the songs you want to capture have checkmarks in the main list. Choose a format for the files you're about to create using the pop-up menu on the iTunes→Preferences→Advanced→Importing tab. Then click the Import CD button at the lower-right corner of the window (see Figure 9-16).

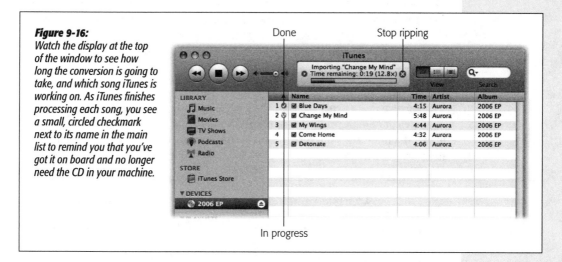

**Figure 9-16:**
*Watch the display at the top of the window to see how long the conversion is going to take, and which song iTunes is working on. As iTunes finishes processing each song, you see a small, circled checkmark next to its name in the main list to remind you that you've got it on board and no longer need the CD in your machine.*

When it's all over, you'll find the imported songs listed in your Library. (Click the Library icon in the left-side Source list.) From there, you can drag them into any other "folder" (playlist), as described next.

## Playlists—and Smart Playlists

When you click the Music icon in the left-side Source list, the main part of the screen displays every music file iTunes knows about (and even every QuickTime movie file; iTunes will play back soundtracks). It's organized much like a Finder window, with columns indicating the song length, singer or band, album, and so on. As always, you can rearrange these columns by dragging their headings, sort your list by one of these criteria by clicking its heading, reverse the sorting order by clicking the heading a second time, and so on. To find a particular song, just type a few letters into the Spotlight-ish Search blank above the list. iTunes hides all but the ones that match.

Apple recognizes that you may not want to listen to *all* your songs every time you need some tunes. That's why iTunes lets you create *playlists*—folders in the Source list that contain only certain songs. In effect, you can devise your own albums, like one called Party Tunes, another called Blind Date Music, and so on.

### Creating playlists

To create a new playlist, click the + button in the lower-left corner of the window, or choose File→New Playlist (⌘-N). Alternatively, if you've already highlighted certain songs—by ⌘-clicking them or Shift-clicking them—you can choose File→New Playlist From Selection.

A new playlist appears as an icon in the Source list. You can rename one by double-clicking it, and add songs to one by dragging them out of the main list.

---

**Tip:** Deleting a song from a playlist doesn't delete it from the Library (or your hard drive). Similarly, it's fine to add the same song to as many different playlists as you like, since you're not actually increasing the size of your Library. (You might be starting to pick up a running theme in Apple's software. Playlists work just like albums in iPhoto, or the Sidebar in the Finder.)

---

### Playing with criteria

*Smart playlists* constantly rebuild themselves according to criteria you specify. You might tell one smart playlist to assemble 45 minutes' worth of songs that you've rated higher than four stars but rarely listen to, and another to list your most-often-played songs from the Eighties.

**Figure 9-17:**
A Smart Playlist is a powerful search command for your iTunes database. You can set up certain criteria, like the hunt for particular Beatles tunes illustrated here. The "Live updating" checkbox makes iTunes keep this playlist updated as your collection changes, as you change your ratings, as your Play Count changes, and so on.

*Tip:* To rate a song, make the window wide enough that you can see the Rating column. (If you don't see this column, right-click any column heading and choose Rating from the list of options.) Then just click the Rating column for a selected song. The appropriate number of stars appears—one, two, three, four, or five—depending on the position of your click. You can change a song's rating as many times as you like—a good thing, considering the short shelf life of a pop hit these days.

To make a smart playlist, choose File→New Smart Playlist (Option-⌘-N)—or just Option-click the + button beneath the source list. The dialog box shown in Figure 9-17 appears. The controls here are designed to set up a search of your music database. Figure 9-17, for example, illustrates how you'd find up to 74 Beatles tunes released between 1965 and 1968—that you've rated three stars or higher and that you've listened to exactly twice.

When you click OK, your smart playlist is ready to show off. When you click its name in the Source list, the main song list updates itself according to your criteria and any changes in your music collection. (Smart playlists get transferred to your iPod or iPhone, but don't continue to update themselves there.)

## iTunes: Burning Music CDs

iTunes can record selected sets of songs, no matter what the original sources, onto a blank CD. When it's all over, you can play the burned CD on almost any standard CD player, just as you would a CD from the record store—but this time, you hear only the songs you like, in the order you like, with all of the annoying ones eliminated.

*Tip:* Use CD-R discs. CD-RW discs are not only more expensive, but may not work in standard CD players. (Not all players recognize CD-R discs either, but the odds are better.)

Start by creating a playlist for the CD you're about to make. Click its icon in the left-side Source list to see the list you've built. Drag songs up or down in the list to reflect their playback order. Keep these points in mind:

- The readout at the bottom of the list shows how much time the songs will take.

- About 74 or 80 minutes of AIFF audio files fit on one CD. But if you make an MP3 CD instead (choose iTunes→Preferences→Advanced→Burning tab, and then choose MP3 CD as the format), you can fit at least ten times as much. Note, though, that MP3 CDs don't play on all CD players—only those advertised with this feature. Also note that your MP3 CD can't include songs you've bought on Apple's iTunes music store; iTunes won't convert them into the non-copy-protected MP3 format.

- You can control how many seconds of silence iTunes leaves between tracks on your custom CD. Choose iTunes→Preferences→Advanced→Burning tab, and make a selection from the Gap Between Songs pop-up menu.

When everything is set up, click the Burn Disc button in the playlist window. Insert a blank CD into the Mac. The burning process takes some time. Feel free to work in other programs while iTunes chugs away.

# DVD Movies

Using DVD Player, Mac OS X's built-in DVD-playing software, your Mac can play Hollywood DVDs as though it was born to do so.

Watching movies on your Mac screen couldn't be simpler: Just insert the DVD. The Mac detects that it's a video DVD (as opposed to, say, one that's just filled with files) and, unless you've fiddled with your preference settings, opens the DVD Player program (Figure 9-18). (It can take awhile.)

If DVD Player doesn't start up automatically when you insert a DVD movie, you can open it yourself. It's sitting there in your Applications folder. (Then fix the problem, using the CDs & DVDs panel of System Preferences.)

## Playing a Movie

Once DVD Player starts playing your movie, you can use the "remote control," which is deconstructed in Figure 9-18. Or just use the keyboard controls:

- By far the easiest way to start and stop Playback is to press the Space bar—once to start, again to pause, again to start again.

**Figure 9-18:**
*Top: DVDs on your screen! Use your mouse to click the buttons, if you like; that's a lot more direct than having to use the arrow keys on a remote control.*

*Bottom: You can orient this controller either horizontally or vertically on your screen by choosing Controls→Use Vertical Controller. You can also do without this remote control altogether, since all of its buttons have keyboard equivalents.*

Slo Mo
Frame Advance
Return to Movie

Subtitles
Language
Angle

Previous chapter/Next chapter
(Hold to scan backward/forward)

- Press Shift-⌘-→ to fast-forward; press that combination repeatedly to cycle from twice to 4, 8, 16, or 32 times normal speed. (Or just choose a speed from the Controls→Scan Rate submenu.)

  Similarly, press Shift-⌘-← to scan backwards. Click Play (or press the Space bar) to resume normal playback.

- You can make the movie louder or quieter by repeatedly tapping ⌘-↑ or -↓. That's a good keystroke to remember when you've hidden the remote control itself.

Or, if you prefer a clip 'n' save cheat sheet of all the keystrokes, here it is:

| Function | Keystroke |
|---|---|
| Play, Pause | Space bar |
| Fast-forward | Shift-⌘-→ |
| Rewind | Shift-⌘-← |
| Skip back 5 seconds | Option-⌘-← |
| Skip forward 5 seconds | Option-⌘-→ |
| Louder | ⌘-↑ |
| Quieter | ⌘-↓ |
| Mute/Unmute | Option-⌘-↓ |
| Next/previous "chapter" | →, ← |
| Main menu | ⌘-~ (upper left of your keyboard) |
| Full-screen mode | ⌘-F |
| Half, normal, maximum size | ⌘-1, -2, -3 |
| Eject | ⌘-E |
| Show/hide remote control | Option-⌘-C |
| Add a bookmark | ⌘-= (equal sign) |

---

**FREQUENTLY ASKED QUESTION**

## Region Changing

*The first time I tried to play a DVD, I got this weird message about initializing the region code. What's up with that?*

Hollywood generally releases a movie in each part of the world at different times. A movie may come out on video in the U.S. when it's just hitting screens in Europe. We certainly can't have people watching a DVD before the movie studio says it's OK! That's why many discs are region-locked, so that they play back only on players in certain geographical regions.

As a DVD player in disguise, your Mac is just doing its duty. You can change its region (you'll be offered the chance to do so when you insert a region-locked DVD from another region), but only five times—and then it's frozen forever in

the fifth version.

The dialog box shows you which region your DVD is designed for: **1** for the U.S. and Canada; **2** for Japan, Europe, South Africa, and the Middle East; **3** for Southeast and East Asia; **4** for Australia, New Zealand, Pacific Islands, Central America, Mexico, South America, and the Caribbean; **5** for Eastern Europe, Africa, and North Korea; **6** for China; and **8** for airplanes, cruise ships, and so on. Any DVD that you burn yourself is assigned region **0**, meaning that it will play anywhere.

(There's no Region 7. Maybe it's reserved for the empty spot in movie executives' hearts.)

*Tip:* Isn't that cool how DVD Player automatically displays the subtitles for the dialog (if subtitles exist on the DVD) when you hit the Mute key?

## Full-Screen Playback

In Leopard, DVD movies begin playing back in in full-screen mode all by themselves (you no longer have to choose View→Enter Full Screen). Even the menu bar disappears. (To make it reappear, move your cursor near the top of the screen.)

As shown in Figure 11-19, though, a new suite of powerful navigation controls is still available, even in full-screen mode.

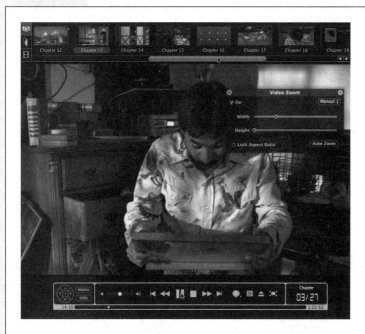

**Figure 9-19:**
*Even in full-screen mode, you can control the playback and navigate the disc using the new, translucent, pop-up control bars.*

*The chapter list appears when you move your cursor to the top of the screen. The "remote control" bar appears when the cursor approaches the bottom.*

*One especially cool feature is the new Player Settings button. It opens the Zoom controls window shown here, which gives you manual control over the width and height of the picture on your screen.*

*Don't miss the scrubber bar at the very bottom, either. It lets you scroll directly to any spot in the DVD.*

## Language Fun

Most Hollywood DVDs have been programmed with onscreen subtitles to help those with hearing impairments and people sitting in noisy bars. Click the Subtitle button (Figure 9-18) to turn on the subtitles, and click again to hide them. (You can specify the language you want—English subtitles, Spanish subtitles, or whatever the DVD offers—by clicking the same button repeatedly. Or choose DVD Player→Preferences, click the Disc Setup icon, and choose a language from the Subtitle pop-up menu.)

Meanwhile, each time you click the Audio button on the remote, the movie's soundtrack switches to a different language (if, in fact, alternate soundtrack languages have been provided). You'll see the name of each language appear briefly in the remote's "display." (You can also use the Audio button as a pop-up menu to choose the language you want directly.)

*Tip:* For real fun, turn on English subtitles but switch the soundtrack to a foreign language. No matter how trashy the movie you're watching, you'll gain much more respect from your friends and family when you tell them that you're watching a foreign film.

## The Big Picture

Now, watching a movie while sitting in front of your Mac is not exactly the great American movie-watching dream. Fortunately, every recent Mac model has a video-output jack; with the proper cables, you can connect the Mac to your TV for a much more comfortable movie-watching experience.

Just be sure to connect the cable *directly* to the TV. If you connect it to your VCR instead, you'll probably get a horrible, murky, color-shifting picture—the result of the built-in copy-protection circuitry of every VCR.

Or what the heck—just ask for an Apple TV for your birthday.

# Keyboard

As you know by now, switching to the Mac entails switching your brain, especially when it comes to the old keyboard shortcuts. All of those Ctrl-key sequences become, on the Mac, ⌘-key sequences. (Check your Macintosh keyboard: The ⌘ key is right next to the Space bar, usually on both sides.)

But plenty of other Mac keys may seem unfamiliar. For your reassurance pleasure, page 19 offers a rundown of what they do.

## Text-Navigation Keystrokes

In Windows, you may have grown accustomed to certain common keystrokes for navigating text—key combinations that make the insertion point jump to the beginning or end of a word, line, or document, for example.

Mac OS X programs offer similar navigation keystrokes, as you can see here:

| Function | Windows keys | Mac keys |
|---|---|---|
| Move to previous/next word | Ctrl+arrow keys | Option-arrow keys |
| Move to beginning/end of line | Home/End | Home/End* |
| Move to previous/next paragraph | Ctrl+up/down arrows* | Option-up/down arrows* |
| Move to top/bottom of window | Home/End | Home/End (but see below) |
| Select all text | Ctrl+A | ⌘-A |
| Select text, one letter at a time | Shift+arrow keys | Shift-arrow keys |
| Select text, one word at a time | Ctrl+Shift+arrow keys | Option-Shift-arrow keys |
| Undo | Ctrl+Z | ⌘-Z |
| Cut, Copy, Paste | Ctrl+X, C, P | ⌘-X, C, P |
| Close window | Alt+F4 | ⌘-W |

| | | |
|---|---|---|
| Switch open programs | Alt+Tab | ⌘-Tab |
| Hide all windows | ▨+D | F11 |

\* in some programs

Incidentally, the keystroke for jumping to the *top or bottom* of a window varies widely on the program. You need ⌘-Home/End in Microsoft Word, ⌘-up/down arrow in TextEdit and Stickies, and Home/End in iPhoto and Finder list windows.

As a consolation prize, though, here's a bit of good news: All *Cocoa* programs (page 141)—TextEdit, Stickies, iPhoto, iDVD, Safari, Keynote, iChat, iCal, Mail, Address Book, and so on—offer an amazing quantity of consistent, Unix-based navigation keystrokes that should last you the rest of your life. Here they are:

- **Control-A.** Moves your insertion point to the beginning of the paragraph. (*Mnemonic:* A = beginning of the alphabet.)

- **Control-E.** Deposits your insertion point at the end of the paragraph. (*Mnemonic:* E = *E*nd.)

- **Control-D.** Forward delete. Deletes the letter to the *right* of the insertion point.

- **Control-K.** Instantly deletes all text from the insertion point to the right end of the line. (*Mnemonic:* K = *K*ills the rest of the line.)

- **Control-O.** Inserts a paragraph break, much like Return, but leaves the insertion point where it was, above the break. This is the ideal trick for breaking a paragraph in half when you've just thought of a better ending for the first part.

- **Control-T.** Moves the insertion point one letter to the right—and along with it, drags whichever letter was to its left. (*Mnemonic:* T = *T*ranspose letters.)

- **Option-Delete.** Deletes the entire word to the left of the insertion point. When you're typing along in a hurry, and you discover that you've just made a typo, this is the keystroke you want. It's much faster to nuke the previous word and retype it than to fiddle around with the mouse and the insertion point just to fix one letter.

Four additional keystrokes duplicate the functions of the arrow keys. Still, as long as you've got your pinky on that Control key…

- **Control-B, Control-F.** Moves the insertion point one character to the left or right, just like the left and right arrow keys. (*Mnemonic:* *B*ack, *F*orward).

- **Control-N, Control-P.** Moves the insertion point one row down or up, like the down and up arrow keys. (*Mnemonic:* *N*ext, *P*revious).

## Mouse

Most USB mice work as soon as you plug them into your Mac—even two-button, scroll-wheel mice. Using System Preferences, you can even program your spare mouse buttons to invoke cool features like Exposé and the Dashboard.

That's not to say, however, that you shouldn't install your mouse's driver software. If your mouse *came* with such software (or if you find it on the manufacturer's Web site), you may well find that your mouse learns a few new tricks—making its "back" and "forward" buttons work properly in Safari, for example. Otherwise, a shareware program like USB Overdrive ($20, from *www.usboverdrive.com*) can unlock those features.

(For more on Mac mice, see page 13.)

# Monitors

Your Mac can use standard monitors of the type found in the Windows world. Every Macintosh can drive *multiple* screens at the same time, too, meaning that you can generally use your old PC screen either as your Mac's main monitor or as a second, external screen.

If one of those arrangements appeals to you, the only complication might be the connector. Most PC screens, of course, have a standard VGA connector (or a more modern DVI connector) at the tip of their tails. Your Mac may or may not have a place to plug in that VGA or DVI cable:

- iMacs, Mac laptops, and the Mac Mini come with a short adapter cable. One end clicks into the Mac; the other end mates with your monitor's VGA cable.

- If you have a Power Mac or Mac Pro, you may have both a proprietary Apple monitor connector *and* a VGA connector, or you may have at least one DVI connector. (If not, you can always buy a second graphics card.)

---

**Tip:** It's even possible to connect *both* your Mac and your PC to the *same* monitor, and switch from one to the other at will. If this arrangement appeals to you, you'll need a so-called KVM switch (which also lets you switch your keyboard and mouse between your two computers). You can find KVM switches for sale at electronics stores, and online from manufacturers like Belkin (*www.belkin.com*).

---

In any case, most recent Mac models let you choose either *mirror mode* (where both screens show the same thing—a handy setup in classroom situations) or *desktop extension mode* (where one screen acts as additional real estate, an annex to the first). You specify which mode you want using the Displays pane of System Preferences, or using the Displays menu-bar icon.

# Time Machine

As the old saying goes, there are two kinds of people: those who have a regular backup system—and those who *will*.

You'll get that grisly joke immediately if you've ever deleted the wrong folder by accident, made changes that you regret, or worst of all, had your hard drive die. All those photos, all that music you've bought online, all your email—gone.

Yet the odds are overwhelming that at this moment, you do not have a complete, current, automated backup of your Mac. Despite a thousand warnings, articles, and cautionary tales a year, guess how many do? About *four percent.* Everybody else is flying without a net.

If you don't have much to back up—you don't have much in the way of photos, music, or movies—you can get by with burning copies of stuff onto blank CDs or DVDs. But that method leaves most of your Mac unprotected: all your programs and settings, not to mention Mac OS X itself.

What you really want, of course, is a backup that's rock-solid, complete, and *automatic.* You don't want to have to remember to do a backup, to insert a tape, to find a cartridge. You just want to know that you're safe.

That's the idea behind Time Machine, a marquee feature of Leopard. It's a silent, set-it-and-forget-it piece of peace of mind. You sleep easy, knowing there's a safety copy of your *entire* system: your system files, programs, settings, music, pictures, videos, document files—*everything.*

Yes, Time Machine has a fabulous, gorgeous, sci-fi, space-themed recovery mode, where it looks like you're flying back in time to retrieve files, folders, or disks from the past. With luck, you'll never need it. But if your luck runs out, you'll be *so* happy you set Time Machine up.

**Figure 9-20:**
*Top: The Mac has just encountered a second hard drive. Time Machine still works if there's other stuff on the drive, but life is simpler if you don't use that drive for anything but Time Machine. The more space Time Machine has to work with, the farther back in time you'll be able to go to recover deleted or mangled files.*

*Bottom: The backup has begun. You know that because you see both a progress message and the ↻ symbol that appears next to the backup drive's name in your Sidebar.*

## Setting up Time Machine

Here's the bad news: Time Machine requires a second hard drive. That's the only way to create a completely safe, automatic backup of your *entire* main hard drive.

That second hard drive can take any of these forms:

- An external USB or FireWire hard drive.

- Another internal hard drive.

- A partition of any one of those drives.

- An Apple *Time Capsule*, which is a Wi-Fi base station and wireless network backup drive in one sleek little case.

- The hard drive of another Leopard Mac on the network. You must first mount its drive on your screen (Chapter 14).

---

**Tip:** It's perfectly OK to back up several Macs onto the same external hard drive, as long as it's got enough room. You can also back up onto a hard drive that has other stuff on it, although of course that means you'll have less room for Time Machine backups.

---

In all cases, the backup disk must be bigger than the drive you're backing up (preferably *much* bigger).

Here's what you *can't* use as the backup disk: iPods, iDisks, your startup disk, CDs, DVDs, flash drives, or any other kind of removable disk.

---

**Note:** If Time Machine doesn't recognize the drive you've given it, the drive might not be a standard Mac-formatted hard drive. That's a gotcha that befalls many a Mac fan who buys a new hard drive for backup purposes; many new drives come in Windows's format, which Time Machine doesn't recognize.

To make a new, empty drive like this ready for Time Machine, open Disk Utility (page 520). Click the drive's name, click the Erase tab, choose "Mac OS Extended (Journaled)" from the Volume Format pop-up menu, and then click Erase.

---

Sure, it sounds like an Apple plot to sell more hard drives. But you'd be surprised at how cheap hard drives are. At this writing, you can buy a 300-gigabyte internal hard drive for under $80, for goodness' sake, or an external 500-gig drive for $120—and hard drive prices-per-gigabyte only go down.

The first time the Mac sees your second hard drive, it invites you to use it as Time Machine's backup drive (Figure 9-20, top). That could be the moment you connect an external USB or FireWire drive, or the first time you turn on the Mac after installing an internal drive.

If you click Use as Backup Disk, you're taken immediately to the Time Machine pane of System Preferences (Figure 9-21, bottom). It shows that Time Machine is now on, your backup disk has been selected, and the copying process has begun. The Mac copies *everything* on your hard drive, including Mac OS X itself, all your programs, and everyone's Home folders.

---

**Note:** Time Machine doesn't use any compression or encoding; it's copying your files exactly as they sit on your hard drive, for maximum safety and recoverability. On the other hand, it does save *some* space on the backup drive, because it doesn't bother copying cache files, temporary files, and other files you'll never need to restore.

---

Your total involvement has been *one click*. And that, ladies and gentlemen, is the easiest setup for a backup program in history.

Now go away and let the Mac do its thing. The first backup can take a *very* long time—hours—as the Mac duplicates your entire internal hard drive onto the second drive. The Mac may feel drugged during this time.

## How the Backups Work

From now on, Time Machine quietly and automatically checks your Mac once per hour. If any file, folder, or setting changes, it gets backed up at the end of the hour. These follow-up backups, of course, take very little time, since Time Machine backs up only what's changed.

So, should disaster strike, the only files you can lose are those that you've changed within the last 59 minutes.

---

**FREQUENTLY ASKED QUESTION**

### The End of Time

*What happens when my backup drive gets full?*

Good question.

The whole idea of Time Machine is that it preserves multiple backups, so that you can rewind a window or a drive not just to *a* backup, but to *any* date in the past. The bigger the hard drive, the farther back those monthly backups are preserved.

Eventually, of course, your backup drive runs out of space. At that point, Time Machine notifies you and offers you a choice.

You can keep using that drive; Time Machine will begin

deleting the oldest backups to make room for newer ones.

Or you can install a new Time Machine backup drive. New backups will go on that one; your older backups will still be available on the original drive.

If you ever need to retrieve files or folders from the older disk, right-click the Time Machine icon in the Dock; from the shortcut menu, choose Browse Other Time Machine Disks. In the list of disks, choose the older one. Then click the Time Machine icon on the Dock to enter the Restore mode.

---

*Tip:* And even then, you can *force* more frequent backups if you want to. Any time you want Time Machine to update its backup before the hour's up, right-click Time Machine's icon on the Dock. From the shortcut menu, choose Back Up Now.

You can pause the backup the same way—if you need to use the backup drive for another quick task, for example. Right-click the Dock icon and then choose Stop Backing Up. (Don't forget to turn the backing-up on again when you're finished.)

---

## Declaring Stuff Off-Limits to Time Machine

The whole point of Time Machine, of course, is to have a backup of your *entire* hard drive. That's how most people use it.

It's conceivable, though, that you might want to exclude some files or folders from the Time Machine treatment. There are two reasons.

First, you might not want certain, ahem, *private* materials to be part of your incriminating data trail.

Second, you might want to save space on the backup drive, either because it's not as big as your main drive or because you'd rather dedicate its space to *more* backups of the *essential* stuff. For example, you might decide not to back up your collection of downloaded TV shows, since video files are enormous. Or maybe you use an online photosharing Web site as a backup for all your photos, so you don't think it's necessary to include those in the Time Machine backup.

To eliminate certain icons from the backup, open the Time Machine panel of System Preferences. Click Options.

In the resulting list, click the + button; navigate your hard drive, and then select the files or folders you don't want backed up. Or just find their actual icons in the Finder and *drag* them into the list here. (Use the – button to *remove* items from the list, thereby excluding them from the excluded list.)

If you're strapped for disk space, one logical candidate to exclude is the System folder on your main hard drive—that is, Mac OS X itself. After all, if you lose your hard drive, you already *have* a copy of Mac OS X: the original installation DVD. (Of course, it doesn't have all the Apple updates that may have come out since the original version.)

When you add the System folder to the exclusion list, Time Machine makes another space-saving offer: "Would you like to also exclude other files installed with Mac OS X, such as system applications and UNIX tools?"

Agreeing (by clicking Exclude All System Files) saves you another several gigabytes of backup space.

**Do not back up:**

| | |
|---|---|
| 📄 500–Gigger | 89.8 GB |
| 📁 Applications | 7.1 GB |
| 📁 Final Cut Pro Documents | 2.9 GB |
| 📁 System Files and Applications | 10.0 GB |
| 📁 Virtual Machines | 8.5 GB |

Total Included: Calculating Size

☐ Warn when old backups are deleted

Cancel    Done

**You've chosen to exclude the System folder.**

Would you like to also exclude other files installed with Mac OS X, such as system applications and UNIX tools?

Exclude System Folder Only    Exclude All System Files

---

By the end of the day, you'll have 24 hourly backups on that second disk, all taking up space. So at day's end, Time Machine replaces that huge stash with a single *daily* backup. You can no longer rewind your system to 3:00 p.m. last Monday, but you can rewind to the way it was at the *end* of that day.

Similarly, after a week, the dailies are replaced by an end-of-week backup; after a month, the weeklies are replaced by a single end-of-the-month backup. Now you can't rewind to October 24, but you can rewind to November 1. (Apple assumes that it won't take you a whole month to notice that your hard drive has crashed.)

*Tip:* You can see these backups, if you want. Open your backup drive, open the Backups.backupdb folder, and open the folder named for your computer. Inside, you'll find a huge list of backup folders, bearing names like 2007-12-22-155831. That's the backup from December 22, 2007 at 15:58 (that is, 3:58 p.m.) and 31 seconds.

The point is that Time Machine doesn't just keep *one* copy of your stuff. It keeps *multiple* backups. It remembers how things were in every folder—not just yesterday, but last week, last month, and so on. It keeps on making new snapshots of your hard drive until the backup drive is full.

At that point, the oldest ones get deleted to make room for new ones.

*Tip:* Ordinarily, Time Machine alerts you when it has to start deleting old backups. If you'd rather have it just do it without bothering you, open System Preferences; click Time Machine; click Options; and finally turn off "Warn when old backups are deleted."

**Figure 9-21:**
*Use the big On/Off switch to shut off all Time Machine activity, although it would be hard to imagine why you'd want to risk it. You can click Choose Backup Disk to choose a different hard drive to represent the mirror of your main drive (after the first one is full, for example).*

By the way, if a backup is interrupted—if you shut down the Mac, put it to sleep, or take your laptop on the road—no big deal. Time Machine resumes automatically the next time you're home and connected.

## Changing Time Machine Settings

Time Machine has three faces in Leopard. There's the application itself, which sits in your Applications folder; click it to enter Restore mode. There's its Dock icon; its shortcut menu has a few commands (like Back Up Now) that aren't available anywhere else.

And then there's its System Preferences pane, where you adjust its settings (Figure 9-21). To see it, choose  →System Preferences, and then click Time Machine. Or choose Time Machine Preferences from Time Machine's Dock icon.

---

**Tip:** If your information is especially important, or if you're especially paranoid, you can rotate among *more than one* backup hard drive. Keep one offsite so you won't be hosed in case of fire, flood, or burglary.

---

## Recovering Lost or Changed Files

All right, you've got Time Machine on the job. You sleep easy at night, confident that your life's in order—and your stuff's backed up.

Then, one day, it happens: Your hard drive crashes. Or you can't find a file or folder you know you had. Or you save a document and then wish you could go back to an earlier draft. Some kind of disaster—sunspots, clueless spouse, overtired self—has befallen your files.

This is Time Machine's big moment.

Start by pinpointing what you're looking for, in one of these two ways:

- Open the disk or folder window where the missing or changed item was.

- Type what you're looking for into the Search box at the top of any Finder window. Click the location button that makes the most sense: "This Mac" or the name of the window you're in.

  In the case of deleted files or folders, the search will probably come up empty; that's totally OK.

Now click the Time Machine icon on the Dock (or in the Applications folder). Don't look away; you'll miss the show.

Your Leopard desktop *slides down the screen* like a curtain that's been dropped from above. And it reveals…outer space. This is it, the ultimate Apple eye candy: an animated starry universe, with bits of stardust and meteors occasionally flying outward from the massive nebula at the center.

Front and center is your Finder window—or, rather, dozens of it, stretching back in time (Figure 9-22). Each is a snapshot of that window at the time of a Time Machine backup.

You have four ways to peruse your backup universe:

- Click individual windows to see what's in them.

- Drag your cursor through the timeline at the right side. It's like a master dial that flies through the windows into the past.

**Figure 9-22:**
*This is the big payoff for all your efforts.*

*Top: The familiar desktop slides down, dropping away like a curtain. For the first time, you get to see what's been behind the desktop all this time. Turns out it's outer space.*

*Bottom: Time Machine shows you dozens of copies of the Finder window, representing its condition at each backup, stretching back to the past.*

- Click one of the two big, flat, perspective arrows. The one pointing into the past means "Jump directly to the most recent window version that's *different* from the way it is right now."

In other words, it's often a waste of time to go flipping through the windows one at a time, because your missing or changed file might have been missing or changed for the last 25 backups (or whatever). What you want to know is the last time the contents of this window *changed*. And that's what the big flat arrows do. They jump from one *changed* version of this window to another. (Or, if you began with a search, the arrow takes you to the most recent version backup with a matching result.)

- Use the Search box in the corner of the window. You can search for whatever you're missing in the current backup.

As you go, the very bottom of the screen identifies where you are in time—that is, which backup you're examining.

In many ways, the recovery mode is just like the Finder. You can't actually open, edit, rename, or reorganize anything here. But you can use Quick Look (page 57) to inspect the documents, to make sure you've got the right version. And you can use icon, list, or Cover Flow view, as well as column view, to sort through the files you're seeing.

If you're trying to recover an older *version* of a file or folder, highlight it, and then click the flat arrow button that's pointing away from you; Time Machine skips back to the most recent version that's *different* from the current one.

If you're trying to restore a deleted file or folder that you've now located, highlight it, and then click Restore (lower-right). The Leopard desktop rises again from the bottom of the screen, there's a moment of copying, and then presto: The lost file or folder is back in the window where it once belonged.

---

**Note:** Time Machine prides itself not just on recovering files and folders, but also on putting them back where they belonged.

If you recover a different version of something that's *still there,* Mac OS X asks if you want to replace it with the recovered version.

And if you're recovering a document whose original folder no longer exists, Time Machine automatically recreates the folder so that the recovered item feels at home.

---

### Recovering from iPhoto, Address Book, and Mail
It turns out that the Finder isn't the only program that's hooked into Time Machine's magic. iPhoto '08, Address Book, and Mail work with Time Machine, too. Other software companies can also revise their own applications to work with it.

In other words, if you want to recover certain photos, addresses, or email messages that have been deleted, you don't start in the Finder; you start in iPhoto, Address Book, or Mail.

Then click the Time Machine icon on the Dock. Once again, you enter the starry recovery mode—but this time, you're facing a strange, disembodied, stripped-down copy of iPhoto, Address Book, or Mail (Figure 9-23).

*Tip:* Alternatively, in iPhoto, you can also choose File→Browse Backups to enter recovery mode.

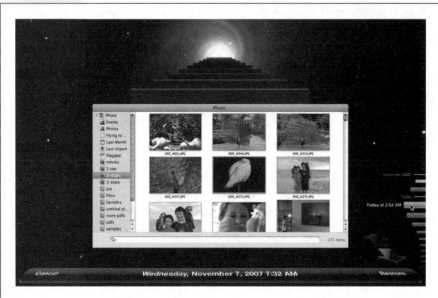

**Figure 9-23:**
*The Time Machine version of iPhoto is a weird, simplified, viewing-only version. You can't do much here besides browse your backups—but when you're in dire straits, that's enough.*

You're ready to find your missing data. Click the Jump Back arrow to open the most recent version of your photo library, address book file, or email stash that's different from what you've got now. (You can also use the timeline on the right if you remember the date when things went wrong.)

*Tip:* If you're looking for something particular, specify that before you start clicking. For example, select the iPhoto event or album first, or type a name into the Address Book search box.

At this point, you can select individual photos (or albums, or events), address book entries, or email messages to restore; just click the Restore button.

Often, though, you'd rather reinstate the *entire* iPhoto library, Address Book file, or email collection from the backup. That's what the Restore All button is for.

If you click it, the experience is slightly different. iPhoto asks if you're sure you want to replace your iPhoto library. Address Book may discover a lot of duplicate name-and-address entries, and invite you to step through them, deciding which one "wins" (the old or the new).

**Note:** When you finish restoring in Mail, you'll find the restored messages in the On My Mac→Time Machine→Recovered folder at the left side of the window.

### Recovering the entire hard drive

Every hard drive will die at some point. You just hope it won't happen while *you* own the computer.

But the great gods of technology have a mean-spirited sense of humor, and hard drives do die. But you, as a Time Machine aficionado, won't care. You'll just repair or replace the hard drive, and then do this:

1. **Connect the Time Machine backup disk to the Mac. Insert the Leopard installation DVD. Double-click the Install Mac OS X icon.**

   The Mac OS X installer opens up as though it's going to lead you through the process of putting Leopard on the new, empty hard drive. But don't fall for it.

2. **At the Welcome screen, choose Utilities→Restore System from Backup.**

   The Restore Your System dialog box appears.

3. **Click Continue. Click your Time Machine backup disk. In the list of backups, click the most recent one.**

   The installer goes about copying *everything* from the backup disk onto your new empty hard drive. When it's all over, you'll have a perfect working system, just the way it was before your series of unfortunate events.

### Recovering to another Mac

Weirdly enough, you can also use Time Machine as a glorified data bucket that carries your world from one computer to another. You can bring over some or part of any Time Machine backup to a totally different Mac.

On the new machine, connect your backup disk. In the Applications→Utilities folder, open the program called Migration Assistant. On the first screen, click "From a Time Machine backup." The subsequent screens invite you to choose which backup, which Home folder, and which elements (applications, settings, files) you want to bring over. (You can use the Leopard installation DVD for this purpose, too, as described above.)

## Frequently Asked Questions

Time Machine is a very different kind of backup program, and a real departure for longtime Mac addicts. A few questions, therefore, are bound to come up—like these.

• **Can I back up more than one Mac onto the same disk?** Yes. Each Mac's backup is stored in a separate folder on that disk.

- **Does the backup disk have to be dedicated to Time Machine?** No. It can have other files and folders on it. Of course, the more space is available, the farther back your backup trail can go.

- **Can I use more than one backup disk—like one at the office and one at home?** Yes. Just use the Time Machine panel of System Preferences (or the Time Machine Dock icon's shortcut menu) to select the new backup drive each time you switch.

- **Can I delete something for good, from all the backups at once?** Yes. Click the Time Machine icon on the Dock to enter the Restore (outer-space) mode. Find and select the file or folder you want to obliterate. From the ✿ menu, choose Delete From All Backups. (Sneaky, huh? That command is never in the ✿ menu *except* when you're in Time Machine restoring mode.)

- **Can Time Machine back up other hard drives besides the main internal one?** Yes. Open System Preferences→Time Machine. Click Options. Your secondary drives are listed here on the excluded-items list. If you want them backed up too, *remove* them from the list (click the drive name and then click the – button.)

- **Anything else you want to get off your chest?** Yes. Time Machine has trouble with three kinds of files:

**Figure 9-24:**
*To set up .Mac sync, open System Preferences. Click .Mac, and then click the Sync tab. Turn on the checkboxes for the information you want synchronized. Use the pop-up menu at the top to set up an automatic sync schedule. While you're at it, turn on "Show status in menu bar," so you'll be able to start or stop the syncing manually, too.*

First, FileVault (page 405). If you've encrypted your Home folder using FileVault, Time Machine can back up only your Home folder *only* when you've logged out. And when things go wrong, it can recover only your *entire* Home folder (not individual files or folders). It scarcely seems worth the trouble.

Second, Aperture. Turn off Time Machine backing-up while you're working in Aperture, Apple's professional photo-organizing program.

Finally, remember that Time Machine backs up *entire* files at a time—not pieces of files. If you edit huge, multigigabyte files like video files, therefore, keep in mind that each giant file gets recopied to the backup drive every time you change it. That is, one 2-gig video file that you work on all day could wind up occupying 48 gigabytes on the backup drive by the end of the day. Consider adding these files to the exclusion list, as described above.

**Figure 9-25:**
*This message lets you decide how to proceed when data on one of the synced Macs is wildly out of sync with what's been "published" by another Mac. You can merge the information from the two (a great way to combine address books or calendars), make this Mac's data wipe out the other's ("Replace data on .Mac"), or make the Internet-based data replace this computer's ("Replace data on computer").*

*You can do this job en masse (top)—or, if you click Options, you can make this choice independently for each data type.*

# .Mac Sync

If you're paying $100 a year for a .Mac account (page 295), Mac OS X has a real surprise in store. In System Preferences, a humble preference pane called .Mac lets you set up automatic syncing between Macs, using the Internet as a conduit to transfer data tidbits like these:

- **Safari Bookmarks.** If a Web site is important enough to merit bookmarking while you're using your laptop, why shouldn't it also show up in the Bookmarks menu on your desktop Mac at home?

- **Calendars, Contacts.** This is a big one. There's nothing as exasperating as realizing that the address book you're consulting on your home Mac is missing somebody you're *sure* you entered—on your Mac at work. This option keeps all your Macs' Address Books and iCal calendars synchronized. Delete a phone number at work, and you'll find it deleted on your Mac at home, too.

- **Dashboard Widgets.** Now the configuration and setup of your widgets on Mac A are synced to Macs B, C, and D, so they all match.

- **Keychains.** In other words, your passwords. All your Macs can have the same passwords memorized. Worth its weight in gold.

- **Mail Accounts, Rules, Signatures, and Smart Mailboxes.** These refer to your account settings and preferences from Mac OS X's Mail programs, not the email messages themselves.

- **Notes.** This option refers to the notes you enter in the Mail Notes feature (Chapter 11). How great to make a reminder for yourself on one Mac, and to have it reminding you later on another one. (If you have Microsoft Office, you'll see an Entourage Notes option here, too.)

- **Preferences.** All your System Preferences settings.

To set up .Mac syncing, turn on the checkboxes for the items you want synced, as shown in Figure 9-24.

After the first sync, you can turn on the checkboxes on the other Macs, too, in effect telling them to participate in the great data-sharing experiment.

The first time they try, they may get confused. "Hold on. *My* address book is empty, but the one I'm downloading from the Internet (from the other Mac) is loaded. Who wins?" You get the dialog box shown in Figure 9-25, which lets you decide how to proceed.

# Part Three:
# The Mac Online

**Chapter 10: Internet Setup**

**Chapter 11: Mail & Address Book**

**Chapter 12: Safari & iChat**

*3*

# Internet Setup

M illions of people still connect to the Internet using a modem that dials out over ordinary phone lines. But the balance is rapidly tipping in favor of people connecting over higher-speed wires, using so-called *broadband* connections that are always on: cable modems, DSL, or corporate networks. This chapter explains how to set up each one (and how to use each with a wireless AirPort system).

## Network Central—and Multihoming

In this chapter, you'll be spending a lot of time in the Network pane of System Preferences (Figure 10-1). (Choose  →System Preferences; click Network.) This list summarizes the ways your Mac can connect to the Internet or an office network—Ethernet, AirPort wireless, Bluetooth, FireWire, cellular modem card, and so on—and how each connection is doing.

### Multihoming

What you may not realize is that the *order* of the network connections listed here is important. That's the sequence the Mac uses as it tries to get online. If one of your programs needs Internet access, and the first method isn't hooked up, the Mac switches to the next available connection automatically.

In fact, Mac OS X can maintain *multiple simultaneous* network connections—Ethernet, AirPort, dial-up, even FireWire—a feature known as *multihoming*.

This feature is especially relevant for laptops. When you open your Web browser, your laptop might first check to see if it's at the office, plugged into a cable modem via an Ethernet cable, which is the fastest, most secure type of connection. If there's no

Ethernet, it looks for an AirPort network. Finally, if it draws a blank there, the laptop reluctantly dials the modem. It may not be the fastest Internet connection, but it's all you've got at the moment.

Here's how to go about setting up the connection attempt sequence you want:

1. **Open System Preferences. Click the Network icon.**

   The Network Status screen (Figure 10-1) brings home the point of multihoming: You can have more than one network connection operating at once.

**Figure 10-1:**
*The network connections listed here are tagged with color-coded dots. A green dot means turned on and connected to a network; yellow means working, but not connected at the moment; red means you haven't yet set up a connection method.*

2. **From the ✿ pop-up menu, choose Set Service Order.**

   Now you see the display shown in Figure 10-2. It lists all the different ways your Mac knows how to get online, or onto an office network.

3. **Drag the items up and down in the list into priority order.**

   If you have a wired broadband connection, for example, you might want to drag Built-in Ethernet to the top of the list, since that's almost always the fastest way to get online.

4. **Click OK.**

You return to the Network pane of System Preferences, where the master list of connections magically re-sorts itself to match your efforts.

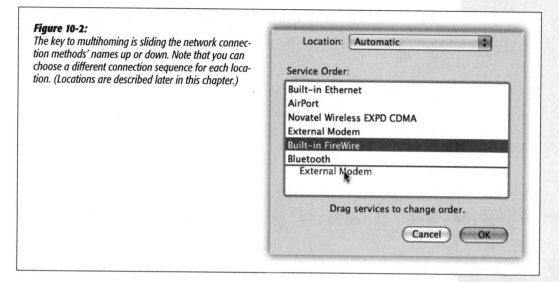

**Figure 10-2:**
*The key to multihoming is sliding the network connection methods' names up or down. Note that you can choose a different connection sequence for each location. (Locations are described later in this chapter.)*

Your Mac will now be able to switch connections even in real time, during a single Internet session. If lightning takes out your Ethernet hub in the middle of your Web surfing, your Mac will seamlessly switch to your AirPort network, for example, to keep your session alive.

All right then: Your paperwork is complete. The following pages guide you through the process of setting up these various connections.

# Broadband Connections

If your Mac is connected wirelessly or, um, *wirefully* to a cable modem, DSL, or office network, you're one of the lucky ones. You have a high-speed broadband connection to the Internet that's always available, always on. You never have to wait to dial, disconnect, or download. You're connected to the Net via your Mac's Ethernet jack or AirPort antenna, leaving the dial-up era behind.

## Automatic Configuration

The real beauty of most broadband connections these days is that they require *no setup whatsoever*. Take a new Mac out of the box, plug in the Ethernet cable to your cable modem (or choose a wireless network from the 🛜 menulet), and you can begin surfing the Web instantly.

That's because most cable modems, DSL boxes, and wireless base stations automatically feed all of the necessary configuration settings to the Mac (including techie specs like

IP address and DNS Server addresses), courtesy of a glorious feature called *DHCP*. This acronym means *dynamic host configuration protocol*, which is tech-ese for: "We'll fill in your Network pane of System Preferences automatically."

## Manual Configuration

If, for some reason, you're not able to surf the Web or check email the first time you try, it's conceivable that your broadband modem or your office network *doesn't* offer DHCP. In that case, you may have to fiddle with the Network pane of System Preferences, preferably with a customer-support rep from your broadband provider on the phone.

On the Network pane, click either AirPort or Built-in Ethernet, depending on how your Mac is connected to the broadband modem. Now you see something like Figure 10-3.

**Figure 10-3:**
*Don't be alarmed by the morass of numbers and periods—it's all in good fun. (If you find TCP/IP fun, that is.)*

In this illustration, you see the setup for a cable-modem account with a static IP address, which means you have to type in all of these numbers yourself, as guided by the cable company. The alternative is a DHCP server account, which fills most of it in automatically.

## Ethernet Connections

The beauty of Ethernet connections is that they're super-fast and super-secure. No bad guys sitting across the coffee shop, armed with shareware "sniffing" software, can intercept your email and chat messages, as they theoretically can when you're on wireless.

As shown in Figure 10-3, clicking the name of an Ethernet connection in the Network pane reveals the geeky settings required for a manual Ethernet setup.

For most people, the correct setting in the Configure pop-up menu is "Using DHCP," which means "Mac OS X fills in the correct settings for you."

If, in the unusual circumstance that you can't get online with "Using DHCP," then you'll have to fill in this control panel manually. You'll have to fill in all the boxes here—Subnet Mask, Router, and so on—with cryptic numbers separated by periods.

To get this information, you can call your Internet provider (cable or TV company) for help—or you can copy your Windows configuration onto the Mac, like this:

### Settings from Windows XP, Windows 2000

If you have Windows XP, choose Start→Control Panel. Open Network Connections. If you have Windows 2000, choose Start→Settings→Network and Dial-up Connections.

Either way, continue by right-clicking the icon for your broadband connection and, from the shortcut menu, choose Properties. Double-click the row that says "Internet Protocol (TCP/IP)."

**Figure 10-4:**
Don't be alarmed by all the numbers and periods—it's all in good fun. (If you find TCP/IP fun, that is.) Here, you see the setup for a cable-modem account with a static IP address, which means you have to type in these numbers yourself, as guided by the cable company.

If the resulting screen says "Obtain an IP address automatically" (see Figure 10-4), then leave "Using DHCP" selected in the Mac's Configure pop-up menu; your Mac should teach itself the correct settings automatically.

If the Windows screen says, "Use the following IP address" instead, select Manually from the Mac's Configure pop-up menu, and copy the relevant numbers into the Mac's Network panel like this (see Figure 10-4).

Similarly, if the Internet Protocol (TCP/IP Properties) dialog box says, "Use the following DNS server addresses," type the numbers from the "Preferred DNS server" and "Alternate DNS server" boxes into the Mac's DNS Servers text box. (Press Return to make a new line for the second number.)

---

**Note:** If your Mac plugs directly into the cable modem (that is, you don't use a router), you'll have to turn the cable modem or DSL box off and then on again when you've switched from the PC to the Mac.

---

### Settings from Windows 98, Windows Me

Choose Start→Settings→Control Panel. In the Control Panel window, double-click Network. Double-click the TCP/IP row that identifies how your PC is connected to the broadband modem. (It may say "TCP/IP→3Com Ethernet Adapter," for example.)

Click the IP Address tab. If it says "Specify an IP address," copy the IP Address and Subnet Mask numbers into the same ones on the Mac's Network panel. Then click the Gateway tab, and copy the "Installed gateway" number into the Mac's Router box.

Finally, click the DNS Configuration tab. Copy the strings of numbers you see here into the Mac's DNS Servers text box. (Press Return to make a new line for the second number, if necessary.)

### Applying the Settings

That's all the setup—click Apply. If your settings are correct, you're online, now and forever. You never have to worry about connecting or disconnecting.

## AirPort (Wi-Fi) Connections

*AirPort* is Apple's term for the 802.11 (Wi-Fi) wireless networking technology. If you have it, your Mac can communicate with a wireless base station up to 300 feet away, much like a cordless phone. Doing so lets you surf the Web from your laptop in the hotel room, for example, or share files with someone across the building from you.

Sometimes you just want to join a friend's Wi-Fi network. Sometimes you've got time to kill in an airport, and it's worth a $7 splurge for half an hour. And sometimes, at some street corners in big cities, Wi-Fi signals bleeding out of apartment buildings might give you a choice of 20 or 30 free hot spots to join.

---

**Note:** Not all attempts to join Wi-Fi hot spots are successful, even the unlocked ones. Sometimes the signal is strong enough to make the hot spot's name show up in your 🛜 menu, but not enough for an actual connection. Sometimes, for security, hot spots are rigged to permit only *specific* computers to join, and yours isn't one of them. And sometimes wireless routers are broadcasting, but their Internet connection is down.

---

Either way, your Mac joins Wi-Fi hot spots like this:

- First, it sniffs around for a Wi-Fi network that you've used before. If it finds one, it connects automatically. You're not asked for a password or anything else; you're just online. For details, see the box on page 286.

- If the Mac can't find a previous hot spot, but it detects a new hot spot or two, a message appears on the screen (Figure 10-5), displaying their names. Double-click one to connect.

- If you missed the opportunity to join a hot spot when the message appeared, or if you joined the wrong one or a non-working one, then you have another chance. You can always choose a hot spot's name from the 🛜 menulet, as shown in Figure 10-5 at bottom. A 🔒 icon indicates a hot spot that requires a password.

---

**Tip:** If you don't *want* your Mac to keep interrupting you with its discoveries of new hot spots—it can get pretty annoying when you're in a taxi driving through a city—you can shut them off. In System Preferences, click Network, click AirPort, and then turn off "Ask to join new networks."

---

**Figure 10-5:**
*Left: Congratulations—your Mac has discovered new Wi-Fi hot spots all around you! Double-click one to join it. But if you see a 🔒 icon next to the hot spot's name, beware: It's been protected by a password. If you don't know it, then you won't be able to connect.*

*Right: Later, you can always switch networks using the AirPort menulet.*

## Commercial Hot Spots

Choosing the name of the hot spot you want to join is generally all you have to do—if it's a *home* Wi-Fi network.

Unfortunately, joining a *commercial* Wi-Fi hot spot—one that requires a credit card number (in a hotel room or airport, for example)—requires more than just connecting to it. You also have to *sign into* it before you can send so much as a single email message.

To do that, open your Web browser. You'll see the "Enter your payment information" screen either immediately or as soon as you try to open a Web page of your choice. (Even at free hot spots, you might have to click OK on a welcome page to initiate the connection.)

Supply your credit card information or (if you have a membership to this Wi-Fi chain, like Boingo or T-Mobile) your name and password. Click Submit or Proceed, try *not* to contemplate how this $8 per hour is pure profit for somebody, and enjoy your surfing.

# Dial-up Modem Connections

If you ask Apple, dial-up modems are dead. Macs don't even come with built-in modems anymore. You can get an external USB modem for $50, but clearly, Apple is trying to shove the trusty dial-up technology into the recycling bin.

---

**POWER USERS' CLINIC**

### The Super-Secret Hot-Spot Management Box

If you open System Preferences→Network, click AirPort in the left-side list, and then click Advanced, you see the cool new dialog box shown here. It lets you manage the list of Wi-Fi hot spots that Mac OS X has memorized on your travels.

For example, you can delete the old ones. You can also double-click a Wi-Fi net's name to type in and store its password. Finally, you can drag the hot spots' names up and down the list to establish a priority for making connections when more than one is available.

Ordinarily, Mac OS X memorizes the names of the various hot spots that you join on your travels. It's kind of nice, actually, because it means you're interrupted less often by the "Do you want to join?" box.

But if you're alarmed at the massive list of hot spots that Leopard has memorized—for privacy reasons, say—here's where you turn off "Remember any network this computer has joined."

---

Still, millions of people never got the memo. If you're among them, you need to sign up for Internet service. Hundreds of companies, large and small, would love to become your *Internet service provider* (ISP), generally charging $20 or so per month for the privilege of connecting you to the great Internet.

Once you've selected a service provider, you plug its settings into the Network pane of System Preferences. You get the necessary information directly from your ISP by consulting either its Web page, the instruction sheets that came with your account, or a help-desk agent on the phone.

> **Note:** The following instructions don't pertain to America Online. It comes with its own setup program and doesn't involve any settings in System Preferences.

## Setting Up the Modem

Open System Preferences and click Network. If your modem isn't already listed, click the + button at lower left; from the Interface pop-up menu that appears, choose External Modem, and then click Create.

Your modem connection now appears in the list at the left side of the pane. Click it. Now fill in the blanks like this:

- **Configuration.** It's called Default at first, which is fine. If you like, you can choose Add Configuration from this pop-up menu and then name it after your ISP (*Earthlink*, for example).

- **Telephone Number.** This is the local access number that your modem is supposed to dial to connect to your ISP.

> **Tip:** If you need your Mac to dial a 9 or an 8 for an outside line (as you would from within a hotel), or *70 to turn off Call Waiting, add it to the beginning of the phone number followed by a comma. The comma means "Pause for 2 seconds." You can also put the comma to good use when typing in the dialing sequence for a calling-card number.

- **Account Name.** This is your account name, as assigned by the ISP. If you're BillG@ earthlink.net, for example, type *BillG* here.

- **Password.** Specify your ISP account password here. Turn on "Save password" if you'd rather not retype it every time you connect.

One quick way to find out this information is to refer to your old Windows machine, assuming it could get online:

- **Windows XP.** Choose Start→Control Panel. Open Network Connections. Double-click the icon for your dial-up connection.

- **Windows 2000.** Choose Start→Settings→Network and Dial-up Connections. Double-click the icon for your Internet connection.

- **Windows Me.** Choose Start→Settings→Dial-Up Networking. In the Control Panel, double-click the icon for your dial-up connection.

• **Windows 98.** Open My Computer→Dial-Up Networking. Double-click the icon for your Internet connection.

In each case, the Connect dialog box appears, with connection information staring you in the face. Copy this information into the corresponding boxes on the Mac. When you're finished making your settings, click Apply Now.

---

**Note:** Only an administrator can make changes to the Internet dial-up settings. To make a change, therefore, you may have to click the little padlock in the lower-left corner of the dialog box to input an administrator's name and password.

---

Incidentally, if you click the Advanced button, you bring up a special dialog box, filled with checkboxes that control your online sessions. On the PPP tab, for example, you can specify how long the Mac waits before hanging up the phone line after your last online activity, and how many times the Mac should dial if the ISP phone number is busy.

One checkbox here that you'll almost certainly want to turn on is "Connect automatically when needed." It makes your Mac dial the Internet automatically whenever you check your email or open your Web browser. (Otherwise, you'd have to establish the Internet call manually, using the Modem menulet shown in Figure 10-7.) Only then could you check your email or use your Web browser.)

**Figure 10-6:**
*Dial-up modems may be fading in the era of high-speed Internet connections, but they're not dead yet. Mac OS X still offers a full panoply of tweaky settings.*

On the Modem tab, some handy settings include:

- **Wait for dial tone before dialing.** This one's for you, North American laptop owners. Because the dial tones in certain foreign countries sound weird to the Mac, it won't dial because it's still listening for that good old North American dial tone. In that case, turning off this checkbox makes the Mac dial bravely even though it hasn't heard the sound it's listening for.

- **Dialing.** Specify what kind of phone service you have—Tone or, in a few rural locations, Pulse.

- **Sound.** By clicking Off, you make your Mac dial the Internet silently, sparing sleeping family members or dorm roommates from having to listen to your modem shriek as it connects.

## Going Online

That's all there is to it. If you've turned on "Connect automatically when needed," your Mac dials and connects to the Internet automatically whenever an Internet-related program tries to connect (a Web browser or email program, for example).

If you didn't turn on that option, then you can make your Mac dial the Internet in one of two ways:

- **Use the Network pane.** Right here in System Preferences, you can click Connect to make the connection.

- **Use the menu-bar icon.** If you were smart, however, you turned on "Show modem status on menu bar" in System Preferences→Network. It adds the 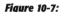 menulet to the upper-right corner of your screen, which lets you get online with one quick menu choice (Figure 10-7).

**Figure 10-7:**
*Life is simplest when you've told your Mac to dial automatically when it needs to get online. But you can also go online on command, using this menulet.*

## Disconnecting

The Mac automatically drops the phone line 15 minutes after your last activity online (or whatever interval you specified on the PPP tab of the Advanced dialog box). In fact, if other people have accounts on your Mac (Chapter 13), the Mac doesn't even hang up when you log out. It maintains the connection so that the next person can surf the Net without redialing.

Of course, if other people in your household are screaming for you to get off the line so they can make a call, you can also disconnect manually. Choose Disconnect from the 📞 menulet.

---

**Tip:** If you have more than one ISP, or if you travel between locations with your laptop, don't miss the Location feature. It lets you switch sets of dial-up modem settings—including the local phone number—with a simple menu selection. It's described on the facing page.

---

## Switching Locations

If you travel with a laptop, you know the drill. You're constantly opening up System Preferences→Network so that you can switch between Internet settings: Ethernet at the office, Wi-Fi at home. Or maybe you simply visit the branch office from time to time, and you're getting tired of having to change the local access number for your ISP each time you leave home (and return home again).

The simple solution is the 🍎→Location submenu, which appears once you have set up more than one Location. As Figure 10-8 illustrates, all you have to do is tell it where you are. Mac OS X handles the details of switching Internet connections.

*Figure 10-8:*
*The Location feature lets you switch from one "location" to another just by choosing its name—either from the 🍎 menu (top) or from this pop-up menu in System Preferences (bottom).*

*The Automatic location just means "the standard, default one you originally set up." (Don't be fooled: Despite its name, Automatic isn't the only location that offers multihoming, described earlier in this chapter.)*

## Creating a New Location

To create a *Location*, which is nothing more than a set of memorized settings, open System Preferences, click Network, and then choose Edit Locations from the Location pop-up menu. Continue as shown in Figure 10-9.

---

***Tip:*** You can use the commands in the ✿ menu to rename or duplicate a Location.

---

When you click Done, you return to the Network panel. Take this opportunity to set up the kind of Internet connection you use at the corresponding location, just as described on the first pages of this chapter.

---

**Figure 10-9:**
*When you choose Edit Locations, this list of existing Locations appears; click the + button. A new entry appears at the bottom of the list. Type a name for your new location, such as Chicago Office or Dining Room Floor.*

---

**GEM IN THE ROUGH**

## Cellular Modems

Wi-Fi hot spots are fast and usually cheap—but they're hot *spots*. Beyond 150 feet away, you're offline.

No wonder laptop luggers across America are getting into *cellular* Internet services. All of the big cellphone companies offer PC cards or ExpressCards that let your laptop get online at high speed *anywhere* in major cities. No hunting for a coffee shop; with a cellular Internet service, you can check your email while zooming down the road in a taxi. (Outside the metropolitan areas, you can still get online wirelessly, though much more slowly.)

Verizon and Sprint offer the fastest cellular Internet networks, using a technology called EV-DO. AT&T's and T-Mobile's offerings are much slower.

So why isn't the world beating a path to this delicious technology's door? Because it's expensive—at this writing, $60 a month on top of your phone bill.

You may also be able to get your laptop online by connecting it to your cellphone with a cable—a lower-priced, slower option. Ask your cellphone carrier.

---

If you travel regularly, you can build a *list* of Locations, each of which "knows" the way you like to get online in each city you visit.

A key part of making a new Location is putting the various Internet connection types (Ethernet, AirPort, Modem, Bluetooth) into the correct order. Your connections will be slightly quicker if you give the modem priority in your Hotel setup, the AirPort connection priority in your Starbucks setup, and so on.

You can even turn off some connections entirely. For example, if you use nothing but a cable modem when you're at home, you may want to create a location in which *only* the Ethernet connection is active. Use the Make Service Inactive command in the ✿ pop-up menu.

Conversely, if your laptop uses nothing but Wi-Fi when you're on the road, your Location could include *nothing* but the AirPort connection. You'll save a few seconds each time you try to go online, because your Mac won't bother hunting for an Internet connection that doesn't exist.

## Making the Switch

Once you've set up your various locations, you can switch among them using either the Location pop-up menu (in System Preferences→Network) or the  →Location submenu, as shown in Figure 10-8. As soon as you do so, your Mac is automatically set to get online the way you like.

*Tip:* If you have a laptop, create a connection called Offline. From the Show pop-up menu, choose Network Port Configurations; make *all* the connection methods in the list inactive. When you're finished, you've got yourself a laptop that will *never* attempt to go online. You've got yourself the laptop equivalent of Airplane Mode on a cellphone.

# Internet Sharing

If you have cable modem or DSL service, you're a very lucky individual. Not only do you benefit from great speed when surfing the Web or processing email, but your connection is on full-time. You never have to wait for some modem to dial (screeching all the way), and wait again for it to disconnect. Too bad only one computer in your household or office can enjoy these luxuries.

Actually, it doesn't have to be that way. You can spread the joy of high-speed Internet to every Mac (and PC) on your network in either of two ways:

- **Buy a router.** A *router* is a little box, costing about $50, that connects directly to the cable modem or DSL box. In most cases, it has multiple Internet jacks so you can plug in several Macs, PCs, and/or wireless base stations. As a bonus, a router provides excellent security, serving as a firewall to keep out unsolicited visits from hackers on the Internet. (If you use a router, *turn off* Mac OS X's own firewall in System Preferences→Security.)

- **Use Internet Sharing.** Mac OS X's Internet Sharing feature is the software version of a router, in that it distributes a single Internet signal to every computer on the network. But unlike a router, it's free. You just fire it up on the one Mac that's connected directly to the Internet—the *gateway* computer. (Windows Me, XP, and Vista offer a similar feature.)

But there's a downside: If the gateway Mac is turned off or asleep, the other machines can't get online.

Most people use Internet Sharing to share a broadband connection like a cable modem or DSL. But in fact, Internet Sharing works if the gateway Mac connects to the Internet via dial-up modem or even a Bluetooth cellphone.

The only requirement is that the gateway Mac *also* has a network connection (Ethernet, AirPort, or FireWire) to the Macs that will share the connection.

## Turning On Internet Sharing

To turn on Internet Sharing on the gateway Mac, open the Sharing panel of System Preferences. Turn on Internet Sharing, as shown in Figure 10-10, and then confirm your decision by clicking Start. (In most setups, you'll want to turn on Internet Sharing *only* on the gateway Mac.)

To set up sharing, you have to specify (a) how the gateway Mac is connected to the Internet, and (b) how it's connected to the other Macs on your office network:

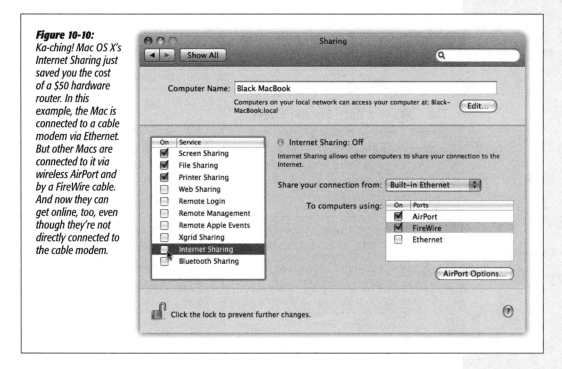

**Figure 10-10:**
*Ka-ching! Mac OS X's Internet Sharing just saved you the cost of a $50 hardware router. In this example, the Mac is connected to a cable modem via Ethernet. But other Macs are connected to it via wireless AirPort and by a FireWire cable. And now they can get online, too, even though they're not directly connected to the cable modem.*

• **Share your connection from.** Using this pop-up menu, identify how *this Mac* (the gateway machine) connects to the Internet—via Built-in Ethernet, AirPort, or whatever. If you select AirPort, you create the *software base station* effect described in the next section.

• **To computers using.** Turn on the checkboxes to teach your Mac how the other Macs are connected to it—via what form of networking, in other words.

---

***Note:*** Which checkboxes appear here depend on which kinds of Internet connections are turned on in the Network pane of System Preferences. If the gateway Mac doesn't have AirPort circuitry, for example, or if AirPort is turned off in the current configuration, the AirPort option doesn't appear.

---

Now visit each of the other Macs on the same network. Open the Network pane of System Preferences. Select AirPort, Built-in Ethernet, or FireWire—whichever reflects how each Mac is connected to your network. Then, from the Configure pop-up menu, choose Using DHCP. Leave everything else blank. Finally, click Apply Now.

As long as the gateway Mac remains turned on, you should find that both it and your other Macs can get onto the Internet simultaneously, all at high speed. (Even Windows PCs on the same network can also get online, as long as you set them up to use DHCP just as you did your "downstream" Macs.)

---

***Note:*** If you're like most people, your gateway Mac has only one Ethernet port. How, you may wonder, can you plug in both the cable modem and the local network?

One approach is to install a second Ethernet card. The more economical approach: Connect the cable modem to the *Uplink* or *WAN* jack on your Ethernet hub or router. (On some models, an ordinary Ethernet port can be turned *into* an Uplink port if you flip a tiny switch.) Your gateway Mac plugs into the hub as usual.

---

## The Software Base Station Effect

If the gateway Mac has AirPort circuitry, turning on Internet Sharing (and "To computers using: AirPort") has another profound effect: It creates a *software* base station. The Mac itself is now the transmitter for Internet signals to and from any other AirPort-equipped Macs within range. You just saved yourself the cost of an Apple base station.

---

***Tip:*** Internet Sharing can create the opposite effect, too: Instead of letting a wireless Mac piggyback on a wired Mac's connection, you can let a wired Mac share a *wireless* connection.

Suppose, for example, that you and a buddy both have laptops in a hotel lobby. You're online, having paid $13 to use the hotel's Wi-Fi network. If you set up Internet Sharing appropriately, your buddy can connect to yours via an Ethernet cable or even a FireWire cable and surf along with you—no extra charge.

---

# .Mac Services

In January 2000, Apple CEO Steve Jobs explained to the Macworld Expo crowds that he and his team had had a mighty brainstorm: Apple controls *both ends* of the connection between a Mac and the Apple Web site. As a result, Apple should be able to create some pretty clever Internet-based features as a reward to loyal Mac fans. Later that same day, the Apple Web site offered a suite of *free* services called iTools.

Then the technology bubble burst.

These days, .Mac (as it's now called) costs $100 a year (Figure 10-11).

**Figure 10-11:**
*The .Mac features appear as buttons on the .Mac Web site. For example, iCards are attractively designed electronic greeting cards that you can send by email. Backup is a basic backup program that you can download from this site. Webmail, HomePage, an antivirus program, and features that synchronize your iCal and iSync data with other computers are the other second-tier features. The best feature, however, is iDisk.*

## Signing Up for .Mac

Open System Preferences and click the .Mac icon. Click Learn More. You now go online, where your Web browser has opened up to the .Mac sign-up screen. Fill in your name and address, make up an account name and password, turn off the checkbox that invites you to get junk mail, and so on.

The final step is to return to the .Mac pane of System Preferences. Fill in the account name and password you just composed, if necessary. You're ready to use .Mac.

## iDisk

The iDisk is an Internet-based hard-drive icon on your desktop, holding up to 10 gigabytes of files. (Your .Mac account comes with 10 gigabytes of storage. In your account settings at *www.mac.com*, you can decide how to divide up that storage between your iDisk and the other .Mac stuff, like mail and your Web sites. And, of course, you can pay more money for more storage.)

Anything you drag into the folders inside this iDisk icon gets copied to Apple's secure servers on the Internet. Meanwhile, on your end, it appears to work just like a hard drive.

In other words, iDisk can be a handy pseudo-hard drive. When you're saving a document from within a program, you can save it directly onto your iDisk. And because this backup disk is offsite, if a fire or thief destroys your office *and* your backup disks, your iDisk is still safe.

Furthermore, you can pull the iDisk onto *any* computer's screen—Mac or Windows—at your office, at your home, at your friend's house, so you don't need to carry around a physical disk to transport important files.

### Pulling it onto your screen

Apple must really love the iDisk concept, because it has devised about 300 different ways to pull the iDisk icon onto your screen (Figure 10-12):

- **Choose Go→iDisk→My iDisk (or press Shift-⌘-I).**

- **Click the iDisk icon in the Sidebar (of a Finder window or a Save or Open dialog box).**

- **Choose Go→Connect to Server.** At the bottom of the resulting dialog box, type *http://idisk.mac.com/casey* (substitute your actual account name for *casey*). Press

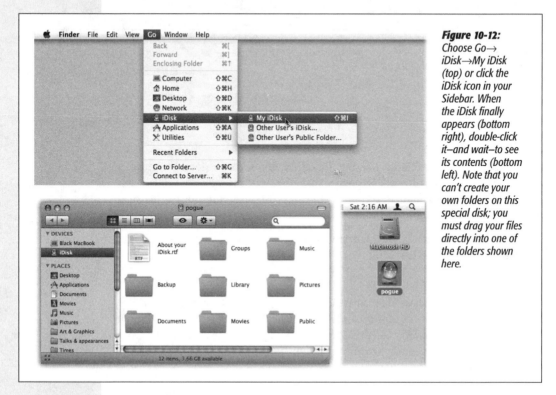

***Figure 10-12:***
*Choose Go→ iDisk→My iDisk (top) or click the iDisk icon in your Sidebar. When the iDisk finally appears (bottom right), double-click it—and wait—to see its contents (bottom left). Note that you can't create your own folders on this special disk; you must drag your files directly into one of the folders shown here.*

Enter. Type your .Mac name and password, if necessary, and then click Connect. (This is the quickest approach if you're using somebody else's Mac.)

- **Visit *www.mac.com* and click the iDisk icon.** Type in your name and password, and then click Enter. Finally, click Open Your iDisk. (Clearly, this is a lot more work than the one-click methods already described. Use this technique when you're using a public machine far from home, for example.)

At this point, the iDisk behaves like an external hard drive. You can drag files or folders from your hard drive into one of the folders that appear on the iDisk.

---

***Note:*** You can't create your own folders in the iDisk's main window. You must put your files and folders into one of the folders *already on the iDisk,* such as Documents or Pictures. If you try to drag an icon directly into the iDisk window, or onto the iDisk icon, you'll get an error message.

---

Thereafter, you can retrieve or open whatever you copied to the iDisk. Open one of the folders on it; you can now open, rename, trash, or copy (to your hard drive) whatever you find inside.

### The Public folder

In general, whatever you put onto your iDisk is private and password-protected. There's one exception, however: Whatever you put into the *Public* folder on any iDisk can be seen, opened, and copied by any other .Mac member. All they need is your member name—not your .Mac password (although you *can* password-protect it, if you like). Think of the iDisk Public folder as the long-lost twin of the Public folder in your own Home folder.

The Public folder is terrific for storing family photos where anyone who's interested can look at them. It's also handy when you're collaborating; just post the latest drafts of your work in the Public folder for your co-workers to review.

To view someone *else's* Public folder, use one of these techniques; suppose the person's .Mac name is SkiBunny23:

- **From Mac OS X 10.3, 10.4, or 10.5.** Choose Go→iDisk→Other User's Public Folder. Type in the person's member name, and hit Return.

- **Mac OS X 10.1 or 10.2.** Choose Go→Connect to Server. At the bottom of the dialog box, type *http://idisk.mac.com/skibunny23/Public.* Click Connect or press Enter. If a password is required, use *public* as the user name and, well, the password as the password.

---

***Tip:*** Actually, there's a simpler way: Use iDisk Utility, described below.

---

- **From Mac OS 9.** Choose  →Chooser, click AppleShare, click the Server IP Address button, type *idisk.mac.com* in the Server Address box, and then click Connect. Type *skibunny23;* for the password, use *public* (unless the folder really is password-protected, in which case you should type the password you were given). Then click Connect. Select the iDisk, and then click OK.

• **From Windows.** See the box below.

After a minute or so, a new iDisk icon appears on your desktop, bearing that member's name. Double-click it to view its contents. You can copy these files to your hard drive, or double-click them to open them directly.

### iDisk options

If you open System Preferences, click the .Mac icon, and click iDisk, you're offered a few interesting options, along with a graph that shows how full your iDisk is getting. Here, you can also make these changes:

• **Let people put stuff in your Public folder.** Ordinarily, other people can deposit stuff into your Public folder as well as copy things out. If you'd rather set it up so that only *you* can drop things in there, click "Read only."

• **Password-protect your Public folder.** Probably a good idea if you decide to make your Public folder available for deposits.

**Note:** These functions are available to pre-Panther/Tiger people (and Windows people too) if they visit *www.mac.com,* click ".Mac Downloads," sign in, and download the program called iDisk Utility (or iDisk Utility for Windows).

---

**POWER USER'S CLINIC**

## The iDisk from Windows

Once, you could get to your iDisk only from a Macintosh. These days, you can bring your iDisk onto the screen of any computer, even one running Windows or Linux. Suddenly the iDisk is a handy transfer station between your Mac and Windows world.

The procedure varies by operating system, but the general idea is the same: You're going to create a new "hard drive" in your My Computer window, whose icon represents the iDisk.

If you have Windows XP and plan to connect regularly, you can download the free iDisk Utility for Windows, which makes pulling up someone's iDisk a simple matter of a couple of clicks. Visit *www.mac.com* and click .Mac Downloads to find it.

Otherwise, here are the steps for different Windows versions:

**Windows Vista:** Open your Web browser. Go to *www.mac.com* and log in; click iDisk in the left column. A new browser window opens. Type your .Mac name and password, and click Log In.

**Windows XP:** Choose Tools→Map Network Drive in any desktop window.

**Windows 2000:** Choose Tools→Map Network Drive. Click "Web folder or FTP site."

**Windows 98:** Open My Computer. Double-click the Web Folders icon; double-click Add Web Folder.

In the XP/2000/98 cases, you should now type in this address as the location to add: *http://idisk.mac.com/casey* (where *casey* is your .Mac member name). When you're asked for a name and password, type in your usual .Mac name and password.

After a minute or two, you'll find the icon for your iDisk in the My Computer window, sitting there as though it's a hard drive attached to the PC. In Windows XP, for example, it's in the Network Drives category, called something like "Frank23 on 'idisk.mac.com.'"

# Email

Apple offers an email address to each .Mac member.

Probably anyone who can *get* to the Apple Web site already *has* an email account. So why bother? The first advantage is the simple address: *YourName@mac.com*. And because .Mac is a Mac-only service, the odds are good that you'll be able to claim the name you want. No longer must you be known as *bgates28514@earthlink.net*. (Cultdom has its privileges.)

Second, Mac.com addresses are integrated into Mac OS X's Mail program, as you'll see in the next chapter. And finally, you can read your .Mac email from any computer anywhere in the world, via the *www.mac.com* Web site.

# HomePage

Creating a Web page (an HTML document) isn't difficult. Using a program like Dreamweaver, GoLive, Netscape Composer, Keynote, or even Microsoft Word, you can design the text and graphics for a simple Web page in a single afternoon.

It's much more difficult, however, to figure out how to *post* that Web page—to hang it on the Internet where the world can see it. To do that, you need special software, several passwords and codes, and a lot of help from your ISP.

The .Mac HomePage feature eliminates all that hassle. All you have to do is drag your Web-page documents and graphics into the Sites folder on your iDisk. Your Web page is instantly available for viewing by everyone on the Internet.

---

***Tip:*** You can create as many Web pages as you want. When you return to the HomePage screen, a list of your existing Web pages appears (complete with Edit Page and Delete Page buttons).

---

If you already know how to design Web pages, great; put the HTML documents and graphics you've created into the Sites folder of your iDisk.

And if you have no experience designing Web pages, Mac OS X itself can help you:

- iPhoto and Image Capture can both turn photos from your digital camera into handsome art-gallery Web pages. After they've done so, drag the resulting HTML documents and image folders into your iDisk's Sites folder. Presto! You've got yourself a photo-gallery Web page.

- Sign into *www.mac.com*. If you click HomePage, you'll find a large gallery of canned Web site design templates that you can easily fill up and post in cyberspace: photo albums, movie players, résumés, baby announcements, and so on.

  When you finally click the Publish button at the top of the screen, new Web page (HTML) documents appear in the Sites folder of your iDisk. Also, your screen now displays your page's URL (Web address), which you can email to anyone who'd be interested.

Finally, your Web page is available for anyone on the Internet to see.

---

## Backup

.Mac membership also includes access to a program called Backup, which gives you automatic backups of your most important files. It doesn't give you as much peace of mind as Time Machine (Chapter 6), which backs up your *entire* computer, though.

For details on Backup, see this chapter's free downloadable appendix. It's on this book's "Missing CD" page at *www.missingmanuals.com.*

## iSync

iSync is a little program that syncs your calendar and address book to your cellphone or Palm organizer.

# Internet Location Files

An Internet location file (Figure 10-14) is like a system-wide bookmark: When you double-click one, your Web browser opens to that page, or your email program generates an outgoing message to a predetermined addressee. You could put a folder full of location files for favorite Web sites into the Dock. Do the same with addresses to which you frequently send email. Thereafter, you save a step every time you want to jump to a particular Web page or send email to a particular person—just choose the appropriate name from the Dock folder's Stack. (It's fine to rename them, by the way.)

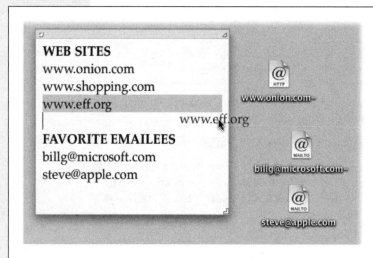

**Figure 10-14:**
*To create an Internet location file, drag a highlighted address from a program like TextEdit to your desktop. Although Web and email addresses are the most popular types, you can also create location files for the ad-dresses of newsgroups (news:// news.apple.com), FTP sites (ftp:// ftp.apple.com), AppleShare servers (afp://at/Engineering:IL5 3rd Floor), AppleTalk zones (at:// IL5 2nd Floor), and even Web pages stored on your Mac (file:// Macintosh HD/Website Stuff/ home.html).*

# Mail & Address Book

Y ou know how every copy of Windows comes with Outlook Express, a basic, free email program? Well, every copy of Mac OS X comes with Mail, a slightly fancier email program that's also free. Mail is a surprisingly complete, refreshingly attractive program, filled with shortcuts and surprises. Together with the high-octane Address Book program included with Mac OS X, you may never pine for your Windows setup again.

**Note:** This chapter assumes that you've already transferred your email, addresses, and email account settings to Mail and the Address Book, as described in Chapter 6.

## Checking Your Mail

You get new mail and send mail you've already written in any of several ways:

- Click Get Mail on the toolbar.
- Choose Mailbox→Get All New Mail (or press Shift-⌘-N).

**Note:** If you have multiple email accounts, you can also use the Mailbox→Get New Mail submenu to pick just *one* account to check for new mail.

- Right-click Mail's Dock icon, and choose Get New Mail from the shortcut menu. (You can use this method from within any program, as long as Mail is already open.)

- Wait. Mail comes set to check your email automatically every few minutes. To adjust its timing or turn this feature off, choose Mail→Preferences, click General, and then choose a time interval from the "Check for new mail" pop-up menu.

Now Mail contacts the mail servers listed in the Accounts pane of Mail's preferences, retrieving new messages and downloading any files attached to those messages. It also *sends* any outgoing messages that couldn't be sent when you wrote them.

---

*Tip:* The far-left column of the Mail window has a tiny Mail Activity monitor tucked away; click the square icon at the bottom of the Mail window to reveal Mail Activity. If you don't want to give up window real estate, or you prefer to monitor your mail in a separate window, you can do that, too. The Activity Viewer window gives you a Stop button, progress bars, and other useful information. Summon it by choosing Window→Activity Viewer, or by pressing ⌘-0.

Also, if you're having trouble connecting to some (or all) of your email accounts, choose Window→Connection Doctor. There, you can see detailed information about which of your accounts aren't responding. If your computer's Internet connection is at fault, you can click Assist Me to try to get back online.

---

**GEM IN THE ROUGH**

## The Mighty Morphing Interface

You don't have to be content with the factory-installed design of the Mail screen. You can control almost every aspect of its look and layout.

For example, you can control the main window's information columns exactly as you would in a Finder list view window—make a column narrower or wider by dragging the right edge of its column heading, rearrange the columns by dragging their titles, and so on.

You can also control *which* columns appear using the commands in the View→Columns menu. Similarly, you can *sort* your email by clicking these column headings, exactly as in the Finder. Click a second time to reverse the sorting order.

The various panes of the main window are also under your control. For example, you can drag the divider bar between the Messages list and the Preview pane up or down to adjust the relative proportions, as shown here. In fact, you can get rid of the Preview pane altogether by double-clicking the divider line, double-clicking just above the vertical scroll

bar, or dragging the divider line's handle all the way to the bottom of the screen. Bring it back by dragging the divider line up from the bottom.

You can also control the Mailboxes pane. Drag its thin vertical line that separates this tinted column from the white messages area to make the column wider or narrower. You can even drag it so tightly that you see only the mailboxes' icons. You can make the column disappear or reappear by choosing View→Hide Mailboxes (or View→Show Mailboxes), or by pressing Shift-⌘-M.

Finally, you have full control over the toolbar, which works much like the Finder toolbar. You can rearrange or remove icon buttons (by ⌘-dragging them); add interesting new buttons to the toolbar (by choosing View→Customize Toolbar); change its display to show *just* text labels or *just* icons—either large or small (by repeatedly ⌘-clicking the white, oval, upper-right toolbar button); or hide the toolbar entirely (by clicking that white button or using the View→Hide Toolbar command).

---

## The Mailboxes List

Mail, like Outlook Express, lists your various email folders in a column on the left-hand side of the window. In this Mailboxes column, you'll find the usual suspects, sometimes hidden by flippy triangles: Inbox, Outbox, Sent, Drafts, and so on. Only a few of these mailboxes may be new to you:

- **Trash** works a lot like the Trash on your desktop, in that messages you put there don't actually disappear. They remain in the Trash folder until you permanently delete them or move them somewhere else—or until Mail's automatic trash-cleaning service deletes them for you (page 320).

- **Junk** appears automatically when you use Mail's spam filter, as described later in this chapter.

- **On My Mac** is a folder on your Mac for your mail-filing convenience. You can set these folders up yourself (page 317).

- **Reminders.** Any Notes you've jotted down while working in Mail are here. (See page 327 for notes on Notes.) To Do items hang out here as well (page 328).

- **RSS Feeds.** Who needs to bop into a Web browser to keep up with the news? Mail brings it right to you while you're corresponding. Page 325 explains how to set up RSS feeds in Mail.

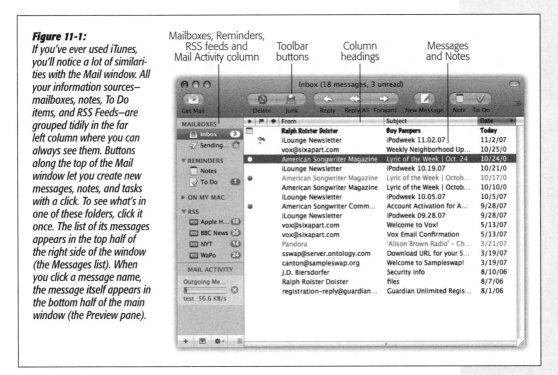

**Figure 11-1:**
*If you've ever used iTunes, you'll notice a lot of similarities with the Mail window. All your information sources—mailboxes, notes, To Do items, and RSS Feeds—are grouped tidily in the far left column where you can always see them. Buttons along the top of the Mail window let you create new messages, notes, and tasks with a click. To see what's in one of these folders, click it once. The list of its messages appears in the top half of the right side of the window (the Messages list). When you click a message name, the message itself appears in the bottom half of the main window (the Preview pane).*

Mailboxes, Reminders, RSS feeds and Mail Activity column | Toolbar buttons | Column headings | Messages and Notes

To see what's in one of these folders, click it once. The list of its messages appears in the top half of the main window. Now, when you click a message name, the message itself appears in the Preview pane.

Figure 11-1 shows the idea.

## Writing Messages

To send email to a recipient, click the New icon on the toolbar. The New Message form, shown in Figure 11-2, opens. If you've ever sent email from a Windows PC, this should all feel familiar. Here are a few notes:

- To send this message to more than one person, separate their addresses in the "To:" box with commas: *bob@earthlink.net, billg@microsoft.com, steve@apple.com.*

- Mail offers Auto-complete. If somebody is in your Address Book (page 331), just type the first couple letters of his name or email address; Mail automatically completes the address. (If the first guess is wrong, type another letter or two until Mail revises its proposal.)

- As in most dialog boxes, you can jump from blank to blank (from the "To:" field to the "Cc:" field, for example) by pressing the Tab key.

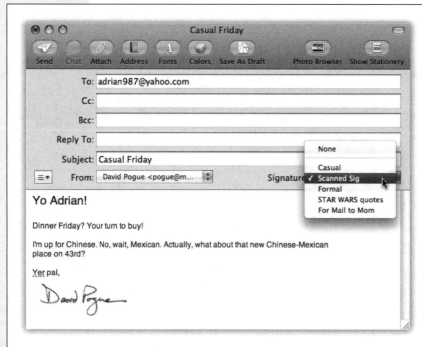

**Figure 11-2:**
*A message has two sections: the* header, *which holds information about the message; and the* body, *the big empty area that contains the message itself. In addition, the Mail window has a toolbar, which offers features for composing and sending messages. The Signature pop-up menu doesn't exist until you create a signature (page 307); the Account pop-up menu lets you pick which email address you'd like to send the message from (if you have more than one email address).*

- A *blind carbon copy* ("Bcc") lets you send a message to someone on the sly (none of the "To" and "Cc" recipients will know that you sent the message to the "Bcc" recipients). If you're sending a message from a different email address than usual, "Reply-to" lets you specify an email address that your recipient should, well, reply to. And a message's Priority lets you tell your recipients how urgent the message is.

  If you would find these fields helpful while composing a message, click the three-lined pop-up menu on the left side of the New Message window. Click Customize. Now just turn on the checkboxes next to whichever fields you want visible, and click OK.

- There are two main kinds of email: *plain text* and *formatted* (what Apple calls Rich Text). Plain text messages are faster to send and open, universally compatible with the world's email programs, and greatly preferred by many veteran computer fans. And even though the message is plain, you can still attach pictures and other files.

  By contrast, formatted messages (see Figure 11-3) sometimes open slowly, and in some email programs the formatting doesn't come through at all.

  To control which kind of mail you send on a message-by-message basis, choose, from the Format menu, either Make Plain Text or Make Rich Text. To change the factory setting for new outgoing messages, choose Mail→Preferences, click the Composing icon, and choose from the Message Format pop-up menu.

- As you type your message, Mail checks your spelling, using a dotted red underline to mark questionable words. To check for alternative spellings for a suspect word, right-click it. From the list of suggestions in the shortcut menu, click the word you really intended, or choose Learn Spelling to add the word to the Mac OS X dictionary shared by all Cocoa programs (page 141).

---

***Tip:*** To turn off automatic spell check, choose Edit→Spelling→Check Spelling→Never. Or, if you'd rather Mail wait until you're *done* composing your messages before spell checking, choose Edit→Spelling→Check Spelling→When You Click Send.

---

- When you click Send (or press Shift-⌘-D), your Mac connects to the Internet and sends the message.

  If you'd rather have Mail place each message you write in the Outbox folder, quietly collecting them instead of connecting to the Net the moment you click Send, choose Mailbox→Go Offline. While you're offline, Mail will refrain from trying to connect, which is a great feature when you're working on a laptop at 39,000 feet. (Choose Mailbox→Go Online to reverse the procedure.)

## Attaching Files to Messages

Sending little text messages is fine, but it's not much help when you want to send somebody a photograph, a sound, or a Word document. To attach a file to a message you've written, use one of these methods:

• Drag the icons you want to attach directly off the desktop (or out of a folder) into the New Message window. There your attachments appear with their own hyperlinked icons (shown in Figure 11-3), meaning that your recipient can simply click to open them.

---

***Tip:*** Exposé was *born* for this moment. Hit the F11 key to make all open windows flee to the edges of the screen, revealing the desktop. Root around until you find the file you want to send. Begin dragging it; without releasing the mouse, press F11 again to bring your message window back into view. Complete your drag into the message window.

---

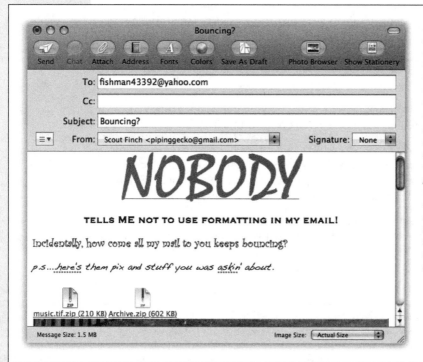

**Figure 11-3:**
*If you really want to use formatting, click the Fonts icon on the toolbar to open the Font panel, or the Colors icon to open the Color Picker (page 148). The Format menu (in the menu bar) contains even more controls: paragraph alignment (left, right, or justify), and even Copy and Paste Style commands that let you transfer formatting from one block of text to another.*

Mail makes it look as though you can park the attached file's icon (or the full image of a graphics file) *inside* the text of the message, mingled with your typing. Don't be fooled, however; on the receiving end, all of the attachments will be clumped together at the end of the message (unless your recipient also uses Mail).

• Drag the icons you want to attach from the desktop onto Mail's Dock icon. Mail dutifully creates a new, outgoing message, with the files already attached.

• Click the Attach icon on the New Message toolbar, choose File→Attach File, or press Shift-⌘-A. The standard Open File sheet now appears, so that you can navigate to and select the files you want to include. (You can choose multiple files simultaneously in this dialog box. Just ⌘-click or Shift-click the individual files you want as though you were selecting them in a Finder window.)

Once you've selected them, click Choose File (or press Enter). You return to the New Message window, where the attachments' icons appear, ready to ride along when you send the message.

To remove an attachment, drag across its icon to highlight it, and then press the Delete key. (You can also drag an attachment icon clear out of the window into your Dock's Trash, or choose Message→Remove Attachments.)

If you have a high-speed connection like a cable modem, by the way, have pity on your recipient. A big picture or movie file might take you only seconds to send, but tie up your correspondent's modem for hours.

## Signatures

*Signatures* are bits of text that get stamped at the bottom of your outgoing email messages. A signature might contain a name, a postal address, a pithy quote, or even a scan of your *real* signature.

You can customize your signatures by choosing Mail→Preferences, and then clicking the Signatures icon. Here's what you should know:

- **To build up a library of signatures that you can use in any of your accounts:** Select All Signatures in the leftmost pane, and then click the + button to add each new signature. Give each new signature a name in the middle pane, and then customize the signatures' text in the rightmost pane.

---

**Tip:** If you ever get tired of a signature, you can delete it forever by selecting All Signatures→[your signature's name], clicking the – button, and then clicking OK.

---

- **To make a signature available in one of your email accounts:** Drag the signature's name from the middle pane onto the name of the account in the leftmost pane. In other words, you can make certain signatures available to only your work (or personal) account, so you never accidentally end up appending your secret FBI contact signature to the bottom of a birthday invitation you send out.

- **To assign a particular signature to one account:** In the left pane, click an account; choose from the Choose Signature pop-up menu. Each time you compose a message from that account, Mail inserts the signature you selected.

---

**Tip:** To make things more interesting for your recipients, pick At Random; Mail selects a different signature each time you send a message. Or, if you're not that much of a risk-taker, choose In Sequential Order; Mail picks the next signature in order for each new message you write.

---

Remember, that you can always change your signature on a message-by-message basis, using the Signature pop-up menu in any new email message.

- **To use the signature feature as a prefix in replies:** Turn on "Place signature above quoted text." If you turn on this setting, your signature gets inserted *above* any of the text that you're replying to, rather than below. You'd use this setting if your "signature" said something like, "Hi there! You wrote this to me—".

---

***Tip:*** If you're into consistent typographical styling, also turn on "Always match my default font." That setting makes sure any messages you send contain the signature in the same font as the rest of the message, lending an air of professionalism to your message.

---

# Stationery

Rich text—and even plain text—messages are fine for your everyday personal and business correspondence. But suppose you have an occasion where you *want* to jazz up your mail, like an electronic invitation to a bridal shower or a mass-mail update as you get your kicks down Route 66.

These messages just cry out for Mail's new *Stationery* feature. Stationery means colorful, predesigned mail templates that you make your own by dragging in photos from your own collection. Those fancy fonts and graphics will certainly get people's attention when they open the message.

---

***Note:*** They will, that is, if their email programs understand HTML formatting. That's the formatting that Mail uses for its stationery. (If the nerd-word *HTML* rings a bell, it's because this HyperText Markup Language is the same used to make many Web pages so lively and colorful.)

It might be a good idea to make sure everyone on your recipient list has a mail program that can handle HTML; otherwise, your message may look like a jumble of code and letters in the middle of the screen.

---

To make a stylized message with Mail Stationery:

1. **Create a new message.**

   Click File→New Message, press ⌘-N, or click the New Message button on the Mail window toolbar. The choice is up to you.

2. **On the right side of the toolbar on the New Message window, click Show Stationery.**

   A panel opens up, showing you all the available templates, in categories like "Birthday" and "Announcements."

3. **Click a category, and then click a stationery thumbnail image to apply it to your message.**

   The body of your message changes to take on the look of the template.

4. **If you like what you see, click the Hide Stationery button on the toolbar to fold up the stationery-picker panel.**

***Tip:*** If you don't like the background color, try clicking the thumbnail; some templates offer a few different color choices.

Apple's canned stationery looks fantastic. The only problem is, the photos that adorn most of the templates are pictures of *somebody else's* family and friends. Unless you work for Apple's modeling agency, you probably have no clue who they are.

Fortunately, it's easy enough to replace those placeholder photos with your *own* snaps.

5. **Add and adjust pictures.**

   Click the Photo Browser icon on the message toolbar to open up a palette that lists all the photos you've stored in iPhoto, Aperture, and Photo Booth (Figure 11-4).

***Tip:*** If you don't keep your pictures in any of those programs, you can drag any folder of pictures onto the Photo Browser window to add them.

**Figure 11-4:**
*To use Stationery, start by clicking a template, then add your own text in place of the generic copy that comes with the template.*

*Click the Photo Browser button at the top of the message window to open your Mac's photo collections (shown at right), and then drag the images you want into the picture boxes on the stationery template. You don't have to know a lick of HTML to use the templates—it's all drag, drop, and type, baby.*

Now you can drag your own pictures directly *onto* Apple's dummy photos on the stationery template. They replace the sunny models.

To resize a photo in the template, double-click it. A slider appears that lets you adjust the photo's size within the message. Drag the mouse around the photo window to reposition the picture relative to its frame.

6. **Select the fake text and type in what you really want to say.**

Unless you're writing to your Latin students, of course, in which case "Duis nonsequ ismodol oreetuer iril dolore facidunt" might be perfectly appropriate.

Once you've got that message looking the way you want it, address it just as you would any other piece of mail, and click the Send button to get it on its way.

---

*Tip:* You're not stuck with Apple's designs for your Stationery templates; you can make your own. Just make a new message, style the fonts and photos the way you want them, and then choose File→Save as Stationery. You can now select your masterwork in the Custom category, which appears down at the end of the list in the stationery-picker panel.

---

If you decide that the message would be better off as plain old text, click Show Stationery on the message window. In the list of template categories, click Stationery and then Original to strip the color and formats out of the message.

## Reading Email

Mail puts all incoming email into your Inbox; the statistic after the word *Inbox* lets you know how many messages you haven't yet read. New messages are also marked with light blue dots in the main list.

---

*Tip:* The Mail icon in the Dock also shows you how many new messages you have waiting; it's the number in the red circle.

---

Click the Inbox folder to see a list of received messages. If it's a long list, press Control-Page Up and Control-Page Down to scroll. Click the name of a message once to read it in the Preview pane, or double-click a message to open it into a separate window. (If a message is already selected, pressing Return or Enter also opens its separate window.)

---

*Tip:* Instead of reading your mail, you might prefer to have Mac OS X read it *to* you, as you sit back in your chair and sip a strawberry daiquiri. Highlight the text you want to hear (or choose Edit→Select All), and then choose Edit→Speech→Start Speaking. You'll hear the message read aloud, in the voice you've selected on the Speech pane of System Preferences.

To stop the insanity, choose Edit→Speech→Stop Speaking.

---

Once you've viewed a message, you can respond to it, delete it, print it, file it, and so on. The following pages should get you started.

### Threading

*Threading* is one of the most useful mail-sorting methods to come along in a long time—and it's available in Mail. When threading is turned on, Mail groups emails with the same subject (like "Raccoons" and "Re: Raccoons") *as a single item* in the main mail list.

To turn on threading, choose View→Organize by Thread. If several messages have the same subject, they all turn light blue to indicate their membership in a thread (Figure 11-5).

Here are some powerful ways to use threading:

**Figure 11-5:**
*Threads have two parts: a heading (the subject of the thread, listed in dark blue when it's not selected) and members (the individual messages in the thread, listed in light blue and indented). Often, the main list shows only a thread's heading; click the flippy triangle to reveal its members.*

- **View a list of all the messages in a thread** by clicking its heading. In the Preview pane, you see a comprehensive inventory of the thread (Figure 11-5). You can click a message's name in this list to jump right to it.

- **Move all the members of a thread to a new mailbox** simply by moving its heading. You might find this useful, for example, when you've just finished a project and want to file away all the email related to it quickly. (As a bonus, a circled number tells you how many messages you're moving as you drag the heading.) You can even delete all the messages in a thread at once by deleting its heading.

- **Examine thread members from multiple mailboxes.** Normally, threads only display messages held in the *same* mailbox, but that's not especially convenient when you want to see both messages (from your Inbox) and your replies (in your Sent box). To work around that problem, click Inbox, and then ⌘-click the Sent mailbox (or any other mailboxes you want to include). Your threads seamlessly combine related messages from all of the selected mailboxes.

- **Quickly collapse all threads** by choosing View→Collapse All Threads. If your main list gets cluttered with too many expanded threads, this is a quick way to force it into order. (If, on the other hand, your main list isn't cluttered *enough*, choose View→Expand All Threads.)

- **Send someone all the messages in a thread** by selecting the thread's heading and clicking Forward. Mail automatically copies all the messages of the thread into a new message, putting the oldest at the top. You might find this useful, for instance, when you want to send your boss all the correspondence you've had with someone about a certain project.

## Adding the Sender to Your Address Book

When you choose the Message→Add Sender To Address Book command, Mail memorizes the email address of the person whose message is on the screen. In fact, you can highlight a huge number of messages and add *all* the senders simultaneously using this technique.

Thereafter, you'll be able to write new messages to somebody just by typing the first few letters of the name or email address.

## Data Detectors

Mail recognizes commonly used bits of information that may appear in a message: a physical address, a phone number, a date and time, and so on. With one quick click, you can send that information into the appropriate Mac OS X program, like iCal, Address Book, or your Web browser (for looking an address up on a map).

Here's how it works. When you spot a name, address, date, or time, point to it without clicking. Mail draws a dotted rectangle around it. right-click inside the rectangle, or right-click, or click the pop-up ▼ at the right side.

As shown in Figure 11-6, a shortcut menu appears. Its contents vary depending on what you're pointing to:

**Figure 11-6:**
*Mail can detect street addresses, phone numbers, dates, and times. When it spots something you may want to add to another program like Address Book or iCal, it draws a dotted line around the info when you point to it without clicking. Click the little ▼ to get a shortcut menu for further options—like automatically adding the address to your Address Book program or seeing the address pinpointed on a Google map.*

- **A mailing address.** You can choose Show Map from the shortcut menu; your Web browser opens automatically and shows you that address on a Google map.

  Alternatively, you can choose Create New Contact (to add an Address Book entry for this address) or Add to Existing Contact (if the *person* is in your Address Book—just not the *address*). Like magic, a little editing box sprouts out of the data-detected rectangle, prefilled with the information from the message, so that you can approve it.

---

***Tip:*** If you highlight some text in the message and *then* click the pop-up ▼ menu, Mail also fills in the Notes field in this person's Address Book entry with the highlighted text. *Wicked* cool.

---

- **A date and time.** The shortcut menu offers two useful commands. Create New iCal Event opens Mac OS X's calendar program and creates a new appointment at the date and time identified in the message. It's up to you to type a name for the date, set an alarm, and do all the other appointment-setting things described in Chapter 16.

---

***Tip:*** If, while working in iCal, you ever forget where this event came from, double-click it. In the Info balloon, you'll see a link that takes you right back to the original Mail message that started it all.

---

If you choose Show This Date in iCal, though, you go to iCal, which opens directly to the specified date and/or time. The logic of this feature is overwhelming; after all, when someone emails you to ask if you're free for drinks next Thursday at 10, what's the first thing you usually want to do? Check your calendar, of course.

## Opening Attachments

Just as you can attach files to a message, so people often send files to you.

---

***Tip:*** Mail doesn't ordinarily indicate the presence of attachments in the Messages list. It can do so, however. Just choose View→Columns→Attachments. A new column appears in the email list—at the far right—where you'll see a paper-clip icon and the number of file attachments listed for each message.

---

Like Outlook Express for Windows, Mail doesn't store downloaded files as normal file icons on your hard drive. They're actually encoded right into Mail's internal *.mbox* mailbox database files. To extract an attached file from this mass of software, you must proceed in one of these ways:

- Click the Quick Look button in the message header. Instantly, you're treated to a nearly full-size preview of the file's contents. Yes, Quick Look has come to email. Its strengths and weaknesses here are exactly as described in Chapter 2.

- Click the Save button in the message header to save it to the Mac's Downloads folder, nestled within easy reach in the Dock.

---

***Tip:*** If you don't want to use the Downloads folder, you can choose a new autosave location for attachments by choosing Mail→Preferences→General→Downloads.

---

- Right-click the attachment's icon, and choose Save Attachment from the shortcut menu. You'll be asked to specify where you want to put it. Or save time by choosing Save to Downloads Folder, meaning the Downloads folder in the Dock.

- Drag the attachment icon out of the message window and onto any visible portion of your desktop (or any visible folder).

- Click the Save button at the top of the email, or choose File→Save Attachments. (If the message has more than one attachment, this maneuver saves all of them.)

---

*Tip:* The Save button at the top of the Preview pane doubles as a pop-up menu; if you click it and keep the mouse button pressed, you can select from several other options for saving the attachments—like importing them into iPhoto or downloading only one of them.

---

- Double-click the attachment's icon, or single-click the blue link underneath the icon. If you were sent a document (a photo, Word file, or Excel file, for example), it now opens in the corresponding program.

---

**POWER USERS' CLINIC**

## Attachment Tricks

Nowadays, what's *attached* to an email message is often more important than the message itself. You might send a PowerPoint file to a co-worker or send your aunt a picture of your new dog, for example, without bothering to write anything more than "See attached" in the body of the message.

That's why it's such a pain when email attachments don't go through properly–or when they're too big to send at all. Luckily, Mac OS X now provides three tools for making attachments smaller and more compatible with Windows, so you'll never get another angry "I *can't* see attached!" reply again.

**If you're sending images along with your message, you can shrink them down right in Mail.** Use the Image Size pop-up menu in the lower-right corner of the window to pick a smaller size for the images (like Medium or Small).

You can keep tabs on the total size of your attachments in the lower-left corner of the window, too. Ideally, you should keep the total under 2 MB, so dial-up users don't get annoyed–and so your message doesn't get rejected by your recipient's ISP for being too big.

**Use the Finder to compress big files before you send them.** As described on page 86, the Finder creates zip-compressed files, which generally take up much less space than the originals.

**You can pick from two different formats for your attachments: normal or Windows-friendly.** Normal attachments open correctly on both Macs and PCs. Trouble is, a normal attachment may show up on a PC accompanied by a useless second attachment whose name starts with "._". (Your recipients should just ignore it.)

Windows-friendly attachments, on the other hand, always work correctly on PCs–but may not open at all on Macs. Unless you work in an all-Windows company, then, stick with the normal setting.

To use the Windows-friendly setting for an open message, choose Edit→Attachments→Send Windows Friendly Attachments. (If no message is open, the command says "*Always Send Windows Friendly Attachments*" instead). You can also adjust the setting on a per-email basis using the Send Windows Friendly Attachments checkbox at the bottom of the attachment dialog box.

---

**Note:** After the attachment is open, use the File→Save As command to save the file into a folder of your choice. Otherwise, any changes you make to the document won't be visible except when you open it from within Mail.

- Right-click the attachment's icon. From the shortcut menu, you can specify which program you want to use for opening it, using the Open With submenu.

## Replying to a Message

To answer a message, click the Reply button on the message toolbar (or choose Message→Reply, or press ⌘-R). If the message was originally addressed to multiple recipients, you can send your reply to everyone simultaneously by clicking Reply All instead.

A new message window opens, already addressed. As a courtesy to your correspondent, Mail places the original message at the bottom of the window, set off by a vertical bar, as shown in Figure 11-7.

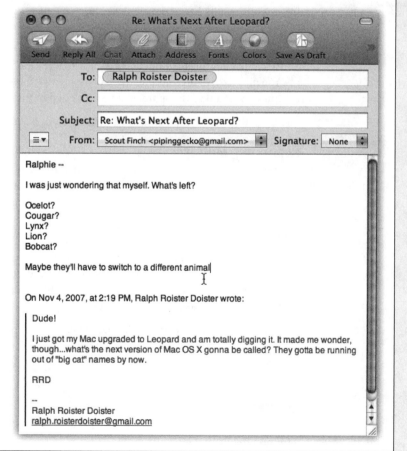

*Figure 11-7:*
*In Rich Text–formatted Mail messages (not to be confused with RTF [Rich Text Format] word processing format, which is very different), a reply includes the original message, marked in a special color (which you can change in Mail→Preferences) and with a vertical bar to differentiate it from the text of your reply.*

*(In plain-text messages, each line of the reply is >denoted >with >brackets, although only your recipient will see them.) The original sender's name is automatically placed in the "To:" field. The subject is the same as the original subject with the addition of Re: (shorthand for Regarding). You're now ready to type your response.*

*Tip:* If you highlight some text before clicking Reply, Mail pastes *only that portion* of the original message into your reply. That's a great convenience to your correspondent, who now knows exactly which part of the message you're responding to.

At this point, you can add or delete recipients, edit the Subject line or the original message, attach a file, and so on.

*Tip:* Use the Return key to create blank lines in the original message. Using this method, you can splice your own comments into the paragraphs of the original message, replying point by point. The brackets preceding each line of the original message help your correspondent keep straight what's yours and what's hers.

When you're finished, click Send. (If you click Reply All in the message window now, your message goes to everyone who received the original note, *even* if you began the reply process by clicking Reply. Mac OS X, in other words, gives you a second chance to address your reply to everyone.)

## Forwarding Messages

Instead of replying to the person who sent you a message, you may sometimes want to pass the note on to a third person.

To do so, click the Forward toolbar button (or choose Message→Forward, or press Shift-⌘-F). A new message opens, looking a lot like the one that appears when you reply. You may wish to precede the original message with a comment of your own, along the lines of: "Frank: I thought you'd be interested in this joke about your mom."

Finally, address it as you would any outgoing piece of mail.

## Redirecting Messages

A redirected message is similar to a forwarded message, with one useful difference: When you forward a message, your recipient sees that it came from you. When you redirect it, your recipient sees the *original* writer's name as the sender. In other words, a redirected message uses you as a low-profile relay station between two other people.

Treasure this feature. Plenty of email programs, including Outlook and Outlook Express for Windows, don't offer a Redirect command at all. You can use it to transfer messages from one of your own accounts to another, or to pass along a message that came to you by mistake.

To redirect a message, choose Message→Redirect, or press Shift-⌘-E. You get an outgoing copy of the message—this time without any quoting marks. (You can edit redirected messages before you send them, too, which is perfect for April Fools' Day pranks.)

## Printing Messages

Sometimes there's no substitute for a printout. Choose File→Print, or press ⌘-P to summon the Print dialog box.

## Filing Messages

Mail lets you create new mailboxes in the Mailboxes pane. You might create one for important messages, another for order confirmations from Web shopping, still another for friends and family, and so on. You can even create mailboxes *inside* these mailboxes, a feature beloved by the hopelessly organized.

Mail in Leopard even offers *smart mailboxes*—self-updating folders that show you all your mail from your boss, for example, or every message with "mortgage" in its subject. It's the same idea as smart folders in the Finder or smart playlists in iTunes: folders whose contents are based around criteria that you specify (Figure 11-8).

*Figure 11-8:*
*Mail lets you create self-populating folders. In this example, the "New Mail from Steve" smart mailbox will automatically display all messages from Steve Jobs at Apple that you've received in the past week.*

The commands you need are all in the Mailbox menu. For example, to create a new mailbox folder, choose Mailbox→New Mailbox, or click the + button at the bottom of the Mailboxes column. To create a smart mailbox, choose Mailbox→New Smart Mailbox.

Mail asks you to name the new mailbox. If you have more than one email account, you can specify which one will contain the new folder. (Smart mailboxes, however, always sit outside your other mailboxes.) When you click OK, a new icon appears in the mailbox column, ready for use.

You can move a message (or group of messages) into a mailbox folder in any of three ways:

- Drag it out of the main list onto the mailbox icon.

- In the list pane, highlight one or more messages, and then choose from the Message→Move To submenu, which lists all your mailboxes.

- Right-click a message, or one of several that you've highlighted. From the resulting shortcut menu, choose Move To, and then, from the submenu, choose the mailbox you want.

Of course, the only way to change the contents of a *smart* mailbox is to change the criteria that it uses to populate itself. To do so, double-click the smart mailbox icon and use the dialog box that appears.

## Flagging Messages

Sometimes you'll receive email that prompts you to some sort of action, but you may not have the time (or the fortitude) to face the task at the moment. ("Hi there... it's me, your accountant. Would you mind rounding up your expenses for 1997 through 2007 and sending me a list by email?")

That's why Mail lets you *flag* a message, summoning a little flag icon in a new column next to a message's name. These indicators can mean anything you like—they simply call attention to certain messages. You can sort your mail list so that all your flagged messages are listed first; click the flag at the top of the column heading.

To flag a message in this way, select the message (or several messages) and then choose Message→Mark→As Flagged, or press Option-⌘-L, or right-click the message's name in the list and, from the shortcut menu, choose Mark→As Flagged. (To clear the flags, repeat the procedure, but use the Mark→As Unflagged command instead.)

## Finding Messages

When you deal with masses of email, you may come to rely on Mail's *dedicated* searching tools. They're fast and convenient, and when you're done with them, you can go right back to browsing your Message list as it was.

### Finding messages within a mailbox

The box in the upper-right corner of the main mail window is Mail's own private Spotlight. You can use it to hide all but certain messages, as shown in Figure 11-9.

---

**Tip:** You can also set up Mail to show you only certain messages that you've *manually* selected, hiding all others in the list. To do so, highlight the messages you want, using the usual selection techniques (Shift-clicking, for example). Then choose View→Display Selected Messages Only. (To see all of them again, choose View→Display All Messages.)

---

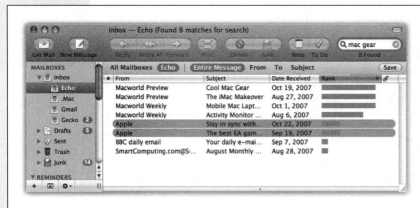

**Figure 11-9:**
*You can jump to the search box by clicking or by pressing Option-⌘-F. As you type, Mail shrinks the list of messages. You can fine-tune your results using the buttons just above the list. To return to the full message list, click the tiny ✕ at the right side of the search box.*

In Leopard, this search field is more powerful than ever. For example:

---

- You have the power of Spotlight charging up your search rankings; the most relevant messages for your search appear high on the list. And Notes and To Do items show up in the search results now, too.

- When you're searching, a thin row of buttons appears underneath the toolbar. You can use these buttons to narrow your results to only messages with your search term in their *subject*, for example, or to only those messages in the currently selected mailbox.

- When you select a message in the search view, the Preview pane pops up from the bottom of the window. If you click Show in Mailbox, on the other hand, you exit the search view and jump straight to the message in whatever mailbox it came from. That's perfect if the message is part of a thread, since jumping to the message also displays all the other messages from its thread.

- If you think you'll want to perform the current search again sometime, click Save in the upper-right corner of the window. Mail displays a dialog box with your search term and criteria filled in; all you have to do is give it a name and click OK to transform your search into a smart mailbox that you can open any time.

### Finding text within an open message

You can also search for certain text *within* an open message. Choose Edit→Find→Find (or press ⌘-F) to bring up the Find dialog box.

## Deleting Messages

Sometimes it's junk mail. Sometimes you're just done with it. Either way, it's a snap to delete a selected message, several selected messages, or a message that's currently before you on the screen. You can press the Delete key, click the Delete button on the toolbar, choose Edit→Delete, or drag messages out of the list window and into your Trash mailbox—or even onto the Dock's Trash icon.

---

**TROUBLESHOOTING MOMENT**

### Rebuilding Your Mail Databases

Mail keeps your messages in a series of mailbox database files in your Home→Library→Mail folder.

Over time, as you add and delete hundreds of messages from these database files, some digital sawdust gets left behind, resulting in peculiarities when addressing messages or general Mail sluggishness. You also wind up with *massive* message files hidden on your hard drive, which can consume hundreds of megabytes of disk space. That's a particular bummer if you like to copy your message databases to your laptop when you go on a trip.

Fortunately, it's easy enough to *rebuild the message databases*. Doing so cleanses, repairs, and purges your message files. As a result, you wind up with a much more compact and healthy database.

To rebuild a mailbox, highlight it in the Mailboxes column in Mail. (Highlight several by ⌘-clicking, if you like.) Then choose Mailbox→Rebuild. Mac OS X takes several minutes (or hours, depending on the size of your mailboxes) to repair and compact your database—but if you're experiencing Mail weirdness or slowness, it's well worth the sacrifice.

---

*Tip:* If you delete a message by accident, the Undo command (Edit→Undo or ⌘-Z) restores it.

All of these commands move the messages to the Trash folder. If you like, you can then click its icon to view a list of the messages you've deleted. You can even rescue messages by dragging them back into another mailbox (back to the Inbox, for example).

### Method 1: Emptying the Trash folder

Mail doesn't vaporize messages in the Trash folder until you "empty the trash," just like in the Finder. You can empty the Trash folder in any of several ways:

- Click a message (or several) within the Trash folder list, and then click the Delete icon on the toolbar (or press the Delete key). Now those messages are *really* gone.

- Choose Mailbox→Erase Deleted Messages (⌘-K). (If you have multiple accounts, choose Erase Deleted Messages→In All Accounts.)

- Right-click the Trash mailbox icon, and then choose Erase Deleted Messages from the shortcut menu. Or choose the same command from the ✿ pop-up menu at the bottom of the window.

- Wait. Mail will permanently delete these messages automatically after a week.

  If a week is too long (or not long enough), you can change this interval. Choose Mail→Preferences, click Accounts, and select the account name from the list at left. Then click Mailbox Behaviors, and change the "Erase deleted messages when"

---

**UP TO SPEED**

## All the Little Symbols

The first column of the main email list shows little symbols that let you know at a glance how you've processed certain messages. The most common one is, of course, the light-blue dot (●), which means "new message." (After reading a message, you can mark it once again as an *unread* message by choosing Message→Mark→As Unread [Shift-⌘-U]—or by right-clicking the message's name and then choosing Mark→As Unread from the shortcut menu.)

You might also see these symbols, which represent messages that you've replied to (↩), forwarded (→), redirected (↱), or flagged 🚩.

A well-guarded secret, however, is that the "replied to" and "forwarded" symbols aren't just indicators—they're *buttons*.

When you see one of these symbols next to your original message, click it to jump straight to your reply (or forwarded message). You're spared the trouble of having to search through all your mailboxes.

Incidentally, you may have noticed that Mail marks a message as having been read the moment you click it. You can change it back to unread by using its shortcut menu—but there's also a more permanent workaround.

If you hide the Preview pane by double-clicking the divider bar just above it, Mail no longer marks messages "read" just because you clicked them in the list. (You can bring back the Preview pane by double-clicking just above the vertical scroll bar, or by dragging the divider bar back up from the bottom.)

---

pop-up menu. If you choose Quitting Mail from the pop-up menu, Mail will take out the trash every time you quit the program.

### Method 2: Deleted mail turns invisible

Mail offers a second—and very unusual—method of deleting messages that doesn't involve the Trash folder at all. Using this method, pressing the Delete key (or clicking the Delete toolbar button) simply hides the selected message in the list. Hidden messages remain hidden, but don't go away for good until you use the Rebuild Mailbox command described in the box on page 319.

If this arrangement sounds useful, choose Mail→Preferences; click Accounts and select the account from the list on the left; click Mailbox Behaviors; and then turn off the checkbox called "Move deleted messages to a separate folder" or "Move deleted messages to the Trash mailbox." (The checkbox's wording depends on what kind of account you have.) From now on, messages you delete vanish from the list.

They're not really gone, however. You can bring them back, at least in ghostly form, by choosing View→Show Deleted Messages (or pressing ⌘-L). Figure 11-10 shows the idea.

**Figure 11-10:**
*To resurrect a deleted message (indicated in light gray type), right-click it and choose Undelete from the shortcut menu.*

Using this system, in other words, you never truly delete messages; you just hide them.

At first, you might be concerned about the disk space and database size involved in keeping your old messages around forever like this. Truth is that Mac OS X is perfectly capable of maintaining many thousands of messages in its mailbox databases—and with the sizes of hard drives nowadays, a few thousand messages aren't likely to make much of a dent.

Meanwhile, there's a huge benefit to this arrangement. At some point, almost everyone wishes they could resurrect a deleted message—maybe months later, maybe years later. Using the hidden-deleted-message system, your old messages are always around for reference. (The downside to this system, of course, is that SEC investigators can use it to find incriminating mail that you thought you'd deleted.)

When you do want to purge these messages for good, you can always return to the Special Mailboxes dialog box and turn the "Move deleted mail to a separate folder" checkbox back on.

## Message Rules

Once you know how to create folders, the next step in managing your email is to set up a series of *message rules* (filters) that file, answer, or delete incoming messages automatically based on their contents (such as their subject, address, and/or size). Message rules require you to think like the distant relative of a programmer, but the mental effort can reward you many times over. Message rules turn Mail into a surprisingly smart and efficient secretary.

### Setting up message rules

Here's how to set up a message rule:

1. Choose Mail→Preferences. Click the Rules icon.

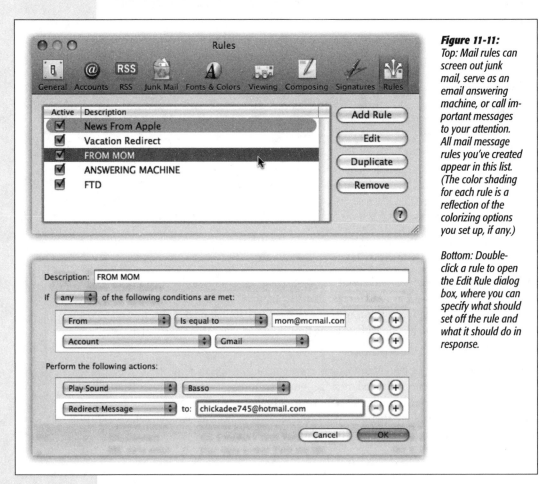

**Figure 11-11:**
*Top: Mail rules can screen out junk mail, serve as an email answering machine, or call important messages to your attention. All mail message rules you've created appear in this list. (The color shading for each rule is a reflection of the colorizing options you set up, if any.)*

*Bottom: Double-click a rule to open the Edit Rule dialog box, where you can specify what should set off the rule and what it should do in response.*

The Rules pane appears, as shown at top in Figure 11-11.

## 2. Click Add Rule.

Now the dialog box shown at bottom in Figure 11-11 appears.

## 3. Use the criteria options (at the top) to specify how Mail should select messages to process.

For example, if you'd like the program to watch out for messages from a particular person, you would set up the first two pop-up menus to say "From" and "Contains," respectively.

To flag messages containing *loan, $$$$, XXXX, !!!!,* and so on, set the pop-up menus to say "Subject" and "Contains."

You can set up *multiple* criteria here, so you flag messages whose subjects contain any one of those common spam triggers. (If you change the "any" pop-up menu to say "all," then *all* of the criteria must be true for the rule to kick in.)

## 4. Specify which words or people you want the message rule to watch for.

In the text box to the right of the two pop-up menus, type the word, address, name, or phrase you want Mail to watch for—a person's name, or *$$$$,* in the previous examples.

## 5. In the lower half of the box, specify what you want to happen to messages that match the criteria.

If, in Steps 1 and 2, you've told your rule to watch for junk mail containing *$$$$* in the Subject line, here's where you can tell Mail to delete it or move it into, say, a Junk folder.

With a little imagination, you'll see how the options in this pop-up menu can do absolutely amazing things with your incoming email. Mail can colorize, delete, move, redirect, or forward messages—or even play a sound when you get a certain message.

By setting up the controls as shown in Figure 11-11, for example, you'll have specified that whenever your mother *(mom@mcmail.com)* sends something to your Gmail account, you'll hear a specific alert noise as the email is redirected to a different email account, *chickadee745@hotmail.com.*

## 6. In the very top box, name your mail rule. Click OK.

Now you're back to the Rules pane (Figure 11-11, top). Here you can choose a sequence for the rules you've created by dragging them up and down. Here, too, you can turn off the ones you won't be needing at the moment, but may use again one day.

*Tip:* Mail applies rules as they appear, from top to bottom, in the list. If a rule doesn't seem to be working properly, it may be that an earlier rule is intercepting and processing some messages before the "broken" rule even sees them. To fix this, try dragging the rule (or the interfering rule) up or down in the list.

# The Anti-Spam Toolkit

Spam, the junk that now makes up more than 80 percent of email, is a problem that's only getting worse. Luckily, you, along with Mail's advanced spam filters, can make it better—at least for *your* email accounts.

## Using the Junk Mail Filter

You'll see the effects of Mail's spam filter the first time you check your mail: A certain swath of message titles appears in color. These are the messages that Mail considers junk.

*Note:* Out of the box, Mail doesn't apply its spam-targeting features to people whose addresses are in your address book, to people you've emailed recently, or to messages sent to you *by name* rather than just by email address. You can adjust these settings in Mail→Preferences→Junk Mail tab.

During your first couple of weeks with Mail, your job is to supervise Mail's coloring job. That is, if you get spam that Mail misses, click the message, and then click the Junk button at the top of its window, or the Junk icon on the toolbar. On the other hand, if Mail flags legitimate mail as spam, slap it gently on the wrist by clicking the Not Junk button. Over time, Mail gets better and better at filtering your mail; it even does surprisingly well against the new breed of image-only spam.

The trouble with this so-called Training mode is that you're still left with the task of trashing the spam yourself, saving you no time whatsoever.

Once Mail has perfected its filtering skills to your satisfaction, though, open Mail's preferences, click Junk Mail, and click "Move it to the Junk mailbox." From now on, Mail automatically files what it deems junk into a Junk mailbox, where it's much easier to scan and delete the messages en masse.

*Tip:* Don't miss the "Trust Junk Mail headers set by your Internet Service Provider" option in the Junk Mail pane of the preference window. If you turn on that checkbox, Mail takes your ISP's word that certain messages are spam, giving you a *double* layer of spam protection.

## More Anti-Spam Tips

The Junk filter goes a long way toward cleaning out the spam from your mail collection—but it doesn't catch everything. If you're overrun by spam, here are some other steps you can take:

- **Don't let the spammers know you're there.** You choose Mail→Preferences, click Viewing, and turn off "Display remote images in HTML messages." This option saves you time, because graphics are big and slow to download. It also shields you from unexpected free samples of pornographers' wares.

But it *also* thwarts a common spammer tactic by blocking graphics that appear to be embedded into a message, but are actually retrieved from a Web site somewhere. Spammers use that embedded-graphics trick to know that their message has fallen on fertile ground—a live sucker who actually looks at these messages—but with that single preference switch, you can fake them out.

- **Rules.** Set up some message rules, as described on page 322, that autoflag messages as spam that have subject lines containing trigger words like "Viagra," "Herbal," "Mortgage," "Refinance," "Enlarge Your"—you get the idea.

- **Create a private account.** If you're overrun by spam, consider sacrificing your address to the public areas of the Internet, like chat rooms, online shopping, Web site and software registration, and newsgroup posting. Spammers use automated software robots that scour every public Internet message and Web page, recording email addresses they find. (In fact, that's probably how they got your address in the first place.)

  Using this technique, at least you're now restricting the junk mail to one, secondary mail account. Reserve a separate email account for person-to-person email.

Here are some suggestions for avoiding landing on spammers' lists in the first place:

- **Don't ask for it.** When filling out forms online, turn off the checkboxes that say, "Yes, send me exciting offers and news from our partners."

- **Fake out the robots.** When posting messages in a newsgroup or message board, insert the letters NOSPAM somewhere into your email address. Anyone replying to you via email must delete the NOSPAM from your email address, which is a slight hassle. Meanwhile, though, the spammers' software robots will lift a bogus email address from your online postings.

- **Never reply to spam.** Doing so identifies your email address as an active one, and can lead to even more unwanted mail. Along the same lines, never click the "Please remove me from your list" link at the bottom of an email unless you know who sent the message.

And for goodness' sake, don't *order* anything sold by the spammers. If only one person in 500,000 does so, the spammer makes money.

# RSS Feeds

The ability to subscribe to those constantly updating news summaries known as *RSS feeds* in your Web browser (page 353) has saved a lot of people a lot of time over the years. After all, why waste precious minutes looking for the news when you can make the news find you?

With Mail, you don't even have to waste the seconds switching from your Inbox to your browser or dedicated RSS program to get a fresh dose of headlines. They can appear right in the main Mail window. You don't even have to switch programs to find out which political candidate shot his foot off while it was still in his mouth.

In fact, if you find it too exhausting to click the RSS icon in the Mailboxes list, you can choose instead to have all your RSS updates land right in your Inbox along with all your other messages.

## Adding RSS Feeds

With just a few clicks, you can bring the news of the world right in with the rest of your mail. Choose File→Add RSS Feeds, and then proceed as shown in Figure 11-12.

*Tip:* As you turn on the feeds you want to see in Mail, ⌘-click to select a bunch of feeds at once.

**Figure 11-12:**
*In the Add RSS Feeds box, you can click to add sites you've already subscribed to in Safari. If you don't already have the feed bookmarked in Safari, click "Specify a custom feed URL" and paste the feed's address into the resulting box. If you've got a ton of feeds and don't want to wade through them all, use the search box to seek out the specific feed you need.*

If you want the RSS headlines to appear in your Inbox like regular email messages, turn on "Show in Inbox." Finally, once you've chosen the feeds you want to see, click Add. Your feeds now appear wherever you told them to go: either the Inbox or the Mailboxes column.

Now, in the RSS category of your Mailboxes list, the names of your RSS feeds show up; the number in the small gray circle tells you how many unread headlines are in the list. If a feed headline intrigues you enough to want more information, click "Read More…" to do just that. Safari pops up and whisks you away to the Web site that sent out the feed in the first place.

After you've read a news item and are done with it, click the Delete button at the top of the window. You can tell Mail to dump all the old articles after a certain amount of time (a day, a week, a month…) in Mail→Preferences→RSS→Remove Articles.

Or, to get rid of an RSS feed altogether, select it and then choose Maibox→Delete Feed. (Right-clicking the name gives you the same option.)

# Notes

No operating system is complete without Notes. You *have* to have a place for little reminders, phone numbers, phone messages, Web addresses, brainstorms, shopping-list hints—anything that's worth writing down, but too tiny to justify heaving a whole word processor onto its feet.

The silly thing is how many people create reminders for themselves by *sending themselves an email message.*

That system works, but it's a bit inelegant. Fortunately, Mac OS X now has a dedicated Notes feature. As a bonus, it syncs automatically to the Notes folder of your iPhone's mail program, or to other computers, as long as you have an IMAP-style email account.

**Figure 11-13:**
*They may look like little pads of scratch paper, but Mail Notes let you paste in Web addresses and photos alongside your typed and formatted text. If you want to share, click the Send button to have the entire Note plop into a new Mail message, ready to be addressed.*

Notes look like actual yellow notepaper with ruled lines, but you can style 'em, save 'em, and even send 'em to your friends. You can type into them, paste into them, and attach pictures to them. And unlike loose scraps of paper or email messages to yourself that may get lost in your mailbox, Notes stay obediently tucked in the Reminders section of the Mailboxes list so you can always find them when you need them.

---

**Tip:** Ordinarily, Notes also appear in your Inbox, at the top. If you prefer to keep your Inbox strictly for messages, though, you can remove the Notes. Choose Mail→Preferences→Accounts→Mailbox Behaviors, and then turn off "Store notes in Inbox." The Notes will still be waiting for you in the side column, down in the Reminders area.

---

To create a note, click the Note button on the Mail toolbar. You can also choose File→New Note or press Control-⌘-N to pop up a fresh piece of onscreen paper.

Once you have your Note, type your text and click the Fonts and Colors buttons at the top of the window to style it. To insert a picture, click the Attach button, and then find the photo or graphic on your Mac you want to use. Figure 11-13 shows an example.

---

**Note:** You can also attach other kinds of files to a Note—ordinary documents, for example. But you can't send such Notes to other people—only Notes with pictures.

---

When you're finished with your Note, click Done to save it. When you look for it in the Reminders category of the Mailboxes list, you'll see that Mail used the first line of the Note as its subject.

To delete a Note for good, select it and press the Delete key.

If you've worked hard on this little Note and want to share it, double-click it to open the note into a new window. Click the Send button on its toolbar. Mail puts the whole thing into a new Mail message—complete with yellow-paper background—so your pal can see how seriously (and stylishly) you take the whole concept of "Note to self."

## To Dos

You've got all this mail piling up with all sorts of things to remember: dinner dates, meeting times, project deadlines, car-service appointments. Wouldn't it be great if you didn't have to remember to look through your mailbox to find out what you're supposed to be doing that day?

It would, and it is, thanks to Mail's To Do feature (Figure 11-14). And the best part is that Mail accesses the *same* To Do list as iCal. The same task list shows up in both programs.

### Creating To Dos

You can use To Dos in several different ways. For example, when you get an email message that requires further action ("I need the photos for the condo association newsletter by Friday"), highlight the important part of the text. Then do any of these things:

- Click To Do in the message window's toolbar.

**Figure 11-14:**
*Top: If a message brings a task that you need to complete, you can give yourself an extra little reminder, right in Mail. Highlight the pertinent text and click the To Do button to add a large, colorful reminder to the top of the message.*

*Bottom: Click the arrow next to the first line of the To Do for a quick and easy way to set a due date/time and alarm, and also choose which calendar you want to use for this particular chore.*

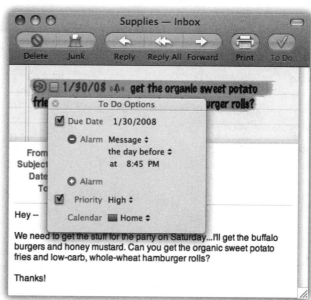

- Choose File→New To Do.

- Press Option-⌘-Y.

- Right-click the highlighted text, and then choose New To Do from the shortcut menu.

In each case, Mail pops a copy of the selected text into a yellow strip of note-style paper at the top of the message, as shown in Figure 11-14.

That task is also listed in the Reminders area of the Mailboxes list. If you need to see *all* the tasks that await you from all your mail accounts, click the flippy triangle to have it spin open and reveal your chores. The number in the gray circle indicates how many To Do items you still need to do.

---

**Tip:** Right-click any item in this To Do list to open a shortcut menu that offers useful controls for setting its due date, priority, and *calendar* (that is, iCal category).

---

When you click the To Do area of the Mailboxes list, all your tasks are listed in the center of the Mail window. Click the gray arrow after each To Do subject line to jump back to the original message it came from.

---

**Tip:** Not all of your life's urgent tasks spring from email messages. Fortunately, you can create standalone To Dos, too. Just click the To Do button at the top of the Mail window when no message is selected. A blank item appears in your To Do list with the generic name "New To Do." Select the name to overwrite it with what this reminder is really about: *Buy kitty litter TODAY* (or whatever).

---

**GEM IN THE ROUGH**

## To Dos and Notes: The Big Sync

Whether you edit your To Do list and Notes in your email program (Mail) or your calendar program (iCal), they're always just one sync away from a Palm organizer, a cellphone, or an iPod.

You do the iPod syncing in iTunes, of all places. Just connect the iPod to the Mac, select its icon in the source list, and click the Contacts tab. Scroll to the Calendars area and turn on the calendars you want to copy to the iPod. Finally, click the Apply button in the corner of the iTunes window. Once you've synchronized iPod with Mac, you can find your calendars and To Do items on the iPod at iPod→Extras→Calendars→To Dos.

And what about the iPhone? If you have that glorious combination of a .Mac account and an iPhone, your To Do items

sync right over from your Mac to the iPhone. Find them on the phone in Mail→Accounts→.Mac→Apple Mail To Do.

Note: To Dos and Notes from .Mac mail accounts sit in their own little area of the Reminders list in Mail. Control-click the .Mac ones; in the shortcut menu, you'll see options for syncing and editing with your shared calendar. If you check your .Mac mail in a Web browser when you're away from home, you can see (but not edit) the Notes you've created on your Mac.

(Your To Do list, however, doesn't show up in the Web-based version of .Mac mail. Yet, anyway. Perhaps *that's* on Apple's own To Do list.)

---

## Completing and Deleting To Dos

When you complete a task, click the small checkbox in front of the To Do subject line—either in the message itself or in the Reminders list. Once you've marked a task as Done this way, the number of total tasks in the Reminders list goes down by one, and that's one less thing you have to deal with.

To delete a big yellow To Do banner from a message, point to the left side of the banner until a red handwritten-looking X appears. Click the X to zap the To Do banner from the message.

You can delete a To Do item from the Reminders list by selecting it and then pressing Delete, among other methods.

## To Do List: Mail/iCal Joint Custody

Seeing your To Do items in Mail is great—when you're working in Mail. Getting them into iCal is even better, though, because you can see the big picture of an entire day, week, or month. As it turns out, Mail and iCal share the exact same To Do list. Create a To Do in one program, and it shows up *instantly* in the other one.

---

**Tip:** You can even set the due date and priority of a task from within Mail. Those controls are in the To Do Options balloon (Figure 11-14). You open this balloon by right-clicking the task and choosing Edit To Do. Later, in iCal, if you double-click a To Do item, and then click "Show in Mail," you get whisked back to the original message, sitting right there in Mail.

---

# Address Book

Address Book is Mac OS X's little-black-book program—an electronic Rolodex where you can stash the names, job titles, addresses, phone numbers, email addresses, and

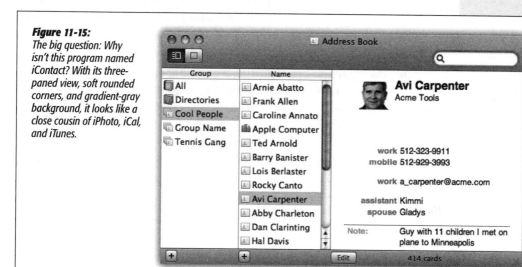

**Figure 11-15:**
*The big question: Why isn't this program named iContact? With its three-paned view, soft rounded corners, and gradient-gray background, it looks like a close cousin of iPhoto, iCal, and iTunes.*

Internet chat screen names of all the people in your life (Figure 11-15). Address Book can also hold related information, like birthdays, anniversaries, and any other tidbits of personal data you'd like to keep at your fingertips.

Once you make Address Book the central repository of all your personal contact information, you can call up this information in a number of convenient ways:

- You can launch Address Book and search for a contact by typing just a few letters in the Search box.

- Regardless of what program you're in, you can use a single keystroke (F12 is the factory setting, or F4 on aluminum keyboards) to summon the Address Book Dashboard widget (page 150). There, you can search for any contact you want, and hide the widget with the same quick keystroke when you're done.

- When you're composing messages in Mail, Address Book automatically fills in email addresses for you when you type the first few letters.

**Tip:** If you choose Window→Address Panel (Option-⌘-A) from within Mail, you can browse all of your addresses without even launching the Address Book program. Once you've selected the people you want to contact, just click the "To:" button to address an email to them—or, if you already have a new email message open, to add them to the recipients.

- When you use iChat to exchange instant messages with people in your Address Book, the pictures you've stored of them automatically appear in chat windows.

- If you've bought a subscription to the .Mac service (page 295), you can synchronize your contacts to the Web, so you can see them while you're away from your Mac (page 275). You can also share Address Books with fellow .Mac members: Choose Address Book→Preferences→Sharing, click the box for "Share your address book," and then click the + button to add the .Mac pals you want to share with. You can even send them an invitation to come share your contact list. If you get an invitation yourself, open your own Address Book program and choose Edit→Subscribe to Address Book.

- Address Book can send its information to an iPod or an iPhone, giving you a "little black book" that fits in your shirt pocket, can be operated one-handed, and comes with built-in musical accompaniment. (To set this up, open iTunes while your iPod or iPhone is connected. Click the iPod/iPhone's icon; on the Contacts or Info tab, turn on "Synchronize Address Book Contacts.")

You can find Address Book in your Applications folder or (in a fresh installation of Mac OS X) in the Dock.

**Tip:** See Chapter 6 for details on importing addresses from other programs into Address Book.

## Creating Address Cards

Each entry in Address Book is called a *card*—like a paper Rolodex card, with predefined spaces to hold all the standard contact information.

To add a new person, choose File→New Card, press ⌘-N, or click the + button beneath the Name column. Then type in the contact information, pressing the Tab key to move from field to field, as shown in Figure 11-16.

---

**Tip:** If you find yourself constantly adding the same fields to new cards, check out the Template pane of Address Book's Preferences (Address Book→Preferences). There, you can customize exactly which fields appear for new cards.

---

**Figure 11-16:**
If one of your contacts happens to have three office phone extensions, a pager number, two home phone lines, a cellphone, and a couple of fax machines, no problem–you can add as many fields as you need. Click the little green + buttons when editing a card to add more phone, email, chat name, and address fields. (The buttons appear only when the existing fields are filled.) Click a field's name to change its label; you can select one of the standard labels from the pop-up menu (Home, Work, and so on) or make up your own labels by choosing Custom, as seen in the lower portion of this figure.

Each card also contains a free-form Notes field at the bottom, where you can type any other random crumbs of information you'd like to store about the person (pet's name, embarrassing nicknames, favorite Chinese restaurant, and so on).

### Editing an address

When you create a new address card, you're automatically in Edit mode, which means you can add and remove fields and change the information on the card. To switch into Browse Mode (where you can view and copy contact information but not change it), click the Edit button or choose Edit→Edit Card (⌘-L). You can also switch *out* of Browse Mode in the same ways.

---

*Tip:* Regardless of which mode you're in—Edit or Browse—you can *always* type, drag, or paste text into the Notes field of an address card.

---

### Adding addresses from Mail

You can also make new contacts in the Address Book right in Mail, saving you the trouble of having to type names and email addresses manually. Select a message in Mail, then choose Message→Add Sender to Address Book (or press ⌘-Y). Presto: Mac OS X adds a new card to the Address Book, with the name and email address fields already filled in. Later, you can edit the card in Address Book to add phone numbers, street addresses, and so on.

## Groups

A *group* is a collection of related address cards, saved under a single descriptive name (as shown in Figure 11-16).

Organizing your contacts into groups can make them much easier to find and use—especially when your database of addresses climbs into the hundreds. For example, if you regularly send out a family newsletter to 35 relatives, you might gather the address cards of all your assorted siblings, cousins, nieces, nephews, uncles, and aunts into a single group called Family. When addressing an outgoing message using Mail, you can type this group name to reach all of your kin at once. A person can be a member of as many different groups as you want.

---

*Tip:* When you send an email message to a group en masse, how does Mail know which email address to use for each person?

Because you've *told* it. Choose Edit→Edit Distribution List. A special dialog box appears, listing everyone in each group, along with each person's complete list of email addresses. (Use the tiny pop-up menu above the list to choose Phone or Address; that way, you can also indicate the preferred phone number and mailing address.)

---

To create a group, click the + button at the bottom of the Group column in the Address Book window, or choose File→New Group (Shift-⌘-N.) Type a name for the newly spawned group icon in the Group column, and then populate it with address cards by dragging entries from the Name list into the group. Clicking a group name automatically locates and displays (in the Names column) all the names that are a part of that group—and hides any that aren't.

---

*Tip:* To turn a set of address cards into a group very quickly, select multiple entries from the Names column—by either Shift-clicking the names (to make contiguous selections) or ⌘-clicking (for non-contiguous selections)—and then choose File→New Group From Selection. You end up with a new group containing all the selected names.

---

### Removing someone from a group

To take someone out of a group, first click the group name, and then click the person's name in the Name column and press the Delete key. If you want to remove the person from Address Book *itself,* click Delete in the resulting dialog box. Otherwise, just click "Remove from Group" or press Return. Address Book keeps the card, but removes it from the currently selected group.

---

**Note:** If you selected All in the Group column, rather than a specific group, you don't get a "Remove from Group" option. Instead, the Mac just asks you to confirm that you do, in fact, want to permanently remove the card.

---

## Pictures

You can dress up each Address Book entry with a photo. Whenever you're editing somebody's address book card, drag a digital photo—preferably 64 pixels square, or a multiple of it—onto the empty headshot square; the image shows up as shown in Figure 11-17. Or double-click the picture well; now you can either browse to a picture on your hard drive by clicking Choose, or, if this person is *with* you, take a new photo by clicking the camera icon. (Don't miss the swirly button next to it, which lets you apply nutty Photo Boothish effects.) At that point, you can enlarge, reposition, and crop the new photo.)

You don't necessarily have to use a photo, of course. You could add any graphic that you want to represent someone, even if it's a Bart Simpson face or a skull and cross-bones. You can use any standard image file in an address card—a JPEG, GIF, PNG, TIFF, or even a PDF.

From now on, if you receive an email from that person, the photo shows up right in the email message.

---

**Tip:** If you've got snapshots in iPhoto, it's particularly easy to add a picture to any address card. Just drag a picture directly from the main iPhoto window to the picture frame on the address card to insert it.

---

### Replacing and removing a picture

To replace a photo on an address card, just drag a new image on top of the old one. If you want to get rid of an existing picture without replacing it, select the card, then choose Card→Clear Custom Image (or, in Edit mode, press Delete).

## Finding an Address

You can search for an Address Book entry inside the currently selected group by typing a few letters of a name (or address, or any other snippet of contact information) in the Search box (Figure 11-17). To search *all* your contacts instead of just the current group, click All in the Group list.

---

**Tip:** You can press ⌘-F to jump directly to the search field and start typing. Your savings: one mouse click.

---

If Address Book finds more than one matching card, use the ↓ and ↑ keys, or Return and Shift-Return, to navigate through them.

Once you've found the card you're looking for, you can perform some interesting stunts. If you click the label of a phone number ("home" or "office", for example), you see the Large Type option: Address Book displays the number in an absurdly gigantic font that fills the entire width of your screen, making it possible to read the number as you dial from across the room. You can also click the label of an email

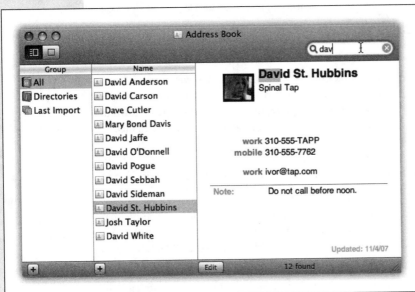

**Figure 11-17:**
*With each letter you type, Address Book filters your social circle and displays the number of matches at the bottom. The matching records themselves appear in the Name column, the first of the matching card entries appears in the far-right pane, and the matching text itself appears highlighted in the matching card.*

**Figure 11-18:**
*The options that become available when you click the field labels on an address card vary according to field type. Pop-up menus let you send email, open a Web page, or view a map, depending on the type of field you've clicked.*

address to create a preaddressed email message, or click a home page to launch your Web browser and go to somebody's site.

You can also copy and paste (or drag) address card info into another program.

---

**Tip:** Once you find a street address in your Address Book, you can find those coordinates on a map by right-clicking the address part of the card and choosing "Map Of" from the shortcut menu, as shown in Figure 11-18. Your Web browser obediently leaps up to display the address on a Google map.

---

## Changing the Address Book Display

You can't do much to customize Address Book's appearance, but the Preferences pane (Address Book→Preferences) gives you at least a couple of options in the General pane that are worth checking out:

- **Display Order.** Choose to have names displayed with the first name followed by the last name, or vice versa.

- **Sort By.** Sort the entries in Address Book by either first or last name.

- **Font Size.** Choose from Regular, Large, or Extra Large. Unfortunately, you can't change anything else about the font used in the Address Book; the color, face, and style are all locked down.

## Printing Options

When you choose File→Print and click the ▼to expand the Print box, the Style pop-up menu offers four ways to print whatever addresses are selected at the moment:

- **Mailing Labels.** This option prints addresses on standard sheets of sticky mailing labels—Avery, for example—that you buy at office-supply stores.

---

**Tip:** As you manipulate settings, you can see your changes in the preview pane on the left. If the preview is too small for you to see, use the Zoom slider. (It doesn't affect your printout.)

If you want to access the *traditional* Print dialog box (to specify paper type, for example), use the unlabeled pop-up menu in the middle of the dialog box top choose Paper Type or whatever. Return to the Labels or Envelopes panes by choosing Address Book from the same pop-up.

---

- **Envelopes.** This feature is great if you have bad handwriting; rather than hand-addressing your envelopes, you can have Address Book print them out for you. Use the Layout pop-up menu to pick the size of your envelopes—it's usually listed on the outside of the envelope box.

---

**Note:** Both the Mailing Labels and Envelopes options print *only* the contacts for which you have, in fact, entered physical mailing addresses.

---

- **Lists.** If all you want is a paper backup of your Address Book entries, use this setting. In the Attributes list, turn on the checkboxes of the fields you want printed—just name and phone number, for example.

- **Pocket Address Book.** This feature prints out a convenient *paper* address book from your virtual one. If you pick Indexed from the Flip Style pop-up menu, each page's edge will even list the first letters of the last names listed on the page, making it a cinch to find the page with the address you want. (Here again, you can pick which fields you'd like to include—phone numbers, addresses, and so on.)

As you fiddle with the options presented here, you get to see a miniature preview, right in the dialog box, that shows what you're going to get.

No matter which mode you choose, the only cards that print are the ones that were selected when you chose File→Print. If you want to print *all* your cards, therefore, click All in the Group column before you print.

---

***Tip:*** You can combine the smart-groups feature with the printing features in one clever way: to print yourself a portable phone book when you're heading off for a visit to a different city. That is, set up a smart group that rounds up everyone you know who lives in Chicago, and then print that as a pocket address book.

---

## Address-Book Backups

When you think about it, the contents of your Address Book may represent *years* of typing and compiling effort. Losing all that information to a corrupted database or a hard drive crash could be devastating. Here are four ways to protect your Address Book data:

- **Turn on .Mac syncing.** As described on page 275, having a .Mac account has its privileges—and one of them is automatic synchronizing with other Macs, or just with the .Mac mothership in the Internet cloud.

- **Back up your entire Address Book database.** Open your Home→Library→Application Support folder. Copy the entire Address Book folder to another disk—burn it to a CD, download it to your iPod, or upload it to a file server, for example. Now your contact data is safe even in the event of a hard drive failure.

- **Back up your whole Mac with Time Machine.** Chapter 9 tells you how.

# Safari & iChat

Apple is obviously intrigued by the possibilities of the Internet. With each new release of Mac OS X, more clever tendrils reach out from the Mac to the world's biggest network.

But Apple's most obvious Internet-friendly creation is Safari, a smartly designed window to the Web (available for both Mac OS X and, believe it or not, Windows). This chapter is all about Safari—the compass icon in the Dock points the way to your Internet adventure—and iChat, the unsung superstar of the chat-and-conferencing universe.

---

**FREQUENTLY ASKED QUESTION**

## Where to Specify Your Preferred Mail and Browser Programs

*Hey! Where the heck do I specify what browser I want to open when, say, I click a link in an email message?*

This is going to sound a little odd. But to indicate that you want some other browser (like Firefox) to be your favorite, you start by opening *Safari.* Choose Safari→Preferences, click the General tab, and choose from the Default Web Browser pop-up menu.

You change email programs using the same twisted logic: You open Mail, and then open its Preferences.

If you'd rather set your default Web browser and email program (and RSS reader, and so on) from System Preferences, try RCDefaultApp, a free System Preference panel that's about 50 times more powerful than the old Internet panel ever was. (You can download it from the "Missing CD" page at *www.missingmanuals.com.*)

---

# Safari

If you want to get something done right, you have to do it yourself.

At least that must be what Apple was thinking when it wrote its own Web browser a few years ago, which so annoyed Microsoft that it promptly ceased all further work on the Mac version of its own Internet Explorer.

Safari is beautiful, very fast, and filled with delicious features. It's not, however, Internet Explorer, and so some Web sites—certain banking sites, for example—refuse to acknowledge its existence. In these situations, you might try the Mac version of Firefox, a free browser available at *www.getfirefox.com*.

To move your Web bookmarks over from Windows to the Mac, see page 167. Then, when you're ready to get going, read on.

## Browsing Basics and Toolbars

You probably know the drill when it comes to Web browsers. When you click an underlined *link (hyperlink)* or a picture button, you're transported from one Web page to another. One page may be the home page of General Motors; another may contain

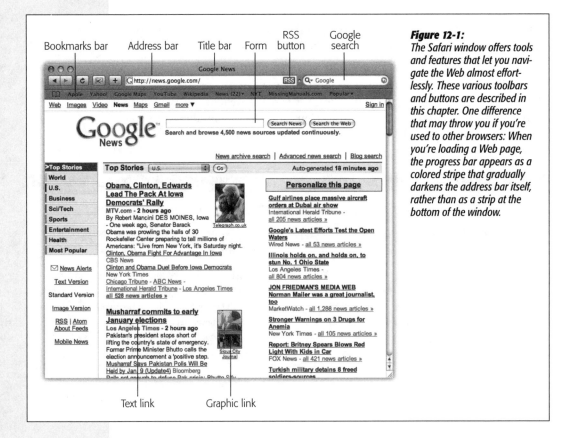

**Figure 12-1:**
*The Safari window offers tools and features that let you navigate the Web almost effortlessly. These various toolbars and buttons are described in this chapter. One difference that may throw you if you're used to other browsers: When you're loading a Web page, the progress bar appears as a colored stripe that gradually darkens the address bar itself, rather than as a strip at the bottom of the window.*

critical information about a bill in Congress; another might have baby pictures posted by a parent in Omaha. Altogether, several billion Web pages await your visit.

*Tip:* Text links aren't *always* blue and underlined. In fact, trendy Web designers sometimes make it very difficult to tell which text is clickable, and which is just text. When in doubt, move your cursor over some text; if the arrow changes to a pointing-finger cursor, you've found yourself a link.

Some of the other Safari tips that may not be obvious:

- **Graphics worth saving.** When you see a picture you'd like to keep, right-click it and choose Save Image to Downloads from the shortcut menu. Safari stores it as a new graphics file in Leopard's Downloads folder on your hard drive. (You can specify where Safari saves downloaded pictures on the Safari→ Preferences→General tab. In that case, the shortcut menu's wording changes to say, for example, "Save Image to 'Pictures.'")

*Tip:* You can also save a graphic to the desktop just by dragging it there, right out of the Safari window. If you're looking at a picture that you'd like to add to your pictures in iPhoto, right-click the image and choose Add Image to iPhoto Library. Sweet!

- **Scroll bars.** Use the scroll bar to move up and down the page—or to save mousing, press the Space bar each time you want to see more. Press Shift-Space to scroll *up.* (The Space bar serves its traditional, space-making function only when the insertion point is blinking in a text box or the address bar.)

  You can also press your up and down arrow keys to scroll one line at a time. Page Up and Page Down scroll in full-screen increments, while Home and End whisk you to the top or bottom of the current Web page. And if your mouse has a scroll wheel, it works, too. (Hold Shift while you're rolling the wheel to scroll *horizontally.*)

## Safari Toolbars

Many of Safari's most useful controls come parked on toolbars and buttons that you summon or hide by choosing their names from the View menu. Here's what they do:

### Address bar

When you type a new Web page address (URL) into this strip and press Enter, the corresponding Web site appears.

Because typing out Internet addresses is so central to the Internet experience and such a typo-prone hassle, the address bar is rich with features that minimize keystrokes. For example:

- You don't have to click the address bar before typing; just press ⌘-L.

- You can highlight the entire address (so it's ready to be typed over with a new one) by clicking the very upper or lower edge of the address bar text box. Alternatively, you can click the small icon just to the left of the current address, or triple-click the address bar, or press ⌘-L.

- You don't have to type out the whole Internet address. You can omit the *http://*, *www*, and *.com* portions; Safari fills in those standard address bits for you. To visit NYTimes.com, for example, a speed freak might press ⌘-L to highlight the address bar, type *nytimes*, and then press Enter.

---

***Tip:*** You're Web surfing, and you suddenly need to look up an appointment in iCal. What do you do?

The power user opens other programs right from within Safari by typing *ical://* in the address bar—or *ichat://*, *addressbook://*, or *sherlock://*—and then pressing Return or Enter. (Unfortunately, those are just about the only Apple programs that work with this URL-launching trick.)

You can also type *mailto:* to open a new outgoing email message in your default email program, or *mailto: steve@apple.com* to preaddress that outgoing message to Steve Jobs. (Of course, remember to replace that email address with someone you'd actually like to contact.)

---

- When you begin to type into the address bar, the AutoComplete feature compares what you're typing against a list of Web sites you've recently visited or that you've saved as bookmarks. Safari displays a drop-down list of Web addresses that seem to match what you're typing. To spare yourself the tedium of typing out the whole thing, click the correct complete address with your mouse, or use the down arrow key to reach the desired listing and then press Enter. The complete address you select then pops into the address bar.

---

**GEM IN THE ROUGH**

## Let AutoFill Do the Typing

Safari can also remember user names, passwords, and other information you type into the text boxes you encounter in your Web travels.

To turn on this great feature, visit the Safari→Preferences→ AutoFill tab. If you turn on "Using info from my Address Book card," whenever you're supposed to fill in your shipping address on a Web form, you can click the AutoFill button in the address bar to have Safari fill in the blanks for you automatically. (If you don't see the AutoFill button—see Figure 12-2—choose its name from the View menu, or use Edit→AutoFill Form to do the deed instead.)

Alternatively, just click a text box—Name, for example—and start typing. As soon as Safari recognizes a familiar scrap of your contact information, it fills out the rest of the word automatically. (If it guessed wrong, just keep typing.)

If, in Preferences, you turn on "User names and passwords," then each time you type a password into a Web page, Safari offers to memorize it for you. It's a great time- and brainsaver, even though it doesn't work on all Web sites. (Of course, use it with caution if you share an account on your Mac with other people.)

When you want Safari to "forget" your passwords—for security reasons, for example—revisit that Safari→ Preferences→AutoFill tab. Click one of the Edit buttons, and then delete the Web site names for which your information has been stored.

Turn on Other Forms if you'd like Safari to remember the terms you've typed into search engines, shopping sites, online gaming sites, and so on.

---

***Tip:*** You might wonder why the View menu even offers you the chance to hide the address bar. If it were hidden, how could you use the Web?

Simple: Even with this bar hidden, you can briefly summon it by pressing ⌘-L. Type the address you want and then press Enter to make the bar disappear again. That's good news for people with small screens—and for Mac trivia collectors.

---

You can summon or dismiss a number of individual buttons on the address bar, in effect customizing it (Figure 12-2):

- **Back/Forward.** Click the ◀ button to revisit the page you were just on. *Keyboard shortcut:* Delete, or ⌘-left arrow, or ⌘-left bracket.

  Once you've clicked ◀, you can then click the ▶ button (or press ⌘-right arrow, or ⌘-right bracket) to return to the page you were on before you clicked the Back button. Click and hold on the ◀ button for a drop-down list of *all* the Web pages you've visited during this online session.

  That pop-up menu lists the sites by name, as in "The New York Times—Breaking News, World News & Multimedia." To view the actual *addresses* instead, Option-click (and hold the mouse down on) the Back or Forward button.

---

***Tip:*** Instead of clicking and holding the ◀ or ▶ button for these tricks, you can save half a second of waiting by just right-clicking.

---

- **Home.** Click to bring up the Web page you've designated as your home page (in Safari→Preferences→General tab).

- **AutoFill.** Click this button to make Safari fill in Web order forms with your name, address, and other information. See the box on the facing page.

- **Text Size.** You can adjust the point size of a Web page's text using these buttons. When you visit a Web site designed for Windows computers—whose text often looks too small on Mac screens—you can use these buttons to bump up the size. *Keyboard shortcut:* ⌘-plus or ⌘-minus.

***Figure 12-2:***
*You summon or hide these buttons by choosing View→ Customize Address bar and dragging buttons onto or off the address bar. Some of them lack text labels, but all offer tooltip labels that you can read by pointing to the button without clicking.*

Backward/Forward    Text Size    Web Clip    Report a bug

Home    Autofill    Reload    Add Bookmark

- **Stop/Reload.** Click the Stop button to interrupt the downloading of a Web page you've just requested (if you've made a mistake, for instance). *Keyboard shortcut:* Esc or ⌘-period.

  Once a page has finished loading, the Stop button turns into a Refresh button. Click this circular arrow if a page doesn't look or work quite right, or if you want to see the updated version of a Web page (such as a breaking-news site) that changes constantly. Safari redownloads the Web page and reinterprets its text and graphics. *Keyboard shortcut:* ⌘-R.

- **Web Clip.** This scissors-clipping-coupon icon is the key to creating Dashboard *Web clips,* as described on page 154. Click this button, and then select the part of the page you want to widgetize.

- **Add Bookmark.** When you find a Web page you might like to visit again, click this button. You can also press ⌘-D, or choose Bookmarks→Add Bookmark, or drag the tiny icon from the address bar directly onto your Bookmarks bar.

  As shown in Figure 12-3, Safari offers to add this Web page's name (or a shorter name that you specify for it) either to the Bookmarks menu or to the Bookmarks *bar* described below. The next time you want to visit that page, just select its name in whichever location you chose.

---

*Tip:* Press Shift-⌘-D to add the bookmark to the menu instantly—no questions asked, no dialog box presented.

---

You can rearrange the names in your Bookmarks menu easily: Choose Bookmarks→ Show All Bookmarks (Option-⌘-B), or click the tiny book icon shown in Figure 12-3. In the resulting organization window, drag the bookmarks up and down.

For more dramatic management tasks—to edit, rename, or delete your bookmarks, for example—also see Figure 12-3.

- **Google Search.** Here's one of Safari's most profoundly useful features—a Search box that automatically sends your search request to Google.com, the world's most popular Web search page. Press Option-⌘-F to deposit your insertion point inside this rounded text box, type something you're looking for—*phony baloney,* say—and then press Enter. Safari takes you directly to the Google results page.

---

*Tip:* The tiny ▾ at the left end of the Google bar is a pop-up menu of your most recent searches.

Bonus Tip: If you right-click a highlighted word or phrase on a Web page, you can choose Google Search from the shortcut menu to search for that text.

---

- **Print.** You can add a printer icon to Safari for point-and-click paper action if you don't want to bother with ⌘-P.

- **Bug.** Ladies and gentlemen, this is Apple at its most humble. This insect-shaped button opens a tiny "Dear Apple" box, where you can tell Apple about a Safari feature or Web page that doesn't work. If you click Options, you can even send Apple a screen illustration of, for example, a screwy Web-page layout that Safari delivered.

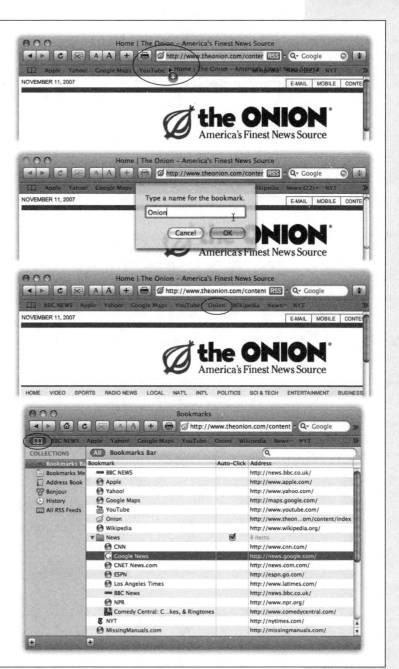

**Figure 12-3:**
*Top: Once you've got a juicy Web page on the screen, you can drag its tiny page-logo icon from the address bar directly onto the Bookmarks bar or menu.*

*Second from top: Safari realizes that you may prefer a shorter name to appear on the space-limited bar, so it offers you the chance to type in a label you prefer.*

*Third from top: When you click OK, the new button appears on the bar, as shown here. (You can also drag any link to the bar, such as a blue underlined phrase from a Web page, or even an icon from your desktop!) To remove a button, drag it off the bar; to rearrange the icons, just drag them.*

*Bottom: Click the little book icon (circled) to open the Organize Bookmarks window. Here, you can drag names up or down to rearrange the list, or drag them into a "folder" that becomes a submenu in the Bookmarks menu. (Create a submenu by clicking the + button below the list.) You can edit a bookmark by clicking once on its name or URL, or delete one by pressing Delete.*

## Status Bar

The Status bar at the bottom of the window tells you what Safari is doing (such as "Opening page…" or "Done"). When you point to a link without clicking, the Status bar also tells you which URL opens if you click it. For those two reasons, it's a very useful strip, but it doesn't appear when you first run Safari. You have to summon it by choosing View→Show Status Bar.

# Tips for Better Surfing

Safari is filled with shortcuts and tricks for better speed and more pleasant surfing. For example:

## SnapBack

The little orange SnapBack button (◄), which sometimes appears at the right end of the address bar or Google search bar, takes you instantly back to the Web page whose address you last typed (or whose bookmark you last clicked), or to your first Google results page.

The point here is that, after burrowing from one link to another in pursuit of some Google result or Amazon listing, you can return to your starting point without having to mash the Back button over and over again. (The SnapBack button doesn't appear until you've actually clicked away from the first page you visited.)

---

***Tip:*** At any time, you can designate your current page as the new SnapBack page. To do so, choose History→ Mark Page for SnapBack (Option-⌘-K).

And you can snap back from the keyboard, too: Option-⌘-P.

---

## Stifle Pop-Ups and Pop-Unders

The world's smarmiest advertisers inundate us with *pop-up* and *pop-under* ads—nasty little windows that appear in front of the browser window or, worse, behind it, waiting to jump out the moment you close your current window. They're often deceptive, masquerading as error messages or dialog boxes, and they'll do absolutely anything to get you to click inside them.

If this kind of thing is driving you crazy, choose Safari→Block Pop-Up Windows, so that a checkmark appears next to the command. It's a war out there—but at least you now have some ammunition.

---

***Note:*** This feature doesn't squelch small windows that pop up when you click a link—only windows that appear unbidden.

Even unbidden windows, however, are sometimes legitimate (and not ads)—notices of new banking features, warnings that the instructions to use a site have changed, and so on. Safari can't tell these from ads and stifles them too. So if a site you trust says "Please turn off pop-up blockers and reload this page," you know you're probably missing out on a *useful* pop-up message.

---

## Impersonating Internet Explorer

Sooner or later, you'll run into a Web site that doesn't work in Safari. Why? When you arrive at a Web site, your browser identifies itself. That's because many commercial Web sites display a different version of the page depending on the browser you're using, thanks to differences in the way various browsers interpret Web layouts.

But because you're one of the minority oddballs using Safari, your otherwise beloved Web site tells you: "Sorry, browser not supported." (Will this problem change now that Apple has released a Windows version of Safari? We can only hope.)

In such times of trouble, you can make Safari *impersonate* any other browser, which is often good enough to fool the picky Web site into letting you in.

The key to this trick is Safari's Debug menu, which is generally hidden. You can make it appear using TinkerTool, a free program available on this book's "Missing CD" page at *www.missingmanuals.com*. It offers a simple checkbox that turns on the Debug menu.

Most of its commands are designed to appeal to programmers, but the submenu you want—User Agent—is useful to everyone. It lets Safari masquerade as a different browser. Choose User Agent→Mac MSIE 5.22, for example, to assume the identity of Internet Explorer for Macintosh.

## Where am I?

As you dig your way down into a Web site, you may wish you could have left a trail of bread crumbs to mark your path. Ah, but Safari has already thought of that. See Figure 12-4.

**Figure 12-4:**
*If you ⌘-click the title bar (centered just above the address bar), Safari displays the "ladder" of pages you descended to arrive at the current one.*

## Faster Browsing Without Graphics

Graphics are part of what makes the Web so compelling. But they're also responsible for making Web pages take so long to arrive on the screen. Without them, Web pages appear almost instantaneously—and you still get fully laid-out Web pages with all their text and headlines.

To turn off graphics, choose Safari→Preferences, and then click the Appearance tab. Turn off "Display images when the page opens," and close the Preferences window. Now try visiting a few Web pages and enjoy the substantial speed boost. (If you wind up on a Web page that's nothing without its pictures, return to Safari→Preferences, turn the same checkbox on, and then reload the page.)

## Expanding Web forms

If the customer-service comment form on that corporate Web site doesn't give you enough room to rant properly, you can resize the text box right on the page—a new, *very* welcome feature in Leopard. Figure 12-5 tells all.

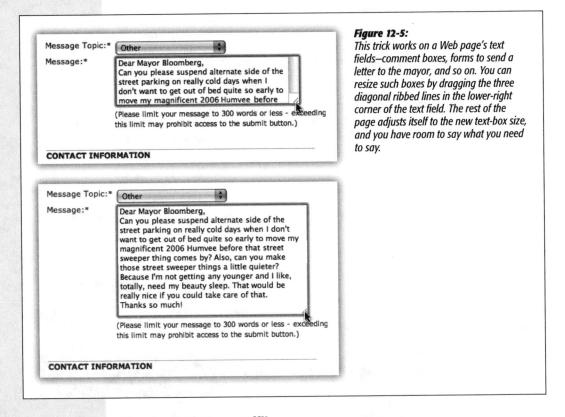

**Figure 12-5:**
*This trick works on a Web page's text fields—comment boxes, forms to send a letter to the mayor, and so on. You can resize such boxes by dragging the three diagonal ribbed lines in the lower-right corner of the text field. The rest of the page adjusts itself to the new text-box size, and you have room to say what you need to say.*

## Viewing Web Pages Offline

You don't have to be connected to the Net to read a favorite Web page. You can save a certain Web page on your hard drive so that you can peruse it later—on your laptop during your commute, for example—just by choosing File→Save As.

To save the *entire* page, along with all its images, movies, and so on, choose Web Archive from the Format pop-up menu.

*Tip:* Whenever you buy something online, don't waste paper by printing out the final "This is your receipt" page. Instead, choose File→Print and, from the PDF pop-up button, choose Save PDF to Web Receipts folder. Safari saves it as a PDF file into a tidy folder (in your Home→Documents folder) called Web Receipts. Nice touch!

## Designate Your Home Page

The first Web site you encounter when Safari connects to the Internet is an Apple Web site. This site is your *home page.* You'll probably find Web browsing more fun, though, if you specify your favorite Web page as your home page.

To do that, navigate your way to the page you prefer. Google, or its news page, *http://news.google.com,* is a good starting place. So is your favorite newspaper home page, or *www.macsurfer.com,* a summary of the day's Mac news coverage around the world, or maybe *www.dilbert.com* for today's Dilbert cartoon.

Then choose Safari→Preferences, click the General tab, and click Set to Current Page (or type the address into the box).

If you can't decide on a home page, or your mood changes from day to day, use the "New windows open with" pop-up menu to choose Empty Page. Some people prefer this setup, which makes Safari load very quickly when you first open it. Once this empty window opens, *then* you can tell the browser where you want to go today.

*Tip:* In the Safari→Preferences→General tab, you can also choose Bookmarks. Then, whenever you open a new window or launch Safari, you can choose exactly which page you want to open by choosing from a list of your bookmarks.

## The History Menu

The History menu lists the Web sites you've visited in the last week or so, neatly organized into subfolders like "Earlier Today" and "Yesterday." (A similar menu appears when you click *and hold* on the Back or Forward button.) These are great features if you can't recall the URL for a Web site that you remember having visited recently.

*Tip:* As illustrated on page 71, the new Help search box searches all of a program's *menus*—including Safari's History menu. You can re-find a site without hunting through all the History submenus manually.

## Finding Text on Web Pages

To find a certain word or phrase on a Web page, press ⌘-F and then type your search word into the Find box. As Safari locates the word or words, it displays them within a bright yellow box and dims the background of the rest of the page. The Find bar also tells you how many times the word or phrase occurs on the page; you can jump to each instance. Click the ⊗ to start over with new search terms, or click Done to close the Find bar and return to your normal browsing activity.

## Zoom in on PDF Pages

PDF files are all over the Web as, among other things, forms to download, online brochures, and scanned book pages. But they aren't always especially readable in a browser window.

Unless, that is, you're using Safari and its PDF viewing and saving tools. The next time you're squinting at a PDF in the window, point to the bottom edge of the document; you'll see a toolbar appear like the one in Figure 12-6. With these four icons, you can zoom out, zoom in, open the file in Preview, or save the PDF file itself to your Downloads folder.

**Figure 12-6:**
*If you're having trouble reading the tiny type in a PDF, move your mouse to the bottom of it to make Safari's PDF toolbar appear. You can zoom out, zoom in, open the file in the Mac's Preview program, or even download it from the Web site with a well-placed click.*

## Tabbed Browsing

Beloved by hardcore surfers the world over, *tabbed browsing* is a way to keep a bunch of Web pages open simultaneously—in a single, neat window. Figure 12-7 illustrates.

Turning on tabbed browsing unlocks a whole raft of Safari shortcuts and tricks, which are just the sort of thing power surfers gulp down like Gatorade:

- If there's a certain set of Web sites you like to visit daily, put the bookmarks into one folder, using Bookmarks→Add Bookmark Folder and the Bookmarks organizer window (Figure 12-3). You can then load all of them at once into a single tabbed window, simply by selecting the resulting "folder" in the Bookmarks menu—or the Bookmarks bar—and choosing Open in Tabs from the submenu.

The beauty of this arrangement is that you can start reading the first Web page while all of the others load into their own tabs in the background.

*Tip:* Click the ⊞ icon at the left end of the Bookmarks bar. In the Bookmarks organizer, click the Bookmarks Bar item in the left-side list. Now you can see an Auto-Click checkbox for each listed folder.

If you turn on this checkmark, then you'll be able to open all the bookmarks in that folder into tabs, all at once, merely by clicking the folder's name in the Bookmarks bar. (If you want to summon the *normal* menu from the folder, just hold the mouse button down.)

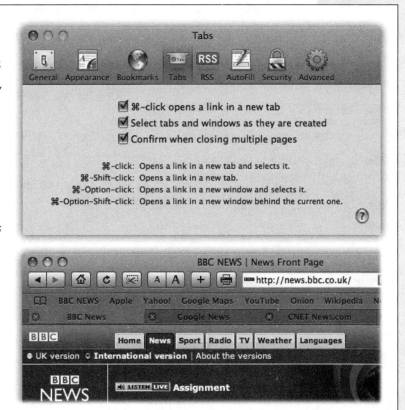

**Figure 12-7:**
*Top: First turn on tabbed browsing in Safari's Preferences→Tabs window. (For best results, also turn on "Select new tabs as they are created.")*

*Bottom: Now, when you ⌘-click a link, or type an address and press ⌘-Return or ⌘-Enter, you open a new tab, not a new window as you ordinarily would. You can now pop from one open page to another by clicking the tabs just under your Bookmarks bar, or close one by clicking its ⊗ button (or pressing ⌘-W).*

- A variation on a theme: When you have a bunch of pages open in tabs, you can drag the tabs across the window to rearrange the order. When you have them the way you want them, right-click a tab, and then choose "Add Bookmark for These

[*Number*] Tabs" from the shortcut menu. You can save your saved tabs to the Bookmarks bar and load all those pages with one click.

- If you Option-click a tab's ⊗ (close) button, you close all tabs *except* the one you clicked. The same thing happens if you hold down Option and choose File→Close Other Tabs, or if you press Option-⌘-W.

- If you Option-⌘-click a link, it opens in a separate window, rather than a new tab. (When tabbed browsing is turned *off*, you just ⌘-click a link to open a new window.)

- If you find yourself with a bunch of separate browser windows all over your screen, you can neatly consolidate them all into one nicely tabbed Safari window by choosing Window→Merge All Windows.

---

**FREQUENTLY ASKED QUESTION**

## Erasing Your Tracks—and Private Browsing

*So, about this History menu: I'd just as soon my wife/husband/boss/parent/kid not know what Web sites I've been visiting. Must that History menu display my movements quite so proudly?*

Some people find it creepy that Safari maintains a complete list of every Web site they've seen recently, right there in plain view of any family member or co-worker who wanders by.

To delete just *one* particularly incriminating History listing, click the book icon at the left end of the Bookmarks bar; in the resulting Bookmarks organizer window, click History. Expand the relevant date triangle, highlight the offending address, and then press your Delete key. Click the book icon again to return to normal browsing. You've just rewritten History!

Or, to erase the *entire* History menu, choose History→Clear History.

Of course, the History menu isn't the only place where you've left footprints. If you choose Safari→Reset Safari instead, you also erase all *other* shreds of your activities: any *cookies* (Web-page preference files) you've accumulated, your list of past downloads, the *cache* files (tiny Web graphics files on your hard drive that a browser stores to save time when you return to the page they came from), and so on. This is good information to know; after all, you might be nominated to the Supreme Court some day.

*That's a lot of work just to cover my tracks; it also erases a lot of valuable cookies, passwords, and History entries I'd like to keep. Is all that really necessary just so I can duck in for an occasional look at the Hot Bods of the Midwestern Tax Preparers' Association Web site?*

No, it's not. A feature called *private browsing* lets you surf without adding any pages to your History list, searches to your Google search box, passwords to Safari's saved password list, or autofill entries to Safari's memory. (Apple says that this feature is intended for use at public Macs, where you don't want to reveal anything personal to subsequent visitors. Ha!)

The trick is to choose Safari→Private Browsing *before* you start browsing. Once you OK the explanation box, Safari records nothing while you surf. (Nothing, that is, except cookies. Your tracks, in other words, are not *completely* hidden. You can erase cookies, if need be, in Safari→Preferences→ Security.)

When you're ready to browse "publicly" again, choose Safari→Private Browsing once more so the checkmark goes away. Safari once again begins taking note of the pages you visit—but it never remembers the earlier ones.

In other words, what happens in Private Browsing stays in Private Browsing.

---

- If you Shift-⌘-click a link, Safari opens that page in a tab *behind* the one you're reading. That's a fantastic trick when you're reading a Web page and see a reference you want to set aside for reading next, but you don't want to interrupt whatever you're reading.

---

**Tip:** Deep in the guts of Safari is a neatly formatted page that lists nearly every keyboard shortcut in Safari. To see it (so you can print it, perhaps), right-click the Safari icon in the Finder. Choose Show Package Contents from the shortcut menu. In the new window, open Contents→Resources. Finally, drag the icon called Shortcuts.html right into the Safari window.

(If you've installed the Debug menu as described on page 347, there's an even easier way: Choose Debug→Keyboard and Mouse Shortcuts.)

---

In the beginning, the Internet was an informational Garden of Eden. There were no banner ads, pop-ups, flashy animations, or spam messages. Back then, people thought the Internet was the greatest idea ever.

Those days, unfortunately, are long gone. Web browsing now entails a constant battle against intrusive advertising and annoying animations. And with the proliferation of Web sites of every kind—from news sites to personal weblogs (*blogs*)—just reading your favorite sites can become a full-time job.

Enter RSS, a technology that lets you subscribe to *feeds*—summary blurbs provided by thousands of sources around the world, from Reuters to Apple to your nerdy next-door neighbor. You use a program like Safari to "subscribe" to updates from such feeds, and then read any new articles or postings at your leisure.

The result: You spare yourself the tedium of checking for updates manually, plus you get to read short summaries of new articles without ads and blinking animations. And if you want to read a full article, you can click its link in the RSS feed to jump straight to the main Web site.

---

**Note:** RSS either stands for Rich Site Summary or Really Simple Syndication. Each abbreviation explains one aspect of RSS—either its summarizing talent or its simplicity.

---

## Viewing an RSS Feed

So how do you sign up for these free, automatic RSS "broadcasts?" Watch your address bar as you're surfing the Web. When you see a blue RSS button appear (identified back in Figure 12-1), Safari is telling you, "This site has an RSS feed available."

To see what the fuss is all about, click that button. Safari switches into RSS-viewing mode, as shown in Figure 12-8.

At this point, you have two choices:

- **Add the RSS feed as a bookmark.** Use the Bookmarks→Add Bookmark command, and add the feed to your Bookmarks menu, Bookmarks bar, or Mail (page 325) as you would any Web page. From now on, you'll be able to see whether the RSS feed has had any new articles posted—without actually having to visit the site.

- **Close the RSS feed altogether.** To do so, just click the RSS button again. You're left back where you started, at whatever Web page you were visiting.

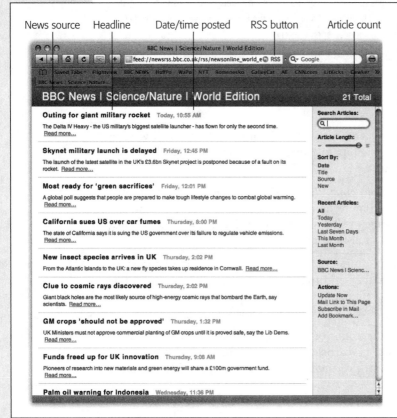

News source · Headline · Date/time posted · RSS button · Article count

*Figure 12-8:*
*The Length slider controls how much text appears for each RSS blurb; if you drag it all the way to the left, you're left with nothing but headlines. To change the number and order of the articles being displayed, use the search options on the right. And if you feel a sudden desire to tell your friends about an amazing RSS feed you've just discovered, use the "Mail Link to This Page" link in the lower-right section of the window.*

## RSS Tricks

RSS is a tremendously flexible and powerful technology, especially in Safari. The fun never ends, as these tricks illustrate.

### Creating RSS summaries

If you create a new bookmark folder (page 344) and fill it with RSS feeds, you can see the *total* number of new articles right next to the folder's name. You might create a folder of Mac news feeds, for instance, so you know whenever there's a important event in the Mac world.

From then on, by clicking the folder's name (and opening its pop-up menu), you can see which feeds have new articles; they're the ones with numbers next to their names. If you ⌘-click a bookmark folder's name—in either the Bookmarks bar or the Bookmarks menu—Safari shows you *all* the feeds, neatly collated into one big, easily digestible list for your perusing pleasure. (If you're billing by the hour, you can also choose View All RSS Articles from the folder's pop-up menu to achieve the same effect.)

*Tip:* To make the merged list more useful, click New under the Sort By heading. Now Safari displays any new articles at the top of the list, regardless of what site they came from, so you don't have to hunt through the list for new articles yourself.

*Tip:* If you find RSS feeds completely addictive in Safari, you'll love them in Mail—where you can display them right in the program's window or have them land in your Inbox like regular messages.

---

**FREQUENTLY ASKED QUESTION**

## Cookie Control

*Help! I'm afraid of cookies! The cookies are trying to watch me!*

Cookies are something like Web page preference files. Certain Web sites—particularly commercial ones like Amazon.com—deposit them on your hard drive like little bookmarks, so that they'll remember you the next time you visit. Most cookies are perfectly innocuous—and, in fact, are extremely helpful, because they help Web sites remember your tastes. Cookies also spare you the effort of having to type in your name, address, credit card number, and so on, every time you visit these Web sites.

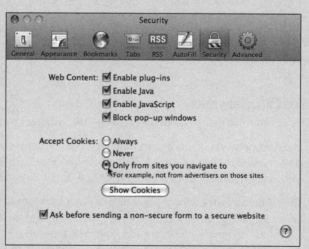

But fear is widespread, and the media fans the flames with tales of sinister cookies that track your movement on the Web. If you're worried about invasions of privacy, Safari is ready to protect you.

Once the browser is open, choose Safari→Preferences→ Security tab. The buttons in this dialog box are like a paranoia gauge. If you click Never, you create an acrylic shield around your Mac. No cookies can come in, and no cookie information can go out. You'll probably find the Web a very inconvenient place; you'll have to re-enter your information upon every visit, and some Web sites may not work properly at all.

A good compromise is "Only from sites you navigate to," which accepts cookies from sites you *want* to visit, but blocks cookies deposited on your hard drive by sites you're not actually visiting—cookies an especially evil banner ad gives you, for example.

Note, too, the Show Cookies button, which reveals the shockingly complete list of every cookie you've accumulated so far—and offers you the chance to delete the ones that don't look so savory.

### The RSS screen saver

In System Preferences→Desktop & Screen Saver→Screen Saver tab, you'll find the RSS Visualizer screen saver, one of the most impressive displays of Mac OS X technology you'll ever see. When you click Options and select an RSS feed (and enable screen savers), you set up Mac OS X to get news from that feed whenever you're away from your Mac. When the screen saver comes on, you're treated to a three-dimensional animation of the news from that site—along with astonished gazes from your co-workers.

If a news story grabs your interest, press the number key mentioned at the bottom of the screen. The screen saver fades out, and Safari comes forward to display the associated article.

*Tip:* But what if the feed you want isn't part of Safari's repertoire? No problem. Add the feed to your Safari bookmarks and relaunch System Preferences.

## iChat

Somewhere between email and the telephone lies a unique communication tool called *instant messaging*. Plenty of instant messenger programs run on the Mac, but guess what? You don't really need any of them. Mac OS X comes with its very own instant messenger program called iChat, built right into the system and ready to connect to your friends on the AIM, Jabber, or GoogleTalk networks.

To start up iChat, go to Applications→iChat, or just click iChat's Dock icon. It looks like a blue speech balloon with a camcorder inside, which is a clue to one of iChat's best and most substantially beefed-up Leopard features: live video chats over the Internet.

### Three Chat Networks

iChat lets you reach out to chat partners on three different networks:

- **The AIM network.** If you've signed up for a .Mac address (the paid kind or the free kind described below) or a free AOL Instant Messenger (AIM) account, you can chat with anyone in the 150-million-member AOL Instant Messenger network.

- **The Jabber network.** Jabber is another chat network, whose key virtue is its *open-source* origins. In other words, it wasn't masterminded by some corporate media behemoth; it's an all-volunteer effort, joined by thousands of programmers all over the world. There's no one Jabber chat program (like AOL Instant Messenger). There are dozens, available for Mac OS X, Windows, Linux, Unix, Palm and PocketPC organizers, and so on. All of them can chat with each other across the Internet in one glorious frenzy of typing.

  And now there's one more program that can join the party: iChat.

- **Google Talk.** Evidently, Google felt that there just weren't enough different chat programs, because it released its own chat program in 2005.

Behind the scenes, it uses the Jabber network, so Google Talk doesn't really count as a different *network*. But it does mean that you can use iChat to converse with all those Google Talkers, too.

- **Your own local network.** Thanks to the Bonjour network-recognition technology, you can communicate with other Macs on your own office network without signing up for anything at all—and without being online. This is a terrific feature when you're sitting around a conference table, idly chatting with colleagues using your wireless laptop (and the boss thinks you're taking notes).

Each network generally has its own separate Buddy List window and its own chat window.

You log into each network separately using the iChat→Accounts submenu, but you can be logged into all of them at once. This is a great option if your friends are spread out among different chat networks.

Otherwise, however, chatting and videoconferencing works identically on all three networks. Keep that in mind as you read the following pages.

## Signing Up

When you open iChat for the first time, you see the "Welcome To iChat" window (Figure 12-9). This is the first of several screens in the iChat setup sequence, during which you're supposed to tell it which kinds of chat accounts you have, and set up your camera, if any.

An *account* is a name and password. Fortunately, these accounts are free, and there are several ways to acquire one.

---

*Tip:* The easiest procedure is to set up your accounts *before* you open iChat for the first time, because then you can just plug in your names and passwords in the setup screens.

You *can* input your account information later, though. Choose iChat→Preferences, click the Accounts button, click the + button, and choose the right account type (Jabber, .Mac, Google Talk, or AIM) from the Account Type pop-up menu.

---

### How to get a free .Mac account

If you're already a member of Apple's .Mac service (page 295), iChat fills in your Mac.com user name and password automatically.

If not, you can get an iChat-only .Mac account for free. To get started, do one of these two things:

- Click the "Get an iChat Account" button that appears on the second Setup Assistant screen.

- Choose iChat→Preferences, click the Accounts button, click the + button, and click Create New .Mac Account.

Either way, you go to an Apple Web page, where you can sign up for a free iChat account name. You'll also get 60 days of the more complete .Mac treatment (usually $100 a year) described in Chapter 10. When your trial period ends, you'll lose all of the other stuff that .Mac provides, but you'll get to keep your iChat name.

**Note:** If your .Mac name is *missingmanualguy,* you'll appear to everyone else as *missingmanualguy@mac. com.* The software tacks on the "@mac.com" suffix automatically.

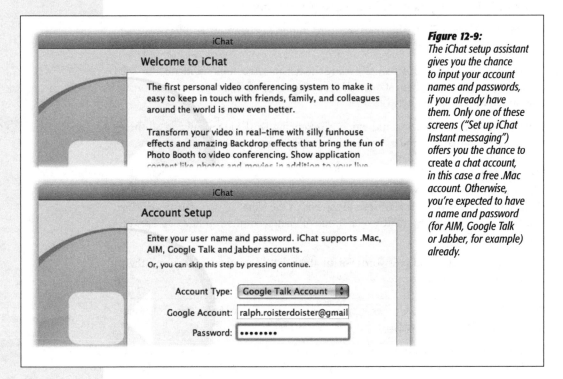

**Figure 12-9:**
*The iChat setup assistant gives you the chance to input your account names and passwords, if you already have them. Only one of these screens ("Set up iChat Instant messaging") offers you the chance to create a chat account, in this case a free .Mac account. Otherwise, you're expected to have a name and password (for AIM, Google Talk or Jabber, for example) already.*

### How to get a free Jabber (or Gmail) account

You can't create a Jabber account using iChat. Apple expects that, if you're that interested in Jabber, you already have an account that's been set up by the company you work for (Jabber is popular in corporations) or by you, using one of the free Jabber programs.

For example, at *www.adiumx.com,* you can download a great chat program for Mac OS X that presents you, the first time you open it, with a Preferences:Accounts screen. Click the + button, choose Jabber, type in any screen name and password you like— and when you're told that your account doesn't exist, mutter, "I know, I know," and click Register. Your account is now created (your account name is *Francis@jabber.org,* for example), and you can plug that screen name and password into iChat.

Alternatively, you can just sign up for a free Google Talk account, which is the same as having a free Gmail account. (Go to Gmail.com to sign up for one.)

Once you've got a Gmail address, choose iChat→Preferences→Accounts, and click the + button. Under Account Type, choose Google Talk and type in your complete Gmail address (like *gwashington@gmail.com)* and password. Your Gmail name pops up on iChat's Jabber list—along with any of your Gmail contacts who are already online and yapping.

### How to get a free AIM account

You can't create an AIM account in iChat, either. If you're an America Online member, your existing screen name and password work; if you've used AIM before, you can use your existing name and password.

If you've never had an AIM account, you can sign up at *https://my.screenname.aol.com.* Click "Create one FREE now" to make up an AIM screen name.

## The Buddy Lists

Once you've entered your account information, you're technically ready to start chatting. All you need now is a chatting companion, or what's called a *buddy* in instant-messaging circles. iChat comes complete with a Buddy List window in which you can house the chat "addresses" for all your friends, relatives, and colleagues out there on the Internet.

Actually, to be precise, iChat comes with *three* buddy lists (Figure 12-10):

- **AIM Buddy List.** This window lists all of your chat pals who have *either* .Mac or AIM accounts; they all share the same buddy list. You see the same list whether you log into your .Mac or your AIM account.

- **Jabber List.** Same idea, except that all of your contacts in this window must have Jabber or Google Talk accounts.

- **Bonjour.** This list is limited to your local network buddies—the ones in the same building, most likely, and on the same network. You can't add names to your Bonjour list; anyone who's on the network and running iChat appears automatically in the Bonjour list.

## Making a List

When you start iChat, your buddy lists automatically appear (Figure 12-10). If you don't see them, choose the list you want from the Window menu: Bonjour, Buddy List, or Jabber. (Or press their keyboard shortcuts: ⌘-1, ⌘-2, or ⌘-3.)

Adding a buddy to this list entails knowing that person's account name, whether it's on AIM, Mac.com, or Jabber. Once you have it, you can either choose Buddies→Add Buddy (Shift-⌘-A) or click the + button at the bottom-left corner of the window.

Down slides a sheet attached to the Buddy List window, offering a window into the Address Book program (Chapter 11).

*Tip:* As you accumulate buddies, your Buddy List may become crowded. If you choose View→Show Offline Buddies (so that the checkmark disappears), only your *currently online* buddies show up in the Buddy List—a much more meaningful list for the temporarily lonely.

If your chat companion is already in Address Book, scroll through the list until you find the name you want (or enter the first few letters into the Search box), click the name, and then click Select Buddy.

If not, click New Person and enter the buddy's AIM address, .Mac address, or (if you're in the Jabber list) Jabber address. You're adding this person to both your Buddy List and your Address Book.

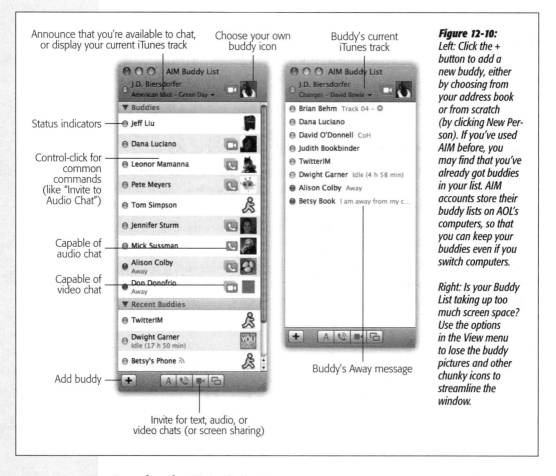

Announce that you're available to chat, or display your current iTunes track

Choose your own buddy icon

Buddy's current iTunes track

Status indicators

Control-click for common commands (like "Invite to Audio Chat")

Capable of audio chat

Capable of video chat

Add buddy

Invite for text, audio, or video chats (or screen sharing)

Buddy's Away message

*Figure 12-10:*
*Left: Click the + button to add a new buddy, either by choosing from your address book or from scratch (by clicking New Person). If you've used AIM before, you may find that you've already got buddies in your list. AIM accounts store their buddy lists on AOL's computers, so that you can keep your buddies even if you switch computers.*

*Right: Is your Buddy List taking up too much screen space? Use the options in the View menu to lose the buddy pictures and other chunky icons to streamline the window.*

## Broadcasting Your Status

Using the pop-up menu just below your name (Figure 12-11, right), you can display your current mental status to *other* people's buddy lists. You can announce that you're Available, Away, or Drunk. (You have to choose Edit Status Menu for that one; see Figure 12-11, left.)

Better yet, if you have music playing in iTunes, you can tell the world what you're listening to at the moment by choosing Current iTunes Track. (Your buddy can even click that song's name to open its screen on the iTunes Store, all for Instant Purchase Gratification.)

For some people, by far the juiciest option is a status called Invisible (available for .Mac and AIM accounts only). It's like a *Star Trek* cloaking device for your onscreen presence (Figure 12-11). Great for stalkers!

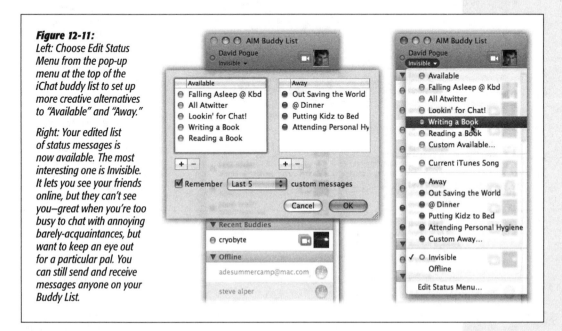

**Figure 12-11:**
*Left: Choose Edit Status Menu from the pop-up menu at the top of the iChat buddy list to set up more creative alternatives to "Available" and "Away."*

*Right: Your edited list of status messages is now available. The most interesting one is Invisible. It lets you see your friends online, but they can't see you—great when you're too busy to chat with annoying barely-acquaintances, but want to keep an eye out for a particular pal. You can still send and receive messages anyone on your Buddy List.*

## Sorting and sizing your friends

In View→Sort Buddies, you can rearrange your buddies as they're listed in the Buddy lists: by availability, first name, last name, or in a manual order that you determine by dragging names up or down.

## Let the Chat Begin

As with any conversation, somebody has to talk first. In chat circles, that's called *inviting* someone to a chat.

### They invite you

To "turn on your pager" so you'll be notified when someone wants to chat with you, run iChat. Hide its windows, if you like, by pressing ⌘-H.

When someone tries to "page" you for a chat, iChat comes forward automatically and shows you an invitation message like the one in Figure 12-12. If the person initiating a chat isn't already in your Buddy List, you'll simply see a note that says "Message from *[name of the person]*."

*Tip:* If you're getting hassled by someone on your AIM/.Mac buddy list, click his screen name and choose Buddies→Block Person. If the person isn't online at the time, go to iChat→Preferences→Accounts→Security and click the button for Block specific people. Click the Edit List button, and then type in the screen name of the person you want out of your IM life.

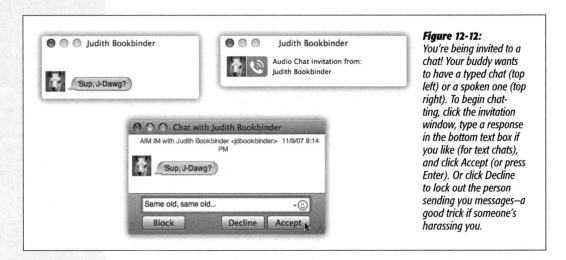

**Figure 12-12:**
*You're being invited to a chat! Your buddy wants to have a typed chat (top left) or a spoken one (top right). To begin chatting, click the invitation window, type a response in the bottom text box if you like (for text chats), and click Accept (or press Enter). Or click Decline to lock out the person sending you messages—a good trick if someone's harassing you.*

## You Invite Them

To invite somebody in your Buddy List to a chat:

- For a text chat, double-click the person's *name*, type a quick invite ("You there?"), and press Enter.

*Tip:* You can invite more than one person to the chat. Each time you click the + button at the bottom of the Participants list, you can choose another person to invite. (Or ⌘-click each name in the buddy list to select several people at once and then click the A button at the bottom of the list to start the text chat.)

Everyone sees all the messages everyone sends.

- To start an audio or video chat, click the microphone or movie-camera icon in your Buddy List (shown in Figure 12-10).

To initiate a chat with someone who *isn't* in the Buddy List, choose File→New Chat With Person. Type the account name of the person, and then click OK to send the invitation.

Either way, you can have more than one chat going at once. In the Olden Days (before October 2007), real iChat nerds often wound up with screens overflowing with individual chat windows. Juggling them all, and keeping them all current, was just part of the fun—and still can be.

But in modern times, you can now contain all your conversations in a single window. If you like the idea of a consolidated chatspace, chose iChat→Preferences→Messages and slap a checkmark in the "Collect chats into a single window" Box. Figure 12-13 has the details.

**Figure 12-13:**
*Now, when you're conversing with several buddies, you can bounce between conversations by clicking the buddy names on the side of the window. It's not as adventurous as keeping all your chats going in separate windows, but it's a lot easier to hide when the boss comes your way.*

## Text Chats

A typed chat works like this: Each time you or your chat partner types something and then presses Enter, the text appears on both your screens. iChat displays each typed comment next to an icon, which can be any of these three things:

- **A picture they added.** If the buddy added her *own* picture—to her own copy of iChat, a Jabber program, or AOL Instant Messenger—it will be transmitted to you, appearing automatically in the chat window. Cool!

- **A picture you added.** If you've added a picture of that person to the Buddy List or Address Book, you see it here instead. (After all, your vision of what somebody looks like may not match his own self-image.)

- **Generic.** If nobody's done icon-dragging of any sort, you get a generic icon—either a blue globe (for .Mac people), a light bulb (for Google Talkers), or the AOL Instant Messenger running man (for AIM people).

To choose a graphic to use as your own icon, click the square picture to the right of your own name at the top of the Buddy, Jabber, or Bonjour list. From the pop-up palette of recently selected pictures, choose Edit Picture to open a pop-up image-selection palette, where you can take a snapshot with your Mac's camera or choose a photo file from your hard drive. Feel free to build an array of different graphics to represent yourself—and to change them in mid-chat, using this pop-up palette, to the delight or confusion of your conversation partner.

---

**Tip:** When you minimize the iChat message window, its Dock icon displays the icon of the person you're chatting with—a handy reminder that she's still there.

---

## In-chat fun

Typing isn't the only thing you can do during a chat. You can also perform any of these stunts:

- **Format your text.** You can press ⌘-B or ⌘-I to make your next typed utterance bold or italic. Or change your color or font by choosing Format→Show Colors or Format→Show Fonts, which summons the standard Mac OS X color or font palettes. (If you use some weird font that your chat partners don't have installed, they won't see the same typeface.)

- **Insert a smiley.** When you choose a face (like Undecided, Angry, or Frown) from this quick-access menu of smiley options (at the right end of the text-reply box), iChat inserts it as a graphic into your response.

  On the other hand, if you know the correct symbols to produce smileys—that :) means a smiling face, for example—you can save time by typing them instead of using the pop-up menu. iChat converts them into smiley icons on the fly, as soon as you send your reply.

- **Send a file.** Choosing Buddies→Send File lets you send a file to *all* the participants in your chat.

  Better yet, just drag the file's icon from the Finder into the box where you normally type. (This trick works well with pictures, because your conversation partner sees the graphic right in his iChat window.)

  This is a fantastic way to transfer a file that would be too big to send by email. A chat window never gets "full," and no attachment is too large to send.

---

**GEM IN THE ROUGH**

### The Chat Transcript

Every now and then, you'll wish you could *preserve* a chat for all time—a particularly meaningful conversation with a friend, lover, or customer-service agent.

On the iChat→Preferences→Messages panel, you can turn on "Automatically save chat transcripts." From now on, the text of your conversations is automatically saved in your Home→Documents→iChats folder. To view a chat later, double-click its icon. It opens within iChat, compete with all colors and formatting.

Even if you don't turn on this "Automatically" checkbox, you can save individual chats in progress by choosing File→Save a Copy As.

---

This method halves the time of transfer, too, since your recipients get the file *as* you upload it. They don't have to wait 20 minutes for you to send the file, and then another 20 minutes to download it, as they would with email or FTP.

Note, though, that this option isn't available in old versions of the AOL Instant Messenger program—only new versions and iChat.

- **Send an Instant Message.** Not everything in a chat session has to be "heard" by all participants. If you choose Buddies→Send Instant Message, you get a *private* chat window, where you can "whisper" something directly to a special someone behind the other chatters' backs.

- **Send Email.** If someone messages you, "Hey, will you email me directions?" you can do so on the spot by choosing Buddies→Send Email. Your email program opens up automatically so you can send the note along; if your buddy's email address is part of his Address Book info, the message is preaddressed.

- **Send an SMS message to a cellphone.** If you're using an AIM screen name or .Mac account, you can send text messages directly to your friends' cellphones (in the United States, anyway). Choose File→Send SMS. In the box that pops up, type the full cellphone number, without punctuation, like this: *2125551212*.

  Press Enter to return to the chat window. Type a very short message (a couple of sentences, tops), and then press Enter.

---

*Tip:* If iChat rudely informs you that your own privacy settings prevent you from contacting "this person," choose iChat→Preferences, click Accounts, click your chat account, and turn on "Allow anyone."

---

Obviously, you can't carry on much of an interactive conversation this way. The only response you get is from AOL's computers, letting you know that your message has been sent. But what a great way to shoot a "Call me!" or "Running late—see you tonight!" or "Turn on channel 4 right now!!!" message to someone's phone.

## Audio Chats

iChat becomes much more exciting when you exploit its AV Club capabilities. Even over a dial-up modem connection, you can conduct audio chats, speaking into your microphone and listening to the responses from your speaker.

If you have a broadband connection, though, you get a much more satisfying experience—and, if you have a pretty fast Mac, up to 10 of you can join in one massive, free conference call from across the Internet.

A telephone icon next to a name in your buddy list tells you that the buddy has a microphone, and is ready for a free Internet "phone call." If you see what appear to be stacked phone icons, then your pal's Mac has enough horsepower to handle a *multiple-person* conference call. (You can see these icons back in Figure 12-10.)

To begin an audio chat, take your pick:

- Click the telephone icon next to the buddy's name, or

- Highlight someone in the Buddy List, and then click the telephone icon at the bottom of the list, or

- If you're already in a text chat, choose Buddies→Invite to Audio Chat.

Once your invitation is accepted, you can begin speaking to each other. The bars of the sound-level meter let you know that the microphone—which you've specified in the iChat→Preferences→Audio/Video tab—is working.

---

**Tip:** Although the audio is *full-duplex* (you can hear and speak simultaneously, like a phone but unlike a walkie-talkie), there may be a delay, like you're calling overseas on a bad connection. If you can't hear anything at all, check out iChat's Help system, which contains a long list of suggestions.

---

## Video Chats

If you and your partner both have broadband Internet connections, even more impressive feats await. You can conduct a free video chat with up to four people, who show up on three vertical panels, gorgeously reflected on a shiny black table surface. This isn't the jerky, out-of-audio-sync, Triscuit-sized video of Windows videoconferencing. If you've got the Mac muscle and bandwidth, your partners are as crisp, clear, bright and smooth as television—and as big as your screen, if you like.

People can come and go; as they enter and leave the "videosphere," iChat slides their glistening screens aside, enlarging or shrinking them as necessary to fit on your screen.

If you see a camcorder icon next to a buddy's name, you can have a full-screen, high-quality video chat with that person, because they, like you, have a suitable camera and a high-speed Internet connection. If you see a *stacked* camcorder icon, then that person has a G5 or a faster Mac that's capable of joining a four-way video chat.

To begin a video chat, click the camera icon next to a buddy's name, or highlight someone in the Buddy List and then click the camcorder icon at the bottom of the list. Or, if you're already in a text chat, choose Buddies→Invite to Video Chat.

A window opens, showing *you*. This Preview mode is intended to show what your buddy will see. (You'll probably discover that you need some kind of light in front of you to avoid being too shadowy.) As your buddies join you, they appear in their own windows (Figure 12-14).

And now, some video-chat notes:

- If your conversation partners seem unwilling to make eye contact, it's not because they're shifty. They're just looking at *you*, on the screen, rather than at the camera—and chances are you aren't looking into your camera, either.

- Don't miss the Video→Full Screen command! Wild.

- You can have video chats with Windows computers, too, as long as they're using a recent version of AOL Instant Messenger. Be prepared for disappointment, though; the video is generally jerky, small, and slightly out of sync. That's partly due to the cheap USB Webcams most PCs have, and partly due to the poor video *codec* (compression scheme) that's built into AOL Instant Messenger.

- You can capture a still "photo" of a video chat by ⌘-dragging the image to your desktop, or by choosing Video→Take Snapshot (Option-⌘-S).

- Don't want to see yourself in the picture-in-picture window during your video chat? Choose Video→Hide Local Video. (That's new in 10.5.)

**Figure 12-14:**
*That's you in the smaller window. To move your own mini-window, click a different corner, or drag yourself to a different corner. If you need to blow your nose or do something else unseemly, Option-click the microphone button to freeze the video and mute the audio. Click again to resume.*

- This cutting-edge technology can occasionally present cutting-edge glitches. The video quality deteriorates, the transmission aborts suddenly, the audio has an annoying echo, and so on. When problems strike, iChat Help offers a number of tips; the Video→Connection Doctor can identify your network speed. (iChat video likes *lots* of network speed.)

- Just as you can save your typed transcripts of instant message conversations, you can record your audio and video chats. Once you start a chat, choose Video→Record Chat. Your buddy is asked if it's OK for you to proceed with the recording (to ward off any question of those pesky wiretapping laws); if permission is granted, iChat begins recording the call.

  When you've got what you want, click Stop. Your recordings are automatically saved into Home→Documents→iChats (AAC files for audio conversations, MPEG-4 files for video chats). From there, you can drag them into iTunes to play or sync them up with an iPod or iPhoto. Yes, you can now relive those glorious iChat moments when you're standing in line at the grocery store.

## Bluescreen Backdrops and Video FX

If your video chats look like a bunch of cubicle-dwellers sitting around chatting at their desks, you can liven things up with one of Leopard's most glamorous and jaw-dropping features: photo or video *backgrounds* for your talking head. Yes, now you can make your video chat partners think you're in Paris, on the moon, or even impersonating a four-panel Andy Warhol silkscreen.

---

*Note:* The iChat and Photo Booth backdrop effects are serious, serious processor hogs; they require, at minimum, a Mac with a Core 2 Duo processor. And bandwidth, man, serious bandwidth—at least 128 Kbps for both upload *and* download speeds.

---

Here's how to prepare your backdrop for a video chat:

1. **Go to iChat→Preferences→Audio/Video.**

**Figure 12-15:**
*Top left: You have plenty of backgrounds to choose from for your next video chat. Click an effect to add it to your chat window. Click the small arrows at the bottom of the window to advance or retreat through the various effects styles. Click the Original square in the middle of the window to erase the effect and start again from scratch.*

*Lower right: Let the live bluescreen action begin!*

A video window opens so you can see yourself.

## 2. Press Shift-⌘-E (or go to Video→Show Video Effects).

The Effects box appears, looking a lot like the one in Photo Booth (Chapter 16); a lot of the visual backdrops are quite similar. Click the various squares of the tic-tac-toe grid to see how each effect will transform you in real time: making your face bulbous, for example, or rendering you in delicate colored pencil shadings.

The first two pages of effects all do video magic on *you* and everything else in the picture. If you want one of those, click it; you're done. There's no step 3. Your video-chat buddies now see you in your distorted or artistic new getup.

The second two pages of effects, however, don't do anything to your image. Instead, they replace the *background.*

This is the really amazing part. In TV and movies, replacing the background is an extremely common special effect. All you have to do is set up a perfectly smooth, evenly lit, shadowless blue or bright green backdrop behind the subject. Later, the computer replaces that solid color with a new picture or video of the director's choice.

iChat, however, creates exactly the same special effect (Figure 12-15) without requiring the bluescreen or the greenscreen. Read on.

## 3. Click the background effect you want.

Suppose, for example, that you've clicked the video loop showing the Eiffel Tower with people walking around. At this point, a message appears on the screen that says, "Please step out of the frame."

## 4. Duck out of camera range (or move off to one side).

See, iChat intends to memorize a picture of the *real* background—without you in it. When you return to the scene, your high-horsepower Mac then compares each pixel of its memorized image with what it's seeing now. Any differences, it concludes, must be *you.* And *that* is how it can create a bluescreen effect without a bluescreen.

***

**Note:** To make this work, both the camera and the background must be perfectly still. If the lighting or the visuals shift or change in any way, you may get some weird, glitchy effects where your real background bleeds through.

***

## 5. When the screen says, "Background detected," step back into the frame.

*Zut alors!* You are now in virtual Paris. Go ahead and start the video chat with your friends, and don't forget your beret.

If you want to clear out the background or change it, click the Original square in the middle of the Effects palette and then choose a different backdrop. (You can also change backdrops in mid-chat by choosing Video→Show Video Effects to open the effects palette.)

***

If things get too weird and choppy onscreen, you can restore the normal background by choosing Video→Reset Background. (That's also handy if you suddenly have to have a video talk with your boss about your excessive use of iChat while he's away on his business trip.)

*Tip:* You can use one of your own photos or video clips as iChat backdrops, too. In the Video Effects box, click the arrows on the bottom until you get to the screen with several blank User Backdrop screens. Next, drag a photo or video from the desktop directly onto one of the blank screens. Click it just like you would any of Apple's stock shots.

## Sharing Your Screen

As you've seen already in this chapter, iChat lets you share your thoughts, your voice, and your image with the people on your buddy lists. And now, for its next trick, it lets you share...*your computer.*

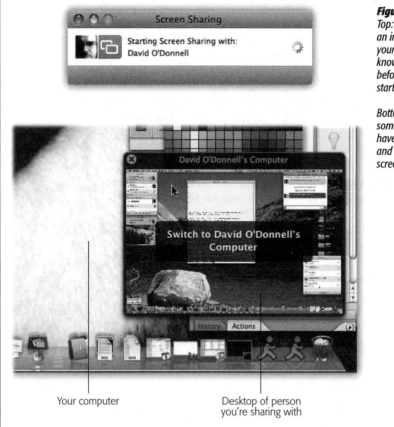

**Figure 12-16:**
*Top: You either send or receive an invitation to start sharing your screen, but make sure you know with whom you're dealing before accepting the offer and starting the sharing process.*

*Bottom: When you're sharing someone else's screen, you have the option to click back and forth between the two Mac screens.*

Your computer

Desktop of person you're sharing with

iChat's screen sharing feature is a close relative of the *network* screen-sharing feature described in Chapter 14. It lets you not only see what's on a far-away buddy's screen, but *control* it, taking command of the distant mouse and keyboard. (Of course, screen sharing can work the other way, too.)

You can open folders, create and edit documents, and copy files on the shared Mac screen. Sharing a screen makes collaborating as easy as working side by side around the same Mac, except now you can be sitting in San Francisco while your buddy is banging it out in Boston.

And if you're the family tech-support specialist—but the family lives all over the country—screen sharing makes troubleshooting a heckuva lot easier. You can now jump on your Mom's shared Mac and figure out why the formatting went wacky in her Word document, without her having to attempt *explaining* it to you over the phone. ("And then the little thingie disappeared and the doohickey got scrambled…")

---

**Note:** Of course, in these days of Big Scary Internet Security Issues, you want to make sure the person you share your screen with is someone you *trust completely*, because he or she is going to have the same access to your Mac as you do. Needless to say, do not accept screen-sharing invitations from people you don't know. Also, be leery of people on your Bonjour list asking you to share your screen, because Bonjour identities can be easily faked.

---

To make iChat screen sharing work, you and your buddy must both be running Macs with Leopard. On the other hand, you can share over any account type: AIM, .Mac, Google Talk, Bonjour, or Jabber.

To begin, click the sharee's name in your Buddy List.

- If you want to share *your* screen with this person, choose Buddies→Share My Screen.

- If you want to see *her* screen (because she has all the working files on her Mac), choose Buddies→Ask to Share.

---

**Note:** Similar commands are available in the Screen Sharing pop-up button—the one that looks like two overlapping squares at the bottom of the Buddy List window. The commands say "Share My Screen with casey234" and "Ask to Share casey234's screen."

---

Once the invitation is accepted, the sharing begins, as shown in Figure 12-16. To help you communicate further, iChat politely opens up an audio chat with your buddy so you can discuss what you're doing on the shared machine.

If you're seeing someone else's screen, you see his Mac desktop in full-screen view, right on your own machine. You also see a small window showing your own Mac; click it to switch back to your own desktop.

---

**Tip:** To copy files from Mac to Mac, drag them between the two windows. Files dragged to *your* Mac wind up in your Downloads folder.

---

If something's not right, or you need to bail out of a shared connection immediately, press Control-Escape on the Mac's keyboard.

## iChat Theater

Talk about the next best thing to being there. The new iChat Theater feature lets you make pitches and presentations to people and committees in faraway cities—without standing in a single airport-security line.

That's because iChat Theater turns the chat window into a presentation screen for displaying and narrating your own iPhoto or Keynote slideshows, QuickTime movie files, and even text documents. Your buddy, on the other end of the iChat line, sees

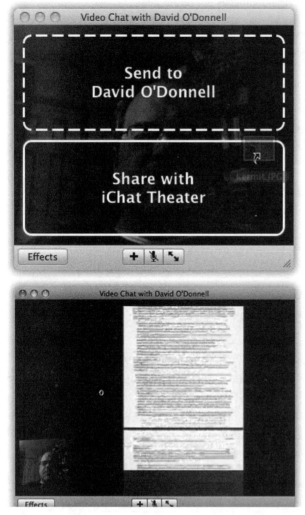

**Figure 12-17:**
Top: You can start an iChat Theater session by choosing File→Share a File with iChat Theater, or as shown here, by simply dropping the file on an open video chat window and going for the iChat Theater option.

Bottom: Once you've started a Theater show in Chat, the shared file takes center stage so you both can look at it and discuss amongst yourselves.

these documents at nearly full size—with you in a little picture-in-picture screen in the corner.

All you need is a fast Mac, fast Internet connection, and some stuff to show off; iChat Theater can display exactly the same kinds of files that Quick Look (Chapter 2) can display: Word, Excel, and PowerPoint documents, photos, text and HTML files, PDF files, audio and movie files, fonts, vCards, Pages, Numbers, Keynote, and TextEdit documents, and so on.

To get the show running, you can take one of two approaches.

- **If a video chat is under way,** you can just drag the file(s) you want to share into the video window. iChat asks if you want to *send* the file to the person or *share* it with iChat Theater (Figure 12-17, top). Click iChat Theater, of course.

- **If no video chat is in progress,** choose File→Share a File in iChat Theater. Locate the file that you want to present on your hard drive. When iChat asks you to start a video chat with the buddy who's going to be your audience, click the video-camera icon next to that person's name (or choose Video→Invite to Video Chat).

When your friend accepts, the curtain goes up, as shown the bottom of Figure 12-17. The file you're sharing takes center stage (er, window) and your buddy appears in a little video window off to the side. Click the ▣ button to expand the view to full screen.

If you have iPhoto '08, sharing picture albums is one menu command away: Choose File→Share iPhoto with iChat Theater. When the Media Browser pops up, pick the album you want to present. The first picture in the selected album appears in the iChat window before iPhoto itself opens, so you can use iPhoto's nice controls for cruising forward (or backward) through your album.

The same thing happens if you're running a Keynote presentation in iChat Theater: The first slide shows up in the chat window while the Keynote program launches to provide you with the proper controls to click through the rest of the slides in the presentation.

When the show is over, close the window to end the iChat Theater session.

# Part Four:
# Putting Down Roots

**Chapter 13: Accounts, Parental Controls, & Security**

**Chapter 14: Networking & Screen Sharing**

**Chapter 15: System Preferences**

**Chapter 16: The Freebie Programs**

4

# Accounts, Parental Controls, & Security

I n an era when *security* is the hottest high-tech buzzword, Apple was smart to make
security a focal point for Leopard. Mac OS X was already virus-free and better
protected from Internet attacks than Windows. But Mac OS X 10.5 is the most
impenetrable Mac system yet, filled with new defenses against the dark arts.

On the premise that the biggest security threat of all comes from other people in
your home or office, though, the most important security feature in Mac OS X is the
*accounts* system.

## Introducing Accounts

The concept of *user accounts* is central to Mac OS X's security approach. Like the Unix
under its skin (and also like Windows XP and Vista), Mac OS X is designed from the
ground up to be a *multiple-user* operating system. You can configure a Mac OS X
machine so that everyone must log in—that is, you have to click or type your name
and type in a password—when the computer turns on (Figure 13-1).

Upon doing so, you discover the Macintosh universe just as you left it, including your
documents, files, and folders; your preference settings (Web browser bookmarks,
desktop picture, screen saver, icons on the desktop and in the Dock, and so on);
email account(s), including personal information and mailboxes; your personally
installed programs and fonts; your choice of programs that launch automatically at
startup; and so on.

This system means that several different people can use it throughout the day, without
disrupting each other's files and settings. It also protects the Mac from getting fouled
up by mischievous (or bumbling) students, employees, and hackers.

If you're the only person who uses your Mac, you can safely skip most of this chapter. The Mac never pauses at startup time to demand the name and password you made up when you installed Mac OS X, because Apple's installer automatically turns on something called *automatic login* (page 396). You *will* be using one of these accounts, though, whether you realize it or not.

Furthermore, when you're stuck in line at the Department of Motor Vehicles, you may find the concepts presented here worth skimming, as certain elements of this multiple-user system may intrude upon your solo activities—and figure in the discussions in this book—from time to time.

---

*Tip:* Even if you don't share your Mac with anyone and don't create any other accounts, you might still be tempted to learn about the accounts feature because of its ability to password-protect the entire computer. All you have to do is to turn *off* the automatic login feature described on page 396. Thereafter, your Mac is protected from unauthorized fiddling when you're away from your desk or when your laptop is stolen.

---

**Figure 13-1:**
*When you set up several accounts, you don't turn on the Mac so much as sign into it. A command in the menu called Log Out summons this sign-in screen, as does the Accounts menu described later in this chapter. Click your own name, and type your password (if any), to get past this box and into your own stuff.*

## The First Account

When you first installed Mac OS X, you were asked for a name and password. You may not have realized it at the time, but you were creating the first *user account* on your Macintosh. Since that fateful day, you may have made a number of changes to your desktop—adjusted the Dock settings, added some favorites to your Web browser, and so on—without realizing that you were actually making these changes only to *your account.*

You've been saving your documents into your own Home folder, which is the cornerstone of your own account. This folder, generally named after you and stashed in the Users folder on your hard drive, stores not only your own work, but also your preference settings for all the programs you use, special fonts that you've installed, your own email collection, and so on.

Now then: Suppose you create an account for a second person. When she turns on the computer and signs in, she finds the desktop exactly the way it was factory-installed by Apple—stunning Earth-in-space desktop picture, Dock along the bottom, the default Web browser home page, and so on. She can make the same kinds of changes to the Mac that you've made, but nothing she does affects *your* environment the next time you log in.

In other words, the multiple-accounts feature has two components: first, a convenience element that hides everyone else's junk; and second, a security element that protects both the Mac's system software and everybody's work.

# Creating an Account

Suppose somebody new joins your little Mac family—a new worker, student, or love interest, for example. And you want to make them feel at home on your Mac.

Begin by opening System Preferences (Chapter 15). In the System Preferences window, click Accounts. You have just arrived at the master control center for account creation and management (Figure 13-2).

To create a new account, start by unlocking the Accounts panel. That is, click the 🔒 at lower-left, and fill in your own account name and password.

Now you can click the + button beneath the list of accounts. The little panel shown at bottom in Figure 13-2 appears.

## Phase 1: Choose an Account Type

As though this business of accounts and passwords isn't complicated enough already, Mac OS X 10.5 offers several *types* of accounts. When you create an account, you're expected to specify *which* type that person gets.

To do that, open the New Account pop-up menu (Figure 13-2, bottom). Its five account types are described on the following pages.

### Administrator accounts

If this is your own personal Mac, just beneath your name on the Accounts pane of System Preferences, it probably says *Admin.* This, as you could probably guess, stands for Administrator.

Because you're the person who originally installed Mac OS X, the Mac assumes that you are its *administrator*—the technical wizard in charge of it. You're the teacher, the parent, the resident guru. You're the one who will maintain this Mac. Only an administrator is allowed to:

- Install new programs into the Applications folder.

- Add fonts that everybody can use.

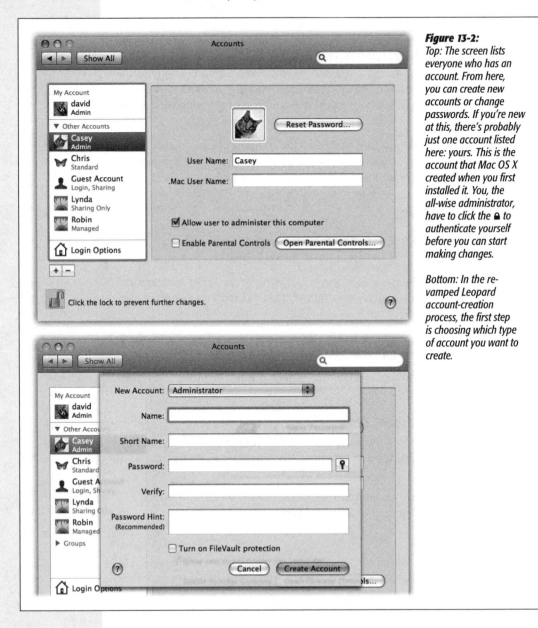

**Figure 13-2:**
*Top: The screen lists everyone who has an account. From here, you can create new accounts or change passwords. If you're new at this, there's probably just one account listed here: yours. This is the account that Mac OS X created when you first installed it. You, the all-wise administrator, have to click the 🔒 to authenticate yourself before you can start making changes.*

*Bottom: In the re-vamped Leopard account-creation process, the first step is choosing which type of account you want to create.*

- Make changes to certain System Preferences panes (including Network, Date & Time, Energy Saver, and Startup Disk).

- Use some features of the Disk Utility program.

- Create, move, or delete folders outside of your Home folder.

- Decide who gets to have accounts on the Mac.

- Open, change, or delete anyone else's files.

You'll find certain settings all over Mac OS X that you can change *only* if you're an administrator—including many in the Accounts pane itself. Administrator status also plays an enormous role when you want to network your Mac to other kinds of computers, as described in the next chapter.

As you create accounts for other people who'll use this Mac, you're offered the opportunity to make each one an administrator just like you. Needless to say, use discretion. Bestow these powers only upon people as responsible and technically masterful as yourself.

### Standard accounts

Most people, on most Macs, are ordinary *Standard* account holders (Figure 13-2). These people have everyday access to their own Home folders and to the harmless panes of System Preferences, but most other areas of the Mac are off limits. Mac OS X won't even let them create new folders on the main hard drive, except inside their own Home folders (or in the Shared folder described on page 400).

A few of the System Preferences panels display a padlock icon (🔒). If you're a Standard account holder, you can't make changes to these settings without the assistance of an administrator. Fortunately, you aren't required to log out so that an administrator can log in and make changes. You can just call the administrator over, click the padlock icon, and let him type in his name and password (if, indeed, he feels comfortable with you making the changes you're about to make).

### Managed accounts with Parental Controls

A Managed account is the same thing as a Standard account—except that you've turned on Parental Controls. (These controls are described later in this chapter.) You can turn a Managed account into a Standard account just by turning off Parental Controls, and vice versa.

That is, this account usually has even fewer freedoms—because you've limited the programs that this person is allowed to use, for example. Use a Managed account for children or anyone else who needs a Mac with rubber walls.

### Sharing Only

This kind of account is extremely useful—*if* your Mac is on a network (Chapter 14).

See, ordinarily, you can log in and access the files on your Mac in either of two ways:

- In person, seated in front of it.

- From across the network.

This arrangement was designed with families and schools in mind: lots of people sharing a *single* Mac.

This setup got a little silly, though, when the people on a network each have their *own* computers. If you wanted your spouse or your sales director to be able to grab some files off of your Mac, you'd have to create full-blown accounts for them on *your* Mac, complete with an utterly unnecessary Home folder that they'd never use.

That's why the *Sharing Only* account is such a great idea. It's available *only* from across the network. You can't get into it by sitting down at the Mac itself—it has no Home folder! Finally, of course, a Sharing Only account holder can't make any changes to the Mac's settings or programs.

In other words, a Sharing Only account exists *solely* for the purpose of file sharing on the network, and people can enter their names and passwords *only* from other Macs.

Once you've set up this kind of account, all the file-sharing and screen-sharing goodies described in Chapter 14 become available.

### Group

A *group* is just a virtual container that holds the names of other account holders. You might create one for your most trusted colleagues, another for those rambunctious kids, and so on—all in the name of streamlining the *file-sharing privileges* feature described on page 418. The box on the facing page covers groups in more detail.

### The Guest account

Mac OS X has always offered a special account called the Guest account. It was great for accommodating visitors, buddies, or anyone else who was just passing through and wanted to use your Mac for awhile. If you let such people use the Guest account, your own account remains private and un-messed-with.

But before Mac OS X 10.5, there was a problem: Any changes your friend made—downloading mail, making Web bookmarks, putting up a raunchy desktop picture—would still be there for the *next* guest to enjoy, unless you painstakingly restored everything back to neutral. The Guest account was like a hotel room shared by successive guests. And *you* were the maid.

In Leopard, any changes your guest makes while using your Mac are automatically erased when she logs out. Files are deleted, email is nuked, setting changes are forgotten. It's like a hotel that gets demolished and rebuilt after each guest departs.

The Guest account isn't listed in the New Account pop-up menu (Figure 13-2). That's because there's only *one* Guest account; you can't actually create additional ones.

So to use the Guest account, bring it to life by turning on "Allow guests to log into this computer." You can even turn on the parental controls described earlier in this chapter by clicking Open Parental Controls, or permit the guest to exchange files with your Mac from across the network (Chapter 14) by turning on "Allow guests to connect to shared folders."

Just remember to warn your vagabond friend that once he logs out, all traces of his visit are wiped out forever. (At least from your *Mac.*)

## Phase 2: Name, Password, and Status

All right. So you click the + button. From the New Account pop-up menu, you choose the type of account you want to create.

Now, on the same starter sheet, you fill in the most critical information about the new account holder:

- **Name.** If it's just the family, this could be Chris or Robin. If it's a corporation or school, you probably want to use both first and last names.

### Creating Groups

Changing permissions settings on a networked Mac, or one with a lot of account holders, is a lot easier if you sweep all your minions into subsets called *groups*.

This process used to require a complicated series of Unixy steps that, if not performed carefully, could seriously foul up your Mac.

But in Mac OS X Leopard, you can create a group as easily as you'd create an account. And in the same place: the Accounts pane of System Preferences.

Click the tiny 🔒 in the lower-left corner. When prompted, type in your administrator's name and password, and then click OK. The Mac is just making sure that somebody with a clue is at the helm.

Now click the + button as though you're about to create a new account. But from the New Account pop-up menu (shown at bottom in Figure 13-2), choose Group. Type a name for the new group (Accounting, Kids, or whatever), and click Create Group.

Now you see something like the list shown here: checkboxes for all of this Mac's account holders. Turn on the checkboxes for the ones you consider worthy of being a part of this group.

You can create as many groups as you like. Later, when it comes time to share a folder or file, you'll save time by choosing a group name instead of setting these permissions one person at a time.

- **Short Name.** You'll quickly discover the value of having a short name—an abbreviation of your actual name—particularly if your name is, say, Alexandra Stephanopoulos.

  When you sign into your Mac in person, you can use either your long or short name. But when you access this Mac by dialing into it or connecting from across the network (as described in the next chapter), use the short version.

  As soon as you tab into this field, the Mac proposes a short name for you. You can replace the suggestion with whatever you like. Technically, it doesn't even have to be shorter than the "long" name, but spaces and most punctuation marks are forbidden.

- **Password, Verify.** Here's where you type this new account holder's password (Figure 13-2). In fact, you're supposed to type it twice, to make sure you didn't introduce a typo the first time. (The Mac displays only dots as you type, to guard against the possibility that somebody is watching over your shoulder.)

  The usual computer book takes this opportunity to stress the importance of a long, complex password—a phrase that isn't in the dictionary, something made up of mixed letters and numbers. This is excellent advice if you create sensitive documents and work in a big corporation.

  But if you share the Mac only with a spouse or a few trusted colleagues in a small office, you may have nothing to hide. You may see the multiple-users feature more as a convenience (keeping your settings and files separate) than a protector of secrecy and security. In these situations, there's no particular urgency to the mission of thwarting the world's hackers with a convoluted password.

  In that case, you may want to consider setting up *no* password—leaving both password blanks empty. Later, whenever you're asked for your password, just leave the Password box blank. You'll be able to log in that much faster each day.

- **Password Hint.** If you gave yourself a password, you can leave yourself a hint in this box. If your password is the middle name of the first person who ever kissed you, for example, your hint might be "middle name of the first person who ever kissed me."

  Later, if you forget your password, the Mac will show you this cue to jog your memory.

- **Turn on FileVault protection.** Page 405 has more on this advanced corporate-security feature. (This option isn't available for Sharing Only accounts.)

When you finish setting up these essential items, click Create Account. If you left the password boxes empty, the Mac asks for reassurance that you know what you're doing; click OK.

You then return to the Accounts pane, where you see the new account name in the list at the left side.

Here, three final decisions await your wisdom:

- **.Mac User Name.** Each account holder might well have her own .Mac account (especially because Apple offers a family-pack deal on these accounts). Since the .Mac service is growing in importance and features—email address, Web site, iDisk, syncing, Back to My Mac, and so on—it's convenient to associate each account with its own .Mac name.

- **Enable Parental Controls.** "Parental controls" refers to the feature that limits what your offspring are allowed to do on this computer—and how much time a day that they're allowed to spend glued to the mouse. (You can turn on parental controls *only* for Standard and Guest accounts, even though the checkbox appears for Admin accounts too.) Details are on page 387.

- **Allow user to administer this computer.** This checkbox lets you turn ordinary, unsuspecting Standard or Managed accounts into Administrator accounts, as described above. You know—when your kid turns 18.

## Phase 3: Choose a Picture

The usual Mac OS X sign-in screen (Figure 13-1) displays each account holder's name, accompanied by a little picture.

When you click the sample photo, you get a pop-up menu of Apple-supplied graphics; you can choose one to represent you. It becomes not only your icon on the sign-in screen, but also your "card" photo in Mac OS X's Address Book program and your icon in iChat.

*Figure 13-3:*
*Once you've selected a photo to represent yourself (left), you can adjust its position relative to the square "frame" (right), or adjust its size by dragging the slider. Finally, when the picture looks correctly framed, click Set. (The next time you return to the Images dialog box, you can recall the new image using the Recent Pictures pop-up menu.)*

If you'd rather supply your *own* graphics file—a digital photo of your own head, for example—then choose Edit Picture from the pop-up menu. As shown in Figure 13-3, you have several options:

- Drag a graphics file directly into the "picture well" (Figure 13-3). Use the cropping slider below the picture to frame it properly.

- Click Choose. You're shown a list of what's on your hard drive. Find and double-click the image you want.

- Take a new picture. If your Mac has a built-in camera above the screen, or if you have an external webcam or a camcorder hooked up, click the little camera button. The Mac counts down from 3 with loud beeps to help you get ready, and then takes the picture.

In each case, click Set to enshrine your icon forever (or until you feel like picking a different one).

## Phase 4: Startup Items

There's one additional System Preferences setting that your account holders can set up for themselves: which programs or documents open automatically upon login. (This is one decision an administrator *can't* make for other people. It's available only to whoever is logged in at the moment.)

To choose your own crew of self-starters, open System Preferences and click the Accounts icon. Click the Login Items tab. As shown in Figure 13-4, you can now build

**Figure 13-4:**
*You can add any icon to the list of things you want to start up automatically. Click the + button to summon the Open dialog box where you can find the icon, select it, and then click Choose. Better yet, if you can see the icon in a folder or disk window (or on the desktop), just drag it into this list. To remove an item, click it in the list and then click the - button.*

a list of programs, documents, disks, and other goodies that automatically launch each time you log in. You can even turn on the Hide checkbox for each one, so that the program is running in the background at login time, waiting to be called into service with a quick click.

Don't feel obligated to limit this list to programs and documents, by the way. Disks, folders, servers on the network, and other fun icons can also be startup items, so that their windows are open and waiting when you arrive at the Mac each morning.

*Tip:* Here's a much quicker way to add something to the Login Items list: right-click its Dock icon and choose "Open at Login" from the shortcut menu.

# Parental Controls

If you're setting up a Standard or Guest account, the Parental Controls checkbox affords you the opportunity to shield your Mac—or its very young, very fearful, or very mischievous operator—from confusion and harm. This is a helpful feature to remember when you're setting up accounts for students, young children, or easily intimidated adults.

You can specify how many hours a day each person is allowed to use the Mac, and declare certain hours (like sleeping hours) off-limits. You can specify exactly who your kids are allowed to communicate with via email (if they use Mail) and instant messaging (if they use iChat), what Web sites they can visit (if they use Safari), what programs they're allowed to use, and even what words they can look up in the Mac OS X Dictionary.

Here are all the ways you can keep your little Standard account holders shielded from the Internet—and themselves. For sanity's sake, the following discussion refers to the Standard account holder as "your child." But some of these controls—notably those in the System category—are equally useful for people of *any* age who feel overwhelmed by the Mac, are inclined to mess it up by not knowing what they're doing, or are tempted to mess it up deliberately.

*Note:* If you use any of these options, the account type listed on the Accounts panel changes from "Standard" to "Managed."

## System

On this tab, you see the options shown in Figure 13-5. Use these options to limit what your Managed-account flock is allowed to do. You can limit them to using certain programs, for example, or prevent them from burning DVDs, changing settings, or fiddling with your printer setups.

(Limiting what people can do to your Mac when you're not looking is a handy feature under any shared-computer circumstance. But if there's one word tattooed on its forehead, it would be "Classrooms!")

On the panel that pops up when you click Configure, you have two options: "Use Simple Finder" and "Only allow selected applications."

**Figure 13-5:**
*In the Parental Controls window, you can control the capabilities of any account holder on your Mac. In the lower half of the System tab window, you can choose applications and even Dashboard widgets by turning on the boxes next to their names. (Expand the flippy triangles if necessary.) Those are the only programs these account holders will be allowed to use. (The new Search box helps you find certain programs without knowing their categories.)*

### Use Simple Finder

If you're *really* concerned about somebody's ability to survive the Mac—or the Mac's ability to survive them—turn on "Use Simple Finder." Then turn on the checkboxes of the programs that person is allowed to use.

Suppose you're the lucky Mac fan who's been given a Simple Finder account. When you log in, you discover the barren world shown in Figure 13-6. There are only three menus (, Finder, and File), a single onscreen window, no hard drive icon, and a bare-bones Dock. The only folders you can see are in the Dock. They include:

• **My Applications.** These are aliases of the applications that the administrator approved. They appear on a strange, fixed, icon view, called "pages." List and column views don't exist. The Simple person can't move, rename, delete, sort, or change the display of these icons—merely click them. If you have too many to fit on one screen, you get numbered page buttons beneath them, which you click to move from one set to another.

- **Documents.** Behind the scenes, this is your Home→Documents folder. Of course, as a Simple Finder kind of soul, you don't *have* a visible Home folder. All your stuff goes in here.

**Figure 13-6:**
*The Simple Finder doesn't feel like home—unless you've got one of those Spartan, space-age, Dr. Evil–style pads. But it can be just the ticket for less-skilled Mac users, with few options and a basic one-click interface. Every program in the My Applications folder is actually an alias to the real program, which is safely ensconced in the off-limits Applications folder.*

- **Shared.** This is the same Shared folder described on page 400. It's provided so that you and other account holders can exchange documents. However, you can't open any of the folders here, only the documents.

- **Trash.** The Trash is here, but you won't use it much. Selecting or dragging any icon is against the rules, so you're left with no obvious means of putting anything into your Trash.

The only programs with their own icons in the Dock are Finder and Dashboard.

Otherwise, you can essentially forget everything else you've read in this book. You can't create folders, move icons, or do much of anything beyond clicking the icons that your benevolent administrator has provided. It's as though Mac OS X moved away and left you the empty house.

- To keep things extra-simple, Mac OS X permits only one window at a time to be open. It's easy to open icons, too, because *one* click opens it, not two.

- The File menu is stunted, offering only a Close Window command. The Finder menu only gives you two options: About Finder and Run Full Finder. (The latter command prompts you for an administrator's user name and password, and then turns back into the regular Finder—a handy escape hatch. To return to Simple Finder, just choose Finder→Return to Simple Finder.)

- The  menu is *really* bare-bones: You can Log Out, Force Quit, or go to Sleep. That's it.

- There's no trace of Spotlight.

Although the Simple Finder is simple, any program (at least, any that the administrator has permitted) can run from Simple Finder. A program running inside the Simple Finder still has all of its features and complexities—only the Finder has been whittled down to its essence.

In other words, Simple Finder is great for streamlining the Finder, but novices won't get far combating their techno-fear until the world presents us with Simple Keynote, Simple Mail, and Simple Microsoft Word. Still, it's better than nothing.

### Only allow selected applications

By tinkering with the checkboxes here, you can declare certain programs off-limits to this account holder, or turn off his ability to remove Dock icons, burn CDs, and so on.

You can restrict this person's access to the Mac in several different ways:

- **Limit the programs.** At the bottom of the dialog box shown in Figure 13-5, you see a list of all the programs in your Applications folder (an interesting read in its own right). Only checked items show up in the account holder's Applications folder.

---

**Tip:** If you don't see a program listed, use the Search box, or drag its icon from the Finder into the window.

---

If, for instance, you're setting up an account for use in the classroom, you may want to turn off access to programs like Disk Utility, iChat, and Tomb Raider.

- **Limit the features.** When you first create them, Standard account holders are free to burn CDs or DVDs, modify what's on the Dock, change their passwords, and view the settings of all System Preferences panels (although they can't *change* all of these settings).

Depending on your situation, you may find it useful to turn off some of these options. In a school lab, for example, you might want to turn off the ability to burn discs (to block software piracy). If you're setting up a Mac for a technophobe, you might want to turn off the ability to change the Dock (so your colleague won't accidentally lose access to his own programs and work).

## Content (Dictionary and Web)

"Content," in this case, means "two options we really didn't have any other place to put." Actually, what it *really* means is Dictionary and Safari.

### Hide profanity in Dictionary

Mac OS X comes with a complete electronic copy of the *New Oxford American Dictionary*. And "complete," in this case, means "it even has swear words."

Turning on "Hide profanity in Dictionary" is like having an Insta-Censor™. It hides most of the naughty words from the dictionary whenever your young account holder is logged in (Figure 13-7).

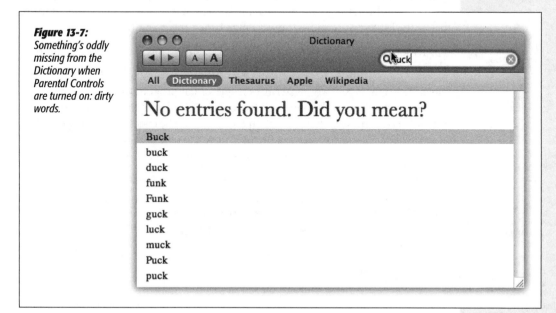

**Figure 13-7:**
*Something's oddly missing from the Dictionary when Parental Controls are turned on: dirty words.*

### Web Site Restrictions

This feature is designed to limit which Web sites your kid is allowed to visit.

Frankly, trying to block the racy stuff from the Web is something of a hopeless task; if your kid doesn't manage to get round this blockade by simply using a different browser, he'll just wind up seeing the dirty pictures at another kid's house. But at least you can enjoy the illusion of taking a stand, using approaches of three degrees of severity:

- **Allow unrestricted access to Web sites.** In other words, no filtering. Anything goes.

- **Try to limit access to adult Web sites automatically.** Those words—"try to"—are Apple's way of admitting that no filter is foolproof.

  In any case, Mac OS X comes with a built-in database of Web sites that it already knows may be inappropriate for children—and these sites won't appear in Safari while this account holder is logged in. By clicking Customize and then editing the "Always allow" and "Never allow" lists, you can override its decisions on a site-at-a-time basis.

• **Allow access to only these Web sites.** This is the most restrictive approach of all: It's a *whitelist*, a list of the *only* Web sites your youngster is allowed to visit. It's filled with kid-friendly sites like Disney and Discovery Kids, but of course you can edit the list by clicking the + and – buttons below the list.

## Mail & iChat

Here, you can build a list of email and chat addresses, corresponding to the people you feel comfortable letting your kid exchange emails and chat with. Click the + button below the list, type the address, press Enter, lather, rinse, and repeat.

For reasons explained in a moment, turn on "Send permission emails to," and plug in your own email address.

Now then: When your youngster uses Apple's Mail program to send a message to someone who's *not* on the approved list, or tries to iChat with someone not on the list, he gets the message shown at top in Figure 13-8. If he clicks Ask Permission, then *your* copy of Mail shortly receives a permission-request message (Figure 13-8, bottom); meanwhile, the outgoing message gets placed in limbo in his Drafts folder.

*Figure 13-8:*
*Top: If your kid tries to contact someone who's not on the Approved list, he can either give up or click Ask Permission.*

*Bottom: In the latter case, you'll know about it. If you're convinced that the would-be correspondent is not, in fact, a stalker, you can grant permission by clicking Always Allow.*

*Your young ward gets the good news the next time he visits his Drafts folder, where the message has been awaiting word from you, the Good Parent.*

If you add that person's address to the list of approved correspondents, then the next time your young apprentice clicks the quarantined outgoing message in his Drafts folder, the banner across the top lets him know that all is well—and the message is OK to go out.

**Note:** This feature doesn't attempt to stop email or chat using *other* programs, like Microsoft Entourage or Skype. If you're worried about your efforts being bypassed, block access to those programs using the Forbidden Applications list described above.

When your underling fires up iChat or Mail, she'll discover that her Buddy List is empty except for the people you've identified.

Handling the teenage hissy fit is your problem.

## Time Limits

Clever folks, those Apple programmers. They must have kids of their own.

**Figure 13-9:**
*Top: If this account holder tries to log in outside of the time limits you specify here, she'll encounter only a box that says, "Computer time limits expired." She'll be offered a pop-up menu that grants her additional time, from 15 minutes to "Rest of the day"—but it requires your parental consent (actually, your parental password) to activate.*

*Bottom: Similarly, if she's using the Mac as her time winds down, she gets this message. Once again, you, the all-knowing administrator, can grant her more time using this dialog box.*

They realize that some parents care about *how much* time their kids spending front of the Mac, and some also care about *which* hours (Figure 13-9):

- **How much time.** In the "Weekday time limits" section, turn on "Limit computer use to," and then adjust the slider. A similar slider appears for Weekend time limits.

- **Which hours.** In the "Bedtime" section, turn on the checkbox for either "School nights" or "Weekend," and then set the hours of the day (or, rather, night) when the Mac is unavailable to your young account holders.

In other words, this feature may have the smallest pages-to-significance ratio in this entire book. Doesn't take long to explain it, but it could bring the parents of Mac addicts a lot of peace.

## Logs

The final tab of the Parental Controls panel is Big Brother Central. Here's a complete rundown of what your kids have been up to. Its four categories—Websites visited, Websites blocked, Applications, and iChat—are extremely detailed. For example, in Applications, you can see exactly which programs your kids tried to use when, and how much time they spent in each one. Figure 13-10 shows the idea.

*Figure 13-10:*
*These logs track everything your kid tried to do; it's spying, sure, but it's for the good of the child. (Right?) Use the pop-up menus at the top to change the time period being reported (Today, This Week, or whatever) and how they're grouped in the list—by date or by application/Web site.*

If you see something that you really think should be off limits—a site in the Websites Visited list, an application, an iChat session with someone—click its name and then click Restrict. You've just nipped *that* one in the bud.

Conversely, if the Mac blocked a Web site that you think is really OK, click its name in the list, and then click Allow. (And if you're wondering what a certain Web page *is,* click it and then click Open.)

# Editing Accounts

If you're an administrator, you can change your own account in any way you like.

If you have any other kind of account, though, you can't change anything but your picture and password. If you want to make any other changes, you have to ask an admin to log in, make the changes you want made to your account, and then turn the computer back over to you.

## Deleting Accounts

Hey, it happens: Somebody graduates, somebody gets fired, somebody dumps you. Sooner or later, you may need to delete an account from your Mac.

When that time comes, click the account name in the Accounts list and then click the minus-sign button beneath the list. Mac OS X asks what to do with all of the dearly departed's files and settings:

- **Save the home folder in a disk image.** This option presents the "I'll be back" approach. Mac OS X preserves the dearly departed's folders on the Mac, in a tidy digital envelope that won't clutter your hard drive, and can be reopened in case of emergency.

  In the Users→Deleted Users folder, you find a disk image file (.dmg). If you double-click it, a new, virtual disk icon named for the deleted account appears on your desktop. You can open folders and root through the stuff in this "disk," just as if it were a living, working Home folder.

  If fate ever brings that person back into your life, you can use this disk image to reinstate the deleted person's account. Start by creating a brand-new account. Then copy the contents of the folders in the mounted disk image (Documents, Pictures, Desktop, and so on) into the corresponding folders of the new Home folder.

- **Do not change the home folder.** This time, Mac OS X removes the *account,* in that it no longer appears in the Login list or in the Accounts panel of System Preferences—but it leaves the *Home folder* right where it is. Use this option if you don't intend to dispose of the dearly departed's belongings right here and now.

- **Delete the home folder.** This button offers the "Hasta la vista, baby" approach. The account and all of its files and settings are vaporized forever, on the spot.

---

***Note:*** If you delete a Shared Only account, you're not offered the chance to preserve the Home folder contents—because a Shared Only account doesn't *have* a Home folder.

---

# Setting Up the Login Process

Once you've set up more than one account, the dialog box shown in Figure 13-1 appears whenever you turn on the Mac, whenever you choose  →Log Out, or whenever the Mac logs you out automatically. But a few extra controls let you, an administrator, set up either more or less security at the login screen—or, put another way, build in less or more convenience.

Open System Preferences, click Accounts, and then click the Login Options button (Figure 13-11). Here are some of the ways you can shape the login experience for greater security (or greater convenience):

- **Automatic login.** This option eliminates the need to sign in at all. It's a timesaving, hassle-free arrangement if only one person uses the Mac, or if one person uses it most of the time.

  When you choose an account holder's name from this pop-up menu, you're prompted for his name and password. Type it and click OK.

  From now on, the dialog box shown in Figure 13-1 won't appear *at all* at startup time. After turning on the machine, you, the specified account holder, zoom straight to your desktop.

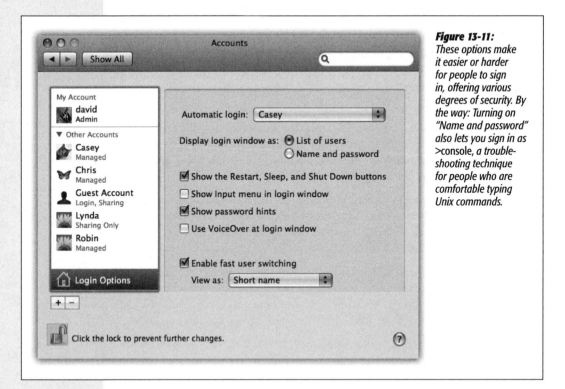

**Figure 13-11:**
*These options make it easier or harder for people to sign in, offering various degrees of security. By the way: Turning on "Name and password" also lets you sign in as* >console, *a trouble-shooting technique for people who are comfortable typing Unix commands.*

Of course, only one lucky person can enjoy this express ticket. Everybody else must still enter their names and passwords. (And how can they, since the Mac rushes right into the Automatic person's account at startup time? Answer: The Automatic thing happens only at startup time. The usual login screen appears whenever the current account holder logs out—by choosing  →Log Out, for example.)

• **Display login window as.** Under normal circumstances, the login screen presents a list of account holders when you power up the Mac, as shown in Figure 13-1. That's the "List of users" option in action.

If you're especially worried about security, however, you might not even want that list to appear. If you turn on "Name and password," each person who signs in must type both his name (into a blank that appears) *and* his password—a very inconvenient, but more secure, arrangement.

• **Show the Restart, Sleep, and Shut Down buttons.** Truth is, the Mac OS X security system is easy to circumvent. Truly devoted evildoers can bypass the standard login screen in a number of different ways: restart in FireWire disk mode, restart at the Unix Terminal, and so on. Suddenly, these no-goodniks have full access to every document on the machine, blowing right past all of the safeguards you've so carefully established.

One way to thwart them is to turn off this checkbox. Now there's no Restart or Shut Down button to tempt mischief-makers. That's plenty of protection in most homes, schools, and workplaces; after all, Mac people tend to be *nice* people. (Another approach: use FileVault, which is descibed on page 405.)

• **Show Input menu in login window.** If the Input menu (page 460) is available at login time, it means that people who use non-U.S. keyboard layouts and alphabets can use the login features without having to pretend to be American. (It also means that you have a much wider universe of difficult-to-guess passwords, since your password can be in, for example, Japanese characters. Greetings, Mr. Bond-san.)

• **Show password hints.** As described earlier, Mac OS X is kind enough to display your password hint ("middle name of the first person who ever kissed me") after you've typed it wrong three times when trying to log in. This option lets you turn off that feature for an extra layer of security. The hint will never appear.

• **Use VoiceOver at login window.** The VoiceOver feature (page 475) is all well and good if you're blind. But how are you supposed to log in? Turn on this checkbox, and VoiceOver speaks the features on the Login panel, too.

• **Enable fast user switching.** This feature lets you switch to another account without having to log out of the first one, as described on page 400.

• **View as.** If you do, in fact, turn on Fast User Switching, a new menu appears at the upper-right corner of your screen, listing all the account holders on the machine. Thanks to this pop-up menu, you can now specify what that menu looks like. It can display the current account holder's full name (Name), the short name (Short

Name), or only a generic torso-silhouette icon (Icon) to save space on the menu bar.

## Signing In, Logging Out

Once somebody has set up your account, here's what it's like getting into, and out of, a Mac OS X machine. (For the purposes of this discussion, "you" are no longer the administrator—you're one of the students, employees, or family members for whom an account has been set up.)

### Identifying Yourself

When you first turn on the Mac—or when the person who last used this computer chooses  →Log Out—the login screen shown in Figure 13-1 appears. At this point, you can proceed in any of several ways:

- **Restart.** Click if you need to restart the Mac for some reason. (The Restart and Shut Down buttons don't appear here if the administrator has chosen to hide them as a security precaution.)

- **Shut Down.** Click if you're done for the day, or if sudden panic about the complexity of user accounts makes you want to run away. The computer turns off.

- **Log In.** To sign in, click your account name in the list. If you're a keyboard speed freak, you can also type the first letter or two—or press the up or down arrow keys—until your name is highlighted. Then press Return or Enter.

  Either way, the password box appears now (if a password is required). If you accidentally click the wrong person's name on the first screen, you can click Back. Otherwise, type your password, and then press Enter (or click Log In).

  You can try as many times as you want to type the password. With each incorrect guess, the entire dialog box shudders violently from side to side, as though shaking its head "No." If you try unsuccessfully three times, your hint appears—if you've set one up. (If you see a strange ⇪ icon in the password box, guess what? You've got your Caps Lock key on, and the Mac thinks you're typing an all-capitals password.)

Once you're in, the world of the Mac looks just the way you left it (or the way an administrator set it up for you).

### Logging Out

When you're finished using the Mac, choose  →Log Out (or press Shift-⌘-Q). A confirmation message appears; if you click Cancel or press Esc, you return to whatever you were doing. If you click Log Out, or press Return, you return to the screen shown in Figure 13-1, and the entire sign-in cycle begins again.

---

***Tip:*** If you press Option as you choose  →Log Out (or as you press ⌘-Q), the confirmation box doesn't appear.

---

# Sharing Across Accounts

It's all fine to say that every account is segregated from all *other* accounts. It's nice to know that your stuff is safe from the prying eyes of your co-workers or family.

But what about collaboration? What if you *want* to give some files or folders to another account holder?

You can't just open up someone else's Home folder and drop it in there. Yes, every account holder has a Home folder (all in the Users folder on your hard drive). But if you try to open anybody else's Home folder, you'll see a tiny red ⊖ icon superimposed on almost every folder inside, telling you "Look, but don't touch."

Fortunately, there are a couple of wormholes between accounts (Figure 13-12):

**Figure 13-12:**
*Top: In other people's Home folders, the Public and Sites folders are available for your inspection. These two folders contain stuff that other people have "published" for the benefit of their co-workers.*

*Middle: In the Public folder is the Drop Box, which serves the opposite purpose. It lets anyone else who uses this Mac hand in files to you; they, however, can't see what's in it.*

*Bottom: Inside the Users folder (to get there from a Home folder, press ⌘-up arrow) is the Shared folder, a wormhole connecting all accounts. Everybody has full access to everything inside.*

- **The Shared folder.** Sitting in the Users folder is one folder that doesn't correspond to any particular person: Shared. Everybody can freely access this folder, inserting and extracting files without restriction. It's the common ground among all the account holders on a single Mac. It's Central Park, the farmer's market, and the grocery-store bulletin board.

- **The Public folder.** In your Home folder, there's a folder called Public. Anything you copy into it becomes available for inspection or copying (but not changing or deleting) by any other account holder, whether they log into your Mac or sign in from across the network.

- **The Drop Box.** And *inside* your Public folder is another cool little folder: the Drop Box. It exists to let *other* people give files to *you,* discreetly and invisibly to anyone else. That is, people can drop files and folders into your Drop Box, but they can't actually *open* it. This folder, too, is available both locally (in person) and from across the network.

# Fast User Switching

The account system described so far in this chapter has its charms. It keeps everyone's stuff separate, it keeps your files safe, and it lets you have the desktop picture of your choice.

Unfortunately, it can go from handy to hassle in one split second. That's when you're logged in, and somebody else wants to duck in just for a second—to check email or a calendar, for example. What are you supposed to do—log out completely, closing all your documents and quitting all your programs, just so the interloper can look something up? Then afterward, you'd have to log back in and fire up all your stuff again, praying that your inspirational muse hasn't fled in the meantime.

Fortunately, that's all over now. Fast User Switching—which works just as it does in Windows—lets Person B log in and use the Mac for a little while. All of *your* stuff, Person A, simply slides into the background, still open the way you had it; see Figure 13-13.

When Person B is finished working, you can bring your whole work environment back to the screen without having to reopen anything. All your windows and programs are still open, just as you left them.

To turn on this feature, open the Accounts panel of System Preferences (and click the 🔒, if necessary, to unlock the panel). Click Login Options, and turn on "Enable fast user switching." (You can see this dialog box in Figure 13-11.)

The only change you notice immediately is the appearance of your own account name in the upper-right corner of the screen (Figure 13-13, top). You can change what this menu looks like by using the "View as" pop-up menu, also shown in Figure 13-11.

That's all there is to it. Next time you need a fellow account holder to relinquish control so that you can duck in to do a little work, just choose your name from the Accounts menu. Type your password, if one is required, and feel guiltless about the interruption.

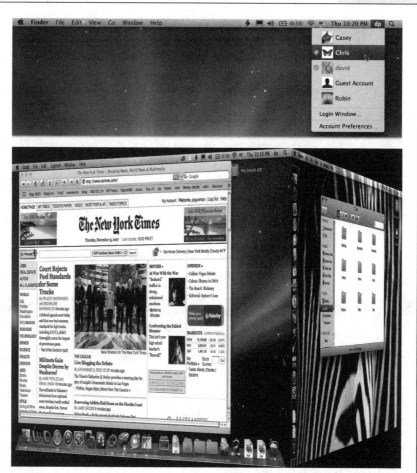

**Figure 13-13:**
Top: The appearance of the Accounts menu lets you know that Fast User Switching is turned on. The circled checkmark indicates people who are already logged in, including those who have been "fast user switched" into the background. The dimmed name shows who's logged in right now.

Bottom: When the screen changes from your account to somebody else's, your entire world slides visibly off-screen as though it's mounted on the side of a rotating cube—a spectacular animation made possible by Mac OS X's Quartz Extreme graphics software.

# Four Mac OS X Security Shields

Mac OS X has a spectacular reputation for stability and security. At this writing, not a single Mac OS X virus has emerged—a spectacular feature that may even have played a part in your decision to go Macward. There's no Windows-esque plague of spyware, either (downloaded programs that do something sneaky behind your back). In fact, there isn't *any* Mac spyware.

The usual rap is, "Well, that's because Windows is a much bigger target. What virus writer is going to waste his time on a computer with eight percent market share?"

That may be part of the reason Mac OS X is virus-free. But Mac OS X has also been built more intelligently from the ground up. Listed below are a few of the many drafty corners of a typical operating system that Apple has solidly plugged:

- The original Windows XP came with five of its *ports* open. Mac OS X has always come from the factory with all of them shut and locked.

  Ports are channels that remote computers use to connect to services on your computer: one for instant messaging, one for Windows XP's remote-control feature, and so on. It's fine to have them open if you're expecting visitors. But if you've got an open port that exposes the soft underbelly of your computer without your knowledge, you're in for a world of hurt. Open ports are precisely what permitted viruses like Blaster to infiltrate millions of PCs. Microsoft didn't close those ports until the Windows XP Service Pack 2.

- Whenever a program tried to install itself in the original Windows XP, the operating system went ahead and installed it, potentially without your awareness.

  In Mac OS X, that never happens. You're notified at every juncture when anything is trying to install itself on your Mac. In fact, you're even notified when you're opening a disk image or .zip file that could *contain* an installable program (Figure 13-14).

- Unlike certain other operating systems, Mac OS X doesn't even let an administrator touch the files that drive the operating system itself without pestering you to pro-

---

**INFREQUENTLY ASKED QUESTION**

## The Case of the Forgotten Password

*Help—I forgot my password! And I never told it to anybody, so even the administrator can't help me!*

No problem. Your administrator can simply open up System Preferences, click Accounts, click the name of the person who forgot the password, and then click Reset Password to re-establish the password.

*But you don't understand. I am the administrator! And I'm the only account!*

Aha—that's a different story. All right, no big deal. At the login screen, type a gibberish password three times. On the last attempt, the Mac will offer you the chance to reset the password. All you have to do is type in your master password (page 408) to prove your credentials.

*Um—I never set up a master password.*

All right then. That's actually good news, because it means you didn't turn on FileVault. (If you had, and you'd also forgotten the master password, your account would now be locked away forever.)

Insert the Mac OS X DVD. Restart the Mac while pressing down the letter C key, which starts up the Mac from the DVD and launches the Mac OS X installer.

On the first installer screen, choose Installer→Reset Password. When the Reset Password screen appears, click the hard drive that contains Mac OS X. From the first pop-up menu, choose the name of your account. Now make up a new password and type it into both boxes. Click Save, close the window, click the installer, and restart.

And next time, be more careful! Write down your password on a Post-it note and affix it to your monitor. (Joke—that's a joke!)

---

vide your password and grant it permission to do so. A Mac OS X virus (if there were such a thing) could theoretically wipe out all of your files, but wouldn't be able to access anyone else's stuff—and couldn't touch the operating system itself.

**Figure 13-14:**
Mac OS X hovers like a stage mother, always informing you when you're at a point where something virusy could be happening. It warns you when you download a compressed file that could contain a runnable program (top), and even when an installer has to run a tiny sub-program before the installation (bottom).

- You may already know about the Finder's Secure Empty Trash option (page 89). But an option on the Erase tab of the Disk Utility program can do the same super-erasing of *all free space* on your hard drive. We're talking not just erasing, but recording gibberish over the spots where your files once were—once, seven times, or *thirty-five* times—utterly shattering any hope any hard-disk recovery firm (or spy) might have had of recovering passwords or files from your hard drive.

- Safari's Private Browsing mode means that you can freely visit Web sites without leaving *any* digital tracks—no history, no Downloads list, nothing (page 352).

- Every time you try to download something, either in Safari or Mail, that contains *executable code* (a program, in other words), a dialog box warns you that it could conceivably harbor a virus—even if your download is compressed as a .zip or .sit file.

Those are only a few tiny examples. Here are a few of Mac OS X's big-ticket defenses.

## The Firewall

If you have a broadband, always-on connection, you're open to the Internet 24 hours a day. It's theoretically possible for some cretin to use automated hacking software to flood you with files or take control of your machine. Mac OS X's *firewall* feature puts up a barrier to such mischief.

Fortunately, it's not a *complete* barrier. One of the great joys of having a computer is its ability to connect to other computers. Living in a cement crypt is one way to avoid getting infected, but it's not much fun.

So if you open the Security panel of System Preferences, and click the Firewall tab, you see something like Figure 13-15 at top. It offers three settings:

• **"Allow all incoming connections"** is the same as having no firewall at all. Now, most of the Internet's cretins are far more interested in tapping into Windows machines than Macs, but you never know. Best to avoid this one.

• **"Allow only essential services"** is the closest thing Leopard has to "block everything." It gives access only to a small, fixed set of deep-seated services that Mac OS X needs to get by.

**Figure 13-15:**
*Top: Apple's new firewall in Mac OS X 10.5 looks like this.*

*It lists the programs that have been given permission to receive communications from the Internet. At any point, you can change a program's Block/Allow setting, as shown here.*

*Bottom: From time to time, some program will ask for permission to communicate with its mother ship. If it's a program you trust, click Always Allow.*

*You can also click the + button to navigate your Applications folder and manually choose programs for inclusion.*

*For more power and flexibility, install a shareware program like Firewalk or Brickhouse (available from www.missingmanuals. com, for example).*

- **"Set access for specific services and applications"** is the best choice for most people. It blocks all incoming pings except those addressed to programs and features that you've approved.

And how do they get approved? Above the horizontal line (Figure 13-15, top), features of Mac OS X itself are listed. They get added to this list automatically when you turn them on in System Preference: File Sharing, Printer Sharing, and so on.

Non-Apple programs can request passage through your firewall, too (Figure 13-15, bottom); if you click Always Allow, they appear below the line in this list.

Now, there are a few footnotes regarding the firewall:

- If you're using Mac OS X's *Internet connection sharing* feature (page 292), then it's important to turn on the firewall only for the *first* Mac—the one that's the gateway to the Internet. Leave the firewall turned off on all the Macs "downstream" from it. You want to protect your Macs from the nasties of the Internet; you don't need them giving each *other* the cold shoulder.

- Similarly, if you've bought a *router* to distribute your Internet connection to multiple computers, it probably has its own firewall circuitry built in. In that case, turn off Mac OS X's own firewall.

- Two useful features are hiding behind the Advanced button (which is visible in Figure 13-15):

  **Enable Stealth Mode** is designed to slam shut the Mac's back door to the Internet. See, hackers often use automated hacker tools that send out "Are you there?" messages. They're hoping to find computers that are turned on and connected full-time to the Internet. If your machine responds, and they can figure out how to get into it, they'll use it, without your knowledge, as a relay station for pumping out spam or masking their hacking footsteps.

  Enable Stealth Mode, then, makes your Mac even more invisible on the network; it means that your Mac won't respond to the electronic signal called a *ping*. (On the other hand, *you* won't be able to ping your machine, either, when you're on the road and want to know if it's turned on and online.)

  **Enable Firewall Logging** creates a little text file where Mac OS X records every attempt that anyone from the outside makes to infiltrate your Mac. (To view the log, click the Open Log button. The file opens in Console for your inspection.)

## FileVault

The Security pane of System Preferences is one of Leopard's most powerful security features. Understanding what it does, however, may take a little slogging.

As you know, the Mac OS X accounts system is designed to keep people out of each other's stuff. Ordinarily, for example, Chris isn't allowed to go rooting through Robin's stuff.

Until FileVault came along, though, there were several ways to circumvent this protection system. A sneak or a showoff could, for example, remove your hard drive and hook it up to a Linux machine or another Mac. He'd then be able to run rampant through everybody's files, changing or trashing them with abandon. For people with sensitive or private files, the result was a security hole bigger than Steve Jobs' bank account.

FileVault is an extra line of defense. When you turn on this feature, your Mac automatically *encrypts* (scrambles) everything in your Home folder, using something called AES-128 encryption. (How secure is that? It would take a password-guessing computer *149 trillion years* before hitting paydirt. Or, in more human terms, slightly longer than two back-to-back Kevin Costner movies.)

This means that unless someone knows (or can figure out) your password, FileVault renders your files unreadable for anyone but you and your computer's administrator— no matter what sneaky tricks they try to pull.

*You* won't notice much difference when FileVault is turned on. You log in as usual, clicking your name and typing your password. Only a slight pause as you log out indicates that Mac OS X is doing some housekeeping on the encrypted files: freeing up some space and/or backing up your home directory with Time Machine.

---

**Tip:** This feature is especially useful for laptop owners. If someone swipes or "borrows" your laptop, they can't get into your stuff without the password.

---

Here are some things you should know about FileVault's protection:

- **It's useful only if you've logged out.** Once you're logged in, your files are accessible. If you want the protection, log out before you wander away from the Mac. (Or let the screen saver close your account for you; see page 409.)

- **It covers only your Home folder.** Anything in your Applications, System, or Library folders is exempt from protection.

- **An administrator can access your files, too.** According to Mac OS X's caste system, anyone with an administrator's account can theoretically have unhindered access to his peasants' files—even with FileVault on—if that administrator has the master password described below.

- **It keeps other people from *opening* your files, not from deleting them.** It's still possible for someone to trash all your files, without ever seeing what they are. There's not much you can do about this with FileVault on *or* off—all a malicious person needs to do is start deleting the encrypted files, and your data is gone. (FileVault works by encrypting your Home folder into eight-megabyte chunks.)

- **Shared folders in your Home folder will no longer be available on the network.** That is, any folders you've shared won't be available to your co-workers *except* when you're at your Mac and logged in.

- **Backup programs may throw a tizzy.** FileVault's job is to "zip" and "unzip" your Home folder as you log in and out. Backup programs that work by backing up files and folders that have changed since the last backup may therefore get very confused.

Even Time Machine (page 263) doesn't always play well with FileVault. For one thing, it can copy the encrypted Home folder only when it's closed—that is, when

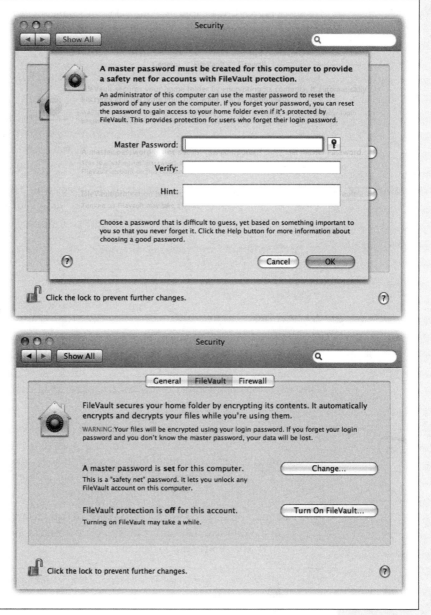

***Figure 13-16:***
*Top: To turn on FileVault for an account, you must start by making up a master password: a skeleton key that can get you into some-body's account even if they forget their password. (You have no idea how often this happens.)*

*Type in your master password twice, and give yourself a hint*

*Bottom: When you click OK, you see that the Security dialog box now says, "A master password is set for this computer." In the event of an emergency, you'll get the hint when you click an account name at the Login screen, and then click Reset Password.*

*Now you can click Turn On FileVault to begin the encryption process.*

you're logged off. So you don't get the continuous hourly backups that everyone else gets.

Second, in times of tragedy, Time Machine can restore only your *entire* Home folder; you can't recover individual documents or folders in it.

- **If you forget your password *and* your administrator forgets the master password, you're toast.** If this happens, your data is *permanently lost.* You'll have no choice but to erase your hard drive and start from scratch.

To turn FileVault on, proceed like this:

1. **In System Preferences, click Security, and then click FileVault. Click Set Master Password.**

   If you're the first person to try to turn on FileVault, you need to create a *master* password first. The master password is an override password that gives an administrator full power to access any account, even without knowing the account holder's password, or to turn off FileVault for any account.

   The thinking goes like this: Yeah, yeah, the peons with Standard accounts forget their *account* passwords all the time. But with FileVault, a forgotten password would mean *the entire Home folder is locked forever*—so Apple gave you, the technically savvy administrator, a back door. (And you, the omniscient administrator, would *never* forget the *master* password—right?)

   When you click Set Master Password, the dialog box shown at top in Figure 13-16 appears.

2. **Click "Turn On FileVault."**

   You're asked to type your account password. A dialog box appears offering some additional security options.

---

***Note:*** You can also turn on FileVault for an account at the moment you create it in System Preferences→ Accounts.

---

3. **Click "Turn On FileVault" again.**

   Now Mac OS X logs you out of your own account. (It can't encrypt a folder that's in use.) Some time passes while it converts your Home folder into a protected state, during which you can't do anything but wait.

   After a few minutes, you arrive at the standard login window, where you can sign in as usual, confident that your stuff is securely locked away from anyone who tries to get at it when you're not logged in.

---

***Note:*** To turn off FileVault, open System Preferences, click Security, and then click Turn Off FileVault. Enter your password and click OK. (The master password sticks around once you've created it, however, in case you ever want to turn FileVault on again.)

---

## Logout Options

As you read earlier in this chapter, the usual procedure for finishing up a work session is for each person to choose  →Log Out. After you confirm your intention to log out, the Login screen appears, ready for the next victim.

But sometimes people forget. You might wander off to the bathroom for a minute, but run into a colleague there who breathlessly begins describing last night's date and proposes finishing the conversation over pizza. The next thing you know, you've left your Mac unattended but logged in, with all your life's secrets accessible to anyone who walks by your desk.

You can prevent that situation using either of two checkboxes, both in the Security panel of System Preferences:

- **Require password to wake this computer from sleep or screen saver.** This option gives you a password-protected screen saver that locks your Mac after a few minutes of inactivity. Now, whenever somebody tries to wake up your Mac after the screen saver has appeared (or when the Mac has simply gone to sleep according to your settings in the Energy Saver panel of System Preferences), the "Enter your password" dialog box appears. No password? No access.

- **Log out after __ minutes of inactivity.** If you prefer, you can make the Mac sign out of your account completely if it figures out that you've wandered off (and it's been, say, 15 minutes since the last time you touched the mouse or keyboard). Instead, it presents the standard Login screen.

*Note:* Beware! If there are open, unsaved documents at the moment of truth, the Mac can't log you out.

## The Keychain

The information explosion of the computer age may translate into bargains, power, and efficiency, but as noted above, it carries with it a colossal annoyance: the proliferation of *passwords* we have to memorize. Shared folders on the network, Web sites, your iDisk, FTP sites—each requires another password.

Apple has done the world a mighty favor with its *Keychain* feature. The concept is brilliant. Whenever you log into Mac OS X and type in your password, you've typed the master code that tells the computer, "It's really me. I'm at my computer now." From that moment on, the Mac *automatically* fills in every password blank you encounter, whether it's a Web site in Safari or Opera, a shared disk on your network, a wireless network, an encrypted disk image, or an FTP program like Transmit or RBrowser. With only a few exceptions, you can safely forget *all* of your passwords except your login password.

These days, all kinds of programs and services know about the Keychain and offer to store your passwords there. For example:

• In Safari, whenever you type your name and password for a certain Web page and then click OK, a dialog box asks: "Would you like to save this password?" (See Figure 13-17, top.)

---

**Note:** This offer is valid only if, in Safari→Preferences, you've clicked the AutoFill tab and turned on "User names and passwords." If not, the "Would you?" message never appears.

Note, too, that some Web sites use a nonstandard login system that also doesn't produce the "Would you?" message. Unless the Web site provides its own "Remember me" or "Store my password" option, you're out of luck; you'll have to type in this information with every visit.

---

• When you connect to a shared folder or disk on the network, the opportunity to save the password in your Keychain is equally obvious (Figure 13-17, bottom).

• You also see a "Remember password (add to Keychain)" option when you create an encrypted disk image using Disk Utility.

• Apple's Mail program stores your email account passwords in your Keychain. Your .Mac account information is stored there, too (on the .Mac pane of System Preferences).

• Microsoft's Entourage program offers to store your passwords. So do FTP (file-transfer) programs like RBrowser and Fetch; check their Preferences dialog boxes.

• A "Remember password" option appears when you type in the password for a wireless network or AirPort base station.

• The iTunes program memorizes your Apple Music Store password, too.

### Locking and unlocking the Keychain

If you work alone, the Keychain is automatic, invisible, and generally wonderful. Logging in is the only time you have to type a password. After that, the Mac figures, "Hey, I know it's you; you proved it by entering your account password. That ID is good enough for me. I'll fill in all your other passwords automatically." In Apple parlance, you've *unlocked* your Keychain just by logging in.

But there may be times when you want the Keychain to *stop* filling in all of your passwords, perhaps only temporarily. Maybe you work in an office where someone else might sit down at your Mac while you're getting a candy bar.

Of course, you can have Mac OS X lock your Mac—Keychain and all—after a specified period of inactivity (page 409).

If you want to lock the Keychain *manually*, so that no passwords are autofilled in until you unlock it again, you can use any of these methods. Each requires the Keychain Access program (in your Applications→Utilities folder):

• **Lock the Keychain manually.** In the Keychain Access program, choose File→Lock Keychain [Your Name] (⌘-L), or just click the big padlock at upper left. Click the Lock button in the toolbar of the Keychain Access window (Figure 13-18).

- **Choose Lock Keychain [Your Name] from the Keychain menulet.** To put the Keychain menulet on your menu bar, open Keychain Access, choose Keychain Access→Preferences. In Preferences, click General, and then turn on Show Status in Menu Bar.

*Figure 13-17:*
*Top: Safari is one of several Internet-based programs that offer to store your passwords in the Keychain; just click Yes. The next time you visit this Web page, you'll find your name and password already typed in.*

*Middle: At any time, you can see a complete list of the memorized Web passwords by choosing Safari→Preferences, clicking AutoFill, and then clicking the Edit button next to "User names and passwords." This is also where you can delete a password, thus making Safari forget it.*

*Bottom: When you connect to a server (a shared disk or folder on the network), just turn on "Remember this password in my keychain."*

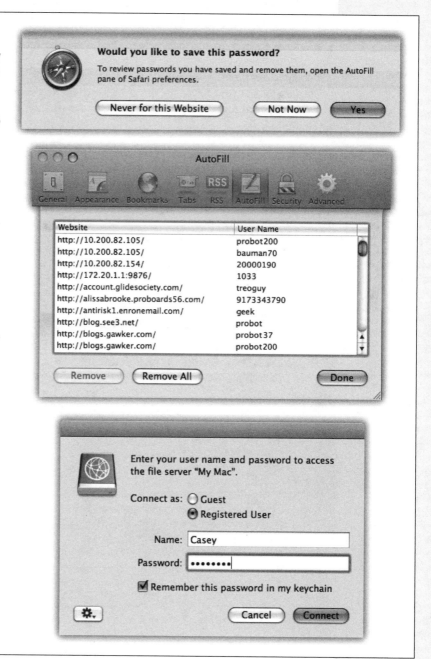

• **Lock the Keychain automatically.** In the Keychain Access program, choose Edit→Change Settings for Keychain [your name]. The resulting dialog box lets you set up the Keychain to lock itself, say, five minutes after the last time you used your Mac, or whenever the Mac goes to sleep. When you return to the Mac, you're asked to re-enter your account password in order to unlock the Keychain, restoring your automatic-password feature.

Whenever the Keychain is locked, Mac OS X no longer fills in your passwords.

### Managing Keychain

To take a look at your Keychain, open the Keychain Access program. By clicking one of the password rows, you get to see its attributes—name, kind, account, and so on (Figure 13-18).

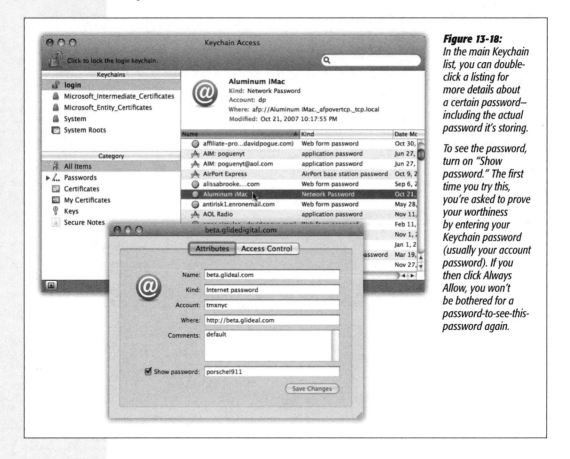

**Figure 13-18:**
*In the main Keychain list, you can double-click a listing for more details about a certain password— including the actual password it's storing.*

*To see the password, turn on "Show password." The first time you try this, you're asked to prove your worthiness by entering your Keychain password (usually your account password). If you then click Always Allow, you won't be bothered for a password-to-see-this-password again.*

# Networking, File Sharing, & Screen Sharing

Just about every Mac ever built is network-ready. Buy a couple of components, and you can connect all the computers in your office together, with or without wires. The process of rigging the hardware and software for a network is somewhat more technical than, say, emptying the Trash, but it's not exactly rocket science.

Once you've got a network, you can copy files from one machine to another—even between Windows PCs and Macs—just as you'd drag files between folders on your own Mac. You can send little messages to each other's screens. Everyone on the network can consult the same database or calendar. You can play games over the network. You can share a single printer, cable modem, or fax modem among all the Macs in the office. You can connect to this network from wherever you are in the world, using the Internet as the world's longest extension cord back to your office.

And in Mac OS X 10.5, you can even do *screen sharing,* which means that you, the wise computer whiz, can see what's on the screen of your pathetic, floundering relative or buddy elsewhere on the network. You can even seize control of the other Mac's mouse and keyboard. You can troubleshoot, fiddle with settings, and so on. It's the next best thing to being there—and often a lot better than being there.

This chapter concerns itself with *local* networking—setting up a network in your home or small office. But don't miss its sibling, Chapter 10, which is about hooking up to the somewhat larger network called the Internet.

## Wiring the Network

Most people connect their computers using one of two connection systems: Ethernet or Wi-Fi (which Apple calls AirPort).

## Ethernet Networks

Almost every Mac, PC, and network-ready laser printer has an Ethernet jack on the back or side panel (see Figure 14-1). If you connect all of the computers and Ethernet printers in your small office to a central *Ethernet hub* or *router*—a compact, inexpensive box with jacks for 5, 10, or even more computers and printers—you've got yourself a very fast, very reliable network. (Most people wind up hiding the hub in a closet, and running the wiring either along the edges of the room or inside the walls.) You can buy Ethernet cables, plus the hub, at any computer store or, less expensively, from an Internet-based mail-order house. (Hubs aren't Mac-specific.)

Ethernet is the best networking system for many offices. It's fast, easy, and cheap.

## AirPort Networks

Wi-Fi, known to the geeks as 802.11 and to Apple fans as AirPort, means wireless networking. It's the technology that lets laptops the world over get online at high speed in any Wi-Fi "hot spot." Hot spots are everywhere these days: in homes, offices, coffee shops (notably Starbucks), hotels, airports, and thousands of other places.

*Tip:* At *www.jiwire.com*, you can type in an address or a city and learn exactly where to find the closest Wi-Fi hot spots.

**Figure 14-1:**
*An Ethernet jack (left) looks like an overweight telephone jack. It connects to an Ethernet router or hub (right) via an Ethernet cable (also known as Cat 5 or Cat 6), which ends in what looks like an overweight telephone-wire plug (also known as an RJ-45 connector).*

Ethernet jack                    Ethernet hub

When you're in a Wi-Fi hot spot, your Mac has a very fast connection to the Internet, as though it's connected to a cable modem or DSL.

AirPort circuitry comes preinstalled every Mac laptop, iMac, and Mac Mini, and you can order it built into a new Mac Pro.

This circuitry lets your machine connect to your network and the Internet without any wires at all. You just have to be within about 150 feet of a *base station* or (in Windows terminology) *access point,* which must in turn be physically connected to your network and Internet connection.

If you think about it, the AirPort system is a lot like a cordless phone, where the base station is, well, the base station, and the Mac is the handset.

The base station can take any of these forms:

- **AirPort base station.** Apple's sleek, white, squarish or rounded base stations ($100 to $180) permit as many as 50 computers to connect simultaneously.

  The less expensive one, the AirPort Express, is so small that it looks like a small white power adapter. It also has a USB jack so you can share a USB printer on the network. It can serve up to 10 computers at once. Another option is Time Capsue, which is both an access point and a hard drive that backs up all your Leopard Macs automatically.

- **A wireless broadband router.** Lots of other companies make less expensive Wi-Fi base stations, including Linksys (*www.linksys.com*) and Belkin (*www.belkin.com*). You can plug the base station into an Ethernet router or hub, thus permitting 10 or 20 wireless-equipped computers, including Macs, to join an existing Ethernet network without wiring. (With all due non-fanboyism, however, Apple's base stations and software are infinitely more polished and satisfying to use.)

---

**UP TO SPEED**

## AirPort a, b, g, and n: Regular or Supersized?

In the short history of wireless networking, Wi-Fi gear has come in several variants, bearing the absurdly user-hostile names *802.11b, 802.11g, 802.11a, 802.11n,* and so on.

The difference involves the technical specs of the wireless signal. Original AirPort uses the 802.11b standard; AirPort Extreme uses 802.11g; the current AirPort cards and base stations use 802.11n.

So what's the difference? Equipment bearing the "b" label transfers data through the air at up to 11 megabits per second; the "g" system is almost five times as fast (54 Mbytes/sec); and "n" is supposed to be four times as fast as *that.*

(Traditionally, geeks measure network speeds in mega*bits*, not mega*bytes*. If you're more familiar with megabytes, though, here's a translation: The older AirPort gear has a top speed of 1.4 megabytes per second, versus more than 6 megabytes per second for the AirPort Extreme stuff.)

(Oh, and while we're using parentheses here: The only place you'll get the quoted speeds out of this gear is when you're on the moon. Here on earth, signal strength is affected by pesky things like air, furniture, walls, floors, wiring, phone interference, and antenna angle. Speed and signal strength diminish proportionally as you move away from the base station.)

Now, each successive version of the Wi-Fi base station/laptop circuitry standard is backward-compatible. For example, you can buy a new, 802.11n base station, and still connect to it from your ancient 802.11g PowerBook. You won't get any greater speed, of course—that would require a laptop with an 802.11n transmitter—but you'll enjoy the greater range in your house.

It's important to understand, though, that even the most expensive, top-tier cable modem or DSL service delivers Internet information at only about *half* a megabyte per second. The bottleneck is the Internet connection, not your network. Don't buy newer AirPort gear thinking that you're going to speed up your email and Web activity.

Instead, the speed boost you get with AirPort Extreme is useful *only* for transferring files between computers and gadgets on your own network (like the bandwidth-hungry Apple TV)—and playing networkable games.

And one more note: All Wi-Fi gear works together, no matter what kind of computer you have. There's no such thing as a "Windows" wireless network or a "Macintosh" wireless network. Macs can use non-Apple base stations, PCs can use AirPort base stations, and so on.

---

*Tip:* It's perfectly possible to plug a Wi-Fi base station into a regular router, too, to accommodate both wired and wireless computers.

• **Another Mac.** Your Mac can also *impersonate* an AirPort base station. In effect, the Mac becomes a software-based base station, and you save yourself the cost of a separate physical base station.

For the easiest AirPort network setup, begin by configuring your Mac so that it can go online the wired way. Once it's capable of connecting to the Internet via wires, you can then use the Airport Utility (in your Applications→Utilities folder) to transmit those Internet settings wirelessly to the base station itself. From then on, the base station's modem or Ethernet jack—not your Mac's—will do the connecting to the Internet.

Whether you've set up your own wireless network or want to hop onto somebody else's, Chapter 10 has the full scoop on *joining* Wi-Fi networks.

## File Sharing

When you're done wiring (or not wiring, as the case may be), your network is ready. Your Mac should "see" any Ethernet or shared USB printers, in readiness to print (Chapter 9). You can now play network games or use a network calendar. And you can now turn on *File Sharing*, one of the most useful features of the Mac OS.

In File Sharing, you can summon the icon for a folder or disk attached to another computer on the network, whether it's a Mac or a Windows PC. It shows up in a Finder window, as shown in Figure 14-3.

At this point, you can drag files back and forth, exactly as though the other computer's folder or disk is a hard drive connected to your own machine.

---

**GEM IN THE ROUGH**

### Networking Without the Network

In a pinch, you can connect two Macs without any real network at all. You can create an Ethernet connection without a hub or a router—or an AirPort connection without a Wi-Fi base station.

To set up the wired connection, just run a standard Ethernet cable between the Ethernet jacks of the two Macs. (You don't need to use an Ethernet *crossover* cable, as you did in days of old.)

To set up a wireless connection, from your 🛜 menulet, choose Create Network. Make up a name for your little

private network, and then click OK. On the second Mac, choose 🛜→Join Network, enter the same private network name, and click Join.

At this point, your two Macs belong to the same *ad hoc* micro-network. But that doesn't mean that you've started accessing their files yet.

To do that, in the Finder on one of the Macs, choose Go→Connect to Server. The Network window opens, showing the icons for all the computers on the local network. Double-click the one you want, enter the account password, if necessary, and you're in.

---

The thing is, it's not easy being Apple. You have to write *one* operating system that's supposed to please *everyone,* from the self-employed first-time computer owner to the network administrator for NASA. You have to design a networking system simple enough for the laptop owner who just wants to copy things to a desktop Mac when returning from a trip, yet secure and flexible enough for the network designer at a large corporation.

Clearly, different people have different attitudes toward the need for security and flexibility.

That's why Leopard offers two ways to share files—a simple and limited way, and a more complicated and flexible way:

- **The simple way: the Public folder.** Every account holder has a Public folder. It's free for anyone else on the network to access. Like a grocery store bulletin board, there's no password required. Super-convenient, super-easy.

  There's only one downside, and you may not care about it: You have to move or copy files *into* the Public folder before anyone else can see them. Depending on how many files you want to share, this can get tedious and eat up disk space.

- **The flexible way: Any folder.** You can also make *any* file, folder, or disk available for inspection by other people on the network. This method means that you don't have to move files into the Public folder, for starters. It also gives you elaborate control over who is allowed to do what to your files. You might want to permit your company's executives to see *and* edit your documents, but allow the peons in Accounting just to see them. And Andy, that unreliable goofball in Sales? You don't want him even *seeing* what's in your shared folder.

  Of course, setting up all those levels of control means more work and more complexity.

## Setup: The Public Folder

Inside your Home folder, there's a folder called Public. Inside *everybody's* Home folder is a folder called Public.

Anything you copy into this folder is automatically available to everyone else on the network. They don't need a password, they don't need an account on your Mac—they just have to be on the same network.

To make your Public folder available to your network mates, you have to turn on the File Sharing master switch. Choose ⬧→System Preferences, click Sharing, and turn on File Sharing (Figure 14-2).

Now round up the files and folders you want to share with all comers on the network, and drag them into your Home→Public folder. That's all there is to it.

---

***Note:*** You may notice that there's already something in your Public folder: a folder called Drop Box. It's there so that other people can give *you* files from across the network, as described later in this chapter.

---

So now that you've set up Public folder sharing, how are other people supposed to *access* your Public folder? See page 422.

## Setup: Sharing Any Folder

If the Public folder method seems too simple and restrictive, then you can graduate to the "share any folder" method. In this scheme, you can make *any* file, folder, or disk available to other people on the network.

This time, you don't have to move your files anywhere; they sit right where you have them. And this time, you can set up elaborate *sharing privileges* (also known as *permissions*) that grant individuals different amount of access to your files.

This method is more complicated to set up than that Public-folder business. In fact, just to underline its complexity, Apple has created two different setup procedures. You can share one icon at a time by opening its Get Info window; or you can work in a master list of shared items in System Preferences.

The following section covers both methods.

***Figure 14-2:***
*Here's the master switch that makes your Public folder (and any other folders you designate) available to other people on the network. You can edit the Computer Name, if you like. Your Mac will appear on the network with this name. Make it nice and descriptive, such as Front Desk iMac.*

### The Get Info method

Here's how to share a Mac file, disk, or folder disk using its Get Info window.

The following steps assume that you've opened  →System Preferences, clicked Sharing, and then turned on File Sharing, as shown in Figure 14-2.

1. **Highlight the file, folder, or disk you want to share. Choose File→Get Info.**

   The Get Info dialog box appears (Figure 14-3). Expand the General panel, if it's not already visible.

---

**Note:** Sharing an entire disk means that every folder and file on it is available to anyone you give access to. On the other hand, by sharing only a folder or two, you can keep *most* of the stuff on your hard drive private, out of view of curious network comrades. Sharing only a folder or two does *them* a favor, too, by making it easier for them to find files you've made available. This way, they don't have to root through your entire drive looking for the folder they actually need.

---

**Figure 14-3:**
*The file-sharing permissions controls are back in the Get Info box for any file, folder, or disk—right back where they were in Mac OS 9 in days of old.*

*By the way: If the Finder quits when you click the + button to fiddle with the permissions, you're not alone. There's a quick fix, though, awaiting on Apple's Help Web site. It's here:*

http://docs.info.apple.com/article.html?artnum=307128

2. **Turn on "Shared folder."**

   Enter your Administrative password, if necessary.

   OK, this disk or folder is now shared. But with whom?

3. **Expand the Sharing & Permissions panel, if it's not already visible. Click the 🔒 icon and enter your administrator's password.**

   The controls in the Sharing & Permissions area spring to life and become editable. You wanted individual control over each account holder's access? You've got it.

   At the bottom of the Info panel is a little table. The first column can display the names of individual account holders, like Casey or Chris, or *groups* of account holders, like Everyone or Accounting Dept. The second column lists the *privileges* each person or group has for this folder.

---

Now, the average person has no clue what "privileges" means, and this is why things get a little hairy when you're setting up folder-by-folder permissions.

4. **Edit the table by adding people's names. Then set their access permissions.**

At the moment, your name appears in the Name column, and it probably says Read & Write in the Privilege column. In other words, you're currently the master of this folder. You can put things in, and you can take things out.

But at the moment, the privileges for "Everyone" is probably "Read only." Other people can see this folder, but can't do anything with it.

Now your job is to work through this list of people, specifying *how much* control each person has over the file or folder you're sharing. To add the name of a person or group, click the + button below the list. The people list shown in Figure 14-4 appears.

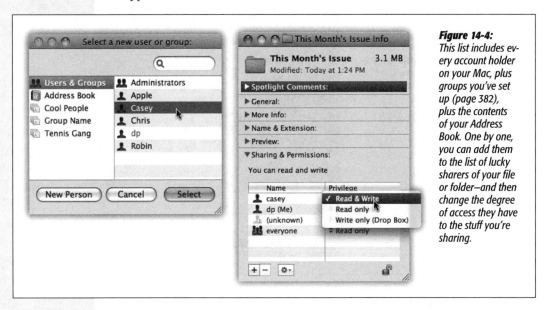

**Figure 14-4:**
*This list includes every account holder on your Mac, plus groups you've set up (page 382), plus the contents of your Address Book. One by one, you can add them to the list of lucky sharers of your file or folder—and then change the degree of access they have to the stuff you're sharing.*

Now click a name in the list. Then, from the Privilege pop-up menu, choose a permissions setting.

**Read & Write** has the most access of all. This person, like you, can add, change, or delete any file in the shared folder, or make any changes you like to a document. Give Read & Write permission to people you trust not to mess things up.

**Read only** means "look, but don't touch." This person can see what's in the folder (or file) and can copy it, but can't delete or change the original. It's a good setting for distributing company documents or making source files available to your minions.

**Write only (drop box)** means that other people can't open the folder at all. They can drop things into it, but it's like dropping icons through a mail slot: The letter disappears into the slot, and then it's too late for them to change their minds. As the folder's owner, you can do what you like with the deposited goodies. This drop-box effect is great when you want students, co-workers, or family members to be able to *turn things in* to you—homework, reports, scandalous diaries—without running the risk that someone else might see those documents.

**No access** is an option only for "Everyone." It means that other people can see this file or folder's icon, but can't do a thing with it.

---

*Tip:* Usually, you'll want the privileges for the folder to also apply to everything *inside* it; it would be a real drag to have to change the sharing privileges of the contents one icon as a time. That's why the ✿ menu at the bottom of the Get Info box has a command called "Apply to enclosed items."

---

5. **Close the Get Info window.**

Now the folder is ready for invasion from across the network.

### The System Preferences method

It's very convenient to turn on sharing one folder at a time, using the Get Info window. But there's another way in, too, one that displays *all* of your shared stuff in one handy master list.

*Figure 14-5:*
*Hiding in System Preferences is a list of every file, disk, and folder that you've shared. To stop sharing something, click it and click the – button. To share something new, drag its icon off the desktop, or out of its window, directly into the Shared Folders list.*

To see it, choose  →System Preferences. Click Sharing. Click File Sharing (and make sure it's turned on).

Now you're looking at a slightly different kind of permissions table, shown in Figure 14-5. It has *three* columns. The first lists the files, folders, and disks you've shared. The second shows *who* gets to work with a certain item from across the network. The third column lets you specify how much access each person in the *second* column has to this folder, as described on page 418.

## Accessing Shared Files

So far in this chapter, you've read about *setting up* a Mac so that people at other computers can access its files.

Now comes the payoff: sitting at another computer and *connecting* to the one you set up. There are two ways to go about it.

### Connection Method A: Use the Sidebar

Suppose, then, that you're seated in front of your Mac, and you want to see the files on another Mac on the network. Proceed like this:

1. **Open any Finder window.**

   In the Shared category of the Sidebar at the left side of the window, icons for all the computers on the network appear. See Figure 14-6.

---

***Tip:*** The same Sidebar items show up in the Save and Open dialog boxes of your programs, too, making the entire network available to you for opening and saving files.

---

**Figure 14-6:**
*Macs often appear in the Sidebar with model-specific names (MacBook, iMac, and so on). Other computers (like PCs) have generic blue monitors. When you click All in the Sidebar, you see both the icons of individual computers and the icons of network chunks (like AppleTalk zones and Windows workgroups).*

If you *don't* see a certain Mac's icon here, it might be turned off, it might not be on the network, or it might have File Sharing turned off.

If there are more than six icons in the Sidebar, or if you're on a corporate-style network that has sub-chunks like *nodes* or *workgroups*, you also see an icon called All. Click it to see the full list of network entities that your Mac can see: not just individual Mac, Windows, and Unix machines, but also any "network neighborhoods" (limbs of your network tree). For example, you may see the names of AppleTalk zones (clusters of machines, as found in big companies and universities).

Or, if you're trying to tap into a Windows machine, open the icon representing the *workgroup* (computer cluster) that contains the machine you want. In small office networks, it's usually called MSHOME or WORKGROUP. In big corporations, these workgroups can be called almost anything—as long as it's no more than 12 letters long with no punctuation. (Thanks, Microsoft.)

If you *do* see icons for workgroups or other network "zones," double-click your way until you're seeing the icons for individual computers.

2. **Click the computer whose files you want to open.**

In the main window, you now see the icons for each account holder on that computer: Mom, Dad, Sissy, whatever. If you have an account on the other computer, you'll see a folder representing *your* stuff, too (Figure 14-7).

**Figure 14-7:**
*Without requiring any name or password on the other Mac, you have full access to anything the other account holders have left in their Public folders. (There's a Public folder in everyone's Home folder.) At this point, you're considered a Guest.*

At this point, the remaining instructions diverge, depending on whether you want to access *other* people's stuff or *your* stuff. That's why there are two alternative versions of step 3 here:

3a. **If you want to access the stuff that somebody *else* has left for you, double-click that person's Public folder.**

Instantly, the icon for that folder appears on your desktop, and an Eject button (⏏) appears beside the computer's name in the Sidebar. (You can turn off both of those visual signals in Finder→Preferences.)

In this situation, you're only a Guest. You don't have to bother with a password. On the other hand, the only thing you can generally see inside the other person's account folder is his Public folder.

If you see anything besides the Drop Box folder in the Public folder you've opened, then it's stuff that the account holder has copied there for the enjoyment of you and your network mates. You're not allowed to delete anything from the other person's Public folder or make changes to them.

You can, however, open those icons, read them, or even copy them to *your* Mac—and then edit *your* copies.

3b. **To access your own Home folder on the other Mac, click it, and then click the Connect As button (Figure 14-8). Sign in as usual.**

When the "Connect to the file server" box appears, you're supposed to specify your account name and password (from the Mac you're tapping into). This is the same name and password you'd use to log in if you were actually sitting at that machine.

**Figure 14-8:**
*Top: You can sign in to your account on another Mac on the network (even while somebody else is actually using that Mac in person). Click Connect As (top right), and then enter your name and password. Turn on "Remember this password" to speed up the process for next time.*

*The Action (✿) pop-up menu offers a Change Password that gives you the opportunity to change your account password on the other machine, just in case you suspect someone saw what you typed.*

*Bottom: No matter which method you use to connect to a shared folder or disk, its icon shows up in the Sidebar. It's easy to disconnect, thanks to the little ⏏ button.*

***Tip:*** The dialog box shown in Figure 14-8 includes the delightful and timesaving "Remember this password in my keychain" option, which makes the Mac memorize your password for a certain disk so you don't have to type it—or even see this dialog box—every darned time you connect.

When you click Connect (or press Return or Enter), your own Home folder on the other Mac appears. Its icon shows up on your desktop, and a little ⏏ button appears next to its name. Click it to disconnect.

In the meantime, you can double-click icons to open them, make copies of them, and otherwise manipulate them exactly as though they were icons on your own hard drive. Depending on what permissions you've been given, you can even edit or trash those files.

## Connection Method B: Connect to Server

The Sidebar method of connecting to networked folders and disks is practically effortless. But it doesn't let you type in a disk's network address. As a result, you can't access any shared disk *on the Internet* (an FTP site, for example), or indeed anywhere beyond your local subnet (your own small network).

Fortunately, there's another way. When you choose Go→Connect to Server, you get the dialog box shown in Figure 14-9. You're supposed to type in the *address* of the shared disk you want.

**Figure 14-9:**
*The Sidebar method of connecting to shared disks and folders is quick and easy, but it doesn't let you connect to certain kinds of disks. The Connect to Server method entails plodding through several dialog boxes and doesn't let you browse for shared disks, but it can find just about every kind of networked disk.*

## Disconnecting Yourself

When you're finished using a shared disk or folder, you can disconnect from it by clicking the ⏏ icon next to its name in the Sidebar.

# Networking with Windows

Mac OS X represents a historic moment in Mac-Windows relations: It lets Macs and Windows PCs see each other on the network, with no special software (or talent) required.

In fact, you can go in either direction. Your Mac can see shared folders on the Windows PCs, and a Windows PC can see shared folders on your Mac. Since a huge number of Mac "switchers" are actually Mac "adders" (meaning that you're keeping the old PC around), you might find these features especially useful.

It goes like this:

## Seated at the Mac, Seeing the PC

Suppose you have a Windows PC and a Mac on the same wired or wireless network. Here's how you get the Mac and PC chatting:

1. **On your Windows PC, share some files.**

   Just as on the Mac, there are two ways to share files in Windows. One of them is super-simple: You just copy the files you want to share into a central, fully accessible folder. No passwords, accounts, or other steps are required.

   In **Windows XP**, that folder is Shared Documents, which you can find by choosing Start→My Computer. Share it on the network as shown in Figure 14-10, top.

   In **Windows Vista,** it's the Public folder, which appears in the Navigation pane of every Explorer window. (In Vista, there's one Public folder for the whole *computer*, not one per account holder.)

   The second, more complicated method is the "share any folder" method, just as in Leopard. In general, you right-click the folder you want to share, choose Properties from the shortcut menu, click the Sharing tab, and turn on "Share this folder on the network" (Figure 14-10, top). Repeat for any other folders you want to make available to your Mac.

---

**GEM IN THE ROUGH**

### Faster Ways to Connect Next Time

If you expect that you might want to access a shared disk or folder again later, take a moment to make an alias of it. (For example, right-click it and choose Make Alias from the shortcut menu.)

Next time, you can bring it back to your screen later just by double-clicking the alias. And if you turned on "Remember this password in my keychain," you won't even be asked for your name and password again.

Similarly, if you drag a shared folder into the Dock, you can bring it back to your screen later just by clicking its icon.

You can even drag its icon into the Login Items window described on page 386. Now the disk appears on your desktop *automatically* each time you log in—the most effortless arrangement of all.

---

**2. On the Mac, open any Finder window.**

The shared PCs may appear as individual computer names in the Sidebar, or you may have to click the All icon to see the icons of their *workgroups* (network clusters—an effect shown on page 422). Unless you or a network administrator changed it, the workgroup name is probably MSHOME or WORKGROUP. Double-click the workgroup name you want.

*Tip:* You can also access the shared PC via the Connect to Server command, as described on page 425. You could type into it *smb://192.168.1.103* (or whatever the PC's IP address is) and hit Return—and then skip to step 5. In fact, using the Connect to Server method often works when the Sidebar method doesn't.

**Figure 14-10:**
*Top: To share a folder in Windows XP, right-click it, choose Properties, and then turn on "Share this folder on the network." In the "Share name" box, type a name for the folder as it will appear on the network. (No spaces are allowed).*

*Bottom: Back in the safety of Mac OS X, click the PC's name in the Sidebar. (If it's part of a workgroup, click All, and then your workgroup name first. And if you still don't see the PC's name, see the box on page 431.)*

*Next, click the name of the shared computer. If the files you need are in a Shared Documents or Public folder, no password is required. You see the contents of the PC's Shared Documents folder or Public folder, as shown here. Now it's just like file sharing with another Mac.*

*If you want access to any other shared folder, click Connect As, and see Figure 14-14.*

Now the names of the individual PCs on the network appear in your Finder window.

**3. Double-click the name of the computer you want.**

If you're using one of the simple file-sharing methods on the PC, as described above, that's all there is to it. The contents of the Shared Documents or Public folder now appear onyour Mac screen. You can work with them just as you wouldyour own files.

If you're not using one of those simple methods, and you want access to individual shared folders, read on.

---

**Note:** In Windows XP Pro, the next step won't work unless you turn *off* Simple File Sharing. To do that, choose Tools→Folder Options in any Explorer window. Click the View tab and turn off "Use simple file sharing."

---

**4. Click Connect As.**

This button appears in the top right corner of the Finder window; you can see it at bottom in Figure 14-10, bottom.

**Figure 14-11:**
*Top: The PC wants to make sure that you're authorized to visit it. If the terminology here seems a bit geeky by Apple standards, no wonder—this is Microsoft Windows' lingo you're seeing, not Apple's. Fortunately, you see this box only the very first time you access a certain Windows folder or disk; after that, you see only the box shown below.*

*Bottom: Here, you see a list of shared folders on the PC. Choose the one you want to connect to, and then click OK. Like magic, the Windows folder shows up on your Mac screen, ready to use!*

Now you're asked for your name and password (Figure 14-11, top).

**5. Enter the name and password for your account on the PC, and then click OK.**

At long last, the contents of the shared folder on the Windows machine appear in your Finder window, just as though you'd tapped into another Mac (Figure 14-11, bottom). The icon of the shared folder appears on your desktop, too, and an Eject button (▲) appears next to the PC's name in your Sidebar.

From here, it's a simple matter to drag files between the machines, open Word documents on the PC using Word for the Mac, and so on—exactly like you're hooked into another Mac.

## Seated at the PC, Seeing the Mac

Cross-platformers, rejoice: Mac OS X lets you share files in *both directions*. Not only can your Mac see other PCs on the network, but they can see the Mac, too.

On the Mac, choose  →System Preferences. Click Sharing, click File Sharing (make sure File Sharing is turned on), and then click Options to open the dialog box shown in Figure 14-12.

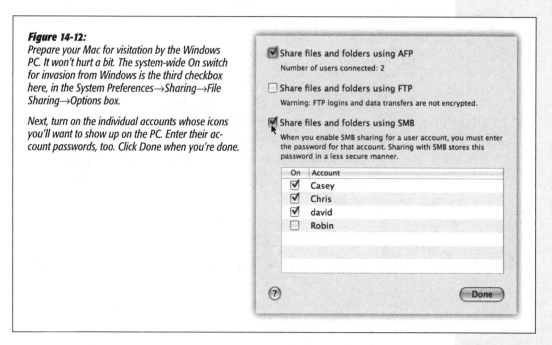

***Figure 14-12:***
*Prepare your Mac for visitation by the Windows PC. It won't hurt a bit. The system-wide On switch for invasion from Windows is the third checkbox here, in the System Preferences→Sharing→File Sharing→Options box.*

*Next, turn on the individual accounts whose icons you'll want to show up on the PC. Enter their account passwords, too. Click Done when you're done.*

Your mission now is to turn on "Share files and folders using SMB." Although Apple can't bring itself to use the term *Windows* in this dialog box, that's what it means by SMB.

Below that checkbox, you see a list of all the accounts on your Mac. Turn on the checkboxes to specify *which* Mac user accounts you want to be able to access. You must type in each person's password, too. Click Done to return to the System Preferences pane.

Before you close System Preferences, study the line near the middle of the window, where it says: "Other users can access your computer at afp://MacBook-Pro" (or whatever your computer's name is). You'll need this name shortly, although not the "afp://" part.

Now, on **Windows XP,** open My Network Places; in **Windows Vista,** choose Start→ Network. If you've sacrificed the proper animals to the networking gods, your Mac's icon should appear by itself in the network window, as shown in Figure 14-13, top.

**Note:** If you *don't* see your Mac here, proceed immediately to the box on the facing page.

*Figure 14-13:*
*Top: Double-click the icon of the Mac you want to visit from your Windows machine (Vista is shown here).*

*Middle: Type your Mac's name in all capitals (or its IP address), then a backslash, and then your Mac account short name. (You can find out your Mac's name on the Sharing pane of System Preferences.)*

*Enter your Mac account's password, too. Turn on "Remember my password" if you plan to do this again someday. Click OK.*

*Bottom: Here's your Mac Home folder—in Windows! Open it up to find all your stuff.*

Double-click the Mac's icon. Public-folder stuff is available immediately. Otherwise, you have to sign in with your Mac account name and password; Figure 14-13, middle, has the details.

In the final window, you see your actual Home folder—on a Windows PC! You're ready to open its files, copy them back and forth, or whatever (Figure 14-13, bottom).

If your Mac's icon *doesn't* appear, and you've read the box below, wait a minute or two. Try restarting the PC. In Windows XP, try clicking "Microsoft Windows Network" or "View workgroup computers" in the task pane.

If your Mac still doesn't show up, you have to add it the hard way. In the address bar of any Windows window, type \\*macbook-pro\chris* (but substitute your Mac's actual computer name and your short account name); use backslashes, not normal / slashes. You can also type your Mac's IP address in place of its computer name.

In the future, you won't have to do so much burrowing; your Mac's icon should appear automatically in the My Network Places or Network window.

## Screen Sharing

The prayers of baffled beginners and exasperated experts everywhere have now been answered. Now, when the novice needs help from the guru, the guru doesn't have to run all the way downstairs or down the hall to assist. Thanks to the new screen-sharing

---

**GEM IN THE ROUGH**

### When Macs and PCs Don't See Each Other

If your Mac's icon doesn't show up on the PC at all, or vice versa, it's probably because the Mac doesn't know anything about Windows *workgroups.* And even a lowly home PC is part of a workgroup (a corporate cluster), whether it knows it or not. And until your Mac is part of that very tiny club, it won't be able to see your PCs, and they won't be able to see it.

So if you're having no luck with this whole Mac-PC thing, try this. Open System Preferences. Click Network. Click whatever connection you're on right now (like AirPort or Ethernet). Click Advanced. Click WINS.

Now you see the peculiar set of controls shown here. The Workgroup pop-up menu already lists the workgroups that your Mac sees. Choose "workgroup" from the pop-up menu. Click OK, and then click Apply.

And marvel as your Windows PCs' names show up in the Sidebar, where they didn't before.

(Of course, your workgroup name might not be "workgroup," but that and mshome are the two most common Windows home-network workgroup names.)

---

feature of Leopard, you can see exactly what's on the screen of another Mac, from across the network—and even seize control of the other Mac's mouse and keyboard (with the newbie's permission, of course).

(Anyone who's ever tried to help someone troubleshoot over the phone knows *exactly* what this means.)

Nor is playing Bail-Out-the-Newbie the only situation when screen sharing is useful. It's also great for collaborating on a document, showing something to someone for approval, or just freaking each other out. It can also be handy when *you* are the owner of both Macs (a laptop and a desktop, for example), and you want to run a program that you don't have on the Mac that's in front of you. You might want to adjust the playlist selection on the upstairs Mac that's connected to your sound system, for example. Or maybe you just want to keep an eye on what your kids are doing on the Macs upstairs in their rooms.

The controlling person can do *everything* on the controlled Mac, including running programs, messing around the folders and files, and even shutting down the controlled Mac.

---

**Note:** Leopard is crawling with different ways to use screen sharing. You can do it over a network, over the Internet, and even during an iChat chat.

That method, described in Chapter 12, is much simpler and better than the small-network method described here. It doesn't require names or passwords, it's easy to flip back between seeing the other guy's screen and your own, and you can transfer files by dragging them from your screen to the other guy's (or vice versa).

Then again, the small-network method described here is built right into the Finder, doesn't require logging into iChat, and doesn't require Leopard running on both computers.

---

As always, trying to understand meta concepts like seeing one Mac's screen on the monitor of another can get confusing fast. So in this example, suppose that you want to take control of Mac #1 while seated at Mac #2.

## Mac #1: Give Permission in Advance

It would be a chaotic world (although greatly entertaining) if any Mac could randomly take control of any other Mac. Fortunately, though, nobody can see your screen without your explicit permission.

To give such permission, choose  →System Preferences→Sharing, and then turn on Screen Sharing.

---

**Note:** If a message appears to the effect that "Screen Sharing is currently being controlled by the Remote Management service," turn off the Remote Management checkbox and then try again.

---

At this point, there are three levels of security to protect your Mac against unauthorized remote-control mischief:

- **Secure.** If you stop here, *anyone with an account on your Mac* will be able to tap in and take control any time they like, even when you're not around. They'll enter the same name and password they'd use if they were sitting at your machine.

If "anyone" means "you and your spouse" or "you and the other two fourth-grade teachers," then that's probably perfectly fine.

- **Securer.** For greater security, though, you can limit who's allowed to stop in. Click "Only these users" and then click the + sign. A small panel appears, listing everyone with an account on your Mac. Choose the ones you trust not to mess things up while you're away from your Mac (Figure 14-14).

- **Securest.** If you click "Only these users" and then don't add *anyone* to the list, then *nobody* can tap into your screen.

Alternatively, if you're only a *little* bit of a Scrooge, you can set things up so that they can request permission to share your screen—as long as you're sitting in front of your Mac at the time and feeling generous.

To set this up, click Computer Settings and turn on "Anyone may request permission to share screen." Now your fans will have to request permission to enter, and you'll have to grant it (by clicking OK on the screen), in real time, while you're there to watch what they're doing.

**Figure 14-14:**
*Your Mac is now ready to be observed and even controlled by other machines across the network. The people listed here are allowed to tap in anytime they like, even when you're not at your machine.*

## Mac #2: Take Control

All right, Mac #1 has been prepared for invasion. Now suppose you're the person on the other end. You're the guru, or the parent, or whoever wants to take control.

Sit at Mac #2 elsewhere on your home or office network. Open a Finder window. Expand the Sharing list in the Sidebar, if necessary, so that you see the icon of Mac #1.

When you click that Mac's icon, the dark strip at the top of the main window displays a button that wasn't there before: Share Screen. Proceed as shown in Figure 14-15.

If you signed in successfully, or if permission is granted, then a weird and wonderful sight appears. As shown in Figure 14-16, your screen now fills with a *second* screen—from the other Mac. You have full keyboard and mouse control to work with that other machine exactly as though you're sitting in front of it.

**Figure 14-15:**
Top: Start by clicking Share Screen in the strip at the top of the other Mac's window.

Middle: If you've been pre-added to the V.I.P. list of authorized screen sharers, as described above, you can sign in with your name and password. If not, you can request permission to share Mac #1's screen. You'll be granted permission only if Mac #1's owner happens to be sitting in front of it at the moment, and has opted to accept such requests.

Bottom: If you request permission, the other person (sitting at Mac #1) sees your request in this form.

Believe it or not, you can actually *copy and paste* material from the remote-controlled Mac to your own—or the other way—thanks to a freaky little wormhole in the time-space continuum.

Just make the toolbar visible (you can see it in Figure 14-16). Click the *second* button on it to copy the faraway Mac's clipboard contents onto *your* Clipboard. Or click the *third* button to put what's on *your* Clipboard onto the *other* Mac's Clipboard. Breathe slowly and drink plenty of fluids, and your brain won't explode.

---

**Note:** Unfortunately, there's no way to transfer *files* while screen sharing–only material you've copied *out* of documents.

---

**Figure 14-16:**
Don't be alarmed. You're looking at the other Mac's desktop in a window on your Mac desktop. You have keyboard and mouse control, and so does the other guy (if he's there); when you're really bored, you can play King of the Cursor. (Note the Screen Sharing toolbar, which has been made visible by choosing View→Show Toolbar.)

- **Quitting.** When you hit the ⌘-Q keystroke, you *don't* quit Screen Sharing; you quit whatever program is *running* on the other Mac! So when you're finished having your way with the other computer, choose Screen Sharing→Quit Screen Sharing to return to your own desktop (and your own sanity).

### Screen Sharing with Back to My Mac

"Back to My Mac" is a Leopard feature that's intended to simplify the nightmare of remote networking. It works only if you're a .Mac member, and you have at least two Macs, both running Leopard. On each one, you've entered your .Mac information into the .Mac pane of System Preferences, and logged in.

Once that's all in place, your Macs behave exactly as though they're on the same home network, even though they're thousands of miles apart across the network.

To set it up, open System Preferences on the first Mac. Click .Mac, and then click Back to My Mac. Click Start. Close System Preferences. Repeat on each Mac, making sure that they all have the same .Mac account information.

Now, on each Mac you'll want to "visit" from afar, open the System Preferences→Sharing pane and turn on File Sharing and/or Screen Sharing.

Then, on your laptop in New Zealand, you'll see an entry for Back to My Mac in the Sharing section of your Sidebar. Click to see the icon of your Mac back at home. At this point, you can connect to it for file sharing by clicking Connect As (page 434), or take control of it by clicking Share Screen (Figure 14-15).

In theory, Back to My Mac spares you an awful long visit to networking hell, because Apple has done all the configuration work for you.

---

*Note:* Lots of people can't get Back to My Mac to work. Apple says that the problems are related to (a) this being a new service with some kinks to be worked out, (b) firewall problems, and (c) router incompatibilities.

All the technical details are available online. Go to *http://search.info.apple.com* and do a search for *306672*. (That's the article number that explains the Back to My Mac issues.)

---

**GEM IN THE ROUGH**

## Screen Sharing with Windows and Other Oddball Machines

The beauty of Leopard's screen-sharing technology is that it isn't *Leopard's* screen-sharing technology. It's a popular, open standard called VNC (Virtual Network Computing).

Once you've turned on Screen Sharing on your Leopard Mac, any computer on earth with a free VNC client program—sort of a viewer program—can pop onto your machine for a screen share. VNC clients are available for Windows, Linux, pre-Leopard Macs, and even some cellphones.

To prepare your Leopard Mac for invasion, open the Sharing pane of System Preferences. Click Screen Sharing, and click

Computer Settings. Turn on "VNC viewers may control screen with password," and make up a password. (VNC doesn't know anything about Mac OS X account passwords, so you're making up one password for sharing your *whole* Mac.)

Give that password to the lucky few who have your trust. Let them plug your Mac's IP address into their VNC clients—or let them connect over your office network, using the address displayed on the Screen Sharing pane ("vnc://Black-MacBook," for example)—and let the sharing begin.

# System Preferences

The hub of Mac customization is System Preferences, the equivalent of the Control Panel in Windows. Some of its panels are extremely important, because their settings determine whether or not you can connect to a network or go online to exchange email. Others handle the more cosmetic aspects of customizing Mac OS X.

This chapter guides you through the entire System Preferences program, panel by panel.

---

***Tip:*** Only a system administrator (page 379) can change settings that affect everyone who shares a certain machine: its Internet settings, Energy Saver settings, and so on. If you see a bunch of controls that are dimmed and unavailable, now you know why.

A tiny 🔒 in the lower-left corner of a panel is the other telltale sign. If you, a nonadministrator, would like to edit some settings, call an administrator over to your Mac and ask him to click the lock, input his password, and supervise your tweaks.

---

## The System Preferences Window

You can open System Preferences by choosing its name from the  menu, clicking its "light-switch" icon in the Dock, or double-clicking its icon in the Applications folder. At first, the rows of icons are grouped according to function: Personal, Hardware, and so on (Figure 15-1, top).

But you can also view them in tidy alphabetical order, as shown at bottom in Figure 15-1. That can spare you the ritual of hunting through various rows just to find a certain panel icon whose name you already know. (Quick, without looking: Which row is Date & Time in?) This chapter describes the various panels following this alphabetical arrangement.

**Figure 15-1:**
*You can view your System Preferences icons alphabetically (top), rather than in rows of arbitrary categories (bottom); just choose View→Organize Alphabetically. This approach not only saves space, but also makes finding a certain panel much easier, because you don't need to worry about which category it's in.*

Either way, when you click one of the icons, the corresponding controls appear in the main System Preferences window. To access a different preference pane, you have a number of options:

- *Fast:* When System Preferences first opens, the insertion point is blinking in the new System Preferences search box. (If the insertion point is *not* blinking there, press ⌘-F.) Type a few letters of *volume, resolution, wallpaper, wireless,* or whatever feature you want to adjust. In a literal illustration of Spotlight's power, the System Preferences window darkens *except* for the icons where you'll find relevant controls (Figure 15-2). Click the name or icon of the one that looks most promising.

- *Fast:* Click the Show All icon in the upper-left corner of the window (or press ⌘-L, a shortcut worth learning). Then click the icon of the new panel you want.

- *Faster:* Choose any panel's name from the View menu—or, if System Preferences is already open, from the System Preferences *Dock icon.*

**Figure 15-2:**
*Even if you don't know what System Prefer- ences panel contains the settings you want to change, Spotlight can help. Type into the box at the top, and watch as the "spotlight" shines on the relevant icons. At that point, you can either click the icon, click the name in the pop-up menu, or arrow down the menu and press Enter to choose. (Apple removed the System Preferences toolbar, but it hopes that this Spotlight business is just as useful.)*

- *Fastest:* Highlight the first System Preferences icon by pressing Tab. (The highlight- ing is very faint, but it's there.) Then type the first couple of letters of the icon you want to highlight—*p* for Print & Fax, *di* for Displays, or whatever—and then press the Space bar to open that panel.

# .Mac

This panel is of no value unless you've signed up for a .Mac account (page 295). It offers four tabs:

- **Account.** This is where you fill in your member name and password for your .Mac account, if you've subscribed.

- **Sync.** Here's where you tell Leopard which elements of your digital world—calendar, address book, email, and so on—you want synchronized, via the .Mac service, among your various Macs.

- **iDisk.** The Disk Space graph indicates how full your electronic iDisk is.

- **Back to My Mac.** This new Leopard feature of .Mac does just what the descrip- tion here says: It lets you, on the road with your laptop (for example), connect to your Mac back home—to retrieve a file you left behind, for example. Details are in Chapter 14.

## Accounts

This is the master list of people who are allowed to log into your Mac. It's where you can adjust their passwords, startup pictures, self-opening startup items, permissions to use various features of the Mac, and other security tools. All of this is described in Chapter 13.

## Appearance

This panel is mostly about how things look on the screen: windows, menus, buttons, scroll bars, and fonts. Nothing you find here lets you perform any *radical* surgery on the overall Mac OS X look—but you can tweak certain settings to match your personal style.

### Changing Colors

Two pop-up menus let you crank up or tone down Mac OS X's overall colorfulness:

- **Appearance.** Choose between Blue or Graphite. Blue refers to Mac OS X's factory setting—bright, candy-colored scroll-bar handles, progress bars,  menu, and pulsing OK buttons—and those shiny red, yellow, and green buttons in the corner of every window. If you, like some graphics professionals, find all this circus-poster coloring a bit distracting, then choose Graphite, which renders all those interface elements in various shades of gray.

- **Highlight color.** When you drag your cursor across text, its background changes color to indicate that you've selected it. Exactly what color the background becomes is up to you—just choose the shade you want using the pop-up menu. The Highlight color also affects such subtleties as the lines on the inside of a window as you drag an icon into it.

If you choose Other, the Color Picker palette appears, from which you can choose any color your Mac is capable of displaying (page 148).

### Tweaking the Scroll Bars

These radio buttons control the scroll-bar arrow buttons of all your windows. You can keep these arrows together at one end of the scroll bar, or you can split them up so that the "up" arrow sits at the top of the scroll bar, and the "down" arrow is at the bottom—a much more Windows-like arrangement. (Horizontal scroll bars are similarly affected.)

---

*Tip:* For details on the "Jump to the next page" and "Scroll to here" options, see page 440.

---

You can also turn on these checkboxes:

- **Use smooth scrolling.** This option affects only one tiny situation: when you click (or hold the cursor down) inside the empty area of the scroll bar (not on the handle, and not on the arrow buttons). And it makes only one tiny change: Instead of jumping abruptly from screen to screen, the window lurches with slight accelerations and decelerations, so that the paragraph you're eyeing never jumps suddenly out of view.

- **Minimize when double-clicking a window title bar.** This option provides another way to minimize a window. In addition to the tiny yellow Minimize button at the upper-left corner of the window, you now have a much bigger target—the entire title bar.

## Number of Recent Items

Just how many of your recently opened documents and applications do you want the Mac to show using the Recent Items command in the  menu? Pick a number from the pop-up menus. For example, you might choose 30 for documents, 20 for programs, and 5 for severs.

## Font Smoothing Style

The Mac's built in text-smoothing (*antialiasing*) feature is supposed to produce smoother, more commercial-looking text anywhere it appears on your Mac: in word processing documents, email messages, Web pages, and so on.

Here, you can control the *degree* to which text gets smoothed. Use the pop-up menu to choose a setting that suits your eyes—and your monitor. For example, Apple offers Standard for CRT screens (cathode-ray tube—that is, traditional, bulky, television-style screens), and Medium for flat-panel screens like laptops and almost all current desktop Macs. Or just leave the setting at Automatic, which gives text on the main screen the appropriate smoothing.

Either way, the differences are fairly subtle. Furthermore, unlike most System Preferences, this one has no effect until the next time you open the program in question. In the Finder, for example, you won't notice the difference until you log out and log back in again.

## Turning Off Smoothing on Tiny Fonts

At smaller type sizes (10-point and smaller), you might find that text is actually *less* readable with font smoothing turned on. It all depends upon the font, the size, your monitor, and your taste. For that reason, this pop-up menu lets you choose a cutoff point. If you choose 12 here, for example, then 12-point (and smaller) type still appears crisp and sharp; only larger type, such as headlines, displays the graceful edge smoothing. You can choose a size cutoff as low as 4 points.

(None of these settings affect your printouts, only the onscreen display.)

# Bluetooth

This panel, radically redesigned for Leopard, shows up only if your Mac is equipped with a Bluetooth transmitter, either built-in or in the form of an external USB gadget.

Bluetooth is a short-range, low-power, wireless *cable-elimination* technology. It's designed to connect gadgets in pairings that make sense, like cellphone+earpiece, wireless keyboard+Mac, Palm organizer+Mac, or Mac+cellphone (to connect to the Internet or to transmit files).

Now, you wouldn't want the guy in the next cubicle to be able to operate *your* Mac using *his* Bluetooth keyboard. So the first step in any Bluetooth relationship is *pairing*,

**Figure 15-3:**
Top: This System Preferences panel reveals a list of every Bluetooth gadget your Mac knows about. Click a Bluetooth device to see details.

Middle: The Bluetooth Setup Assistant scans the area for Bluetooth gadgets, and, after a moment, lists them. Click one, and then click Continue.

Bottom: Where security is an issue, the Assistant offers you the chance to pair your Bluetooth device with the Mac. To prove that you're really the owner of both the laptop and the phone, the Mac displays a one-time password, which you have 30 seconds to type into the phone. Once that's done, you're free to use the phone's Internet connection without any further muss, fuss, or passwords.

where you formally introduce the two gadgets that will be communicating. Here's how that goes:

1. **Open System Preferences→Bluetooth.**

   Make sure Bluetooth Power is turned on. (The only reason to turn it off is to save laptop battery power.) Also make sure Discoverable is turned on; that makes the Mac "visible" to other Bluetooth gadgets in range.

2. **Click the + button below the list at left.**

   The Bluetooth Setup Assistant opens, offering a list of typical Bluetooth equipment that your Mac can talk to: Mobile Phone, Headset, Printer, etc.

3. **Click the kind of gear you have, and then click Continue.**

   The Mac whirs for a moment, and then displays the names of all Bluetooth gadgets that it can sniff out. Usually, it finds the one you're trying to pair.

4. **Click the name of the phone/headset/keyboard/whatever, and then click Continue.**

   If you're pairing a mobile phone or something else that has a keypad or keyboard, the Mac now displays a large, eight-digit *passcode*. It's like a password, except you'll have to input it only this once, to confirm that *you* are the true owner of both the Mac and the phone. (If it weren't for this passcode business, some guy next to you at the airport could enjoy free laptop Internet access through the cellphone in *your* pocket.)

   At this point, your phone or palmtop displays a message to the effect that you have 30 seconds to type that passcode. Do it. When the gadget asks if you want to pair with the Mac and connect to it, say yes.

   If you're pairing a phone or palmtop, the Mac now asks *which* sorts of Bluetooth syncing you want to do. For example, it can copy your iCal appointments, as well as your Address Book address book, to the phone or palmtop.

   (Or, if there are *no* kinds of Bluetooth syncing that your Mac can do with the gadget—for example, there's nothing an iPhone can accomplish by talking to your Mac, since it doesn't offer Bluetooth file transfers, for example—an error message tells you that, too.)

---

***Tip:*** A few Bluetooth phones can even get your laptop onto the Internet via the cellular airwaves. No Wi-Fi required–the phone never even leaves your pocket, and your laptop can get online wherever there's a cellphone signal.

This is a special setup, however, involving signing up with your cell carrier (and paying an additional monthly fee). If you've signed up, then turn on the third option here ("Access the Internet").

---

When it's all over, the new gadget is listed in the left-side panel, in the list of Bluetooth cellphones, headsets, and other stuff that you've previously introduced to this Mac.

Click the + button to open the Bluetooth Setup Assistant again, or the – button to delete one of the listed items.

And then there's the ✿ button. On first click, it's a pop-up menu that says only, "Show More Info." If you select that item and then click ✿ again, you get a pop-up menu with a few Bluetooth utility commands.

## CDs & DVDs

This handy pane (Figure 15-4) lets you tell the Mac what it should do when it detects you've inserted a CD or DVD. For example, when you insert a music CD, you probably want iTunes (Chapter 9) to open automatically so you can listen to the CD or convert its musical contents to MP3 or AAC files on your hard drive. Similarly, when you insert a picture CD (such as a Kodak Photo CD), you probably want iPhoto to open in readiness to import the pictures from the CD into your photo collection.

**Figure 15-4:**
*You can tell the Mac exactly which program to launch when you insert each kind of disc, or tell it to do nothing at all.*

And when you insert a DVD from Blockbuster, you want the Mac's DVD Player program to open.

For each kind of disc (blank CD, blank DVD, music CD, picture CD, or video DVD), the pop-up menu lets you choose options like these:

- **Ask what to do.** A dialog box appears that asks what you want to do with the newly inserted disc.

- **Open (iDVD, iTunes, iPhoto, DVD Player...).** The Mac can open a certain program automatically when you insert the disc. When the day comes that somebody writes a better music player than iTunes, or a better digital shoebox than iPhoto, you can use the "Open other application" option.

- **Run script.** If you've become handy writing or downloading AppleScript programs (Chapter 16), you can schedule one of your own scripts to take over from here. For example, you can set things up so that inserting a blank CD automatically copies your Home folder onto it for backup purposes.

- **Ignore.** The Mac won't do anything when you insert a disc except display its icon on the desktop. (If it's a blank disc, the Mac does nothing at all.)

# Date & Time

Your Mac's conception of what time it is can be very important. Every file you create or save is stamped with this time, and every email you send or receive is marked with this time. As you might expect, setting your Mac's clock is what the Date & Time pane is all about.

## Date & Time Tab

Click the Date & Time tab. If your Mac is online, turn on "Set date & time automatically," and be done with it. Your Mac sets its own clock by consulting a highly accurate scientific clock on the Internet. (No need to worry about Daylight Saving Time, either; the time servers take that into account.)

---

*Tip:* If you have a full-time Internet connection (cable modem or DSL, for example), you may as well leave this checkbox turned on, so your Mac's clock is always correct. If you connect to the Internet by modem, however, turn *off* the checkbox, so your Mac won't keep trying to dial spontaneously at all hours of the night.

---

If you're not online and have no prospect of getting there, you can also set the date and time manually. To change the month, day, or year, you can click the digit that needs changing and then either (a) type a new number or (b) click the little arrow buttons. Press the Tab key to highlight the next number. (You can also specify the day of the month by clicking a date on the minicalendar.)

To set the time of day, use the same technique—or, for more geeky fun, you can set the time by dragging the hour, minute, or second hands on the analog clock. Finally, click Save. (If you get carried away with dragging the clock hands around and lose track of the *real* time, click the Revert button to restore the panel settings.)

---

*Tip:* If you're frustrated that the Mac is showing you the 24-hour "military time" on your menu bar (that is, *17:30* instead of *5:30 p.m.*)—or that it *isn't* showing military time when you'd like it to—click the Clock tab and turn "Use a 24-hour clock" on or off.

Note, however, that this affects only the menu bar clock. If you'd like to reformat the menu bar clock *and* all other dates (like the ones that show when your files were modified in list views), click the Open International button at the bottom of the Date & Time pane. Once there, click the Formats tab. There you'll see a Customize button for Times, which leads you to a whole new world of time-format customization. You can drag elements of the current time (Hour, Minute, Second, Millisecond, and so on) into any order you like, and separate them with any desired punctuation.

---

## Time Zone Tab

You'd be surprised how important it is to set the Time Zone for your Mac. If you don't do so, the email and documents you send out—and the Mac's conception of what documents are older and newer—could be hopelessly skewed. Teach your Mac where it lives using the Time Zone map, as shown in Figure 15-5.

## Clock Tab

In the Clock pane, you can specify whether or not you want the current time to appear, at all times, at the right end of your menu bar. You can choose between two different clock styles: digital (3:53 p.m.) or analog (a round clock face). You also get several other options that govern this digital clock display: the display of seconds, whether or not you want to include designations for a.m. and p.m., the day of the week, a blinking colon, and the option to use a 24-hour clock.

**Figure 15-5:**
*To set your time zone the quick and dirty way, just click on a section of the map to indicate your general region of the world. You'll see the vertical stripe showing your time zone.*

*If you want to teach the Mac more precisely where you are in that time zone, now use the pop-up menu to specify the closest big city in that time zone. (Or, instead of using the pop-up menu with the mouse, you can also highlight the text in the Closest City box. Then start typing your city name until the Mac gets it.)*

**Tip:** At the bottom of the dialog box, you'll find a feature called "Announce the time." At the intervals you specify, the Mac can speak, out loud, the current time: "It's ten o'clock." If you tend to get so immersed in "working" that you lose track of time, Mac OS X just removed your last excuse.

And by the way, your menu bar clock always shows the current *time*. When you need to know today's *date*, just click the clock. A menu drops down revealing the complete date. The menu also lets you switch between digital and analog clock types and provides a shortcut to the Date & Time preferences pane.

# Desktop & Screen Saver

This panel offers two ways to show off Mac OS X's glamorous graphics features: *desktop pictures* and *screen savers*.

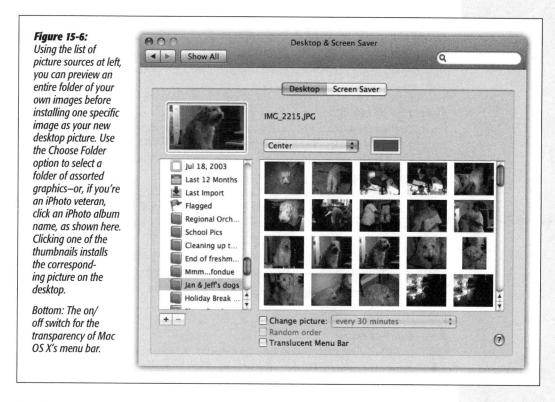

**Figure 15-6:**
*Using the list of picture sources at left, you can preview an entire folder of your own images before installing one specific image as your new desktop picture. Use the Choose Folder option to select a folder of assorted graphics—or, if you're an iPhoto veteran, click an iPhoto album name, as shown here. Clicking one of the thumbnails installs the corresponding picture on the desktop.*

*Bottom: The on/off switch for the transparency of Mac OS X's menu bar.*

## Desktop

Mac OS X comes with several ready-to-use collections of desktop pictures, ranging from *National Geographic*–style nature photos to plain solid colors. To install a new background picture, first choose one of the image categories in the list at the left side of the window, as shown in Figure 15-6.

Your choices include Apple Images (muted, soft-focus swishes and swirls), Nature (bugs, water, Leopard outer space), Plants (flowers, soft-focus leaves), Black & White (breathtaking monochrome shots), Abstract (swishes and swirls with wild colors), or Solid Colors (simple grays, blues, and greens).

### Using your own pictures

Of course, you may feel that decorating your Mac desktop is much more fun if you use one of your *own* pictures. You can use any digital photo, scanned image, or graphic you want in almost any graphics format (JPEG, PICT, GIF, TIFF, Photoshop, and—just in case you hope to master your digital camera by dangling its electronic instruction manual in front of you each morning—even PDF).

That's why icons for your own Pictures folder and iPhoto Albums collections also appear here, along with a button that lets you choose *any* folder of pictures. When you click one of these icons, you see thumbnail versions of its contents in the main screen to its right. Just click the thumbnail of any picture to apply it immediately to the desktop. (There's no need to remove the previously installed picture first.)

---

*Tip:* If there's one certain picture you like, but it's not in any of the listed sources, you can drag its image file onto the *well* (the miniature desktop displayed in the Desktop panel). A thumbnail of your picture instantly appears in the well and, a moment later, the picture is plastered across your monitor.

---

### Making the picture fit

No matter which source you use to choose a photo of your own, you have one more issue to deal with. Unless you've gone to the trouble of editing your chosen photo so that it matches the precise dimensions of your screen (1280 x 854 pixels, for example), it probably isn't exactly the same size as your screen.

---

*Tip:* The top 23 pixels of your graphic are partly obscured by Leopard's translucent menu bar—something to remember when you prepare the graphic.

---

Fortunately, Mac OS X offers a number of solutions to this problem. Using the pop-up menu just to the right of the desktop preview well, you can choose Fit to Screen, Fill Screen, Stretch, Center, or Tile, each of which enlarges the picture (relative to your screen) in a different way.

### Auto picture-changing

The novelty of any desktop picture, no matter how interesting, is likely to fade after several months of all-day viewing. That's why the randomizing function is so delightful.

Turn on "Change picture" at the bottom of the dialog box. From the pop-up menu, specify when you want your background picture to change: "every day," "every 15 minutes," or, if you're *really* having trouble staying awake at your Mac, "every 5 seconds." (The option called "when waking from sleep" refers to the *Mac* waking from sleep, not its owner.)

Finally, turn on "Random order," if you like. If you leave it off, your desktop pictures change in alphabetical order by file name.

That's all there is to it. Now, at the intervals you specified, your desktop picture changes automatically, smoothly cross-fading between the pictures in your chosen source folder like a slideshow. You may never want to open another window, because you'll hate to block your view of the show.

# Screen Saver

On the Screen Saver panel, you can create your own screen-saver slideshows—an absolute must if you have an Apple Cinema Display and a cool Manhattan loft apartment.

---

*Tip:* Of course, a screen saver doesn't really save your screen. LCD flat-panel screens, the only kind Apple sells, are incapable of "burning in" a stationary image of the sort that originally inspired the creation of screen savers years ago.

No, these screen savers offer two unrelated functions. First, they mask what's on your screen from passersby whenever you leave your desk. Second, they're a blast.

---

When you click a module's name in the Screen Savers list, you see a mini version of it playing back in the Preview screen. Click Test to give the module a dry run on your full monitor screen.

When you've had enough of the preview, just move the mouse or press any key. You return to the Screen Saver panel.

Apple provides a few displays to get you started, in two categories: Apple and Pictures.

## Apple

- **Arabesque.** Your brain will go crazy trying to make sense of the patterns of small circles as they come and go, shrink and grow. But forget it; this module, new in Leopard, is all just drugged-out randomness.

- **Computer Name.** This display shows nothing more than the Apple logo and the computer's name, faintly displayed on the monitor. (These elements shift position every few minutes—it just isn't very fast.) Apple probably imagined that this feature would let corporate supervisors glance over at the screens of unattended Macs to find out who was not at their desks.

- **Flurry.** You get flaming, colorful, undulating arms of fire, which resemble a cross between an octopus and somebody arc welding in the dark. If you click the Options button, you can control how many streams of fire appear at once, the thickness of the arms, the speed of movement, and the colors.

- **iTunes Artwork.** Somebody put a lot of work into the album covers for the CDs whose music you own—so why not enjoy them as art? This module builds a gigantic mosaic of album art from *your* music collection, if you have one. The tiles periodically flip around, just to keep the image changing. (The Options button lets you specify how many rows of album-art squares appear, and how often the tiles flip.)

- **RSS Visualizer.** Here, buried 43 layers deep in the operating system, is one of Leopard's most spectacular and useful features: the RSS Visualizer. When this screen saver kicks in, it displays a jaw-dropping, 3-D display of headlines (news and other items) slurped in from the Safari Web browser's *RSS reader.* (RSS items, short for Really Simple Syndication or Rich Site Summary, are like a cross between email messages and Web pages—they're Web items that get sent directly to you. Details in Chapter 12.)

After the introductory swinging-around-an-invisible-3-D-pole-against-a-swirling-blue-sky-background sequence, the screen saver displays one news blurb at a time. Each remains on the screen just long enough for you to get the point of the headline. Beneath, in small type, is the tantalizing instruction, "Press the '3' key to continue." (It's a different number key for each headline.) If you do, indeed, tap the designated key, you leave the screen saver, fire up Safari, and wind up on a Web page that contains the complete article you requested.

The whole thing is gorgeous, informative, and deeply hypnotic. Do not use while operating heavy equipment.

*Tip:* Click Options to specify which Web site's RSS feed you want displayed.

- **Spectrum.** This one's for people who prefer not to have anything specific on their screens, like photos or text; instead, it's just a gradually shifting parade of glowing rainbow hues.

- **Word of the Day.** Here's a parade of interesting words drawn from the Mac OS X Dictionary program. Every minute or so, one of these words stops, parks itself on your screen, and displays its dictionary definition. You're invited to tap the D key to open the dictionary to that entry to read more. Build your word power!

*Tip:* Click Options to specify *which* dictionary you want: the standard Oxford English, or the new Japanese one.

### Pictures

The second category of screen savers are all based on the slideshowy presentation of photos. In Leopard, you can choose from three presentations of pictures in whatever photo group you choose, as represented by the three Display Style buttons just below the screen-saver preview.

- **Slideshow** displays one photo at a time; they slowly zoom and softly cross-fade into each other.

*Tip:* If you click Options, you get choices like "Present slides in random order" (instead of the order they appear in Apple's photo folder, or yours); "Cross-fade between slides" (instead of just cutting abruptly); "Zoom back and forth" (that is, slowly enlarge or shrink each photo to keep it interesting); "Crop slides to fit on screen" (instead of exposing letterbox bars of empty desktop if the photo's shape doesn't match the screen's); and "Keep slides centered" (instead of panning gracefully across).

- **Collage** sends individual photos spinning randomly onto the "table," where they lie until the screen is full.

***Tip:*** This time, the Options button offers the "Present slides in random order" button, plus a "Collage style" pop-up menu that lets you add each photo's name and date to its white, Polaroid-style border.

• **Mosaic** will blow your mind; see Figure 15-7.

***Tip:*** Click the Options button to specify the speed of the receding, the number of photos that become pixels of the larger photo, and whether or not you want the composite photos to appear in random order.

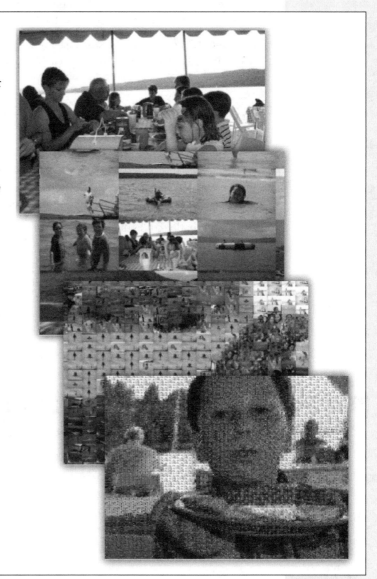

***Figure 15-7:***
*This feeble four-frame representative sample will have to represent, on this frozen page, the stunning animated pullout that is the Mosiac screen saver.*

*It starts with one photo (top); your "camera" pulls back farther and farther, revealing that that photo is just one in a grid—a huge grid— that's composed of all your photos.*

*As you pull even farther back, each photo becomes so small that it becomes only one dot of another photo—from the same collection!*

*And then that one starts shrinking, and the cycle repeats, on and on into infinity. How could Apple not have mentioned Mosaic in its Leopard advertising?*

In any case, all of these photo-show options are available for whatever photo set you choose from the list at left. Your choices include:

- **Abstract, Beach, Cosmos, Forest, Nature Patterns, Paper Shadow.** These sets include Abstract, which features psychedelic swirls of modern art. In the Beach, Cosmos, Forest, and Nature screen savers, you see a series of tropical ocean scenes, deep space objects, lush rain forests, and leaf/flower shots. Paper Shadow is a slideshow of undulating, curling, black-and-white shadowy abstract forms.

  Each creates an amazingly dramatic, almost cinematic experience, worthy of setting up to "play" during dinner parties like the lava lamps of the Seventies.

- **.Mac and RSS.** One of the perks for paying $100 per year for a .Mac membership is the ability to create slideshows online, which can play back either on your own Mac or (if you opted to make it public) on anybody else's.

  Yes, that's right: You can now enjoy a screen saver composed of photos taken by *somebody else on the Internet.* ("Oh, look, honey, here's some shots of Uncle Jed's crops this summer!")

  Click the Options button to specify, by clicking the + button, which member's slideshow collection you want to view and how you want it to appear. (For example, you can turn off the crossfade between slides, crop the slides so that they fit on the screen, opt to present the slides in random order, and so on.)

  As a bonus, in this configuration screen, you can also specify an RSS feed's address (page 353). The idea, of course, is that you'd specify a *photo* RSS feed's address here, like the ones generated by iPhoto.

- **Pictures Folder, Choose Folder.** This is one of the coolest modules. It lets you transform your *own* collection of pictures—whatever you've got in your Home→Pictures folder—into a self-playing slideshow, complete with spectacular zooming and dissolving effects. (If you keep your photos elsewhere, click Choose Folder instead.)

- **Library, Last Roll, Last 12 Months, Events list, Album list.** If you're using iPhoto to organize your digital photos, you'll see its familiar album and event lists here,

---

**FREQUENTLY ASKED QUESTION**

## The Password-Protected Screen Saver

*I like the fact that when I wander away from my desk, the screen saver protects whatever I was doing from prying eyes. But whoever walks by can just press a key to exit the screen saver, so big deal! I looked all over, and couldn't find any way to make the Mac require a password before exiting the screen saver.*

You had the right idea—you were just looking in the wrong place.

In System Preferences, click Security. There's the checkbox you're looking for: "Require password to wake this computer from sleep or screen saver."

You're welcome.

---

making it a snap to choose any of your own photo collections for use as a screen saver.

- **Use random screen saver.** If you can't decide which one of the modules to use, turn on this checkbox. The Mac chooses a different module each time your screen saver kicks in.

- **Show with clock.** This option, new in Leopard, just superimposes the current time on whatever screen saver you've selected. You'd be surprised at how handy it can be to use your Mac as a giant digital clock when you're getting coffee across the room.

### Activating the screen saver

You can control when your screen saver takes over your monitor in a couple of ways:

- **After a period of inactivity.** Using the "Start screen saver" slider, you can set the amount of time that has to pass without keyboard or mouse activity before the screen saver starts. The duration can be as short as three minutes or as long as two hours, or you can drag the slider to Never to prevent the screen saver from ever turning on by itself.

**Figure 15-8:**
*Click the Hot Corners button to open this "sheet," which lets you designate certain corners of your screen as instant-activation spots, or never-come-on spots. Sliding the mouse to the Start Screen Saver corner, for example, turns on your screen saver right away.*

- **When you park your cursor in the corner of the screen.** If you click the Hot Corners button, you'll see that you can turn each corner of your monitor into a *hot corner* (Figure 15-8).

---

***Tip:*** You can find dozens more screen saver modules from Apple at *www.apple.com/downloads/macosx/ icons_screensavers,* and from other people at *www.epicware.com/macosxsavers.html.*

---

# Displays

Displays is the center of operations for all your monitor settings. Here, you set your monitor's *resolution*, determine how many colors are displayed onscreen, and calibrate color balance and brightness.

---

***Tip:*** You can open up this panel with a quick keystroke from any program on the Mac. Just press Option as you tap one of the screen-brightness keys on the top row of your keyboard.

---

The specific controls you'll see here depend on the kind of monitor you're using, but here are the ones you'll most likely see:

***Figure 15-9:***
*In the early days of the Mac, higher color settings required a sacrifice in speed, since the Mac had to compute the color for thousands of individual pixels. Today, there's little downside to leaving your screen at its maximum depth setting ("Millions" of colors). Photos, especially, look best at higher depth settings. (The Detect Displays button appears primarily on laptops; it means "Check for an external monitor or projector.")*

## Display Tab

This tab is the main headquarters for your screen controls. It governs these settings:

- **Resolutions.** All Mac screens today can make the screen picture larger or smaller, thus accommodating different kinds of work. You perform this magnification or reduction by switching among different *resolutions* (measurements of the number of dots that compose the screen). The Resolutions list displays the various resolution settings your monitor can accommodate: 800 x 600, 1024 x 768, and so on (Figure 15-9).

    When you use a low-resolution setting, such as 800 x 600, the dots of your screen image get larger, thus enlarging (zooming in on) the picture—but showing a smaller slice of the page. Use this setting when playing a small QuickTime movie, for example, so that it fills more of the screen. (Lower resolutions usually look blurry on flat-panel screens, though.) At higher resolutions, such as 1280 x 800, the screen dots get smaller, making your windows and icons smaller, but showing more overall area. Use this kind of setting when working on two-page spreads in your page-layout program, for example.

- **Colors.** Today's Mac monitors offer different *color depth* settings, each of which permits the screen to display a different number of colors simultaneously. The Colors pop-up menu generally offers only three choices: 256 Colors, Thousands, and Millions.

*Tip:* You can still make your monitor gray scale (shades of gray), even if no choice for it appears here. The trick is to visit the Universal Access panel, described later in this chapter.

- **Refresh Rate.** This pop-up menu (available for CRT screens only—that is, not flat panels) lets you adjust how many times per second your screen image is repainted by your monitor's electron gun. Choose a setting that minimizes flicker.

- **Brightness, Contrast.** Use these sliders to make the screen look good in the pre-vailing lighting conditions. The Contrast control appears only on CRT monitors, and you'll usually want it all the way up. The Brightness slider is usually best near the middle.

Of course, most Apple keyboards have brightness-adjustment *keys,* so these software controls are included just for the sake of completeness.

*Tip:* You can adjust the color depth and resolution of your monitor without having to open System Preferences. Just turn on "Show displays in menu bar," which adds a Monitors pop-up menu (a *menulet*) to the right end of your menu bar for quick adjustments.

- **Automatically adjust brightness as ambient light changes.** This option appears only if you have a Mac laptop with a light-up keyboard. In that case, your laptop's light sensor also dims the screen automatically in dark rooms—*if* this checkbox is turned on.

## Arrangement Tab

From the dawn of the color-monitor era, Macs have had a terrific feature: the ability to exploit multiple monitors all plugged into the computer at the same time. Any Mac with a video-output jack (laptops, iMacs, eMacs), or any Mac with a second or third video card (Power Macs, Mac Pros), can project the same thing on both screens (*mirror mode*); that's useful in a classroom when the "external monitor" is a projector.

*Tip:* The standard video card in a MacPro has jacks for two monitors. By installing more video cards, you can get up to *six* monitors going at once.

But it's equally useful to make one monitor act as an extension of the next. For ex-ample, you might have your Photoshop image window on your big monitor, but keep all the Photoshop controls and tool palettes on a smaller screen. Your cursor passes from one screen to another as it crosses the boundary.

You don't have to shut down the Mac to hook up another monitor—just put it to sleep. Or just hook up the monitor or projector and then choose Detect Displays from the Displays *menulet.*

When you open System Preferences, you see a different Displays window on each screen, so that you can change the color and resolution settings independently for each. Your Displays menulet shows two sets of resolutions, too, one for each screen.

If your Mac can show different images on each screen, your Displays panel offers an Arrangement tab, showing a miniature version of each monitor. By dragging these icons around relative to each other, you can specify how you want the second monitor's image "attached" to the first. Most people position the second monitor's image to the right of the first, but you're also free to position it on the left, above, below, or even directly on top of the first monitor's icon (the last of which produces a video-mirroring setup). For the least likelihood of going insane, consider placing the real-world monitor into the corresponding position—to the right of your first monitor, for example.

For committed multiple-monitor fanatics, the fun doesn't stop there. See the microscopic menu bar on the first-monitor icon? You can drag that tiny strip onto a different monitor icon, if you like, to tell Displays where you'd like your menu bar to appear. (And check out how most screen savers correctly show different stuff on each monitor!)

## Color Tab

When you click Calibrate, the Display Calibrator Assistant opens to walk you through a series of six screens, presenting various brightness and color-balance settings in each screen. You pick the settings that look best to you; at the end of the process, you save your monitor tweaks as a ColorSync profile that ColorSync-savvy programs can use to adjust your display for improved color accuracy.

## Dock

See Chapter 2 for details on the Dock and its System Preferences pane.

## Energy Saver

The Energy Saver program helps you and your Mac in a number of ways. By blacking out the screen after a period of inactivity, it prolongs the life of your monitor. By putting the Mac to sleep half an hour after you've stopped using it, Energy Saver cuts down on electricity costs and pollution. On a laptop, Energy Saver extends the length of the battery charge by controlling the activity of the hard drive and screen.

Best of all, this pane offers the option to have your computer turn off each night automatically, and turn on again at a specified time in anticipation of your arrival at the desk.

## Sleep Tab

The Energy Saver controls are very different on a laptop Mac and a desktop.

On a desktop Mac, you see a pair of sliders; on a laptop, you have to click Show Details to see them (Figure 15-10).

*Figure 15-10:*
*Top: Here's what Energy Saver looks like in its expanded condition on a laptop. (On a desktop machine, it's far simpler.) In the "Put the display to sleep" option, you can specify an independent sleep time for the screen.*

*Bottom: Here are the Schedule controls—a welcome return of the Mac's self-scheduling abilities.*

In any case, the top slider controls when the Mac will automatically go to sleep—anywhere from one minute after your last activity to Never. (Activity can be mouse movement, keyboard action, or Internet data transfer; Energy Saver won't put your Mac to sleep in the middle of a download.)

At that time, the screen goes dark, the hard drive stops spinning, and your processor chip slows to a crawl. Your Mac is now in *sleep* mode, using only a fraction of its usual electricity consumption. To wake it up when you return to your desk, press any key. Everything you were working on, including open programs and documents, is still onscreen, exactly as it was. (To turn off this automatic sleep feature entirely, drag the slider to Never.)

---

**Note:** On Macs of old, the beauty of the independent "Put the display to sleep" slider was that you could make the screen go dark *before* the Mac itself. That way, the Mac would awaken *instantly* when you touched a key or clicked the mouse.

In Mac OS X, the Mac *always* wakes almost instantly from sleep—one of the great payoffs of Mac OS X. In other words, there's only one good reason left to set the screen to sleep independently of the Mac itself: so that your Mac can run its standard middle-of-the-night maintenance routines, even while the screen is off to save power.

---

**GEM IN THE ROUGH**

## Mysteries of the Battery Menulet

If you've got a laptop, don't miss the checkbox in Energy Saver called "Show battery status in the menu bar." It puts a handy status indicator in the menu bar (⊏⊐) that keeps you informed of your battery's life.

When used as a menu, this menulet lets you choose between displaying the actual number of minutes left until a battery is depleted, the percentage of battery life that remains, or a visual emptying-battery icon. (You can also switch among energy-conservation presets—like Better Energy Savings and Better Performance—from this menulet.)

If you've opted to view the numeric version, you may notice that sometimes the number, or the percentage, is in parentheses, like this: (78%). That's your signal that the laptop is plugged in and charging; you're seeing the number of minutes left until the battery is fully recharged (or the percentage of full charge you've achieved so far). Either way, the readout is counting down (or up) to that joyous moment.

If you're viewing only the battery icon in the menu bar, here's what the readouts mean:

**Power-cord-in-the-battery:** The laptop is plugged in, and the battery is 100 percent charged. Ready to roll, captain!

**Lightning-bolt-in-the-battery:** The laptop is plugged in, but the battery is still charging.

**Superimposed X:** The laptop is plugged in, but the battery isn't in right, it's missing, or it isn't getting a charge for some other reason.

**Emptying black battery:** The laptop is running off of battery power, and has at least 25 percent power left. (The width of the bar reveals how much charge is left.)

**Emptying red battery:** You're running off of battery power, and you have less than 25 percent charge remaining.

A nearly invisible red bar means you have less than nine minutes left. Save those documents, buddy.

Finally, "Put the hard disk(s) to sleep when possible" saves even more juice—and noise—by letting your drives stop spinning when not in use. The downside is a longer pause when you return to work and wake the thing up, because it takes a few seconds for your hard drive to "spin up" again.

## Laptop Options

As noted above, Energy Saver on a laptop offers quite a few additional controls (see Figure 15-10). That's because power management is ten times more important on a laptop, where every drop of battery power counts.

The pop-up menus at the top of the dialog box, for example, let you create different settings for the two states of life for a laptop, when it's plugged in (Power Adapter) and when it's running on battery power (Battery).

Once you've indicated which setting you want to adjust, you can then use the Optimization pop-up menu to choose a canned Energy Saver setting, depending on where you want to fall on the speed-vs.-battery-life spectrum. For example, when you're adjusting the settings for battery-only operation, you can choose Better Battery Life (screen and laptop go to sleep relatively quickly, your processor chip slows down, and the screen brightness dims) or Better Performance (screen sleeps after five minutes, laptop after fifteen, processor runs at top speed).

The Custom option just means "none of the above." Whenever you adjust one of the sliders or checkboxes, Energy Saver automatically changes the pop-up menu to say Custom. Mac OS X remembers your settings here. If you choose one of the presets and then choose Custom again, your hand-adjusted settings remain in place.

## Scheduled Startup and Shutdown

Here's a cool feature your PC never had: By clicking the Schedule button, you can set up the Mac to shut itself down and turn itself back on automatically (Figure 15-10, bottom).

If you work 9 to 5, for example, set the office Mac to turn itself on at 8:45 a.m., and shut itself down at 5:30 p.m.—an arrangement that conserves electricity, saves money, and reduces pollution, but doesn't inconvenience you in the least. In fact, you may come to forget that you've set up the Mac this way, since you'll never actually see it turned off.

---

**Note:** The Mac doesn't shut down automatically if you've left unsaved documents open onscreen. It will go to sleep, though.

---

## Waking and Other Options

Click the Options tab button to summon a few more controls, including "Wake when the modem detects a ring" (handy if you use your Mac as a fax machine), "Restart automatically after a power failure," and "Processor Performance." This last item is the quick fix for the thigh-scalding heat of a PowerBook's metal case: Choose Reduced from this pop-up menu. Your chip doesn't run nearly as fast now, but it's still plenty fast for email, word processing, and so on—and it runs at about half the temperature. (You'll gain some battery life, too.)

# Exposé & Spaces

Exposé and Spaces, the two ingenious window- and screen-management features of Mac OS X, are described in detail in Chapter 4—and so is this joint-venture control panel.

# International

The International pane's primary job is to set up your Mac to work in other languages. If you bought your Mac with a *localized* operating system—a version that already runs in your own language—and you're already using the only language, number format, and keyboard layout you'll ever need, then you can ignore most of this panel.

But at the very least, check it out. When it comes to showing off Mac OS X to your friends and loved ones, the "wow" factor on the Mac's polyglot features is huge.

### Another Language—Instantly

In Mac OS X, you can shift from language to language in certain programs on the fly, without reinstalling the operating system or even restarting the computer.

On the Language tab, you see a listing of the different languages the Mac can switch into, in the corresponding languages—Français, Español, and so on. Just drag one of the languages to the top of the list to select it as the target language, as shown in Figure 15-11.

Now launch Safari, TextEdit, or Stickies. Every menu, button, and dialog box is now in the new language you selected! If you log out and back in (or restart) at this point, the entire Finder will be in the new language, too.

---

***Note:*** *Programs differ widely in their "language awareness." If you use a language beyond the 16 in the list, adding it (use the Edit button) ensures that its relevant features will be available in all programs. (You may still have to add additional language software to make your menus and dialog boxes change.)*

---

### Formats Tab

Of course, if you're *really* French (for example), you'll also want to make these changes:

- On the Formats tab, choose your French-speaking country from the Region pop-up menu, so that time and date formats, number punctuation, and currency symbols also conform to your local customs. (Turn on "Show all regions," if necessary.)

  For example, the decimal and thousands separator characters for displaying large numbers differ from country to country. (The number 25,600.99, for example, would be written as 25 600,99 in France, and as 25.600,99 in Spanish.) And what appears to an American to be July 4 (the notation 7/4), to a European indicates April 7.

If, for some reason, Apple's preprogrammed settings aren't right for your region, you'll see Customize buttons that let you override them.

• Choose the French *keyboard layout* from the Input Menu tab, as explained in Figure 15-11.

**Figure 15-11:**
*Top: This is the list of the 19 "system localizations" that you get with a standard Mac OS X installation.*

*Bottom: Here's Safari running in Dutch. Actually understanding Dutch would be useful at a time like this—but even if you don't, it can't help but brighten up your work day to choose commands like Spraakfunctie or Knip. (Alas, your success with this trick varies by program.)*

***Tip:*** Every program capable of switching languages is also clogging up your hard drive with a lot of language files you'll never use. A program like DeLocalizer can sweep through all your programs and delete those files, leaving your software in perfect condition but more svelte. You can get DeLocalizer from this book's "Missing CD" page at *www.missingmanuals.com*.

## Input Menu Tab

While the Mac can display many different languages, *typing* in those languages is another matter. The symbols you use when you're typing Swedish aren't the same as when you're typing English. Apple solved this problem by creating different *keyboard layouts*, one for each language. Each rearranges the letters that appear when you press the keys. For example, when you use the Swedish layout and press the semicolon key, you don't get a semicolon (;)—you get an ö.

Apple even includes a Dvorak layout—a scientific rearrangement of the standard layout that puts the most common letters directly under your fingertips on the home row. Fans of the Dvorak layout claim greater accuracy, better speed, and less fatigue.

Use the list in the Input Menu pane to indicate which keyboard layout you want. If you select anything in the list, "Show input menu in menu bar" turns on automatically. A tiny flag icon appears in your menu bar—a keyboard *menulet* that lets you switch from one layout to another just by choosing its name. (To preview a certain keyboard arrangement, launch the Keyboard Viewer program described next.)

***Figure 15-12:***
*How do you make a π symbol?*

*Top: Open Keyboard Viewer by choosing its name from the keyboard (flag) menulet.*

*Bottom: Keyboard Viewer reveals the answer. When you press the Option key, the Keyboard Viewer keyboard shows that the pi character (π) is mapped to the P key.*

*To insert the symbol into an open document, just click it in the Keyboard Viewer window.*

# Keyboard Viewer

Keyboard Viewer consists of a single window containing a tiny onscreen keyboard (Figure 15-12). When you hold down any of the modifier keys on your keyboard (like ⌘, Option, Shift, or Control), you can see exactly which keys produce which characters. The point, of course, is to help you learn which keys to press when you need special symbols or non-English characters, such as © or ¢, in each font.

*Note:* Keyboard Viewer shows only the symbols you can produce by typing *keystrokes*. A font may contain thousands of other characters; the Character Palette (see the box below) is the only way to access them.

---

## The Character Palette

There you are, two-thirds of the way through your local matchmaker newsletter, when it hits you that you need a heart symbol. Right now.

You know there's one in one of your symbol fonts, but you're not about to type every single key combo until you produce the heart symbol. You can't help wishing there was an easier way to find those special symbols that hide among your fonts—fancy brackets, math symbols, special stars and asterisks, and so on.

The Keyboard Viewer (described above) is one solution. But there's a better one: the Character Palette. To make it appear, choose Edit→Special Characters.

Most Cocoa programs have this command. If yours doesn't, here's the long way: Open System Preferences, click the International icon, click the Input Menu tab, and turn on the Character Palette checkbox.

You've just installed the Keyboard menulet.

Next time you're word processing or doing page layout, choose Show Character Palette from this menu.

The resulting window rounds up all symbols from all your fonts at once. To find a particular symbol, click the "by Category" tab, and then click the various category headings: Arrows, Stars/Asterisks, Math, and so on. Or, for an even more mind-blowing assortment (musical notes, Braille...), choose All Characters from the View pop-up menu.

You can preview variations of the same symbol by opening the Font Variation triangle. You can also use the Search box to find a symbol by name: "heart" or "yen" or "asterisk," for example. When you find the symbol you want, double-click it.

If you're using a Cocoa program, the correct symbol pops into your document. (If not, you may get the correct character in the wrong font. In that case, change the font of the inserted character manually. To find out what font it came from, click the Font Variation flippy triangle to see the font name.)

---

Here's how. Open the International panel of System Preferences, click Input Menu, and turn on the Keyboard Viewer checkbox. The window shown at top in Figure 15-12 appears. (Thereafter, you'll be able to choose its name from the flag menulet at the top of the screen, as shown at top in Figure 15-12.)

To see the effect of pressing the modifier keys, either click the onscreen keys or press them on your actual keyboard. The corresponding keys on the onscreen keyboard light up as they're pressed.

---

**Note:** Keyboard Viewer shows only the symbols you can produce by typing *keystrokes.* A font may contain thousands of other characters that can't actually be typed; the Character Palette (page 463) is the only way to access these other symbols.

---

# Keyboard & Mouse

This panel lets you do some frivolous fine-tuning of your mouse, keyboard, and (for laptops) trackpad. It also unlocks Mac OS X's strange and remarkable Full Keyboard Access feature, which lets you control your Mac's menus, windows, dialog boxes, buttons, the Dock, and the toolbar—all from the keyboard (page 135). Here's a tour of the Keyboard & Mouse tabs.

## Keyboard Tab

The changes you make are tiny, but can have a cumulatively big impact on your daily typing routine.

- **Key Repeat Rate, Delay Until Repeat.** You're probably too young to remember the antique once known as the *typewriter.* On some electric versions of this machine, you could hold down the letter X key to type a series of XXXXXXXs—ideal for crossing something out in a contract, for example.

  On the Mac, *every* key behaves this way. Hold down any key long enough, and it starts spitting out repetitions, making it easy to type, for example, "No WAAAAAAAY!" or "You go, girrrrrrrrrl!" These two sliders govern this behavior. On the right: a slider that determines how long you must hold down the key before it starts repeating (to prevent triggering repetitions accidentally, in other words). On the left: a slider that governs how fast each key spits out letters once the spitting has begun.

- **Use all F1, F2, etc. keys as standard function keys.** This option appears *only* on laptops and aluminum-keyboard Macs. It's complicated, so read slowly.

  On Mac laptops, many of the F-keys on the top row perform laptop-related functions. For example, the F1 and F2 keys adjust the screen brightness, F3, F4, and F5 control the speaker volume, and so on. (You have the same setup on the aluminum Apple keyboard. Many of its F-keys have special hardware-control functions, too.)

So what if you want to use those keys for other functions? For example, the F1 key is the Help key in many programs. How can you open Help, if F1 makes the screen dimmer?

In those situations, you're supposed to trigger the F-key's second personality by pressing the Fn key simultaneously. So if F1 opens Help on a desktop Mac, Fn-F1 does it on a laptop.

If you find yourself using the software features (like Help) more often than the hardware features (like brightness), you can reverse this logic. Turning on "Use all F1, F2, etc. keys as standard function keys" lets the F-keys be F-keys, so they have no hardware-control functions. Now F1 by itself opens Help. Now, however, you add the Fn key for the *hardware* functions like brightness and volume.

- **Illuminate keyboard in low light conditions.** This setting appears only if your Mac's keyboard does, in fact, light up when you're working in the dark—a showy feature of the high-end Mac laptops. You can specify that you want the internal lighting to shut off after a period of activity (to save power when you've wandered away, for example), or you can turn the lighting off altogether.

**Figure 15-13:**
*This enormous photographic display shows up only if you have the Mighty Mouse, Apple's "two-button" mouse. The pop-up menus let you program the right, left, and side buttons of this mouse. It offers functions like opening Dashboard, triggering Exposé, and so on.*

*This is also where you can turn the right-clicking feature on (just choose Secondary Button from the appropriate pop-up menu)—or swap the right- and left-click buttons' functions.*

- **Modifier Keys.** This button lets you turn off, or remap, the functions of the Option, Caps Lock, Control, and ⌘ keys. It's for Unix programmers whose pinkies can't adjust to the Mac's modifier-key layout—and for anyone who keeps hitting Caps Lock by accident during everyday typing.

## Mouse Tab

It may surprise you that the cursor on the screen doesn't move five inches when you move the mouse five inches on the desk. Instead, the cursor moves farther when you move the mouse faster.

How *much* farther depends on how you set the first slider here. The Fast setting is nice if you have an enormous monitor, since you don't need an equally large mouse pad to get from one corner to another. The Slow setting, on the other hand, forces you to pick up and put down the mouse frequently as you scoot across the screen. It offers very little acceleration, but it can be great for highly detailed work like pixel-by-pixel editing in Photoshop.

The Double-Click Speed setting specifies how much time you have to complete a double-click. If you click too slowly—beyond the time you've allotted yourself with this slider—the Mac "hears" two *single* clicks instead.

If you have an Apple Mighty Mouse—the white mouse that has come with desktop Macs since 2005—then the Mouse tab is a much fancier affair (Figure 15-13).

## Trackpad Tab

This panel shows up only if you have a laptop. At the top, you find duplicates of the same Tracking Speed and Double-Click Speed sliders described above—but these let you establish independent tracking and clicking speeds for the *trackpad*.

### Trackpad Gestures

You may love your Mac laptop now, but wait until you find out about these special features. They make your laptop *crazy* better. It turns out you can point, click, scroll, and right-click—all on the trackpad itself, without a mouse and without ever having to move your fingers.

- **Use two fingers to scroll.** This one is *sweet.* You have to try it to believe it.

  When you turn this option in, dragging *two* fingers across your trackpad scrolls whatever window is open, just as though you had slid over to the scroll bar and clicked there. Except doing it with your two fingers, right in places, is infinitely faster and less fussy. In Leopard, you even get a Scrolling *Speed* slider.

---

***Tip:*** You'll be allowed to scroll only up or down—unless you also turn on "Allow horizontal scrolling."

---

- **Zoom while holding Control.** Here's another irresistible feature. Once you learn it, you'll never look back.

When this checkbox is turned on, you can zoom into the screen image, magnifying the whole thing, just by dragging two fingers up or down the trackpad while you're pressing the Control key. You can zoom in so far that the word "zoom" in 12-point type fills the entire monitor.

This feature comes in handy with amazing frequency. It's great for reading Web pages in tiny type, or enlarging Web movies, or studying the dot-by-dot construction of a button or icon that you admire. Just Control-drag upward to zoom in, and Control-drag downward to zoom out again.

You can customize this feature to within an inch of its life. For example, you can substitute the Option or ⌘ key, if Control isn't working out for you (use the pop-up menu).

---

**Tip:** If you *don't* have a laptop—and therefore you don't have a trackpad—you can get the same effect by Control-scrolling using any mouse that has a trackwheel or trackpea on top, like Apple's standard Mighty Mouse. See "Universal Access" later in this chapter.

---

If you click Options, you get even more choices. First, you can specify how you want to scroll around within your zoomed-in screen image. The factory setting, "Continuously with pointer," is actually pretty frustrating; the whole screen shifts around whenever you move the cursor. ("So the pointer is at or near the center of the image" is very similar.) "Only when the pointer reaches an edge" is a lot less annoying, and lets you *use* the cursor (to click buttons, for example) without sending the entire screen image darting away from you.

---

**Tip:** Also in the Options box: the ability to turn off the pixel-smoothing feature that adds a certain blurriness to the zoomed-in image—and a reminder that you can press Option-⌘-\ (backslash) to turn it on or off at any time.

---

- **Clicking.** Under normal circumstances, you touch your laptop's trackpad exclusively to move the cursor. For clicking and dragging, you're supposed to use the clicking button *beneath* the trackpad.

  Many people find, however, that it's more direct to tap and drag directly on the trackpad, using the same finger that's been moving the cursor. That's the purpose of this checkbox. When it's on, you can tap the trackpad surface to register a mouse click at the location of the cursor. Double-tap to double-click.

- **Dragging.** This option lets you move icons, highlight text, or pull down menus—in other words, to drag, not just click—using the trackpad.

  Start by tapping twice on the trackpad, then *immediately* after the second tap, begin dragging your finger. (If you don't start moving promptly, the laptop assumes that you were double-clicking.) You can stroke the trackpad repeatedly to continue your movement, as long as your finger never leaves the trackpad surface for more than about one second. When you "let go," the drag is considered complete.

• **Drag Lock.** If you worry that you're going to "drop" what you're dragging if you stop moving your finger, turn on this option instead. Once again, begin your drag by double-clicking, then move your finger immediately after the second click.

When this option is on, however, you can take your sweet time in continuing the movement. In between strokes of the trackpad, you can take your finger off the laptop for as long as you like. You can take a phone call, a shower, or a vacation; the Mac still thinks that you're in the middle of a drag. Only when you tap *again* does the laptop consider the drag a done deal.

• **For secondary clicks, place two fingers on the trackpad then click the button.** What Apple's punctuation-challenged programmers are trying to say here is, "You can right-click now!"

And sure enough: If you click with your thumb while your index and middle fingers are resting on the trackpad, you get a right-click (or a Control-click). Right-clicking, of course, opens a shortcut menu filled with useful commands pertaining to whatever you're clicking.

This technique is a lot more natural than it sounds. But like trackpad scrolling and trackpad zooming, it soon becomes an indispensable skill.

---

**Tip:** If you've turned on "Clicking," as described above, then the wording of this option changes to say, "Tap trackpad using two fingers for secondary click." In this case, right-clicking is even easier: whenever you want a right click, just tap the trackpad with two fingers! It gets addictive fast.

---

If you have a MacBook Air, this panel contains some additional gesture options—for rotating images in iPhoto or Preview, for example. Let the little embedded movies be your guide.

### Trackpad options

• **Ignore accidental trackpad input.** This option addresses a chronic syndrome of laptop owners who turn on the Clicking option. When you type along and a finger accidentally brushes the trackpad, it sends the insertion point onto a different line of text. Before you even notice, you've typed over, or typed into, some random part of your document.

This ingenious option locks out the click-and-drag trackpad functions when you're actually typing on the keyboard—an elegantly simple solution.

• **Ignore trackpad when mouse is present.** Here's another ingenious advance in laptop technology. When you hook up a mouse, trackball, or tablet to your laptop, the trackpad is deactivated. If you're using a mouse, then you probably won't want to use the trackpad—and by turning on this checkbox, you're no longer susceptible to brushing it accidentally.

## Bluetooth Tab

People have named their Macs for years (Voyager, Li'l Abner, PowerThang G5). Now they can name their keyboards and mice—and, indeed, must—to accommodate Apple's cordless Bluetooth keyboard and mouse. Here's where you type in their names (so your Mac knows which wireless keyboard and mouse it's "listening" to in a room full of them) and monitor their battery levels.

## Keyboard Shortcuts

Mac OS X comes loaded with keyboard shortcuts for common tasks—and now you can reassign them to shortcuts you prefer. For a full discussion of the options on this pane, see page 135.

# Network

The Network panel is the brain of your Mac's Internet and local networking connections. See Chapter 10 for the settings you need to plug in.

# Parental Controls

These controls, new in Leopard, are described at length in Chapter 13.

# Print & Fax

Chapter 9 describes printing and faxing in detail. This panel's purpose in life is to offer a centralized list of the printers you've introduced to the Mac, to specify the one you use most of the time, and to report on their status.

# QuickTime

The settings in the QuickTime panel affect the way movies are played back on your Mac, including movies that stream to you from a Web page and movies that you watch using QuickTime Player (page 507). Very few of these settings are worth tweaking.

# Security

Mac OS X turns out to be one of the most secure operating systems on earth—and this panel helps to explain why. See Chapter 13 for details on locking up your Mac.

# Sharing

Mac OS X is an upstanding network citizen, flexible enough to share its contents with other Macs, Windows PCs, people dialing in from the road, people dialing in from the Internet, and so on. On this totally overhauled panel, you'll find on/off switches for each of these sharing channels. In this book, many of these features are covered in other chapters:

• **Screen Sharing, File Sharing.** Chapter 14.

• **Printer Sharing.** Chapter 9.

• **Web Sharing.** This single checkbox turns your Mac into a full-fledged Web server—a computer that provides Web pages to any visitors on the Internet.

Place the actual Web pages (in HTML format) into your Home→Sites folder. Then give out the URL at the bottom of the Sharing pane to any prospective visitors: family members, neighbors, and so on.

---

**Note:** Unless you have an Internet connection that's on all the time (like a DSL or cable connection), your visitors will only be able to access the Web site when you are *also* online.

---

• **Remote Login.** Warning: This checkbox is for Unix nerds only. When turned on, it enables you to tap into your Mac's Unix underbelly from anywhere in the world, using a cryptic command called *ssh*. If you have no aspirations of ever becoming a command-line user, you can safely ignore this checkbox.

**Figure 15-14:**
*When Software Update finds an appropriate software morsel, it presents this dialog box that offers to install it automatically. (If you see a smaller version of this dialog box, with no visible list of the new components, click the Details button.)*

*Apple has always created updated and bug-fixing versions of its software components, but they don't do you any good if you don't know about them. You no longer have to scour Mac news Web sites to discover that one of these components has been released and then hunt down the software itself.*

- **Remote Management.** Lets someone else control your Mac using Apple Remote Desktop, a popular add-on program for teachers.

- **Remote Apple Events.** Lets AppleScript gurus (page 480) send commands to Macs across the network.

- **Xgrid Sharing.** Xgrid is powerful software that lets you divide up a complex computational task—like computer animation or huge scientific calculations—among a whole bunch of Macs on your network, so that they automatically work on the problem when they're otherwise sitting idle. If you're intrigued, visit *http://developer.apple.com/hardware/hpc/xgrid_intro.html*.

- **Internet Sharing.** Chapter 10.

- **Bluetooth Sharing.** This pane lets you set up Bluetooth file sharing, a way for other people near you to shoot files over to (or receive files from) your laptop—without muss, fuss, or passwords. Page 441 has the details.

## Software Update

Few operating-system ideas are simpler or better than this one: Whenever Apple improves or fixes some piece Mac OS X or some Apple-branded program, the Software Update program can notify you, download the update, and install it into your system automatically. These updates may include new versions of programs like iPhoto and iMovie; drivers for newly released printers, scanners, cameras, and such; bug fixes and security patches; and so on. It is, in other words, just like Windows Update.

Software Update doesn't run rampant through your system software, however. It's quietly respectful. For example, Software Update doesn't download the new software without asking your permission first and explicitly telling you what it plans to install, as shown in Figure 15-14.

For maximum effortlessness, turn on the "Check for updates" checkbox and then select a frequency from the pop-up menu—daily, weekly, or monthly. If you also turn on "Download important updates in the background," you'll still be notified before anything gets installed, but you won't have to wait for the downloading—the deed will already be done.

(If you've had "Check for updates" turned off, you can always click the Check Now button to force Mac OS X to report in to see if new patches are available.)

## Sound

Using the panes of the Sound panel, you can configure the sound system of your Mac in any of several ways.

---

***Tip:*** Here's a quick way to jump directly to the Sound panel of System Preferences—from the keyboard, without ever having to open System Preferences or click Sound. Just press Option as you tap one of the volume-adjustment keys on the top row of your Apple keyboard.

---

## Sound Effects Tab

"Sound effects" means *error beeps*—the sound you hear when the Mac wants your attention, or when you click someplace you shouldn't.

Just click the sound of your choice to make it your default system beep. Most of the canned choices here are funny and clever, yet subdued enough to be of practical value as alert sounds (Figure 15-15).

As for the other controls on the Sound Effects panel, they include:

- **Alert volume slider.** Some Mac fans are confused by the fact that even when they drag this slider all the way to the left, the sound from games and music CDs still plays at full volume.

    The actual *main* volume slider for your Mac is the "Output volume" slider at the bottom of the Sound pane. The "Alert volume" slider is *just* for error beeps; Apple was kind enough to let you adjust the volume of these error beeps independently.

- **Play user interface sound effects.** This option produces a few subtle sound effects during certain Finder operations: when you drag something off of the Dock, into the Trash, or into a folder, or when the Finder finishes a file-copying job.

**Figure 15-15:**
*You can adjust your overall speaker volume independently from the alert-beep volume, thank goodness. Tip nerds should note that you can also adjust the alert volume by holding down the Option key as you drag the handle in the speaker-volume menulet (on your menu bar).*

- **Play feedback when volume is changed.** Most Mac keyboards have little volume-adjustment keys on the top row that, when pressed, adjust the overall speaker level.

Each time you press one of these keys, the Mac beeps to help you gauge the current volume.

That's all fine when you're working at home. But more than one person has been humiliated in an important meeting when the Mac made a sudden, inappropriately loud sonic outburst—and then amplified that embarrassment by furiously and repeatedly pressing the volume-down key, beeping all the way.

If you turn off this checkbox, the Mac won't make any sound at all as you adjust its volume. Instead, you'll see only a visual representation of the steadily decreasing (or increasing) volume level.

---

*Tip:* If you like the little volume-adjustment clicks *most* of the time, you can shut them up on a one-shot basis by pressing Shift as you tap the volume keys.

---

- **Play Front Row sound effects.** You can read about Front Row, which turns your Mac screen into a giant multimedia directory for your entire Mac, in Chapter 16. All this option does is silence the little clicks and whooshes that liven up the proceedings when you operate Front Row's menus.

## Output Tab

"Output" means speakers or headphones. For 99 percent of the Mac-using community, this pane offers nothing useful except the Balance slider, with which you can set the balance between your Mac's left and right stereo speakers.

## Input Tab

This panel lets you specify which sound source you want the Mac to "listen to," if you have more than one connected: external microphone, internal microphone, line input, USB headset, or whatever. It also lets you adjust the sensitivity of that microphone—its *input volume*—by dragging the slider and watching the real-time Input level meter above it change as you speak.

---

*Tip:* The new "Use ambient noise reduction" is great if you make podcasts or use dictation software. It turns any mike into what amounts to a noise-canceling microphone, deadening the background noise while you're recording.

---

# Speech

Although it may surprise many Mac users, the Mac is quite talented when it comes to speech. Its abilities fall into two categories: reading text aloud, using a synthesized voice; and taking commands from your voice.

## Speech Recognition

The Apple marketing machine may have been working too hard when it called this feature "speech recognition"—the Mac OS feature called PlainTalk doesn't take dictation, typing out what you say. (For that, you need a program like MacSpeech Dictate, *www.macspeech.com*, which is based on the same recognition technology as Dragon NaturallySpeaking for Windows.)

Instead, PlainTalk is a *command-and-control* technology. It lets you open programs, trigger AppleScripts, choose menu commands, trigger keystrokes, and click dialog box buttons and tabs—just by speaking their names.

Few people use PlainTalk speech recognition. But if your Mac has a microphone, PlainTalk is worth at least a 15-minute test drive. It may become a part of your work routine forever. Complete details are in the free downloadable Appendix for this chapter, PlainTalk Speech Recognition.pdf. It's available on this book's "Missing CD" at *www.missingmanuals.com*.

## The Mac Reads to You

The conversation doesn't have to be one-way; it's even easier to make the *Mac* talk.

The Mac can read almost anything you like: text that you pass your cursor over, alert messages, menus, and *any text document in any program*. It can speak in your choice of 24 synthesizer voices, ages 8 to 50. Most read with a twangy, charmingly Norwegian accent—all but Alex, who makes his debut in Leopard and sounds scarily like a professional human voice-over artist.

**Figure 15-16:**
*At the outset, you see only six voices— the ones that sound the most human. Choose More Voices to see the complete list of 22.*

*Then, for 15 minutes of hilarity, try clicking the voices in turn to hear sample sentences. Drag the slider to affect how fast each one speaks. (Clearly, Apple's programmers had some fun with this assignment.)*

To set this up, click the Text to Speech tab (Figure 15-16), Here, you can control which voice your Mac uses, as well as how fast it should speak. Click "Speak selected text when the key is pressed"; you'll be asked to press the keys you want to use as a trigger (like Option-S). From now on, the Mac will read aloud any highlighted text, in any program, when you press Option-S!

# Spotlight

Here's how you tell the Mac (a) which categories of files and information you want the Spotlight search feature to search, (b) which folders you *don't* want searched, for privacy reasons, and (c) which key combination you want to use for summoning the Spotlight menu or dialog box. Details appear are in Chapter 3.

# Startup Disk

Use this panel to pick the System Folder your Mac will use the next time it starts up—when you're swapping between Mac OS X and Windows (running with Boot Camp), for example.

# Time Machine

Here's the master on/off switch and options panel for Time Machine, which is described on page 263.

# Universal Access

The Universal Access panel is designed for people who type with one hand, find it difficult to use a mouse, or have trouble seeing or hearing. (These features can also be handy when the mouse is broken or missing.)

## Seeing Tab (Magnifying the Screen)

If you have trouble seeing the screen, then boy, does Mac OS X have features for you.

### VoiceOver

The Mac has always been able to read stuff on the screen out loud. But in Leopard, Apple took this feature light-years farther, turning it into a full-blown *screen reader* for the benefit of people who can't see. VoiceOver doesn't just read every scrap of text it finds on the screen, it also lets you control everything on the screen (menus, buttons, and so on) without ever needing the mouse.

As you can guess, learning VoiceOver means learning a *lot* of new keyboard shortcuts. (Most of them involve the same two modifier keys pressed together: Control-Option.) Click "Open VoiceOver Utility" to configure this feature's settings. You'll want to spend a good deal of time with the online help screens reading about how VoiceOver works (choose Help→Mac Help, and search for *voiceover*).

### *Zoom*

Another quick solution is to reduce your monitor's *resolution*—thus magnifying the image—using the Displays panel described earlier in this chapter. If you have a 17-inch or larger monitor set to, say, 640 x 480, the result is a greatly magnified picture.

That method doesn't give you much flexibility, however, and it's a hassle to adjust. If you agree, then try the Zoom feature that appears here; it lets you enlarge the area surrounding your cursor in any increment.

To make it work, press Option-⌘-8 as you're working. Or, if the Seeing panel is open, click On in the Zoom section. That's the master switch.

No zooming actually takes place, however, until you press Option-⌘-plus sign (to zoom in) or Option-⌘-minus sign (to zoom out). With each press, the entire screen image gets larger or smaller, creating a virtual monitor that follows your cursor around the screen.

---

**Tip:** If you have a laptop, just using the Control-key trackpad trick described on page 466 is a far faster and easier way to magnify the screen.

And if you have a mouse with a scroll wheel on top (or a scroll-pea, like Apple's standard Mighty Mouse), you can also zoom in or out by pressing Control while you turn *that.*

---

If you click Options, you'll find acres of options that control when the enlarged screen image pans (all the time, or only when the pointer hits a screen edge), the maximum or minimum degree of enlargement, and so on.

### *Display (inverted colors)*

While you're at it, pressing Control-Option-⌘-* (asterisk), or clicking the "Switch to Black on White" button, inverts the colors of the screen, so that text appears white on black—an effect that some people find easier to read. (This option also freaks out many Mac fans who turn it on by mistake, somehow pressing Control-Option-⌘-* by accident during everyday work. They think that the Mac's expensive monitor has just gone loco. Now you know better.)

No matter which color mode you choose, the "Enhance contrast" slider is another option that can help. It makes blacks blacker and whites whiter, further eliminating in-between shades and thereby making the screen easier to see. (If the Universal Access panel doesn't happen to be open, you can always use the keystrokes Control-Option-⌘-< and -> to decrease or increase contrast.)

## Hearing Tab (Flashing the Screen)

If you have trouble hearing the Mac's sounds, the obvious solution is to increase the volume, which is why this panel offers a direct link to the Sound preferences pane. (If your Mac doesn't have external speakers, consider getting some.)

Fortunately, hearing your computer usually isn't critical (except when working in music and audio, of course). The only time audio is especially important is when the Mac tries to get your attention by beeping. For those situations, turn on "Flash the screen when an alert sound occurs" (an effect you can try out by clicking the Flash Screen button). Now you'll see a white flash across the entire monitor whenever the Mac would otherwise beep—not a bad idea on laptops, actually, so that you don't miss beeps when you've got the speakers muted.

**Figure 15-17:**
*Whenever you want to press a multiple-key keystroke like Shift-⌘-D, press them one at a time. You'll see ghost images of these keys superimposed on your screen, as though to show you which keystrokes you've added to your temporary collection. To "un-press" a key you've already pressed, press it again twice.*

## Keyboard Tab (Typing Assistance)

This panel offers two clever features designed to help people who have trouble using the keyboard.

- **Sticky Keys** lets you press multiple-key shortcuts (involving keys like Shift, Option, Control, and ⌘) one at a time instead of all together.

  To make Sticky Keys work, first turn on the master switch at the top of the dialog box. Then go to work on the Mac, triggering keyboard commands as shown in Figure 15-17.

  If you press a modifier key *twice,* meanwhile, you lock it down. (Its onscreen symbol gets brighter to let you know.) When a key is locked, you can use it for several commands in a row. For example, if a folder icon is highlighted, you could double-press ⌘ to lock it down—and then type O (to open the folder), look around, and then press W (to close the window). Press the ⌘ key a third time to "un-press" it.

---

***Tip:*** The checkbox called "Press the Shift key five times to turn Sticky Keys on or off" gives you the flexibility of turning Sticky Keys on and off at will, without even taking a trip to System Preferences. You'll hear a special clacking sound effect alerting you that you just turned on Sticky Keys. (Repeat the five presses to turn Sticky Keys off again.)

---

- **Slow Keys** doesn't register a key press at all until you've held down the key for more than a second or so, to screen out accidental key presses.

If "Use click key sounds" is turned on, you'll hear a little typing sound each time you press a key—but none of these key presses registers unless you hold the key down for a moment. You hear a different sound when the Mac actually accepts the key press—and, of course, you'll see the letter you typed appear onscreen.

## Mouse & Trackpad Tab (Cursor Control from the Keyboard)

Mouse Keys is designed to help people who can't use the mouse—or who want more precision in graphics programs. It lets you click, drag, and otherwise manipulate the cursor by pressing the keys on your numeric keypad. (It's not very useful on keyboards that don't *have* separate numeric keypads, including laptops.)

When Mouse Keys is turned on, the 5 key acts as the clicker—hold it down for a moment to "click the mouse," do that twice to double-click, and so on. Hold down the 0 key to lock down the mouse button, and the period key to unlock it. (The amount of time you have to hold them depends on how you've set the Initial Delay slider.)

Move the cursor around the screen by pressing the eight keys that surround the 5 key. (For example, hold down the 9 key to move the cursor diagonally up and to the right.) If you hold one of these keys down continuously, the cursor, after a pause, begins to move smoothly in that direction—according to the way you have adjusted the sliders called Initial Delay and Maximum Speed.

---

**Tip:** The checkbox called "Press the Option key five times to turn Mouse Keys on or off" saves you the trouble of opening System Preferences.

---

The Cursor Size slider is a godsend not only to people with failing vision, but also to anyone using one of Apple's large, super-high-resolution screens; as the pixel density increases, the arrow cursor gets smaller and smaller. This slider lets you make the arrow cursor larger—much larger, if you like—making it much easier to see.

# The Free Programs

R ight out of the box, Mac OS X comes with a healthy assortment of nearly 50 freebies: programs for sending email, writing documents, doing math, even playing games. Some are dressed-up versions of Mac programs that have been around for years. Others, though, are new programs that not only show off some of Mac OS X's most dramatic new technologies, but also let you get real work done without having to invest in additional software.

These programs reside in two important folders on your hard drive: Applications (in the main hard drive window) and Utilities (within the Applications folder). The Applications folder houses the productivity programs; Utilities holds a couple of dozen maintenance programs for setting up printers and network connections, fixing problems on your hard disk, and so on.

---

*Tip:* You can jump straight to the Applications folder in the Finder by pressing Shift-⌘-A, or by clicking the Applications button in the Finder Sidebar (it's the icon that looks like an *A*). Similarly, Shift-⌘-U takes you to the Utilities folder.

You might consider adding the Application and Utilities folders' icons to the right side of your Dock, too, so that you can access them no matter what program you're in.

---

This chapter guides you through the most important items in your new software library, one program at a time. (Depending on your Mac model, you may find other programs in your Applications folder; Apple occasionally licenses software from other companies to spice up the collection for certain Mac models.)

# Address Book

The Address Book is a database that stores names, addresses, email addresses, phone numbers, and other contact information. Chapter 6 covers the process of importing your Windows contacts into Address Book, and Chapter 11 can help you use them once they're there.

# AppleScript

This folder contains all of the scripts and tools pertaining to the Mac's remarkable AppleScript langauge.

Now, AppleScript may be hard for a Windows switcher to grasp right away, because there's simply nothing like it in Windows. It's a programming language that's both very simple and very powerful, because it lets Mac programs send instructions or data to *each other.*

A simple AppleScript program might perform some simple daily task for you: backing up your Documents folder, for example. A more complex script can be pages long. In professional printing and publishing, where AppleScript enjoys its greatest popularity, a script might connect to a photographer's hard drive elsewhere on the Internet, download a photo from a predetermined folder, color-correct it in Photoshop, import it into a specified page-layout document, print a proof copy, and send a notification email to the editor—automatically.

## Ready-made AppleScripts

Mac OS X comes with several dozen prewritten scripts that are genuinely useful—and all you have to do is choose their names from a menu. "Playing back" an AppleScript in this way requires about as much technical skill as pressing an elevator button.

To sample some of these cool starter scripts, you must first bring the Script menu to your menu bar. To do so, see Figure 16-1.

Some of the scripts in this menu operate on familiar components of the Mac OS, like the Finder; others show off applications or features that are new in Mac OS X. Here are a few of the best:

- **Basics→Open Script Editor** launches Script Editor, a program that you can use to edit and write your own AppleScript programs.

- **Finder Scripts→Add to File Names, Finder→Add to Folder Names.** These scripts tack on a prefix or suffix to the name of every file or folder in the frontmost Finder window (or, if no windows are open, on the desktop). Now you're starting to see the power of AppleScript: You could use this script to add the word *draft* or *final* or *old* to all of the files in a certain folder.

- **Finder Scripts→Replace Text in Item Names** lets you do a search-and-replace of text bits inside file names, folder names, or both. When one publisher rejects your 45-chapter book proposal, you can use this script to change all 45 chapter files from, for example, "A History of Mouse Pads—A Proposal for Random House, Chapter 1" to "A History of Mouse Pads—A Proposal for Simon & Schuster, Chapter 1."

- **Info Scripts→Font Sampler** is designed to show you what all your fonts look like.

- **Mail Scripts→Crazy Message Text** is Apple at its wackiest. When you run it, a dialog box asks you what message you want to send ("Happy Birthday," for example). Mail then creates a colorful, zany, outgoing formatted message in which each letter has a random typeface, style, color, and size. It's ideal for making people think you spent a long time with your Format menu for their entertainment.

---

**Tip:** If you're interested in learning to write your own scripts on the Mac–to control Photoshop, Word, and iChat automatically, for example–a book like *AppleScript: The Missing Manual* is a near-necessity.

---

**Figure 16-1:**
*Left: Leopard's starter scripts appear in categories.*

*Right: To make the Script Menu appear, open Applications→ AppleScript→Apple-Script Utility; turn on "Show Script Menu in menu bar." Apple-Script Utility puts all of the AppleScript options in one place.*

# Automator

Automator is another program that lets you teach your Mac what to do, step by step. But it's easier to use than AppleScript, because you don't have to type any commands. Instead, you assemble a series of visual building blocks called *actions*. Drag actions into the right order, click a big Run button, and your Mac faithfully runs through the list of steps you've given it.

This, too, is a program that most Mac fans will rarely explore. But if you're curious, by all means download the free appendix to this chapter, called "Automator.pdf." It's available on this book's "Missing CD" at *www.missingmanuals.com*.

# Calculator

The Mac OS X Calculator is useful for performing quick arithmetic without having to open a spreadsheet, but it can also act as a scientific calculator for students and scientists, a conversion calculator for metric and U.S. measures, even a currency calculator for world travelers.

Here's everything you need to know for basic math:

- The calculator has three modes: Basic, Advanced (Figure 16-2), and Programmer. Switch among them by choosing the appropriate commands from the View menu (or, more conveniently, using the keyboard shortcuts ⌘-1, ⌘-2, and ⌘-3).

**Figure 16-2:**
*The Calculator program offers a four-function Basic mode, a full-blown scientific calculator mode, and a programmer's calculator (shown here, and capable of hex, octal, decimal, and binary notation). The first two modes offer a "paper tape" feature (View→Show Paper Tape) that lets you correct errors made way back in a calculation.*

*To edit one of the numbers on the paper tape, drag through it, retype, and then click Recalculate Totals. You can also save the tape as a text file by choosing File→Save Tape As, or print it by selecting File→Print Tape.*

- You can operate the Calculator by clicking the onscreen buttons, but it's much easier to press the corresponding number and symbol keys on your keyboard.

***Tip:*** *If you have a Mac laptop, don't miss the embedded numeric keypad, superimposed on the right side of the keyboard and labeled on the keys in a different color ink. When you press the Fn key in the lower-left corner of the keyboard, typing these keys produces the numbers instead of the letters.*

- As you go, you can make your calculator speak each key you press. This is a sensational feature; the Mac's voice ensures that you don't mistype as you keep your eyes on the receipts in front of you, typing by touch.

Just choose Speech→Speak Button Pressed to turn this feature on or off. (You can choose the voice in the Speech pane of System Preferences.)

- Once you've calculated a result, you can copy it (using File→Copy, or ⌘-C) and paste your answer directly into another program.

- If you don't need anything more than a basic calculator, just use the calculator Dashboard widget instead (page 150). You can access it from any program by pressing F12 (and, if the calculator isn't already on the screen, dragging it there from the bar that appears when you click the + button).

### Conversions

Calculator is more than a calculator; it's also a conversion program for meters, grams, inches, miles per hour, and so on. Proceed like this:

1. **Clear the calculator. Type in the starting measurement.**

   To convert 48 degrees Celsius to Fahrenheit, for example, type *48.*

2. **From the Convert menu, choose the kind of conversion you want.**

   In this case, choose Temperature. A little dialog box appears.

3. **Use the pop-up menus to specify which units you want to convert to and from.**

   To convert Celsius to Fahrenheit, for example, choose Celsius from the first pop-up menu, and Fahrenheit from the second.

4. **Click OK.**

   That's it. The calculator displays the result—in Fahrenheit, in this example.

Calculator is especially amazing when it comes to *currency* conversions—from pesos to American dollars, for example—because it does its homework. It goes online to download up-to-the-minute currency rates to ensure that the conversion is accurate. All you have to do is choose Convert→Update Currency Exchange Rates. Then, when you use the Convert→Currency command, your numbers will be the very latest.

---

*Tip:* Again, the Dashboard offers a unit-converter widget that's more useful, because you can access it from any program with a single keystroke (F12).

---

- The Calculator even offers Reverse Polish Notation (RPN), a system of entering numbers that's popular with some mathematicians, programmers, and engineers, because it lets them omit parentheses. Choose View→RPN to turn it on and off.

---

*Tip:* How cool is this? In most programs, you don't need Calculator or even a Dashboard widget. Just highlight an equation (like 56*32.1-517) right in your document, and press ⌘-Shift-8. Presto–Mac OS X replaces the equation with the right answer. This trick works in TextEdit, Mail, Entourage, FileMaker, and many other programs.

And if you ever find that it *doesn't* work, remember that the Spotlight menu is now a calculator, too. Type or paste an equation into the Spotlight search box; instantly, the answer appears in the results menu.

---

# Chess

Mac OS X comes with only one game, but it's a beauty (Figure 16-3). Chess is a traditional chess game played on a gorgeously rendered board with a set of realistic 3-D pieces. You can rotate the board in space, as described in Figure 16-6.

The program is actually a 20-year-old Unix-based chess program, GNU Chess, that Apple packaged up in a new wrapper.

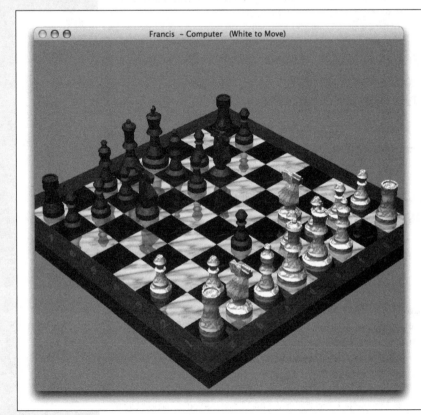

Francis – Computer  (White to Move)

**Figure 16-3:**
*You don't have to be terribly exact about grabbing the chess pieces when it's time to make your move. Just click anywhere within a piece's current square to drag it into a new position on the board (shown here in its Marble incarnation). And how did this chess board get rotated like this? Because you can grab a corner of the board and rotate it in 3-D space. Cool!*

## Playing a Game of Chess

When you launch Chess, you're presented with a fresh, new game that's set up in Human vs. Computer mode—meaning that you (the Human, with the light-colored pieces) get to play against the Computer (your Mac, on the dark side). Drag the chess piece of your choice into position on the board, and the game is afoot.

If you choose Game→New Game, however, you're offered a pop-up menu with choices like Human vs. Computer, Human vs. Human, and so on. If you switch the pop-up menu to Computer vs. Human, you and your Mac trade places; the Mac takes the white side of the board and opens the game with the first move, and you play the black side.

**Tip:** The same New Game dialog box also offers a pop-up menu called Variant, which offers three other chess-like games: Crazyhouse, Suicide, and Losers. The Chess help screens (choose Help→Chess Help, click "Starting a new chess game") explain these variations.

On some night when the video store is closed and you're desperate for entertainment, you might also want to try the Computer vs. Computer option, which pits your Mac against itself. Pour yourself a beer, open a bag of chips, and settle in to watch until someone—either the Mac or the Mac—gains victory.

## Dashboard

In Leopard, Dashboard is a true-blue, double-clickable application. Its behavior doesn't actually change much as a result—it works exactly as described in Chapter 5, and exactly as it always has. But one perk is that you can remove its icon from your Dock, which you couldn't do in the pre-Leopard days.

## Dictionary

For word nerds everywhere, the Dictionary (and Thesaurus) is a blessing—a handy way to look up word definitions, pronunciations, and synonyms. To be precise, Leopard now comes with electronic versions of *seven* reference works in one:

- The entire *New Oxford American Dictionary.*
- The complete *Oxford American Writers Thesaurus.*
- A new dictionary of Apple terms, from A/UX to widget. (Apparently there aren't any Apple terms that begin with X, Y, or Z.)
- Wikipedia. Of course, this famous open-source, citizen-created encyclopedia isn't actually on your Mac. All Dictionary does is give you an easy way to search the *online* version, and display the results right in the comfy Dictionary window.
- A Japanese dictionary, thesaurus, and Japanese-to-English translation dictionary.

**Tip:** You don't ordinarily see the Japanese reference books. You have to turn them on in Dictionary→ Preferences.

Mac OS X also comes with about a million ways to look up a word:

- **Double-click the Dictionary icon.** You get the window shown at top in Figure 16-4. As you type into the Spotlight-y search box, you home in on matching words; double-click a word, or highlight it and press Enter, to view a full, typographically elegant definition, complete with sample sentence and pronunciation guide.

***Tip:*** And if you don't recognize a word in the definition, click *that word* to look up *its* definition. (Each word turns blue and underlined when you point to it, as a reminder.) You can then double-click again in *that* definition—and on, and on, and on.

(You can then use the History menu, the ◄ and ► buttons on the toolbar, or the ⌘-[ and ⌘-] keystrokes to go back and forward in your chain of lookups.)

It's worth exploring the Dictionary→Preferences dialog box, by the way. There, you can choose U.S. or British pronunciations and adjust the font size.

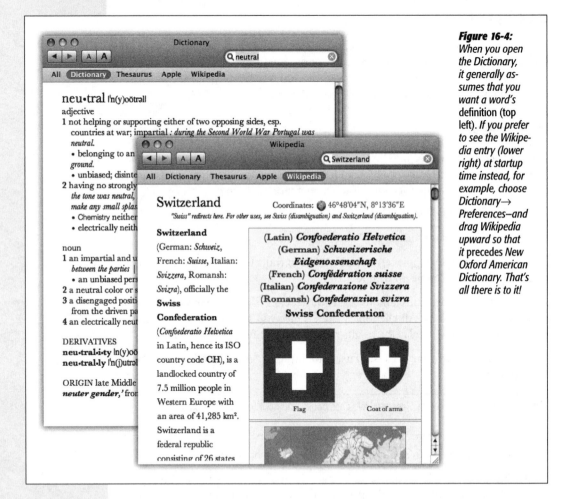

*Figure 16-4:*
*When you open the Dictionary, it generally assumes that you want a word's definition (top left). If you prefer to see the Wikipedia entry (lower right) at startup time instead, for example, choose Dictionary→ Preferences—and drag Wikipedia upward so that it precedes New Oxford American Dictionary. That's all there is to it!*

- **Press F12.** Yes, the Dictionary is one of the widgets in Dashboard (page 150).

- **Right-click a highlighted word in a Cocoa program.** From the shortcut menu, choose Look Up in Dictionary. The Dictionary program opens to that word. (Or visit the Dictionary's Preferences box and choose "Open Dictionary panel." Now you get a panel that pops out of the highlighted word instead.)

- **Point to a word in a Cocoa program, and then press Control-⌘-D.** That keystroke makes the definition panel sprout right from the word you were pointing to. (The advantage here, of course, is that you don't have to highlight the word first.)

---

*Tip:* Here's a trick for the informationally thirsty Mac fan (or speed reader). Once you've invoked the Control-⌘-D keystroke, keep the Control and ⌘ keys pressed. Now drag the cursor across the text. As you push the mouse around, the definition pops up for every word you touch.

Got a big screen or poor eyesight? Then bump up the type size. Dictionary's toolbar has bigger/smaller buttons, and there's a Font Size pop-up menu in the Preferences window.

---

# DVD Player

DVD Player, your Mac's built-in movie projector, is described in Chapter 9.

# Exposé

Like Dashboard, Exposé (page 116) has an icon all its own in Applications. Double-clicking it triggers the F9 effect, which means shrinking and moving *all* open windows around so you can see them simultaneously.

# Font Book

This delightful program lets you install or uninstall fonts, or sets of fonts, as the whim suits you. It's also great for examining your fonts to see what they look like. Details on page 238.

# Front Row

For the last few years, most new Mac models have come with a peculiar accessory: a slim white remote control, looking for all the world like an iPod that's lost too much weight. If you point it at the Mac and press the remote's Menu button, you're catapulted into the magic world of Front Row, a special overlay that provides access to your music, photos, movies, and DVD player—with super-big fonts and graphics that are visible from the couch across the room.

It might seem a little bit weird, then, to hear that Front Row, the software, now comes on *all* Macs, even the ones that didn't come with a remote control and don't have an infrared sensor.

That's because you can operate Front Row entirely from the keyboard—even from across the room, if you have a Bluetooth wireless one. So now even infrared-less Macs like the Mac Pro are invited to the Front Row party.

As shown in Figure 16-5, Front Row is all about drilling down from one menu into another.

Use the arrow keys or the + and – buttons on the remote to choose the activity you're interested in: Music, Photos, DVD, or Videos. Use the Space bar or the ▶ button as the Enter key to choose that kind of entertainment. You'll find, to your delight, that Front Row lets you fire up not only all the music you've got in iTunes, all the photos in iPhoto, and so on, but also all the music, photos, and videos stored on other Macs on your network (assuming you've left iPhoto and iTunes running on those Macs).

Your Mac is now an entertainment center that can be operated from across the room.

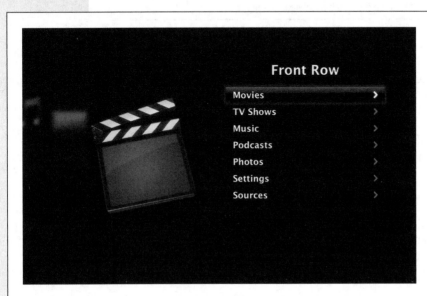

**Figure 16-5:**
*Front Row is all about drilling down through the menu screens, exactly as on an iPod. Start here, on the main menu. Use the center button on the remote, or the Space bar on your keyboard, to select a command or category and open the next screen. Keep going like that until you're watching your movies or slideshows, or listening to your music.*

Here, then, is the cheat sheet for navigating your Mac's entertainment collections—whether you have a Front Row remote or not.

| How to | Using the Remote | Using the Keyboard |
|---|---|---|
| Open and close Front Row | Menu | ⌘-Esc |
| Navigate menus and lists | +, – | ↑, ↓ |
| Return to a previous menu | Menu | Esc |
| Select an item in a menu or list | ▶ɪɪ | Space bar or Return |
| Play and pause audio or video | ▶ɪɪ | Space bar or Return |
| Change volume | +, – | ↑, ↓ |
| Go to the next/previous song, photo, or DVD chapter | ◄◄/►►ɪ | →, ← |
| Rewind/fast-forward (DVD or movie) | ◄◄/►►ɪ (press and hold the button) | →, ← (hold down) |

# GarageBand

GarageBand, Apple's do-it-yourself music construction kit, isn't actually part of Mac OS X. If you have a copy, that's because it's part of the iLife suite that comes on every new Mac (GarageBand, iMovie, iPhoto, iWeb). It's described in the free 85-page iLife appendix to this chapter, available on this book's "Missing CD" page at *www. missingmanuals.com.*

# iCal

In many ways, iCal is not so different from those "Hunks of the Midwest Police Stations" paper calendars people leave hanging on the walls for months past their natural life span. But iCal offers several advantages over paper calendars. For example:

- It can automate the process of entering repeating events, such as weekly staff meetings or gym workout dates.

- iCal can give you a gentle nudge (with a sound, a dialog box, or even an email) when an important appointment is approaching.

- iCal can share information with your Address Book program, with Mail, with your iPod or iPhone, with other Macs, with "published" calendars on the Internet, or with a Palm organizer. Some of these features require one of those .Mac accounts described on page 295. But iCal also works fine on a single Mac, even without an Internet connection.

- iCal can subscribe to other people's calendars. For example, you can subscribe to your spouse's calendar, thereby finding out when you've been committed to after-dinner drinks on the night of the big game on TV.

---

***Tip:*** iCal's Dock icon now displays today's date—even when iCal isn't running. That's reason enough to upgrade to Leopard right there, *n'est-ce pas?*

---

## Working with Views

When you open iCal, you see something like Figure 16-6. By clicking one of the View buttons above the calendar, you can switch among these views:

- **Day** shows the appointments for a single day in the main calendar area, broken down by time slot.

  If you choose iCal→Preferences, you can specify what hours constitute a workday. This is ideal both for those annoying power-life people who get up at 5 a.m. for two hours of calisthenics and the more reasonable people who sleep until 11 a.m.

---

***Tip:*** iCal provides a quick way to get to the current day's date—choose View→Go to Today, or press ⌘-T.

---

- **Week** fills the main display area with seven columns, reflecting the current week. (You can establish a five-day work week instead in iCal→Preferences.)

---

***Tip:*** If you double-click the date above the calendar, you open the day view for that day.

• **Month** shows the entire month that contains the current date (Figure 16-9). Double-click a date number to open the day view for that date.

To save space, iCal generally doesn't show you the *times* of your appointments in Month view. If you'd like to see them anyway, choose iCal→Preferences, click General, and turn on "Show time in month view."

***Tip:*** If your mouse has a scroll wheel, you can use it to great advantage in iCal. For example, when entering a date, turning the wheel lets you jump forward or backward in time. It also lets you change the priority level of a To Do item you're entering, or even tweak the time zone as you're setting it.

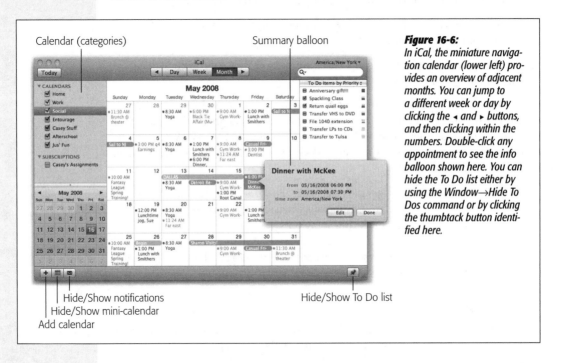

**Figure 16-6:**
*In iCal, the miniature naviga-tion calendar (lower left) pro-vides an overview of adjacent months. You can jump to a different week or day by clicking the ◄ and ► buttons, and then clicking within the numbers. Double-click any appointment to see the info balloon shown here. You can hide the To Do list either by using the Window→Hide To Dos command or by clicking the thumbtack button identi-fied here.*

In any of the views, *double-click* an appointment to see more about it. The very first time you do that, you get the full-blown editing panel shown in Figure 16-7.

After that, double-clicking an event produces only the summary balloon shown in Figure 16-6. If you want to make changes, you can then click the Edit button.

## Making an Appointment

The basic iCal calendar is easy to figure out. After all, with the exception of one un-fortunate Gregorian incident, we've been using calendars successfully for centuries.

Even so, there are two ways to record a new appointment: a simple way and a more flexible, elaborate way.

### The easy way

You can quickly record an appointment using any of several techniques, listed here in order of decreasing efficiency:

- Double-click the appointed time on the calendar, in any view. A colored box appears; this is where you type the name for your new appointment.

- When viewing a day or week view, drag vertically through the time slots that represent the appointment's duration, and then type inside the newly created colored box.

- Using the month view, double-click in a blank area of the appropriate date's square, and then type in the newly created colored bar.

- Choose File→New Event (or press ⌘-N). A new appointment appears on the currently selected day, regardless of the current view.

- In any view, right-click a date and choose New Event from the shortcut menu.

Unless you use the drag-over-hours method, a new event believes itself to be one hour long. But in Day or Week view, you can adjust its duration by dragging the bottom edge vertically. Drag the dark top bar up or down to adjust the start time.

In many cases, that's all there is to it. You have just specified the day, time, and title of the appointment. Now you can get on with your life.

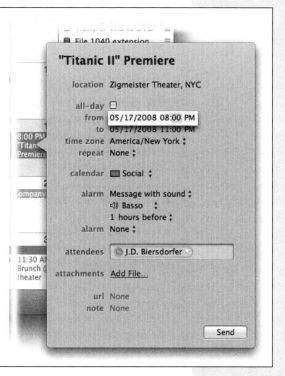

**Figure 16-7:**
*In Leopard, all the details for an appointment sprout right out of the appointment itself. Tab your way to an organized life.*

*Tip: If this Edit balloon is blocking a part of the calendar you need to see, no biggie: just drag the balloon out of the way, using any blank spot as a handle.*

### The long way

The information balloon shown in Figure 16-7 contains much more detailed information about a certain appointment. It appears when you double-click a newly created appointment.

---

**Tip:** After you've already edited an appointment once, the full info balloon is a little more effort to open; double-clicking an event produces only the summary balloon shown in Figure 16-6.

The short way to open the full balloon is to click the appointment, and then press ⌘-E (which is short for Edit→Edit Event). The long way is to double-click the appointment to get the *summary* balloon, and click Edit inside it.

---

For each appointment, you can Tab your way to the following information areas:

- **Subject.** That's the large, bold type at the top—the name of your appointment. For example, you might type *Fly to Phoenix.*

- **Location.** This field makes a lot of sense; if you think about it, almost everyone needs to record *where* a meeting is to take place. You might type a reminder for yourself like *My place,* a specific address like *212 East 23,* or some other helpful information like a contact phone number or flight number.

- **All-day.** An "all-day" event, of course, refers to something that has no specific time of day associated with it: a holiday, a birthday, a book deadline. When you turn on this box, you see the name of the appointment jump to the top of the iCal screen, in the area reserved for this kind of thing; see Figure 16-6.

- **From, to.** You can adjust the times shown here by typing, clicking buttons, or both. Press Tab to jump from one setting to another, and from there to the hours and minutes of the starting time.

  For example, start by clicking the hour, then increase or decrease this number either by pressing your up and down arrow keys or by typing a number. Press Tab to highlight the minutes and repeat the arrow-buttons-or-keys business. Finally, press Tab to highlight the AM/PM indicator, and type either *A* or *P*—or press the up or down arrow key—to change it, if necessary.

---

**Tip:** If you specify a different ending date, a *banner* appears across the top of the calendar.

---

- **Time zone.** This option appears only after you choose iCal→Preferences→ Advanced, and then turn on "Turn on time zone support." And you would do *that* only if you plan to be traveling on the day that this appointment comes to pass.

  Once you've done that, a "time zone" pop-up menu appears. It starts out with "America/New York" (or whatever your Mac's usual time zone is); if you choose Other, a tiny world map appears. Click the time zone that represents where you'll be when this appointment comes due. From the shortcut menu, choose the major city that's in the same zone you'll be in.

**Tip:** The "time zone" pop-up menu remembers each new city you select. The next time you travel to a city you've visited before, you won't have to do that clicking-the-world-map business.

Now, when you arrive in the distant city, use the Time Zone pop-up menu at the top-left corner of the iCal window to tell iCal where you are. You'll see all of iCal's appointments jump, like magic, to their correct new time slots.

- **Repeat.** The pop-up menu here contains common options for recurring events: every day, every week, and so on. It starts out saying None.

Once you've made a selection, you get an **end** pop-up menu that lets you specify when this event should *stop* repeating. If you choose "Never," you're stuck seeing this event repeating on your calendar until the end of time (a good choice for recording, say, your anniversary, especially if your spouse might be consulting the same calendar). You can also turn on "After" (a certain number of times), which is a useful option for car and mortgage payments. And if you choose "On date," you can specify the date that the repetitions come to an end; use this option to indicate the last day of school, for example.

"Custom" lets you specify repeat schedules like "First Monday of the month" or "Every two weeks."

- **Calendar.** A *calendar,* in iCal's confusing terminology, is a subset—a category— into which you can place various appointments. You can create one for yourself, another for family-only events, another for book-club appointments, and so on. Later, you'll be able to hide and show these categories at will, adding or removing them from the calendar with a single click.

**Tip:** Use this same pop-up menu to *change* an appointment's category. If you filed something in "Company Memos" that should have been in "Sweet Nothings for Honey-Poo," open the event's information balloon and reassign it. Quick.

- **Alarm.** This pop-up menu tells iCal how to notify you when a certain appointment is about to begin. iCal can send any of four kinds of flags to get your attention. It can display a message on the screen (with a sound, if you like), send you an email, run a script (page 480), or open a file on your hard drive. (You could use this unusual option to ensure that you don't forget a work deadline by flinging the relevant document open in front of your face at the eleventh hour.)

Once you've specified an alarm mechanism, a new pop-up menu appears to let you specify how much advance notice you want for this particular appointment. If it's a TV show you like to watch, you might set up a reminder only five minutes before airtime. If it's a birthday, you might set up a two-day warning to give yourself enough time to buy a present. In fact, you can set up more than one alarm for the same appointment, each with its own advance-warning interval.

- **Attendees.** If the appointment is a meeting or some other gathering, you can type the participants' names here. If a name is already in your Address Book program, iCal proposes autocompleting the name for you.

  If you separate several names with commas, iCal automatically turns each into a shaded oval pop-up button. You can click it for a pop-up menu of commands like Remove Attendee and Send Email. (That last option appears only if the person in your Address Book has an email address, or if you typed a name *with* an email address in brackets, like this: *Chris Smith <chris@yahoo.com>.*)

  Once you've specified some attendees, a Send button appears in the Info balloon. If you click it, iCal fires up Mail and prepares ready-to-send messages, each with an *iCal.ics* attachment: a calendar-program invitation file. See the box below.

- **Attachment.** This new option lets you fasten a file to the appointment. It can be anything: a photo of the person you're meeting, a document to finish by that deadline, the song that was playing the first time you met this person—whatever.

- **Url.** What Apple really means here, of course, is *URL*—a Uniform Resource Locator, better known as a Web address like *www.apple.com*. If there's a URL relevant to this appointment, by all means type it here. Type more than one, if it'll help you; just be sure to separate each with a comma.

- **Note.** Here's your chance to customize your calendar event. You can type, paste, or drag any text that you like in the note area—driving directions, contact phone numbers, a call history, or whatever.

  Your newly scheduled event now shows up on the calendar, complete with the color coding that corresponds to the calendar category you've assigned.

## What to Do with an Appointment

Once you've entrusted your agenda to iCal, you can start putting it to work. iCal is only too pleased to remind you (via pop-up messages) of your events, reschedule them, print them out, and so on. Here are a few of the possibilities.

### Editing events

To edit an event's details, open its Info balloon, as described in Figure 16-7.

**Tip:** If you just want to change an event's *name,* Option-double-click it right in place.

And if you want to change only an appointment's "calendar" category, right-click anywhere on the appointment, and, from the resulting shortcut menu, choose the category you want.

In both cases, you bypass the need to open the Info balloon.

You don't have to bother with this if all you want to do is *reschedule* an event, however, as described next.

### Rescheduling events

If an event in your life gets rescheduled, you can drag an appointment block vertically in a day- or week-view column to make it later or earlier the same day, or horizontally to another date in any view. (If you reschedule a recurring event, iCal asks if you want to change only *this* occurrence, or this *and* all future ones.)

If something is postponed for, say, a month or two, you're in trouble, since you can't drag an appointment beyond its month window. You have no choice but to open the Info balloon and edit the starting and ending dates or times—or just cut and paste the event to a different date.

### Lengthening or shortening events

If a scheduled meeting becomes shorter or your lunch hour becomes a lunch hour-and-a-half (in your dreams), changing the length of the representative calendar event is as easy as dragging the bottom border of its block in any column view (see Figure 16-8).

---

*Tip:* In week view, if you've grabbed the *bottom* edge of an appointment's block so that the cursor changes, you can drag *horizontally* to make an appointment cross the midnight line and extend into a second day.

---

**Figure 16-8:**
*You can resize any iCal calendar event just by dragging its bottom border. As your cursor touches the bottom edge of a calendar event, it turns into a double-headed arrow. You can now drag the event's edge to make it take up more or less time on your calendar.*

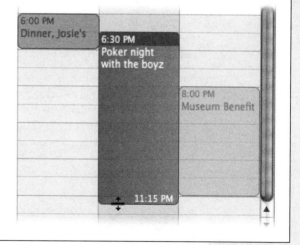

### Printing events

To commit your calendar to paper, choose File→Print, or press ⌘-P. The resulting Print dialog box lets you include only a certain range of dates, only events on certain calendars, with or without To Do lists or mini-month calendars, and so on.

### Deleting events

To delete an appointment, just select it and then press the Delete key. If you delete a recurring event (like a weekly meeting), iCal asks whether you want to delete only that particular instance of the event, or the whole series from that point forward.

## Searching for Events

You should recognize the oval text box at the top of the iCal screen immediately: It's almost identical to the Spotlight box. This search box is designed to let you hide all appointments except those matching what you type into it.

## The "Calendar" Category Concept

Just as iTunes has *playlists* that let you organize songs into subsets, and iPhoto has *albums* that let you organize photos into subsets, iCal has *calendars* that let you organize appointments into subsets. They can be anything you like. One person might have calendars called Home, Work, and TV Reminders. Another might have Me, Spouse 'n' Me, and Whole Family. A small business could have categories called Deductible Travel, R&D, and R&R.

To create a calendar, double-click any white space in the Calendar list (below the existing calendars), or click the + button at the lower-left corner of the iCal window. Type a name that defines the category in your mind.

---

*Tip:* Click a calendar name *before* you create an appointment. That way, the appointment will already belong to the correct calendar.

---

To change the color-coding of your category, right-click its name; from the shortcut menu, choose Get Info. The Calendar Info box appears. Here, you can change the name, color, or description of this category—or turn off alarms for this category.

You assign an appointment to one of these categories using the pop-up menu on its Info balloon, or by right-clicking an event and choosing a calendar name from the shortcut menu. After that, you can hide or show an entire category of appointments at once just by turning on or off the appropriate checkbox in the Calendars list.

---

*Tip:* iCal also has calendar *groups:* calendar containers that consolidate the appointments from several *other* calendars. Super-calendars like this make it easier to manage, hide, show, print, and search subsets of your appointments.

To create a calendar group, choose File→New Calendar Group. Name the resulting item in the Calendar list; for the most part, it behaves like any other calendar. Drag other calendar names onto it to include them. Click the flippy triangle to hide or show the component calendars.

---

## To Do Lists

iCal's Tasks feature lets you make a To Do list and shepherds you along by giving you gentle reminders, if you so desire (Figure 16-9). What's nice is that Mac OS X maintains a single To Do list, which shows up both in iCal and in Mail.

To see the list, click the pushpin button at the lower-right corner of the iCal screen. Add a new task by double-clicking a blank spot in the list that appears, or by choosing File→New To Do. After the new item appears, you can type to name it.

To change the task's priority, alarm, repeating pattern, and so on, double-click it. An Info balloon appears, just as it does for an appointment.

---

**Tip:** Actually, there's a faster way to change a To Do item's priority—click the tiny three-line ribbed handle at the right side of the list. Turns out it's a shortcut menu that lets you choose Low, Medium, or High priority (or None).

---

To sort the list (by priority, for example), use the pop-up menu at the top of the To Do list. To delete a task, click it and then press the Delete key.

---

**Tip:** You have lots of control over what happens to a task listing *after* you check it off. In iCal→Preferences, for example, you can make tasks auto-hide or auto-delete themselves after, say, a week or a month. (And if you asked them to auto-hide themselves, you can make them reappear temporarily using the Show All Completed Items command in the pop-up menu at the top of the To Do list.)

---

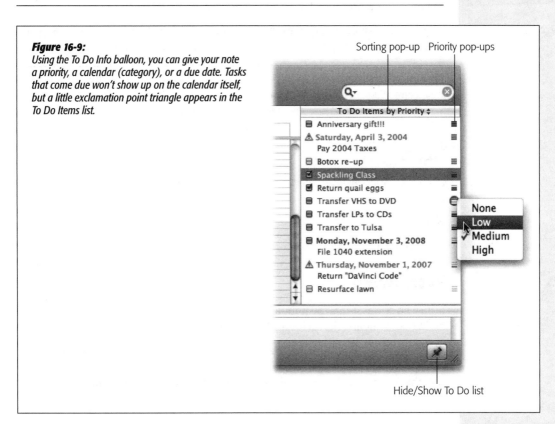

**Figure 16-9:**
*Using the To Do Info balloon, you can give your note a priority, a calendar (category), or a due date. Tasks that come due won't show up on the calendar itself, but a little exclamation point triangle appears in the To Do Items list.*

Sorting pop-up   Priority pop-ups

To Do Items by Priority ⬍

- Anniversary gift!!!
- ⚠ Saturday, April 3, 2004
  Pay 2004 Taxes
- Botox re-up
- Spackling Class
- Return quail eggs
- Transfer VHS to DVD
- Transfer LPs to CDs
- Transfer to Tulsa
- Monday, November 3, 2008
  File 1040 extension
- ⚠ Thursday, November 1, 2007
  Return "DaVinci Code"
- Resurface lawn

None
Low
✓ Medium
High

Hide/Show To Do list

# iChat

Details on the iChat instant-messaging program are in Chapter 12.

# iDVD

iDVD isn't really part of Mac OS X, although you probably have a copy of it; as part of the iLife software suite, iDVD comes free on every new Mac. iDVD lets you turn your digital photos or camcorder movies into DVDs that work on almost any DVD player, complete with menus, slideshow controls, and other navigation features. iDVD handles the technology; you control the style.

For a primer on iDVD, see the free, downloadable iLife appendix to this chapter, available on this book's "Missing CD" page at *www.missingmanuals.com.*

# iMovie, iPhoto

Here's another pair of the iLife apps—not really part of Mac OS X, but probably kicking around on your Mac because iLife comes with all new Macs.

A basic getting-started chapter for these programs awaits, in free downloadable 85-page PDF form, on this book's "Missing CD" page at *www.missingmanuals.com.*

---

*Tip:* If that basic guide isn't enough for you, keep in mind that masterfully written, in-depth guides are available in the form of *iMovie '08 & iDVD: The Missing Manual* and *iPhoto '08: The Missing Manual.* (Corresponding Missing Manual titles are available for earlier versions of these programs, too.)

---

# iTunes

iTunes is Apple's beloved digital music–library program. Chapter 9 tells all.

# Mail

See Chapter 11 for the whole story.

# Photo Booth

It may be goofy, it may be pointless, but the Photo Booth program is a bigger time drain than Solitaire, the Web, and *Dancing with the Stars* put together.

It's a match made in heaven for Macs that have a tiny video camera above the screen, but you can also use it with a camcorder, external iSight camera, or Webcam. Just be sure that the camera is turned on and hooked up *before* you open Photo Booth.

Open this program and then peer into the camera. Photo Booth acts like a digital mirror, showing whatever the camera sees—that is, you.

But then click the Effects button. You enter a world of special visual effects—and we're talking *very* special. Some make you look like a pinhead, or bulbous, or a Siamese twin; others simulate Andy Warhol paintings, fisheye lenses, and charcoal sketches (Figure 16-10). In the Leopard version, in fact, there are *five pages* of effects, nine previews on a page; click the left or right arrow buttons, or press ⌘-left or right arrow key, to see them all. (The last two pages hold *backdrop* effects, described below.)

**Figure 16-10:**
*The Photo Booth effects must have been dreamed up one night at Apple in the midst of a serious beer party. They're truly, disturbingly creative. If you decide that you really look best without any help from Apple's warped imagery, click the Normal icon in the center.*

Click an effect

Still  4-Up  Movie      Effects pages   Finished shots (still, 4-up, movie)

Some of the effects have sliders that govern their intensity; you'll see them appear when you click the preview.

## Still Photos

When you find an effect that looks appealing (or unappealing, depending on your goals here), click the camera button, or press ⌘-T. You see and hear a three-second countdown, and then *snap!*—your screen flashes white to add illumination, and the resulting photo appears on your screen. Its thumbnail joins the collection at the bottom.

*Tip:* If that countdown is getting on your nerves, *Option*-click the camera button. You can get rid of the screen flash, too, by *Shift*-clicking. Needless to say, if you press Option *and* Shift, you get neither the countdown nor the flash.

## 4-Up Photos

If you click the 4-Up button identified in Figure 16-10, then when you click the Camera icon (or press ⌘-T), the 3-2-1 countdown begins, and then Photo Booth snaps *four*

---

**GEM IN THE ROUGH**

### Still and Video Backdrops

In Mac OS X 10.5, Photo Booth and iChat are cousins, and they're closer than ever. One particular feature, in fact, is identical in each: custom backdrops. You can replace the actual, mundane background of your office or den with something far more exciting: a rushing waterfall, for example, or a rider's-eye view of a roller coaster. In fact, you can use any photo or video you want as the background. It's just like the blue-screen or green-screen technology that Hollywood uses to put their actors someplace they're not—but without the bluescreen or greenscreen.

To replace your background in Photo Booth, click Effects. The third page of effects offers eight *canned* backgrounds, prepared by Apple for your enjoyment: various spectacular stills (cloudscape, color dots, the moon) and videos (Eiffel Tower plaza, aquarium, roller coaster, tropical beach, Yosemite waterfall).

The final page offers eight *empty* preview squares. You're supposed to drag a still or a video from your desktop (or iPhoto) into these empty squares, making them not so empty.

In any case, prepare the backdrop by clicking one of the preview squares. Photo Booth says, "Please step out of the frame." Do it. Photo Booth is going to memorize what its field of view looks like *without* you in it, so that when you reappear, it can tell *you* apart from your boring office background.

Now, when you record the movie or take the photo, you'll be amazed to discover that Photo Booth has just transplanted you to the far more exotic locale you selected. (Alas, blotches may result if the background includes movement or highly contrasting elements.)

---

consecutive photos in two seconds. You can exploit the timing just the way you would in a real photo booth—make four different expressions, horse around, whatever.

The result is a single graphic with four panes. (In Photo Booth, they appear rakishly assembled at an angle; but when you export the image, they appear straight, like panes of a window.) Its icon plops into the row of thumbnails at the bottom of the window, just like the single still photos.

## Movies

Here's another Leopard twist: Photo Booth can now record *videos,* complete with those wacky distortion effects. Click the third icon below the screen, the Movie icon (Figure 16-10), and then click the camera button (or press ⌘-T). You get the 3-2-1 countdown—but this time, Photo Booth records a video, with sound, until you click the Stop button or the hard drive is full, whichever comes first. (The little digital counter at left reminds you that you're still filming.) When it's over, the movie's icon appears in the row of thumbnails, ready to play or export.

## Exporting Shots and Movies

To look at a photo or movie you've captured, click its thumbnail in the scrolling row at the bottom of the screen. (To return to camera mode, click the camera button.)

Fortunately, these masterpieces of goofiness and distortion aren't locked in Photo Booth forever. You can share them with your adoring public in any of four ways:

- Drag a thumbnail out of the window to your desktop. Or use the File→Reveal in Finder command to see the actual picture or movie files.

---

***Tip:*** They're in your Home→Pictures→Photo Booth folder. You'll find one JPEG apiece for single shots, four JPEG files for a 4-up, and a .MOV movie file for videos.

---

- Click Mail to send the photo or movie as an outgoing attachment in Mail.

- Click the iPhoto button to import the shot or movie into iPhoto.

- Click Account Picture to make this photo represent you on the Login screen.

---

***Tip:*** You can choose one frame of a Photo Booth movie to represent you. As the movie plays, click the Pause button, then drag the scroll-bar handle to freeze the action on the frame you want. Then click Account Picture.

Similarly, you can click your favorite *one pane* of a 4-up image to serve as your account photo—it expands to fill the Photo Booth screen—before clicking Account Picture.

And speaking of interesting headshots: If you export a 4-up image and choose it as your buddy icon in iChat (Chapter 12), you'll get an *animated* buddy icon. That is, your tiny icon cycles among the four images, creating a crude sort of animation. It's sort of annoying, actually, but all the kids are doing it.

---

As you set off on your Photo Booth adventures, a note of caution: Keep it away from children. They won't move from Photo Booth for the next 12 years.

# Preview

Preview is Mac OS X's built-in graphics viewer, fax viewer, and PDF reader. It's always been teeming with features that most Mac owners never even knew were there—but in Leopard, it's a real powerhouse.

## Preview as Graphics Viewer

Preview's hallmark is its surprising versatility. It can display and manipulate pictures saved in a wide variety of formats, including common graphics formats like JPEG, TIFF, PICT, and GIF; less commonly used formats like BMP, PNG, SGI, TGA, and MacPaint; and even Photoshop, EPS, and PDF graphics. You can even open animated GIFs by adding a Play button to the toolbar, as described below.

### Bunches o' graphics

If you highlight a group of image files in the Finder and open them all at once (for example, by pressing ⌘-O), Preview opens the first one, but lists the thumbnails of the whole group in the Sidebar. You can walk through them with the ↑ and ↓ keys, or you can choose View→Slideshow (Shift-⌘-F) to begin a full-screen slideshow.

---

*Tip:* Use the ✿ menu below the Sidebar group to change the sorting order of these thumbnails.

---

### Cropping graphics

To crop graphics in Preview, drag across the part of the graphic that you want to keep. To redraw, drag the round handles on the dotted rectangle; or, to proceed with the crop, choose Tools→Crop. (The keyboard shortcut is ⌘-K.)

If you don't think you'll ever need the original again, save the document. Otherwise, choose File→Save As to spin the cropped image out as a separate file, preserving the original in the process.

---

*Tip:* You can also rotate an image—even a PDF document—in 90-degree increments and then flip it vertically or horizontally, using the commands in the Tools menu. In fact, if you select several thumbnails in the Sidebar first, you can rotate or flip them all simultaneously.

---

### Fixing up photos

Preview is no Photoshop, but it's getting closer. Let us count the ways:

- **Choose Tools→Inspector.** A floating palette appears. Click the first tab to see the photo's name, when it was taken, its pixel dimensions, and so on. Click the second one for even more geeky photo details, including camera settings like the lens type, ISO setting, focus mode, whether the flash was on, and so on.

• **Choose Tools→Adjust Color.** A translucent, floating color-adjustment palette appears, teeming with sliders for brightness, contrast, exposure, saturation (color intensity), temperature and tint (color cast), sharpness, and more. See Figure 16-11.

**Figure 16-11:**
*Humble little Preview has grown up into a big, strong mini-Photoshop. You can really fix up a photo if you know what you're doing, using these sliders. Or you can just click the Auto Levels button. It sets all those sliders for you, which generally does an amazing job of making almost any photo look better.*

• **Choose Tools→Adjust Size.** This command, new in Leopard, lets you adjust a photo's resolution, which comes in handy a lot. For example, you can scale an unwieldy 10-megapixel, gazillion-by-gazillion-pixel shot down to a nice 640-by-480 JPEG that's small enough to send by email. Or you can shrink a photo down so it fits within a desktop window, for use as a window background.

There's not much to it. Type in the new print dimensions you want for the photo, in inches or whatever units you choose from the pop-up menu. If you like, you can also change the resolution (the number of pixels per inch) by editing the Resolution box.

### Converting file formats

Preview doesn't just open all these file formats—it can also convert between most of them. You can pop open some old Mac PICT files and turn them into BMP files for a Windows user, pry open some SGI files created on a Silicon Graphics workstation and turn them into JPEGs for use on your Web site, and so on.

**Tip:** What's even cooler is you can open raw PostScript files right into Preview, which converts them into PDF files on the spot. You no longer need a PostScript laser printer to print out high-end diagrams and page layouts that come to you as PostScript files. Thanks to Preview, even an inkjet printer can handle them.

All you have to do is open the file you want to convert and choose File→Save As. In the dialog box that appears, choose the new format for the image using the Format pop-up menu (JPEG, TIFF, PNG, or Photoshop, for example). Finally, click Save to export the file.

## The Sidebar

The Sidebar slides out from the side of the main Preview window whenever (a) you open a multipage PDF or TIFF file, (b) you highlight a bunch of graphics files in the Finder and open them all at once, or (c) you click the Sidebar button in the Preview toolbar, or choose View→Sidebar. (If your PDF file has been prepared with a table of contents, the Sidebar shows that.)

The idea is that these thumbnails let you navigate pages or graphics without having to open a rat's nest of individual windows. Figure 16-12 expands on the idea.

**Figure 16-12:**
Left: To open or close the Sidebar (right), choose View→Sidebar, press Shift-⌘-D, or click the Sidebar button on the toolbar. If the toolbar isn't visible, press ⌘-B. Drag the central scroll bar to make the Sidebar bigger.

Right: Some PDF files fill the Sidebar with a ready-made table of contents instead.

## Preview as PDF Reader

Preview is a nearly full-blown equivalent of Acrobat Reader, the free program used by millions to read PDF documents. It lets you search PDF documents, copy text out of them, add comments, fill in forms, and click live hyperlinks—features that used to be available only in Adobe's Acrobat Reader.

Here are the basics:

- Zoom in and out using ⌘-plus and ⌘-minus.

- Use the View→PDF Display submenu to control how the PDF document appears: as two-page spreads; as single scrolling sheets of "paper towel"; with borders that indicate ends of pages; and so on.

- Use ⌘-left arrow and ⌘-right arrow to page through a document. (Your Page Up and Page Down keys aren't quite the same thing; they shift to the previous or next part of the *same* page, if it wasn't already visible.)

---

**Tip:** Some PDF documents include a table of contents, which you'll see in Preview's Sidebar, complete with flippy triangles that denote major topics or chapter headings (Figure 16-12, right). You can use the up arrow and down arrow keys alone to walk through these chapter headings, and then expand one that looks good by pressing the right arrow key. Collapse it again with the left arrow key.

In other words, you expand and collapse flippy triangles in Preview just as you do in a Finder list view.

---

- Bookmark your place by choosing Bookmarks→Add Bookmark (⌘-D); type a clever name. In future, you'll be able to return to that spot by choosing its name from the Bookmarks menu.

- Type in notes, add clickable links (to Web addresses or other spots in the document), or use circles and rectangles to draw your reader's attention to certain sections, as shown in Figure 16-13. (Those circles and rectangles even work on image files.)

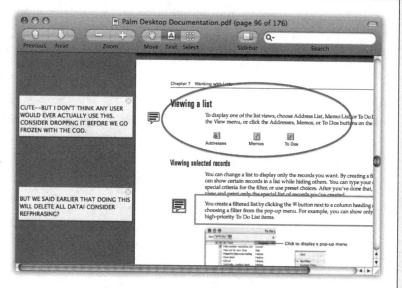

**Figure 16-13:**
*Learn the keystrokes for the PDF markings you can make: Oval (Control-⌘-O), Rectangle (Control-⌘-R), Note (Control-⌘-N), or Link (Control-⌘-L). That's a lot faster than using the Tools→Annotate submenu every time.*

*Hit that keystroke, then drag diagonally to define a rectangle, oval, or link. Or click to place a Note icon, and edit that note in the left margin. You can drag or delete the annotation's little icon, or adjust its look using the Tools→ Inspector palette.*

**Note:** These are full-blown Acrobat annotations; they'll show up when your PDF document is opened by Acrobat Reader or even on Windows PCs.

- Use the Tools→Mark Up submenu to add highlighting, ~~strikethrough~~, or underlining on whatever text you select.

- Turn antialiasing (font smoothing) on or off to improve readability. To find the on/off switch, choose Preview→Preferences, and click the PDF tab. (Though antialiased text generally looks great, it's sometimes easier to read very small type with antialiasing turned off. It's a little jagged, but clearer nonetheless.)

- Turn on View→PDF Display→Continuous to scroll through multipage PDF documents in one continuous stream, instead of jumping from page to page when you use the scroll bars.

- If you want to copy some text out of a PDF document—for pasting into a word processor, for example, where you can edit it—click the Text tool (the letter A on the toolbar) or choose Tools→Text Tool. Now you can drag through some text and then choose Edit→Copy, just as though the PDF document is a Web page. You can even drag across page boundaries.

**Tip:** Ordinarily, dragging across text selects the text from one edge of the page to the other. But if you want to copy only the first column of several, for example, *Option*-drag. Preview now lets you drag out any arbitrary selection rectangle, thereby highlighting any block of text you like, ready for copying.

- You can save a single page from a PDF as a TIFF file in order to use it in other graphics, word processing, or page layout programs that don't recognize PDF.

    To extract a page, use the usual File→Save As command, making sure to choose the new file format from the pop-up menu. (If you choose a format like Photoshop or

**Figure 16-14:**
*Left: Type into the Search or Find box. Matches appear in the Sidebar, with page numbers; click one to go there.*

*Right: In longer documents, it helps to turn on "Group by section." You now see only the names of the document sections, ranked by relevance.*

JPEG, Preview converts only the currently selected page of your PDF document. That's because there's no such thing as a multipage Photoshop or JPEG graphic. But you already knew that.)

• To find a word or phrase somewhere in a PDF document, press ⌘-F (or choose Edit→Find→Find) to open the Find box—or just type into the Q box at the top of the Sidebar, if it's open. Proceed as shown in Figure 16-14.

• Add keywords to a graphic or PDF (choose Tools→Inspector, click the Q tab, click the + button). Later, you'll be able to call up these documents with a quick Spotlight search for those details.

## QuickTime Player

Dozens of Mac OS X programs can play digital movies in Apple' s QuickTime format (the rough equivalent of .AVI files in Windows): Word, FileMaker, AppleWorks, PowerPoint, Safari, America Online, and so on.

But the cornerstone of Mac OS X's movie-, sound-, and photo-playback software is QuickTime Player, which sits in your Applications→QuickTime folder (and comes factory-installed on the Dock). It does exactly what you'd expect: show pictures, play movies, and play sounds. You might think of it as Apple's take on Windows Media Player.

**Figure 16-15:**
Some of the controls shown here are available only in the Pro version of QuickTime Player. They appear as soon as you type in your registration code (which you get when you pay $30).

Counter — 00:02:14

Volume

Playhead

Audio level meters

Resize handle

Rewind to start | Play/Stop  Scroll bar  Jump to end

Selection handle

## Playing Movies

You can open a movie file by double-clicking it, dragging it onto the QuickTime Player icon, or by launching QuickTime Player and then choosing File→Open File (⌘-O). The most important controls (Figure 16-15) are:

- **Scroll bar.** Drag the playhead to jump to a different spot in the movie.

- **Play/Stop button.** Click once to start, and again to stop. You can also press the Space bar, Return key, or ⌘-right arrow for this purpose. (Or avoid the buttons altogether and double-click the movie itself to start or stop playback.)

*Tip:* You can make any movie automatically play when opened, so that you avoid clicking the Play button. To do so, choose QuickTime Player→Preferences→Player Preferences, and turn on "Automatically play movies when opened."

- **Selection handles.** These tiny black triangles appear only in the $30 Pro version. You use them to highlight stretches of footage.

- **Volume.** If you like, you can make the soundtrack louder or softer by dragging this slider with your mouse or clicking in its "track." You may find it easier, however, to press the up or down arrow keys.

*Tip:* Try minimizing a QuickTime Player window while a movie is playing. It shrinks to the Dock—and *keeps on playing.* Do this enough times, and you'll know what it's like to be Steve Jobs on stage.

## QuickTime Pro

If you've spent the $30 to upgrade your free copy of QuickTime Player to the Pro version—and to shut up the "Upgrade Now!" advertisement that appears the first time you open QuickTime Player each day—you've unlocked a number of useful features. For example:

- Your Movie menu contains additional playback options, including full-screen playback.

- When you find a QuickTime movie on a Web page, you can usually save it to your hard drive. (Click on the movie; hold down the mouse button until a pop-up menu appears; choose Save Movie to Disk, or the equivalent in your browser.)

- Using the commands in the Edit menu, you can view, turn on and off, add, or delete the individual *tracks* in a particular movie. (Most movies have nothing but a video track and a soundtrack. But a few specialized movies may also contain a text track, an animation track, alternate soundtracks, and so on.)

By far the most powerful feature you gain in the Pro version, however, is its ability to *edit* QuickTime movies. You can rearrange scenes, eliminate others, and save the result as a new movie with its own name. (Even QuickTime Player Pro doesn't let you *create* live-action QuickTime movies with your camcorder. For that, you need iMovie or a more complex editing program like Final Cut Express. QuickTime Player Pro simply lets you edit *existing* movies.)

## Safari

Apple's first and only Web browser feels decidedly faster and more modern than Internet Explorer, and there are enough tips and tricks lurking inside to last you a lifetime. Details in Chapter 12.

## Stickies

Stickies (Figure 16-16) lets you create virtual Post-it notes that you can stick anywhere on your screen—a triumphant software answer to the thousands of people who stick notes on the edges of their *actual* monitors. If you're a fan of the Windows Notepad, you might find yourself getting heavily into Stickies instead.

**Figure 16-16:**
*In the old days of the Mac, the notes you created with Stickies were text-only, single-font deals. Today, however, you can use a mix of fonts, text colors, and styles within each note. You can even paste in graphics, sounds, and movies (like PICT, GIF, JPEG, QuickTime, AIFF, whole PDF files, and so on), creating the world's most elaborate reminders and to-do lists.*

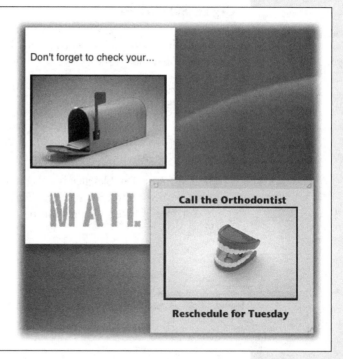

You can use Stickies to type quick notes and to-do items, paste in Web addresses or phone numbers you need to remember, or store any other little scraps and snippets of text you come across. Your electronic Post-its show up whenever the Stickies program is running.

You can use a mix of fonts, text colors, and styles within each note. You can even copy and paste (or drag) *pictures, movies, and sounds* into your notes, producing the world's most elaborate reminders and to-do lists. You can even spell check your notes and search-and-replace text.

## Creating Sticky Notes

The first time you launch Stickies, a few sample notes appear automatically, describing some of the program's features. You can quickly dispose of each sample by clicking the close button in the upper-left corner of each note or by choosing File→Close (⌘-W). Each time you close a note, a dialog box asks if you want to save the note. If you click Don't Save, the note disappears permanently.

---

**Note:** The Stickies module that's part of Dashboard (page 150) is extremely similar, and it's arguably quicker to open (just press F12). But it's also far more limited.

---

To create a new note, choose File→New Note (⌘-N) and start typing, pasting, or dragging text (or graphics, movies, or sounds) in from other programs.

## Organizing Stickies

Once you start plastering your Mac with notes, it doesn't take long to find yourself plagued with desktop clutter. Fortunately, Stickies includes a few built-in tricks for managing a deskful of notes:

- There's a small resize handle on the lower-right corner of each note. Drag it to make notes larger or smaller onscreen.

- Use the small triangle in the upper-right corner of each note to zoom and shrink note windows with a single click. The first click collapses a note down to a more compact size. Another click pops the note back open to normal size.

- The best option: Double-click anywhere along the dark strip at the top of each note to miniaturize it into a compact one-line mini-note, as shown in Figure 16-17. You also can miniaturize a selected note by choosing Window→Miniaturize Window (⌘-M).

**Figure 16-17:**
*If the first line of text gets truncated, as in the third note shown here, you can tug the right corner of the note and drag it wider without de-miniaturizing it.*

- If your notes are scattered randomly across the desktop, you can bring them all forward with the Window→Bring All to Front command.

*Tip:* The most efficient way to use Stickies is to keep the notes in their miniaturized state, as shown in Figure 16-17. When a note is miniaturized, the first line of text shows up in tiny type right in the collapsed title bar of the note, so you don't have to expand the note to remember what's in it. And since many—if not most—of your notes can probably be summed up in a couple of words ("pick up dry cleaning," "call mom"), it's perfectly possible to keep your sticky notes in their miniaturized state permanently.

## Formatting Notes

The Stickies menus offer several word processor–like commands for creating designer sticky notes, with any combination of fonts, colors, and styles. (You can also choose from six different background colors from the Color menu.)

## Saving Sticky Notes

The notes you create in Stickies last only as long as you keep them open. If you close a note to get it out of the way, it vanishes permanently.

If you want to preserve the information you've stuffed into your notes in a more permanent form, use File→Export Text to save each note as a standalone text document. When you use the Export Text command, you can save the file as a plain text file, RTF (a special format recognized by most word processors), and RTFD (a strange and powerful variant of RTF that can contain *attachments*—graphics, files, and even programs you've dragged into the note).

# System Preferences

This program opens the door to the nerve center of Mac OS X's various user preferences, settings, and options. Chapter 15 covers every option in detail.

# TextEdit

TextEdit is a word processor (Figure 16-18)—a pretty darn powerful one, at that, considering you didn't have to pay a cent extra for it. You can create real documents with real formatting, using style sheets, colors, automatic numbering and bullets, tables, and customized line spacing, and—get this—even save the result as a Microsoft Word document. If you need to use Word files, but you can't stand bloated Microsoft interfaces, welcome.

*Tip:* Not only can TextEdit open and save Microsoft Word documents, but it even recognizes some of the very same keyboard shortcuts. For example, you can advance through documents one word at a time by pressing Option-left arrow or Option-right arrow. Adding the Shift key to those key combinations lets you *select* one whole word at a time. You can also use the ⌘ key in conjunction with the right and left arrow keys to jump to the beginning or end of a line.

### TextEdit's Two Personalities

The one confusing aspect of TextEdit is that it's both a *plain text editor* (no formatting; globally compatible) and a true *word processor* (fonts, sizes, styles; compatible with other word processors). You need to keep your wits about you as you edit, because the minute you add formatting to your document, TextEdit no longer lets you save it as a plain text file.

Here's the scheme:

- You can change a plain text document to a formatted one by choosing Format→ Make Rich Text. The ruler appears automatically to remind you that a new world of formatting has just become available.

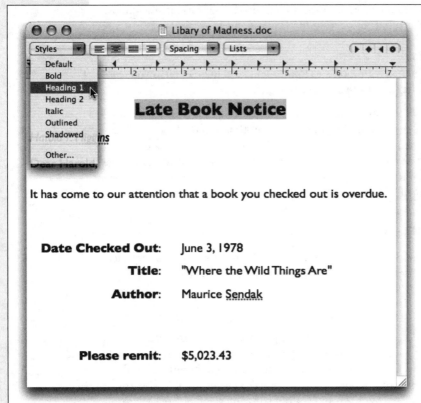

**Figure 16-18:**
*The text ruler gives you control over tab stops, line spacing, paragraph justification, and so on. Pressing ⌘-R makes it appear and disappear. The Style pop-up menu lists canned sets of character and paragraph formatting, so you can apply them consistently throughout a document.*

- Conversely, you can change a formatted document (a Word file you've opened, for example) to a plain text document by choosing Format→Make Plain Text. An alert message appears to point out that you're about to lose all formatting.

- If you know what kind of document you *always* want to open, go to the TextEdit→Preferences dialog box; on the New Document tab, select Rich Text or Plain Text. That's what you'll get each time you choose File→New.

## Working in TextEdit

As you begin typing, all the usual word processing rules apply, with a few twists:

- Choose Bold, Italic, and font sizes using the Format→Font submenu, or choose Format→Font→Show Fonts (⌘-T) to open up the standard Mac OS X Font panel. You can even create subscript or superscript, change the color of the text (Format→Font→Show Colors), and so on.

- Common paragraph-alignment options—Align Left, Align Right, Center, Justify—are all available as ruler buttons and also reside in the Format→Text submenu. Adjust the line spacing (single, double, or any fraction or multiple) using the Spacing pop-up menu in the ruler.

- The ruler also offers automatic bulleting and numbering of paragraphs. Just choose the numbering style you prefer from the Lists pop-up menu.

- You can select several non-adjacent bits of text *simultaneously*. To pull this off, highlight your first piece of text by dragging, and then press ⌘ as you use the mouse to select more text. Bingo: You've highlighted two separate chunks of text.

    When you're done selecting bits of text here and there, you can operate on them en masse. For example, you can make them all bold or italic with one fell swoop. You can even use the Cut, Copy, and Paste commands, as described in the next section. When you cut or copy, the command acts upon all your selections at once.

    You can also drag any *one* of the highlighted portions to a new area, confident that the other chunks will come along for the ride. All of the selected areas wind up consolidated in their new location.

*Tip:* If you *Option*-drag one of the highlighted bits, you *copy* it, leaving the original in place.

---

**UP TO SPEED**

## The Deal with Microsoft Word

Yes, you read that correctly: Humble TextEdit can open and create Microsoft Word documents! Your savings: the $400 price of Microsoft Office!

Well, sort of.

When you open a Microsoft Word document in TextEdit, most of the formatting comes through alive: bold, italic, font choices, colors, line spacing, alignment, and so on. Even very basic tables make it into TextEdit, although with different column widths.

A lot of Word-specific formatting does not survive crossing the chasm, however: borders, style sheets, footnotes, and the like. Bullets and numbered lists don't make it, either, even though TextEdit can create its own versions of these. And TextEdit doesn't recognize the comments and change tracking that your collaborators might use to mark up your manuscript. And forget about the new .docx format.

Saving a TextEdit document as a Word document (File→Save As) is a better bet, because Word understands the many kinds of formatting that TextEdit can produce—including bullets, numbering, and tables. The one disappointment is that Word doesn't recognize any style sheets you've set up in TextEdit. The formatting applied by those style names survives—just not the style names themselves.

Even so, a built-in Word-document editor is a huge, huge step for the Mac OS. It means that in many cases, you can be a first-class citizen on the playing field of American business. Nobody ever needs to know that you're (a) using a Mac, and (b) not using the real Microsoft Word.

---

- Similarly, you can use the Find command to highlight a certain term everywhere it appears in a document. To do that, choose Edit→Find→Find (or just press ⌘-F). Fill in the "Find" and "Replace with" boxes—and then press the Control key. The Replace All button changes to say Select All.

- If you Option-drag vertically, you can freely select an arbitrary column of text (not necessarily the entire page width). This technique is very useful when you want to select only one column in a multicolumn layout, or when you want to select the numbers in a list ("1.," "2.," and so on) and format them all at once. (As noted earlier, this trick also works in Preview PDF documents.)

## Style Sheets

A *style* is a prepackaged collection of formatting attributes that you can apply and reapply with a click of the mouse (bold, 24-point Optima, double-spaced, centered, for instance). You can create as many styles as you need: chapter headings, sidebar styles, and so on. You end up with a collection of custom-tailored styles for each of the repeating elements of your document.

Once you've created your styles, you can apply them as you need them, safe in the knowledge that they'll be consistent throughout the document. During the editing process, if you notice you accidentally styled a *headline* using the *Subhead* style, you can fix the problem by simply reapplying the correct style.

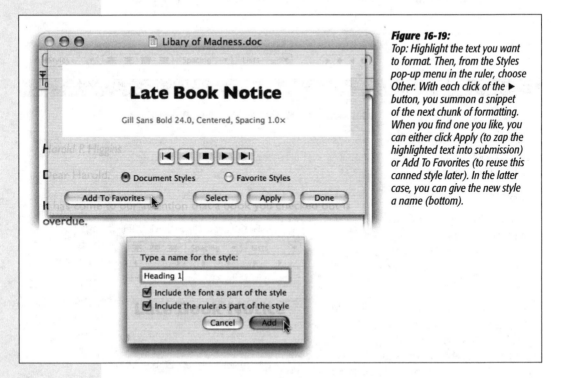

**Figure 16-19:**
*Top: Highlight the text you want to format. Then, from the Styles pop-up menu in the ruler, choose Other. With each click of the ▶ button, you summon a snippet of the next chunk of formatting. When you find one you like, you can either click Apply (to zap the highlighted text into submission) or Add To Favorites (to reuse this canned style later). In the latter case, you can give the new style a name (bottom).*

*Note:* Unlike a real word processor, TextEdit doesn't let you *change* a style's formatting and thereby update every occurrence of it. You can't search and replace by style, either.

- **Creating a named style.** To create a style, format some text so that it looks the way you like it, complete with font, color, line spacing, tab settings, and so on.

  Then, from the Styles pop-up menu in the ruler, choose Other (Figure 16-19, top). Click Add to Favorites, type a name for the style, turn on both checkboxes (Figure 16-19, bottom), and click Add.

- **Applying a style.** Later, when you want to reuse the formatting you set up, highlight some text and then choose the appropriate name from the Styles pop-up menu. TextEdit applies the formatting immediately.

*Tip:* If you simply click *inside a paragraph,* applying a style affects only *paragraph* attributes like line spacing, tab stops, and alignment. If you *highlight a random chunk of text* instead, applying a style affects only *character* attributes like the font and type size. If you highlight an *entire* paragraph, however, both text and paragraph formatting appear.

- **Deleting a style.** To delete a superfluous style, choose Other from the Styles pop-up menu on the ruler. Click the Favorite Styles button, choose the unwanted style's name from the pop-up menu, and then click Remove From Favorites. (Deleting a style doesn't affect any formatting that's already in your document; it just removes the name from the Styles menu.)

- **Copying by example.** In Word and most other "serious" word processors, the routines above correctly describe how you use styles. In TextEdit, however, you can use Option-⌘-C and Option-⌘-V (Format→Copy Style and Format→Paste Style) to grab formatting from one place in your document and reuse it elsewhere. (Of course, you can't apply styles in text-only documents.)

## Tables

*Tables* can make life a heck of a lot easier when you want to create a résumé, agenda, program booklet, list, multiple-choice test, Web page, or another document where numbers, words, and phrases must be aligned across the page. In the bad old days, people did it by pressing the Tab key to line up columns—a technique that turned into a nightmare as soon as you tried to add or delete text. But using a word processor's *table* feature is light-years easier and more flexible, because each row of a table expands infinitely to contain whatever you put into it. Everything else on its row remains aligned.

*Tip:* Tables are also critical for designing Web pages, as any Web designer can tell you. Even though you can't see the table outlines, many a Web page is filled with columns of text that are aligned invisibly by tables. And now that TextEdit can save your work as an HTML document, it's suddenly a viable candidate for designing basic Web pages.

- **Create a table** by choosing Format→Text→Table. The floating Table palette appears (Figure 16-20). Use it to specify how many rows and columns you want. The placeholder table in your document adjusts itself in real time.

- **Format the table** using the other controls in the Table palette. The Alignment controls let you specify how the text in one of the table cells hugs its border. Cell Border controls the thickness of the line around the selected cells' borders (or, if you enter 0, makes the table walls invisible). The color swatch next to Cell Border specifies the color of the solid lines. The Cell Background controls let you color in the table cells with colors of your choice. (Choose Color Fill from the pop-up menu, and then click the color swatch.) This is an especially valuable option for Web designers.

- **Adjust the rows and columns** by dragging the cell borders.

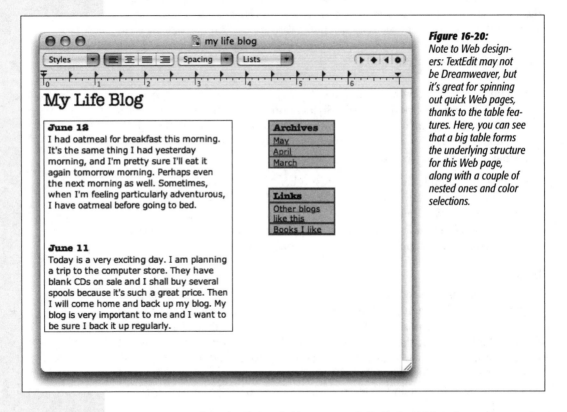

*Figure 16-20:*
*Note to Web design-*
*ers: TextEdit may not*
*be Dreamweaver, but*
*it's great for spinning*
*out quick Web pages,*
*thanks to the table fea-*
*tures. Here, you can see*
*that a big table forms*
*the underlying structure*
*for this Web page,*
*along with a couple of*
*nested ones and color*
*selections.*

- **Merge two selected cells** by clicking Merge Cells in the Table palette. Once you've done that, you can use the Split Cell button to split them apart again. (Split Cell doesn't work except in cells you've previously merged.)

- **Nest one table inside a cell of another** by clicking in the cell and then clicking Nest Table. Change the numbers in the Rows and Columns boxes to set up its dimensions (Figure 16-20).

## TextEdit as Web Designer

The Table palette isn't the only clue that Apple intends TextEdit to be a quick-and-dirty Web page design program. Consider these other tools:

- You can easily add graphics to the page by dragging or pasting them into a document. The program understands TIFF, PICT, JPG, and GIF formats.

- You can add Web-style hyperlinks by highlighting "Click here" (or whatever the link says), choosing Format→Text→Link, and entering the Web address in the resulting dialog box. Or just drag a link in from Safari, Mail, or another program. (To edit the link later, right-click it, and then choose Edit Link.)

- To save a document as an HTML (Web page) file, choose File→Save As; from the File Format pop-up menu, choose Web Archive.

- Don't miss the HTML options in TextEdit→Preferences. On the "Open and Save" tab, you can specify what kind of HTML document you want to produce, what cascading style sheets (CSS) setting you want, and whether or not you want TextEdit to include code to preserve blank areas (white space) in your layout.

---

*Tip:* When you *open* a Web page document—that is, an HTML document—TextEdit is faced with a quandary. Should it open up the page as though it's a Web page, interpreting the HTML code as though it's a browser? Or should it reveal the underlying HTML code itself?

Actually, that's up to you. When you choose File→Open, turn on "Ignore rich text commands" to make the document open up as HTML code. (To make this change permanent, turn on the same checkbox on the "Open and Save" pane of the TextEdit→Preferences dialog box.)

---

## Time Machine

This marquee feature of Leopard is described in Chapter 9.

## Utilities: Your Mac OS X Toolbox

The Utilities folder (inside your Applications folder) is home to another batch of freebies: another couple of dozen tools for monitoring, tuning, tweaking, and troubleshooting your Mac.

The truth is, you're likely to use only a few of these utilities. The rest are very specialized gizmos primarily of interest to network administrators or Unix geeks who are obsessed with knowing what kind of computer-code gibberish is going on behind the scenes.

---

*Tip:* Even so, Apple obviously noticed that as the sophistication of Mac OS X fans grows, more people open the Utilities folder more often. That's why there's a menu command and a keystroke that can take you there. In the Finder, choose Go→Utilities (Shift-⌘-U).

---

## Activity Monitor

Activity Monitor is designed to let the technologically savvy Mac fan see how much of the Mac's available power is being tapped at any given moment.

### The Processes table

Even when you're only running a program or two on your Mac, dozens of computational tasks (*processes*) are going on in the background. The top half of the dialog box, which looks like a table, shows you all the different processes—visible and invisible—that your Mac is handling at the moment.

Check out how many items appear in the Process list, even when you're just staring at the desktop. It's awesome to see just how busy your Mac is! Some are easily recognizable programs (such as Finder), while others are background system-level operations you don't normally see. For each item, you can see the percentage of CPU being used, who's using it (either your account name, someone else's, or *root,* meaning the Mac itself), and how much memory it's using.

Or use the pop-up menu above the list to see:

- **All Processes.** This is the complete list of running processes; you'll notice that the vast majority are little Unix applications you never even knew you had.

- **My Processes.** This list shows only the programs that pertain to *your* world—your login. There are still plenty of unfamiliar items, but they're all running to serve *your* account.

- **Windowed Processes.** Now *this* is probably what you were expecting: a list of actual programs with actual English names, like Activity Monitor, Finder, Safari, and Mail. These are the only ones running in actual windows, the only ones that are *visible,* which is what most people probably think of as programs.

### The System monitor tabs

At the bottom of Activity Monitor, you're offered five tabs that reveal intimate details about your Mac and its behind-the-scenes efforts (Figure 16-21):

- **CPU.** As you go about your usual Mac business, opening a few programs, dragging a playing QuickTime movie across the screen, playing a game, and so on, you can see the CPU graph rise and fall, depending on how busy you're keeping the CPU. On multiple-processor Macs, you see a different bar for each chip, enabling you to see how efficiently Mac OS X is distributing the work among them.

---

***Tip:*** You may also want to watch this graph right in your Dock (choose View→Dock Icon→Show CPU History) or in a bar at the edge of your screen (choose Window→Floating CPU Window→ Horizontally).

Finally, there's the weirdly uncapitalized command View→"Show CPU monitors on top of other windows." It makes the little bar float on top of all your other programs, so you can't miss it.

---

- **System Memory.** Here's a colorful graph that reveals the state of your Mac's RAM at the moment.

The number below the graph shows how much memory is installed in your Mac. If, when your Mac is running a typical complement of programs, the Wired number plus the Active number nearly equals your total RAM amount, it's time to consider buying more memory. You're suffocating your Mac.

- **Disk Activity.** Even when you're not opening or saving a file, your Mac's hard drive is frequently hard at work, shuffling chunks of program code into and out of memory, for example. Here's where the savvy technician can see exactly how frantic the disk is at the moment.

**Figure 16-21:**
*The many faces of Activity Monitor.*

*Top: It can be a graph of your processor (CPU) activity, your RAM usage at the moment, your disk capacity, and so on. For most people, only the processes listed here with tiny icons beside their names are actual windowed programs—those with icons in the Finder, the ones you actually interact with.*

*Don't miss the top-left Quit button. It's a convenient way to jettison a locked-up program when all else fails.*

*Bottom: If you double-click a process's name, you get a three-tab dialog box that offers stunningly complete reams of data (mostly of interest only to programmers) about what that program is up to. (The Open Files and Ports tab, for example, shows you how many files that program has opened, often invisibly.)*

- **Disk Usage.** This little graph offers one of the quickest ways to check out how full your hard drive is at the moment. (If you have more than one drive—say, a flash drive, tape-backup drive, or whatever—choose another drive's name from the pop-up menu.)

- **Network.** Keep an eye on how much data is shooting across your office network with this handy EKG-ish graph.

## AirPort Utility

You use the AirPort Utility to set up and manage AirPort base stations (Apple's line of wireless Wi-Fi networking routers).

If you click Continue, it presents a series of screens, posing one question at a time: what you want to name the network, what password you want for it, and so on. Once you've followed the steps and answered the questions, your AirPort hardware will be properly configured and ready to use.

## Bluetooth File Exchange

One of the luxuries of using a Mac that has Bluetooth is the ability to shoot files (to colleagues who own similarly clever gadgets) through the air, up to 30 feet away. Bluetooth File Exchange makes it possible, as described on page 441.

## Disk Utility

This important program serves two key functions:

- It serves as Mac OS X's own little Norton Utilities: a powerful hard drive administration tool that lets you repair, erase, format, and partition disks. In everyday life, you'll probably use Disk Utility most often for its *Repair Permissions* feature, which solves an uncanny number of weird little Mac OS X glitches. But it's also worth keeping in mind, in case you ever find yourself facing a serious disk problem.

- Disk Utility also creates and manages *disk images,* electronic versions of disks or folders that you can exchange electronically with other people.

The following discussion tackles the program's two personalities one at a time.

### Disk Utility, the hard drive–repair program

Here are some of the tasks you can perform with this half of Disk Utility:

- Repair folders, files, and program that don't work because you supposedly don't have sufficient "access privileges." This is by far the most common use of Disk Utility, not to mention the most reliable and satisfying. Using the Repair Disk Permissions button fixes an *astonishing* range of bizarre Mac OS X problems, from programs that won't open to menulets that freeze up the works.

- Get size and type information about any disks attached to your Mac.

- Fix disks that won't appear on your desktop or behave properly.

- Completely erase disks—including rewritable CDs and DVDs (such as CD-RW and DVD-RW discs).

- Partition a disk into multiple *volumes* (that is, subdivide a drive so that its segments appear on the desktop with separate disk icons).

---

**Tip:** In Leopard, for the first time in Mac history, Disk Utility can create or enlarge disk partitions without requiring you to erase the entire hard drive. Details below.

---

- Set up a *RAID array* (a cluster of separate disks that acts as a single volume).

---

**Note:** Disk Utility can perform *some* of its magic on the startup disk—the disk that's running Mac OS X at the moment. For example, it can check the disk for damage, fix the *permissions* of the disk, or even adjust its partitions.

But any other operation, like reformatting, erasing, or actually repairing the disk, still requires the Mac to start up from a different disk (your Leopard DVD, for example). Otherwise, it'd be like a surgeon performing an appendectomy on himself—not a great idea.

---

The left Disk Utility panel lists your hard drive and any other disks in or attached to your Mac at the moment. When you click the name of your hard drive's mechanism, like "74.5 GB Hitachi iC25N0…" (not the "Macintosh HD" partition label below it), you see a panel with five tabs, one for each of the main Disk Utility functions:

- **First Aid**. This is the disk-repair part of Disk Utility, and it does a terrific job at fixing many disk problems. When you're troubleshooting, Disk Utility should always be your first resort.

  To use it, click the icon of a disk and then click either Verify Disk (to get a report on the disk's health) or Repair Disk (which fixes whatever problems the program finds). In other words, First Aid attempts to perform the same healing effects on a sick hard drive as, say, a program like Norton Utilities.

  If Disk First Aid reports that it's unable to fix the problem, *then* it's time to invest in a program like DiskWarrior (*www.alsoft.com*).

---

**Tip:** If Disk Utility finds nothing wrong with a disk, it reports, "The volume appears to be OK." Don't be alarmed at the not-so-congratulatory wording of that message—that's the strongest vote of confidence Disk Utility can give.

---

You may wind up using the Verify and Repair Disk *Permissions* buttons even more often. Their function is to straighten out problems with the invisible Unix file permissions that keep you from moving, changing, or deleting files or folders. (The occasional software installer can create problems like this.) You'd be surprised how often running one of these permission checks solves little Mac OS X glitches.

Chapter 14 has a much more detailed discussion of permissions.

- **Erase.** Select a disk, choose a format (*always* Mac OS Extended [Journaled], unless you're formatting a disk for use on a Windows machine or an ancient Mac running Mac OS 8.1 or earlier), give it a name, and click Erase to wipe a disk clean.

- **Partition.** With the Partition tools, you can erase a hard drive in such a way that you subdivide its surface. Each chunk is represented on your screen by another hard drive icon (Figure 16-22).

**Figure 16-22:**
*Partitioning your drive with Disk Utility no longer involves erasing it completely. Select the drive you want to partition from the list on the left, and click the Partition tab. Click the + button for each new partition you want.*

*Now drag the horizontal dividers in the Volumes map to specify the relative sizes of the partitions you want to create. Assign a name and format for each partition in the Volume Information area, and then click Apply.*

There are some very good reasons *not* to partition a drive these days: A partitioned hard drive is more difficult to resurrect after a serious crash, requires more navigation when you want to open a particular file, and offers no speed or safety benefits.

On the other hand, there's one very good reason *to* do it: Partitioning is the only way to use Boot Camp, described as Chapter 8. Your Mac is a Mac when running off of the first partition, and a Windows PC when starting up from the second one.

- **RAID.** RAID stands for Redundant Array of Independent Disks, and refers to a special formatting scheme in which a group of separate disks are configured to work together as one very large, very fast drive. In a RAID array, multiple disks share the job of storing data—a setup that can improve speed and reliability.

Most Mac users don't use or set up RAID arrays, probably because most Mac users only have one hard drive (and Disk Utility can't make your startup disk part of a RAID array).

If you're using multiple external hard disks, though, you can use Apple RAID to merge them into one giant disk. Just drag the icons of the relevant disks (or disk partitions) from the left-side list of disks into the main list (where it says, "Drag disks or volumes here to add to set"). Use the RAID Type pop-up menu to specify the RAID format you want to use (Stripe is a popular choice for maximizing disk speed), name your new mega-disk, and then click Create. The result is a single "disk" icon on your desktop that actually represents the combined capacity of all the RAID disks.

- **Restore.** This tab lets you make a perfect copy of a disk or a disk image, much like the popular shareware programs CarbonCopy Cloner and SuperDuper. You might find this useful when, for example, you want to make an exact copy of your old Mac's drive on your new one. You can't do that just by copying your old files and folders manually. If you try, you won't get the thousands of *invisible* files that make up Mac OS X. If you use the Restore function, they'll come along for the ride.

---

**POWER USERS' CLINIC**

## Partition Adjustments on the Fly

In Leopard, for the first time, you can expand, shrink, or create partitions without having to erase the whole hard drive. If you're into partitioning at all, this is a *huge* convenience.

**Expanding a partition.** Suppose, for example, that your main hard drive has two partitions: a main one (200 gigs) and a secondary one (50 gigs) that used to hold all your photos and movies. But you've outgrown the second partition, and have moved all those photos and movies to their own external hard drive. Wouldn't it be nice to add the newly unoccupied 50 gigs to your main partition?

You can do that without having to erase the whole hard drive. (This process, however, nukes everything on the *second* partition, so make sure you're prepared to lose it all.)

Open Disk Utility. Click the name of the hard drive (for example, "Hitachi HTS541616J9SA00"–*not* "Macintosh HD"). Click Partition. You see a display like the one in Figure 16-29.

Click the second partition (or third, or whatever partition is *just after* the one you want to expand) and then click the – button below the list. Poof! It's gone.

Now you can drag the main partition's bottom edge downward (or type a new size into the Size box), expanding it into the free area. Take a deep breath, and then click Apply.

**Shrinking a partition.** In Figure 16-29, you can see that a portion of the first partition is lightly shaded. (It's blue in real life.) The blue represents data; you can't shrink a partition so much that it crowds out your files. You can, however, shrink the partition to eliminate empty space. Just drag the lower edge of its map chunk upward.

**Creating new partitions.** Any time there's leftover space on the drive, you can create *new* partitions from it.

To do that, click the + button, and proceed as described in Figure 16-29.

---

Start by dragging the disk or disk image you want to copy *from* into the Source box. Then drag the icon of the disk you want to copy *to* into the Destination box.

---

***Tip:*** If you want to copy an *online* disk image onto one of your disks, you don't have to download it first. Just type its Web address into the Source field. You might find this trick convenient if you keep disk images on your iDisk, for example.

---

If you turn on Erase Destination, Disk Utility obliterates all the data on your target disk before copying the data. If you leave this checkbox off, however, Disk Utility simply copies everything onto your destination, preserving all your old data in the process. (The Skip Checksum checkbox is available only if you choose to erase your destination disk. If you're confident that all of the files on the source disk are 100% healthy and whole, turn on this checkbox to save time. Otherwise, leave it off for extra safety.)

Finally, click the Restore button. (You might need to type in an administrator password.) Restoring can take a long time for big disks, so go ahead and make yourself a cup of coffee while you're waiting.

---

***Tip:*** Instead of clicking a disk icon and then clicking the appropriate Disk Utility tab, you can just right-click a disk's name and choose Information, First Aid, Erase, Partition, RAID, or Restore from the shortcut menu.

---

### Disk Utility, the disk-image program

The world's largest fan of *disk images* is Apple itself; the company often releases new software in disk-image form. A lot of Mac OS X add-on software arrives from your Web download in disk-image form, too, as shown below.

Disk images are popular for software distribution for a simple reason: Each image file precisely duplicates the original master disk, complete with all the necessary files in all the right places. When a software company sends you a disk image, it ensures that you'll install the software from a disk that *exactly* matches the master disk.

It's important to understand the difference between a *disk-image file* and the *mounted disk* (the one that appears when you double-click the disk image). If you flip back to page 147 and consult Figure 4-19, this distinction should be clear.

---

***Tip:*** After you double-click a disk image, click Skip in the verification box that appears. If something truly got scrambled during the download, you'll know about it right away—your file won't decompress correctly, or it'll display the wrong icon, for example.

In fact, you can make Disk Utility *always* skip that verification business, which is a relic from the days of floppy disks. To do so, choose Disk Utility→Preferences, and turn off "Check images on locked media."

---

*You* can create disk images, too. Doing so can be very handy in situations like the following:

- You want to create a backup of an important CD. By turning it into a disk-image file on your hard drive, you'll always have a safety copy, ready to burn back onto a *new* CD. (This is an essential practice for educational CDs that kids will be handling soon after eating peanut butter and jelly.)

- You want to replicate your entire hard drive—complete with all of its files, programs, folder setups, and so on—onto a new, bigger hard drive (or a new, better Mac), using the Restore feature described earlier.

- You want to back up your entire hard drive, or maybe just a certain chunk of it, onto an iPod or another disk. (Again, you can later use the Restore function to complete the transaction.)

- You bought a game that requires its CD to be in the drive at all times. Many programs like these run equally well off of a mounted disk image that you made from the original CD.

- You want to send somebody else a copy of a disk via the Internet. You simply create a disk image, and then send *that*—preferably in compressed form.

Here's how you make a disk image.

- **To image-ize a disk or partition.** Click the name of the disk in the left-panel list, where you see the disks currently in, or attached to, your Mac. (The topmost item is the name of your *drive,* like "484.0 MB MATSHITA DVD-R" for a DVD drive or "74.5 GB Hitachi" for a hard drive. Beneath that entry, you generally see the name of the actual partition, like "Macintosh HD," or the CD's name as it appears on the screen.)

  Then choose File→New→Disk Image from [the disk or partition's name].

- **To image-ize a folder.** Choose File→New→Disk Image from Folder. In the Open dialog box, click the folder you want and then click Image.

---

*Tip:* Disk Utility can't turn an individual *file* into a disk image. But you can put a single file into a folder, and then make a disk image of *it*.

---

Either way, the next dialog box (Figure 16-23) offers some fascinating options.

**Figure 16-23:**
*These two pop-up menus let you specify (a) what kind of disk image you want, and (b) whether or not you want it password-protected. The latter option is great when you want to password-protect one folder, without bothering with your entire Home folder.*

• **Image Format.** If you choose "read/write," your disk image file, when double-clicked, turns into a superb imitation of a hard drive. You can drag files and folders onto it, drag them off of it, change icons' names on it, and so on.

If you choose "read-only," however, the result behaves more like a CD. You can copy things off of it, but not make any changes to it.

The "compressed" option is best if you intend to send the resulting file by email, post it for Web download, or preserve the disk image on some backup disk for a rainy day. It takes a little longer to create a simulated disk when you double-click the disk image file, but it takes up a lot less disk space than an uncompressed version.

Finally, choose "DVD/CD master" if you're copying a CD or a DVD. The resulting file is a perfect mirror of the original disc, ready for copying onto a blank CD or DVD when the time comes.

• **Encryption.** Here's an easy way to lock private files away into a vault that nobody else can open. If you choose one of these two AES encryption options (choose AES-128, if you value your time), you're asked to assign a password to your new image file. Nobody can open it without the password—not even you. On the other hand, if you save it into your Keychain (page 409), it's not such a disaster if you forget the password.

• **Save As.** Choose a name and location for your new image file. The name you choose here doesn't need to match the original disk or folder name.

When you click Save (or press Enter), if you opted to create an encrypted image, you're asked to make up a password at this point.

Otherwise, Disk Utility now creates the image and then *mounts* it—that is, turns the image file into a simulated, yet fully functional, disk icon on your desktop.

When you're finished working with the disk, eject it as you would any disk (right-click it and choose Eject, for example). Hang onto the .dmg disk image file itself, however. This is the file you'll need to double-click if you ever want to recreate your "simulated disk."

### Turning an image into a CD

One of the other most common disk-image tasks is turning a disk image *back* into a CD or DVD—provided you have a CD or DVD burner on your Mac, of course.

All you have to do is drag the .dmg file into the Disk Utility window, select it, and click the Burn icon on the toolbar (or, alternatively, right-click the .dmg icon and choose Burn from the shortcut menu). Insert a blank CD or DVD, and then click Burn.

## Grab

Grab takes pictures of your Mac's screen, for use when you're writing up instructions, illustrating a computer book, or collecting proof of some secret screen you found buried in a game. You can take pictures of the entire screen (press ⌘-Z, which for once in its life does *not* mean Undo) or capture only the contents of a rectangular selection (press Shift-⌘-A). When you're finished, Grab displays your snapshot in a new window, which you can print, close without saving, or save as a TIFF file, ready for emailing or inserting into a manuscript.

Now, as experienced Mac enthusiasts already know, the Mac OS has long had its *own* built-in shortcuts for capturing screenshots: Press Shift-⌘-3 to take a picture of the whole screen, and Shift-⌘-4 to capture a rectangular selection.

(Page 208 has a complete list of the variations.)

So why use Grab instead? In many cases, you shouldn't. The Shift-⌘-3 and Shift-⌘-4 shortcuts work like a dream. But there are some cases in which it might make more sense to opt for Grab. Here are three:

- Grab can make a *timed* screen capture (choose Capture→Timed Screen, or press Shift-⌘-Z), which lets you enjoy a 10-second delay before the screenshot is actually taken. After you click the Start Timer button, you have an opportunity to activate windows, pull down menus, drag items around, and otherwise set up the shot before Grab shoots the picture.

- When you capture a screenshot using Grab's Selection command, the *size* of your selection is displayed, in pixels, right under the pointer as you drag. If you need to capture a 256-pixel-wide square, for example, you can do so with pinpoint accuracy. (Choose Edit→Inspector to read the dimensions of a screenshot *after* you capture it.)

- With Grab, you have the option of including the cursor in the picture, which is extremely useful when you're showing a menu being pulled down or a button being clicked. (Mac OS X's screenshot keystrokes, by contrast, always eliminate the pointer.) Use the technique described in Figure 16-24 to add the pointer style of your choice to a Grab screenshot.

**Figure 16-24:**
*Unlike the Shift-⌘-3 or Shift-⌘-4 keystrokes, Grab lets you include the pointer/cursor in the picture—or hide it. Choose Grab→Preferences and pick one of the eight different pointer styles, or choose to keep the pointer hidden by activating the blank button in the upper-left corner.*

**Tip:** Actually, if you're going to write a book or manual about Mac OS X, the program you really need is Snapz Pro X; a trial version is available from this book's "Missing CD" at *www.missingmanuals.com,* among other places. It offers far more flexibility than any of Mac OS X's own screenshot features. For example, you have a choice of file format, you can neatly snip out just one dialog box or window with a single click, and you can even capture *movies* of screen activity.

## Grapher

This equation grapher is an *amazing* piece of work.

When you first open Grapher, you're asked to choose what kind of virtual "graph paper" you want: two-dimensional (standard, polar, logarithmic) or three-dimensional (cubic, spherical, cylindrical). Click a name to see a preview; when you're happy with the selection, click Open.

Now the main Grapher window appears (Figure 16-25). Do yourself a favor: Spend a few wow-inducing minutes choosing canned equations from the Examples menu, and watching how Grapher whips up gorgeous, colorful, sometimes animated graphs on the fly.

**Figure 16-25:**
*In general, you type equations into Grapher just as you would on paper (like z=2xy). If in doubt, check the online help, which offers enough hints on functions, constants, differential equations, series, and periodic equations to keep the* A Beautiful Mind *guy busy for days.*

When you're ready to plug in an equation of your own, type it into the text box at the top of the window. (If you're not such a math hotshot, or you're not sure of the equation format, work from the canned equations and mathematical building blocks that appear when you choose Equation→New Equation from Template or Window→Show Equation Palette.)

Once the graph is up on the screen, you can tailor it like this:

- To move a 2-D graph in the window, choose View→Move Tool and then drag; to move a 3-D graph, ⌘-drag it.

- To rotate a 3-D graph, drag it around.

- To change the colors, line thicknesses, 3-D "walls," and other graphic elements, click the ❶ button (or choose Window→Show Inspector) to open the formatting palette. The controls you find here vary by graph type, but rest assured that Grapher can accommodate your every visual whim.

- To change the fonts and sizes, choose Grapher→Preferences. On the Equations panel, the four sliders let you specify the relative sizes of the text elements. If you click the sample equation, the Font panel appears (page 241), so you can fiddle with the type.

- Add your own captions, arrows, ovals, or rectangles using the Object menu.

## Keychain Access

Keychain Access memorizes and stores all your secret information—passwords for network access, file servers, FTP sites, Web pages, and other secure items. For instructions on using Keychain Access, see Chapter 13.

## Migration Assistant

This little cutie automates the transfer of all your stuff from one Mac to another—your Home folder, network settings, programs, and more. This comes in extremely handy when you buy a newer, better Mac—or when you need Time Machine to recover an entire dead Mac's worth of data. (It can also copy everything over from a secondary hard drive or partition.)

The instructions on the screen guide you through the setup process; then the Assistant automates the transfer.

## System Profiler

System Profiler is a great tool for learning exactly what's installed on your Mac and what's not—in terms of both hardware and software. The people who answer the phones on Apple's tech-support line are particularly fond of System Profiler, since the detailed information it reports can be very useful for troubleshooting nasty problems.

There are now three ways to open System Profiler:

- **Slow.** Burrow into your Applications→Utilities folder; double-click System Profiler.

- **Medium.** Choose  →About This Mac. In the resulting dialog box, click More Info.

---

*Tip:* If you click your Mac OS X version number twice in the About box, you get to see your Mac's serial number!

---

- **Fast.** Hold down the Option key, which makes the  →About This Mac command *change* to say System Profiler. Choose it.

When you launch System Profiler, it reports information about your Mac in a categorized list down the left side (Figure 16-26).

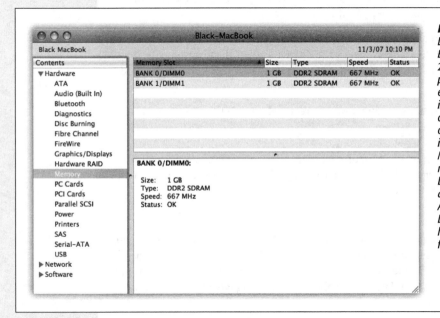

**Figure 16-26:**
*Does your Mac-Book's chip run at 2 Ghz or 2.6? What percentage of your external hard drive is filled up? Want a comprehensive list of every program installed on your Mac, with version numbers? Can your DVD burner burn dual-layer discs? And (shown here): Does your laptop have any open slots for extra RAM?*

## Terminal

Mac OS X's resemblance to an attractive, mainstream operating system like Windows is just an optical illusion; the engine underneath the pretty skin is Unix, one of the oldest and most respected operating systems in use today. And Terminal is the rabbit hole that leads you—if you're technically bold—straight down into the Mac's powerful Unix world.

The first time you see it, you'd swear that Unix has about as much in common with the Mac OS X illustrated in the other chapters of this book as a Jeep does with a watermelon. It's a *command line interface:* a place where you can type out instructions to the computer itself. This is a world without icons, menus, or dialog boxes; even the mouse is almost useless.

Surely you can appreciate the irony: The brilliance of the original 1984 Macintosh was that it *eliminated* the command line interface that was still the ruling party on the computers of the day (like Apple II and DOS machines). Most non-geeks sighed with relief, delighted that they'd never have to memorize commands again. Yet here's Mac OS X, Apple's supposedly ultramodern operating system, complete with a command line! What's going on?

Actually, the command line never went away. At universities and corporations worldwide, professional computer nerds kept right on pounding away at the little *C:* or % prompts, appreciating the efficiency and power such direct computer control afforded them.

Now, you never *have* to use Mac OS X's command line. In fact, Apple has swept it far under the rug, obviously expecting that most people will use the beautiful icons and menus of the regular desktop.

For intermediate or advanced computer fans with a little time and curiosity, however, the command line opens up a world of possibilities. It lets you access corners of Mac OS X that you can't get to from the regular desktop. It lets you perform certain tasks with much greater speed and efficiency than you'd get by clicking and dragging icons. And it gives you a fascinating glimpse into the minds and moods of people who live and breathe computers.

### A Terminal crash course

The first time you open Terminal, you'll notice that there's not much in its window except the date and time of your last login, a welcome message, and the "$" (the command line prompt).

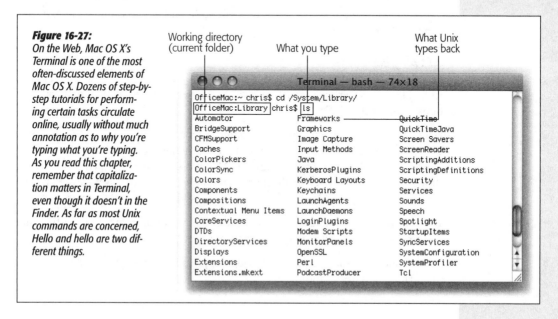

**Figure 16-27:**
*On the Web, Mac OS X's Terminal is one of the most often-discussed elements of Mac OS X. Dozens of step-by-step tutorials for performing certain tasks circulate online, usually without much annotation as to why you're typing what you're typing. As you read this chapter, remember that capitalization matters in Terminal, even though it doesn't in the Finder. As far as most Unix commands are concerned, Hello and hello are two different things.*

For user-friendliness fans, Terminal doesn't get off to a very good start—this prompt looks about as technical as computers get. It breaks down like this (see Figure 16-27):

- **office-mac:** is the name of your Mac (at least, as Unix thinks of it), as recorded in the Sharing panel of System Preferences.

- **~.** The next part of the prompt indicates what folder you're "in" (Figure 16-27). It denotes the *working directory*—that is, the current folder. (Remember, there are no icons in Unix.) Essentially, this notation tells you where you are as you navigate your machine.

The very first time you try out Terminal, the working directory is set to the symbol ~, which is shorthand for "your own Home folder." It's what you see the first time you start up Terminal, but you'll soon be seeing the names of other folders here— *[office-mac: /Users]* or *[office-mac: /System/Library]*, for example. (The slashes show you which folders are inside which other folders.)

---

**Note:** Before Apple came up with the user-friendly term *folder* to represent an electronic holding tank for files, folders were called *directories*. (Yes, they mean the same thing.) But in any discussion of Unix, "directory" is the correct term.

---

- **chris$** begins with your short user name. It reflects whoever's logged into the *shell* (the current terminal "session"), which is usually whoever's logged into the *Mac* at the moment. As for the $ sign: Think of it as a colon. In fact, think of the whole prompt shown in Figure 16-36 as Unix's way of asking, "OK, Chris, I'm listening. What's your pleasure?"

The insertion point looks like a tall rectangle at the end of the command line. It trots along to the right as you type.

### Unix programs

Each Unix command generally calls up a single application (or *process,* as geeks call it) that launches, performs a task, and closes. Many of the best-known such applications come with Mac OS X.

Here's a fun one: Just type *uptime* (capitalization counts in Unix) and press Enter. That's how you run a Unix program: just type its name and press Enter. On the next line, Terminal shows you how long your Mac has been turned on continuously. It shows you something like: "6:00PM up 8 days, 15:04, 1 user, load averages: 1.24, 1.37, 1.45"—meaning your Mac has been running for 8 days, 15 hours nonstop.

You're finished running the *uptime* program. The $ prompt returns, suggesting that Terminal is ready for whatever you throw at it next.

Try this one: Type *cal* at the prompt, and then press Enter. Unix promptly spits out a calendar of the current month.

```
office-mac:~ chris$ cal
        May 2008
Su Mo Tu We Th Fr Sa
             1  2  3
 4  5  6  7  8  9 10
11 12 13 14 15 16 17
18 19 20 21 22 23 24
25 26 27 28 29 30 31

office-mac:~ chris$
```

This time, try typing *cal 6 2008, cal -y,* or *cal -yj.* These three commands make Unix generate a calendar of June 2008, a calendar of the current year, and a calendar of *Julian* days of the current year, respectively.

### Navigating in Unix

If you can't see any icons for your files and folders, how are you supposed to work with them?

You use Unix commands like *pwd* (tells you what folder you're looking at), *ls* (lists what's *in* the current folder), and *cd* (changes to a different folder).

---

***Tip:*** As you can tell by these examples, Unix commands are very short. They're often just two-letter commands, and an impressive number of those use *alternate hands* (ls, cp, rm, and so on).

---

### Getting help

Mac OS X comes with over 1,200 Unix programs. How are you supposed to learn what they all do? Fortunately, almost every Unix program comes with a help file. It may not appear within an elegant, gradient-gray Leopard window—in fact, it's pretty darned plain—but it offers much more material than the regular Mac Help Center.

These user-manual pages, or *manpages,* hold descriptions of virtually every command and program available. Mac OS X, in fact, comes with manpages on almost 9,000 topics—over 30,000 printed pages' worth.

Unfortunately, manpages rarely have the clarity of writing or the learner-focused approach you'll find in the Mac Help Center. They're generally terse, just-the-facts descriptions. In fact, you'll probably find yourself needing to reread certain sections again and again. The information they contain, however, is invaluable to new and experienced users alike, and the effort spent mining them is usually worthwhile.

To access the manpage for a given command, type *man* followed by the name of the command you're researching. For example, to view the manpage for the *ls* command, enter: *man ls.* Now the manual appears, one screen at a time.

For more information on using *man,* view its *own* manpage by entering—what else?—*man man.*

---

*Tip:* The free program ManOpen, available for download from the "Missing CD" page of *www.missing manuals.com,* is a Cocoa manual-pages reader that provides a nice-looking, easier-to-control window for reading manpages.

### Learning more

Unix is, of course, an entire operating system unto itself. If you get bit by the bug, here are some sources of additional Unix info:

- *www.ee.surrey.ac.uk/Teaching/Unix.* A convenient, free Web-based course in Unix for beginners.

- *www.megazone.org/Computers/manual.shtml.* A fast-paced, more advanced introduction.

- *Learning Unix for Mac OS X Tiger,* by Dave Taylor & Brian Jepson (O'Reilly Media). A compact, relatively user-friendly tour of the Mac's Unix base.

*Tip:* Typing *unix for beginners* into a search page like Google.com nets dozens of superb help, tutorial, and reference Web sites. If possible, stick to those that feature the *bash shell.* That way, everything you learn online should be perfectly applicable to navigating Mac OS X via Terminal.

# Part Five: Appendixes

5

**Appendix A: Installation & Troubleshooting**

**Appendix B: The "Where'd It Go?" Dictionary**

**Appendix C: The Master Mac OS X Secret Keystroke List**

# Installation & Troubleshooting

I f you're lucky, this is a wasted chapter. After all, you'll probably never have to install Mac OS X (assuming it came preinstalled on your Mac), and in the best of all technological worlds, you won't have to do much troubleshooting, either. But here's this appendix, anyway—just in case.

## Getting Ready to Install

For starters, you need to make sure that you and your Mac have what it takes to handle Mac OS X—specifically:

- **A Macintosh with a G4, G5, or Intel processor.** Basically, most Macs manufactured since the end of 2004 are eligible, which isn't bad at all.

- **Plenty of free hard disk space.** You need 9 GB free to install the full Mac OS X 10.5—less if you decline to install all the optional languages and printer drivers (more on this in a moment).

- **A lot of memory.** Apple recommends at least 512 MB of memory, but for the greatest speed, install 1 gigabyte—2 or more if you can afford it. (And these days, you probably can.)

- **The latest firmware.** *Firmware* describes the low-level, underlying software instructions that control the actual circuitry of your Mac. Every now and then, Apple updates it for certain Mac models, and it's very important that your Mac has the absolute latest. If yours doesn't, a message will appear to let you know during the Leopard installation. Some Macs might just spit the DVD right out. Quit the installer and grab the latest updater from *www.apple.com/support/downloads*.

• **A copy of Leopard to install.** Apple sells Leopard in several ways. There's the regular Leopard DVD, for example, and there's the Family Pack, which authorizes you to install Leopard on up to five Macs in the same household. (Neither version is copy-protected or requires any kind of serial number, which is a nice change from Windows; only the honor system stops you from installing on a sixth Mac.)

And then there's the version that comes with every new Mac. It's labeled Mac OS X Leopard Disc 1, but it's the same thing as the sold-separately DVD. (Disc 2, in this case, contains all the other programs that come with a new Mac, like the iLife software suite.)

## Three Kinds of Installation

The Mac OS X installer can perform a number of different installations. For example, it can put a copy of Mac OS X 10.5 onto a hard drive that currently has:

• **Nothing on it.** If you one day have to erase your hard drive completely—because it's completely hosed, or, less drastically, because you've bought a new, empty external hard drive—this is how to do it. See "Erase & Install," on page 541, for a step-by-step guide.

• **Mac OS X 10.0 through 10.4.** The Leopard installer can turn your older copy of Mac OS X *into* the 10.5 version, in the process maintaining all of your older preferences, fonts, documents, accounts, and so on. See "The Upgrade Installation" on page 540.

On the other hand, a substantial body of evidence (specifically, hundreds of moaning Mac fans online) points to the wisdom of performing a *clean install,* rather than an upgrade installation. (Apple calls the clean install the "Archive & Install" option.) A clean installation provides a healthier, more glitch-proof copy of 10.5. See "The Clean Install" on page 540.

• **Mac OS X 10.5.** In times of dire troubleshooting, when nothing in Appendix B has helped, you can actually give yourself a *fresh copy* of 10.5, even though it's already on the hard drive. See "The Clean Install" on page 540.

## The Basic Installation

The installation process takes about 45 minutes, but for the sake of your own psyche, you'll probably want to set aside a whole afternoon. Once the installation is over, you'll want to play around, organize your files, and learn the lay of the land.

### Phase 1: The Installer

Here's how you install Leopard onto a drive that doesn't have a version of Mac OS X on it already:

1. **Insert the Mac OS X DVD. Double-click the Install Mac OS X icon in the disc's main window. When the Restart button appears, click it.**

The Mac starts up from the disc and takes you directly to the first Installer screen.

The installer soon falls into a pattern: Read the instructions, make a couple of choices, and click Continue to advance to the next screen. As you go, the list on the left side of the screen reveals where you are in the overall procedure.

---

**Tip:** You can back out of the installation at any time before step 5, just by choosing Installer→Quit Installer. When the Restart button appears, click it. Then eject the Mac OS X disc, either by holding down the mouse button while the computer restarts or, if you have a tray-loading CD drive, by pushing its Eject button during the moment of darkness during the restart.

---

2. **Work your way through the Select Language screen, Welcome screen, and Software License Agreement screens, clicking Continue each time.**

Note that once you're past the Select Language screen, the Mac OS X Installer menu bar becomes available. In the Utilities menu are some very useful commands; they let you jump directly into programs like Disk Utility (to erase or partition your hard drive), Terminal (to do some Unixy preparatory steps), System Profiler (to see how much memory this machine has), Reset Password (if you've forgotten yours), and more.

If you do decide to take that detour to another program, when you quit it, you'll return to the Installer program, right where you left off.

The Software License Agreement requires you to click a button confirming that you agree with whatever Apple's lawyers say.

3. **On the Select a Destination screen, click the disk or partition on which you want to install Mac OS X.**

Icons for all of your disks (or partitions) appear on the screen, but ones that are off-limits to Mac OS X (like CDs and USB hard drives) appear dimmed, if at all. Click the icon of the drive—or the partition, if you've created one to hold Mac OS X—that will be your new main startup drive.

---

**Note:** If a yellow, triangular exclamation point logo appears on a drive, it probably has a *newer* version of Mac OS X 10.5 on it. (Read the message at the bottom of the dialog box to find out.) That's the case if you're trying to install from the original 10.5 DVD, but you already have 10.5.2 on the hard drive, for example. No problem; you should be reading "The Clean Install" instructions on page 540 anyway.

---

4. **Click Continue.**

You arrive at the Easy Install screen. The easiest way to proceed here is to click Install. But don't.

Instead, take the time to click Customize.

The Installer shows you a list of the various chunks that constitute Mac OS X. A few of them are easily dispensable. For example, if you turn off Additional Fonts,

Language Translations (for Japanese, German, French, and so on), the drivers for printer models that you don't own, and the X11 Unix kit, you save *5.5 gigabytes*. It's like getting a whole mini-hard drive for free (ka-ching!). Click Done when you're finished gloating.

5. **Click Install.**

    Now you're in for a 25-minute wait as the Installer copies software onto your hard drive. When the installer's finished, you see a message indicating that your Mac will restart in 30 seconds. If you haven't wandered off to watch TV, click the Restart button to end the countdown and get on with it.

Mac OS X 10.5 is now installed on your Mac—but you're not quite ready to use it yet. See "The Setup Assistant" on the facing page.

## The Upgrade Installation

If Mac OS X version 10.0 through 10.4-point-anything is on your hard drive, the Leopard installer can neatly nip and tuck its software code, turning it *into* version 10.5. Everything remains just as you had it: your accounts, folders, files, email, network settings, everything-else settings, and so on.

This sophisticated surgery *occasionally* leaves behind a minor gremlin here and there: peculiar cosmetic glitches, a checkbox that doesn't seem to work, and so on. If that possibility concerns you, a clean install is a safer way to go. (A clean install does, however, require a little more post-installation fiddling to reinstate your settings, notably your Internet and network preferences.)

If you're still game to perform the upgrade installation, follow the previously outlined steps 1 through 3. On the Select Destination screen, however, click Options.

Now you're offered several variations of the basic installation. The one you want is Upgrade Mac OS X. Click it, and then click OK. Proceed with the previous step 4. (The button described there now says Upgrade, though, instead of Install.)

## The Clean Install ("Archive and Install")

In Windows, the *clean install* is considered an essential troubleshooting technique. It entails installing a second System Folder or Windows folder—a fresh one, uncontaminated by the detritus left behind by you and your software programs.

In general, though, you and your software *can't* invade the Mac OS X System folder. The kind of gradual corruption that could occur in those older operating systems is theoretically impossible in Mac OS X, and therefore the need to perform a clean install is almost completely eliminated.

That's the theory, anyway. In fact, somehow or other, things do go wrong with your Mac OS X installation. Maybe you or somebody else has been fiddling around in Terminal and wound up deleting or changing some important underlying files. Certain shareware programs can perform deep-seated changes like this, too.

The point is that eventually, you may wish you could just start over with a new, perfect copy of Mac OS X. And thanks to the clean install ("Archive and Install") option, you can—without having to erase the hard drive first.

Start by following steps 1 through 3 in "The Basic Installation" section. On the Select Destination screen, though, click Options. Now you're offered four kinds of installation. Turn on "Archive and Install." ("Preserve Users and Network Settings" should be on, too.)

This powerful option leaves all of your accounts (Home folders, documents, pictures, movies, Favorites, email, and so on) *untouched*. As the option's name implies, it also leaves your network and Internet settings alone. But it deactivates your old System folder (you'll find it, later, in a new folder called Previous System Folders) and puts a new one in its place. And that's exactly what you want.

Click OK and then continue with step 4 (page 539). When it's all over, you'll be confident that your Mac OS X installation is clean, fresh, and ready for action.

## Erase & Install

The final installation option is called Erase & Install (known to the geek community as "Nuke 'n' Pave"). As you can guess, it erases your entire hard drive and installs the ultimate clean, fresh, sparkling new copy of Leopard and its applications there. Use this "nuke-and-pave" option when you're about to sell your Mac and want to ensure that no trace of your former stuff is still there.

If you're absolutely certain that you won't regret *completely erasing the computer* (or you have a brand-new, virgin hard drive), follow the previously described steps 1 through 3. On the Select Destination screen, though, click Options, and select Erase & Install. Continue with step 4.

## The Setup Assistant

When the Mac restarts after the installation, the first thing you experience is one of the most visually stunning post-installation OS startup movies in history: a flythrough of deep space, accompanied by scooby-dooby music and a fancy parade of 3-D, computer-generated translations of the word "Welcome." Once Apple has quite finished showing off its multimedia prowess, you arrive at a Welcome screen.

---

**Note:** You also hear a man's voice letting you know that if you're blind, you can press Esc to hear audio guidance for setting up the Mac and learning VoiceOve.

If you do so, you're treated to a crash course in VoiceOver, the screen-control/screen-reading software described on page 475. This, by the way, is the only time you'll be offered this tutorial, so pay attention. (Hint: Here are the basics. Hold down the Control and Option keys and press the arrow keys to highlight different elements of the screen, hearing them pronounced. When a new window opens, press Control-Option-Shift-W to read the contents of the window. Press Control-Option-Space bar to "click.")

---

Once again, you're in for a click-through-the-screens experience, this time with the aim of setting up your Mac's various options. After answering the questions on each screen, click Continue.

The number and sequence of information screens you'll encounter depend on whether you've upgraded an existing Mac or started fresh, but here are some of the possibilities:

- **Welcome.** Click the name of the country you're in.

- **Select Your Keyboard.** Different countries require different keyboard layouts. For example, if you choose the Canadian layout, pressing the ] key on a U.S. keyboard produces the ç symbol. Click Continue.

- **Do you already own a Mac?** If you choose "Transfer my information from another Mac," the installer will assist you in sucking all of your old programs, files, folders, and settings from the old Mac to the new one.

  You have to help *it*, however, by connecting a FireWire cable between the two Macs, and then restarting the old Mac while holding down its T key. ("FireWire connection established.") Yes, that's right: the installer is putting you into FireWire Disk Mode (page 168) for super-high-speed transfer.

  You're using the Mac OS X Migration Assistant, shown in Figure A-1. The bottom of the screen lets you know how much stuff you've tagged for transferring, and how much disk space remains on the new Mac.

  When you click Transfer, the data-copying process begins.

- **Select a Wireless Service.** This is your chance to introduce the Mac to any wireless networks in the vicinity. Click the network name you want to join, if you see it. If you don't see it, click Rescan to make the Mac sniff again in an attempt to locate the network. Or if there's no wireless hot spot at all—hey, it could happen—click Different Network Setup.

  In that event, you're offered choices like Airport wireless, Cable modem/DSL modem, Local network (Ethernet), and "My computer does not connect to the Internet." (Bummer!) When you click Continue, you may be asked for specific information—the local access number, account name, and password, and so on—regarding your Internet account. See Chapter 10 for advice on filling in these settings.

- **Enter Your Apple ID.** Here, you're offered the chance to type in, or create, an Apple ID—which is your email address. An Apple ID doesn't cost anything, but it makes life easier if you want to buy songs from the Apple Music Store, order gift books or prints from iPhoto, and so on. (If you have a .Mac account—see page 295—put that account info here.)

- **Registration Information.** This is your chance to become a grain of sand on the great beach of the Apple database (and to set up your own "card" in Mac OS X's Address Book program).

**Tip:** If you're not interested in providing your personal information to Apple, or if you've already done so during a previous installation, press ⌘-Q. A message offers you Skip, Shut Down, and Cancel buttons. If you click Skip, you jump straight ahead to "Create Your Account," below.

**Figure A-1:**
*The Migration Assistant is actually pretty amazing. It brings over to your new Mac (or new Mac OS X installation) all of the files, settings, folders, and even installed programs from an older Mac—or, in times of tragedy, from a Time Machine backup (see Chapter 6).*

*Along the way, you'll be asked whose account folder(s) you want brought over, which other stuff (like applications, files, and folders) to copy, and which sorts of settings.*

*When it's all over, you might have to reactivate a couple of Adobe programs, but otherwise, you should be ready to roll on your new (or new-feeling) Mac.*

- **A Few More Questions.** Where will you primarily use this computer? What best describes what you do? Do you want to get junk mail from Apple?

- **Create Your Account.** Most of the steps up to this point have been pretty inconsequential, but this is a big moment. You're about to create your *account*—your Administrator account, in fact, as described in Chapter 13.

  All you have to do is make up a name, usually a short variation of your name and a password. Choose carefully, because you can't easily change your account name later.

  What you come up with here is extremely important, especially if several different people use this Mac at different times, or if other people connect to it on a network. See page 383 for details on creating a password and a hint that will help you remember it.

If you're the only one who uses your Mac, it's perfectly OK to leave the password blank empty.

- **Select a Picture For This Account.** If your Mac has a built-in camera (most models do), you can take a photo of yourself to use as your account icon. Just click "Take a video snapshot." You get a three-second countdown, and then the Mac snaps your photo. (You can always reshoot it.) Adjust the cropping by dragging inside the photo, and adjust the size by dragging the slider beneath it.

  If you're camera-shy, of course, you can choose "Choose from the picture library" instead, and find an Apple-provided icon instead.

- **Your .Mac Billing Information.** If you have a .Mac membership, Apple cheerfully lets you know when it will expire.

- **Thanks For being a .Mac member.** Aw, shucks.

- **Thank You.** When you click Go, you wind up at the Mac OS X desktop, just as described in Chapter 1.

# Troubleshooting

Whether it's a car engine or an operating system, anything with several thousand parts can develop the occasional technical hiccup. Mac OS X is far more resilient than its predecessors, but it's still a complex system with the potential for occasional glitches.

It's safe to say that you'll have to do *less* troubleshooting in Mac OS X than in Mac OS 9 or Windows, especially considering that most freaky little glitches go away if you just try these two steps, one at a time:

- Quit and restart the wayward program.
- Log out and log back in again.

It's the *other* problems that'll drive you batty.

## Minor Eccentric Behavior

All kinds of glitches may befall you, occasionally, in Mac OS X. Your desktop picture doesn't change when you change it in System Preferences. A menulet doesn't open when you click it. A program won't open—it just bounces in the Dock a couple of times and then stops.

When a single program is acting up like this, but quitting and restarting it does no good, try the following steps, in the following sequence.

## First Resort: Repair Permissions

An amazing number of mysterious glitches arise because the *permissions* of either that item or something in your System folder—that is, the complex mesh of interconnected Unix permissions described in Chapter 14—have become muddled.

When something doesn't seem to be working right, therefore, open your Applications→ Utilities folder and open Disk Utility. Proceed as shown in Figure A-2.

This is a really, *really* great trick to know.

---

**Tip:** Many Mac mavens, in fact, believe in running this Repair Permissions routine after running *any kind of installer*, just to nip nascent problems in the bud. That includes both installers of new programs and of Apple's own Mac OS X updates.

---

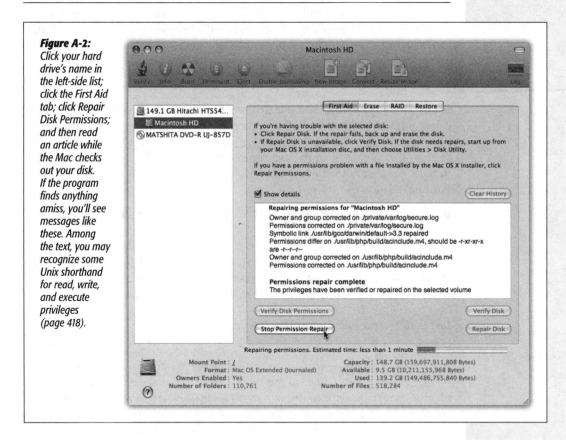

**Figure A-2:**
*Click your hard drive's name in the left-side list; click the First Aid tab; click Repair Disk Permissions; and then read an article while the Mac checks out your disk. If the program finds anything amiss, you'll see messages like these. Among the text, you may recognize some Unix shorthand for read, write, and execute privileges (page 418).*

## Second Resort: Look for an Update

If a program starts acting up immediately after you've installed or upgraded to Mac OS X 10.5, chances are good that it has some minor incompatibility. Chances are also good that you'll find an updated version on the company's Web site.

---

### Third Resort: Toss the Prefs File

A corrupted preference file can bewilder the program that depends on it.

Before you go on a dumpfest, however, take this simple test. Log in using a *different account* (perhaps a dummy account that you create just for testing purposes). Run the problem program. Is the problem gone? If so, then the glitch exists only when *you* are logged in—which means it's a problem with *your* copy of the program's preferences.

Return to your own account. Open your Home folder→Library→Preferences folder, where you'll find neatly labeled preference files for all of the programs you use. Each ends with the file name suffix *.plist*. For example, com.apple.finder.plist is the Finder's preference file, com.apple.dock.plist is the Dock's, and so on.

Put the suspect preference file into the Trash, but don't empty it. The next time you run the recalcitrant program, it will build itself a brand-new preference file that, if you're lucky, lacks whatever corruption was causing your problems.

If not, quit the program. You can reinstate its original .plist file from the Trash, if you'd find that helpful as you pursue your troubleshooting agenda.

Remember, however, that you actually have *three* Preferences folders. In addition to your own Home folder's stash, there's a second one in the Library folder in the main hard drive window (which administrators are allowed to trash), and a third in the System→Library folder in the main hard drive window (which nobody is allowed to trash—at least not without one of the security-bypass methods described in the box on the next page).

In any case, the next time you log in, the Mac creates fresh, virginal preference files.

### Fourth Resort: Restart

Sometimes you can give Mac OS X or its programs a swift kick by restarting the Mac. It's an inconvenient step, but not nearly as time-consuming as what comes next. And it can fix problems that cropped up when you started up the computer.

### Last Resort: Trash and Reinstall the Program

Sometimes reinstalling the problem program clears up whatever the glitch was.

First, however, throw away all traces of it. Open the Applications folder and drag the program's icon (or its folder) to the Trash. In most cases, the only remaining pieces to discard are its .plist file (or files) in your Home→Library→Preferences folder, and any scraps bearing the program's name in your Library→Application Support folder. (You can do a quick Spotlight search to round up any other pieces.)

Then reinstall the program from its original disc or installer—after first checking the company's Web site to see if there's an updated version, of course.

## Frozen Programs (Force Quitting)

The occasional unresponsive application has become such a part of Mac OS X life that, among the Mac cognoscenti online, the dreaded, endless "please wait" cursor has been given its own acronym: SBOD (Spinning Beachball of Death). When the SBOD strikes, no amount of mouse clicking and keyboard pounding will get you out of the recalcitrant program.

Here are the different ways you can go about *force quitting* a stuck program (the equivalent of pressing Control-Alt-Delete in Windows), in increasing order of desperation:

- **Use the Dock.** If you can't use the program's regular File→Quit command, try right-clicking its Dock icon and choosing Quit from the pop-up menu.

- **Force quit the usual way.** Choose  →Force Quit to terminate the stuck program, or use one of the other force-quit methods described on page 114.

- **Force quit the sneaky way.** Some programs, including the Dock, don't show up at all in the usual Force Quit dialog box. Your next attempt, therefore, should be to open the Activity Monitor program (in Applications→Utilities), which shows *everything* that's running. Double-click a program and then, in the resulting dialog box, click Quit to force quit it.

---

*Tip:* If you find yourself having to quit the Dock more than once, here's an easier way: Make yourself a little AppleScript (Chapter 16) consisting of a single line: *tell application "Dock" to quit.* Save it as an application. Whenever you feel that the Dock (or Spaces or Exposé, which technically belong to the Dock) needs a good kick in the rear, double-click your little AppleScript.

---

If all of this seems like a lot to remember, you can always force restart the Mac. On most Macs, you do that by holding down the power button for five seconds. If that doesn't work, press Control-⌘-power button.

## Can't Move or Rename an Icon

If you're not allowed to drag an icon somewhere, the error message that appears almost always hits the nail on the head: You're trying to move a file or folder that *isn't yours*. The box on the facing page explains the solutions to this problem.

## Application Won't Open

If a program won't open (if its icon bounces merrily in the Dock for a few seconds, for instance, but then nothing happens), begin by trashing its preference file, as described on the facing page. If that doesn't solve it, reinstalling the program usually does.

## Startup Problems

Not every problem you encounter is related to running applications. Sometimes trouble strikes before you even get that far. The following are examples.

### Kernel Panic

When you see the cheerful, multilingual dialog box shown in Figure A-3, you've got yourself a *kernel panic*—a Unix nervous breakdown.

(In such situations, *user panic* might be the more applicable term, but that's programmers for you.)

If you experience a kernel panic, it's almost always the result of a *hardware* glitch—most often a bad memory (RAM) board, but possibly an accelerator card, graphics card, SCSI gadget, or USB hub that Mac OS X doesn't like. A poorly seated AirPort

You need to restart your computer. Hold down the Power button for several seconds or press the Restart button.

Veuillez redémarrer votre ordinateur. Maintenez la touche de démarrage enfoncée pendant plusieurs secondes ou bien appuyez sur le bouton de réinitialisation.

Sie müssen Ihren Computer neu starten. Halten Sie dazu die Einschalttaste einige Sekunden gedrückt oder drücken Sie die Neustart-Taste.

コンピュータを再起動する必要があります。パワーボタンを
数秒間押し続けるか、リセットボタンを押してください。

**Figure A-3:**
*A kernel panic is almost always related to some piece of add-on hardware. And look at the bright side: At least you get this handsome dialog box in Leopard. That's a lot better than the Mac OS X 10.0 and 10.1 effect—random text gibberish super-imposing itself on your screen.*

card can bring on a kernel panic, too, and so can a bad USB or FireWire cable.

If simply restarting the machine doesn't help, detach every shred of gear that didn't come from Apple. Restore these components to the Mac one at a time until you find out which one was causing Mac OS X's bad hair day. If you're able to pinpoint the culprit, seek its manufacturer (or its Web site) on a quest for updated drivers, or at least try to find out for sure whether the add-on is compatible with Mac OS X.

---

**Tip:** This advice goes for your Macintosh itself. Apple periodically updates the Mac's *own* "drivers" in the form of a *firmware update.* You download these updates from the Support area of Apple's Web site (if indeed Mac OS X's own Software Update mechanism doesn't alert you to their existence).

---

There's one other cause for kernel panics, by the way, and that's moving, renaming, or changing the access permissions for Mac OS X's essential system files and folders—the Applications or System folder, for example. (See Chapter 14 for more on permissions.) This cause isn't even worth mentioning, of course, because nobody would be that foolish.

### Safe Mode (Safe Boot)

In times of troubleshooting, Mac OS 9 fans used to press the Shift key at startup to turn off the extensions. Windows fans press an F-key to start up in Safe Mode. Either way, the idea is the same: to turn off all nonessential system-software nubbins in an effort to get a sick machine at least powered up.

Although not one person in a hundred knows it, Mac OS X offers the same kind of emergency keystroke. It can come in handy when you've just installed some new piece of software and find that you can't even start up the machine, or when one of your fonts is corrupted, or when something you've designated as a Login Item turns out to be gumming up the works. With this trick, you can at least turn on the computer so that you can uninstall the cranky program.

The trick is to *press the Shift key* as the machine is starting up. Hold it down from the startup chime until you see the words "Safe Boot," in red lettering, on the login screen.

Welcome to Safe Mode.

What have you accomplished?

- **Checked your hard drive.** The Shift-key business makes the startup process seem to take a very long time; behind that implacable Apple logo, Mac OS X is actually scanning your entire hard drive for problems. It's running the same disk check that's described on page 779x.

- **Brought up the login screen.** When you do a safe boot, you must click your name and enter your password, even if you normally have Automatic Login turned on.

- **Turned off your kernel extensions.** All kinds of software nuggets load during the startup process. Some of them, you choose yourself: icons you add to the Login Items list in the System Preferences→Accounts pane. Others are normally hidden: a large mass of *kernel extensions,* which are chunks of software that add various features to the basic operating system. (Apple's kernel extensions live in your System→Library→Extensions folder; others may be in your Library→StartupItems folder.)

  If you're experiencing startup crashes, some non-Apple installer may have given you a kernel extension that doesn't care for Mac OS X 10.5—so in Safe Mode, they're all turned off.

- **Turned off your fonts.** Corrupted fonts are a chronic source of trouble—and because you can't tell by looking, they're darned difficult to diagnose. So just to make sure you can at least get into your computer, Safe Mode turns them all off (except the authorized, Apple-sanctioned ones that it actually needs to run, which are in your System→Library→Fonts folder).

- **Trashed your font cache.** The font cache is a speed trick. Mac OS X stores the visual information for each of your fonts on the hard drive, so that the system won't have to read in every single typeface off your hard drive when you open your Font menus or the Font panel.

  When these files get scrambled, startup crashes can result. That's why a Safe Boot moves all of these files into the Trash. (You'll even see them sitting there in the Trash after the startup process is complete, although there's not much you can do with them except walk around holding your nose and pointing.)

• **Turned off your login items.** Safe Mode also prevents any Finder windows from opening *and* prevents your own hand-picked startup items from opening—that is, whatever you've asked Leopard to auto-open by adding them to the System Preferences→Accounts→Login Items list.

This, too, is a troubleshooting tactic. If some login item crashes your Mac every time it opens, you can squelch it just long enough to remove it from your Login Items list.

---

*Tip:* If you don't hold down the Shift key until you click the Log In button (after entering your name and password at the login screen), you squelch *only* your login items but *not* the fonts and extensions.

---

Once you reach the desktop, you'll find a long list of standard features inoperable. You can't use DVD Player, capture video in iMovie, use a wireless network, use certain microphones and speakers, or use your modem. (The next time you restart, all of this goodness will be restored, assuming you're no longer clutching the Shift key in a sweaty panic.)

In any case, the beauty of Safe Mode is that it lets you get your Mac going. You have access to your files, so at least the emergency of crashing-on-startup is over. And you can start picking through your fonts and login items to see if you can spot the problem.

### Gray Screen During Startup

Confirm that your Mac has the latest firmware, as described earlier. Detach and test all your non-Apple add-ons. Finally, perform a disk check (see below).

### Blue Screen During Startup

Most of the troubleshooting steps for this problem (which is usually accompanied by the Spinning Beachball of Death cursor) are the same as those described under "Kernel Panic" above.

### Forgotten Password

If you or one of the other people who use your Mac have forgotten the corresponding account password, no worries: Just read the box on page 402.

## Fixing the Disk

The beauty of Mac OS X's design is that the operating system itself is frozen in its perfect, pristine state, impervious to conflicting system extensions, clueless Mac users, and other sources of disaster.

That's the theory, anyway. But what happens if something goes wrong with the complex software that operates the hard drive itself?

Fortunately, Mac OS X comes with its own disk-repair program. It takes the form of a program in Applications→Utilities called Disk Utility.

In any case, running Disk Utility is a powerful and useful troubleshooting tool that can cure all kinds of strange ills, including these problems, among others:

• Your Mac freezes during startup, either before or after the Login screen.

• The startup process interrupts itself with the appearance of the text-only command line.

• You get the "applications showing up as folders" problem.

Disk Utility can't fix the disk it's *on* (except for permissions repairs, described at the beginning of this appendix).That's why you have to restart the computer from the Leopard installation disc (or another startup disk), and run Disk Utility from there. The process goes like this:

1. **Start up the Mac from the Leopard DVD.**

   The best way to do that is to insert the disc and then restart the Mac while holding down the C key.

   You wind up, after some time, at the Mac OS X Installer screen. Don't be fooled—installing Mac OS X is *not* what you want to do here. Don't click Continue!

2. **Choose Utilities→Disk Utility.**

   That's the unexpected step. After a moment, the Disk Utility screen appears.

3. **Click the disk or disk partition you want to fix, click the First Aid tab, and then click Repair Disk.**

   The Mac whirls into action, checking a list of very technical disk-formatting parameters.

If you see the message, "The volume 'Macintosh HD' appears to be OK," that's meant to be *good* news. Believe it or not, that cautious statement is as definitive an affirmation as Disk Utility is capable of making about the health of your disk.

Disk Utility may also tell you that the disk is damaged, but that it can't help you. In that case, you need a more heavy-duty disk-repair program like Drive 10 (*www. micromat.com*) or DiskWarrior (*www.alsoft.com*).

## Where to Get Troubleshooting Help

If the basic steps described in this chapter haven't helped, the universe is crawling with additional help sources.

In general, this is the part in any Mac book where you're directed to Apple's help Web site, to various discussion forums, and so on—and, indeed, those help sources are listed below.

But the truth is, the mother of all troubleshooting resources is not any of those—it's Google. You'll find more answers faster using Google than you ever will by starting at any of the individual help sites below. That's because Google includes all of those help sites in its search!

Suppose, for example, that you've just installed the 10.5.1 software update for Leopard, and it's mysteriously turned all your accounts (including your own) into Standard accounts. And without any Administrator account, you can't install new programs, change network settings, add or edit other accounts, and so on.

You could go to one Web site after another, hunting for a fix, repeating your search—or you could just type *Leopard 10.5.1 standard accounts* into Google and hit Enter. See Figure A-4.

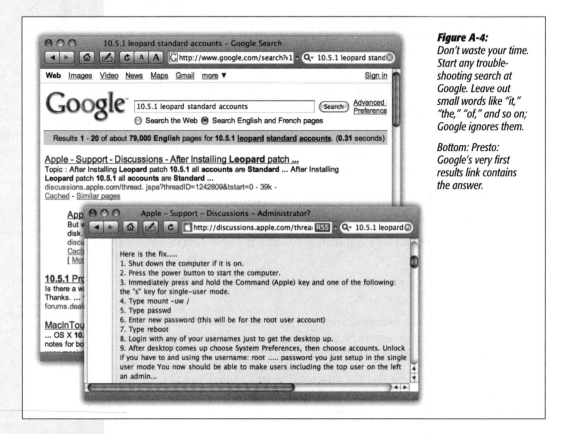

*Figure A-4:*
*Don't waste your time. Start any trouble-shooting search at Google. Leave out small words like "it," "the," "of," and so on; Google ignores them.*

*Bottom: Presto: Google's very first results link contains the answer.*

## Help Online

These Web sites contain nothing but troubleshooting discussions, tools, and help:

- **Apple Discussion Groups** (*http://discussions.info.apple.com*). The volume and quality of question-and-answer activity here dwarfs any other free source. If you're polite and concise, you can post questions to the multitudes here and get more replies to them than you'll know what to do with.

- **Apple's help site** (*www.apple.com/support*). Apple's help Web site includes downloadable manuals, software updates, frequently asked questions, and many other resources.

It also has a Search box, which may look mild-mannered but is actually the mother of all troubleshooting resources: the Knowledge Base. This is the collection of 50,000 individual technical articles, organized in a searchable database, that the Apple technicians themselves consult when you call for help. You can search it either by typing in keywords or by using pop-up menus of question categories.

- **MacFixIt** (*www.macfixit.com*). The world's one-stop resource for Mac trouble-shooting advice; alas, you have to pay to access the good stuff.

### Help by Telephone

Finally, consider contacting whoever sold you the component that's making your life miserable: the printer company, scanner company, software company, or whatever.

If it's a Mac OS problem, you can call Apple at 800-275-2273 (that's 800-APL-CARE). For the first 90 days following your purchase of Mac OS X (which, as far as Apple knows, is the date of your first call), the technicians will answer your questions for free.

After that, unless you've paid for AppleCare for your Mac (a three-year extended warranty program), Apple will charge you to answer your questions. Fortunately, if the problem turns out to be Apple's fault, they won't charge you.

# The "Where'd It Go?" Dictionary

All the words and pictures so far in this book are just great for leisure reading. But in a crisis of helplessness on your new Mac, this appendix may be more useful. It's an alphabetical listing of every common Windows function and where to find it in Mac OS X. After all, an operating system is an operating system. The actual functions are pretty much the same—they're just in different places.

## About [This Program]

To find out the version number of the program you're using, don't look in the Help menu. Instead, look in the *application* menu next to the  menu—the one that bears the name of the program you're in. That's where you find the About command for Macintosh programs.

## Accessibility Options Control Panel

The special features that let you operate the computer even with impaired vision, hearing, or motor control are called Universal Access in Mac OS X. It's in System Preferences (Chapter 15).

## Active Desktop

The Mac never displays Web pages directly on the desktop—and knowing Apple, that's probably a point of pride. But Dashboard (Chapter 4) keeps Internet information only a keystroke away.

## Add Hardware Control Panel

The Mac requires no program for installing the driver for a new external gadget. The drivers for most printers, mice, keyboards, cameras, camcorders, and other accessories are preinstalled. If you plug something into the Mac and find that it doesn't work immediately, just install the driver from the included CD (or the manufacturer's Web site).

## Add or Remove Programs Control Panel

Here's another one you just don't need on the Macintosh. Installing a program onto the Mac is described on page 146. Removing a program simply involves dragging its icon to the Trash. (For a clean sweep, inspect your Home→Library→Preferences and Library→Application Support folders to see if any preference files got left behind.)

## All Programs

There's no Programs menu built into Mac OS X, like the one on the Windows Start menu. If you'd like one, drag your Applications folder into the end of the Dock. Now its icon is a tidy pop-up menu of every program on your machine.

## Alt Key

On the Mac, it's the Option key. You can substitute Option for Alt in any keystroke in most popular programs. The Option key has a number of secondary features on the Mac, too: It hides the windows of one program when you click into another, for example. (As for operating the Mac's menus from the keyboard, see page 134.)

## Automatic Update

On the Mac, it's called Software Update, and it does exactly the same thing (page 470).

## Backspace key

It's in the same place on the Macintosh keyboard, but it's called the Delete key.

## Battery Level

The status of the battery in your Mac laptop appears in the menu bar. (If you don't see it, open System Preferences→Energy Saver and turn it on.)

## BIOS

You'll never have to update or even think about the ROM of your Macintosh (the approximate equivalent of the BIOS on the PC). It's permanent and unchanging. The very similar *firmware* of your Macintosh does occasionally have to be updated in order to work with a new version of the Mac operating system or some dramatic new feature—once every four years, perhaps. You'll be notified on the screen when the time comes.

## Briefcase

Mac OS X doesn't have anything like the Briefcase, a Windows invention designed to help you keep your files in sync between a laptop and a desktop computer. On the other hand, if you sign up for a .Mac account (page 295), you get something even better: automatic syncing between multiple Macs, using the Internet as an intermediary (page 275).

## Calculator

The calculator program in Mac OS X is almost identical to the one in Windows XP, except that it can also perform conversions (temperature, distance, currency, and so on) and features an editable "paper tape." It sits in your Applications folder and is described in Chapter 16. (There's a simpler Calculator in Dashboard, too, and of course you can do quick computations right in the Spotlight box in your menu bar [page 483]).

## Camera and Scanner Wizard

When you connect a digital camera or scanner to your Mac, iPhoto opens automatically and prepares to download the pictures automatically. Details on iPhoto are in this book's free online iLife Appendix.

## CDs

Hold down the ⏏ key on your Mac keyboard for a moment to open the CD/DVD drawer, or, if you have a slot-loading CD drive, to spit out the disc that's in it. There are various other ways to eject a disk, but the point is that you never do so by pushing the Eject button on the disk drive itself.

## Character Map

This Windows program helps you find out what keys you need to press to trigger trademark symbols, copyright symbols, and other special characters. The equivalent on the Mac is called Keyboard Viewer (page 462)—but the Character Palette (page 557) is even easier to use.

## Clean Install

The Mac OS X installer can give you a fresh, virginal copy of the operating system, just as the Windows installer can. Instructions are in Appendix A.

## Clipboard

The Macintosh clipboard works almost exactly like the one in Windows. In the Finder, you can choose Edit→Show Clipboard to see whenever you have most recently copied or cut.

## Command Line

In Mac OS X, the command line is alive and well—but it speaks Unix, not DOS. You get to it by opening Terminal (page 530).

## Control Panel

The Control Panel in Mac OS X is called System Preferences, and it's represented on the Dock by a little light-switch icon. As in Windows XP/Vista, you can view these icons either by category or in a simple alphabetical list: Just choose either Organize by Categories or Organize Alphabetically from the View menu.

## Copy, Cut, Paste

When you're editing in a word processor or graphics program, the Mac OS X Cut, Copy, and Paste commands work exactly as they do in Windows.

At the desktop, however, there are a few differences. You can indeed copy icons and paste them into a new window using the Copy and Paste commands—you just can't *cut* them out of a window, as you can in Windows. On the other hand, Mac OS X offers a handy secondary feature: If you paste into a word or text processor instead of into another desktop window, you get a tidy list of the names of the icons you copied.

## Ctrl Key

On the Macintosh, you generally substitute the ⌘ key in keystrokes that would normally involve the Control key. In other words, the Save command is now ⌘-S instead of Ctrl-S, Open is ⌘-O instead of Ctrl-O, and so on.

## Date and Time

You set your Mac's calendar and clock in the Date & Time pane of System Preferences.

## Delete Key (Forward Delete)

Desktop Mac keyboards have a forward-delete key (labeled *Del*) exactly like the ones on PCs. On Mac laptops, you trigger the forward-delete function by pressing the regularly scheduled Delete key while pressing the Fn key in the lower-left corner of the keyboard.

## Desktop

The Macintosh desktop is pretty much the same idea as the Windows desktop, with a few key differences:

- Disk icons show up on the Mac desktop as soon as they are inserted or connected. You don't have to open a window to see their icons.

- You change the desktop picture using the Desktop & Screen Saver pane of System Preferences.

- The Trash is an icon on the Dock, not loose on the desktop.

## Directories

Most people call them *folders* on the Mac.

## Disk Defragmenter

There's no such utility included with Mac OS X; the Mac defragments important files on its own hard drive automatically. (A *defragmenting* program moves around the pieces of files on your hard drive in an effort to optimize their placement and speed of opening.)

## Disks

Working with disks is very different on the Mac. Every disk inside, or attached to, a Macintosh is represented on the screen by an icon. Mac OS X does have something like the My Computer window (choose Go→Computer), but the icons on the desktop, the Sidebar, and the Computer window reflect only the disks currently inserted in your Mac. You'll never see an icon for an empty drive, as you do on Windows, and there's no such thing as drive letters (because the Mac refers to *disks*, not to *drives*—and refers to them by name).

## Display Control Panel

The functions of the Windows Display Control Panel lurk in the Mac OS X System Preferences program—just not all in one place. You set a desktop picture and choose a screen saver using the Desktop & Screen Saver pane, and adjust your monitor settings using the Displays pane. (Mac OS X offers no equivalent to the Appearance tab in Windows, for changing the system-wide look of your computer.)

## DLL Files

The Macintosh equivalent of DLL files—shared libraries of programming code—are invisible and off-limits. As a result, no Macintosh user ever experiences DLL conflicts or out-of-date DLL files.

## DOS Prompt

There's a command line in Mac OS X, but it's Unix, not DOS. See page 530.

## Drivers

See "Add or Remove Programs."

## End Task Dialog Box

If some Macintosh program is hung or frozen, you escape it pretty much the same way you would in Windows: by forcing it to quit. To bring up the Force Quit dialog box, you press Option-⌘-Esc, or choose Force Quit from the  menu.

## Exiting Programs

You can quit a program either by choosing Quit from the menu bearing its name (next to the  menu), or by right-clicking its Dock icon and then choosing Quit from the pop-up menu.

## Explorer

The Mac has its own "tree" view of the files and folders on your hard drive: list view. By expanding the "flippy triangles" of your folders, you build a hierarchy that shows you as much or as little detail as you like.

If you prefer the Explorer effect of clicking a folder in *one* pane to see its contents in the next, try column view instead. Both views are described in Chapter 2.

## Favorites

In Mac OS X, there isn't one single Favorites menu that lists both favorite Web sites and favorite icons. The Bookmarks menu of Safari, the Web browser, lists only Web sites. In the Finder, you can use the Sidebar to list favorite files.

## Faxing

Faxing is built into Mac OS X; it's described on page 232. (Hint: Choose File→Print; from the PDF button at the bottom of the print dialog box, choose Fax PDF.)

## File Sharing

See Chapter 14 for an in-depth look at the Macintosh networking and file-sharing system.

## Floppy Disks

Floppy drives on Macs disappeared in about 1998. According to Apple, it's much more efficient to transfer files between machines using an Ethernet cable, a wireless network, a CD that you burned, a flash drive, or email.

Of course, you can buy an external USB floppy drive for any Mac for about $45.

## Folder Options

The Folder Options control panel in Windows is a crazy collection of unrelated settings that boil down to this:

- **General tab.** Exactly as in Windows, it's up to you whether or not double-clicking a folder opens up a second window—or just changes what's in the first one. On the Mac, you make these changes using the Finder→Preferences command. There you'll find the option called "Always open folders in a new window."

- **View tab.** Most of the options here don't exist on the Mac. For example, you can't opt to make all the invisible system files visible (at least not without add-on shareware). You can, however, choose whether or not you want to see the file name extensions in your desktop windows (like .doc and .html). Choose Finder→Preferences, and turn "Show all file extensions" on or off.

- **File Types tab.** Just as in Windows, you can reassign certain document types so that double-clicking opens them up in the program of your choice. But on the Mac, you can reassign either a whole class of files at once, as on Windows, *or* one file at a time. To do it, use the Get Info window as described on page 129.

- **Offline Files.** The closest equivalent feature on the Mac is the .Mac syncing feature described on page 275.

## Fonts

The Mac and Windows both use TrueType, PostScript, and Open Type fonts. (In fact, your Mac can even use the exact font files you had on Windows.) A complete discussion is on page 237.

## FTP (File Transfer Protocol)

You can pull up FTP servers right on your screen (just type their addresses into the Go→Connect to Server dialog box). To put files *onto* an FTP server, though, you need a shareware program like RBrowser or Fetch.

## Help and Support

At the desktop, choose Help→Mac Help. In other programs, the Help command is generally at the right end of your menus, exactly as in Windows.

## Hibernation

The Mac can't hibernate at all, as modern PCs do, cutting all power but remembering what programs and documents you had open for a faster restart later. Sleep mode is the closest it gets (see "Standby Mode" in this appendix).

## Internet Explorer

Microsoft abandoned Internet Explorer for Mac several years ago—right after Apple introduced its own, better, faster browser called Safari. If you come across a site that *requires* Internet Explorer, you can still download the ancient Mac version of this program from *www.mactopia.com*.

## Internet Options

You find the options for your Web browser by choosing Safari→Preferences.

## IRQs

They don't exist on the Mac.

## Java

This interpreter of tiny programs written in the Java programming language is alive and well in Mac OS X. Java programs run fine in all Mac Web browsers.

## Keyboard Control Panel

You can make exactly the same kinds of settings—and more—on the Keyboard pane of System Preferences.

## Logging In

As it turns out, the multiple-accounts feature of Mac OS X is extremely similar to that of Windows 2000, XP, and Vista. In either case, you can, if you wish, create a requirement to login with a name and password before using the computer. This arrangement keeps separate the documents, email, and settings of each person who uses the computer. (Chapter 13 tells all.)

## Mail Control Panel

Mac OS X comes with its own email program (see Chapter 11); all of its settings are contained within the program.

# Maximize Button

On the Mac, clicking the Zoom button (the green button at the upper-left corner of a window) does something like the Maximize button in Windows: It makes your window larger. On the Mac, however, clicking the Zoom button rarely makes the window expand to fill the entire screen. Instead, the window grows—or *shrinks*—precisely enough to enclose its contents.

# Menus

Here's one of the biggest differences between the Mac and Windows: On the Macintosh, there's only one menu bar, always at the very top of the screen. The menus change depending on the program and the window you're using, but the point is that the menu bar is no longer inside each window you open.

---

*Tip:* Just because you don't see the little underlines in the menus doesn't mean you can't operate all of the menus from the keyboard, as in Windows. See page 134 for details.

---

# Minimize Button

You can minimize a Mac OS X window to the Dock, just the way you would minimize a Windows window to the taskbar. You do so by double-clicking its title bar, pressing ⌘-M, choosing Window→Minimize Window, or clicking the yellow Minimize button at the top left of a window. (Restore the window by clicking its icon on the Dock.)

# Mouse Control Panel

The equivalent settings await you in the Keyboard & Mouse pane of system Preferences.

# My Computer

The Mac's Computer window is very similar (choose Go→Computer), in that it shows the icons of all disks (hard drive, CD, and so on). On the other hand, it shows *only* the disks that are actually inserted or connected (see "Disks").

# My Documents, My Pictures, My Music

The equivalent buckets for your everyday documents, music files, and pictures are the Documents, Pictures, and Music folders in your Home folder.

# My Network Places

To see your "network neighborhood," just open any Finder window; all of the Macs and PCs on your network show up in the Sidebar at the left side.

# Network Neighborhood

See the previous entry.

# Notepad

There's no Mac OS X Notepad program. But give Stickies a try (page 509).

# Personal Web Server

If you're technically proficient, you can turn your Mac into a Web site. On the Sharing pane of System Preferences, turn on Personal Web Sharing. Any HTML documents you put into your Home→Sites folder are now available on your network or the Web.

# Phone and Modem Options Control Panel

To find the modem settings for your Mac, open System Preferences. Click Network, click Internal Modem (or External Modem) in the list at left, and then click Advanced.

# Power Options

To control when your Mac goes to sleep and (if it's a laptop) how much power it uses, use the Energy Saver panel of System Preferences (Chapter 15).

# Printer Sharing

To share a USB inkjet printer with other Macs on the network, open the Sharing pane of System Preferences on the Mac with the printer. Turn on Printer Sharing.

To use the shared printer from across the network, open the document you want to print, choose File→Print, and choose the name of the shared printer from the first pop-up menu.

# Printers and Faxes

For a list of your printers, open the Printer Setup Utility in your Aplications→Utilities folder. For details on faxing, see "Faxing."

# PrntScrn Key

You capture pictures of your Mac screen by pressing Shift-⌘-3 (for a full-screen grab) or Shift-⌘-4 (to grab a selected portion of the screen). Details on page 208.

# Program Files Folder

The Applications folder (Go→Applications) is like the Program Files folder in Windows—except that you're not discouraged from opening it and double-clicking things. On the Macintosh, every program bears its true name. Microsoft Word is called Microsoft Word, not WINWORD.EXE.

# Properties Dialog Box

You can call up something very similar for any *icon* (file, folder, program, disk, printer) by highlighting its icon and then choosing File→Get Info. But objects in Macintosh *programs* generally don't contain Properties dialog boxes.

# Recycle Bin

Mac OS X has a Trash icon at the end of the Dock. In general, it works exactly like the Windows Recycle Bin—and why not, since the Macintosh Trash was Microsoft's inspiration?—but there are a couple of differences. The Macintosh never auto-empties it, for example. That job is up to you (the simplest way is to right-click it and choose Empty Trash from the shortcut menu).

The Mac never bothers you with an "Are you sure?" message when you throw something into the Trash, either. In fact, it doesn't even ask for confirmation when you *empty* the Trash (at least, not when you empty it by right-clicking). The Mac interrupts you for permission only when you choose File→Empty Trash—and you can even turn that confirmation off, if you like (in Finder→Preferences).

To put icons into the Trash, drag them there, or just highlight them and then press ⌘-Delete.

### Regional and Language Options Control Panel

The equivalent is the International pane of System Preferences.

### Registry

There is no registry. Let the celebration begin!

### Run Command

The equivalent command line is Terminal (page 530).

### Safe Mode

You can press the Shift key during startup to suppress the loading of certain software libraries, but Mac OS X's "safe mode" (page 548) isn't quite as stripped-down as Windows' Safe Mode.

### ScanDisk

Just like Windows, the Mac automatically scans and, if necessary, repairs its hard drive every time your machine starts up. To run such a check on command, open Disk Utility (located in the Applications→Utilities folder), and then click the First Aid tab.

### Scheduled Tasks

To schedule a task to take place unattended, use the *launchd* command in Terminal (geeks only), or one of the scheduling programs listed at *www.versiontracker.com*.

### Scrap Files

On the Mac, they're called *clipping files,* and they're even more widely compatible. You create them the same way: Drag some highlighted text, or a graphic, out of a program's window and onto the desktop. There it becomes an independent clipping file that you can drag back in—to the same window, or a different one.

### Screen Saver

The Mac's screen savers are impressive. Open System Preferences and click the Desktop & Screen Saver icon.

## Search

In Mac OS X, you have the ultimate file-searching tool: Spotlight (page 94). Get psyched!

To find Web sites, use the Google Search box at the top of the Safari browser.

## Shortcut Menus

They work exactly the same as they do in Windows. You produce a shortcut menu by right-clicking things like icons, list items, and so on.

## Shortcuts

On the Mac, they're known as *aliases*. See page 84.

## Sounds and Audio Devices

Open System Preferences; click the Sound icon. You may also want to explore the Audio MIDI Setup program in Applications→Utilities.

## Speech Control Panel

The Mac's center for speech recognition and text-to-speech is the Speech pane of System Preferences. As Chapter 15 makes clear, the Mac can read aloud any text in any program, and it lets you operate all menus, buttons, and dialog boxes by voice alone.

## Standby Mode

On the Mac, it's called Sleep, but it's the same idea. You make a Mac laptop sleep by closing the lid. You make a Mac desktop sleep by choosing  →Sleep, or just walking away; the Mac will go to sleep on its own, according to the settings in the Energy Saver pane of System Preferences.

## Start Menu

There's no Start menu in Mac OS X. Instead, you stash the icons of the programs, documents, and folders you use frequently onto the Dock at the edge of the screen, or into the Sidebar at the left edge of every Finder window.

Exactly as with the Start menu, you can rearrange these icons (drag them horizontally), or remove the ones you don't use often (drag them away from the Dock and then release). To add new icons of your own, just drag them into place (applications go to the left of the Dock's divider line, documents and folders to the right).

## StartUp Folder

To make programs launch automatically at startup, include them in the list of Login Items in the System Preferences→Accounts pane.

## System Control Panel

The Mac has no central equivalent of the System window on a Windows PC. But its functions have analogs here:

- **General tab.** To find out your Mac OS X version number and the amount of memory on your Mac, choose  →About This Mac.

- **Computer Name tab.** Open System Preferences, click Sharing, and edit your computer's network names here.

- **Hardware tab.** The closest thing the Mac has to the Device Manager is System Profiler (in your Applications→Utilities folder). See page 529.

- **Advanced tab.** In Mac OS X, you can't easily adjust your virtual memory, processor scheduling, or user profile information.

- **System Restore tab.** This feature isn't available in Mac OS X.

- **Automatic Updates tab.** Open System Preferences and click Software Updates.

- **Remote tab.** Mac OS X Leopard excels at remote control of other computers. See the description, for example, of screen sharing on pages 370 and 431.

## System Tray

The perfect Mac OS X equivalent of the System Tray (also called the notification area) is the row of *menulets* at the upper-right corner of your screen; see page 16.

## Taskbar

Mac OS X doesn't have a taskbar, but it does have something very close: the Dock (Chapter 2). Open programs are indicated by a small glowing dot beneath their icons on the Dock. If you hold down your cursor on one of these icons (or or right-click it), you get a pop-up list of the open windows in that program, exactly as in Windows XP.

Clicking a folder or disk icon on the Dock is even more useful. It produces a pop-up display of everything inside that disk or folder—a terrific form of X-ray vision that has no equivalent in Windows.

On the other hand, some conventions never die. Much as on Windows, you cycle through the various open programs on your Dock by holding down the ⌘ key and pressing Tab repeatedly.

## Taskbar and Start Menu Control Panel

To configure your Dock (the equivalent of the taskbar and Start menu), choose  →Dock→Dock Preferences, or click the Dock icon in System Preferences.

## "Three-Fingered Salute"

Instead of pressing Ctrl-Alt-Delete to jettison a stuck program on the Mac, you press Option-⌘-Esc. A Force Quit dialog box appears. Click the program you want to toss, click Force Quit, confirm your choice, and then relaunch the program to get on with your day.

## ToolTips

Small, yellow identifying balloons pop up on the Mac just as they do in Windows. Just point to a toolbar icon or truncated file name without clicking. (There's no way to turn these labels off.)

## TweakUI

The closest equivalent for this free, downloadable, but unsupported Microsoft utility for tweaking the look of your PC is TinkerTool for Mac OS X. You can find it at, and download it from, *www.versiontracker.com.*

## User Accounts Control Panel

Like Windows 2000, XP, and Vista, Mac OS X was designed from square one to be a multiuser operating system, keeping the files, mail, and settings of each person separate. You set up and manage these accounts in System Preferences→Accounts (Chapter 13).

## Window Edges

You can enlarge or shrink a Mac OS X window only by dragging its lower-right corner—not its edges.

## Windows (or WINNT) Folder

Mac OS X's operating system resides in a folder simply called System, which sits in your main hard drive window. Exactly as in recent Windows versions, you're forbidden to add, remove, or change anything inside. Also as in Windows, most of it is invisible anyway.

## Windows Logo Key

The Mac has no equivalent for the ⊞ key on most PC keyboards.

---

*Tip:* If you hook up a USB Windows keyboard to your Mac, the ⊞ key behaves like the Mac's ⌘ key.

---

## Windows Media Player

The Mac comes with individual programs for playing multimedia files:

- **QuickTime Player** (Chapter 16) to play back movies and sounds.

- **iTunes** (Chapter 9) to play CDs, Internet radio, MP3 files, and other audio files. (iTunes for Mac, like its Windows brother, can even *create* MP3 files.)

- **DVD Player** (Chapter 9) for playing DVDs. If your Mac does, in fact, have a DVD player built in, this program is in the Applications folder.

Windows Media Player *is*, however, available in a Macintosh version, paradoxical though that may sound. For details, see page 209.

---

## Windows Messenger

Mac OS X's voice and videoconferencing software is called iChat, and it's described in Chapter 12. But if you really want the actual Microsoft experience, Windows Messenger is available in a Mac version. You can download it from *www.microsoft.com/mac*.

## WordPad

The TextEdit program (in the Applications folder) is a barebones word processor like WordPad. It can even open and save Word files, as WordPad can.

## Zip Files

Zip files exist on the Mac, too, and you create them almost the same way: right-click a file or folder and choose Compress from the shortcut menu.

# The Master Mac OS X Secret Keystroke List

H ere it is, by popular, frustrated demand: The master list of every secret (or not-so-secret) keystroke in Mac OS X Leopard, including all of the keys you can press during startup. Clip and post to your monitor (unless, of course, you got this book from the library).

---

**Note:** For the most part, the following list doesn't include the keystrokes that are already listed in your menus, like ⌘-P for Print, ⌘-S for Save, and so on.

---

## Startup Keystrokes

| Keys to Hold Down | Effect |
|---|---|
| C | Starts up from a CD |
| D | Starts up from the first partition |
| N | Starts up from network server |
| R | Resets the laptop screen |
| T | Puts the Mac into FireWire Target Disk mode |
| X | Starts up in Mac OS X (if 9 is on the same disk) |
| Option | Shows icons of all startup disks and partitions, so you can choose one for starting up. |
| Shift-Option-⌘-Delete | Starts up from external drive (or CD) |
| Option-⌘-P-R | Zaps the parameter RAM (PRAM). (Hold down until you hear the second chime.) |

| | |
|---|---|
| Option-⌘-O-F | Brings up Open Firmware screen (pre-Intel Macs). |
| ⌘-V | Shows Unix console messages during startup, logout, and shutdown |
| ⌘-S | Starts up in single-user (Unix command-line) mode |
| Mouse down | Ejects a stuck CD or DVD |
| Shift | Just after powering up: Turns off *kernel extensions* (page 835) |
| Shift | Just after logging in: Prevents Finder windows and startup items from opening. (They'll return the next time you start up.) |

## In the Finder

| | |
|---|---|
| ⌘-Space | Highlights Spotlight box |
| Option-⌘-Space | Opens Spotlight window |
| →, ← | Expands or collapses a selected folder in list view |
| Option-→ | Expands a folder in a list view *and* all folders inside it |
| Option-← | Collapses folder *and* all folders inside it |
| ⌘-↑ | Opens parent folder |
| Shift-Option-⌘-↑ | Selects the Desktop |
| ⌘-↓ (or ⌘-O) | Opens the selected icon |
| Option-click the flippy triangle | Expands or collapses all folders within that window |
| Tab | Selects next icon alphabetically |
| Shift-Tab | Selects previous icon alphabetically |
| Space bar | Opens Quick Look preview of highlighted icon(s) |
| Space bar | (During a spring-loaded folder drag) Opens the disk or folder under mouse immediately |
| Option-⌘-drag | Scrolls a Finder window in any direction (list or icon view) |
| Option-click the Zoom button | Enlarges the window to full screen |
| Option-click Close button | Closes all Finder windows |
| ⌘-drag an icon | Moves it into, or out of, the System folder (administrator password required) |
| Option | Changes Quick Look button to Slideshow button |

| ⌘-drag | Rearranges or removes menulets or toolbar icons |
| ⌘-click window title | Opens a pop-up menu showing the folder path |
| Option-click the Minimize button | Minimizes all windows (works in most programs) |

## ⌘ Menu

| Option | Changes "About This Mac" to "System Profiler" |
| Option | Eliminates confirmation box from Restart, Shut Down, and Log Out |

## Finder Menu

| Option | Eliminates confirmation box from Empty Trash and Secure Empty Trash |
| Shift-⌘-Q | Logs out |
| Shift-Option-⌘-Q | Logs out without confirmation box |
| Shift-⌘-Delete | Empties the Trash |
| Shift-Option-⌘-Delete | Empties the Trash without confirmation box |
| Option-"Empty Trash" | Empties the Trash without confirmation box |
| ⌘-comma | Opens Preferences |
| ⌘-H | Hide This Program |
| Shift-⌘-H | Hide Other Programs |

## File Menu

| ⌘-N | New Finder Window |
| Shift-⌘-N | New Folder |
| Option-⌘-N | New Smart Folder |
| ⌘-O or ⌘-↓ | Open |
| Control-⌘-O | Open in New Window |
| Option-click File menu | Changes "Open With" to "Always Open With" |
| ⌘-W | Close Window |
| Option-⌘-W | Close All |
| ⌘-I | Get Info |
| Option-⌘-I | Show Inspector |
| Control-⌘-I | Summary Info (of selected icons) |
| ⌘-D | Duplicate |

| | |
|---|---|
| ⌘-L | Make Alias |
| ⌘-Y | Quick Look |
| Option-⌘-Y | Slideshow (of selected icons) |
| ⌘-R | Show Original (of alias) |
| ⌘-T | Add to Sidebar |
| Shift-⌘-T | Add to Favorites |
| Shift-Delete | Move to Trash |
| ⌘-E | Eject |
| ⌘-F | Find |
| Shift-⌘-F | Find by Name |

## Edit Menu

| | |
|---|---|
| ⌘-Z | Undo |
| ⌘-C, ⌘-X, ⌘-V | Copy, Cut, Paste |
| ⌘-A | Select All |
| Option-⌘-A | Deselect All |

## View Menu

| | |
|---|---|
| ⌘-1, -2, -3, -4 | Icon, List, Column, Cover Flow views |
| Control-⌘-1, -2, -3, -4, -5, -6 | Arrange by Name, Date Modified, Date Created, Size, Kind, Label |
| Option | Changes "Clean Up Selection" to "Clean Up" |
| Option | Changes "Keep Arranged By" to "Arrange By" |
| Option-⌘-T | Show/Hide Toolbar |
| ⌘-J | Show/Hide View Options palette |

## Go Menu

| | |
|---|---|
| ⌘-[, ⌘-] | Back, Forward |
| ⌘-↑ | Enclosing folder |
| Control-⌘-↑ | Enclosing folder in new window |
| Shift-⌘-C | Computer window |
| Shift-⌘-H | Home window |
| Shift-⌘-D | Desktop window |
| Shift-⌘-K | Network window |
| Shift-⌘-I | Open iDisk |
| Shift-⌘-A | Applications window |
| Shift-⌘-G | Go to Folder |
| ⌘-K | Connect to Server |

## Window Menu

| | |
|---|---|
| ⌘-M | Minimize |
| Option-⌘-M | Minimize All |
| Option | Changes "Bring All to Front" to "Arrange in Front" |

## Help Menu

| | |
|---|---|
| Shift-⌘-? | Opens Help search box |

## Power Keys

| | |
|---|---|
| Control-⏏ | Brings up dialog box for shutdown, sleep, or restart |
| Option-⌘-⏏ | Sleep |
| Control-Option-⌘-⏏ | Shut Down |
| Control-⌘-power | Restart |

## The Dock

| | |
|---|---|
| Option-click a Dock icon | Switches to new program and hides previous one |
| Option-⌘-D | Hides/shows the Dock |
| ⌘-click a Dock or Stacks icon | Reveals its actual Finder icon |
| Option-⌘-click a Dock icon | Switches to this program and hides all others |
| Control-click a Dock icon | Opens a shortcut menu |
| ⌘-drag an icon onto a Dock icon | Prevents Dock icons from moving, so you can drop your icon onto one of them |
| ⌘-drag a Dock icon | Drags the actual item |
| Option-⌘-drag an icon onto the Dock | Forces Dock program icon to open the icon you're dropping |

## Managing Programs

| | |
|---|---|
| Option-click a Dock icon | Switches to new program and hides previous one |
| Option-click in a window | Switches to new program and hides previous one |
| ⌘-H | Hide this program's windows (works in most apps) |
| Option-⌘-H | Hide all *other* programs' windows (most apps) |
| F8 | Spaces: Enters "big picture" view of your virtual screens (if you've turned on Spaces) |
| Shift-F8 | Spaces: Enters "big picture" view in slow motion |

| | |
|---|---|
| Control-1, 2, 3, 4… | Jump to a specific Spaces screen |
| Control-↑, ↓, ←, → | Next Spaces screen in this direction |
| F9 | Exposé: Shrinks and tiles all windows in all programs |
| Shift-F9 | Exposé: Shrinks and tiles all windows in slow motion |
| F10 | Exposé: Shrinks and tiles all windows in frontmost program |
| F11 | Exposé: Flings all windows in all programs to edges of screen, revealing desktop |
| F12 | Dashboard widgets |
| ⌘-Tab | Press and release: Switches back and forth between current and previous open program |
| ⌘-Tab | Hold down ⌘: Displays floating icons of open programs. Press Tab repeatedly to cycle through them. (Add Shift to cycle *backward* through open programs on the Dock.) |
| ⌘-~ | Switches to next open window in this program. (Add Shift to cycle in the opposite direction.) |
| Option-⌘-Esc | Opens the Force Quit dialog box (to close a stuck program) |
| Shift-⌘-3 | Captures the screen image as a PDF file on your desktop |
| Shift-⌘-4 | Produces a crosshair; drag to capture a selected portion of the screen as a PDF graphics file. (Press Space to get the "camera" cursor that snips out just a menu, icon, or window.) |
| ⌘-Space | Switches keyboard layout (if more than one is installed). (If you use Spotlight, you must choose a different keystroke for this function.) |

## Dialog Boxes

| | |
|---|---|
| ⌘-comma | Opens Preferences dialog box (any Apple program) |
| Esc | "Clicks" the Cancel button in a dialog box |
| Enter | "Clicks" the OK button (or other blue, highlighted button) in a dialog box |
| Option-⌘-F | Moves insertion point to the Search box in most Apple programs |
| ⌘-D, ⌘-R | "Clicks" the Don't Save or Replace button |

# Index

# Index

 menu, 39
⌘ key, 23
   disabling, 465
   purpose of, 19
⌘-tab, 115-116
⏏ (Eject)
   Menulet, 18
   key, 22, 24-25
⌦ (forward delete) key, 23
◀◀, ▶/❚❚, and ▶▶ keys, 24
◔ menu *see* Spotlight
◀, ◁), ◁)) keys, 22
⊞ key, 20
.dmg (disk image) files, 146-147
.gz files, 146-147
.Mac accounts, 295-300
   Back to My Mac, 435-436
   backup, 300
   defined, 295
   email, 299
   free (for iChat use), 357-358
   Home Page, 299
   iDisk, 295-296
   signing up, 295
   syncing feature, 275-276
   System Preferences, 439
.sit files, 146-147
.tar files, 146-147
.zip files, 146-147

## A

About This Program command, 555
Accessibility Options control panel, 555
accounts, 377-395
   account groups, 382-383
   account photos, 385-386
   administrator vs. standard, 379-383
   creating, 379-387
   creating the first account, 543
   defined, 377-378
   deleting, 395
   Drop Box folder, 400
   editing, 395
   Fast User Switching, 400-401
   File Vault, 405-409
   guest accounts, 382-383
   logging in, 37-38, 396-398
   logging out, 15, 398
   Menulet, 19
   name, 383-385
   parental controls, 385, 387-395
   passwords, 383-385
   Public folder, 400
   settings, 379-397
   Shared folder, 400
   sharing folders among, 399-400
   sharing-only, 381
   startup items, 386-387
   types of, 379-383
ACDSee, 191-192
Acrobat Reader, 192
ACT, 192-193
Active Desktop, 555
Activity Monitor, 517-519
ad hoc networks, 416
Add Hardware control panel, 555
Add/Remove Programs control panel, 556
Address Book, 331-338
   adding from email messages, 312
   backing up, 338
   creating and editing contacts, 332-333
   groups, 334

pictures in, 335
printing, 337-338
searching for addresses, 335-336
syncing between Macs, 275-276
tips and tricks, 332
**Adobe programs**, 194
**AdSubtract**, 193-194
**AIM (AOL Instant Messenger)**, 195
**AIM network**, 356-359
**AirPort** *see* **Wi-Fi connections**
**AirPort Utility**, 520
**aliases**, 84-85
benefits of, 84
defined, 84
**All Programs menu**, 556
**Alt key**, 20, 556
**Alt-tab**, 115-116
**antivirus software**, 200
**AOL**, 194-195
**Apache**, 27
**Appearance settings**, 440-441
Desktop color scheme, 440
font smoothing, 441
highlight color, 440
scroll bar settings, 440
**Apple Store file transfers**, 160-161
email and address book, 172
**AppleCare**, 553
**AppleScript**, 480-481
script menu, 18
**applications** *see* **programs**
**Application menu**, 113
**Applications folder**, 25
**archiving files and folders**, 86
**arrow notation**, 7
**audio chats**, 365-366
**Automatic Update**, 556
**Automator**, 481

**B**

**Back to My Mac**, 435-436
**Backspace key**, 20, 556
**backups,** 263-274 *see also* **Time Machine**
.Mac program, 300
Address Book, 338
**battery**
menu-bar gauge, 17, 458
power settings, 458-459
**BIOS**, 556
**Bluetooth**
Menulet, 17
pairing with other gear, 442-443
settings, 441-443

**bookmarks (Favorites)**
adding, 344
managing, 344-345
syncing between Macs, 275-276
transferring from pc, 167
**Boolean searches**, 99-100
**Boot Camp**, 211-220
familiar Windows keystrokes in, 217
installing, 213-217
removing Windows, 219
requirements, 212
right-clicking in, 216
switching between Mac and Windows, 217-218
tips and tricks, 219-220
**Briefcase**, 556
**broadband connections**, 281-284
**burning CDs and DVDs**, 245-250
-RW (rewritable disks), 249
with a disk, 248-250
without a disk (burn folder), 246-247

**C**

**Calculate All Sizes option**, 50
**Calculator**, 482-483, 557
calculations in Spotlight menu, 483
calculations within a document, 483
using Spotlight menu, 98
**calendar**, 489-497
**Camera & Scanner Wizard**, 557
**Caps Lock key**
disabling, 465
**Carbon programs**, 111, 141
**CDs and DVDs**, 24-25, 557
auto-playing music CDs, 249
burning, 245-250
burning music CDs, 257
Desktop icons, 39
ripping in iTunes, 255
**CDs and DVDs** *see also* ⏏ **key; DVD Player**
settings, 444
System Profiler, 529-530
**Character Map**, 557
**Character Palette**, 463
**chatting** *see* **iChat**
**Chess**, 484-485
**children's software**, 195
**Clear key**, 23
**clicking**, 8
double-click settings, 465-466
**Clipboard**, 557
**clipping files**, 169

**clock**
  Menulet, 17
  settings, 444-446
**Close button**, 30-31
  "unsaved" dot, 137
**Cocoa programs**, 111, 141-145
  advantages of, 142-145
  Font panel, 142
  Services menu, 142-143
**Color Picker dialog box**, 148
**column view**, 52-55
  column widths, 53
  defined, 52
  icon previews, 54
  preview column, 54
  sorting, 53
  text size, 54
**columns (list view)**
  adjusting width, 49-51
  hiding and showing, 49-51
**command line**, 530-534
**compressing files and folders**, 86
**Connect to Server command**, 425
**Control-clicking**, 8, 13
**Control key**, 19, 23
  disabling, 465
  Spaces, 125-127
**Control Panel** *see* **System Preferences**
**converting documents to Mac format**, 167-168
**cookies**, 355
  Safari, 355
**copy and paste**, 558
  icons, 80-81
  text and graphics, 169
**Cover Flow view**, 55-57
  defined, 55
  movies in, 56
  PDF documents in, 56
  size of, 56
**control panel**, 557
**CPU monitor**, 518
**CrossOver**, 222
**Ctrl key**, 558

## D

**Dashboard**, 150-156, 485
  defined, 150-152
  making your own Widgets, 154-156
  moving and closing Widgets, 152
  tips and tricks, 153-154
  syncing widgets between Macs, 275-276
**data detectors**, 312-313

**Date & Time**
  settings, 444-446
  Menulet, 17
**Del key**, 20
**Delete key**, 20, 23, 558
**Desktop**, 26, 558
  background picture, 166
  elements of, 38-39
**Desktop** *see also* **Exposé**
**Desktop pictures**, 166, 447-448
  auto-changing, 448
  choosing, 447
**dial-up modems**, 286-290
  connecting and disconnecting, 289-290
  Menulet, 18
  setting up accounts, 287
**dialog boxes**
  keyboard control, 136, 573-574
**dictionary**, 485-487
  using Spotlight menu, 98
**digital cameras**, 242
**directories**, 558
**disability assistance**, 475-478
**disk activity monitor**, 518-519
**Disk Defragmenter**, 558
**disk images**, 149-150, 524-525
  creating, 525
  encrypting, 526
  formatting, 525
  mounting, 526
**Disk Utility**, 520-526
  cloning disks, 523
  disk images, 524-525
  disk repair, 550-551
  disk repair functions, 520-523
  partitioning, 523
  RAID arrays, 522-523
**disks**, 243-245, 559
  Desktop icons, 39
  disk activity monitor, 518-519
  ejecting, 243-245
  erasing, 245, 521
  partitioning, 521-522
  startup disks, 218, 243-245
  working with, 24-25
**Display control panel**, 559
**displays** *see* **monitors**
**DLL files**, 559
**Dock**, 39, 60-69
  adding and removing icons, 60-61
  as Taskbar replacement, 16
  auto-hiding, 64
  defined, 16

dragging and dropping onto, 130
dragging to, 68
keyboard control, 135
keyboard shortcuts, 573
moving to side of screen, 65
shortcut menus, 66-68
shrinking and enlarging, 64
Stacks, 62-64
switching applications, 66
three ways to display folder contents, 62
turning off Stacks, 62
**document-program relationships**, 129-134
**documents**
converting from PC to Mac, 167-168
reassigning program using Dock, 130
**Documents folder**, 27
**DOS**, 557, 559
**double-clicking**, 8
**drag and drop**
icons, 79-81
text and graphics, 169
to the Dock, 68
**dragging**, 8
**Dragon NaturallySpeaking**, 203
**Drop Box folder**, 400
**DVD Player**, 257-261
full-screen playback, 260
keyboard shortcuts, 259
movie playback, 258-260
subtitles and languages, 260

## E

**Earthlink Total Access**, 196
**EasyCD Creator**, 196
**ejecting disks**, 24-25
**email** *see* **Mail**
**Encarta**, 196
**End key**, 22
**End Task dialog box**, 559
**Energy Saver**, 456-459
laptop settings, 458-459
scheduled startup and shutdown, 459
Sleep settings, 456-458
**Enter key**, 20
**erasing disks**, 245
**Esc key**, 23
**Ethernet connections**, 282-283
setting up a network, 414
**Eudora**, 197
**Exchange Servers**, 179-180
**exiting programs**, 114, 559
**Explorer**, 559 *see also* **Finder**

**Exposé**, 116-122
choosing a trigger, 120-122
finding one window in current program, 118
keyboard shortcuts, 120-122
on aluminum Apple keyboards, 116
reducing window clutter, 116-117
revealing Desktop, 118-120
settings, 120-125

## F

**F1, F2, F3... keys**, 23, 464
**Fast User Switching**, 400-401
**Favorites**, 560
**faxing**, 232-235
Menulet, 18
receiving faxes, 235
sending the fax, 233-234
setting up, 233
**file associations**, 129-134
forcing using Dock, 130
reassigning, 132-134
**file sharing**, 416-431
accessing shared folders (Connect to Server), 425
accessing shared folders (using sidebar), 422-425
any-folder method, 418-422
between Mac and PC, 426-431
permissions, 418-422
Public folder, 417-418
setting up, 417-422
**file sizes**, 47, 93
showing folder sizes, 50
sorting by, 48
**File Vault**, 405-409
**filename extensions**, 131
**filenames**, 75-77
**files** *see also* **icons**
**FileVault**
and Time Machine, 274
**Finder**, 15-16 *see also* **Dock; icons; windows**
keyboard shortcuts, 570
Sidebar, 32-33
Simple Finder, 388-389
window views, 39-57
**finding files**, 94-110
**Firefox**, 197
**firewall**, 403-405
**Firewire disk mode**, 168-170
**flippy triangles**, 49
**floppy disks**, 560
**Fn key**, 21
**folder options**, 560

**folder proxy icon**, 30
**folders**
  aliases, 84-85
  Calculate All Sizes option, 50
  color labels, 85-88
  flippy triangles, 49
  in the Dock: three views, 62
  locked files, 90-91
  spring-loaded, 81-83
  Stacks, 62-64
**Font Book,** 236-241
**Font panel**, 142, 241-242
**fonts**, 237-242
  Character Palette, 463
  deleting and hiding, 240-241
  font libraries, 241
  Font panel, 142, 241-242
  installing and managing, 238-239
  Keyboard Viewer, 462-463
  smoothing settings, 441
  type size for icon labels, 42
  where they live, 237-238
**force quitting programs**, 114-115, 546-547
**Forward delete key**, 20, 558
**Front Row**, 487-488
  keyboard shortcuts, 488
  sound effects, 473
**FTP**, 561

**G**

**gadgets** *see* **Dashboard**
**games**, 197
**GarageBand**, 489
**Get Info window**, 91-94
  defined, 91
  panels of, 92-93
  reassigning file associations, 132-134
  sharing folders, 418-420
**Go To Folder command**, 46
**Google Desktop Search**, 197
**Google Talk network**, 356-359
**Grab**, 526-527
**Grab command**, 142-143
**Grapher**, 527-529
**graphics**, 502-507
**grid of icons** *see* **Stacks**
**grid spacing**, 42
**guest accounts**, 382-383

**H**

**hard drives**
  cloning, 523
  diagnosing and repairing, 520-523

disk activity monitor, 518-519
  disk repair, 550-551
  FireWire disk mode, 168-170
  partitioning, 523
  RAID arrays, 522-523
**hard drives** *see also* **Disk Utility**
**hardware**, 223-276
**"heads-up" program switcher,** 121
**help**, 70-73
**help for the disabled**, 475-478
**Help key**, 23
**Hibernation**, 561
**hibernation** *see* **sleep mode**
**Home folder**, 26-27
  defined, 26
**Home key**, 22
**HomePage**, 299

**I**

**iCal**, 489-497
  calendar categories, 496
  data detectors, 312-313
  day/week/month views, 489-490
  making an appointment, 490-494
  printing from, 495
  reminder alarms, 493
  rescheduling events, 494-495
  searching for events, 496
  syncing between Macs, 275-276
  To Do list, 328-331, 496-497
**iChat**, 356-373
  audio chats, 365-366
  available networks, 356-359
  blue screen effects, 367-368
  Buddy List, 359-361
  iChat Theater (exhibiting documents),
    372-373
  Menulet, 18
  parental controls, 392-393
  screen sharing, 370-371
  sending files, 364-365
  smilies, 364-365
  SMS messages to phones, 364-365
  text chats, 361-365
  text formatting, 364-365
  transcripts, 364-365
  video chats, 366-370
**icon view**, 41-47 *see also* **icons**
**icons**
  aliases, 84-85
  color labels, 85-88
  copy and paste, 80-81
  copying, 79-81

defined, 8
designing your own, 83
finding, 94-110
grid spacing, 42
icon size, 41
label font size, 42
label position, 42
locked files, 90-91
moving, 79-81
previews of, 42-43
printing list of, 80
renaming, 75-76
selecting, 77-79
Show Item Info option, 42-43
sorting and aligning, 45-47
**ICQ**, 198
**iDisk**, 295-298
defined, 296
password protection, 298
Public folder, 297-298
pulling onto your screen, 296-297
summoning from Windows, 297-298
**iMovie**, 498
**input menu**, 18, 460
**installing Mac OS X**, 537-544
basic installation, 538-540
clean install, 540-541
erase & install, 541
setup assistant, 541-544
system requirements, 537
three kinds of installation, 538
upgrade installation, 540
**installing programs**, 146-150
**instant messaging** *see* **iChat**
**International**
Character Palette, 463
Keyboard Viewer, 462-463
language settings, 460
number formats, 460
**Internet**
broadband connections, 281-284
dial-up modems, 286-290
Ethernet connections, 282-283
firewall, 403-405
Internet connection sharing, 292-294
locations, 290-292
setting up, 279-300
specifying preferred browser, 339
transferring Internet settings from PC, 279-290
Wi-Fi connections, 284-286
**Internet connection sharing**, 292-294
**Internet Explorer**, 198, 561

**Internet location files**, 300
**Internet options**, 561
**iPhoto**, 498
**IRQs**, 561
**iTornado**, 161
**iTunes**, 198, 250-257
burning music CDs, 257
defined, 250
graphic equalizer, 254
iPod and iPhone, 251
iTunes Store, 252
keyboard shortcuts, 254
playback tricks, 253-254
playing across the network, 252
playing audio CDs, 250-251
playlists, 255-257
ripping CDs, 255
smart playlists, 256
Sound Check, 254

## J

**Jabber network**, 356-359
**Java**, 561

## K

**Kazaa**, 198
**kernel panic**, 547-548
**keyboard**
Mac vs. PC differences, 19-24
**Keyboard Viewer**, 462-463
**keyboards**
aluminum Apple keyboards, 116
Bluetooth options, 468
F1, F2, etc. functions, 464
illumination settings, 464-465
international layouts, 460
key repeat rate, 464
numeric keypad, 22
settings, 464-468
typing assistance (Sticky Keys), 476-477
various Apple types, 21
**keychain**, 409-412
locking and unlocking, 410
managing, 412
syncing between Macs, 275-276
**keyboard shortcuts**, 8
changing Spotlight keystroke, 108
Cover Flow view, 57
dialog boxes, 573-574
Dock, 573
DVD Player, 259
Expose, 120-122
Finder, 570

folder shortcuts, 79
force quitting, 546-547
Front Row, 488
Home folder, 26
iTunes, 254
master list, 569-574
menus, 571-573
menus, Dock, windows, etc., 134-136
on aluminum Apple keyboards, 116
power button, 573
programs, 573-574
Spotlight, 100
switching programs, 115-116
window views, 40
word processing, 261-262

## L

**labels**, 85-88
  benefits of, 85-87
  defined, 85
  editing names and colors, 87-88
**language settings**, 459-463
**laptops**
  ⌦ (Forward Delete) key, 23
  auto brightness, 455
  battery gauge, 17
  Fn key, 21
  illumination settings, 464-465
  power settings, 458-459
  shutting down, 12
  trackpad settings, 466-468
  two-finger scrolling, 166
**Library folder**, 27
**Limewire**, 198
**list view**, 47-52
  columns, 49-51
  flippy triangles, 49
  sorting, 48-49
**locations**, 290-292
  creating, 291
  defined, 290
  switching, 292
**locked files**, 90-91
**logging in**, 37-38, 561
  accounts, 377-395
  automatic, 396
  configuring, 396-398
  Safe mode, 548-550
**logging out**, 15, 398
  automatic, 409
**login items**, 386-387

## M

**MacAfee VirusScan**, 198
**Mail**, 300-338
  adjusting panes, 302
  capturing addresses, 312
  checking your mail, 301-302
  composing and sending, 304-310
  data detectors, 312-313
  deleting messages, 319-321
  file attachments (receiving), 313-315
  file attachments (sending), 305-307
  filing, 317
  finding messages, 318-319
  flagging, 317-318
  forwarding, 316
  mailbox list, 303
  message rules, 322-323
  notes, 327-328
  parental controls, 392-393
  plain text vs. formatted, 305
  printing, 316
  reading and processing, 310-323
  redirecting, 316
  replying, 315-316
  RSS feeds, 325-326
  signatures, 307
  spam filter, 324-325
  spelling checker, 305
  stationery, 308-310
  syncing settings between Macs, 275-276
  threading, 310-311
  To Do list, 328-331
**Mail command**, 143
**Mail control panel**, 561
**Maximize button (Zoom button)**, 31, 562
**Macintosh** *see also* documents; icons; keyboards;
        programs
  disks on, 24-25
  FireWire disk mode, 168-170
  Intel processors, 145-146
  keyboard differences vs. PC, 19-24
  keyboard, 19-24
  logging out, 15
  on, off, sleep, 13-15
  restarting, 14
  secret two-button mouse, 12-13
  shutting down, 14
  sleep mode, 13-14
  System Preferences, 437-478
  System Profiler, 529-530
  terminology differences, 36
  troubleshooting, 544-553
  turning on, 11-12

**memory**
  monitor, 518
  System Profiler, 529-530
**menulets**, 16-19
  battery gauge, 458
  described individually, 17-19
  Wi-Fi connections, 285
**menus**
  complete keyboard control, 134-136
  defined, 8
  keyboard-shortcut symbols in, 19
  keyboard shortcuts, 571-573
  Mac vs. Windows, 562
  menu bar, 39
  menu-bar clock, 444-446
  searching for a command, 71
  turning off the translucence, 447
  where to find them, 15
**messenger** *see* **iChat**
**Microsoft Access**, 199
**Microsoft Money**, 200-201
**Microsoft Office**, 201-202
**Microsoft Outlook** *see* **Outlook**
**Microsoft Publisher**, 203
**Microsoft Visio**, 203
**Migration Assistant**, 529
**Minesweeper**, 203
**minimizing windows**, 127-129
  all simultaneously, 29
  Minimize button, 31, 562
**modems**, 286-290
  cellular, 291
  dial-up, 286-290
**monitors**, 263
  adjusting resolution, 18
  adjusting screen zoom and contrast, 475-476
  brightness and contrast, 455
  changing resolution, 454
  color calibration, 456
  connecting projectors, 263
  Display settings, 453-456
  Menulet, 18
  mirroring, 263
  multiple, 455-456
  multiple monitors, 263 *see also* Spaces
  refresh rate, 455
  virtual *see* Spaces
**mouse**
  basics, 8
  double-click settings, 465-466
  how to right click, 12-13
  installing non-Apple mice, 262-263
  keyboard control of, 478
  left-handers, 13

Mighty Mouse, 13
  motion settings, 465-466
  multi-button (Expose), 122
  replacing, 13
  settings, 464-468
**movies** *see* **QuickTime Player**
**Movies folder**, 27
**mp3 files** *see* **iTunes**
**MSN Messenger**, 203
**multiple monitors**, 263, 455-456 *see also* **Spaces**
**music** *see* **iTunes**
**Music folder**, 27
**MusicMatch**, 209
**Mac OS X**
  accounts, 377-395
  advantages of, 3-5
  clean install, 540-541
  Dashboard, 150-156
  explanation of Leopard name, 2
  Expose, 116-122
  finding files, 94-110
  Help system, 70-73
  included programs, 479-534
  installing, 537-544
  installing programs, 146-150
  master keyboard shortcuts list, 569-574
  networking, 413-436
  reasons to switch, -5
  running Windows on, 211-222
  Safari, 339-356
  System Preferences, 437-478
  Spaces, 122-127
  troubleshooting, 544-553
  Utilities folder, 517-534
  window elements, 28-36
**My Documents, My Pictures...** 562

## N

**NaturallySpeaking**, 203
**Netscape**, 204
**Network Neighborhood**, 562
**networking**, 413-436
  Activity Monitor, 519
  ad hoc networks, 416
  between Mac and PC, 426-431
  broadband connections, 281-284
  Ethernet connections, 282-283
  file sharing, 416-431
  Internet connection sharing, 292-294
  locations, 290-292
  multihoming, 279-281
  playing iTunes across the network, 252
  printing sharing, 230-232
  screen sharing, 431-436

setting up a network, 413-416
Wi-Fi connections, 284-286
**newsgroup readers**, 204
**Norton AntiVirus**, 204
**Norton Utilities**, 204
**Notepad**, 204, 562
**Notes**
in Mail, 327-328
syncing between Macs, 275-276
**Notification Area**, 566 *see also* **Menulets**
**number formats**, 460
**numeric keypad**, 22

## O

**Old Finder Mode**, 33-35
**Open dialog box**, 139-140
**Option-clicking**, 8
**Option key**, 23
disabling, 465
minimize all windows, 29
purpose of, 20
**Outlook**, 204
transferring mail to the Mac, 172-180
**Outlook Express**, 204
**Outlook vs. Outlook Express**, 171
**O2M (Outlook2Mac)**, 172-180

## P

**Page Down key**, 22
**Page Up key**, 22
**Paint Shop Pro**, 205
**Palm Desktop**, 205
**Parallels**, 212, 220-222
tips and tricks, 221-222
**parental controls**, 385, 387-395
activity logs, 394-395
hiding profanity in dictionary, 390-392
limited mail and chat partners, 392-393
limiting programs and activities, 387-390
restricting adult Web sites, 391-392
Simple Finder, 388-389
time limits, 393-394
**partitioning**, 521-523
for Boot Camp, 213-214
**passwords**
for accounts, 383-385
forgotten, 402
keychain, 409-412
master password, 408
password hints, 383-385
**path bar**, 35
**PDF files**
adding keywords to, 507

advantages of, 236-237
annotating, 505
bookmarking, 505
copying from, 506
creating, 236
exporting pages from, 506
from any program, 228
in Cover Flow, 56
in Preview, 504-507
in Quick Look, 58
navigating, 505
opening, 236
saving to iPhoto, 237
saving web receipts, 237
searching in, 507
sending by email, 237
**peripherals**, 223-276
**permissions**, 418-422
repairing, 545
**Personal Web Server**, 563
**Phone & Modem Options control panel**, 563
**Photo Booth**, 498-502
4-up photos, 500-501
blue screen background effects, 500
exporting from, 501
movies, 501
still photos, 499-500
**Picasa**, 205
**Pictures folder**, 27
**playlists**, 255-257
**PocketPC**, 205
**Power Options control panel**, 563
**power settings** *see* **Energy Saver**
**powering on**, 11-12
keyboard shortcuts, 573
**PowerPoint**, 206
**PPP menulet**, 18
**Preview**, 502-507
as graphics editor, 502-504
as PDF reader, 504-507
**Printer Sharing**, 563
**printing**, 223-232
Address Book, 337-338
choosing a default printer, 225
making the printout, 226-229
managing the print queue, 229-230
Page Setup, 226
preview, 228
printing sharing, 230-232
saving as PDF, 228
scheduled, 229
setting up a printer, 223-225
**printing sharing**, 230-232
**privileges**, 418-422

**PrntScrn key**, 563
**processors**
    System Profiler, 529-530
**Program Files folder**, 563
**program-document relationships**, 129-134
**programs** *see also* **Address Book; Calculator;**
    **Exposé; etc.**
    application menu, 113
    Carbon vs. Cocoa, 111
    Dashboard, 150-156
    exiting, 559
    finding Mac equivalents of PC programs,
        191-210
    force quitting, 114-115
    frozen, 546-547
    included with Mac OS X, 479-534
    installing, 146-150
    keyboard shortcuts, 573-574
    open at login, 67
    Open dialog box, 139-140
    opening, 112-113
    quitting, 114
    quitting from the Dock, 68
    switching, 115-116
    switching with Dock, 66
    System Profiler, 529-530
    troubleshooting, 544-553
    uninstalling, 150
    Universal (Intel Macs), 145-146
    Utilities folder, 517-534
    window management, 127-129
    won't open, 547
**Programs folder** *see* **Applications folder**
**projectors**
    Menulet, 18
**Properties Get Info window**
**Properties dialog box**, 563
**Public folder**, 27, 400
    file sharing, 417-418

## Q

**Quick Look**, 57-60
    defined, 57
    full screen, 59-60
    recognized document types, 58-59
    slideshows, 60
    zooming in, 59-60
**QuickBooks**, 206
**Quicken**, 206
**QuickTime Player**, 507-508
    editing in, 508
    playback tricks, 507-508
    Pro version, 508
**quitting programs**, 114

## R

**RAID arrays**, 522-523
**RealPlayer**, 207
**Recycle Bin**, 563-564 *see also* **Trash**
**Registry**, 563-564
**remote control**, 487-488
**remote login**, 470
**renaming icons**, 75-77
**repairing broken aliases**, 85
**resize box**, 35
**restarting**, 14
    troubleshooting, 546
**right-clicking**, 13
    defined, 12
    how to, 12-13
**Rosetta**, 145
**routers**, 292, 414-415
**RSS feeds**
    Mail, 325-326
    screensaver, 356
    Safari, 353-356
**RssReader**, 207
**Run command**, 564

## S

**Safari**, 339-356
    address bar, 341-342
    autocomplete, 342
    bookmarks (adding), 344
    bookmarks (managing), 344
    browsing basics, 340-341
    cookies (erasing), 352
    Debug menu, 347
    designating start page, 349
    embedded PDF documents, 350
    expanding Web forms, 348
    finding text, 349
    Google Search box, 344
    history (erasing), 352
    History menu, 349
    impersonating Internet Explorer, 347
    making your own Widgets, 154-156
    pop-up ads, 346
    private browsing, 352
    reload button, 344
    RSS feeds, 353-356
    saving graphics to hard drive, 341
    saving Web pages to disk, 348-349
    SnapBack, 346
    specifying preferred browser, 339
    tabbed browsing, 350-353
    text size, 343
    toolbars, 341-346

turning off graphics, 347
URL tips and tricks, 341-342
Web clips, 344
Web receipts, 237
**Safe mode**, 548-550, 564
**Save dialog box**, 136-140
navigating, 138
Spotlight in, 139
tour of, 136-137
**ScanDisk**, 564
**Scheduled Tasks**, 564
**scrap files**, 169, 564
**screen sharing**
Back to My Mac, 435-436
between Mac and PC, 436
iChat, 370-371
on local network, 431-436
setting up permissions, 431-433
taking control of another Mac, 434
**screensavers**, 448-453
activating, 453
choosing, 449-452
password protection, 452
password required, 409
RSS feeds, 356
using your own photos, 452
**screenshots (screen captures)**, 208
built-in keystrokes, 208
Grab, 526-527
Grab command, 142-143
timed, 527
**Script menu**, 18, 480-481
**scroll bars**, 35
settings, 440
**search**, 94-110
in Address Book, 335-336
**Search with Google command**, 144
**security**
accounts, 377-395
Apple philosophy, 402-403
auto-logout, 409
File Vault, 405-409
firewall, 403-405
keychain, 409-412
password-protected screensaver, 452
private browsing, 352
Secure Empty Trash, 89-90
secure hard drive erase, 403
special Mac OS X features, 400-412
warning messages, 402-403
**selecting icons**, 77-79
**Services menu**, 142-143
Grab command, 142
Mail command, 143

Make New Sticky Note, 143
Search with Google command, 144
Summarize command, 144
**setup assistant**, 541-544
**Shared folder**, 400
**Sharing preferences**, 292
**Shift clicking**, 8
**Shortcut menus**, 565
**shortcuts (icons)** *see* **aliases**
**shutting down**, 14
scheduled, 459
**Sidebar**, 32-33
accessing shared folders, 422-425
adjusting and rearranging, 33
dragging and dropping onto, 130
**signatures**, 307
**Simple Finder**, 388-389
**Sites folder**, 27, 469
**Skype**, 207
**Spotlight**, 94-110
advanced searches, 97-100
as calculator, 98
as dictionary, 98
basics of, 94-95
Boolean searches, 99-100
customizing search categories, 107-108
Finder window, 100-107
limiting by date, 98, 104
limiting by kind, 97, 104
limiting by metadata, 98-99
memorized searches, 109-110
menu, 94-95
multi-criteria searches, 101-106
privacy settings, 109
quote marks in, 97
search by filename, 102
Services menu, 144
smart folders, 109-110
tips and tricks, 95-97
what to do with the results, 106-107
where to look, 102
**Sleep mode**, 13-14
password required, 409
timing settings, 456-458
**slideshows in Quick Look**, 60
**smart folders**, 109-110
**SnagIt**, 207
**software** *see* **programs**
**Software Update**, 470-471
**Solitaire**, 208
**sorting icons**
column view, 53
icon view, 45-47
list view, 48-49

**sounds**
error beeps, 471-472
Front Row sound effects, 473
input/output options, 473
settings, 471-473
sound effects, 471-472
transferring from pc, 166
volume slider, 472
**Sounds & Audio Devices**, 565
**System Preferences**, 437-478
.Mac, 439
Accounts, 379-397, 440
Appearance, 440-441
Bluetooth, 441-443
CDs and DVDs, 444
Date & Time, 444-446
Desktop & Screen Saver, 446-453
Displays, 453-456
Dock, 64-65
Energy Saver, 456-459
Exposé & Spaces, 120-125
International, 459-463
Keyboard & Mouse, 464-468
Network, 279-288
opening and arranging, 437-439
parental controls *see* **parental controls**
Print & Fax *see* **faxing; printing**
QuickTime, 469
security *see* **security**
Sharing, 292, 469-471
Spotlight *see* **Spotlight**
Software Update, 470-471
Sound, 471-473
Speech, 473-474
Startup Disk, 218, 475
Time Machine *see* **Time Machine**
Universal Access, 475-478
**Spaces**, 122-127
big-picture view, 126-127
defined, 122-123
moving windows between, 127
setting up, 123-125
tips and techniques, 125-127
**speaker volume** *see* **volume**
**speech**
dictation software, 203
speech recognition (command and control), 473-474
text to speech (the Mac reads), 474
**spelling checker**
Mail, 305
**spring-loaded folders**, 81-83
on the Dock, 68

**ssh**, 470
**Stacks**, 62-64
turning off, 62
**standby mode** *see* **sleep mode**
**Start menu**, 565
**starting up**
keyboard shortcuts, 569
Safe mode, 548-550
scheduled, 459
troubleshooting, 547-551
**startup disks**, 243-245
booting in Windows, 218
**StartUp folder**, 565
**status bar**, 36
**Stickies**, 509-511
creating, 510
defined, 509
formatting, 511
Make New Sticky Note, 143
organizing, 510
saving and exporting, 511
**Street Atlas USA**, 209
**Summarize command**
Services menu, 144
**switching**
reasons for, 5
**switching programs ("Alt-tab")**, 115-116
**symbols**, 463
**sync**
.Mac sync, 275-276
Menulet, 18
**System control panel**, 565-566
**System folder**, 27-28
**System Preferences**
syncing between Macs, 275-276
**System Profiler**, 529-530
**System tray**, 566
**System Tray** *see* **menulets**

**T**

**target disk mode** *see* **FireWire disk mode**
**task manager**, 114-115
**Taskbar**, 566
**Taskbar** *see* **Dock**
**TaxCut**, 209
**troubleshooting**, 544-553
Apple Tech Support, 553
blue screen at startup, 550
disk repair, 550-551
force quitting, 546-547
frozen programs, 546-547
getting troubleshooting help, 551-553
gray screen at startup, 550

kernel panic, 547-548
minor glitches, 544-546
online resources, 552
preferences file, 546
program won't open, 547
reinstalling software, 546
repairing permissions, 545
restarting, 546
Safe mode, 548-550
sharing between Mac and PC, 431
startup problems, 547-551
updating programs, 545
**Terminal**, 530-534
basics of, 531-532
defined, 530
getting help, 533
navigating, 533
Unix programs, 532-533
**text chats**, 361-365
**TextEdit**, 511-517
basic web design, 516-517
editing in, 512-513
Microsoft Word compatibility, 513
style sheets, 514-515
tables, 515-516
**thesaurus**, 485-487
**"three-fingered salute,"** 114-115, 566
**time zone**, 444-446
**title bar**, 28-29
folder proxy icon, 30
secret hierarchical menu, 29
**Time Machine**, 263-274
and FileVault, 274
changing settings, 268-269
defined, 264
deleting items from all backups, 273-274
excluding folders from, 267
frequently asked questions, 273-274
full backup drive, 266
how it works, 266-268
multiple backup disks, 273-274
multiple Macs, 273-274
recovering entire hard drive, 272-273
recovering files, 269-273
recovering from iPhoto, Mail, and Address
    Book, 271-272
setting up, 264-266
**To Do lists**
iCal, 496-497
Mail, 328-331
**toolbar**
buttons on, 69-70
hiding and showing, 33-35

keyboard control, 135
Old Finder Mode, 33-35
shrinking or hiding, 70
**ToolTips**, 567
**trackpads**, 466-468
drag lock, 467
dragging on pad, 467
gestures, 466-468
keyboard control of, 478
options, 468
right-clicking, 467
two-finger scrolling, 166
**transferring address book from Eudora**,
    184-186
**transferring address book from Outlook**,
    180-184
CSV method, 182-183
Outlook2Mac method, 180
Thunderbird method, 180-182
**transferring email and contacts from Outlook
    Express**, 184-187
**transferring email from Outlook to the Mac**
Eudora method, 179
Exchange Servers, 179-180
Outlook2Mac method, 172-173
Thunderbird method, 174-179
**transferring email settings from PC**, 188-190
**transferring email, contacts, and settings from
    PC**, 171-190
**transferring files from pc**, 159-170
by Apple Store, 160-161
iTornado, 161
over the network, 163
via Bluetooth, 164
via CD or DVD, 162-163
via email, 164
via file-sending web site, 163-164
via hard drive or flash drive, 162-163
via iDisk, 164
where to put the files, 165
**transferring Internet settings from PC**, 279-290
**Trash**, 88-91
defined, 88
emptying, 89-90
in Mail, 319-321
locked files, 90-91
rescuing from, 88-89
Secure Empty Trash, 89-90
**Tray**, 566
**Tray** *see* **Menulets**
**TurboTax**, 209
**turning on the Macintosh**, 11-12
**TweakUI**, 567

# U

**uninstalling programs**, 150
**unit conversions**, 482-483
**Universal (Intel Macs)**, 145-146
**Universal Access**, 475-478
   adjusting screen zoom and contrast, 475-476
   flashing for error beeps, 476
   mouse assistance, 478
   typing assistance (Sticky Keys), 476-477
   VoiceOver (screen reader), 475
**Unix**, 530-534
   learning more, 533-534
   navigating in, 533
   Unix programs, 532
**user accounts** *see* **accounts**
**Utilities folder**, 517-534

# V

**video chats**, 366-370
**views (windows)**, 39-57
**virtual monitors** *see* **Spaces**
**VirtualBox**, 222
**virtualization software**, 220-222
**viruses**, 200
**VMWare Fusion**, 212, 220-222
   tips and tricks, 221-222
**VoiceOver**, 475
**volume**, 472
   ◀, ◀◦, ◀◦) volume keys, 22
   Menulet, 19

# W

**wallpaper**, 447-448
   transferring from the PC, 166
**Web** *see also* **Safari**
   building your own site, 299
   designing pages in TextEdit, 516-517
   restricting adult Web sites, 391-392
   Safari, 339-356
   specifying preferred browser, 339
**Web clips**, 154-156
   Dashboard, 344
   Safari, 344
**Web receipts**, 237
**Web server**, 27
**Web sharing**, 469
**Wi-Fi connections**, 284-286
   AirPort Utility, 520
   commercial hot spots, 286
   menulets, 285
   setting up a network, 414-415
**Widgets** *see* **Dashboard**
**Wikipedia**, 485-487
**WinAmp**, 209

**window edges**, 567
**windows** *see also* **Exposé**
   background colors and photos, 44
   Close button, 30-31
   elements of, 28-36
   folder proxy icon, 30
   four views of, 39-57
   hiding and showing, 127-129
   keyboard control, 135
   management, 127-129
   managing and shuffling, 33-35
   Minimize button, 31
   multiple simultaneous, 54
   Old Finder Mode, 33-35
   path bar, 35
   printing list of contents, 80
   resize box, 35
   scroll bars, 35
   Sidebar, 32-33
   status bar, 36
   title bar, 28-29
   toolbar, 33-35
   toolbar buttons, 69-70
   Zoom button, 31
**Windows Explorer** *see* **Finder**
**Windows folder** *see* **System folder**
**Windows Media Player**, 209
**Windows on the Mac**, 211-222
   Boot Camp, 212-220
**WINNT folder**, 567
**WinZip**, 210
**word processing** *see also* **TextEdit**
   keyboard shortcuts, 261-262
**WordPad**, 568
**WordPerfect**, 210
**Windows (Microsoft Windows)**
   terminology differences, 36
**Windows Explorer**, 559
**Windows folder**, 567
**Windows Media Player**, 567
**Windows Messenger**, 568

# X

**Xgrid sharing**, 470

# Y

**Yahoo Messenger**, 210

# Z

**zipping files and folders**, 86, 568
**Zoom button**, 31

## Colophon

This book was written on a black MacBook laptop that remained attached to David Pogue like an appendage. It was typed in Microsoft Word, with substantial assistance from the typing-shortcut program TypeIt4Me (*www.typeit4me.com*) and the macro program QuicKeys (*www.quickeys.com*).

The screenshots were captured with Snapz Pro X (*www.ambrosiasw.com*), edited in Adobe Photoshop CS3 (*www.adobe.com*), and overlaid with labels, lines, and circles in Macromedia Freehand Mac OS X (*www.adobe.com*).

The author wrote the index, entry by entry, using a highly tweaked FileMaker database (*www.filemaker.com*) and a clever Perl script that converted FileMaker's output into a fully formatted index.

The book was designed and laid out in Adobe InDesign CS3 on a PowerBook G4 and Power Mac G5. The fonts include Formata (as the sans-serif family) and Minion (as the serif body face). To provide the symbols (, , , and so on), Phil Simpson designed two custom fonts using Macromedia Fontographer.

The book was then exported as Adobe Acrobat PDF files for final transmission to the printing plant in Michigan.

## The iTornado Discount

As mentioned in Chapter 5, one of the simplest and fastest ways to transfer your stuff from your PC to your Mac (or back again) is the retractable iTornado. The microprocessor-controlled cable plugs into the USB ports on both your computers; built-in software opens automatically on both screens. It shows you a complete "folder tree" of the contents of both machines. You can start transferring files in either direction—at 25 megabits per second—just by dragging and dropping.

Because we both know good things when we see 'em, Data Drive Thru and this book's creators have conspired to offer you, the reader of this book, a tasty deal on the iTornado:

- **20 percent off, and**

- **Free shipping and handling.**

To take advantage of this offer, order the iTornado from *www.thetornado.com*—and in the Promo Code box, type *missingmanuals.*

The discount, and the free shipping, will be applied automatically.

Happy transferring!

# THE MISSING MANUALS
## The books that should have been in the box

## Answers found here!

Missing Manuals deliver complete and comprehensive coverage of the most popular operating systems, applications and multimedia devices. Written in a unique, witty style that helps you learn quickly, these entertaining books explain every feature clearly and thoroughly, helping you master every aspect of your software.

Look for these and other Missing Manuals at your favorite bookstore or online.

**Visit www.missingmanuals.com for the latest books, screencasts, tips, and more.**

## POGUE PRESS™
## O'REILLY®